An Introduc

Theatre & Drama

Marshall Cassady & Pat Cassady

National Textbook Company
NTC a division of *NTC Publishing Group* • Lincolnwood, Illinois USA

To Dr. Robert Price

1991 Printing

Published by National Textbook Company, a division of NTC Publishing Group.
©1975 by NTC Publishing Group, 4255 West Touhy Avenue,
Lincolnwood (Chicago), Illinois 60646-1975 U.S.A.

0 1 2 3 4 5 6 7 8 9 VP 19 18 17 16 15 14 13 12

Introduction

Theatre is one of the world's oldest art forms. Even before there was written language, there were plays. And while other forms of entertainment come and go, the theatre remains an integral part of our lives.

There are many reasons for this. Most important, people go to the theatre to be entertained. Drama offers us escape. It enriches our lives. It teaches us about ourselves and others. It records our heritage. By reading or seeing plays produced, we better understand the attitudes, beliefs, and feelings of people in different cultures and in different times throughout history. Drama is a reflection of society; if it were not, it would have no appeal.

The primary purpose of this book is to acquaint you with the many forms of theatre in the Western world. The plays included range from ancient tragedy to the modern musical, from those that are concerned with morality to those that dramatize the absurdity of man's condition. From classic to avante garde, the reader will find more than enough to whet the palate.

Besides offering entertainment, theatre is an enriching experience. It makes our own lives more meaningful, as well as the lives of others, regardless of time and place.

In order to acquaint you with as many forms of theatre and drama as possible, we have organized this book chronologically. Each complete selection is prefaced with an overview of the time frame in which it was written and produced, so that you will better understand how the play was produced and what economic, religious or social conditions influenced its writing as well as production. That done, we present a profile of the playwright to give you a better idea or picture of the person, as well as his or her ideas.

At the end of each play are questions designed for you to reflect on what you have read and projects to further increase your enjoyment and understanding of theatre and drama.

Any collection of plays has to be selective. A single volume, at best, can only represent a fraction of the world's great drama. Therefore, each section in this book ends with a suggested reading list that will allow you to pursue whatever strikes your fancy, be it a playwright, a particular historical period, or a type of drama.

One final word. The section on modern theatre is by far the largest in this book simply because theatre has undergone such dramatic changes in the last 100 years. We have also included a number of American playwrights, first to show the diversity within our own theatre; second to demonstrate how American drama has reflected changes in our own society. And so we not only have included Eugene O'Neill and Tennessee Williams, but also a young man named Kopit who tends to see our lives through much the same lenses as a Beckett or a Pinter or an Ionesco. And we have included *West Side Story*, not only because the musical is a unique American contribution to the theatre, but because it dramatizes the problems this country faces in assimilating new cultures. Finally, we have included Lorraine Hansberry because she wrote for *everyone* with compassion and poignance. That is what the theatre has always been about, and that is what we trust it will continue to be about for all times.

Contents

CONTENTS

I

The Beginnings of Theatre

Theatre in the Western world had its beginnings in two sources: the need to imitate and the need to worship. The need to imitate, or the mimetic instinct, is one of man's oldest and most basic characteristics. Children learn to walk by seeing others walk, and learn to talk by making the sounds that others do. We learn to play musical instruments through example. We imitate the actions of others when we are unsure how to act in social situations. We then expand our areas of learning or accomplishment by imitating what we did previously and trying to perfect it. It is this practice and imitation that makes some of us good basketball players or good dancers. We also use imitation in our play. Young children love to play pretending games, acting the roles of nurses, doctors, firemen, cowboys, or astronauts. They are imitating others whom they have observed.

Imitation or action can also be a means of communication. When a person tells others about an experience he has had, he often pantomimes some of the actions he took. Thus, he is imitating a previous situation to make it clear to others. When you are angry at someone and tell another person about the situation that caused the anger, your voice often imitates that of the person who made you angry. However, your imitation is selective in that the worst qualities of the person's voice are used. Then they are heightened. In other words, you caricaturize that person's voice, much as a political cartoonist exaggerates certain facial features when he draws a public figure.

It is believed that before spoken language was developed, primal man communicated largely through action and imitation. In this way, he could tell others about situations of which he was a part, and he could demonstrate to others what he planned to do or what he wanted them to do. From this basic instinct to imitate, storytelling was born. Man not only could imitate what actually *did* happen to him, but what *could* happen. In primitive tribes of today, we still can see the rituals that developed. One member of the tribe plays an animal with horns and a mask, while another assumes the appearance of a supernatural being. Out of such ritual or imitation came worship of a god. The medicine man assumed a nonhuman appearance to ward off evil spirits, and the priest of the tribe imitated the actions of the gods to please them and to show that the people feared and loved them. The need for ritual survives to the present day in our culture, as can be seen in wedding ceremonies and other church services, and even in the pageantry of sports events like football games.

The Greek Theatre

Theatre in the Western world, or the theatre from which that of today developed, was a blending of ritual and imitation. It began some time before the sixth century B.C. in Greece, with dithyrambs in honor of the god Dionysus. Dithyrambs were hymns that related episodes from the life of the god of wine and harvest. Dionysus was the son of Zeus, the greatest of Greek gods, and of Semele, who was a mortal. According to legend, he was killed, dismembered, and then resurrected. Thus his life was related to the cycle of life: birth, maturation, death, and rebirth. This in turn suggested the seasons of spring, summer, fall, winter, and again spring; and he was worshipped to ensure the return of spring.

The dithyramb, which means "twice born," was performed by a chorus of fifty men, led by a priest. As the festivals honoring Dionysus continued, the dithyramb developed and changed. Later, the chorus dressed as satyrs, creatures that were half-goat and half-man. The worship then became known as the "goat song" or *tragoedia*, from which we get our word "tragedy," and after a time a single actor would usually deliver lines. The first of these actors for whom we have record was Thespis, whose name gave us "thespians," a synonym for actors.

The introduction of the actor added dialogue to the plays. However, there was still no conflict, and the actor played many roles by changing masks. The chorus itself remained the unifying force of the plays and served both as a narrator and a character. There is record that Thespis first performed in 534 B.C. because it was in that year that he was credited with winning the prize at the first tragedy contest in Greece.

The three festivals at which drama in Greece actually developed were the City Dionysia, held in Athens at the end of March each year: the Lenaia, held in January; and the Rural Dionysia, held each year in December. Each of these festivals had a master of revels, called the *archon,* who was in charge of all the arrangements. He selected the plays and the order in which they would be presented. It was also his job to choose wealthy citizens to bear the expense of room and board for the chorus members. These citizens, called the *choregi,* served for one day each and paid for the training of the chorus, for the costumes, for the musicians, and for any additional expenses. While the *archon* was elected, the *choregi* were appointed to this prestigious position. The playwright applied to the *archon* and was granted rights to present plays. If he was selected and given a chorus, he was expected to present three tragedies and a satyr play, as well as music. Many playwrights also directed the plays and appeared in them. The actors themselves were paid by the state. Admission to the festivals was free, and everyone was expected to attend.

The most important of the festivals was the City Dionysia. During the time it was being held, all prisoners were freed and no legal proceedings were allowed to continue. The festival was frequently attended by dignitaries of other states. It began with a processional and pageant in which the statue of Dionysus was taken from the temple at the foot of the Acropolis, carried outside the city of Athens, and then carried back inside the city to the accompaniment of great celebration. Following the processional, the dithyrambs were presented. Ten were given each year, five composed of choruses of boys and five composed of choruses of men. For the next three days, plays were presented.

Included were trilogies, or three separate plays, always tragedies and tied together by the inclusion of some of the same characters. Of less importance were the satyr plays, plays with a comic tone which burlesqued one of the Greek myths. The tragedies and satyr plays were presented during the mornings, comedies during the afternoons. The festival ended with the awarding of prizes and a meeting of governmental leaders to discuss affairs of state. The prizes were shared by the *choregi* and the writers. Later, actors also received prizes.

The first important Greek dramatist of whom we have record is Aeschylus, who lived from 525 to 456 B.C. In his plays he relied largely on the chorus, which, like the dithyrambic chorus, contained fifty members. He wrote largely about traditional themes, based on myths and Olympian law. Although his plays had a plot line, they were mostly choral. His important contribution, however, was the introduction of a second actor into the plays—not yet to provide dramatic conflict but only variety. Listening to a chorus recite for hours at a time could become very monotonous! Aeschylus' best work is considered the *Orestian Trilogy,* which is based on Greek mythology. The plays which make up the trilogy all deal with the concept of revenge: *Agamemnon,* which is the one most frequently produced today; the *Libation Bearers,* and *Eumenides.* Aeschylus often is regarded as the founder of Western drama.

The next writer of major importance in Greece was Sophocles, who lived from 496 to 406 B.C. Usually considered the greatest Greek dramatist, he wrote more than one hundred plays, seven of which still exist. He is credited with introducing a third actor into his plays and with reducing the size of the chorus from fifty to twelve. He was more interested in the interplay between characters than with the telling of religious myths in the style of Aeschylus. His plots are much more realistic than those of Aeschylus, and he is concerned with man as the determiner of his own fate, rather than being ruled by the gods. His characters are complex, strong, and believable, the central character always having a "tragic flaw" which brings about his downfall. Sophocles' plays are much better developed than are the plays of Aeschylus, with skillful and believable climaxes.

The third major writer of Greek tragedy was Euripides, who lived from 480 to 406 B.C. He is credited with ninety-two plays, of which seventeen tragedies and a satyr play survive. The one produced most often is *The Trojan Women*. Euripides was concerned largely with the human being as an individual. His plays dealt with the inner conflict of good and evil—that is, man against his conscience—and questioned many of the ideals of Greek society and religion. He was admired for his ideas and the presentation of realistic characters, but criticized for the structure of his plays, which was often melodramatic and contrived.

Throughout all Greek drama, the chorus continued to serve as the unifying force. Although its size fluctuated, it still acted as a character, or sometimes two characters discussing events with each other, or as the narrator. The chorus also sometimes played the role of a messenger bringing news of someone's violent death, perhaps in battle, because it was against Greek religious beliefs to present violence on the stage. The chorus usually entered just after the opening of the play and remained on stage until the end.

In Greece, plays were presented out of doors on a flat place, or *orchestra*, at the base of a hill. At first, this was really only an open space, with no walls or ceiling. The auditorium, or *theatron*, was the hillside itself where the audience stood to watch the plays. Seats were gradually added, and in time permanent seats were constructed of stone.

An altar to Dionysus, called the *themele*, was always located in the middle of each site. Later, some time during the fifth century B.C., a *skene* building, or scene house, was added. Its original purpose was to provide a place where the actors might dress and where they could wait before going on stage, but as time went on it began to be used as a background for the dramatic action. The theatre of Dionysus, the most famous Greek theatre, seated about 14,000 spectators.

The scene house still later became a two-story building with various openings on both stories. The second story was used for the appearance of the gods, while the doors below were for the protagonist and the other characters. One of the openings, the *thyromata*, framed action which occurred within the building. It is believed that the *thyromata* may have been the predecessor of our proscenium or picture-frame stage.

Since most of the action in Greek plays takes place out of doors, very little scenery was used. It is believed, however, that painted flats were sometimes leaned against the exterior walls of the scene house. Another later form of scenery was the *periaktoi*, or tall prisms with three sides on which different scenes were painted. These prisms, mounted on poles at each side of the stage, could be rotated to show the appropriate scenes. The paintings probably were simple, only suggesting changes rather than supplying realistic backgrounds.

Stage machinery was also used. One device, called simply the *mechane*, or machine, was a crane that raised and lowered the gods as they appeared in plays where the endings were contrived and gods intervened to solve human problems. Another piece of machinery, the *eccyclema*, a cart which rolled out of the *thyromata*, was used to carry the bodies of actors portraying warriors killed in battle. The Greeks, as mentioned, did not show violence on stage, but after the violence occurred, the wounded or dying might be brought before the audience.

The actors in the Greek theatre were highly respected. They were trusted as diplomats, were exempt from military service, and were considered servants of Dionysus. The Greek actor had to be skillful because he was expected to assume many different roles. For each role he wore a different mask. Every type of character that appeared in a Greek play had a specific mask. Thus it was easy for the audience to recognize a servant, a young woman, or an old man just by the mask he wore. This was particularly important because all the performers were men. The tragic actor also wore a high boot, or *cothurnus,* to give him added stature. It also is believed that most of the tragic characters wore *chitons,* or ankle-length embroidered robes. However, various other costumes were worn, too.

There are no recorded accounts, but it is believed that the Greek style of acting was very artificial by modern standards. The actors always moved in straight lines. If they wanted to turn, they would execute the movement with almost military precision. Every turn or gesture was angular. The arms were held straight, or bent only at the elbows. Part of the reason for this angularity was that the costumes were too heavy to allow graceful, curved movements. The delivery of the lines also would have sounded unnatural to our ears, since the masks included cone-shaped pieces, like small megaphones, in front of the mouth to project the sound. Since the early theatres were large, and the acoustics probably were not good, there could be no subtle changes in vocal inflection. The actors' movements and their rate of speaking were both slow.

Perhaps the most important contribution of the Greek theatre to that of our own era was the writings of a man who was neither a playwright nor an actor. His name was Aristotle, and his writings have influenced every major period of theatrical history from ancient Greek times to the present. In his book *The Poetics,* written in 350 B.C., he discussed the elements he considered important to drama. Drawing largely on the plays of Sophocles, he formulated rules for the writing of tragedy.

Although Greek comedy developed later than tragedy and was considered inferior to it, comedy was important to Greek citizens, who stressed the concept of "a well-balanced man in a well-balanced state." The Greeks felt that humor was important because man has a need to laugh as well as to cry in order to maintain a "well-balanced state."

Although Greek comedies were presented at the City Dionysia, they were given more support at one of the other festivals, the Lenaia. Choruses of twenty-four members were used, and often there were more individual actors than appeared in tragedies. The subject matter differed from that of tragedy. Comedy dealt with contemporary matters, and many times was not much more than political satire. The actor's costume usually consisted of a short *chiton* worn over tights. The chorus often represented animals, such as frogs or birds.

Although the comic plots were more complicated, there was actually less emphasis on plot than in tragedy, and more on the characters themselves. Rather than basing their stories on mythology, the playwrights invented their own plots. In essence, tragedy dealt with what man should be, while comedy dealt with what he actually is.

Comedy in ancient Greece is usually divided into two categories, Old and New. Old Comedy is characterized by its emphasis on an idea rather than on a cause-effect relationship of events. The plays have many episodes, which often seem unrelated to each other. However, they do build in comic intensity.

The major writer of Old Comedy was Aristophanes, who wrote about forty plays, eleven of which still exist. A few of these, *The Clouds, The Birds,*

Lysistrata, and *The Wasps,* are produced often today. Aristophanes lived from about 448 to 380 B.C.

New Comedy is associated with Menander, who lived from about 342 to 292 B.C. This form of comedy dealt with middle-class citizens because playwrights were no longer free to satirize their leaders. The characters were now more stereotyped. New Comedy was important because it provided the model for Roman comedy which was to follow. In the third century B.C., as the Romans began their conquest of Greece, they came into contact with its theatre. Thus, the classical theatre gradually changed and grew to suit Rome's own tastes and needs.

Roman Theatre

Drama in Rome stemmed directly from Greek drama and theatrical practice, via Sicily. Greek citizens who had settled on that island performed loosely improvised plays called mimes, which had begun in Greece in the sixth century B.C. These mimes, with their suggestive action and dialogue, sensational elements, and stereotyped characters, were imported into Rome in the third century. Like later forms of drama, they were presented as a part of the Roman games, the *ludi romani.*

The presentation of plays was not associated with the worship of a god. In fact, there was no real connection between plays and religion, although shrines to various gods often were part of the theatre buildings. Drama was presented strictly for entertainment, at first during festivals held only four times a year, but later on other occasions, such as military victories or the funerals of noted citizens. In addition to the plays, the festivals featured chariot races, gladiatorial displays, enactments of sea battles, boxing and public crucifixions. Slaves were forced to participate in gladiatorial battles to the death, often with the promise of freedom if they fought well and were victorious. Jugglers, acrobats, trained animal acts, and pantomimes in which dancing played the most important part could also be seen at the festivals.

At first the actors in the *ludi romani* were amateurs, but as time went on, professional companies were formed. The festivals were in charge of a magistrate and were financed in much the same way as they had been in Greece. The magistrate received aid from the state, but might contribute some of his own money. He then contracted with an acting company and a manager for the plays, which it is believed were bought outright from the writers. (In Greece the playwright often directed, and acted in, his own plays.) Several acting companies participated in each festival, and admission was free. It was back in Rome, centuries ago, that the practice of bribing audiences to applaud certain plays began. The reason was simple: in addition to receiving money for acting, the companies that were judged the best (i.e., received the most applause) were given prizes.

At first the Roman theatres were temporary structures, made of wood, with only a platform and a scene (Greek *skene*) building. Not until 55 B.C. was the first permanent theatre erected at Pompeii. Many such buildings then followed at various locations in the empire, each more elaborate than those preceding it. There were stone columns and arches and intricate statues and friezes. The buildings were often covered to protect the artistry as well as the actors.

The Roman theatres differed in many respects from those of Greece. First, rather than being constructed on a hillside, they were built on a level spot with stadium-type seating. The auditorium and orchestra area were semi-circular, and the stages were lower and deeper. The orchestra area was not used for scenes, but usually for the seating of distinguished members of the audience. The Roman theatre buildings were more of an architectural whole than were the theatres of Greece, the entire structure being composed of high walls. In this respect they resembled later indoor theatres in Europe, particularly since an awning was often stretched over the top. In some of the later theatres, the orchestra area was enclosed by a wall for gladiatorial contests, or flooded for the enactment of sea battles or water ballets. In some of the theatres there was a front curtain, which could either be dropped into the orchestra area or into slots. The stages had trapdoors for the shifting of properties.

Scenery for the comedies would show houses on a street. Some historians believe that a back curtain was used both as scenery and to mask the back-stage area, while others think that the scenery was three-dimensional. *Periaktoi* were used to indicate changes in location, since the same street scene was used for all comedy and a palace scene was used for all tragedy.

As the Roman theatre progressed, the actors began to lose prestige—in fact to be despised—because the troupes were generally composed of slaves under a manager. If these actors displeased the manager, they would be beaten or put to death. However, there are also records of citizens of wealth being actors. One of these was Roscius, who died in 62 B.C. As Rome's most famous actor, he was made a knight.

Roman actors, known as *histriones,* usually specialized in playing certain types of characters, although it is recorded that Roscius played in both comedy and tragedy. There is evidence that after the first century B.C. certain actors became stars and had a large following. The actors in both comedy and tragedy wore masks made of linen, with attached wigs, so that they covered the entire head. Mime actors, considered inferior to those playing in comedy and tragedy, did not wear masks, and their gestures were more animated than those of comic and tragic actors.

It is believed that the acting style of Rome was more improvisational in nature than that of Greece. The movements were broad and exaggerated because in large theatres many spectators could not discern small movements. Costumes for tragedy were similar to those worn by Greek actors. Costumes for comedy were Greek if the play was based on Greek life, or Roman if it dealt with everyday Roman life. Female roles were played by men, except in the mimes, and certain colors in costuming represented certain occupations. No chorus was used in Roman plays.

Along with several types of mimes presented in Rome was another very popular form, the Atellan farce, which is believed to have originated in the town of Atella, possibly in the marketplace. One of the oldest forms of Roman comedy, this was characterized by improvisation and stock characters, who included the braggart, the gluttonous fool, and the old miser—the model for Shakespeare's Shylock in *The Merchant of Venice* and Molière's Harpagon in *The Miser.* The plots consisted of ludicrous situations involving such things as drunkenness and trickery. Unlike the mime, the Atellan farce used no women in the cast. Early mimes were entirely improvised, but later ones were written. They were short and during the latter stages of their popularity became indecent and obscene.

It was during the First Punic War (264–241 B.C.) that the Romans became exposed to the drama of Greece and began importing Greek plays. In 240 B.C., Livius Andronicus produced at the Roman games the first Greek play which had been translated into Latin. Others followed. The performances began in the morning, and each play was finished by noon. New plays were usually presented at the festivals, but some were revived, especially comedies.

The first Roman dramatist of whom there is record and the first to adapt

Greek plays to Roman life, was Gnaeus Naevius, who lived from 270 to 201 B.C. He also wrote original plays and was most noted for his comedies.

Titus Maccius Plautus, Rome's first major playwright (254 to 184 B.C.), wrote a large number of comedies, twenty-one of which still exist. He borrowed his plots from Menander, the fourth-century Greek dramatist, but made some changes in adapting them. Two of his best-known works are *The Menaechmi* and *Amphitryon,* both of which deal with the complications of mistaken identity. Shakespeare based his *Comedy of Errors* on *The Menaechmi.* Plautus' plays differed from Greek comedies in that they did not satirize the government, since that practice was frowned upon by the leaders of Rome. Instead, they pointed up the idiosyncrasies of individual characters, often dealing with misunderstood motives and deceptions. A prologue outlined the plot for the audience.

The other Roman comic writer of major importance, though not as popular as Plautus, was Publius Terentius Afer, known as Terence (about 195 to 159 B.C.). His style was too literary to have a wide appeal. His dialogue, however, was written in the style of everyday conversation, and his plays showed a sympathetic treatment of character. A black slave who had lived in Athens, Terence wrote six plays, all of which survive. *The Brothers* is one of his better known works. He based his writings on the so-called New Comedy of Menander but attempted to improve the form and structure, often combining several Greek plays into one drama of his own. Each of the plays had a double plot, and they were more polished and more skillfully written than those of Plautus. In effect, Plautus wrote comedies of situation, while Terence wrote romantic comedies.

The only Roman tragedies still in existence were written by Lucius Anneus Seneca, who lived from 4 B.C. to 65 A.D., and were intended only to be read aloud, never performed. Nevertheless, Seneca exerted a great influence on the later development of drama, particularly during the Renaissance. Although all of his plays were adaptations of Greek tragedies, they differed markedly from their sources. Because they were written to be recited rather than produced, they contained much violence that would have been nearly impossible to present on the stage. They were characterized by elaborate speeches, soliloquies, asides, and sensationalism in general.

Although the drama of Rome is inferior to that of Greece, both its comedy and tragedy had a great influence in later historical periods. Almost all the rules for tragedy formulated in medieval Italy were based on the writings of Seneca, and Roman comedy led to the emergence of the *commedia dell'arte* troupes during the Renaissance.

After a time, written drama began to decline in Rome and was replaced by gladiatorial contests, mimes, poetry readings, mock sea battles, and dancing. After the fourth century A.D., largely because of the influence of the Christian Church, the theatre declined, existing only in a very limited way until the tenth century, when it once more began to gain popularity.

PROJECTS

1. Report on the acting style of the Greeks from the viewpoint of a modern drama critic. Or present a short section of a Greek play following the acting style of the Greeks.
2. Investigate the origins of the Greek comic and tragic masks (or make one out of papier-maché).

3. Costuming has always been important in the theatre. Prepare an illustrated report on Greek theatrical costumes (or make a typical costume of the period).
4. Compare or contrast a Greek or Roman theatre with a twentieth century theatre. You may want to make a model of a theatre to illustrate your report.
5. Investigate in depth Aristotle's theories of drama. Do you agree or disagree with his theories? Explain.
6. Choose a Greek play and trace its basis in mythology.
7. Investigate more fully the religious festivals of Greece or the festivals and games of Rome.
8. Prepare a report on the use of stage machines used in classical theatre (or construct a model of one).
9. Write and present a short scene in the style of a Greek dithyramb or choral reading.
10. Prepare a report showing the influence of Greek history on the plays of that era.
11. Report on the Roman Empire at the time of Plautus and Terence.
12. Read a Roman play. How does it reflect the state of society at the time it was written?

Sophocles lived during Greece's Golden Age.

Born in 496 B.C. in Colonus, a small village near Athens, Sophocles was the son of a merchant. He was well educated and a member of the best Athenian society. A handsome man, he is said to have had a good voice and to be an accomplished musician. Having shown an interest in drama at an early age, Sophocles was an actor until his voice became too weak to be heard in the Theatre of Dionysus, where all plays in Athens were given.

When he started writing, he patterned his plays after those of Aeschylus. He was twenty-eight years old when he won his first playwriting contest, defeating Aeschylus among others. Altogether Sophocles wrote more than a hundred plays and won more first prizes for his writing than any other Greek playwright, not to mention many second prizes. His seven surviving plays are *Ajax*, written in about 450 B.C.; *Antigone*, in about 442 B.C.; *Trachiniae*, in 409 B.C.; *Oedipus Rex*, in about 425 B.C.; *Electra* and *Philoctetes*, both in 409 B.C., and *Oedipus at Colonus*, written shortly before his death.

Sophocles lived during Greece's Golden Age, when Athens was the intellectual capital of the Western world. In 440 B.C., he was elected, for a year, to a board of ten generals, and it is believed he held other public offices, such as minister of finance. Sophocles' death in 406 B.C. came just two years before the fall of Athens to Sparta in the Peloponnesian War. His last play was written when he was about ninety years old.

Not only did Sophocles' plays embody the grandeur and attainment of his age, but they brought Greek drama to maturity. They are the epitome of tragic writing because they lift the audience's emotions. They affirm man's good, not his evil, and though they end in tragedy, they are not depressing. Sophocles was the playwright who carried Greek drama to its highest plane, removing it furthest from the mere ritual of Dionysiac worship.

Whereas the plays of Aeschylus show human beings as the puppets of the gods or victims of a preordained fate, in Sophocles' plays man rises above his fate. He himself has a large measure of control over his life. His own character and inner being cause him to act as he does. Because of this, the audience can identify with the tragic hero and can relate him to their own lives. We are interested in Oedipus or Antigone because they are human. They are real people who take action to solve their problems. It is this strong characterization that makes us feel with them. Rather than presenting a myth or a religious concept, Sophocles tries to have the audience discover the true nature of human beings, with all their complexities, thoughts, and emotions. In his plays we see how human error can bring about evil and suffering. Sophocles' tragic figure, always basically good and reasonable, falls only when he allows himself to be overcome by circumstance and abandons his reasoning faculties. Still, man rises above his fate. He has certain ideals, which he may violate in the course of the play but which he nevertheless continues to hold.

Because man is the master of his own fate, he is thus free. When the

11

audience sees man portrayed as basically good, they are able to see nobility in others, and therefore to feel a certain nobility in themselves. Although the tragic hero has involved himself in a course of action that will bring about his downfall, the audience does not feel depressed when he comes to a tragic end. Because he is noble, he must accept responsibility for his fate. In other words, Sophocles was a truly humanistic playwright. He loved order and moderation, and his characters uphold the ideal of "a well-balanced man in a well-balanced state".

Structurally, his plays are an improvement over earlier Greek drama for several reasons. His dialogue is more natural and concise. His plays follow a plot-line, which holds the audience's interest. He also uses extensively a third actor, allowing for a greater believability in characterization as well as providing more suspense and interest. Then, too, he cuts down on the use of the chorus, and includes more complications in the plot.

Oedipus Rex is Sophocles' best play. First of all, it is complete within itself. Unlike some of the earlier trilogies, which lead directly from one play into the next, *Oedipus Rex* includes in its structure everything that needs to be known in order to understand and appreciate it. Much of the exposition is woven into the play. Although it takes place in less than a day's time, we learn of all the preceding events which have caused the plague in Thebes. In other words, it meets nearly all the standards that Aristotle, the dramatic theorist, said were important for a play.

As a matter of fact, Aristotle based his theories of drama largely on *Oedipus Rex*. He said that a play must have a beginning, a middle, and an end. First of all, this means that the play must have a problem introduced at the beginning. Second, this problem must be developed, and last, before the ending, the problem must be resolved. Aristotle said the audience should experience a purging of the emotions of pity and fear—definitely a part of the story of Oedipus—and should feel exalted after the play has ended. If we see a production of the play, we pity Oedipus and suffer because of his downfall, but we know that his tragic end is the only possible outcome the play could have. The end is inevitable, but inevitable because of the hero himself and not because the gods ordained it. The play proceeds logically from the opening confrontation between Oedipus and the priest to Oedipus' blinding of his eyes.

The story on which Sophocles based his play was well known to the audiences of the time. Laius, the king of Thebes, who was Oedipus' father, was told in a prophecy that only if he had no children would his kingdom be saved from ruin. If he had children, he would die at the hand of his son, who would then marry Laius' wife, or the son's own mother. Laius was promised this fate as punishment for a sin he had earlier committed: kidnapping a boy.

King Laius and his wife, Queen Jocasta, did have a son, whom they quickly abandoned. The baby was found and then cared for by the king of Corinth, Polybus, and his wife Merope. When they discovered him, his feet were tied and thus injured, so he was given the name Oedipus, which means "swollen foot". As Oedipus grew older, he was teased because he did not resemble his "parents". Disturbed by this, he visited the oracle at Delphi, where he was told he would kill his father and marry his mother. To avoid this fate, he fled from Polybus and Merope and started toward Thebes. Along the way he met a stranger, really Laius, who ordered him out of the road. Oedipus became angry and killed Laius, thus bringing to pass the first part of the prophecy. Continuing on his way to Thebes, he had to pass the Sphinx, a creature that had the head of a woman, the body of a lion, the wings of an eagle, and the tail of a snake. The Sphinx had been refusing to let those pass who could not solve a riddle. If they failed to give the right answer, the creature devoured them. The riddle, was: What walks on four legs in the morning, two in the afternoon, and three in the evening? Oedipus solved it. The answer was "man", who in his infancy crawls, then walks, and then, in old age, uses a cane. Because he outwitted the Sphinx, Oedipus was offered the kingship of Thebes, which with Laius dead, now lacked a ruler. Along with receiving the kingdom, he was expected to marry the widowed Queen Jocasta. Then, by unknowingly marrying his own mother, he became an unclean person and a plague befell the city. This is where Sophocles' play opens, and only in the exposition throughout the play do we find out the events which brought about the plague.

The same myth had been dramatized by earlier playwrights, but there the story showed that the gods made Laius and his family suffer for Laius' sin. Sophocles' play, however, seems to state that the events are not preordained by the gods. The oracle only forsees what will happen to Oedipus because of the type of person he is—a person who would kill another in an argument. Also, Oedipus is free to pursue the goal of finding out who murdered the king or dropping the matter, even though there is a plague in Thebes. In other words, his character is responsible for Oedipus' destiny, and the gods are in the background.

If Oedipus had remained reasonable, he need not have suffered tragedy. He is reasonable in pursuing the facts of his father's murder, but unreasonable when he discovers what he himself has done unknowingly. If he had led an entire life of reason and moderation, his end would not have been tragic. He is the victim of his self-confidence and pride, and of his intensity. A strong person, he assumes responsibility for the entire city, and saves all the inhabitants from death by the plague.

The play is divided into a prologue and five episodes, each separated from the next by a choral passage. The prologue is largely expository, while each episode grows logically out of what has preceded it. The choral passages comment on what has already occurred and speculate about what will happen in the course of the play. The resolution scene is longer than any other and deals not so much with the discovery of the murderer, but with what Oedipus will do after he discovers the truth.

In the final scene, the audience feels most deeply for Oedipus, since now he is no longer the self-righteous ruler but only a concerned father who has been made an outcast. His blinding himself is logical in view of the high moral standards he has set for his life. Although he killed Laius unknowingly, he still assumes full responsibility for the murder of his father.

The action of the play begins with the problem of the plague and how it can be ended and goes on to the ultimate resolution and the blinding of Oedipus. There are no subplots. Thus, unity of action, considered of great importance by Aristotle, is maintained. There is unity of time, also recommended by Aristotle, in that the play takes place in less than one day. There also is unity of place, in that the action does not shift locale. Unity of place was not mentioned by Aristotle but was attributed to him in later periods of theatrical history, particularly during the Italian Renaissance.

Oedipus Rex is a simple and concentrated play. Its power lies in an integration of many elements, including its truly tragic hero, its unity, its subject matter, its dialogue, and its potential for audience identification. Thus it has survived as a nearly perfect example of tragedy.

Oedipus Rex

CHARACTERS

OEDIPUS   *King of Thebes*

A PRIEST OF ZEUS

CREON   *brother-in-law of Oedipus and Jocasta's brother*

TEIRESIAS   *blind prophet or seer of Thebes*

JOCASTA   *Queen of Thebes wife of Oedipus and widow of Laius, the former king*

A MESSENGER FROM CORINTH   *an old shepherd*

A SHEPHERD   *formerly a slave in the palace of Thebes*

A SERVANT FROM THE PALACE   *who acts as a second messenger*

CHORUS   *senators or elders of the Theban State*

NONSPEAKING CHARACTERS

SUPPLIANTS   *old men, youths, and children*

ANTIGONE   *daughters of Oedipus*

ISMENE   *and Jocasta*

ATTENDANTS, SERVANTS, SUPPLIANTS

14

Oedipus Rex

SCENE: *The royal palace of Thebes.*
In front of the columns, Suppliants *of various ages sit around the altars holding wreaths of branches.* Priests *stand among them, and at the main altar stands the most reverend of these, the* Priest of Zeus.[1] *And now* Oedipus, *King of Thebes, comes out majestically through the central door.*

OEDIPUS: Children, youngest brood of Cadmus the old,[2]
why do you sit here with branches in your hand
while the air is heavy with incense
and the town rings with prayer and lament?
Deeming it unfit to hear the reason from a messenger,
I, Oedipus, on whom men rely,
have come myself to hear you out.

(*Turning to the* Priest of Zeus)

Tell me, venerable priest of Zeus,
you who can speak for these,
what do you want or fear?
Be sure I shall gladly help,
for hard of heart would I be
to have no pity for such suppliants.

PRIEST: Oedipus, ruler of my land,
you see our generations at the altar—
the nestlings here too weak to fly far,
the priesthood bent with age,
and the chosen young.
The rest sit with branches in the market-place,
before the twin altars to Pallas,[3]
and by Ismenus[4] who answers with fire.
Our city—you yourself have seen!—
can no more lift prow out of the wave of death.
The blight lies on the blossom,
on the herds in pasture,
and on the women barren in labor.
The god who carries fire through the land,

[1] chief Greek god [2] legendary founder of Thebes [3] daughter of Zeus [4] an oracle

the ferocious plague,
swoops down to empty the home of Cadmus
while the Grave grows more opulent with our weeping.
We, these children and I, do not call you a god.
But you are first among men
in the common chances of men,
and even when the contest
is with more than man.
For you came to Thebes and lifted the toll
we paid to the songstress sphinx:
we could tell you nothing, and no one taught you;
yet you prevailed—with the help, we think, of a god.
Now, Oedipus, the greatest of mortals,
we supplicate you to be savior again,
whether with the help of some god who whispers to you
or by your own wisdom as a man;
for I have learned this thing—
when men have proved themselves by former deeds,
they also prevail in present counsel.
Best of mortals,
lift up our estate once more.
Live up to your noble fame,
for now the land you rescued
calls you Savior.
Never let us remember of your reign
that as high as we rose with you
so low we were cast down thereafter.
Oh no, raise up our fallen city,
that it fail no more,
and bring us good fortune again.

If you are to rule this land, as you rule it now,
surely it is better to be the lord of men
than of a waste;
nor walled town nor ship has any worth
when no men live in it.

OEDIPUS: Oh my poor children, known,
well known to me what brought you here!
I know you suffer,
and yet none among you can suffer as I:
Your pain comes to each one alone for himself,
and for none else, but I suffer for all:
for the city, for myself, and for you.
You do not rouse me, then, as one sunk in sleep;
be sure I have given many tears to this
and gone wide ways in the wandering of thought.
But the only recourse I knew I took:
I sent Menoeceus' son, Jocasta's brother,
to the Pythian house,[5] to hear from Apollo
by what word or deed I am to deliver you.
It troubles me to count the days Creon has been gone,

---

[5] the oracle Phoebus Apollo's palace at Delphi

but when he comes I am no man of worth
if I fail to perform what God has ordered.
PRIEST: In good season you have spoken, lord; your servants signal that
he is near.

(Oedipus *turns to see* Creon *approaching*)

OEDIPUS: Yes, and his face is bright.
O King Apollo, may the words he brings shine on us, too.
PRIEST: He brings good news; else he would not come
crowned with sprigs of bay.
OEDIPUS: He can hear me now: Prince and kinsman,
Menoecceus' son, what news from the God?

(Creon *approaches* Oedipus)

CREON: Favorable news.—For even trouble hard to bear
is well, all well, if the issue be good.
OEDIPUS: What says the oracle?
So far your words give us cause
for neither confidence nor despair.
CREON:—If you will hear me now, I am ready;
else let us go within.
OEDIPUS: No, speak before them,
for the grief I bear is most for them.
CREON: What the God has told I will then tell.
Phoebus, our lord, speaks plainly:
Drive out, he says, pollution,
defilement harbored in the land;
drive it out nor cherish it
until it prove past cure.
OEDIPUS: And by what rite?
CREON: Banish the guilty man, or let blood be shed
for bloodshed, since blood it is that brought
this storm of death upon the state.
OEDIPUS: Who is the man for whom God decrees doom?
CREON: King Laius was lord of Thebes before you held the helm—
OEDIPUS: I know of him by hearsay;
I never knew him.
CREON: He was slain.
The God commands punishment
for those who slew the King.
OEDIPUS: And where are they? Where shall be found
the dim trace of an ancient crime?
CREON: In this land, the God says.
What is sought can be found;
only unheeded things escape.
OEDIPUS: Was it in house, in field, or abroad
that Laius met death?
CREON: To Delphi he went who never came home.
OEDIPUS: Had he companions who witnessed the deed?
CREON: No, they perished, all but one
who fled; and of what he saw he had
but one thing to report as certain.

OEDIPUS: The one thing might be the means
to discover all; if but a small beginning were made—
    CREON: He said that many robbers fell on them;
the deed was not done by a single hand.
    OEDIPUS: And how could robbers dare so far
unless bribed by someone in the city?
    CREON: We thought of that, ourselves.
But Laius was dead, and our trouble,
our *other* trouble, distracted us.
    OEDIPUS: What trouble was so great to hinder your search
when royalty was slain?
    CREON: The riddling sphinx. It made us seek
an instant remedy for the instant thing
and let dark things go.
    OEDIPUS: Well, I will start afresh
and make dark things clear.
Right was Phoebus and right are you
to give this care to the dead man's cause,
and, as is meet, you shall find me
with you avenging country and God besides.
Not on behalf of one unknown but in my own interest,
as King, will I erase this stain,
for one who slew the old might slay the new;
I help myself in helping Laius.
Come, then, my children, rise from the altar-steps
and lift up your suppliant boughs,
and let the rest of Cadmus' seed be summoned here.
Say, nothing will be untried;
say, I will make a cleansing
and find for all Thebes, as God wills,
prosperity or grief.

(Oedipus *goes into the palace with* Creon)

PRIEST: My children, let us rise!
We came for this that the King promises,
and may God Phoebus, sender of the word, deliver us.

(The Chorus, *composed of the* Elders of Thebes, *now enters*)

CHORUS (1ST STROPHE):[6]   Oh, message of Zeus, whose words are sweet,
with what strange portent have you come
from the golden seat of Pytho[7]
to our glorious Theban home?
I am stretched as on the rack, and terror shakes me,
O Delian Healer,[8] to whom our pleas for help are sent,
and I stand in fear of what you may bring to pass:
new things unknown or doom renewed in the cycle of years.
Speak to me of golden hope,
Immortal Voice.

---

[6] a rhythmic system of verse used by the chorus   [7] Apollo   [8] Apollo

CHORUS (1ST ANTISTROPHE):[9]   I call upon you first, divine Athene, daughter
of Zeus!
Then on your sister Artemis,[10] the guardian of our land
who sits on her throne of fame
above the circled precinct of our market-place;
and on Phoebus, whose darts fly far.
Oh shine forth, averters of fate!
If ever before when destruction struck the state you came,
if ever you drove the fire of evil beyond our borders,
come to us now.
CHORUS (2ND STROPHE):   Numberless, alas, the griefs I bear,
the plague on all our host,
with no resource of mind a shield for our defense.
The fruit no longer sprung from the glorious land
and no woman rising relieved from birth-labor
by issue of a child.
And one by one you may see
flying away, like birds on swift wing,
life after life that hastens to the Evening Land.
CHORUS (2ND ANTISTROPHE):   By such unnumbered death the great town
perishes:
unpitied her children lie upon the ground, spreading pestilence,
while the young wives and gray-haired mothers
uplift a wailing, some here, some there,
bent over the altar-edge suppliant and moaning.
Prayer to God the Healer rises
but intermingled with lament.
O golden Daughter of Zeus,
send bright-faced deliverance.
CHORUS (3RD STROPHE):   And grant that Ares the Destroyer,[11]
who neither with brass shield nor clamor of war racks me,
may speed from our land to the caverns of Amphitrite[12]
below the wave
or to the Thracian sea where no haven is,
for whosoever escape the night
may find relief at last when the day-break comes.
O Zeus, Father, who wields the fire-fraught lightening,
destroy Death with your bolt.
CHORUS (3RD ANTISTROPHE):   Next, Lycean King, Apollo, I were glad too
that the arrows from your bow-string of woven gold
winged forth in their might to confound the foe.
Yes, and that the beams of fire
Artemis sends through the hills brought aid.
And I call the God
whose hair is bound with gold, flushed Bacchus[13] with Maenad[14] band,
to draw near with his torch and defeat
the god unhonored among the gods.

(Oedipus *returns*)

[9] the exact answering to the strophe   [10] sister of Apollo and goddess of the moon   [11] the war
god   [12] a sea nymph and wife of Poseidon, god of the sea   [13] another name for Dionysus
[14] women who worshipped Dionysus

OEDIPUS: You are at prayer, and in answer,
if you will heed my words
and minister to your own disease,
you may hope for help and win relief.
These words I say who have been a stranger
to your report and to the deed,
for I were not now on the track of it
without your aid.
But made a citizen among you after the deed,
I now proclaim to all of Thebes:
Whoever among you knows the murderer
at whose hand King Laius died,
I command he tell the truth.
For though he fear blame, I say,
exempt shall he be from punishment
and leave the land unhurt,
enduring no other harm.
Or if anyone know the assassin
to be alien, of a foreign state,
let him not be silent,
for I will pay him a reward
and favor him forever.

But if he hold back from fear,
attempt to screen another or himself,
give ear to what I intend:
I order that no one in this land I rule
give shelter or speak word to the murderer
whoever he be,
nor make him partner to a prayer or a sacrifice,
nor serve him with water for his hand
in lustral rite.[15]
And I command that the slayer
Whosoever he be,
whether he alone be guilty or had confederates,
evilly, as he is evil, wear out his life
unblest in misery.
And for myself I pray:
If knowingly I succor him
as inmate of my household,
let me too endure the curse invoked on you.

This charge I lay upon you:
Make good my words—
for my sake,
for the sake of the God,
and for the sake of the land
so blasted and barren under wrathful Heaven.
For even without ordinance from God,
it was not right to leave the guilt unpurged
when one so noble, your own king, was dead.

[15] purification

You must search it out!
And now, since I hold the power he once held,
possess his marriage bed and wife,
and since, had his hope of issue not miscarried,
he and I would have had children from one mother
and so been bound by more ties still,
except that Fate came heavy upon his head—
on this account I, as for my own father,
will leave nothing unattempted
to ferret our those who shed his blood.
I will fight for the scions of Labdacus[16] and Polydorus[17]
and for the earlier ancestors, Cadmus and Agenor[18] of old.
And for those who disobey me, I pray
the gods give them no harvest of earth and no fruit of the womb;
waste be their lot—and a destiny still more dire.
But you, the loyal men of Cadmus who my intent approve,
may Justice, our ally, and all the gods
forever proffer you their blessings.

    CHORUS: As you have put an oath upon me,
on oath, my King, I say:
I am not the slayer, nor knew him who slew.—
From Phoebus, himself, who set the quest, should come the answer.

    OEDIPUS: You speak well,
but against their will
no man has the power to constrain the gods.

    CHORUS: I would propose, if I may, a second course—

    OEDIPUS: and I should listen to a third course, too,
if it were proposed.

    CHORUS: Teiresias above all men
is known to see what Phoebus sees.
The clearest answer could come from him,
if one sought it.

    OEDIPUS: Not even this chance have I overlooked:
Advised by Creon, I have twice sent for the seer;
I am perturbed he has not come.

    CHORUS: There are other reports besides:
faint, fading rumors to explore.

    OEDIPUS: What rumors? I am ready to weigh every tale.

    CHORUS: Certain wayfarers, it was said, killed Laius.

    OEDIPUS: That, too, I heard,
but he who saw it is himself unseen.

    CHORUS: But if he has a grain of fear in his heart
he will step forth, knowing your curse.

    OEDIPUS: My words will not frighten a man
who was not afraid to perform the deed.

    CHORUS: Then there is one to expose him, and he comes:
Here they bring the godlike prophet
in whom truth lives.

    (Teiresias, *led by a* Boy, *arrives*)

---

[16] Laius' father [17] son of Cadmus [18] father of Cadmus

OEDIPUS: Teiresias, whose mind can search all things,
the utterable and the unutterable alike,
secret of heaven and what lies on earth,
though you cannot see, you must know how the plague
afflicts the land.
Our prophet, in you alone we find a protector,
the only savior.
Perhaps you have not been told,
but Phoebus, when consulted, declared
we must discover the slayers of Laius
and slay or drive them out.
Do not, then, spare augury of birds
or any other form of divination you possess
to save yourself and the state,
and to save me and all who are defiled by the deed.
Man's noblest deed is to bring aid by what means he has,
and you alone can help.
   TEIRESIAS: O fate! How terrible it is to know
When nothing good can come of knowing.
I knew of the matter but it slipped out of mind;
else I would not have come.
   OEDIPUS: What now? How can you regret your coming?
   TEIRESIAS: Let me go home. You will bear your burden easier then,
and I mine, too.
   OEDIPUS: What! You have not spoken loyally or kindly,
giving no answer with strange words.
   TEIRESIAS: Because your own words miss the mark,
do not expect mine to hit it safely.
   OEDIPUS: For the love of God, if you know,
do not turn away.
We bend before you; we are your suppliants.
   TEIRESIAS: You ask only because you know nothing.
I will not reveal my grief—I call it mine, not yours.
   OEDIPUS: What do you know and refuse to tell?
You are a traitor if you allow the state to be destroyed.
   TEIRESIAS: Since I want no harm for you or myself,
why do you ask vain questions?
I will tell you nothing.
   OEDIPUS: Worst of traitors,
you would rouse a stone to wrath!
Will you never speak out, be stirred by nothing,
be obstinate to the end?
   TEIRESIAS: You see the fault in me but not in yourself.
So it is me you blame?
   OEDIPUS: Who would not take offense
hearing you flout the city?
   TEIRESIAS: It will come of itself—
the thing that must,
although I breathe no word.
   OEDIPUS: Since it must come,
surely you can tell me what it is!
   TEIRESIAS: I say no more. Storm at me if you will, you'll hear no more.
   OEDIPUS: And being in such anger, I, for my part,
will hold back nothing, be sure.

I'll speak my thought:
Know then I suspect you of having plotted the deed yourself
and of having done it
short of killing with own hand;
and if you had eyesight,
I would declare the doing too your own.
    TEIRESIAS: Was it so?
Well then I charge you to abide by your own decree
and from this day on speak neither to me nor them,
being *yourself* the defiler of the land.
    OEDIPUS: So this is your taunt!
And you expect to go scot-free?
    TEIRESIAS: I *am* free,
for the truth has made me so.
    OEDIPUS: Tell me at least who is in league with you?
For surely this lie was not of your own making!
    TEIRESIAS: Yours is the blame,
who spurred me on to speak against my will.
    OEDIPUS: Speak again:
Perhaps I did not understand you.
    TEIRESIAS: Did you not understand at first hearing?
Or are you bent on provoking me again?
    OEDIPUS: No, I did not grasp your meaning.
Speak again!
    TEIRESIAS: I say that *you* are the murderer—
he whom you seek.
    OEDIPUS: Now at last, now you have spoken twice,
you shall rue your words.
    TEIRESIAS: Shall I speak on
and incense you more?
    OEDIPUS: Say what you will; it will be said in vain.
    TEIRESIAS: I say, then, you have lived in unsuspected shame
with one who is your nearest,
and you do not yet see the plight you are in.
    OEDIPUS: And you expect to go on ranting
without smarting for it?
    TEIRESIAS: Yes, certainly, if there is strength in truth.
    OEDIPUS: Why, so there is—
except for you; you have no truth,
blind as you are in ears, in mind—and eyes.
    TEIRESIAS: Wretched man,
you utter taunts that everyone will soon heap
upon none other than yourself.
    OEDIPUS: Night, an endless night is your prison;
you cannot hurt me or any man who can see the sun.
    TEIRESIAS: No, it is not your doom to be hurt by me;
Apollo's is the work ahead,
and Apollo's work is enough.
    OEDIPUS: Are these inventions yours or Creon's?
    TEIRESIAS: Creon is not your enemy;
you are your own foe.
    OEDIPUS: Oh riches and dominion and the craft
surpassing others' craft in an envied life,
how deep is the souce of jealousy

if for the sake of the power the city put into my hand,
a gift unsought by me.
Trusty Creon, my old friend, creeps by stealth upon me,
seeks to unseat me,
and has suborned this quack and scheming juggler
who has an eye only for gain but whose divining skill is blind!

Yes, blind, I say:
For tell me, my prophet, when have you ever seen clear?
Where was your deliverance when the monster-woman wove dark song?
Surely the unriddling of the riddle
was not for a chance traveler like me
but for you with your skill of divination!
Yet no help came from you, neither from watching the flight of birds
nor talking to any god.

No, I came,
I the ignorant who had no miraculous aid.
I, by my own wit, made answer, untaught of birds,
and I stopped the monster's breath.
And now it is me you would thrust out,
thinking to stand by Creon's side when he takes the throne.
But I think you will regret your proffered purge for the land,
you and that other plotter;
and, dotard, you would have been punished already
if I had no regard for age however arrogant.

   CHORUS: O, Oedipus, to our mind,
both this man's words and your own
have been spoken in anger.
Our need is not for these recriminations,
but for guidance on how best to abide by God's command.

   TEIRESIAS: King though you be,
the right of reply, at least, belongs to us both;
I am your peer,
for I am Apollo's servant, not yours.
Now will you find me in Creon's service.
And I tell you, who have taunted me with blindness,
you that have sight
do not see your plight, where you dwell,
and with whom.
You do not even know what stock you came from,
nor that, unknowing, you have been
foe to your own kin
both above the earth
and below, among the shades.[19]
You, the double curse of mother and father,
shall leave your land one day in painful haste
with darkness on the eyes that now see so straight.

And what are the places that shall not hear your cry,
what Cithaeron-crag shall not resound with it soon,
when you have learned what marriage-song

---

[19] Hades

wafted you on a fair voyage to a foul haven
in your own house!
What multitudinous evils you cannot guess
shall level you down to yourself
and to your own brood of children!
So heap all your scorn on Creon and my words,
but know this: no man shall be crushed
more utterly than you.
    OEDIPUS: Is this to be endured? Go quickly,
and my curse go with you.
Back from these walls of my home,
back to your own.
    TEIRESIAS: I should never have come had you not sent for me.
    OEDIPUS: You would have waited long to be called
if I had known you for a fool.
    TEIRESIAS: Yes, I am a fool to you
whose parents thought me wise.
    OEDIPUS: Parents, you say? Don't go!
Who were they? Who gave me birth?
    TEIRESIAS: This day shall give you both birth and ruin.
    OEDIPUS: Riddles, always riddles! You darken everything.
    TEIRESIAS: Does that disturb you
who were so adept at unriddling?
    OEDIPUS: Yes, cast it in my teeth,
that which lifted me high—
    TEIRESIAS: —and will soon bring you low!
Your fortune, Oedipus, has been your misfortune.
    OEDIPUS: If misfortune must befall me
for having saved the city,
I say I do not care.
    TEIRESIAS: Well, I will go then.
You, boy, lead me home.
    OEDIPUS: Yes, let him take you out of my sight.
Here you are only a hindrance and a trouble,
and when you are gone you will vex me no more.
    TEIRESIAS: I will go, having said what I came to say,
and not because I fear your anger, for you possess
no power to destroy me. But I tell you this now, King:
The man you have sought with threats and proclamation,
that man is here!
Believed to be of foreign birth, he shall soon be found
Theban-born, and he shall take no joy in the discovery.
Blind, he who still has sight,
a beggar, he who is still wealthy,
he shall turn his face toward an alien land,
tapping the ground before him with a staff.
And he shall be found at once
brother and father to the children in his house,
son and husband to the woman who bore him,
and fellow-sower in the bed of his father,
who he slew.
Go into your palace and ponder upon all this—
and if I am proved wrong,
henceforth say that I have no skill in prophecy.

(Teiresias departs, led by the Boy, while Oedipus goes into the palace)

CHORUS (1ST STROPHE):   Who is he whom the divine voice of the Delian rock
has pronounced guilty with red hands,
perpetrator of horrors no tongue dare name?
Now is his time to run faster than steeds that gallop with the wind.
For upon him leaps the son of Zeus,
armed with flame of lightning
and followed by the dread unerring Fates
that never tire in pursuit.

CHORUS (1ST ANTISTROPHE):   For a word but now blazed from snow-covered Parnassus[20]
orders us to look for the unknown man who,
hidden in the wild-grown forest, slinks or roams,
fierce as a bull and forlorn, on a joyless path
through cave and crag to avoid
the doom pronounced at earth's central seat.
Yet that never-ending doom continues to follow and to beat wings
over him in pursuit.

CHORUS (2ND STROPHE):   In truth I am in dread with darkest thought
aroused by the seer, the wise,
though I cannot approve or deny what he said.
I do not know what to say,
but I am uneasy with foreboding,
having no clear vision in the present or into the future.
For never in past years or now did I hear
the house of Labdacus had reason
to fear hurt from a son of Polybus
that I should arraign the good repute of Oedipus
to avenge the line of Labdacus for an unknown crime.

CHORUS (2ND ANTISTROPHE):   True, Zeus indeed and Apollo are wise
and know the things of human concern,
but that a mere mortal man, though he be a seer,
can have certain knowledge above mine—
of this there is no clear proof.
One man may surpass another in wisdom,
yet until I see the prophet's word proved true
never will I agree when Oedipus is blamed;
for once the winged maiden[21] came against him
and he showed himself wise by the test and good to the state.
So never shall verdict of mine turn against him to accuse him of crime.

(Creon appears and addresses the Chorus)

CREON: My fellow-citizens, having heard that Oedipus makes a charge
against me that is vile, I come here indignant:
if in the present trouble he believes he was wronged

[20] sacred mountain near the oracle of Delphi   [21] sphinx

by me in some word or action,
then I willingly forego my term of years to come
rather than bear this blame.
For the rumor, having spread, wrongs me in all respects
if I am considered a traitor by the populace,
by you and by all friends.

CHORUS: The reproach came, we think, under the stress of anger,
not from the heart.

CREON: Has it not been said that I counseled the seer to
deliver falsehoods?

CHORUS: So it was said, though I cannot understand to what
purpose.

CREON: Did the king make his charge directly,
with steady eyes and a steadfast mind?

CHORUS: That I could not tell; it is my rule not to look closely
at what my masters do. But here he is,
the lord of the house.

(Oedipus *comes out, in a rage*)

OEDIPUS: So, you have come with a bold face to my house
who would make yourself assassin of its master
and brazen pilferer of his crown?
Come, tell me, in the name of all the gods,
what cowardice or dotage you found in Oedipus
that you dared to lay a plot against him.
How could you believe I would fail to notice
your creeping upon me by stealth
or, discovering your designs, I would not defend myself?
Now was it not folly, this attempt of yours,
without a following, without a troop of friends, to seize the throne?
It is a thing to be achieved, as you ought to know,
with followers and with support of wealth.

CREON: I beg you fairly to hear a fair reply and then decide.

OEDIPUS: Are you so quick, then, to explain? You should be forewarned.
I shall be slow to understand you;
I have found you a malignant enemy.

CREON: But hear my explanation—

OEDIPUS: Explain but this—this one thing:
Tell me you are not a villain.

CREON: You are not wise if you believe
unreasoning obstinacy is good.

OEDIPUS: And you are not sane if you believe
kinsmen who wrong kinsmen are not punished.

CREON: What you say is just, of course,
but what is my offense?

OEDIPUS: Did you or did you not advise me
to send for the canting prophet?

CREON: Yes, and I still believe I did right.

OEDIPUS: How long ago is it since Laius—

CREON: —Since Laius . . . ? I do not understand—

OEDIPUS: —disappeared from men's sight by violence?

CREON: The count of years goes far into the past.

OEDIPUS: This seer of yours, did he practice his craft
even then?
CREON: Yes, He was honored, as he is now.
OEDIPUS: Did he mention me at that time even once?
CREON: He did not. Never, certainly, in my presence.
OEDIPUS: And you never searched for the man who died?
CREON: We searched, of course; we discovered nothing.
OEDIPUS: Why did not this wise seer tell his story then?
CREON: It is not my wont to speak of things I do not know.
OEDIPUS: This much at least you know and will declare if
you are wise—
CREON: What? If I know, I will make no denial.
OEDIPUS: That if he had not conspired with you,
he would never have declared the King was slain by *me*!
CREON: You must know best whether this was said by him;
but here I require enlightenment of you as you have required of me.
OEDIPUS: Learn this then:
Never shall I be found guilty of the blood of Laius.
CREON: Learn this then!
You have my sister to wife?
OEDIPUS: That there is no denying.
CREON: And she has equal rights with you in the state?
OEDIPUS: Yes, and she obtains everything she desires.
CREON: And I as a third owner of the land, am I not the
equal of you two?
OEDIPUS: Ah!—and there, in that thought, appears the
falseness of your friendship!
CREON: Not if you reason with yourself as I reason!
Weigh this first:
Would I rather choose burdensome sovereignty like yours
and be uneasy with fear
than equal power but power shared in untroubled peace?
I am not by nature covetous of kingly rule
but only of kingly worth, as befits a sober mind.

At present I have all needful things from you and none of your anxieties.
But were I the ruler of the city, as you are now,
I should have to do many things against my inclination.
How would a throne, then, be pleasanter to me
than painless sovereignty?
I am not yet so bemused to want honors that afford no profit.
Every man is my friend now. He greets me,
and wishes me well. And whosoever has a boon to ask of you
first he speaks with me to favor his cause.
Why, then, should I exchange my life for yours?
I should have to take leave of sense to want to dethrone you;
I have no love for such designs at all,
nor could I bear to act with one who plotted them.
And for proof of this, first, go to Delphi
and inquire if I did not report the oracle
as it was given.
Next, if you discover I plotted with the seer,
seize me and slay me,—
and do this, not with your sentence alone,

but with mine, here given.
But do not place guilt on me by conjecture,
lacking all proof.
It is not just to judge a bad man good
and a good man bad;
and to cast away a friend is like throwing away
one's own life, which one values most.
Ah well! only in time will you learn this thing,
for time alone reveals the honest man
while a single day is long enough to disclose the knave.
    CHORUS: His words ring true, my King.
Quick judgment is unsafe.
    OEDIPUS: Quick? When a plotter moves against me
I must be quick with counterplot;
if I delay until he acts, he gains his ends
and I miss mine.
    CREON: What is it, then, you want?
To expel me from my country?
    OEDIPUS: By no means:
I want your death, not banishment;
to teach the world what danger there is in jealousy.
    CREON: You speak as one resolved to believe nothing.
    OEDIPUS: Because you deserve no belief.
    CREON: You talk as one bereft of sense.
    OEDIPUS: I have sense enough where my interest lies.
    CREON: You should consider my interest too.
    OEDIPUS: Never! You are false.
    CREON: But if your judgment is mistaken?
    OEDIPUS: Be that as it may, I must remain the ruler of this city.
    CREON: But not if you rule wrongly.
    OEDIPUS: This city is my city!
    CREON: Yours only? The city is mine too.
    CHORUS: Have done, my lords, have done!
Here is Jocasta in good time; I see her coming
whose voice will compose your quarrel.

    (Jocasta *arrives*)

    JOCASTA: Misguided men, for shame,
what has stirred up trouble among you
with strife of tongues while the land is so afflicted?

    (*To* Oedipus)

Come into the palace,
and you, Creon, go home, go home;
push no mere nothing into a calamity.
    CREON: Sister, your Oedipus threatens me:
he has only to decide whether to drive me from the city or kill me!
    OEDIPUS: That is true! For I have found him out, finding him
conspiring against my person.
    CREON: May I never know happiness and die accursed by God
if there is any truth in what you charge against me!

JOCASTA:　Oedipus, in Heaven's name believe him,
first for the awful oath he has sworn by the gods,
and next for my sake and for the sake of all these men.

CHORUS:　Hear her, our King. With wisdom reflect upon this
and be gracious, we pray you. Grant it.

OEDIPUS:　What shall I grant?

CHORUS:　Accept his word; he was never before found in folly,
and his oath is a weighty one.

OEDIPUS:　Do you know what you ask?

CHORUS:　Yes.

OEDIPUS:　Declare it then.

CHORUS:　Use no unproved conjecture against the man
who has been your friend and who has given his oath.

OEDIPUS:　Then be very sure you know that in asking this
you call destruction or exile upon myself.

CHORUS:　Oh no! By God the Sun, who stands
foremost in the heavens.
unblessed and accursed may I be,
cast in utter darkness, my lord,
if I have any such thought!
But the withering of the land wears down my unhappy heart
and this new trouble, strife between you,
is too heavy to bear.

OEDIPUS:　Then let him go free,
though his freedom work my death or my doom
to be thrust out dishonored from Thebes.
Your lips, not his, have moved me to compassion.
But wherever he is he shall still have my hatred.

CREON:　How sullen you are in yielding
and vehement in temper when moved!
Such natures are, not without justice,
the heaviest burden to themselves.

OEDIPUS:　Will you not leave in peace and go away!

CREON:　I will; but though you misjudge me, these men know
I am innocent.

(Creon *leaves*. Oedipus *stands shaken with rage*)

CHORUS:　O Lady, will you take him within?

JOCASTA:　I will when I have learned what chanced.

CHORUS:　A blind conjecture arose on one side,
bred of rash words;
and on the other side, the sting of injustice
brough strife.

JOCASTA:　So both sides were wrong?

CHORUS:　We think so.

JOCASTA:　What was the story that started this?

CHORUS:　Enough, enough!
Let it rest, now it has ended;
our land is vexed enough without it.

OEDIPUS:　But do you see where your good purpose
has now carried you in blunting my anger?

CHORUS: King, I have said this before, and I say again:
I should be a madman, devoid of counsel, to put away
the man who steered a good course in my country's trouble
and who shall yet, my God grant it, lead us again to safety.
JOCASTA: In the name of the gods,
husband, I beg of you, what was the tale?
What put you in a rage? Tell me.
OEDIPUS: I will; I honor you more than I honor them:
Creon has laid a plot against me.
JOCASTA: Husband, be plainer—
OEDIPUS: He declares I am guilty of the blood of Laius.
JOCASTA: So? Did he say he heard it,
or does he claim to know it himself?
OEDIPUS: Neither: *He* keeps his own mouth unsoiled;
he made the rogue of a seer his mouthpiece.
JOCASTA: If that is all, prepare yourself to put it out of mind
at once. Listen to me and learn
that no one born of woman is capable of divination—
as I myself discovered:

To Laius once came an oracle—
I will not say directly from Apollo,
but from his ministers—
that he should die by the hand of a son
born of him and me.
But you must know that Laius, as reported,
was waylaid by robbers
where three highways meet,
and our child, who should have slain him,
if the oracle was true,
was barely three days old when Laius
pinned its ankles together
and had it cast out by servants
on a pathless mountain.
So Apollo did not bring it to pass
that the child should be the slayer of the man
and that Laius should suffer
the thing he dreaded—
death from the hand of the son.
The oracle was clear, yet was proven false, as you see.
So much then for the power of the seers!
What God desires us to know,
be sure he will reveal it himself.
OEDIPUS: Oh wife, wife!
you cannot know what your report has done to me.
What anguish—
JOCASTA: What disturbs you now?
OEDIPUS: I thought I heard you say
Laius was slain where three roads meet—
JOCASTA: Yes, so the report went and so it goes still.
OEDIPUS: And where is this place, Jocasta?
JOCASTA: In Phocis
Two roads, one from Delphi and one from Daulia, meet.
OEDIPUS: How long ago did all this happen?

JOCASTA: The news was brought to the city
a short time before you became the king.
OEDIPUS: O Zeus! what fate have you stored up for me?
JOCASTA: What is troubling you?
OEDIPUS: No! No questions yet! Tell me only
what sort of man was he? How tall was Laius?
How old?
JOCASTA: He was no longer young—his hair was turning white,
and he was tall, his figure not unlike your own.
OEDIPUS: I am a miserable man.
An ignorant man, Jocasta, I fear
I have laid myself under my own curse.
JOCASTA: You terrify me, Oedipus. What are you saying?
OEDIPUS: I have a misgiving the seer can see. Just that!
But you can make something plainer. Tell me—
JOCASTA: What? Something makes me tremble,
yet I must answer.
OEDIPUS: Did Laius have few attendants,
or did he travel with a host, as a prince should?
JOCASTA: There were five of them, one a herald;
there was one carriage, for the King.
OEDIPUS: All plain—too plain!
Who told you this, Jocasta?
JOCASTA: The survivor who returned alone. A servant.
OEDIPUS;   Is he still in service?
JOCASTA: No longer. When he found you king here on his return
in the place of Laius,
he touched my hand and petitioned me
to send him to the fields to pasture flocks.
He asked it as one who found himself ill at ease
in the city and would be far from it.
He deserved more than this consideration,
for, as slaves go, he was a worthy man.
I could not refuse his request.
OEDIPUS: If only we could have him back here quickly!
JOCASTA: He can be brought,
but why do you wish to see him?
OEDIPUS: I fear, Jocasta, I have already said too much;
I must see him first.
JOCASTA: He shall come, then.
But unburden your heart to me first;
I deserve your confidence.
OEDIPUS: I shall not keep anything from you
since my forebodings have carried me so far.
In whom should I confide more,
passing through such a peril,
than you, my wife, who are dear to me?

My father, as you know, was Polybus of Corinth,
my mother, Merope, the Dorian,
and I was counted the first in the city.
Then something occurred—a startling thing,
although it should not have put me into such a passion:

At the banquetboard, a man in his cups[22]
said I was no true son of my mother and father.
For all my fury I checked my temper,
but the morning after, I went to my parents
and taxed them with it.
Their anger at the fellow who flung the taunt
was so great that I felt reassured;
yet the thing still galled me, for the rumor crept on.
So, unknown to father and mother, I went to Delphi.
Phoebus, it is true, left dark what I came to know,
but his answer was full of other things terrible to hear;
I was fated, he said, to defile my mother's bed
and bring forth a progeny intolerable to the light,
and to be my natural father's slayer, too.

So, having heard, I put Corinth far behind me,
thereafter measuring the way where the city lies
by the stars only,
seeking a place where I could never expect
the foretold infamies to be fulfilled.
But as I journeyed on
I found myself upon the very spot where, you say, Laius perished.

Worse still, when I was near those three roads,
I saw a herald advancing and a man in a carriage drawn by colts;
and both, the man in front and the old man,
wanted to edge me rudely off the road.
Enraged, I struck the man who thrust me aside,
whereupon the seated elder, biding time as I passed him,
leaned out and brought his goad[23] with two toothpoints
down hard on my head.
I repaid the blow at once,
striking him with my staff so hard that with one stroke
I rolled him out of the carriage into the road;
and then with my sword I struck down every man of them.
So, if there is reason to connect this nameless man with Laius,
you see before you a man more miserable than any man before,
For, then, what man could be more hated by the gods?—
a man whom no citizen and no stranger in Thebes may receive,
whom no man may welcome but must drive out of doors.
And none other than I, laid this curse on myself.

And hear me once more: If this is so,
with the hands that slew I pollute the bed
of him who was slain.
Am I not then loathsome and all unclean?

And think of it, it was only to be driven out of Thebes
that I had to flee before
in self-banishment, forsake my own people,

[22] man who is drunk   [23] pointed rod used to urge on animals

and never set foot again in Corinth my native city
lest I be fated to be yoked with my mother
and kill my father, the good Polybus who begot and reared me.

Would not a man then speak correctly who in judging of this said
that a god of evil is my enemy?
Never, you pure and sacred majesties of Heaven, never
may I behold that day. Let me pass out of men's sight
before I see myself brought low by a destiny so vile.

CHORUS: We, too, are fearful, Prince. Yet do not lose hope.
Await the man who saw the deed and can reveal all.

OEDIPUS: Yes, I still hold on to hope until he arrives.

JOCASTA: (*Troubled*) And when—when he appears,
what will you ask him?

OEDIPUS: I will tell you:
If his tale will tally with yours
I am clear at least of *this* disaster.

JOCASTA: How so? What did you hear me say
that must tally?

OEDIPUS: You were saying that he spoke of *robbers*.
Why, then, if he still speaks of several men,
I am not the slayer!
One is not the same as *many*.
But if he speaks of one man traveling alone,
then veritably the guilt leans toward me.

JOCASTA: Of this be assured at least,
so the tale was told by him; he cannot revoke it
when the city, not I alone, heard him tell it so.
Yet even if he shifts from it, of this be sure—
he cannot make the death of Laius square with the prophecy.
Plain were Apollo's words:
Laius was to be slain by a son born of me.
And, after all, the poor thing never killed him
but died itself before! So henceforth
I do not mean to look to left or right
for fear of divination.

OEDIPUS: You have reassured me, I think; yet send for the
slave, I pray you.
See that it is done.

JOCASTA: Since you desire this,
I will send someone quickly, to please you, as in everything.
And now let us go within.

(Oedipus *and* Jocasta *go into the palace*)

CHORUS (1ST STROPHE): Mine be a way of life that keeps
the holy purity of word and deed,
prescription of the laws that are sublime,
born in the regions of the sky,
whose only begetter is Olympian Zeus.

No mortal begot the laws
and no forgetfulness shall put them to sleep.

Ever-wakeful, the God lives great in them,
and He never grows old.

    CHORUS (1ST ANTISTROPHE):   Pride begets the tyrant,
and Insolence, puffed with vain wealth,
climbs and climbs to the topmost height
only to be flung down to horrible doom
where no foothold serves.
Only ambition that serves the whole state
is ever worthy and propitious,
and only rivalry that benefits all may God,
our defender, never quell.

    CHORUS (2ND STROPHE):   But may an evil fate afflict
him who in ill-starred pride
proceeds with his arrogance by word or deed,
despising Justice
and the holy images of God.
May he be doomed
who seeks an advantage unfairly
and does not abstain from unholiness,
profaning inviolable things.

When such things are done what mortal may boast
he shall ward off the shafts of God from his life?
When such behavior is honored,
why, then, should we keep our sacred dance?

    CHORUS (2ND ANTISTROPHE):   Never to the inviolate hearth
at the navel of the world,
nor to Abae's shrine or Olympia
will I go in prayer,
if the oracles are proved untrue
for each man's finger to point at with scorn.
No, Zeus, if you are rightly called King
of the world, let not this issue
leave your ever-deathless hands.

For already men set at nought
the old prophecy for Laius, now faded,
and nowhere does Apollo receive his due honor:
Worship vanishes from the earth.

    (Jocasta *comes out of the palace with* Attendants)

    JOCASTA: Princes of the land, it occurred to me
to visit the temples of the deities,
bringing in my hand these garlands and this incense.
For Oedipus lends his mind too much to alarms,
nor, like a sober person, measures
a new conjecture by past experience,
but is at the mercy of whoever speaks to him
of terrors at hand. I can do nothing with him.
So to Apollo I mean to go,
to you, Lycean God, to us the nearest,
a suppliant with offerings,
that you afford us some deliverance.

For now we are all frightened, seeing him, Oedipus,
helmsman of our ship, in fright.

(A Messenger *appears*)

MESSENGER: Strangers, may I learn of you, where is the palace
of Oedipus the King? or better, where
is he himself, if you know?
AN ELDER OF THE CHORUS: Stranger, this is his dwelling
and he is within;
and this lady is the mother of his children.
MESSENGER: May she be blessed in a happy home
since she is his queen.
JOCASTA: May you be blessed too for the kind greeting.
Say what you have to seek or tell.
MESSENGER: Good news, my lady, to your house and husband.
JOCASTA: What is your news? And from whom have you come?
MESSENGER: From Corinth. What I am to say
will please you, if not without some pain.
JOCASTA: What can this mean, a double-faced report?
MESSENGER: The people of the Isthmus, the Corinthians,
intend to make him king.
JOCASTA: What! Does not Polybus, the old king, still rule?
MESSENGER: No longer; he is death's subject in the pit.
JOCASTA: The father of Oedipus is dead?
MESSENGER: May I be reft[24] of life myself if my report is untrue.
JOCASTA: (*To an* Attendant) Run, girl; tell your master
instantly.

(The Attendant *goes into the palace*)

O oracles of the gods, where are you now?
Oedipus fled long since from the man's presence,
fearing to become his murderer, and instead
the man has died a natural death; he was not killed by Oedipus.

(Oedipus *appears*)

OEDIPUS: (*Anxiously*) Jocasta, dear wife, why have you sent
for me?
JOCASTA: To hear this man speak.
And as you listen, mark well to what a pass
your dark oracles have come.
OEDIPUS: Who is this? And what does he say?
JOCASTA: He comes from Corinth
to report that Polybus, your father, is gone.
OEDIPUS: Is this true? Stranger,
let me have your news from your own mouth!
MESSENGER: To make the report plainer,
I tell you, King, that our king is dead.

[24] robbed

OEDIPUS: Oh! Did he die by traitorous assault or by illness?
MESSENGER: A light thing in the scale of life
brings the old to their rest.
OEDIPUS: Then he died, it seems, of illness.
MESSENGER: Yes, and of the long years he had lived.
OEDIPUS: (*Triumphantly*) Oh, oh! Why should one look to the hearth of
Pytho
and to the birds that scream overhead
on whose showing I was to slay my father?
He is dead and already under earth,
and I have been here, not there, and have not put my hand to the spear.—
Unless he died through longing
and in this sense is dead because of me.
So Polybus is gone,
and all those oracles as they stood
have been alid to rest with him in Hades,
and have been proved of no account.
JOCASTA: Did I not foretell all this?
OEDIPUS: You did, but my fear led me astray.
JOCASTA: And so let none of these predictions weigh you
down further.
OEDIPUS: Yet—yet how can I help still dreading my mother's bed?
JOCASTA: Now, why should a man be so fearful
when he knows that Chance rules everything
and man foreknows nothing on earth?
To have a carefree mind is therefore best.
As for that mother marriage-bed—
have no fear of it, my dear.
Many men before have dreamed of such a marriage,
but he who gives no weight to these fantasies
is most at ease in his life.
OEDIPUS: All that you say would be well
if my mother were not living. But since she is alive
I have reason for my fears.
JOCASTA: Your father's death—does not this allay them?
OEDIPUS: But my fear concerns the living.
MESSENGER: (*Puzzled*) Who is this, the woman you dread?
OEDIPUS: Merope, old man, the consort of Polybus.
MESSENGER: But what disturbs you?
OEDIPUS: ˙An oracle from the gods, appalling in import.
MESSENGER: May it be told?
Or is it unlawful for another to know?
OEDIPUS: I may tell it.
The gods declared that I should marry my mother,
and with my own hands shed the blood of my father.
Corinth, my home, has not seen me for no other reason:
I have won great happiness here,
yet, you know, it is sweet to see the face of one's parents.
MESSENGER: This, then, was the fear that kept you away?
OEDIPUS: Old man, I did not want to slay my father!
MESSENGER: Why should I not then free you of this fear, my King,
since my coming here was well meant?
OEDIPUS: And a good reward would be yours.
MESSENGER: In truth, it was for this I came; mainly

that I should reap some favor on your return to the city.

Oedipus: (*Frantically*) Return? Oh, no! Never!
I'll never go anywhere near my parents.

Messenger: O son, it is plain
you cannot know what you are doing.

Oedipus: In what way, old man? In God's name, tell me.

Messenger: That is, if I understand your reasons.

Oedipus: Yes, old man, these reasons hold me back—
I fear that Phoebus may somehow prove a true prophet.

Messenger: You fear to stain yourself with guilt through parents?

Oedipus: Even so—the thought appalls me.

Messenger: Then know your fears to be baseless.

Oedipus: But how—If I am their son?

Messenger: Because there is no blood-tie.

Oedipus: What are you saying: Was not Polybus my begetter?

Messenger: No more than I who speak to you,
or so much as I, in fact, and no more.

Oedipus: How, my own sire no more to me than a hireling?

Messenger: Yes. He did not beget you, no more than I.

Oedipus: Then why did he call me his son?

Messenger: Know this; he had you as a gift from me.

Oedipus: And he could love me so much, though I came from another's
hand!

Messenger: His many seasons of childlessness drew him to you.

Oedipus: Was I an infant you found—or purchased?

Messenger: In Cithaeron's wooded valley—there I found you.

Oedipus: What took you up there?

Messenger: I tended flocks on the mountain.

Oedipus: You were a shepherd then, wandering for hire?

Messenger: But your preserver, my son, and I came in good time.

Oedipus: In good time? What was my plight?

Messenger: Your ankles might tell you.

Oedipus: Yes, that is an old affliction.

Messenger: I loosed you;
your ankles had been pierced and were pinned together.

Oedipus: Yes, I have borne a shameful mark on them from my cradle.

Messenger: And it is from this you bear the name of Oedipus
given to your for your swollen feet.

Oedipus: Tell me this, by Heaven! Was it done by my father—or my
mother?

Messenger: I have no knowledge of the deed.
He that gave you to me can tell you, I think.

Oedipus: What! You had me from another? You did not light on me
yourself?

Messenger: Another shepherd gave you to me.

Oedipus: What was he? Do you know him?

Messenger: I think the man belonged to Laius.

Oedipus: The king who ruled this city?

Messenger: The same. The man was a shepherd in his service.

Oedipus: Do you know whether he is alive? Can I see the man?

Messenger: You must know the best who live in this land.

Oedipus: (*Addressing the crowd*) Is there anyone present
who knows the herdsman of whom he speaks,
who has seen him in pasture or in the city?

If, anyone knows, let him answer:
the hour has come for everything to be made clear.

CHORUS: The Corinthian speaks of no other, I think,
than the peasant you asked to see;
but Jocasta is the one who would know best.

OEDIPUS: Jocasta, do you remember him you sent for?
Are he and this herdsman one man?

JOCASTA: (*Greatly troubled*) Why ask of whom the Corinthian speaks?
Give no heed to this—waste no thought on it—
it is of no importance—

OEDIPUS: Importance? Can anything be more important!
With the clue close at hand,
should I not pursue the matter of my parentage
and let it come to light?

JOCASTA: Oedipus, for the sake of all the gods,
if you have any care for your own life, let the old things alone;
I am sick of all this—I have had enough!

OEDIPUS: Have no fear, Jocasta. Even if I am proved a slave,
three times a slave, and if my mother were three-deep a slave,
you will not be considered a slave too.

JOCASTA: Dearest, let me persuade you
I beseech you, nor more questions!

OEDIPUS: Do not beseech me
to let the occasion slide; I must have light!

JOCASTA: (*Desperately*) I have your interest at heart—my fears are for
you—
my adivce, my dear, is best.

OEDIPUS: Then this best advice—
I am out of patience with it.

JOCASTA: O Oedipus, Oedipus,
God keep you, ill-fated one, from learning who you are.

OEDIPUS: Will someone go at once and fetch the herdsman,
and leave this woman to glory in her noble stock!

JOCASTA: O miserable one, unhappy one—
that is all I can say—now and forever.

(Jocasta *rushes into the palace in desperation*)

CHORUS: Why has our lady run into the palace
wild with grief?
A premonition shakes me:
it was terror that sealed her lips.

OEDIPUS: Let come what will.
Be my descent ever so lowly, I still must know.
Perhaps the woman, who is proud with a woman's towering pride,
finds my origin too humble for her.
As for me,
I hold myself to be the child of gracious Fortune,
and take no dishonor from this:
Fortune is the mother from whom I sprang,
and I call the months my brothers,
they that sometimes found me cast down
and then set high again.

With such a lineage,
I shall never be found ashamed
and falter in searching into my birth.

(The Chorus *is filled with confidence on hearing him)*

CHORUS (STROPHE):   If I am a seer or wise of heart at all,
mountain nurse, Cithaeron,
you shall not fail by Heaven
to know at tomorrow's full moon
that Oedipus honors you as his foster-mother
and that you are honored in the dance by us
as one favored by our monarch.
Phoebus, to whom we call, favor these things too!
    CHORUS (ANTISTROPHE):   Who was it, child? which of the
ageless goddesses
bore you to Pan[25] the father,
who roams the pasture hills?
Or was she bride to Phoebus? *He* the father?
Or to Cyllene's[26] lord? Or the Bacchantes'[27] god,
a dweller on the hill-tops, was it *He*
who received you his new-born joy from one
of the oreads[28] with whom he mostly sports?

(Attendants appear, leading a Shepherd, *an old man)*

OEDIPUS: *(To the Corinthian* Messenger) If I may guess, who
never saw him,
here is your herdsman.
His ripe years measure with yours,
and the men who bring him are of my household.
But you, if you have seen him before, can tell me.
    CHORUS: I recognize him—
trustiest of the servants Laius had in his house.
    OEDIPUS: Now, Corinthian stranger: Is it he?
MESSENGER: This is the man.
    OEDIPUS: *(To the old* Shepherd) Well then—old man! Look at me!
Tell me—you served Laius?
    SHEPHERD: I was his slave.
Not bought by him, but reared in his house.
    OEDIPUS: Doing what work? What was your way of life?
    SHEPHERD: For the best part of my life I tended flocks.
    OEDIPUS: Where did they graze?
    SHEPHERD: Sometimes *on* Cithaeron, sometimes *near* the mountain.
    OEDIPUS: *(Pointing out the* Messenger) This man—do you recall having
ever met him there?
    SHEPHERD: Not to say off-hand, from memory.
    MESSENGER: And no wonder, master!
But he will when I remind him. We kept pasture there
three half-years,
he with his two flocks, I with one.

---

[25] goatherd's god   [26] the mountain where Hermes (Mercury) was born   [27] Worshippers of Bacchus   [28] nymphs of the mountains

They grazed together from spring-time to the rise of Arcturus in the fall.
Then I drove my sheep to our fold at home
and he brought his back to Laius.

(To the Shepherd*)*

Was this so as I tell it or not?
  SHEPHERD: It was—but it was a long time ago.
  MESSENGER: And tell me now, do you remember giving me a boy,
an infant then, to rear as my own?
  SHEPHERD: *(Frightened)* What do you mean? Why do you ask me that?
  MESSENGER: *(Pointing to* Oedipus) Here is the man, my friend, who was
then the child.
  SHEPERD: *(Violently)* The plague take you! Hold your tongue!
  OEDIPUS: How now? You have no right to blame him.
The words that offend are yours.
  SHEPHERD: Offend? How have I offended, master?
  OEDIPUS: In not telling us about the child.
  SHEPHERD: He busies himself with no business of his own.
He speaks without knowing.
  OEDIPUS: Herdsman! If you will not speak to please me,
you shall be forced.
  SHEPHERD: For god's love, master, do not harm an old man!
  OEDIPUS: *(To his* Servants) Hold him fast; twist his arms
behind him!
  SHEPHERD: Wretch that I am! What do you want to know?
  OEDIPUS: You gave him a child? The child he asks about?
  SHEPHERD: I gave it. Would I had died before!
  OEDIPUS: You will now, if you do not speak the truth.
  SHEPHERD: And it will be worse with me if I speak it.
  OEDIPUS: The fellow trifles with us still—evades the
question. . .
  SHEPHERD: *(As the* Servants *twist his arms)* No, no! I
have told you that I gave him the child.
  OEDIPUS: From whom did you have it?
Did someone give it to you,
or was it your own?
  SHEPHERD: It was not mine.
Another gave it to me.
  OEDIPUS: Which of these citizens? From whose home?
  SHEPHERD: Master, I beg of you—
I beg you, do not ask it.
  OEDIPUS: You are a dead man if I ask again.
  SHEPHERD: It was a child, then—of the house of Laius.
  OEDIPUS: A slave's child? Or born of the King's own family?
  SHEPHERD: I stand on the knife-edge of dreadful words; I fear to speak.
  OEDIPUS: And I, to hear. Yet I must!
  SHEPHERD: The child was called his son;
but she within, your lady, could best say how that was.
  OEDIPUS: Did she then give it to you?
  SHEPHERD: So it was, my King.
  OEDIPUS: For what purpose? Speak!

SHEPHERD: That I should do away with it.
OEDIPUS: Wretched woman! Her own child?
SHEPHERD: Yes, from fear of the evil prophecies.
OEDIPUS: What prophecies?
SHEPHERD: That he should kill his parents, it was said.
OEDIPUS: Why, then, did you give him to this old man?
SHEPHERD: Through pity, master.

I gave him the child,
thinking he would take it to another land, his own.
He did so but, alas, he saved it for the worst of sorrows.
For, if you are the man he says you are,
then surely you were born to great misery!

OEDIPUS: (*Uttering the cry of a wounded animal*) Oh—oh—oh!
Everything is proved true—everything has come to pass!
Light of the sun.
never shall I look on you again,
I who am revealed
damned by the light I saw at birth,
damned by my marriage,
damned by the blood I shed.

(*Oedipus rushes frantically into the palace*)

CHORUS (1ST STROPHE):   O generations of men,
how I account your lives no better
than not living at all!
Where is to be found the man
who attains more happiness, than a mere seeming
and after the seeming, a falling away!
Yours is the fate that warns me—
luckless, unhappy Oedipus!—
to call no creature living on earth enviable.

CHORUS (1ST ANTISTROPHE):   For this is he, o Zeus,
who speeding his bolt far beyond the rest
won the prize of all-engrossing prosperity.
He slew the darkly singing maiden,
her of the crooked talons;
he stood as a tower between death and our land,
and thereafter was called king,
received unrivaled honor
and next to none ruled great Thebes.

CHORUS (2ND STROPHE):   But now, O Zeus, whose is the story more grievous
to hear,
and who is more yoked to misfortune
now his entire life is reversed?
O, renowed' prince Oedipus,
who, on the nuptial bed,
sought the same source
as father that you had as son,
how could the soil your father sowed before
suffer you, unhappy one, in peace so long!

CHORUS (2ND ANTISTROPHE):   Time, all-revealing, that has found you
guilty without intent,

arraigns you now for a monstrous marriage
in which begetter and begotten are one.
O child of Laius,
I wish that I had never beheld your face!
True, I must lament your fate
with a dirge that pours from my lips,
and yet, though I got new life from you at first,
you have dropped a great darkness on my eyes.

(A Servant rushes out of the palace)

SERVANT: O you, most honored in the land,
what things you have to hear, what sights to see,
what sorrow to endure, if you still cherish
the house of Labdacus, true to your oath!
For neither the waves of Ister, I fear, nor Phasis
can wash this house clean,
so many evils it covers and shall soon disclose.
Yes, evils self-inflicted,
which are the worst to bear.
   CHORUS: There was no lack of suffering before;
what report can cause more lamentation?
   SERVANT: To tell the shortest tale,
our royal lady, Jocasta, is dead.
   CHORUS: Unhappy woman! How did she die?
   SERVANT: By her own hand.
it cannot be so terrible to you as to one who witnessed it,
but as far as I can tell, you shall hear:
When she passed into the vestibule, frantic,
she ran straight to the bedchamber
with her fingers tearing at her hair.
She dashed the doors shut behind her,
called upon dead Laius,
mindful of the begotten son
by whom, she said, he died
and by whom she bore unholy offspring.
So she bewailed the nuptial bed
on which she had brought forth a twofold brook—
a husband by her husband, and children by her son.
What happened next, how she died,
is more than I can tell, for Oedipus burst in
and we could not behold her end,
our eyes being fixed on him. For he went about raging
calling for a sword, and demanding
where he could find the wife who was no wife
but the mother-soil of both himself and his children.
And while he was raging, some power guided him to her;
for with a dreadful cry, as though led on,
he flung himself at the closed doors,
unhinging their bolts with his bare hands.

Going in after him, we saw the lady, her neck
in a twisted rope and swinging.

Then he, giving a dreadful cry,
loosed her halter and when she lay on the ground,
how awful the sequel we saw!
For tearing from the raiment the golden brooches of her robe,
he raised them high and stuck them into his eyes,
calling out, as he smote:
"No longer, my eyes, shall you behold the horror
I suffered and performed! Too long
have you looked on those on whom you should not have looked
while failing to see what you should have seen.
Henceforth, therefore, be dark!"
With words like these, not once but many times
he struck at his eyes with the lifted pins,
and at each blow the eyes streamed blood on his beard
like crimson rain.

These are the evils that from a two-fold source,
not one alone, but from woman and husband,
have burst forth. The fortune of the old house
was once a rare happiness, but in this hour
of shame and ruin, lamentation and death,
of all earthly suffering that can be named
nothing was spared.

    CHORUS: Is he eased of his misery now and quiet?
    SERVANT: He calls for someone to unbar the doors
and show him to all the Thebans as his father's slayer
and his mother's—but no, the unholy word shall not pass my lips.
He proposes to cast himself out of the land
and no longer to burden the house with his curse.
Yet he lacks strength and has no one to guide his steps,
for no one can bear to go near him.
But you will see for yourselves now, for the bolts are being drawn,
and he will come out, revealing
what even he who shrinks from the horror will pity.

    (Oedipus comes out of the palace, his eyes bloodstained and horrible)

    CHORUS: O dreadful sight,
most dreadful that my eyes have ever looked upon!
Unhappy one, what madness came upon you?
Who is the demon, the foe to man,
that with a spring beyond mortal power
leaped upon your ill-fated life as its prey
Hapless one, although there is more I would ask you
and I am drawn to you with pitying sorrow,
I cannot even bring myself to look again;
you fill me with such shuddering.
    OEDIPUS: Wretched that I am! Oh! Oh!
Where am I going in my misery,
and where is my voice borne on the wings of air?
Fate, have you brought me so far?
    CHORUS: To a destiny terrible to men's ears
and terrible to their sight!

OEDIPUS: Horror of darkness that envelops me!
Dreadful visitant, resistless and unspeakable,
whom a too fair breeze of fortune sped against me,
how my soul is stabbed, first by the present pain
and again by the memory of fearful deeds!
CHORUS: (Sympathetically) A mind troubles so many
you may well bear and mourn a two-fold pain.
OEDIPUS: Oh friend, you still are steadfast,
still ready to tend and to endure me,
a blind man!
Your presence is not hidden from me;
in my darkness I know your voice.
CHORUS: Yet, man of dreadful deed,
how could you bear to extinguish your sight?
What inhuman power drive you?
OEDIPUS: Apollo, friends,
Apollo brought these woes to pass;
but it was my own hand that struck.
My own hand alone, man of misery that I am!
I did not want to see when sight could show me nothing good.
CHORUS: It is true, alas.
OEDIPUS: What was left to see?
What to love?
What greeting to hear with pleasure?
Hurry, lead me out of the land,
lead away the lost one, the most damned of men,
the man most abhorred by the gods.
CHORUS: Unhappy equally in misfortune
and in too keen consciousness of horror,
it were better that you had never lived.
OEDIPUS: A curse on the man who freed me in the pasture,
who unbound my feet
and saved me from death
and brought me to a life such as this.
Had I died then, on Cithaeron's slope,
I should have brought no grief
both to my friends and myself.
CHORUS: I, too, could wish it had been so.
OEDIPUS: I would not have come to shed my father's blood,
nor been known among men as my mother's husband.
But now I am forsaken by the gods,
the son of a defiled mother, and successor
in the bed of him who gave me miserable life.
If there is any evil that exceeds all evil,
that has been the fate of Oedipus.
CHORUS: Yet I cannot say you have done well.
To have died would have been better than to be blind and living.
OEDIPUS: I have done what I thought best; I'll have no counsel in this.
Had I retained my sight, with what eyes
in the land of shades underground
could I have looked on my father and my wretched mother—
those two against whom I have done such things
that no halter could punish the crime.
And would the children born of me

have been an endurable sight? Not to these eyes—never.
Nor could I look upon this city, with its citadel and shrines,
from which I cut myself off, I of Thebes the greatest,
when I myself pronounced the doom to drive *him* out,
the criminal revealed now by the gods as the hateful seed of Laius.
Bearing this stain upon me,
could I have looked with unaverted eyes on my people?
Never. And had there been some way
to seal the fountain of hearing, too,
I should have cast this wretched body into a still closer prison,
secure from all sound as well as sight,
for it is sweet to be beyond the stab of pain.

Oh, Cithaeron, why did you shelter me
who came to you an infant?
Why not have destroyed me at once,
leaving my birth unrevealed?
And you Polybus and Corinth
and the ancient house I called the home of my fathers,
how fair a nursling you fostered
and how foul a man
festered within the child,
doomed to be found evil and of evil birth.

And you crossroads—
hidden glen, thicket and narrow way
where the three paths met,
you that drank from my murdering hands
a father's blood,
do you still remember what you saw me do?

And, then, the deeds I went on to perform!
O, marriage, marriage,
You brought me forth,
then brought children to your child.
In a kinship of fathers, brothers, sons,
and of brides, wives, and mothers,
you compounded the foulest shame a man can know,
ghastly incest.
But no, it is unfit to utter what it is unfit to do!
Hurry, friends, and in God's name, hide me somewhere beyond
this land.
Or kill me;
or cast me into the sea where you may never look upon me again.

Approach; take hold of me.
Have no fear of contamination;
my plague will touch no one else.

(Creon *is seen approaching*)

Chorus: No! Creon approaches in good time

to advise and perform what must be.
He is left sole guardian of the land.
    OEDIPUS: Creon! How shall I speak?
How can I request anything from him,
having proved unjust in what passed between us?

    (Creon *appears with* Attendants)

    CREON: I have come, Oedipus, not in mockery
nor with intended reproaches for past words.
But if you have no regard for the children of men,
respect, at least, the all-sustaining flame
of our Lord the Sun!
Spare Him the sight of naked pollution
that not earth, nor holy rain, nor light can welcome.

    (To the Attendants)

Come! Take him inside quickly.
It is seemly that kinsfolk alone
should see and hear a kinsman's grief.
    OEDIPUS: For the God's sake, since you have come to me,
a man so vile, with so noble a spirit,
grant me one request.
For your own good I ask it, not for mine.
    CREON: Ask what you wish.
    OEDIPUS: Cast me out of this land,
speed me to a land where no man may greet me.
    CREON: I should have done this, be sure
if I had not wanted to learn first what the God decrees.
    OEDIPUS: Surely his oracle was clear—
to let the parricide and defiler die.
    CREON: That was said.
But in our present plight it is well to ask the God again.
    OEDIPUS: How can you expect a response from God
on behalf of so frightful a man as Oedipus?
    CREON: Even you must now put your faith in the God.
    OEDIPUS: Even so! And I entreat you
to order a burial that befits her who lies within;
she is your own,
for whom you should properly perform the rites.
But for me, never should my father's city
have to behold me dwelling in it while I live.

Let me go to the hills,
there where my mountain Cithaeron rises,
once appointed to be my tomb by mother and father.
Dying there,
I shall die as by their decree who rightly doomed me at my birth.

Yet i also know there is more to come.
Neither an illness nor anything else will destroy me.
I should never have been snatched from death there

but for a strange, still uncompleted, destiny.
Well, then, let my fate, whatever it be,
take me where it will! But my children, Creon!
My sons require none of your care,
being grown men who will not lack the means to live.
Creon, I pray you, take care of my daughters,
my two poor unhappy girls,
who never ate at a separate table away from me or lacked my presence
and ever shared all things with me.
Grant them your protection.
And suffer me, if you will, to touch them
And share my grief with them.
Grant me this, Prince,
grant it, noble one,
that in touching them I may feel
they are with me, as when I still had my sight.

(Led out by Servants, Antigone and Ismene, the young daughters,
  come out of the palace, sobbing)

OEDIPUS: (Hearing them) O heavenly powers, are those my children sobbing?
Can it be that Creon, pitying me,
sends me the children, the dear ones?
Have you done that?
    CREON: I have, seeing what joy you took in them before.
May they give you comfort.
    OEDIPUS: Then a blessing be your reward.
May heaven prove a kinder guide on your road of life
than it was to me.
Oh, my children, where are you?
Come here—here to the hands of him
whose mother was your own,
the hands that put out your father's once clear eyes,
which seeing nothing, understanding nothing,
brought him to her from whom he sprang
to become your father.
For you, too, I weep,
though I cannot see your faces,
knowing the bitter life men will make for you
in the days to come. For,
to what gathering of citizens will you go,
to what festival,
from which you will not come back in tears?
Where will be found the man
willing to assume the disgrace that clings to my offspring
and that would to yours?
For what reproach is lacking?
"Your father slew his father,
and planted you in the womb of his own being."
Such will be the taunts you must hear!
The man who would marry you does not live;
you must wither away in barrenness.

O Creon, son of Menoeceus, hear me!
You are the only father left to them,
both their parents lost—both!
Do not allow my children, who are your kinswomen too,
to wander about in beggary, unwed.
Do not let them sink down to my misery.
Pity them when you see them forlorn,
so utterly forlorn in their young years.
Give me your promise with the touch of your hand!

And to you, my children,
I could give much counsel if you were older.
As it is, I can only make this prayer:
May you find some place where you can live in quiet,
and may you have a better life than your father's.

CREON: Enough lamentation! Pass into the house, Oedipus.
OEDIPUS: I must obey, though it is hard.
CREON: To everything there is a season.
OEDIPUS: Know, then, on what conditions I go within.
CREON: Name them, and I shall know.
OEDIPUS: See to it that I am cast out of Thebes. Banish me!
CREON: That must be as the God decrees.
OEDIPUS: But surely you understand that I am hateful to the God!
CREON: If so, you will obtain your desire soon enough.
OEDIPUS: So you consent.
CREON: I have said as I mean.
OEDIPUS: (Still holding on to his daughters) Then it is
time for me to be led within.
CREON: Go then, but let the children go.
OEDIPUS: (Clinging passionately to them) No, do not take
them from me.
CREON: (Severely) Do not seek to be the master in everything,
for everything you mastered fell away from you.

(Oedipus is led into the palace by an Attendant. Then
Creon goes in with Antigone and Ismene, leaving the Chorus
outside)

CHORUS: Dwellers in Thebes,
behold, this is Oedipus,
who unriddled the famous riddle
and was a man most notable.
What Theban did not envy his good fortune?
Yet behold into what a whirlwind of trouble he was hurled!

Therefore, with eyes fixed on the end destined for all,
count no one of the race of man happy
until he has crossed life's border free from pain.

(The Chorus retires)

FOR DISCUSSION

1. The theme of *Oedipus Rex* could be that life is uncertain. How is this illustrated in the play? Another theme could be that man often sees better with inner vision than with physical sight. Find examples in the play that support this statement. Can you think of any other themes?
2. *Oedipus Rex* is considered a great play because it lifts the audience emotionally. Do you agree or disagree that it does? Why?
3. Discuss how the plot of *Oedipus Rex* progresses both forward and backward at the same time.
4. Residents of ancient Greece believed that man is basically good and noble. How does the character of Oedipus illustrate this belief?
5. In what way was Oedipus a man of reason? In what way was he ruled by his emotions? What specific actions in the play relate either to his reasoning or to his emotional nature?
6. Greek philosophy stated that there should be constant order in an orderly world. How is this belief brought out in *Oedipus Rex?*
7. To what degree was Oedipus controlled by fate? How much were his own actions responsible for what happened to him?
8. What character traits do you think caused Oedipus' downfall?
9. Do you think that the chorus was used effective in telling the story of Oedipus? Is the language effective? The poetic style?
10. What do you think was the true reason why Oedipus blinded himself?
11. Why do you think the gods decreed that Oedipus should be banished?
12. Do you think that Oedipus' blinding and banishment is the only logical outcome the play could have? Why?

SUPPLEMENTARY READING

Aeschylus   *Agamemnon*
Sophocles   *Ajax, Antigone, Electra*
Euripides   *Medea, The Trojan Women*
Aristophanes   *The Birds, The Clouds, The Frogs*
Plautus   *The Menaechmi*
Terence   *The Brothers*

II

The Medieval Theatre

After the fall of the Roman Empire, little in the way of drama was presented for several hundred years. Some isolated entertainments were given by traveling minstrels, acrobats, singers, jugglers, and animal trainers. There were a few presentations of mimes and pantomimes, and some pagan rites and festivals. However, it was difficult for drama to exist because of the opposition of the church, which forbade actors the sacraments and issued frequent orders that theatrical performances could not be presented or attended.

Surprisingly enough, when drama was finally reborn, it was as a part of the church service. Such liturgical drama came into existence to teach and to provide visual examples of biblical stories. The first drama consisted of "tropes," or short playlets, presented at the time of church's major yearly events, such as Easter, Advent, and Christmas. The first to be dramatized was Easter. There is record of such a dramatization being given around 925 A.D. The play included only three lines and took place during a meeting of the angel and the three Marys at Christ's tomb. The angel asks whom the Marys seek. They reply that it is Jesus. The angel tells them that he has risen and that they should proclaim that fact.

Gradually, the playlets were expanded, became more elaborate, and were included extensively in church services. Delivered at first in Latin, in later presentations each line was spoken first in Latin, then repeated in the language of the country. Later still, beginning in the eleventh century, the Latin was dropped, and the lines were spoken in the language of the people. These tropes were not confined to any single country, but spread over most of continental Europe and England as well.

In the beginning, the plays were presented only by clergymen and only in the larger churches and cathedrals. Their settings consisted of "mansions," or *sedes,* and *platea,* the acting area. A mansion represented a specific place, such as Christ's tomb, which was most often the altar of the church. After the dramatizations became more lengthy and elaborate, the mansions represented several different locales and were placed at various points around the interior of the church. Since each mansion was small, the platea could be an unlocalized area or the entire open space. The action would start at one mansion, then move into the platea, while the audience was expected to imagine that it was still taking place at the mansion. When the play switched to a different mansion, the same unlocalized area was used, and the audience now recognized the action as taking place at the new mansion.

By the thirteenth century, the drama began to move outdoors because the plays became so elaborate that they began to interfere with the services. Usually the play, still acted by clergymen, was presented on the west side of the church. Since the west side often had a raised porch which opened onto the town square, it provided a ready-made stage. The spectators could stand in the square and watch.

Gradually laymen began acting in the plays, and by the fourteenth and fifteenth centuries, all the responsibilities of the production were assumed by secular groups. By this time, the dialogue was spoken entirely in the local everyday language. The secular play-producing groups were largely trade guilds, or else special societies formed particularly for this purpose. In France, one such group was the *Confrérie de la Passion.* Although the church did not participate to any great extent, its approval for production was still necessary. Each guild had a patron saint, its own priest, and a chapel. Sometimes several small guilds would join together to produce a single play.

Still later, the drama moved from the west door of the church to other locations. Various types of structures were used. Some plays were produced on a platform pushed against a building, while others were presented in old Roman amphitheatres or in the town square. In England there were two major methods of production. One was to present plays in "rounds" or ancient amphitheatres, and the other was to use "pageant wagons" as stages. Each wagon carried two or more mansions, and some historians believe that at times several wagons were placed together. The acting may have taken place entirely on the wagons or on the ground in front of them. At any rate, the wagons could be moved from one place to another.

Typically, the mansions were placed so as to represent the planes of heaven, earth, and hell. Heaven was usually at one end and hell at the other, with a series of mansions between. The more mansions there were, the longer and more elaborate the presentation. It is recorded, for instance, that at Mons, France, in 1501, a play was given with sixty-seven mansions. It took forty-eight days to rehearse, and one performance lasted four days.

The dramas were really short episodes that had no connection with each other except that they dealt with biblical subject matter. Each episode was complete in itself, and the overall presentation had no continuing plot.

Of great concern were special effects. There are records of men being hired to invent all sorts of startling "secrets" to be revealed to the audience. Some of these secrets are unknown to this day. The effects included such things as Christ's walking on the water, and smoke and fire billowing from the mouth of hell. Actors and subjects were raised and lowered by means of ropes and pulleys. In this manner, for instance, a large number of monsters could fly freely through hell. Mechanical animals were used, and there is one record of an effigy being filled with bones and animal entrails to provide a more realistic scene for the audience. Trapdoors were employed extensively. Fountains sprang up, water turned into wine, and the miracle of the loaves and fishes was enacted.

Many of these special effects were used even before the drama moved out of the church, and the mansions were constructed to resemble more and more closely the places they represented. Unlike the drama of Greece, the religious drama of the medieval period involved much violence.

Most of the actors dressed in contemporary costumes, which they supplied themselves, but angels wore white robes with wings, and God was dressed as an official of the church. No pains were spared to make the devil at the same time awesome and funny. He wore wings, horns, claws, and a tail, and was a great hit with his audiences. In fact, the plays contained many comic elements, which were not permitted by the church until the sixteenth century. The list of properties for a play was often quite extensive, and they often cost a great deal of money.

Unfortunately, not many of the texts of these plays survive. Of the hundreds given in England, the only ones that exist in complete form are from Chester, York, Coventry, and Wakefield.

By the end of the fourteenth century, a new trend had developed: the several plays that had been presented throughout the church year were combined into a single presentation, or cycle. Such cycles lasted until the middle of the sixteenth century, during which time the plays changed in content, with old sections being dropped and new ones added. However, they were still episodic and concerned biblical stories, church history, or sermons by clergymen.

The guilds or town councils hired directors who were in charge of the technical aspects of the production as well as the acting. A director was also responsible for collecting any admission fees and welcoming the audience.

Until laymen began appearing extensively in the plays, the actors chanted their lines. Later, however, their speech became more natural. They were, for the most part, amateurs. Some received minimal pay, although at times actors playing leading roles were paid large sums of money. All were given food and drink during the rehearsal and performance periods. The performers at first were all men, but later women and children appeared in some of the plays. Most often the actors were local citizens of the working class.

Along with the liturgical drama and cycle plays, other less desirable forms developed within the church. For example, the Feast of Fools, presented on New Year's Day, allowed minor clergy to ridicule the mass and church officials. The Feast of Asses had a choir braying like donkeys, and the Festival of the Boy Bishop featured the "ordaining" of a boy with mock formality. Such performances sometimes involved the presentation of obscene songs and dances and the playing of games of chance.

The three most important forms of drama to evolve from the church presentations were mystery plays, miracle plays, and morality plays. The mystery play, which got its name from the French word *mystère*, meaning trade or occupation, dealt with the life of Christ and often depicted scenes from the creation to the second coming. These plays were first presented inside the church but later moved outdoors. Miracle plays dealt with the lives of saints and martyrs, but could also include topical scenes involving family troubles. They emphasized such things as miraculous power and divine intervention in the lives of men.

The morality plays, Which developed later than the other two forms, were most popular between the beginning of the fifteenth century and the mid-sixteenth century. The subject matter was concerned with moral instruction, particularly man's attempt to save his soul. All the characters were allegorical. The central figure usually was called Everyman, and such characters as Virtue and Vice fought over his soul. The first morality play of which there is record was the *Play of The Lord's Prayer*, presented in York, England, in 1384. Morality plays were more popular in England than anywhere else, although they also were presented on the continent of Europe. Unlike the cycle plays, morality plays were generally performed by professional actors.

Along with the church plays, Several forms of secular drama developed during the Middle Ages. The most important was the farce, typically presented in France, Germany, and England. It was usually bawdy and risqué, being concerned with man's depravity, and not more than a few hundred lines in length. One writer of medieval farce was Hans Sachs of Germany, who is credited with writing more than two hundred plays. A second secular form was the interlude, a comic play performed by traveling players for wealthy citizens at celebrations. The interlude became popular at the end of the fifteenth century. The least important of the secular forms was the folk play, presented by amateur actors who went from house to house enacting stories of heroes or legendary figures.

Medieval drama began to decline during the sixteenth century for several reasons. The social structure of Europe was changing, and the plays no longer could be presented effectively as community undertakings. There was an increased interest in classical learning, and new forms of drama were beginning to develop, which combined both medieval and classical influences. Perhaps most important, there was dissension in the church. Queen Elizabeth I of England forbade religious plays in 1559, and the church itself forbade such plays in continental Europe. Thus, by the beginning of the seventeenth century, medieval drama was at an end—except in Spain, where it continued well past the middle of the eighteenth century.

PROJECTS

1. Investigate the use of stage machinery in the medieval theatre. How does it compare with the use of stage machines in classical theatre?
2. Find out as much as you can about the *Feast of Fools*, the *Feast of Asses*, and the *Festival of the Boy Bishop*.
3. Investigate the production of a specific cycle play.
4. Prepare a report on the pageant wagon (or make a model of one).
5. Investigate the staging of English "rounds."
6. Contrast the representation of the planes of heaven, earth, and hell in the

medieval theatre with the planes as they might be represented today (or build a model of the planes as they might have been represented after drama was removed from the church).

7. Investigate more fully the factors that contributed to the decline of medieval drama.

The morality play was a medieval form

of drama. In all morality plays the characters are abstractions. They are not individualized, but represent all people. Therefore, the audience is expected to identify with the central character, most often called Everyman or Mankind.

The purpose of the morality play was to teach a moral lesson. Unlike the earlier liturgical drama, however, morality plays did not deal with biblical scenes or with the lives of the saints. Instead, they sought to teach the importance of leading a moral life. Later, such plays also were written to spread the propaganda of either Protestantism or Catholicism.

The play *Everyman* is purely religious in its presentation of the central character's meeting with death. It was written during the last few years of the fifteenth century, before the conflict between Catholics and Protestants began to influence the writing of morality plays. It is believed that *Everyman* is derived from the Dutch play, *Elckerlijk,* written in 1495 by Peter Dorlandus, although we do not know who was responsible for translating and adapting it into English. The first English version was printed by Richard Pynson during the early part of the sixteenth century.

Everyman is somewhat different from many of the other morality plays in that it is short and contains no humor. Often morality plays dealt with a man's whole life and presented mischievous characters in the person of the Devil and Vice. In all cases, however, the plots were constructed by the author. The form is important in that it was a step toward the secularization of drama. Morality plays were presented all over Europe.

Everyman has survived because of its simplicity and its subject matter. It presents a central character, who, like all of us, must face death and is thus overwhelmed and bewildered. It illustrates the fact that death must be faced alone. As he meets with his life's associates, Everyman ultimately sees the meaning of his life and is redeemed from an eternity in hell.

The morality play continues to exert an influence on the theatre. Christopher Marlowe relied heavily upon it for his play *The Tragical History of Doctor Faustus.* Not only other Elizabethan writers, such as Thomas Dekker, but even twentieth-century playwrights have been influenced by the form. Two examples are *The Servant in the House,* by Charles Rann Kennedy, and the *The Death of Everymom,* an Absurdist play written in 1967 by Arnold Powell. *Everyman* itself has been produced many times throughout history.

Everyman

CHARACTERS

MESSENGER
GOD
DEATH
EVERYMAN
FELLOWSHIP
COUSIN
KINDRED
GOODS
GOOD-DEEDS

KNOWLEDGE
CONFESSION
BEAUTY
STRENGTH
DISCRETION
FIVE-WITS
ANGEL
DOCTOR

Everyman

Here Beginnith a Treatise How the High Father of Heaven Sendeth Death to Summon Every Creature to Come and Give Account of Their Lives in This World and Is in Manner of a Moral Play.

(*Enter* Messenger.)

MESSENGER: I pray you all give your audience,
And hear this matter with reverence,
By figure[1] a moral play—
The Summoning of Everyman called it is,
That of our lives and ending shows.
How transitory we be all day.
This matter is wondrous precious,
But the intent of it is more gracious,
And sweet to bear away.
The story saith, —Man, in the beginning,
Look well, and take good heed to the ending,
Be you never so gay.
Ye think sin in the beginning full sweet,
Which in the end causeth thy soul to weep,
When the body lieth in clay.
Here shall you see how *Fellowship* and *Jollity*,
Both *Strength, Pleasure,* and *Beauty,*
Will fade from thee as flower in May.
For ye shall hear how our heaven king
Calleth *Everyman* to a general reckoning:
Give audience, and hear what he doth say. (*Exit.*)

(*God speaketh.*)

GOD: I perceive here in my majesty,
How that all creatures be to me unkind,
Living without dread in worldly prosperity:
Of ghostly sight[2] the people be so blind,
Drowned in sin, they know me not for their God;
In worldly riches is all their mind,

[1] In form   [2] spiritual matters

59

They fear not my rightwiseness,[3] the sharp rod;[4]
My law that I shewed, when I for them died,
They forget clean, and shedding of my blood red;
I hanged between two,[5] it cannot be denied;
To get them life I suffered to be dead;
I healed their feet, with thorns hurt was my head;
I could do no more than I did truly,
And now I see the people do clean forsake me.
They use the seven deadly sins[6] damnable;
As pride, covetise,[7] wrath, and lechery,
Now in the world be made commendable;
And thus they leave of angels the heavenly company;
Everyman liveth so after his own pleasure,
And yet of their life they do nothing sure:
I see the more that I them forbear
The worse they be from year to year;
All that liveth appaireth[8] fast,
Therefore I will in all the haste
Have a reckoning of Everyman's person
For and[9] I leave the people thus alone
In their life and wicked tempests,
Verily they will become much worse than beasts;
For now one would by envy another up eat;
Charity they all do clean forget.
I hoped well that Everyman
In my glory should make his mansion,[10]
And thereto I had them all elect;[11]
But now I see, like traitors deject,
They thank me not for the pleasure that I to them meant,
Nor yet for their being that I them have lent;
I proffered the people great multitude of mercy,
And few there be that asketh it heartily;
They be so cumbered with worldly riches,
That needs on them I must do justice,
On Everyman living without fear.
Where art thou, *Death*, thou mighty messenger?

    (Enter Death.*)*

    DEATH: Almighty God, I am here at your will,
Your commandment to fulfil.
    GOD: Go thou to *Everyman*,
And show him in my name
A pilgrimage he must on him take.
Which he in no wise may escape;
And that he bring with him a sure reckoning
Without delay or any tarrying. *(Exit.)*
    DEATH: Lord, I will in the world go run over all,
And cruelly outsearch both great and small;

---

[3] righteousness [4] symbol of Christian discipline [5] Christ was crucified between two thieves.
[6] The seven sins also include Envy, Gluttony, and Sloth. [7] covetousness [8] becomes more evil
[9] if [10] live [11] chosen

Every man will I beset that liveth beastly
Out of God's laws, and dreadeth not folly:
He that loveth riches I will strike with my dart,
His sight to blind, and from heaven to depart,[12]
Except that alms be his good friend,
In hell for to dwell, world without end.

(Enter Everyman.)

Lo, yonder I see *Everyman* walking;
Full little he thinketh on my coming;
His mind is on fleshly lusts and his treasure,
And great pain it shall cause him to endure
Before the Lord Heaven King.
Everyman, stand still; wither art thou going
Thus gaily? Hast thou thy Maker forget?
    EVERYMAN: Why askst thou?
Wouldest thou wete?[13]
    DEATH: Yea, sir, I will show you;
In great haste I am sent to thee
From God out of his majesty.
    EVERYMAN: What, sent to me?
    DEATH: Yea, certainly.
Though thou have forget him here,
He thinketh on thee in the heavenly sphere,
As, or[14] we depart, thou shalt know.
    EVERYMAN: What desireth God of me?
    DEATH: That shall I show thee;
A reckoning he will needs have
Without any longer respite.
    EVERYMAN: To give a reckoning longer leisure I crave;
This blind matter troubleth my wit.
    DEATH: On thee thou must take a long journey:
Therefore thy book of count with thee thou bring;
For turn again thou cannot by no way,
And look thou be sure of thy reckoning:
For before God thou shalt answer, and show
Thy many bad deeds and good but a few;
How thou hast spent thy life, and in what wise,[15]
Before the chief lord of paradise.
Have ado that we were in that way,
For, wete thou will, thou shalt make none attournay.[16]
    EVERYMAN: Full unready I am such reckoning to give.
I know thee not: what messenger art thou?
    DEATH: I am *Death,* that no man dreadeth.[17]
For every man I rest[18] and no man spareth;
For it is God's commandment
That all to me should be obedient.
    EVERYMAN: O *Death,* thou comest when I had thee least in mind;
In thy power it lieth me to save,

---

[12] keep from heaven   [13] know   [14] ere   [15] way   [16] have no one to plead your case   [17] Death fears
no man.   [18] take

Yet of my good[19] will I give thee, if ye will be kind,
Yea, a thousand pound shalt thou have,
And defer this matter till another day.

DEATH: *Everyman, it may not be by no way;*
I set not by gold, silver, nor riches,
Ne[20] by pope, emperor, king, duke, ne princes.
For and I would receive gifts great,
All the world I might get;
But my custom is clean contrary.
I give thee no respite: come hence, and not tarry.

EVERYMAN: Alas, shall I have no longer respite?
I may say *Death* giveth no warning:
To think on thee, it maketh my heart sick,
For all unready is my book of reckoning.
But twelve year and I might have abiding,[21]
My counting book I would make so clear,
That my reckoning I should not need to fear.
Wherefore, *Death,* I pray thee, for God's mercy,
Spare me till I be provided of remedy.

DEATH: Thee availeth not to cry, weep, and pray:
But haste thee lightly[22] that you were gone the journey,
And prove thy friends if thou can.
For, wete thou will, the tide abideth no man,
And in the world each living creature
For *Adam's* sin must die of nature.

EVERYMAN: *Death,* if I should this pilgrimage take,
And my reckoning surely make,
Show me, for saint *charity,*[23]
Should I not come again shortly?

DEATH: No, *Everyman;* and thou be once there,
Thou mayest never more come here,
Trust me verily.

EVERYMAN: O gracious God, in the high seat celestial,
Have mercy on me in this most need;
Shall I have no company from this vale terrestrial
Of mine acquaintance that way me to lead?

DEATH: Yea, if any be so hardy.
That would go with thee and bear thee company.
Hie thee that you were gone to God's magnificence
Thy reckoning to give before his presence.
What weenest thou thy life[24] is given thee,
And thy worldly goods also?

EVERYMAN: I had wend[25] so, verily.

DEATH: Nay, nay; it was but lent thee;
For as soon as thou art go,
Another awhile shall have it, and then go therefro
Even as thou hast done.
Everyman, thou art mad; thou hast thy wits five,
And here on earth will not amend thy life,
For suddenly I do come.

---

[19] possessions   [20] nor   [21] If I could have twelve years   [22] quickly   [23] holy love   [24] Do you think your life   [25] thought

EVERYMAN: O wretched caitiff,[26] whither shall I flee,
That I might scape this endless sorrow!
Now, gentle *Death,* spare me till tomorrow,
That I may amend me
With good advisement.
DEATH: Nay, thereto I will not consent,
Nor no man will I respite,
But to the heart suddenly I shall smite
Without any advisement.
And now out of thy sight I will me hie;
See thou make thee ready shortly,
For thou mayst say this is the day
That no man living may scape away. (*Exit* Death.)
EVERYMAN: Alas, I may well weep with sighs deep;
Nor have I no manner of company
To help me in my journey, and me to keep;
And also my writing[27] is full unready.
How shall I do now for to excuse me?
I would to God I had never be gete.[28]
To my soul a full great profit it had be;
For now I fear pains huge and great.
The time passeth; Lord, help that all wrought:
For though I mourn it availeth nought.
The day passeth, and is almost a-go;[29]
I wot[30] not well what for to do.
To whom where I best my complaint to make?
What, and I to *Fellowship* thereof spake,
And showed him of this sudden chance?
For in him is all mine affiance;[31]
We have in the world so many a day
Be on[32] good friends in sport and play.
I see him yonder, certainly;
I trust that he will bear me company;
Therefore to him will I speak to ease my sorrow.
Well met, good *Fellowship,* and good morrow!

(Fellowship *speaketh.*)

FELLOWSHIP: *Everyman,* good morrow by this day.
Sir, why lookest thou so piteously?
If any thing be amiss, I pray thee, me say,
That I may help to remedy.
EVERYMAN: Yea, good *Fellowship,* yea,
I am in great jeopardy.
FELLOWSHIP: My true friend, show to me your mind;
I will not forsake thee, unto my life's end,
In the way of good company.
EVERYMAN: That was well spoken, and lovingly.
FELLOWSHIP: Sir, I must needs know your heaviness;
I have pity to see you in any distress;
If any have you wronged ye shall revenged be,

---

[26] captive   [27] account   [28] been born   [29] gone   [30] know   [31] trust   [32] been

Though I on the ground be slain for thee,—
Though that I know before that I should die.
   EVERYMAN: Verily, *Fellowship,* gramercy.[33]
   FELLOWSHIP: Tush! by thy thanks I set not a straw.
Show me your grief, and say no more.
   EVERYMAN: If I my heart should to you break,
And then you to turn your mind from me,
And would not me comfort, when you hear me speak,
Then should I ten times sorrier be.
   FELLOWSHIP: Sir, I say as I will do in deed.
   EVERYMAN: Then be you a good friend at need:
I have found you true here before.
   FELLOWSHIP: And so ye shall evermore;
For, in faith, and thou go to hell,
I will not forsake thee by the way!
   EVERYMAN: Ye speak like a good friend; I believe you well;
I shall deserve it, and I may.
   FELLOWSHIP: I speak of no deserving, by this day.
For he that will say and nothing do
Is not worthy with good company to go;
Therefore show me the grief of your mind.
As to your friend most loving and kind.
   EVERYMAN: I shall show you how it is;
Commanded I am to go on a journey,
A long way, hard and dangerous,
And give a strait count without delay
Before the high judge Adonai.
Wherefore I pray you, bear me company,
As ye have promised, in this journey.
   FELLOWSHIP: That is matter indeed! Promise is duty,
But, and I should take such a voyage on me,
I know it well, it should be to my pain:
Also it make me afeard, certain.
But let us take counsel here as well as we can,
For your words would fear a strong man.
   EVERYMAN: Why ye said, if I had need,
Ye would me never forsake, quick[34] nor dead,
Though it were to hell truly.
   FELLOWSHIP: So I said, certainly,
But such pleasures be set aside, thee sooth[35] to say:
And also, if we took such a journey,
When should we come again?
   EVERYMAN: Nay, never again till the day of doom.
   FELLOWSHIP: In faith, then will not I come there!
Who hath you these tidings brought?
   EVERYMAN: Indeed, *Death* was with me here.
   FELLOWSHIP: Now, by God that all hath bought,
If *Death* were the messenger,
For no man that is living today
I will not go that loath journey—
Not for the father that begat me!

[33] thanks   [34] living   [35] truth

EVERYMAN: Ye promised other wise, pardie.[36]
FELLOWSHIP: I wot[37] well I say so truly;
And yet if thou wilt eat, and drink, and make good cheer,
Or haunt to women, the lusty company,
I would not forsake you, while the day is clear,
Trust me verily!
EVERYMAN: Yea, thereto ye would be ready;
To go to mirth, solace, and play,
Your mind will sooner apply
Than to bear me company in my long journey.
FELLOWSHIP: Now, in good faith, I will not[38] that way.
But and thou wilt murder, or any man kill,
In that I will help thee with a good will!
EVERYMAN: O that is a simple advice indeed!
Gentle *Fellow*, help in my necessity;
We have loved long, and now I need,
And now, gentle *Fellowship*, remember me.
FELLOWSHIP: Whether ye have loved me or no,
By Saint John, I will not with thee go.
EVERYMAN: Yet I pray thee, take the labor, and do so much for me
To bring me forward,[39] for saint charity.
And comfort me till I come without the town.
FELLOWSHIP: Nay, and thou would give me a new gown,
I will not a foot with thee go;
But and you had tarried I would not have left thee so.
And as now, God speed thee in thy journey,
For from thee I will depart as fast as I may.
EVERYMAN: Whither away, *Fellowship?* will you forsake me?
FELLOWSHIP: Yea, by my fay,[40] to God I betake[41] thee.
EVERYMAN: Farewell, good *Fellowship;* for this my heart is sore;
Adieu for ever, I shall see thee no more.
FELLOWSHIP: In faith, *Everyman,* farewell now at the end;
For you I will remember that parting is mourning. (*Exit* Fellowship.)
EVERYMAN: Alack! shall we thus depart indeed?
Our Lady, help, without any more comfort,
Lo, *Fellowship,* forsaketh me in my most need;
For help in this world whither shall I resort?
Fellowship herebefore with me would merry make;
And now little sorrow for me doth he take.
It is said, in prosperity men friends may find,
Which in adversity be full unkind.
Now whither for succor shall I flee,
Sith[42] that *Fellowship* hath forsaken me?
To my kinsmen I will truly,
Praying them to help me in my necessity;
I believe that they will do so,
For "kind will creep where it may not go."[43]
I will go say,[44] for yonder I see them go.
Where be ye now, my friends and kinsmen?

---

[36] a mild oath   [37] know   [38] I don't want to go   [39] go with me   [40] faith   [41] commit   [42] since
[43] Relatives will creep where they can't walk.   [44] test it

(Enter Kindred *and* Cousin*)*

KINDRED: Here be we now at your commandment.
Cousin, I pray you show us your intent
In any wise, and not spare.
    COUSIN: Yea, *Everyman,* and to us declare
If ye be disposed to go any whither,
For wete you well, we will live and die together.
    KINDRED: In wealth and woe we will with you hold,
For over his kin a man may be bold.
    EVERYMAN: Gramercy, my friends and kinsmen kind.
Now shall I show you the grief of my mind:
I was commanded by a messenger,
That is an high king's chief officer;
He bade me go a pilgrimage to my pain,
And I know well I shall never come again;
Also I must give a reckoning straight,
For I have a great enemy,[45] that hath me in wait,[46]
Which intendeth me for to hinder.
    KINDRED: What account is that which ye must render?
That would I know.
    EVERYMAN: Of all my works I must show
How I have lived and my days spent;
Also of ill deeds, that I have used
In my time, sith life was me lend;
And of all virtues that I have refused.
Therefore I pray you go thither with me,
To help to make mine account, for saint *charity.*
    COUSIN: What, to go thither? Is that the matter?
Nay, *Everyman,* I had liefer[47] fast bread and water
All this five year and more.
    EVERYMAN: Alas, that ever I was bore![48]
For now shall I never be merry
If that you forsake me.
    KINDRED: Ah, sir; what, ye be a merry man!
Take good heart to you, and make no moan.
But one thing I warn you, by Saint Anne.
As for me, ye shall go alone.
    EVERYMAN: My *Cousin,* will you not with me go?
    COUSIN: No, by our Lady; I have the cramp in my toe.
Trust not to me, for, so God me speed,
I will deceive you in your most need.
    KINDRED: It availeth not us to tice.[49]
Ye shall have my maid with all my heart;
She loveth to go to feasts, there to be nice,[50]
And to dance, and abroad to start:
I will give her leave to help you in that journey,
If that you and she may agree.
    EVERYMAN: Now show me the very effect of your mind.
Will you go with me, or abide behind?
    KINDRED: Abide behind? yea, that I will and I may!

[45] Satan   [46] waits for me   [47] rather   [48] born   [49] entice   [50] merry

Therefore farewell until another day. (*Exit* Kindred.)

EVERYMAN: How should I be merry or glad?
For fair promises to me make,
But when I have most need, they me forsake.
I am deceived; that maketh me sad.

COUSIN: Cousin *Everyman*, farewell now,
For verily I will not go with you;
Also of mine own an unready reckoning
I have to account; therefore I make tarrying.
Now, God keep thee, for now I go. (*Exit* Cousin.)

EVERYMAN: Ah, *Jesus*, is all come hereto?
Lo, fair words maketh fools feign;[51]
They promise and nothing will do certain.
My kinsmen promised me faithfully
For to abide with me steadfastly,
And now fast away do they flee:
Even so *Fellowship* promised me.
What friend were best me of to provide?
I lose my time here longer to abide.
Yet in my mind a thing there is;—
All my life I have loved riches;
If that my good now help me might,
He would make my heart full light.
I will speak to him in this distress.—
Where art thou, my *Goods* and riches?

GOODS: (*Within*) Who calleth me? *Everyman?* What haste thou hast!
I lie here in corners, trussed and piled so high,
And in chests I am locked so fast,
Also sacked in bags, thou mayst see with thine eye,
I cannot stir; in packs low I lie.
What would ye have, lightly me say.

EVERYMAN: Come hither, *Good*, in all the haste thou may,
For of counsel I must desire thee.

(*Enter* Goods.)

GOODS: Sir, and ye in the world have trouble or adversity,
That can I help you to remedy shortly.

EVERYMAN: It is another disease[52] that grieveth me;
In this world it is not, I tell thee so.
I am sent for another way to go,
To give a straight account general
Before the highest Jupiter of all;
And all my life I have had joy and pleasure in thee.
Therefore I pray thee go with me,
For, peradventure, thou mayst before God Almighty
My reckoning help to clean and purify;
For it is said ever among,[53]
That money maketh all right that is wrong.

GOODS: Nay, *Everyman*, I sing another song,
I follow no man in such voyages;

51 pretend   52 trouble   53 always said

For and I went with thee
Thou shouldst fare much the worse for me;
For because of me thou did set thy mind,
Thy reckoning I have made blotted and blind,
That thine account thou cannot make truly;
And that hast thou for the love of me.
   EVERYMAN: That would grieve me full sore,
When I should come to that fearful answer.
Up, let us go thither together.
   GOODS: Nay, not so, I am too brittle, I may not endure;
I will follow no man one foot, be ye sure.
   EVERYMAN: Alas, I have thee loved, and had great pleasure
All my life-days on good and treasure.
   GOODS: That is to thy damnation without lesing,[54]
For my love is contrary to the love everlasting
But if thou had me loved moderately during,
As, to the poor give part of me,
Then shouldst thou not in this dolor be,
Nor in this great sorrow and care.
   EVERYMAN: Lo, now was I deceived or[55] I was ware,[56]
And all I may wyte[57] my spending of time.
   GOODS: What, weenest[58] thou that I am thine?
   EVERYMAN: I had wend[59] so.
   GOODS: Nay, *Everyman,* I say no;
As for a while I was lent thee,
A season thou hast had me in prosperity;
My condition is man's soul to kill;
If I save one, a thousand I do spill;[60]
Weenest thou that I will follow thee?
Nay, from this world, not verily.
   EVERYMAN: I had went otherwise.
   GOODS: Therefore to thy soul *Good* is a thief;
For when thou art dead, this is my guise[61]
Another to deceive in the same wise
As I have done thee, and all to his soul's reprief.[62]
   EVERYMAN: O false *Good,* cursed thou be!
Thou traitor to God, that hast deceived me,
And caught me in thy snare.
   GOODS: Mary, thou brought thyself in care,
Whereof I am glad,
I must needs laugh, I cannot be sad.
   EVERYMAN: Ah, *Good,* thou hast had long my hearty love;
I gave thee that which should be the Lord's above.
But wilt thou not go with me in deed?
I pray thee truth to say.
   GOODS: No, so God me speed,
Therefore farewell, and have good day. (*Exit* Goods.)
   EVERYMAN: O, to whom shall I make my moan
For to go with me in that heavy journey?
First *Fellowship* said he would with me gone;
His words were very pleasant and gay,

---

[54] lying   [55] before   [56] aware   [57] blame   [58] think   [59] thought   [60] lay waste   [61] manner   [62] shame

But afterward he left me alone.
Then spake I to my kinsmen all in despair,
And also they gave me words fair,
They lacked no fair speaking,
But all forsake me in the ending.
Then went I to my *Goods* that I loved best,
In hope to have comfort, but there had I least;
For my *Goods* sharply did me tell
That he bringeth many into hell.
Then of myself I was ashamed,
And so I am worthy to be blamed;
Thus may I myself hate.
Of whom shall I now counsel take?
I think that I shall never speed
Till that I go to my *Good-Deeds,*
But, alas, she is so weak,
That she can neither go nor speak;
Yet will I venture on her now.—
My *Good-Deeds,* where be you?

(Good-Deeds *speaks from the ground.)*

GOOD-DEEDS: Here I lie cold in the ground;
Thy sins hath me sore bound,
That I cannot stir.
    EVERYMAN: O, *Good-Deeds,* I stand in fear;
I must you pray of counsel,
For help now should come right well.
    GOOD-DEEDS: *Everyman,* I have understanding
That ye be summoned account to make
Before *Messias,* of Jerusalem King;
And you do by me[63] that journey with you will I take.
    EVERYMAN: Therefore I come to you, my moan to make;
I pray you, that ye will go with me.
    GOOD-DEEDS: I would full fain, but I cannot stand verily.
    EVERYMAN: Why, is there anything on you fall?
    GOOD-DEEDS: Yea, sir, I may thank you of all;[64]
If ye had perfectly cheered[65] me,
Your book of account now full ready had be.
Look, the books of your works and deeds eke;
Oh, see how they lie under the feet,
To your soul's heaviness.
    EVERYMAN: Our Lord *Jesus,* help me!
For one letter here I cannot see.[66]
    GOOD-DEEDS: There is a blind reckoning in time of distress!
    EVERYMAN: *Good-Deeds,* I pray you, help me in this need,
Or else I am for ever damned indeed;
Therefore help me to make reckoning
Before the redeemer of all thing,
That king is, and was, and ever shall.
    GOOD-DEEDS: *Everyman,* I am sorry of your fall,

---

[63] If you listen to me   [64] everything?   [65] cherished   [66] I can't see even one letter.

And fain would I help you, and I were able.

EVERYMAN: *Good-Deeds,* your counsel I pray you give me.

GOOD-DEEDS: That shall I do verily;
Though that on my feet I may not go,
I have a sister that shall with you also,
Called *Knowledge,* which shall with you abide,
To help you to make that dreadful reckoning.

(*Enter* Knowledge.)

KNOWLEDGE: *Everyman,* I will go with thee, and be thy guide,
In thy most need to go by thy side.

EVERYMAN: In good condition I am now in every thing,
And am wholly content with this good thing;
Thanked be God my Creator.

GOOD-DEEDS: And when he hath brought thee there,
Where thou shalt heal thee of thy smart,
Then go you with your reckoning and your *Good-Deeds* together
For to make you joyful at heart
Before the blessed Trinity.

EVERYMAN: My *Good-Deeds,* gramercy;
I am well content, certainly,
With your words sweet.

KNOWLEDGE: No go we together lovingly,
To *Confession,* that cleansing river.

EVERYMAN: For joy I weep; I would we were there;
But, I pray you, give me cognition
Where dwelleth that holy man, *Confession.*

KNOWLEDGE: In the house of salvation:
We shall find him in that place,
That shall us comfort by God's grace. (*They approach* Confession.)
Lo, this is *Confession;* kneel down and ask mercy,
For he is in good conceit[67] with God almighty.

EVERYMAN: O glorious fountain that all uncleanness doth clarify,
Wash from me the spots of vices unclean,
That on me no sin may be seen;
I come with *Knowledge* for my redemption,
Repent with hearty and full contrition;
For I am commanded a pilgrimage to take,
And great accounts before God to make.
Now, I pray you, *Shrift,*[68] mother of salvation,
Help my good deeds for my piteous exclamation.

CONFESSION: I know your sorrow well, *Everyman;*
Because with *Knowledge* ye come to me,
I will you comfort as well as I can,
And a precious jewel I will give thee,
Called penance, wise voider[69] of adversity;
Therewith shall your body chastised be,
With abstinence and perseverance in God's service:
Here shall you receive that scourge of me,
Which is penance strong, that ye must endure,

---

[67] favor   [68] confession   [69] discharger

To remember thy Savior was scourged for thee
With sharp scourges, and suffered it patiently;
So must thou, or thou scape that painful pilgrimage;
Knowledge, keep him in this voyage,[70]
And by that time *Good-Deeds* will be with thee.
But in any wise, be sure of mercy,
For your time draweth fast, and ye will saved be;
Ask God mercy, and He will grant truly,
When with the scourge of penance man doth him bind,
The oil of forgiveness then shall he find.

EVERYMAN: Thanked be God for his gracious work!
For now I will my penance begin;
This hath rejoiced and lighted my heart,
Though the knots be painful and hard within;

KNOWLEDGE: *Everyman,* look your penance that ye fulfil,
What pain that ever it to you be.
And *Knowledge* shall give you counsel at will,
How your accounts ye shall make clearly.

EVERYMAN: O eternal God, O heavenly figure,
O way of rightwiseness, O goodly vision,
Which descended down in a virgin pure
Because he would *Everyman* redeem,
Which Adam forfeited by his disobedience:
O blessed Godhead, elect and high-divine,
Forgive my grievous offence;
Here I cry thee mercy in this presence.
O ghostly treasure, O ransomer and redeemer
Of all the world, hope and conductor,
Mirror of joy, and founder of mercy,
Which illumineth heaven and earth thereby,
Hear my clamorous complaint, though it late be;
Receive my prayers; unworthy in this heavy life,
Though I be, a sinner most abominable,
Yet let my name be written in Moses' table;[71]
O Mary, pray to the Maker of all thing,
Me for to help at my ending,
And save me from the power of my enemy,
For *Death* assaileth me strongly;
And, Lady, that I may by means of thy prayer
Of your Son's glory to be partaker,
By the means of his passion I it crave,
I beseech you, help my soul to save.—
Knowledge, give me the scourge of penance;
My flesh therewith shall give a quittance:
I will now begin, if God give me grace.

KNOWLEDGE: *Everyman,* God give you time and space:
Thus I bequeath you in the hands of our Saviour,
Thus may you make your reckoning sure.

EVERYMAN: In the name of the Holy Trinity,
My body sore punished shall be:
Take this body for the sin of the flesh;

---

[70] course   [71] The tables of stone on which the ten commandments were recorded.

Also thou delightest to go gay and fresh,
And in the way of damnation thou did me bring;
Therefore suffer now strokes and punishing.
Now of penance I will wade the water clear,
To save me from purgatory, that sharp fire.

(Good-Deeds *rises.*)

GOOD-DEEDS: I thank God, now I can walk and go;
And am delivered of my sickness and woe.
Therefore with *Everyman* I will go, and not spare;
His good works I will help him to declare.
    KNOWLEDGE: Now, *Everyman,* be merry and glad;
Your *Good-Deeds* cometh now; ye may not be sad;
Now is your *Good-Deeds* whole and sound,
Going upright upon the ground.
    EVERYMAN: My heart is light, and shall be evermore;
Now will I smite faster than I did before.
    GOOD-DEEDS: *Everyman,* pilgrim, my special friend,
Blessed be thou without end;
For thee is prepared the eternal glory.
Ye have me made whole and sound,
Therefore I will bide by thee in every stound.[72]
    EVERYMAN: Welcome, my *Good-Deeds;* now I hear thy voice,
I weep for very sweetness of love.
    KNOWLEDGE: Be no more sad, but ever rejoice,
God seeth thy living in his throne above;
Put on this garment to thy behoof,[73]
Which is wet with your tears,
Or else before God you may it miss,
When you to your journey's end come shall.
    EVERYMAN: Gentle *Knowledge,* what do you it call?
    KNOWLEDGE: It is a garment of sorrow:
From pain it will you borrow;[74]
Contrition it is,
That getteth forgiveness;
It pleaseth God passing well.
    GOOD-DEEDS: *Everyman,* will you wear it for your heal?
    EVERYMAN: Now blessed be Jesu, Mary's Son!
For now have I on true contrition.
And let us go now without tarrying:
Good-Deeds, have we clear our reckoning?
    GOOD-DEEDS: Yea, indeed I have it here.
    EVERYMAN: Then I trust we need not fear;
Now, friends, let us not part in twain.
    KNOWLEDGE: Nay, Everyman, that will we not, certain.
    GOOD-DEEDS: Yet must thou lead with thee
Three persons of great might.
    EVERYMAN: Who should they be?
    GOOD-DEEDS: *Discretion* and *Strength* they hight,[75]
And thy *Beauty* may not abide behind.

---

[72] all the same   [73] advantage   [74] save   [75] are called

KNOWLEDGE: Also ye must call to mind
Your *Five-Wits* as for your counselors.
GOOD-DEEDS: You must have them ready at all hours.
EVERYMAN: How shall I get them hither?
KNOWLEDGE: You must call them all together,
And they will hear you incontinent.[76]
EVERYMAN: My friends, come hither and be present,
Discretion, Strength, my *Five-Wits,* and *Beauty.*

(*Enter* Discretion, Strength, Five-Wits, *and* Beauty.)

BEAUTY: Here at your will we be all ready.
What will ye that we should do?
GOOD-DEEDS: That ye would with *Everyman* go,
And help him in his pilgrimage,
Advise you,[77] will ye with him or not in that voyage?
STRENGTH: We will bring him all thither,
To his help and comfort, ye may believe me.
DISCRETION: So will we go with him all together.
EVERYMAN: Almighty God, loved thou be,
I give thee laud that I have hither brought
Strength, Discretion, Beauty, and *Five-Wits;* lack I nought;
And my *Good-Deeds,* with *Knowledge* clear,
All be in my company at my will here;
I desire no more to my business.
STRENGTH: And I, *Strength,* will by you stand in distress,
Though thou would in battle fight on the ground.
FIVE-WITS: And though it were through the world round,
We will not depart for sweet nor sour.
BEAUTY: No more will I unto death's hour,
Whatsoever thereof befall.
DISCRETION: *Everyman,* advise you first of all;
Go with a good advisement and deliberation;
We all give you virtuous monition[78]
That all shall be well.
EVERYMAN: My friends, hearken[79] what I will tell:
I pray God reward you in his heavenly sphere.
Now hearken, all that be here,
For I will make my testament
Here before you all present.
In alms half my good I will give with my hands twain
In the way of charity, with good intent,
And the other half still shall remain
In bequest to be returned there[80] it ought to be.
This I do in despite of the fiend of hell
To go quite out of his peril
Ever after and this day.
KNOWLEDGE: *Everyman,* hearken what I say;
Go to priesthood, I you advise,
And recieve of him in any wise

---

[76] immediately   [77] consider   [78] warning   [79] listen   [80] where

The holy sacrament and ointment[81] together;
Then shortly see ye turn again hither;
We will all abide you here.
   FIVE-WITS: Yea, *Everyman,* hie you that ye ready were,[82]
There is no emperor, king, duke, nor baron,
That of God hath commission,
As hath the least priest in the world being;
For of the blessed sacraments pure and benign,
He beareth the keys and thereof hath the cure
For man's redemption, it is ever sure;
Which God for our soul's medicine
Gave us out of his heart with great pain;
Here in this transitory life, for thee and me
The blessed sacraments seven there be,
Baptism, confirmation, with priesthood good,
And the sacrament of God's precious flesh and blood,
Marriage, the holy extreme unction, and penance;
These seven be good to have in remembrance,
Gracious sacraments of high divinity.
   EVERYMAN: Fain would I receive that holy body[83]
And meekly to my ghostly father I will go.
   FIVE-WITS: *Everyman,* that is the best that ye can do:
God will you to salvation bring,
For priesthood exceedeth all other thing;
To us Holy Scripture they do teach,
And converteth man from sin heaven to reach;
God hath to them more power given,
Than to any angel that is in heaven;
With five words he may consecrate
God's body in flesh and blood to make,
And handleth his maker between his hands;
The priest bindeth and unbindeth all bands,
Both in earth and in heaven;
Thou ministers all the sacraments seven;
Though we kissed thy feet thou were worthy;
Thou art surgeon that cureth sin deadly:
No remedy we find under God
But all only priesthood.
Everyman, God gave priests that dignity,
And setteth them in his stead among us to be;
Thus be they above angels in degree. (*Exit* Everyman.)
   KNOWLEDGE: If priests be good it is so surely;
But when Jesus hanged on the cross with great smart
There he gave, out of his blessed heart,
The same sacrament in great torment:
He sold them not to us, that Lord Omnipotent.
Therefore Saint Peter the apostle doth say
That Jesu's curse hath all they
Which God their Saviour do buy or sell,[84]

---

[81] communion and extreme unction for the dying   [82] are   [83] communion wafer   [84] give communion for pay

Or they for any money do take or tell.[85]
Sinful priests giveth the sinners example bad;
Their children sitteth by other men's fires, I have heard;
And some haunteth women's company,
With unclean life, as lusts of lechery:
These be with sin made blind.

   FIVE-WITS: I trust to God no such may we find;
Therefore let us priesthood honor,
And follow their doctrine for our souls' succor;
We be their sheep, and they shepherds be
By whom we all be kept in surety.
Peace, for yonder I see *Everyman* come,
Which hath made true satisfaction.

   GOOD-DEEDS: Methinketh it is he indeed.

   (Re-enter Everyman.)

   EVERYMAN: Now Jesu be your alder speed.[86]
I have received the sacrament for my redemption,
And then mine extreme unction:
Blessed be all they that counseled me to take it!
And now, friends, let us go without longer respite;
I thank God that ye have tarried so long.
Now set each of you on this rod[87] your hand,
And shortly follow me:
I go before, there I would be; God be our guide.

   STRENGTH: *Everyman*, we will not from you go,
Till ye have gone this voyage long.

   DISCRETION: I, *Discretion*, will bide by you also.

   KNOWLEDGE: And though this pilgrimage be never so strong,[88]
I will never part you fro:
Everyman, I will be as sure by thee
As ever I did by Judas Maccabee. (*They approach the grave.*)

   EVERYMAN: Alas, I am so faint I may not stand,
My limbs under me do fold;
Friends, let us not turn again to this land,
Not for all the world's gold,
For into this cave must I creep
And turn to the earth and there to sleep.

   BEAUTY: What, into this grave? alas!

   EVERYMAN: Yea, there shall you consume, more and less.[89]

   BEAUTY: And what, should I smother here?

   EVERYMAN: Yea, by my faith, and never more appear.
In this world live no more we shall,
But in heaven before the highest Lord of all.

   BEAUTY: I cross out all this; adieu by Saint John;
I take my tap in my lap[90] and am gone.

   EVERYMAN: What, Beauty, whither will ye?

   BEAUTY: Peace, I am deaf;[91] I look not behind me,
Not and thou would give me all the gold in thy chest.

---

[85] account [86] aid us all [87] cross [88] hard [89] those of both high and low station [90] my leave quickly [91] I won't listen.

EVERYMAN: Alas, whereto may I trust?
Beauty goeth fast away hie;
She promised with me to live and die.
STRENGTH: *Everyman,* I will thee also forsake and deny;
Thy game liketh[92] me not at all.
EVERYMAN: Why, then ye will forsake me all.
Sweet *Strength,* tarry a little space.
STRENGTH: Nay, sir, by the rood of grace[93]
I will hie from thee fast,
Though thou weep till thy heart brast.[94]
EVERYMAN: Ye would ever bide by me, ye said.
STRENGTH: Yea, I have you far enough conveyed;
Ye be old enough, I understand,
Your pilgrimage to take on hand;
I repent me that I higher came.
EVERYMAN: *Strength,* you to displease I am to blame;
Will you break promise that is debt?
STRENGTH: In faith, I care not;
Thou art but a fool to complain,
You spend your speech and waste your brain;
Go thrust thee into the ground. (*Exit* Strength.)
EVERYMAN: I had wend surer I should you have found.
He that trusteth in his *Strength*
She him deceiveth at the length.
Both *Strength* and *Beauty* forsaketh me,
Yet they promised me fair and lovingly.
DISCRETION: *Everyman,* I will after *Strength* be gone,
As for me I will leave you alone.
EVERYMAN: Why, *Discretion,* will ye forsake me?
DISCRETION: Yea, in faith, I will go from thee,
For when *Strength* goeth before
I follow after evermore.
EVERYMAN: Yet, I pray thee, for the love of the Trinity,
Look in my grave once piteously.
DISCRETION: Nay, so nigh will I not come.
Farewell, everyone! (*Exit* Discretion.)
EVERYMAN: O all thing faileth, save God alone;
Beauty, Strength, and *Discretion;*
For when *Death* bloweth his blast,
They all run from me full fast.
FIVE-WITS: *Everyman,* my leave now of thee I take;
I will follow the other, for here I thee forsake.
EVERYMAN: Alas! then may I wail and weep,
For I took you for my best friend.
FIVE-WITS: I will no longer thee keep;
Now farewell, and there an end. (*Exit* Five-Wits.)
EVERYMAN: O Jesu, help, all hath forsaken me!
GOOD-DEEDS: Nay, *Everyman,* I will abide with thee,
I will not forsake thee indeed;
Thou shalt find me a good friend at need.
EVERYMAN: Gramercy, *Good-Deeds;* now may I true friends see;

[92] pleases   [93] Christ's cross   [94] break

They have forsaken me every one;
I loved them better than my *Good-Deeds* alone.
Knowledge, will ye forsake me also?

    KNOWLEDGE: Yea, *Everyman,* when ye to death do go:
But not yet for no manner of danger.

    EVERYMAN: Gramercy, *Knowledge,* with all my heart.

    KNOWLEDGE: Nay, yet I will not from hence depart,
Till I see where ye shall be come.

    EVERYMAN: Methinketh, alas, that I must be gone,
To make my reckoning and my debts pay,
For I see my time is nigh spent away.
Take example, all ye that this do hear or see,
How they that I loved best do forsake me,
Except my *Good-Deeds* that bideth truly.

    GOOD-DEEDS: All earthly things is but vanity:
Beauty, Strength, and *Discretion* do man forsake,
Foolish friends and kinsmen, that fair spake,
All fleeth save *Good-Deeds,* and that am I.

    EVERYMAN: Have mercy on me, God most mighty;
And stand by me, thou Mother and Maid, holy Mary.

    GOOD-DEEDS: Fear not I will speak for thee.

    EVERYMAN: Here I cry God mercy.

    GOOD-DEEDS: Short our end, and minish[95] our pain;
Let us go and never come again.

    EVERYMAN: Into thy hands, Lord, my soul I commend;
Receive it, Lord, that it be not lost;
As thou me boughtest, so me defend,
And save me from the fiend's boast,
That I may appear with that blessed host
That shall be saved at the day of doom.
In manus tuas—of might's most
Forever—*commendo spiritum meum.*[96]

    *(*Everyman *and* Good-Deeds *descend into the grave.)*

    KNOWLEDGE: Now hath he suffered that we all shall endure;
The *Good-Deeds* shall make all sure.
Now hath he made ending;
Methinketh that I hear angels sing
And make great joy and melody,
Where *Everyman's* soul received shall be.

    ANGEL: *(Within)* Come, excellent elect spouse to Jesu;
Hereabove thou shalt go
Because of thy singular virtue:
Now the soul is taken the body fro;
Thy reckoning is crystal-clear.
Now shalt thou into the heavenly sphere,
Unto the which all ye shall come
That liveth well before the day of doom. *(Exit* Knowledge.)

    (Enter Doctor *as* Epilogue.)

---

[95] diminish [96] "Into thy hands I commend my spirit." Luke 23:46.

DOCTOR: This moral men may have in mind;
Ye hearers, take if of worth,[97] old and young,
And forsake pride, for he deceiveth you in the end,
And remember *Beauty, Five-Wits, Strength,* and *Discretion,*
They all at the last do *Everyman* forsake,
Save his *Good-Deeds,* there doth he take.
But beware, and[98] they be small
Before God, he hath no help at all.
None excuse may be there for *Everyman:*
Alas, how shall he do then?
For after death amends may no man make,
For then mercy and pity do him forsake.
If his reckoning be not clear when he do come,
God will say—*ite maledicti in ignem aeternum.*[99]
And he that hath his account whole and sound,
High in heaven he shall be crowned;
Unto which place God bring us all thither
That we may live body and soul together.
Thereto help the Trinity,
Amen, say ye, for saint *Charity.*

Thus Endeth This Moral Play of Everyman.

---

[97] if you think it's worthwile   [98] if   [99] "Go, ye accused into everlasting fire." Matthew 25:41.

FOR DISCUSSION

1. *Everyman* is said to be a dramatized allegory. What is an allegory? Does this play fit your definition?
2. Does the play have a plot? What actually happens in *Everyman?* Discuss the action.
3. Where do you think the setting for the play could be? Could it be in the mind of man? Discuss.
4. Who are the main characters in the play? What characters play supporting roles?
5. *Everyman* is a morality play. What is morality? Do you think the definition has changed any since the play was written?
6. What characters deserted Everyman? Who stayed with him? How do you interpret this?
7. Do you think you would enjoy seeing this play on stage? Why or why not?
8. Try to state the theme of this play.
9. *Everyman* seems to preach a sermon. Does this add to or detract from its dramatic effect? Why?
10. Everyman is asked to account for his life. Why does he try to gain the help of the other characters?
11. How was Everyman able to heal Good-Deeds?

SUPPLEMENTARY READING

Author unknown   *Abraham and Isaac*
Author unknown   *The Second Shepherds' Play*

III

The Renaissance Theatre

Italian Theatre

For most of Europe, we may say that the Renaissance began in 1453 with the fall of Constantinople to the Turks. After the Turks took control, the Christian monks and scholars fled to Italy, taking all the manuscripts they could carry. Italy at that time was a collection of independent states which had courts and academies where the arts were patronized. In addition to the renewed study of the classics, the interest in learning was further spurred by the invention of the printing press.

Because Latin was understood by all scholars of the time and because classical learning was greatly admired, the plays of the Roman playwrights Plautus, Terence, and Seneca influenced the beginnings of drama in Italy. The first plays were adaptations on translations of these three writers, of whom Seneca was the most admired. Largely due to the influence of his plays, rigid rules were formulated for the writing of drama. This inflexible framework was called neoclassicism. One rule was that all plays must be written in five acts. Tragedies had to teach a moral lesson, and all drama was viewed as a vehicle for instruction. The events depicted had to be those which could happen in everyday life. Tragedy had to deal with nobility, and comedy with the middle and lower classes. There could be no mixing of comic and tragic elements.

In addition to the Roman dramatists, other influences affected the formulation of the rules of neoclassicism. Most important were Aristotle's *Poetics* and Horace's *Art of Poetry,* written during the first century B.C. One of the most binding rules, was that every drama had to adhere strictly to the unities of time, place, and action. Unity of time meant that a play had to occur in the space of one day. Unity of place meant that the setting could not change from one location to another. Unity of action, the only true classical element insisted upon by Aristotle, meant that there could be no subplots.

During the period of the Italian Renaissance, very little good drama was written because of the hampering effect of these rules. One of the first writers of comedy was Lodovico Ariosto, who lived from 1474 to 1533. His two plays, *Cassaria* (1508) and *I Suppositi* (1509), are often considered to mark the true beginnings of Italian drama. They dealt with the playwright's own time period and were concerned with the Italian court and bureaucracy. Another playwright was Niccolò Machiavelli, perhaps more familiar for his writings on political philosophy. His play *La Mandragola,* written between 1513 and 1520, followed the classic format, but was highly cynical in its subject matter, which was taken from the farces of the medieval period.

For the most part, neoclassic plays were too strictly structured to provide much entertainment. So, since people wanted to be entertained, several new forms of drama began to develop. One was the pastoral, which was widely popular during the sixteenth century. The characters were shepherds and shepherdesses, nymphs and fauns, and the plots involved romantic love. One of the best known is *The Faithful Shepherd,* written in 1590 by Giambattista Guarini, which greatly influenced the later development of romantic literature in France and England.

Another form was the *intermezzi,* originally a series of short scenes or plays, with singing and dancing, which were presented between the acts of a neoclassic tragedy. The subject matter was often drawn from mythology, there were elaborate stage effects, and the *intermezzi* became highly popular. At first, the *intermezzi* between the acts at a single performance were playlets unrelated to each other. However, as time passed, all the scenes were somewhat tied together, and were often related to the neoclassic tragedy in which they appeared.

The *intermezzi* began to decline in favor early in the seventeenth century, with the rise of opera, which began to be written and produced in the last decade of the sixteenth century. Opera was developed as an attempt to add music, dancing, and choral singing to the tragedies, in much the same way (the Italians believed) as had been done in ancient Greece. The popularity of the opera increased so rapidly that by 1650 it had spread throughout much of Europe.

The most important contribution of the Italian Renaissance to the theatre was not the writing of drama but the staging of it. There was a strong movement toward the presentation of spectacles and spectacular effects. This trend was influenced by a man named Vitruvius, who centuries before, in the early part of the first century A.D. had written a book about constructing buildings, *De Architectura*. The book was rediscovered in 1414 and translated into Italian in 1521. It led another man, Sebastiano Serlio, to write the book *Architettura* in 1545, in which he showed how a theatre should be planned and how scenery was to be erected and used. He assumed that theatres would be constructed in existing buildings and recommended following the Roman style, with seating arrangements at one end of a hall and a stage at the other.

Serlio described three settings that could be used for all plays: the tragic, the comic, and the pastoral. Both the comic and the tragic settings were street scenes, while the pastoral was a wooded area. The settings combined false perspective with the three-dimensional elements. The floor of the stage was to be painted in squares which became smaller and smaller toward the back. The stage floor itself was to be raked upward, so that the back part would be higher than the front. It is from this description of stages by Serlio that we have the terms "upstage" and "downstage." The reason for all this—for raking the stage, or sloping it up toward the back, and for painting squares of decreasing size—was to give the impression of distance. Such use of false perspective became an important part of all the theatres constructed in Italy during the Renaissance. Even today there are still stages in existence that are raked.

As the theatre gained in popularity in Italy, a need was felt to erect permanent theatre buildings, rather than to continue producing plays in existing buildings. The architecture that was developed was based on Roman models. The oldest theatre that still exists is the Teatro Olimpico, constructed for the Olympic Academy in Vicenza and first used in 1585. It was started by a man named Andrea Palladio in 1580. Before it was completed, however, Palladio died, and the theatre was finished by his pupil Vincenzo Scamozzi, who added his own ideas. It followed the plan of Roman theatres but added the use of perspective in the raked floors and the background, which shows openings for streets. These aisle-ways or streets decrease in size the farther back they go, giving the effect of great distance. The rest of the building contains thirteen rows of seats in an elliptical pattern, providing excellent sightlines for viewing the plays from any place in the audience area. The orchestra floor is flat, and the stage itself is raised several feet above the orchestra level.

Another important theatre of the period was the Teatro Farnese, built by Giovanni Battistia Aleotti in 1618 at Parma. The building is particularly important because it was the first to use the proscenium arch, or the framing device, which is common in most modern theatres. The proscenium arch is much like the matting around a painting, and masks the back-stage and side-stage areas, called the wings. It also masks the top of the stage, where objects to be flown in and out are stored and where, in modern theatres, many groups of lights are hung. Another advantage of the proscenium arch is that it facilitates the use of a front curtain, which can be closed to mask changes of scenery and properties.

With the proscenium arch, the settings of the Italian theatre consisted of a backdrop, borders across the top of the stage and wings (so-called because they extend into the wing areas of the stage). The wings were flats at each side of the stage to further frame the action and to present the illusion of a specific place. The action, however, could not be portrayed realistically because of the false or forced perspective. Since the stage was raked and the scenery was smaller toward the upstage area, an actor had to play in front of the scenery. If he walked too far upstage, he dwarfed the buildings, which were shorter than he was. This, of course, would prove to be comic and would ruin the effects of the play. What the proscenium arch did was to provide a definite separation of audience and action.

The scenery and effects in the theatre of the Italian Renaissance were quite elaborate. In addition to the use of borders and backdrop (upstage curtain), methods were worked out to show changes in location or setting. One method was based on Serlio's work and involved a modified use of the Greek *periaktoi*. The Serlian wings were two flats fastened together in a V shape. Later a third side was added. Each three-sided wing was then placed slightly more toward the center of the stage than the one in front of it. The side facing the audience could be painted to give the effect of walls or any specific location. To change the scene, another side, painted a different way, could be rotated and exposed to the audience. Another method of changing scenes was developed by Nicola Sabbattini. He used the two-sided, V-shaped wings, one very close behind the other, in groups. The painted portion, or one of the sides, faced the audience. The other piece was angled upstage to support the wing so it could stand alone. Since the wings were in groups, it was a simple task to pull away the front wing of each group to reveal a new scene behind. From these two devices the wing and drop system was further refined, spreading throughout Europe and to the United States in the years that followed. One variation was called the "chariot and pole" system. This meant that the wings or flats were mounted on poles which extended down to the chariots, or wagons with wheels. The wheels fit into slots in the stage floor. One set of wings could thus be moved offstage easily while another was moved on. Such systems of shifting scenery remained virtually unchanged in European theatres until the middle of the nineteenth century.

Stage machinery provided almost miraculous effects. Buildings rose and descended through trapdoors, and mechanical animals and chariots flew around the stage, manipulated by ropes and pulleys. The animals and chariots were constructed of wooden frames covered with canvas. These special flying effects, known as "glories," involved great expense in their construction. The scenery was painted in great detail by professional artists, among the best of their day. Because the plays were presented indoors, artificial lighting in the form of candles was used. Special lighting effects could be achieved by placing candles behind colored bottles. The practice of using candles lasted well into the nineteenth century and accounted for many theatre fires.

In addition to the drama that was presented in buildings, another form developed in Renaissance Italy—the *comedia dell'arte,* believed to have evolved either from ancient pantomimes or from the plays of Plautus and Terence. It remained one of the most popular forms of theatre from the mid-fifteenth to the mid-sixteenth century. *Commedia dell'arte* was adaptable to changing situations and locations. It was performed by professional troupes and involved the use of an outline, called a *scenario,* rather than a script. The characters built their lines and actions from the basic outline, but were free to add what they wished. Because the troupes moved from village to village, they would adapt their material to a specific place by referring to current events and residents of each locale.

Certain stock characters were used, much like those in Roman comedy. They were divided into three groups: the lovers, who were straight characters, the professional types, and the servants. The latter two types were always comic. Some of these stock characters were Pantalone, the old miser; Il Capitano, the braggart soldier, and Il Dottore, the academic doctor, of Ph.D., who used a kind of gibberish in substituting incorrect words and phrases for the proper ones. The comic servants were a group called the *zanni*, from which our word "zany" derives. One of these servants was Pulcinella, a hunchback with a hooked nose similar to the character Punch in Punch and Judy shows. Another was Arlecchino, who performed comedy similar to that of the Three Stooges.

Once a person was accepted as a member of a *commedia dell'arte* troupe, he played the same character for the rest of his life. Because of this specialization in character portrayal, a young lover might remain the romantic figure in a presentation well into his seventies. The troupes went from town to town to play in the marketplace, although the best troupes, such as the Gelosi or the Accesi, sometimes were invited to play for nobility in the court theatres. The plays were presented on wagons with only a piece of cloth as background. A major part of the show consisted of *lazzi*, which was either verbal or visual business. A character would go into a certain comedy routine whenever he felt it necessary. By agreed-on signals the members of the troupe could let him know when they wanted him to end the routine and go on with the story of the play. The *commedia dell'arte* had a strong and marked influence on later forms of drama, as did other Italian theatre practices.

Spanish Theatre

During the time that neoclassicism was gaining a foothold in Italy, drama and the theatre were also developing in Spain. Although influenced to a certain degree by neoclassicism, Spain, because of its independence and isolation from the rest of Europe, developed a drama of greater literary value than that of Italy. Since a great number of plays were written between 1580 and 1680, this era became known as Spain's Golden Age.

Native Spanish drama began to develop between 1500 and 1550. The first playwright, and the founder of Spanish drama, was Juan del Encina, who lived from about 1468 to about 1537. His plays were secular and were similar to Italian pastorals. The first popular dramatist of Spain was Lope de Rueda, who toured with his own company. His plays were comedies and showed to a certain extent the influence of the *commedia dell'arte*. Rueda is credited with inventing the *paso,* or comic and sketch presented as an interlude. Some of the plays of Spain were written following classical models and were presented at the palaces and universities in both Latin and Spanish.

The most popular drama was greatly influenced by medieval cycle plays. These early plays, called *auto sacramentales,* showed reenactments of biblical scenes or scenes from the lives of saints. However, they differed from the mystery plays in that they used allegorical characters, somewhat similar to those in morality plays.

The drama of Spain, although it developed later than that of other countries, was at first produced by guilds and later by city councils. The first actors were amateurs. Three productions were presented each year until 1592. After that there were four a year until 1647, then only two. Some of the plays were repeated from year to year, but new ones also were produced. All included dancing at the end of each performance. The early dramas were presented in the church, but after a time the actors traveled around the city, giving the plays, in various locations and using pageant wagons, called *carros,* to carry their scenery. These productions included songs, comic sketches, and juggling. Interludes of comedy and obscenity sometimes accompanied even the religious plays.

Some of the early plays dealt with religious themes, but also contained references to contemporary events. Later plays dealt only with contemporary life. Unlike other European countries, Spain's religious drama continued until 1765, when it was finally forbidden. The only writer of religious drama in the city of Madrid between 1647 and 1681 was Pedro Calderón de la Barca, whose plays totaled more than two hundred. He stole many of his ideas from other sources, but made his writings more poetic and spiritual than the originals.

Secular drama began to be written and produced by the beginning of the sixteenth century, and all the comedies of Spain's Golden Age were written in verse. The best known and most prolific playwright of Spain was Lope de Vega, who lived from 1562 to 1635 and is believed to have written more than 1,800 plays. His drama was characterized by a mixing of form, vigorous action, and suspense. Most of his characters were drawn from historical sources or mythology. However, he was by no means the only playwright. It is estimated that by the end of the Golden Age, more than 30,000 plays had been written, a large percentage of which dealt with the themes of love and honor.

The plays were presented either in the court theatres or in *corrales*. Most of the court plays were produced between 1623 and 1654, during the reign of Philip IV, both in palaces and on the palace grounds. The *corrales*, typical of northern Spain, were open courtyards formed by the outer walls of houses. Spectators filled the balconies and rooms of the houses or sat on benches in the courtyard. Those who wanted to pay a smaller admission fee stood behind the rows of benches. The stage itself was wide and contained no curtain. There was some crudely painted scenery, but most of the changes of locale were indicated through dialogue. The stage had a large apron, or front portion, which extended into the courtyard. A balcony above the acting area also could be used for scenes from the plays. At first the theatres were temporary structures, but later, after the first permanent theatre was erected in Madrid in 1579, more and more permanent theatres were built. In the southern part of Spain, there were no courtyards and plays were presented in patios.

As permanent theatres were erected, the number of acting companies increased. In 1603 the government sought to have some control over them by restricting their number to eight; but the attempt at regulation was unsuccessful. Some of the companies were "sharing" troupes; that is, they shared equally in the expense and profit of a production. Others were organized with actors under salary to a manager. Each troupe contained sixteen to twenty members. The companies generally bought plays outright from the authors.

Actors were considered undesirable members of society. However, despite opposition from the church, they were generally tolerated. One difference between dramatic productions in Spain and other European countries was that there were actresses in some of the troupes, although not until 1587 were women licensed to appear in plays.

By 1700, Spain's power began to decline and so did the theatre. By the middle of the eighteenth century, its Golden Age was a thing of the past.

The Theatre of Elizabethan England

The Elizabethan era in England is named for Queen Elizabeth I, who was the ruling monarch from 1558 to 1603. Although there were traveling players in England before this period, their performances were infrequent and scattered, and in the fifteenth century they were defined by law as vagabonds and rogues. But in the reign of Elizabeth, actors were legally recognized, when a law was passed in 1572 stating that, in order to perform, actors needed a license from two justices of the peace or the patronage of a nobleman. Two years later a Master of Revels was appointed to license acting companies.

Patronage by a nobleman did not guarantee success, since no financial support was involved. It meant only that he protected the troupe, who in return were expected to present entertainments for him. In general, despite legal recognition, actors were little more than tolerated by the middle class, which distrusted the theatre. As a matter of fact, one reason why public theatres were placed outside the city of London is that there they were less accessible to apprentices who might sneak away from their jobs to attend a performance.

The development of the theatre under Elizabeth was influenced by several factors. Because of the religious discontent brought about by the conflict between Catholics and Protestants, the queen sought to unite the country by making the citizens aware of their cultural heritage. This spirit of nationalism in turn affected the theatre, and plays began to be written with patriotic themes. Both playwrights and play producers were influenced by the medieval theatre and Renaissance forms of drama established in Italy.

The queen and other members of the nobility did much to establish the theatre as a respectable form of entertainment for everyone, not just the upper classes. It took some time before the larger public ceased to regard it as immoral and only a means of camouflaging more undesirable activities. Even after the protection of acting companies by the central government assured the actors that they could legally perform, there was still strong opposition from the local government leaders in smaller towns, and actors sometimes were actually paid *not* to perform. Despite that fact, the theatre was firmly established in England by the 1580's.

The English theatre had several early origins. First were the schools, where plays were read, and sometimes performed, in Latin. Students then wrote plays in imitation of the models. Although they were influenced by the classical style of writing, these new plays dealt with English locations and subject matter. A second source was the Inns of Court, which were schools and places of residence for lawyers. Because the residents were from the upper class, they were exposed to classical learning and influenced by the plays of ancient Rome. Professional acting companies were a third source. The plays they presented were a mixture of various elements, some of which came from classical drama and from the medieval period. However, the playwrights were no longer bound by the unities of time, place, and action, as can be seen in Shakespeare's plays, which have subplots, switch time and place, and even mix comic and tragic elements.

One of the earliest English playwrights was John Heywood, who lived from 1497 to 1578. A musician at the court of Henry VIII, he is known principally for his development of the interlude—a short sketch, much like the medieval morality play, but with English characters. Another playwright was Nicholas Udall, who lived from 1505 to 1556 and was greatly influenced by the classics. His play *Ralph Roister Doister*, written sometime between 1534 and 1541, is believed to have been performed while he was headmaster at Eton, a famous British school. The play had five acts, took place in a single setting, and, though based on Roman comedy, used British characters. The first truly British tragedy, and the first play in England to be written in blank verse, was *Gorboduc*, by Thomas Sackville and Thomas Norton. Produced in 1561, it used traditional allegorical characters and a chorus.

Although the drama of the Elizabethan era originated with these early plays, it did not fully achieve greatness until such men as Thomas Kyd, who wrote *The Spanish Tragedy* around 1587, prepared the way. His play served as an example for the gripping "revenge" tragedies that were to follow. One superb example is Shakespeare's *Hamlet,* with its sensational and suspenseful plot, startling, melodramatic situations, and insightful characterizations. Wholly different was the work of John Lyly, England's first writer of sophisticated comedy, who was noted for his use of mythological themes and pastoral settings.

The three greatest writers of Elizabethan drama were Ben Jonson, Christopher Marlowe, and William Shakespeare. Jonson's first comedy, *Every Man in His Humor,* written in 1598, presented the eccentricities of the English middle class. *Every Man Out of His Humor,* written in 1599, was a satire of all that Jonson detested in society. In fact, he used comedy to denounce middle-class vices and foolish actions and thus to correct the social ills of England. His most widely read play, *Volpone, or the Fox,* written in 1606, bitterly satirizes human greed.

Christopher Marlowe is often called the father of English tragedy. His *Tamburlaine the Great,* (about 1587) can be said to have ushered in the first great age of drama in England. It was written in blank verse, a forerunner of Shakespeare's immortal blank verse tragedies. He wrote only four plays, including *Dr. Faustus,* and was considered a greater poet than a dramatist. His early death prevented the full development of his powers. However, he did much to free Elizabethan drama from the restrictions of medieval forms.

The greatest Elizabethan dramatist was of course William Shakespeare. Not much is known about his early life other than that he was born in 1564 and was the son of John and Mary Shakespeare. The record of his life shows that he was married, probably to Anne Hathaway, in 1582. By the 1590's he was a dramatist and actor in London. In 1595 he was a shareholder or part owner in the Lord Chamberlain's Company, later called the King's Men, at the Globe Theatre. He began writing around 1590 and wrote thirty-eight plays before he died in 1616. Although he borrowed many of his plots from other sources, the plays were highly original and entertaining, the memorable achievements of a unique dramatic genius. He wrote comedies, tragedies, and history plays, but his tragedies are considered his best.

During the Elizabethan era there were two types of theatres, public (outdoor) and private (indoor), although the private theatres were open to anyone who could afford the admission fee. The public theatres operated during the summer, the private theatres during the winter. The first private theatre was built in 1576 in Blackfriars, a residential section of London. The indoor theatres, which played to more exclusive audiences, accommodated only one-fourth to one-half as many spectators as did the public theatres. Audience members sat either in the pit (the main floor of the auditorium), or in galleries, or in private boxes. Usually the stage was three to four feet above the level of the pit, and there was no proscenium arch or front curtain.

All the popular public theatres, such as the Swan, the Fortune, and the Globe, had to be located outside the city of London, which at that time was disease-ridden. They varied in size but usually held two thousand to three thousand spectators. The playhouses were constructed in various shapes from circles to squares. The Globe, where Shakespeare's plays were performed, is believed to have been eight-sided. In the public theatre, the pit was a large, unroofed, open space where the groundlings, or those paying the lowest admission fee, stood to watch the plays. Around the pit (or yard, as it was sometimes called) were galleries, which formed the outer portion of the building and contained boxes for spectators who paid a higher admission fee. The stage projected into the pit, so that spectators could view the action from three sides. It was not unusual for some spectators to sit on the stage itself, forcing the actors to move around them.

Action could take place on three levels. At the rear of the stage was an area called the "inner below"—a large room to conceal or reveal characters and locations. There also was an upper stage where, for example, the balcony scene in the play *Romeo and Juliet* could have been performed. A third level was for musicians. It is generally believed that scenery was not used in public theatres, and there was no artificial lighting, since the plays were presented in the afternoon. Night scenes were suggested by having the actors carry lanterns or candles. There were trapdoors in the stage, used, for instance, in the gravediggers' scene in *Hamlet*.

Acting companies at the public theatres consisted of ten to twenty men and three to five boy apprentices. The boys played female parts until they reached maturity, then were taken in as permanent members of the company. Each actor specialized in a certain type of role, but almost all wore contemporary costumes unless they played unusual roles such as foreigners or supernatural beings. About half the members were shareholders, while the boys were apprenticed to learn the trade of acting.

Each playwright wrote for a specific company. Some were salaried, while others sold their plays outright. The playwright thus often wrote for particular actors and often helped with the rehearsals of the plays. The companies all had a repertoire of plays they had rehearsed, and hence could change the bill frequently.

After the death of Elizabeth, the English theatre lost popularity for a time; then, nearly sixty years later, it again began to emerge as a lively form of entertainment.

PROJECTS

1. Investigate the factors that led to the beginnings of the Renaissance in Italy.
2. Find out more about Serlio's writings on theatres and staging.
3. Contrast the *Teatro Olimpico* or the *Teatro Farnese* with either a Greek or modern theatre. (Or build a model of either the *Teatro Olimpico* or the *Teatro Farnese*.)
4. Report on the staging methods and/or the Italian theatres. Find photographs or illustrations to accompany your report.
5. How was scenery changed in the Renaissance theatres? Prepare a demonstration or an illustrated report on the three methods of shifting scenery.
6. Investigate more fully the "glories" of Renaissance Italy. What is meant by "Renaissance man?" Do you consider yourself to be a "Renaissance person?" Explain.
7. Trace the history of the *commedia dell'arte*.
8. Write and present a scene in the style of the *commedia dell'arte*.
9. Discover as much as you can about the production of *auto sacramentales* in Spain.
10. Investigate the origin of the *corrales* in Spain. Describe how they are

similar to or different from a Greek, Roman, or medieval theatre (or build a model of a *corral* and discuss it).

11. Almost everyone has heard of the Globe Theatre. Investigate the history of the theatre (or build a model of it).

12. Investigate the Elizabethan acting companies. How were they paid? For whom did they perform? Choose an Elizabethan acting company and follow it through a typical week's work.

13. Find out about one or two well-known actors in Elizabethan England. What was the actor's social status?

14. Find out as much as you can about Shakespeare's life after he became involved in the theatre. Do you agree or disagree that he was a genius? Do you think he wrote all of the plays attributed to him? Explain.

15. Make an investigation of theatrical productions in Elizabethan public playhouses.

Shakespeare dominated Elizabethan drama.

He was born in 1564, probably on April 23, to John and Mary Shakespeare. He was married in 1582 and had three children. Although there were few records of Shakespeare's early adulthood, in 1592 the dramatist Robert Greene wrote a pamphlet which indicates that by that time Shakespeare was probably already established as a playwright and actor in London. In 1593 and 1594, Shakespeare dedicated poems to the Earl of Southampton, suggesting that he was on familiar terms with the earl. In 1595, he was apparently a shareholder or part owner in the Lord Chamberlain's company, an acting troupe for which he both performed and wrote plays. After 1599, he was part owner of the Globe Theatre building. He died in 1616.

It is believed that Shakespeare started writing in about 1590. He wrote at least thirty-six plays, including histories, comedies, and tragedies. His first plays were histories dealing with England's past. Very early in his career he also started writing comedies which show a wide range in style. Among the earliest were *Love's Labour's Lost* and *The Comedy of Errors*. Among his early tragedies, considered the best of the three types of drama he wrote, were *Romeo and Juliet,* written about 1595, and *Julius Caesar.* In addition to the plays, Shakespeare wrote many poems, notably his sonnets.

Ever since the Elizabethan era, Shakespeare has been regarded as the greatest English dramatist. One reason for his immortality is that his plays have a reality that appeals to people of all ages and thus a meaning for everyone. Even though Shakespeare often borrowed his plots and ideas from others, his presentation of characters and situations with which we can identify has made him one of the most enduring of playwrights.

It is believed that *As You Like It* was written between 1598 and 1600. The play was derived from a contemporary novel written by Thomas Lodge. Shakespeare kept the basic plot but made changes necessary to make the story more playable on the stage, and added more realistic characters such as Jaques, Touchstone, William, and Audrey.

The play also has many of the aspects of the pastoral romance, one of the most popular forms of literature during the Renaissance. Pastoral works, including poetry, novels, and plays, dealt with the countryside and country people, often shepherds. The play suggests a Robin Hood kind of existence in the living conditions of the banished duke and his followers.

The central plot, as developed by Shakespeare rather than Lodge, deals with the romance of Rosalind and Orlando. Rosalind loves Orlando but masquerades as a boy until she is sure of his love. Then she removes her disguise, and the play ends with these two getting married. There are various subplots involving the two dukes and the love stories of the other characters. However, Rosalind and Orlando are the focus of attention.

One of the most interesting characters in the play is the comic Touchstone, who as a "city dweller" is contrasted with the shepherds and rustics whom he meets. Touchstone is witty and conceited, but we learn to like him because of his faithfulness and honesty. Another interesting character is Jaques, who contributes nothing to the plot but whose personality is very well developed.

Although not considered one of Shakespeare's greatest plays, *As You Like It* has always been popular because of its lightness and charm.

As You Like It

DRAMATIS PERSONAE

DUKE, *living in banishment.*
FREDERICK, *his brother, and*
   usurper of
   his dominions.

AMIENS, *lords attending on the*
JAQUES,   *banished duke.*
LE BEAU, *a courtier attending*
   upon
   Frederick.

CHARLES, *wrestler to Frederick.*
OLIVER,
JAQUES, *sons of Sir Rowland de*
   Boys.
ORLANDO,
ADAM,   *servants to Oliver.*
DENNIS,
TOUCHSTONE, *a clown.*

SIR OLIVER MARTEXT, *a vicar.*

CORIN, *shepherds.*

SILVIUS,
WILLIAM, *a country fellow, in*
love with
   Audrey.
A person representing Hymen.

ROSALIND, *daughter to the*
banished
   duke.
CELIA, *daughter to Frederick.*

PHEBE, *a shepherdess.*
AUDREY, *a country wench.*
Lords, pages, and attendants, &c.

SCENE: *Oliver's house; Duke*
Frederick's
   court; and the Forest of Arden.

As You Like It

ACT I.

SCENE I. *Orchard of* Oliver's *house.*

(Enter Orlando *and* Adam.)

ORLANDO: As I remember, Adam, it was upon this fashion; bequeathed me by will[1] but poor a thousand crowns, and, as thou sayest, charged my brother, on his blessing,[2] to breed[3] me well: and there begins my sadness. My brother Jaques he keeps at school, and report speaks goldenly of his profit:[4] for my part, he keeps me rustically at home, or, to speak more properly, stays me[5] here at home unkept; for call you that keeping for a gentleman of my birth, that differs not from the stalling of an ox? His horses are bred better; for, besides that they are fair with their feeding, they are taught their manage,[6] and to that end riders dearly[7] hired: but I, his brother, gain nothing under him but growth; for the which his animals on his dunghills are as much bound to him as I.[8] Besides this nothing that he so plentifully gives me, the something that nature gave me his countenance[9] seems to take from me: he lets me feed with his hinds,[10] bars me[11] the place of a brother, and, as much as in him lies, mines my gentility with my education.[12] This is it, Adam, that grieves me; and the spirit of my father, which I think is within me, begins to mutiny against this servitude: I will no longer endure it, though yet I know no wise remedy how to avoid it.

ADAM: Yonder comes my master, your brother.

ORLANDO: Go apart, Adam, and thou shalt hear how he will shake me up.[13]

(Enter Oliver.)

OLIVER: Now, sir! what make you here?

ORLANDO: Nothing: I am not taught to make anything.

OLIVER: What mar you then, sir?

---

[1] my father bequeathed   [2] if he wanted his blessing   [3] to educate   [4] progress   [5] makes me stay
[6] to pace   [7] expensively   [8] owe him as much as I (which is nothing)   [9] patronage   [10] servants
[11] excluded me from   [12] His lack of education is inconsistent with his social rank.   [13] be violent with me

ORLANDO: Marry,[14] sir, I am helping you to mar that which God made, a poor unworthy brother of yours, with idleness.

OLIVER: Marry, sir, be better employed, and be naught awhile.[15]

ORLANDO: Shall I keep your hogs and eat husks with them? What prodigal portion[16] have I spent, that I should come to such penury?[17]

OLIVER: Know you where you are, sir?

ORLANDO: O, sir, very well: here in your orchard.

OLIVER: Know you before whom, sir?

ORLANDO: Ay, better than him I am before knows me. I know you are my eldest brother; and, in the gentle condition of blood,[18] you should so know me. The courtesy of nations[19] allows you my better, in that you are the first-born; but the same tradition takes not away my blood, were there twenty brothers betwixt us: I have as much of my father in me as you; albeit, I confess, your coming before me is nearer to his reverence.[20]

OLIVER: What, boy!

ORLANDO: Come, come, elder brother, you are too young[21] in this.

OLIVER: Wilt thou lay hands on me, villain?

ORLANDO: I am no villain; I am the youngest son of Sir Rowland de Boys; he was my father, and he is thrice a villain that says such a father begot villains. Wert thou not my brother, I would not take this hand from thy throat till this other had pulled out thy tongue for saying so: thou hast railed on thyself.

ADAM: Sweet masters, be patient: for your father's remembrance, be at accord.

OLIVER: Let me go, I say.

ORLANDO: I will not, till I please: you shall hear me. My father charged you in his will to give me good education: you have trained me like a peasant, obscuring and hiding from me all gentleman-like qualities. The spirit of my father grows strong in me, and I will no longer endure it: therefore allow me such exercises[22] as may become a gentleman, or give me the poor allottery[23] my father left me by testament; with that I will go buy my fortunes.

OLIVER: And what wilt thou do? beg, when that is spent? Well, sir, get you in: I will not long be troubled with you; you shall have some part of your will: I pray you, leave me.

ORLANDO: I will no further offend you than becomes me for my good.

OLIVER: Get you with him, you old dog.

ADAM: Is 'old dog' my reward? Most true, I have lost my teeth in your service. God be with my old master! he would not have spoke such a word. (*Exeunt Orlando and Adam.*)

OLIVER: Is it even so? begin you to grow upon[24] me? I will physic your rankness,[25] and yet give no thousand crowns neither. Holla, Dennis!

(*Enter Dennis.*)

DENNIS: Calls your worship?

OLIVER: Was not Charles, the duke's wrestler, here to speak with me?

DENNIS: So please you, he is here at the door and importunes access[26] to you.

---

[14] Virgin Mary [15] pull away [16] I haven't wasted my position like the prodigal son of the Bible did. [17] poverty [18] since you are my brother [19] because we are civilized [20] makes you more worthy of respect [21] inexperienced [22] training [23] share [24] bother me [25] insolence [26] wants urgently to see you

OLIVER: Call him in. (*Exit* Dennis.) 'Twill be a good way; and to-morrow the wrestling is.

(*Enter* Charles.)

CHARLES: Good morrow to your worship.

OLIVER: Good Monsieur Charles, what's the new news at the new court?

CHARLES: There's no news at the court, sir, but the old news: that is, the old duke is banished by his younger brother the new duke; and three or four loving lords have put themselves into voluntary exile with him, whose lands and revenues enrich the new duke; therefore he gives them good leave to wander.

OLIVER: Can you tell if Rosalind, the duke's daughter, be banished with her father?

CHARLES: O, no; for the duke's daughter, her cousin, so loves her, being ever from their cradles bred together, that she would have followed her exile, or have died to stay²⁷ behind her. She is at the court, and no less beloved of her uncle than his own daughter; and never two ladies loved as they do.

OLIVER: Where will the old duke live?

CHARLES: They say he is already in the forest of Arden,²⁸ and a many merry men with him; and they there live like the old Robin Hood of England: they say many young gentlemen flock to him every day, and fleet the time carelessly,²⁹ as they did in the golden world.³⁰

OLIVER: What, you wrestle to-morrow before the new duke?

CHARLES: Marry, do I, sir; and I came to acquaint you with a matter. I am given, sir, secretly to understand that your younger brother Orlando hath a disposition to come in disguised against me to try a fall. To-morrow, sir, I wrestle for my credit; and he that escapes me without some broken limb shall acquit him well.³¹ Your brother is but young and tender; and, for your love, I would be loath to foil³² him, as I must, for my own honour, if he come in: therefore, out of my love to you, I came hither to acquaint you withal,³³ that either you might stay him from his intendment³⁴ or brook³⁵ such disgrace well as he shall run into, in that it is a thing of his own search and altogether against my will.

OLIVER: Charles, I thank thee for thy love to me, which thou shalt find I will most kindly requite.³⁶ I had myself notice of my brother's purpose herein and have by underhand means³⁷ laboured to dissuade him from it, but he is resolute. I'll tell thee, Charles: it is the stubbornest young fellow of France, full of ambition, an envious emulator³⁸ of every man's good parts, a secret and villanous contriver³⁹ against me his natural brother: therefore use thy discretion; I had as lief thou didst break his neck as his finger. And thou wert best look to 't; for if thou dost him any slight disgrace or if he do not mightily grace himself on thee,⁴⁰ he will practise against thee by poison, entrap thee by some treacherous device and never leave thee till he hath ta'en thy life by some indirect means or other; for, I assure thee, and almost with tears I speak it, there is not one so young and so villanous this day living. I speak but brotherly of him; but should I anatomize⁴¹ him to thee as he is, I must blush and weep and thou must look pale and wonder.

---

²⁷ would die if she had to stay ²⁸ Ardennes in Belgium ²⁹ waste time ³⁰ the days before evil entered the world ³¹ shall distinguish himself ³² overthrow ³³ thereby ³⁴ purpose ³⁵ endure ³⁶ return ³⁷ in a reasonable way ³⁸ envious hater ³⁹ plotter ⁴⁰ distinguish himself at your expense ⁴¹ analyze

CHARLES: I am heartily glad I came hither to you. If he come to-morrow, I'll give him his payment:[42] if ever he go alone again, I'll never wrestle for prize more: and so God keep your worship!

OLIVER: Farewell, good Charles. (*Exit* Charles.) Now will I stir this gamester:[43] I hope I shall see an end of him; for my soul, yet I know not why, hates nothing more than he. Yet he's gentle, never schooled and yet learned, full of noble device,[44] of all sorts enchantingly beloved, and indeed so much in the heart of the world, and especially of my own people, who best know him, that I am altogether misprised:[45] but it shall not be so long; this wrestler shall clear all: nothing remains but that I kindle[46] the boy thither; which now I'll go about. (*Exit.*)

SCENE II. *Lawn before the* Duke's *palace.*

(*Enter* Celia *and* Rosalind.)

CELIA: I pray thee, Rosalind, sweet my coz,[47] be merry.

ROSALIND: Dear Celia, I show more mirth than I am mistress of; and would you yet I were merrier? Unless you could teach me to forget a banished father, you must not learn[48] me how to remember any extraordinary pleasure.

CELIA: Herein I see thou lovest me not with the full weight that I love thee. If my uncle, thy banished father, had banished thy uncle, the duke my father, so thou hadst been still with me, I could have taught my love to take thy father for mine: so wouldst thou, if the truth of thy love to me were so righteously tempered as mine is to thee.[49]

ROSALIND: Well, I will forget the condition of my estate, to rejoice in yours.

CELIA: You know my father hath no child but I, nor none is like to have: and, truly, when he dies, thou shalt be his heir, for what he hath taken away from thy father perforce,[50] I will render thee again in affection; by mine honour, I will; and when I break that oath, let me turn monster: therefore, my sweet Rose, my dear Rose, be merry.

ROSALIND: From henceforth I will, coz, and devise sports. Let me see; what think you of falling in love?

CELIA: Marry, I prithee,[51] do, to make sport withal: but love no man in good earnest; nor no further in sport neither than with safety of a pure blush[52] thou mayst in honour come off[53] again.

ROSALIND: What shall be our sport, then?

CELIA: Let us sit and mock the good housewife Fortune from her wheel,[54] that her gifts may henceforth be bestowed equally.

ROSALIND: I would we could do so, for her benefits are mightily misplaced, and the bountiful blind woman doth most mistake in her gifts to women.

CELIA: 'Tis true; for those that she makes fair she scarce makes honest, and those that she makes honest she makes very ill-favouredly.[55]

ROSALIND: Nay, now thou goest from Fortune's office to Nature's: Fortune reigns in gifts of the world, not in the lineaments[56] of Nature.

(*Enter* Touchstone.)

---

[42] punishment   [43] fun-loving person   [44] noble thoughts   [45] despised   [46] incite   [47] cousin   [48] teach   [49] if you love me as much as I love you   [50] through necessity   [51] pray thee   [52] safety that costs no more than a blush   [53] escape   [54] Fortune was thought of as a blind woman who spun men's fate.   [55] ugly   [56] characteristics

CELIA: No? when Nature hath made a fair creature, may she not by Fortune fall into the fire? Though Nature hath given us wit to flout[57] at Fortune, hath not Fortune sent in this fool[58] to cut off the argument?

ROSALIND: Indeed, there is Fortune too hard for Nature, when Fortune makes Nature's natural the cutter-off of Nature's wit.

CELIA: Peradventure this is not Fortune's work neither, but Nature's; who perceiveth our natural wits too dull to reason of such goddesses and hath sent this natural for our whetstone; for always the dulness of the fool is the whetstone of the wits. How now, wit! whither wander you?

TOUCHSTONE: Mistress, you must come away to your father.

CELIA: Were you made the messenger?[59]

TOUCHSTONE: No, by mine honour, but I was bid to come for you.

ROSALIND: Where learned you that oath, fool?

TOUCHSTONE: Of a certain knight that swore by his honour they were good pancakes[60] and swore by his honour the mustard was naught:[61] now I'll stand to it, the pancakes were naught and the mustard was good, and yet was not the knight forsworn.[62]

CELIA: How prove you that, in the great heap of your knowledge?

ROSALIND: Ay, marry, now unmuzzle your wisdom.

TOUCHSTONE: Stand you both forth now: stroke your chins, and swear by your beards that I am a knave.

CELIA: By our beards, if we had them, thou art.

TOUCHSTONE: By my knavery, if I had it, then I were; but if you swear by that that is not, you are not forsworn: no more was this knight, swearing by his honour, for he never had any; or if he had, he had sworn it away before ever he saw those pancakes or that mustard.

CELIA: Prithee, who is't that thou meanest?

TOUCHSTONE: One that old Frederick, your father, loves.

CELIA: My father's love is enough to honour him: enough! speak no more of him; you'll be whipped for taxation[63] one of these days.

TOUCHSTONE: The more pity, that fools may not speak wisely what wise men do foolishly.

CELIA: By my troth, thou sayest true; for since the little wit that fools have was silenced, the little foolery that wise men have makes a great show. Here comes Monsieur Le Beau.

ROSALIND: With his mouth full of news.

CELIA: Which he will put[64] on us, as pigeons feed their young.

ROSALIND: Then shall we be news-crammed.

CELIA: All the better; we shall be the more marketable.

(Enter Le Beau.)

CELIA: Bon jour, Monsieur Le Beau: what's the news?

LE BEAU: Fair princess, you have lost much good sport.

CELIA: Sport! of what colour?[65]

LE BEAU: What colour, madam! how shall I answer you?

ROSALIND: As wit and fortune will.

TOUCHSTONE: Or as the Destinies decree.

CELIA: Well said: that was laid on with a trowel.[66]

TOUCHSTONE: Nay, if I keep not my rank,—

---

[57] mock   [58] idiot or fool   [59] policeman   [60] probably fritters which could use mustard   [61] bad   [62] lying   [63] satire   [64] tell us   [65] kind   [66] heavily

ROSALIND: Thou losest thy old smell.[67]

LE BEAU: You amaze me, ladies: I would have told you of good wrestling, which you have lost the sight of.

ROSALIND: Yet tell us the manner of the wrestling.

LE BEAU: I will tell you the beginning; and, if it please your ladyships, you may see the end; for the best is yet to do; and here, where you are, they are coming to perform it.

CELIA: Well, the beginning, that is dead and buried.

LE BEAU: There comes an old man and his three sons,—

CELIA: I could match this beginning with an old tale.

LE BEAU: Three proper[68] young men, of excellent growth and presence.

ROSALIND: With bills[69] on their necks, 'Be it known unto all men by these presents.'

LE BEAU: The eldest of the three wrestled with Charles, the duke's wrestler; which Charles in a moment threw him and broke three of his ribs, that there is little hope of life in him: so he served the second, and so the third. Yonder they lie; the poor old man, their father, making such pitiful dole[70] over them that all the beholders take his part with weeping.

ROSALIND: Alas!

TOUCHSTONE: But what is the sport, monsieur, that the ladies have lost?

LE BEAU: Why, this that I speak of.

TOUCHSTONE: Thus men may grow wiser every day: it is the first time that ever I heard breaking of ribs was sport for ladies.

CELIA: Or I, I promise thee.

ROSALIND: But is there any else longs to see this broken music[71] in his sides is there yet another dotes upon rib-breaking? Shall we see this wrestling, cousin?

LE BEAU: You must, if you stay here; for here is the place appointed for the wrestling, and they are ready to perform it.

CELIA: Yonder, sure, they are coming: let us now stay and see it.

(Flourish. Enter Duke Frederick, Lords, Orlando, Charles, and Attendants.)

DUKE FREDERICK: Come on: since the youth will not be entreated, his own peril[72] on his forwardness.

ROSALIND: Is yonder the man?

LE BEAU: Even he, madam.

CELIA: Alas, he is too young! yet he looks successfully.[73]

DUKE FREDERICK: How now, daughter and cousin![74] are you crept hither to see the wrestling?

ROSALIND: Ay, my liege, so please you give us leave.

DUKE FREDERICK: You will take little delight in it, I can tell you; there is such odds in the man.[75] In pity of the challenger's youth I would fain[76] dissuade him, but he will not be entreated. Speak to him, ladies; see if you can move him.

CELIA: Call him hither, good Monsieur Le Beau.

DUKE FREDERICK: Do so: I'll not be by.

---

[67] Note the pun on "rank" and "smell."   [68] handsome   [69] advertisement   [70] sorrow   [71] comparing the broken body to a broken musical instrument   [72] He does it at his own risk.   [73] as if he would be a success   [74] Cousin means any close relative.   [75] Charles has a much greater advantage.   [76] gladly

LE BEAU: Monsieur the challenger, the princesses call for you.
ORLANDO: I attend[77] them with all respect and duty.
ROSALIND: Young man, have you challenged Charles the wrestler?
ORLANDO: No, fair princess; he is the general challenger: I come but in, as others do, to try with him the strength of my youth.
CELIA: Young gentleman, your spirits are too bold for your years. You have seen cruel proof of this man's strength: if you saw yourself with your eyes or knew yourself with your judgement,[78] the fear of your adventure would counsel you to a more equal enterprise. We pray you, for your own sake, to embrace your own safety and give over this attempt.
ROSALIND: Do, young sir; your reputation shall not therefore be misprised:[79] we will make it our suit to the duke that the wrestling might not go forward.
ORLANDO: I beseech you, punish me not with your hard thoughts; wherein I confess me much guilty, to deny so fair and excellent ladies any thing. But let your fair eyes and gentle wishes go with me to my trial: wherein if I be foiled, there is but one shamed that was never gracious; if killed, but one dead that is willing to be so: I shall do my friends no wrong, for I have none to lament me, the world no injury, for in it I have nothing; only in the world I fill up a place, which may be better supplied when I have made it empty.
ROSALIND: The little strength that I have, I would it were with you.
CELIA: And mine, to eke out hers.
ROSALIND: Fare you well: pray heaven I be deceived in you!
CELIA: Your heart's desires be with you!
CHARLES: Come, where is this young gallant that is so desirous to lie with his mother earth?
ORLANDO: Ready, sir; but his will hath in it a more modest working.[80]
DUKE FREDERICK: You shall try but one fall.
CHARLES: No, I warrant your grace, you shall not entreat him to a second, that have so mightily persuaded him from a first.
ORLANDO: An you mean to mock me after, you should not have mocked me before: but come your ways.[81]
ROSALIND: Now Hercules be thy speed,[82] young man!
CELIA: I would I were invisible, to catch the strong fellow by the leg.

(*They wrestle.*)

ROSALIND: O excellent young man!
CELIA: If I had a thunderbolt in mine eye, I can tell who should down.

(*Shout. Charles is thrown.*)

DUKE FREDERICK: No more, no more.
ORLANDO: Yes, I beseech your grace: I am not yet well breathed.[83]
DUKE FREDERICK: How dost thou, Charles?
LE BEAU: He cannot speak, my lord.
DUKE FREDERICK: Bear him away. What is thy name, young man?
ORLANDO: Orlando, my liege; the youngest son of Sir Rowland de Boys.
DUKE FREDERICK: I would thou hadst been son to some man else:
The world esteem'd thy father honourable,
But I did find him still mine enemy:
Thou shouldst have better pleased me with this deed,
Hadst thou descended from another house.
But fare thee well; thou art a gallant youth:

[77] wait on [78] if you saw yourself as you are [79] despised [80] intent [81] come on [82] help
[83] beginning to tire

I would thou hadst told me of another father.

    (Exeunt Duke Frederick, *train, and* Le Beau.*)*

    CELIA: Were I my father, coz, would I do this?
    ORLANDO: I am more proud to be Sir Rowland's son,
His youngest son; and would not change that calling,[84]
To be adopted heir to Frederick.
    ROSALIND: My father loved Sir Rowland as his soul,
And all the world was of my father's mind:
Had I before known this young man his son,
I should have given him tears unto[85] entreaties,
Ere he should thus have ventured.
    CELIA: Gentle cousin,
Let us go thank him and encourage him:
My father's rough and envious disposition
Sticks me at heart.[86] Sir, you have well deserved:
If you do keep your promises in love
But justly, as you have exceeded all promise,
Your mistress shall be happy.
    ROSALIND: Gentleman,

    (Giving him a chain from her neck.)

Wear this for me, one out of suits with fortune,[87]
That could give more, but that her hand lacks means.
Shall we go, coz?
    CELIA: Ay. Fare you well, fair gentleman.
    ORLANDO: Can I not say, I thank you? My better parts
Are all thrown down,[88] and that which here stands up
Is but a quintain,[89] a mere lifeless block.
    ROSALIND: He calls us back: my pride fell with my fortunes;
I'll ask him what he would. Did you call, sir?
Sir, you have wrestled well and overthrown
More than your enemies.
    CELIA: Will you go, coz?
    ROSALIND: Have with you.[90] Fare you well.
                     (Exeunt Rosalind *and* Celia.*)*
    ORLANDO: What passion hangs these weights upon my tongue?
I cannot speak to her, yet she urged conference.[91]
O poor Orlando, thou art overthrown!
Or Charles or something weaker masters thee.

    (Re-enter Le Beau.*)*

    LE BEAU: Good sir, I do in friendship counsel you
To leave this place. Albeit you have deserved
High commendation, true applause and love,
Yet such is now the duke's condition
That he misconstrues all that you have done.

---

[84] name [85] in addition to [86] pierces me to the heart [87] one out of luck [88] I am acting as if I had no manners [89] figure of a man [90] come on [91] me to speak

The duke is humorous:[92] what he is indeed,
More suits you to conceive[93] than I to speak of.
    ORLANDO: I thank you, sir: and, pray you, tell me this;
Which of the two was daughter of the duke
That here was at the wrestling?
    LE BEAU: Neither his daughter, if we judge by manners;
But yet indeed the lesser[94] is his daughter:
The other is daughter to the banish'd duke,
And here detain'd by her usurping uncle,
To keep his daughter company; whose loves
Are dearer than the natural bond of sisters.
But I can tell you that of late this duke
Hath ta'en displeasure 'gainst his gentle niece.
Grounded upon no other argument
But that the people praise her for her virtues
And pity her for her good father's sake;
And, on my life, his malice 'gainst the lady
Will suddenly break forth. Sir, fare you well:
Hereafter, in a better world than this,
I shall desire more love and knowledge of you.
    ORLANDO: I rest much bounden[95] to you: fare you well. (*Exit* Le Beau.)
Thus must I from the smoke into the smother;[96]
From tyrant duke unto a tyrant brother:
But heavenly Rosalind! (*Exit.*)

SCENE III. *A room in the palace.*

    (*Enter* Celia *and* Rosalind.)

    CELIA: Why, cousin! why, Rosalind! Cupid have mercy! not a word?
    ROSALIND: Not one to throw at a dog.
    CELIA: No, thy words are too precious to be cast away upon curs; throw
some of them at me; come, lame me with reasons.
    ROSALIND: Then there were two cousins laid up; when the one should be
lamed with reasons and the other mad without any.
    CELIA: But is all this for your father?
    ROSALIND: No, some of it is for my child's father. O, how full of briers
is this working-day world!
    CELIA: They are but burs, cousin, thrown upon thee in holiday foolery:
if we walk not in the trodden paths, our very petticoats will catch them.
    ROSALIND: I could shake them off my coat: these burs are in my heart.
    CELIA: Hem them away.
    ROSALIND: I would try, if I could cry 'hem'[97] and have him.
    CELIA: Come, come, wrestle with thy affections.
    ROSALIND: O, they take the part of a better wrestler than myself!
    CELIA: O, a good wish upon you! you will try in time, in despite of[98] a
fall. But, turning these jests out of service, let us talk in good earnest: is it
possible, on such a sudden, you should fall into so strong a liking with old
Sir Rowland's youngest son?
    ROSALIND: The duke my father loved his father dearly.

[92] touchy   [93] imagine   [94] shorter   [95] oblige   [96] go from the frying pan into the fire   [97] could clear
my throat   [98] spite

CELIA: Doth it therefore ensue that you should love his son dearly? By this kind of chase,[99] I should hate him, for my father hated his father dearly; yet I hate not Orlando.

ROSALIND: No, faith, hate him not, for my sake.

CELIA: Why should I not? doth he not deserve well?[100]

ROSALIND: Let me love him for that, and do you love him because I do. Look, here comes the duke.

CELIA: With his eyes full of anger.

(Enter Duke Frederick, *with* Lords.*)*

DUKE FREDERICK: Mistress, dispatch you with your safest haste
And get you from our court.

ROSALIND: Me, uncle?

DUKE FREDERICK: You, cousin:
Within these ten days if that thou be'st found
So near our public court as twenty miles,
Thou diest for it.

ROSALIND: I do beseech your grace,
Let me the knowledge of my fault bear with me:
If with myself I hold intelligence[101]
Or have acquaintance with mine own desires,
If that I do not dream or be not frantic,—
As I do trust I am not—then, dear uncle,
Never so much as in a thought unborn
Did I offend your highness.

DUKE FREDERICK: Thus do all traitors:
If their purgation[102] did consist in words,
They are as innocent as grace itself:
Let it suffice thee that I trust thee not.

ROSALIND: Yet your mistrust cannot make me a traitor:
Tell me whereon the likelihood depends.

DUKE FREDERICK: Thou art thy father's daughter; there's enough.

ROSALIND: So was I when your highness took his dukedom;
So was I when your highness banish'd him:
Treason is not inherited, my lord;
Or, if we did derive[103] it from our friends,[104]
What's that to me? my father was no traitor:
Then, good my liege, mistake me not so much
To think my poverty is treacherous.

CELIA: Dear sovereign, hear me speak.

DUKE FREDERICK: Ay, Celia; we stay'd her for your sake,
Else had she with her father ranged along.[105]

CELIA: I did not then entreat to have her stay;
It was your pleasure and your own remorse:[106]
I was too young that time to value her;
But now I know her: if she be a traitor,
Why so am I; we still have slept together,
Rose at an instant, learn'd, play'd, eat together,
And wheresoe'er we went, like Juno's swans,
Still we went coupled and inseparable.

---

[99] reasoning   [100] deserve to be hated   [101] If I understand my own thoughts   [102] proof of innocence   [103] inherit   [104] relatives   [105] gone along with her father   [106] love

DUKE FREDERICK: She is too subtle for thee; and her smoothness,
Her very silence and her patience
Speak to the people, and they pity her.
Thou art a fool: she robs thee of thy name;
And thou wilt show more bright and seem more virtuous
When she is gone. Then open not thy lips:
Firm and irrevocable is my doom
Which I have pass'd upon her; she is banish'd
   CELIA: Pronounce that sentence then on me, my liege:
I cannot live out of her company.
   DUKE FREDERICK: You are a fool. You, niece, provide yourself:
If you outstay the time, upon mine honour,
And in the greatness of my word, you die.

   (Exeunt Duke Frederick and Lords.)

   CELIA: O my poor Rosalind, whither wilt thou go?
Wilt thou change fathers? I will give thee mine.
I charge thee, be not thou more grieved than I am.
   ROSALIND: I have more cause.
   CELIA: Thou hast not, cousin;
Prithee, be cheerful: know'st thou not, the duke
Hath banish'd me, his daughter?
   ROSALIND: That he hath not.
   CELIA: No, hath not? Rosalind lacks then the love
Which teacheth thee that thou and I am one:
Shall we be sunder'd? shall we part, sweet girl?
No: let my father seek another heir.
Therefore devise with me how we may fly,
Whither to go and what to bear with us;
And do not seek to take your change[107] upon you?
To bear your griefs yourself and leave me out;
For, by this heaven, now at our sorrows pale,
Say what thou canst, I'll go along with thee.
   ROSALIND: Why, whither shall we go?
   CELIA: To seek my uncle in the forest of Arden.
   ROSALIND: Alas, what danger will it be to us,
Maids as we are, to travel forth so far!
Beauty provoketh thieves sooner than gold.
   CELIA: I'll put myself in poor and mean attire.
And with a kind of umber smirch[108] my face;
The like do you: so shall we pass along
And never stir assailants.
   ROSALIND: Were it not better,
Because that I am more than common tall,
That I did suit me all points[109] like a man?
A gallant curtle-axe[110] upon my thigh,
A boar-spear in my hand; and—in my heart
Lie there what hidden woman's fear there will—
We'll have a swashing and a martial outside,

---

[107] change of luck   [108] put brown makeup on   [109] dress completely   [110] a broad sword

As many other mannish cowards have
That do outface it with their semblances.[111]
    CELIA: What shall I call thee when thou art a man?
    ROSALIND: I'll have no worse a name than Jove's own page;
And therefore look you call me Ganymede.
But what will you be call'd?
    CELIA: Something that hath a reference to my state;
No longer Celia, but Aliena.
    ROSALIND: But, cousin, what if we assay'd[112] to steal
The clownish fool out of your father's court?
Would he not be a comfort to our travel?
    CELIA: He'll go along o'er the wide world with me;
Leave me alone to woo him. Let's away,
And get our jewels and our wealth together,
Devise the fittest time and safest way
To hide us from pursuit that will be made
After my flight. Now go we in content
To liberty and not to banishment. (*Exeunt.*)

ACT II.

SCENE I. *The Forest of Arden.*

(*Enter* Duke senior, Amiens, *and two or three* Lords, *like foresters.*)

    DUKE SENIOR: Now, my co-mates and brothers in exile,
Hath not old custom[113] made this life more sweet
Than that of painted[114] pomp? Are not these woods
More free from peril than the envious-court?
Here feel we but the penalty of Adam,
The seasons' difference, as the icy fang
And churlish chiding of the winter's wind,
Which, when it bites and blows upon my body,
Even till I shrink with cold, I smile and say
'This is no flattery: these are counsellors
That feelingly persuade me what I am.'
Sweet are the uses[115] of adversity,
Which, like the toad, ugly and venomous,
Wears yet a precious jewel in his head;
And this our life exempt from public haunt[116]
Finds tongues in trees, books in the running brooks,
Sermons in stones and good in every thing.[117]
I would not change it.
    AMIENS: Happy is your grace,
That can translate the stubbornness of fortune
Into so quiet and so sweet a style.
    DUKE SENIOR: Come, shall we go and kill us venison?
And yet it irks me the poor dappled fools,
Being native burghers[118] of this desert city,

---

[111] will look very masculine   [112] tried   [113] long experience   [114] artificial   [115] advantages
[116] away from crowds   [117] Nature is full of lessons. [118] citizens

Should in their own confines[119] with forked heads[120]
Have their round haunches gored.
  FIRST LORD: Indeed, my lord,
The melancholy Jaques grieves at that,
And, in that kind, swears you do more usurp
Than doth your brother that hath banish'd you.
To-day my Lord of Amiens and myself
Did steal behind him as he lay along[121]
Under an oak whose antique root peeps out
Upon the brook that brawls along this wood:
To the which place a poor sequester'd stag,
That from the hunter's aim had ta'en a hurt,
Did come to languish, and indeed, my lord,
The wretched animal heaved forth such groans
That their discharge did stretch his leathern coat
Almost to bursting, and the big round tears
Coursed one another down his innocent nose
In piteous chase; and thus the hairy fool,
Much marked of the melancholy Jaques,
Stood on the extremest verge of the swift brook,
Augmenting it with tears.
  DUKE SENIOR: But what said Jaques?
Did he not moralize this spectacle?
  FIRST LORD: O, yes, into a thousand similes.
First, for his weeping into the needless stream;
'Poor deer,' quoth he, 'thou makest a testament
As worldings do, giving thy sum of more
To that which had too much:' then, being there alone,
Left and abandon'd of his velvet friends,
' 'Tis right,' quoth he; 'thus misery doth part
The flux[122] of company:' anon a careless herd,
Full of the pasture, jumps along by him
And never stays to greet him; 'Ay,' quoth Jaques,
'Sweep on, you fat and greasy citizens;
'Tis just the fashion: wherefore do you look
Upon that poor and broken bankrupt there?'
Thus most invectively[123] he pierceth through
The body of the country, city, court,
Yea, and of this our life, swearing that we
Are mere usurpers, tyrants and what's worse,
To fright the animals and to kill them up
In their assign'ed and native dwelling-place.
  DUKE SENIOR: And did you leave him in this contemplation?
  SECOND LORD: We did, my lord, weeping and commenting
Upon the sobbing deer.
  DUKE SENIOR: Show me the place:
I love to cope[124] him in these sullen fits,
For then he's full of matter.[125]
  FIRST LORD: I'll bring you to him straight.

                                 (*Exeunt.*)

---

[119] territories [120] arrows [121] stretch at full length [122] flow [123] abusively [124] meet [125] good
sense

SCENE II. *A room in the palace.*

(Enter Duke Frederick, *with* Lords.*)*

DUKE FREDERICK: Can it be possible that no man saw them?
It cannot be: some villains of my court
Are of consent and sufferance[126] in this.
   FIRST LORD: I cannot hear of any that did see her.
The ladies, her attendants of her chamber,
Saw her a-bed, and in the morning early
They found the bed untreasured of their mistress.
   SECOND LORD: My lord, the roynish[127] clown, at whom so oft
Your grace was wont to laugh, is also missing.
Hisperia, the princess' gentlewoman,
Confesses that she secretly o'erheard
Your daughter and her cousin much commend
The parts and graces of the wrestler
That did but lately foil the sinewy Charles;
And she believes, wherever they are gone,
That youth is surely in their company.
   DUKE FREDERICK: Send to his brother; fetch that gallant hither;
If he be absent, bring his brother to me;
I'll make him find him: do this suddenly,
And let not search and inquisition quail[128]
To bring again[129] these foolish runaways.

(Exeunt.)

SCENE III. *Before* Oliver's *house.*

(Enter Orlando *and* Adam, *meeting.)*

ORLANDO: Who's there?
   ADAM: What, my young master? O my gentle master!
O my sweet master! O you memory
Of old Sir Rowland! why, what make you[130] here?
Why are you virtuous? why do people love you?
And wherefore are you gentle, strong and valiant?
Why would you be so fond[131] to overcome
The bonny priser[132] of the humorous duke?
Your praise is come too swiftly home before you.
Know you not, master, to some kind of men
Their graces serve them but as enemies?
No more do yours: your virtues, gentle master,
Are sanctified and holy traitors to you.
O, what a world is this, when what is comely
Envenoms him that bears it!
   ORLANDO: Why, what's the matter?
   ADAM: O unhappy youth!
Come not within these doors; within this roof
The enemy of all your graces lives:
Your brother—no, no brother; yet the son—

---

[126] accomplices   [127] scurvy   [128] don't stop looking   [129] back   [130] what are you doing   [131] foolish
[132] prizefighter

Yet not the son, I will not call him son
Of him I was about to call his father—
Hath heard your praises, and this night he means
To burn the lodging where you use to lie
And you within it: if he fail of that,
He will have other means to cut you off.
I overheard him and his practices.[133]
This is no place;[134] this house is but a butchery:
Abhor it, fear it, do not enter it.

ORLANDO: Why, whither, Adam, wouldst thou have me go?

ADAM: No matter whither, so you come not here.

ORLANDO: What, wouldst thou have me go and beg my food?
Or with a base and boisterous[135] sword enforce
A thievish living on the common road?
This I must do, or know not what to do:
Yet this I will not do, do how I can;
I rather will subject me to the malice
Of a diverted blood[136] and bloody brother.

ADAM: But do not so. I have five hundred crowns,
The thrifty hire[137] I saved under your father,
Which I did store to be my foster-nurse
When service should in my old limbs lie lame
And unregarded age in corners thrown:
Take that, and He that doth the ravens feed,
Yea, providently caters for the sparrow,
Be comfort to my age! Here is the gold;
All this I give you. Let me be your servant:
Though I look old, yet I am strong and lusty;
For in my youth I never did apply
Hot and rebellious liquors in my blood,
Nor did not with unbashful forehead[138] woo
The means of weakness and debility;
Therefore my age is as a lusty winter,
Frosty, but kindly:[139] let me go with you;
I'll do the service of a younger man
In all your business and necessities.

ORLANDO: O good old man, how well in thee appears
The constant service[140] of the antique world,
When service sweat for duty, not for meed![141]
Thou art not for the fashion of these times,
Where none will sweat but for promotion,
And having that, do choke their service up
Even with the having: it is not so with thee.
But, poor old man, thou prunest a rotten tree,
That cannot so much as a blossom yield
In lieu[142] of all thy pains and husbandry.[143]
But come thy ways; we'll go along together,
And ere we have thy youthful wages spent,
We'll light upon some settled low content.[144]

---

[133] plots   [134] home   [135] threatening   [136] alienated relative   [137] money   [138] boldness   [139] proper
[140] faithful servants   [141] reward   [142] in return for   [143] economy   [144] will find a humble and
contented living

ADAM: Master, go on, and I will follow thee,
To the last gasp, with truth and loyalty.
From seventeen years till now almost fourscore
Here lived I, but now live here no more.
At seventeen years many their fortunes seek;
But at fourscore it is too late a week:[145]
Yet fortune cannot recompense me better
Than to die well and not my master's debtor. (*Exeunt.*)

SCENE IV. *The Forest of Arden.*

(*Enter* Rosalind *for* Ganymede, Celia *for* Aliena, *and* Touchstone.)

ROSALIND: O Jupiter, how weary are my spirits!
TOUCHSTONE: I care not for my spirits, if my legs were not weary.
ROSALIND: I could find in my heart to disgrace my man's apparel and to
cry like a woman; but I must comfort the weaker vessel,[146] as doublet and
hose ought to show itself courageous to petticoat: therefore courage, good
Aliena!
CELIA: I pray you, bear with me; I cannot go no further.
TOUCHSTONE: For my part, I had rather bear with you than bear you; yet
I should bear no cross[147] if I did bear you, for I think you have no money in
your purse.
ROSALIND: Well, this is the forest of Arden.
TOUCHSTONE: Ay, now am I in Arden; the more fool I; when I was at home,
I was in a better place: but travellers must be content.
ROSALIND: Ay, be sc, good Touchstone.

(*Enter* Corin *and* Silvius.)

Look you, who comes here; a young man and an old in solemn talk.
CORIN: That is the way to make her scorn you still.
SILVIUS: O Corin, that thou knew'st how I do love her!
CORIN: I partly guess; for I have loved ere now.
SILVIUS: No, Corin, being old, thou canst not guess,
Though in thy youth thou wast as true a lover
As ever sigh'd upon a midnight pillow:
But if thy love were ever like to mine—
As sure I think did never man love so—
How many actions most ridiculous
Hast thou been drawn to by thy fantasy?[148]
CORIN: Into a thousand that I have forgotten.
SILVIUS: O, thou didst then ne'er love so heartily!
If thou remember'st not the slightest folly
That ever love did make thee run into,
Thou hast not loved:
Or if thou hast not sat as I do now,
Wearying thy hearer in thy mistress' praise,
Thou hast not loved:
Or if thou hast not broke from company
Abruptly, as my passion now makes me,
Thou hast not loved.

---

[145] much too late   [146] woman   [147] coin with a figure of a cross on it   [148] love

O Phebe, Phebe, Phebe! (*Exit.*)

ROSALIND: Alas, poor shepherd! searching of thy wound,
I have by hard adventure[149] found mine own.

TOUCHSTONE: And I mine. I remember, when I was in love I broke my sword upon a stone and bid him take that for coming a-night[150] to Jane Smile; and I remember the kissing of her batlet[151] and the cow's dugs that her pretty chopt[152] hands had milked; and I remember the wooing of a peascod[153] instead of her, from whom I took two cods[154] and, giving her them again, said with weeping tears 'Wear these for my sake.' We that are true lovers run into strange capers; but as all is mortal in nature, so is all nature in love mortal[155] in folly.

ROSALIND: Thou speakest wiser than thou art ware of.

TOUCHSTONE: Nay, I shall ne'er be ware of mine own wit till I break my shins against it.

ROSALIND: Jove, Jove! this shepherd's passion
Is much upon my fashion.

TOUCHSTONE: And mine; but it grows something stale with me.

CELIA: I pray you, one of you question yond man
If he for gold will give us any food:
I faint almost to death.

TOUCHSTONE: Holla, you clown!

ROSALIND: Peace, fool: he's not thy kinsman.

CORIN: Who calls?

TOUCHSTONE: Your betters, sir.

CORIN: Else are they very wretched.

ROSALIND: Peace, I say. Good even to you, friend.

CORIN: And to you, gentle sir, and to you all.

ROSALIND: I prithee, shepherd, if that love or gold
Can in this desert place buy entertainment,[156]
Bring us where we may rest ourselves and feed:
Here's a young maid with travel much oppress'd
And faints for succour.

CORIN: Fair sir, I pity her
And wish, for her sake more than for mine own,
My fortunes were more able to relieve her;
But I am shepherd to another man
And do not shear the fleeces that I graze:
My master is of churlish[157] disposition
And little recks[158] to find the way to heaven
By doing deeds of hospitality:
Besides, his cote,[159] his flocks and bounds of feed[160]
Are now on sale, and at our sheepcote now,
By reason of his absence, there is nothing
That you will feed on; but what is, come see,
And in my voice most welcome shall you be.

ROSALIND: What is he that shall buy his flock and pasture?

CORIN: That young swain[161] that you saw here but erewhile,
That little cares for buying any thing.

ROSALIND: I pray thee, if it stand[162] with honesty,

---

[149] painful chance   [150] by night   [151] club used for beating clothes when washing them   [152] chapped   [153] pea pod   [154] pods   [155] great   [156] accommodation   [157] miserly   [158] cares   [159] cottage   [160] pastures   [161] man in love

Buy thou the cottage, pasture and the flock,
And thou shalt have to pay for it of us.
    CELIA: And we will mend thy wages.[163] I like this place,
And willingly could waste my time in it.
    CORIN: Assuredly the thing is to be sold:
Go with me: if you like upon report
The soil, the profit and this kind of life,
I will your very faithful feeder[164] be
And buy it with your gold right suddenly.

                                                      (*Exeunt.*)

SCENE V. *The forest.*

        (*Enter* Amiens, Jaques, *and others.*)

                            Song.

        AMIENS: Under the greenwood tree
        Who loves to lie with me,
        And turn his merry note
        Unto the sweet bird's throat,
Come hither, come hither, come hither:
        Here shall he see
        No enemy
But winter and rough weather.
        JAQUES: More, more, I prithee, more.
        AMIENS: It will make you melancholy, Monsieur Jaques.
        JAQUES: I thank it. More, I prithee, more. I can suck melancholy out of a
song, as a weasel sucks eggs. More, I prithee, more.
        AMIENS: My voice is ragged: I know I cannot please you.
        JAQUES: I do not desire you to please me; I do desire you to sing. Come,
more; another stanzo: call you 'em stanzos?
        AMIENS: What you will, Monsieur Jaques.
        JAQUES: Nay, I care not for their names; they owe me nothing. Will you
sing?
        AMIENS: More at your request than to please myself.
        JAQUES: Well then, if ever I thank any man, I'll thank you; but that they
call compliment is like the encounter of two dog-apes,[165] and when a man
thanks me heartily, me thinks I have given him a penny and he renders me
the beggarly thanks.[166] Come, sing; and you that will not, hold your tongues.
        AMIENS: Well, I'll end the song. Sirs, cover[167] the while; the duke will
drink under this tree.
He hath been all this day to look you.
        JAQUES: And I have been all this day to avoid him. He is too disputable[168]
for my company: I think of as many matters as he, but I give heaven thanks
and make no boast of them. Come, warble, come.

                            Song.

---

[162] is consistent   [163] improve   [164] serve it   [165] male baboons   [166] lavish thanks   [167] set the table
in the meantime   [168] argumentative

Who doth ambition shun (*All together here.*)
And loves to live i' the sun,
Seeking the food he eats
And pleased with what he gets,
Come hither, come hither, come hither:
Here shall he see
No enemy
But winter and rough weather.

JAQUES: I'll give you a verse to this note[169] that I made yesterday in despite
of my invention.[170]

AMIENS: And I'll sing it.

JAQUES: Thus it goes:—
If it do come to pass
That any man turn ass,
Leaving his wealth and ease,
A stubborn will to please,
Ducdame, ducdame, ducdame:
Here shall he see
Gross fools as he,
An if he will come to me.

AMIENS: What's that 'ducdame'?

JAQUES: 'Tis a Greek invocation, to call fools into a circle. I'll go sleep, if
I can; if I cannot, I'll rail against all the first-born of Egypt.

AMIENS: And I'll go seek the duke: his banquet is prepared. (*Exeunt sever-*
ally.)

SCENE VI. *The forest.*

(*Enter* Orlando *and* Adam.)

ADAM: Dear master, I can go no further: O, I die for food! Here lie I down,
and measure out my grave. Farewell, kind master.

ORLANDO: Why, how now, Adam! no greater heart in thee? Live a little;
comfort a little; cheer thyself a little. If this uncouth[171] forest yield any thing
savage, I will either be food for it or bring it for food to thee. Thy conceit[172]
is nearer death than thy powers.[173] For my sake be comfortable;[174] hold death
awhile at the arm's end: I will here be with thee presently; and if I bring thee
not something to eat, I will give thee leave to die: but if thou diest before
I come, thou art a mocker of my labour. Well said! thou lookest cheerly, and
I'll be with thee quickly. Yet thou liest in the bleak air: come, I will bear thee
to some shelter; and thou shalt not die for lack of a dinner, if there live any
thing in this desert. Cheerly, good Adam! (*Exeunt.*)

SCENE VII. *The forest.*

(*A table set out. Enter* Duke senior, Amiens, *and* Lords *like* outlaws.)

DUKE SENIOR: I think he be transform'd into a beast;
For I can no where find him[175] like a man.

FIRST LORD: My lord, he is but even now gone hence:
Here was he merry, hearing of a song.

---

[169] tune   [170] despite the fact that it's not really good   [171] wild   [172] imagination   [173] strength
[174] comforted   [175] in the shape of

DUKE SENIOR: If he, compact of jars,[176] grow musical,
We shall have shortly discord in the spheres.
Go, seek him: tell him I would speak with him.

(Enter Jaques.)

FIRST LORD: He saves my labour by his own approach.
DUKE SENIOR: Why, how now, monsieur! what a life is this,
That your poor friends must woo your company?
What, you look merrily!
JAQUES: A fool, a fool! I met a fool i' the forest,
A motley fool;[177] a miserable world!
As I do live by food, I met a fool;
Who laid him down and bask'd him in the sun,
And rail'd on Lady Fortune in good terms,
In good set terms and yet a motley fool.
'Good morrow, fool,' quoth I. 'No, sir,' quoth he,
'Call me not fool till heaven hath sent me fortune:'
And then he drew a dial[178] from his poke,[179]
And, looking on it with lack-lustre eye,
Says very wisely, 'It is ten o'clock:
Thus we may see,' quoth he, 'how the world wags:
'Tis but an hour ago since it was nine,
And after one hour more 'twill be eleven;
And so, from hour to hour, we ripe and ripe,
And then, from hour to hour, we rot and rot;
And thereby hangs a tale.' When I did hear
The motley fool thus moral[180] on the time,
My lungs began to crow like chanticleer,[181]
That fools should be so deep-contemplative,
And I did laugh sans intermission[182]
An hour by his dial. O noble fool!
A worthy fool! Motley's the only wear.[183]
DUKE SENIOR: What fool is this?
JAQUES: O worthy fool! One that hath been a courtier,
And says, if ladies be but young and fair,
They have the gift to know it: and in his brain,
Which is as dry as the remainder[184] biscuit
After a voyage, he hath strange places cramm'd
With observation, the which he vents[185]
In mangled forms. O that I were a fool!
I am ambitious for a motley coat.
DUKE SENIOR: Thou shalt have one.
JAQUES: It is my only suit;
Provided that you weed your better judgements
Of all opinion that grows rank[186] in them
That I am wise. I must have liberty
Withal, as large as a charter as the wind,

---

[176] made of discords [177] professional jester [178] watch [179] pocket [180] moralize [181] like a rooster
[182] without stopping [183] The clown's outfit is the only thing to wear. [184] leftover [185] states
[186] abundantly

To blow on whom I please; for so fools have;
And they that are most galled with my folly,
They most must laugh. And why, sir, must they so?
The 'why' is plain as way to parish church:
He that a fool doth very wisely hit
Doth very foolishly, although he smart,
Not to seem senseless of the bob: if not,
The wise man's folly is anatomized
Even by the squandering glances of the fool.
Invest me in my motley; give me leave
To speak my mind, and I will through and through
Cleanse the foul body of the infected world,
If they will patiently receive my medicine.
    DUKE SENIOR: Fie on thee! I can tell what thou wouldst do.
    JAQUES: What, for a counter,[187] would I do but good?
    DUKE SENIOR: Most mischievous foul sin, in chiding sin:
For thou thyself hast been a libertine,
As sensual as the brutish sting itself;
And all the embossed sores[188] and headed evils,
That thou with license of free foot hast caught,
Wouldst thou disgorge into the general world.
    JAQUES: Why, who cries out on pride,[189]
That can therein tax any private party?
Doth it not flow as hugely as the sea,
öTill that the weary very means do ebb?
What woman in the city do I name,
When that I say the city-woman[190] bears
The cost of princes on unworthy shoulders?
Who can come in and say that I mean her,
When such a one as she such is her neighbour?
Or what is he of basest function[191]
That says his bravery is not on my cost,
Thinking that I mean him, but therein suits
His folly to the mettle[192] of my speech?
There then; how then? what then? Let me see wherein
My tongue hath wrong'd him: if it do him right,[193]
Then he hath wrong'd himself; if he be free,[194]
Why then my taxing like a wild-goose flies,
Unclaim'd of any man. But who comes here?

(Enter Orlando, *with his sword drawn.)*

    ORLANDO: Forbear, and eat no more.
    JAQUES: Why, I have eat none yet.
    ORLANDO: Nor shalt not, till necessity[195] be served.
    JAQUES: Of what kind should this cock come of?
    DUKE SENIOR: Art thou thus bolden'd, man, by thy distress,
Or else a rude despiser of good manners,
That in civility thou seem'st so empty?

---

[187] a thing of no value   [188] boils and carbuncles   [189] attacking the sin of pride, not the individual person   [190] citizen's wife   [191] office   [192] material   [193] if my charges are just   [194] guiltless   [195] those who must have food

ORLANDO: You touch'd my vein[196] at first: the thorny point[197]
Of bare distress hath ta'en from me the show
Of smooth civility: yet am I inland bred[198]
And know some nurture.[199] But forbear, I say:
He dies that touches any of this fruit
Till I and my affairs are answered.[200]
        JAQUES: An[201] you will not be answered with reason, I must die.
        DUKE SENIOR: What would you have? Your gentleness shall force
More than your force move us to gentleness.
        ORLANDO: I almost die for food; and let me have it.
        DUKE SENIOR: Sit down and feed, and welcome to our table.
        ORLANDO: Speak you so gently? Pardon me, I pray you:
I thought that all things had been savage here;
And therefore put I on the countenance
Of stern commandment. But whate'er you are
That in this desert inaccessible,
Under the shade of melancholy boughs,
Lose and neglect the creeping hours of time;
If ever you have look'd on better days,
If ever been where bells have knoll'd[202] to church,
If ever sat at any good man's feast,
If ever from your eyelids wiped a tear
And know that 'tis to pity and be pitied,
Let gentleness my strong enforcement be:
In the which hope I blush, and hide my sword.
        DUKE SENIOR: True is it that we have seen better days,
And have with holy bell been knoll'd to church
And sat at good men's feasts and wiped our eyes
Of drops that sacred pity hath engender'd:
And therefore sit you down in gentleness
And take upon command[203] what help we have
That to your wanting may be minister'd.
        ORLANDO: Then but forbear your food a little while,
Whiles, like a doe, I go to find my fawn
And give it food. There is an old poor man,
Who after me hath many a weary step
Limp'd in pure love: till he be first sufficed,
Oppress'd with two weak[204] evils, age and hunger,
I will not touch a bit.
        DUKE SENIOR: Go find him out,
And we will nothing waste till you return.
        ORLANDO: I thank ye; and be blest for your good comfort! (*Exit.*)
        DUKE SENIOR: Thou seest we are not all alone unhappy:
this wide and universal theatre
Presents more woeful pageants than the scene
Wherein we play in.
        JAQUES: All the world's a stage,
And all the men and women merely players:
They have their exits and their entrances;
And one man in his time plays many parts,

---

[196] disposition   [197] accuteness   [198] civilized   [199] education   [200] satisfied   [201] if   [202] tolled
[203] at pleasure   [204] evils causing weakness

His acts being seven ages. At first the infant,
Mewling[205] and puking in the nurse's arms.
And then the whining school-boy, with his satchel
And shining morning face, creeping like snail
Unwillingly to school. And then the lover,
Sighing like furnace, with a woeful ballad
Made to his mistress' eyebrow. Then a soldier,
Full of strange oaths and bearded like the pard,[206]
Jealous in honour, sudden and quick in quarrel,
Seeking the bubble reputation[207]
Even in the cannon's mouth. And then the justice,
In fair round belly with good capon lined,[208]
With eyes severe and beard of formal cut,
Full of wise saws[209] and modern instances[210]
And so he plays his part. The sixth age shifts
Into the lean and slipper'd pantaloon,[211]
With spectacles on nose and pouch on side,
His youthful hose, well saved, a world too wide
For his shrunk shank; and his big manly voice,
Turning again toward childish treble, pipes
And whistles in his sound. Last scene of all,
That ends this strange eventful history,
Is second childishness and mere oblivion,
Sans teeth, sans eyes, sans taste, sans every thing.

(Re-enter Orlando, *with* Adam.*)*

DUKE SENIOR: Welcome. Set down your venerable burden
And let him feed.
   ORLANDO: I thank you most for him.
   ADAM: so had you need:
I scarce can speak to thank you for myself
   DUKE SENIOR: Welcome; fall to: I will not trouble you
As yet, to question you about your fortunes.
Give us some music; and, good cousin, sing.

Song.

AMIENS: Blow, blow, thou winter wind,
Thou art not so unkind[212]
   As man's ingratitude;
Thy tooth is not so keen,
Because thou art not seen,
   Although thy breath be rude.
Heigh-ho! sing, heigh-ho! unto the green holly:
Most friendship is feigning, most loving mere folly:
   Then, heigh-ho, the holly!
      This life is most jolly.

---

[205] crying weakly   [206] sensitive in honor   [207] fleeting fame   [208] full of good food obtained through bribes   [209] wise sayings   [210] commonplace illustrations   [211] feeble old man   [212] unnatural

Freeze, freeze, thou bitter sky,
That dost not bite so nigh
   As benefits forgot:
Though thou the waters warp.[213]
Thy sting is not so sharp
   As friend remember'd not.
Heigh-ho! sing, &c.
DUKE SENIOR: If that you were the good Sir Rowland's son,
As you have whisper'd faithfully you were,
And as mine eye doth his effigies[214] witness
Most truly limn'd[215] and living in your face,
Be truly welcome hither: I am the duke
That loved your father: the residue of your fortune,[216]
Go to my cave and tell me. Good old man,
Thou art right welcome as thy master is.
Support him by the arm. Give me your hand,
And let me all your fortunes understand.

                                               (*Exeunt.*)

ACT III.

SCENE I. *A room in the palace.*

   (Enter Duke Frederick, Lords, *and* Oliver.*)*

   DUKE FREDERICK: Not see him since? Sir, sir, that cannot be:
But were I not the better[217] part made mercy,
I should not seek an absent argument
Of my revenge, thou present.[218] But look to it:
Find out thy brother, wheresoe'er he is;
Seek him with candle; bring him dead or living
Within this twelvemonth, or turn thou no more
To seek a living in our territory.
Thy lands and all things that thou dost call thine
Worth seizure do we seize into our hands,
Till thou canst quit[219] thee by thy brother's mouth[220]
Of what we think against thee.
   OLIVER: O that your highness knew my heart in this!
I never loved my brother in my life.
   DUKE FREDERICK: More villain thou. Well, push him out of doors;
And let my officers of such a nature
Make an extent upon[221] his house and lands:
Do this expediently and turn him going.[222] (*Exeunt.*)

SCENE II. *The forest.*

   (Enter Orlando, *with a paper.)*

   ORLANDO: Hang there, my verse, in witness of my love:

---

[213] freeze   [214] image   [215] painted   [216] the remainder of your life   [217] greater   [218] I should not look for your brother but take vengence on you.   [219] acquit   [220] evidence   [221] seize   [222] start him moving

And thou, thrice-crowned queen of night,[223] survey
With thy chaste eye, from thy pale sphere above,
   Thy huntress' name that my full life doth sway.
O Rosalind! these trees shall be my books
   And in their barks my thoughts I'll character;[224]
That every eye which in this forest looks
   Shall see thy virtue witness'd every where.
Run, run, Orlando; carve on every tree
The fair, the chaste and unexpressive[225] she. (*Exit.*)

    (*Enter* Corin *and* Touchstone.)

    CORIN: And how like you this shepherd's life, Master Touchstone?
    TOUCHSTONE: Truly, shepherd, in respect of itself, it is a good life; but in respect that it is a shepherd's life, it is naught.[226] In respect that it is solitary, I like it very well; but in respect that it is private,[227] it is a very vile life. Now, in respect it is in the fields, it pleaseth me well; but in respect it is not in the court, it is tedious. As it is a spare life, look you, it fits my humour well; but as there is no more plenty in it, it goes much against my stomach. Hast any philosophy in thee, shepherd?
    CORIN: No more but that I know the more one sickens the worse at ease he is; and that he that wants money, means and content is without three good friends; that the property of rain is to wet and fire to burn; that good pasture makes fat sheep, and that a great cause of the night is lack of the sun; that he that hath learned no wit by nature nor art may complain of good breeding or comes of a very dull kindred.
    TOUCHSTONE: Such a one is a natural philosopher. Wast ever in court, shepherd?
    CORIN: No, truly.
    TOUCHSTONE: Then thou art damned.
    CORIN: Nay, I hope.
    TOUCHSTONE: Truly, thou art damned, like an ill-roasted egg all on one side.
    CORIN: For not being at court? Your reason.
    TOUCHSTONE: Why, if thou never wast at court, thou never sawest good manners; if thou never sawest good manners, then thy manners must be wicked; and wickedness is sin, and sin is damnation. Thou art in a parlous[228] state, shepherd.
    CORIN: Not a whit, Touchstone: those that are good manners at the court are as ridiculous in the country as the behaviour of the country is most mockable at the court. You told me you salute not at the court, but you kiss your hands: that courtesy would be uncleanly, if courtiers were shepherds.
    TOUCHSTONE: Instance, briefly; come, instance.
    CORIN: Why, we are still handling our ewes, and their fells,[229] you know, are greasy.
    TOUCHSTONE: Why, do not your courtier's hands sweat? and is not the grease of a mutton as wholesome as the sweat of a man? Shallow, shallow. A better instance, I say; come.
    CORIN: Besides, our hands are hard.

---

[223] the goddess Diana   [224] write   [225] inexpressible love   [226] worthless   [227] solitary   [228] perilous
[229] skins

TOUCHSTONE: Your lips will feel them the sooner. Shallow again. A more sounder instance, come.

CORIN: And they are often tarred over with the surgery of our sheep; and would you have us kiss tar? The courtier's hands are perfumed with civet.[230]

TOUCHSTONE: Most shallow man! thou wormsmeat, in respect[231] of a good piece of flesh indeed! Learn of the wise, and perpend:[232] civet is of a baser birth than tar, the very uncleanly flux of a cat. Mend the instance, shepherd.

CORIN: You have too courtly a wit for me: I'll rest.

TOUCHSTONE: Wilt thou rest damned? God help thee, shallow man! God make incision in thee! thou art raw.[233]

CORIN: Sir, I am a true labourer: I earn that I eat, get that I wear, owe no man hate, envy no man's happiness, glad of other men's good, content with my harm,[234] and the greatest of my pride is to see my ewes graze and my lambs suck.

TOUCHSTONE: That is another simple sin in you, to bring the ewes and the rams together and to offer to get your living by the copulation of cattle; to be bawd[235] to a bell-wether, and to betray a she-lamb of a twelvemonth to a crooked-pated, old, cuckoldly ram, out of all reasonable match.[236] If thou beest not damned for this, the devil himself will have no shepherds; I cannot see else how thou shouldst 'scape.

CORIN: Here comes young Master Ganymede, my new mistress's brother.

(Enter Rosalind, with a paper, reading.)

ROSALIND: From the east to western Ind,
    No jewel is like Rosalind.
    Her worth, being mounted on the wind,[237]
    Through all the world bears Rosalind.
    All the pictures fairest lined[238]
    Are but black to Rosalind.
    Let no fair be kept in mind
    But the fair[239] of Rosalind.

TOUCHSTONE: I'll rhyme you so eight years together, dinners and suppers and sleeping-hours excepted: it is the right butter-women's rank to market.

ROSALIND: Out, fool!

TOUCHSTONE: For a taste:
    If a hart[240] do lack a hind,[241]
    Let him seek out Rosalind.
    If the cat will after kind,
    So be sure will Rosalind.
    Winter garments must be lined,
    So must slender Rosalind.
    They that reap must sheaf and bind;
    Then to cart with Rosalind.
    Sweetest nut hath sourest rind,
    Such a nut is Rosalind.
    He that sweetest rose will find
    Must find love's prick and Rosalind.

This is the very false gallop of verses: why do you infect yourself with them?

ROSALIND: Peace, you dull fool! I found them on a tree.

---

[230] perfume from the glands of a civet cat   [231] in comparison with   [232] consider   [233] inexperienced   [234] ill fortune   [235] go-between   [236] mating   [237] blown by the wind   [238] drawn   [239] beauty   [240] male deer   [241] female deer

TOUCHSTONE: Truly, the tree yields bad fruit.

ROSALIND: I'll graff[242] it with you, and then I shall graff it with a medlar:[243] then it will be the earliest fruit i' the country; for you'll be rotten ere you be half ripe, and that's the right virtue of the medlar.

TOUCHSTONE: You have said; but whether wisely or no, let the forest judge.

(Enter Celia, with a writing.)

ROSALIND: Peace!
Here comes my sister, reading: stand aside.

CELIA: *(Reads)*
    Why should this a desert be?
      For it is unpeopled? No;
    Tongues I'll hang on every tree,
      That shall civil sayings show:
    Some, how brief the life of man
      Runs his erring[244] pilgrimage,
    That the stretching of a span[245]
      Buckles[246] in his sum of age;
    Some, of violated vows
      'Twixt the souls of friend and friend:
    But upon the fairest boughs,
      Or at every sentence end,
    Will I Rosalinda write,
      Teaching all that read to know
    The quintessence of every sprite
      Heaven would in little show.
    Therefore Heaven Nature charged
      That one body should be fill'd
    With all graces wide-enlarged:
      Nature presently distill'd
    Helen's cheek, but not her heart,
      Cleopatra's majesty,
    Atalanta's better part,
      Sad Lucretia's modesty.
    Thus Rosalind of many parts
      By heavenly synod[247] was devised,
    Of many faces, eyes and hearts,
      To have the touches[248] dearest prized.
    Heaven would that she these gifts
      should have,
    And I to live and die her slave.

ROSALIND: O most gentle pulpiter! what tedious homily[249] of love have you wearied your parishioners withal, and never cried 'Have patience, good people'!

CELIA: How now! back, friends! Shepherd, go off a little. Go with him, sirrah.

TOUCHSTONE: Come, shepherd, let us make an honourable retreat; though not with bag and baggage, yet with scrip and scrippage. *(Exeunt Corin and Touchstone.)*

---

[242] graft   [243] small brown fruit   [244] wandering   [245] so that   [246] encompasses   [247] assembly
[248] traits   [249] sermon

CELIA: Didst thou hear these verses?

ROSALIND: O, yes, I heard them all, and more too; for some of them had in them more feet than the verses would bear.

CELIA: That's no matter: the feet might bear the verses.

ROSALIND: Ay, but the feet were lame and could not bear themselves without the verse and therefore stood lamely in the verse.

CELIA: But didst thou hear without wondering how thy name should[250] be hanged and carved upon these trees?

ROSALIND: I was seven of the nine days out of the wonder[251] before you came; for look here what I found on a palm-tree. I was never so berhymed[252] since Pythagoras,[253] time, that I was an Irish rat,[254] which I can hardly remember.

CELIA: Trow[255] you who hath done this?

ROSALIND: Is it a man?

CELIA: And a chain,[256] that you once wore, about his neck. Change you colour?

ROSALIND: I prithee, who?

CELIA: O Lord, Lord! it is a hard matter for friends to meet; but mountains may be removed with earthquakes and so encounter.

ROSALIND: Nay, but who is it?

CELIA: Is it possible?

ROSALIND: Nay, I prithee now with most petitionary vehemence, tell me who it is.

CELIA: O wonderful, wonderful, and most wonderful wonderful! and yet again wonderful, and after that, out of all hooping![257]

ROSALIND: Good my complexion![258] dost thou think, though I am caparisoned[259] like a man, I have a doublet and hose in my disposition? One inch of delay more is a South-sea of discovery;[260] I prithee, tell me who is it quickly, and speak apace. I would thou couldst stammer, that thou mightst pour this concealed man out of thy mouth, as wine comes out of a narrow-mouthed bottle, either too much at once, or none at all. I prithee, take the cork out of thy mouth that I may drink thy tidings.

CELIA: So you may put a man in your belly.

ROSALIND: Is he of God's making? What manner of man? Is his head worth a hat, or his chin worth a beard?

CELIA: Nay, he hath but a little beard.

ROSALIND: Why, God will send more, if the man will be thankful: let me stay[261] the growth of his beard, if thou delay me not the knowledge of his chin.

CELIA: It is young Orlando, that tripped up the wrestler's heels and your heart both in an instant.

ROSALIND: Nay, but the devil take mocking: speak, sad brow[262] and true maid.

CELIA: I' faith, coz, 'tis he.

ROSALIND: Orlando?

CELIA: Orlando.

---

[250] was said to be [251] It was believed a wonder lasted nine days. [252] rhymed to death [253] He taught the belief that souls, after death, went into the bodies of animals. [254] It was believed that in Ireland rats could be killed by rhyming them to death. [255] know you [256] And with a chain [257] beyond any exclamation of surprise [258] She doesn't want her blushing to betray her. [259] dressed [260] as endless as a South Sea voyage [261] wait for [262] in earnest

ROSALIND: Alas the day! what shall I do with my doublet and hose? What did he when thou sawest him? What said he? How looked he? Wherein went[263] he? What makes he here? Did he ask for me? Where remains he? How parted he with thee? and when shalt thou see him again? Answer me in one word.

CELIA: You must borrow me Gargantua's[264] mouth first: 'tis a word too great for any mouth of this age's size. To say ay and no to these particulars is more than to answer in a catechism.

ROSALIND: But doth he know that I am in this forest and in man's apparel? Looks he as freshly as he did the day he wrestled?

CELIA: It is as easy to count atomies[265] as to resolve the propositions of a lover;[266] but take a taste of my finding him, and relish it with good observance. I found him under a tree, like a dropped acorn.

ROSALIND: It may well be called Jove's tree,[267] when it drops forth such fruit.

CELIA: Give me audience, good madam.

ROSALIND: Proceed.

CELIA: There lay he, stretched along,[268] like a wounded knight.

ROSALIND: Though it be pity to see such a sight, it well becomes the ground.

CELIA: Cry 'holla'[269] to thy tongue, I prithee; it curvets[270] unseasonably. He was furnished[271] like a hunter.

ROSALIND: O, ominous! he comes to kill my heart.

CELIA: I would sing my song without a burden.[272] thou bringest[273] me out of tune.

ROSALIND: Do you not know I am a woman? when I think, I must speak. Sweet, say on.

CELIA: You bring me out. Soft! comes he not here?

(*Enter* Orlando *and* Jaques.)

ROSALIND: 'Tis he: slink by, and note him.

JAQUES: I thank you for your company; but, good faith, I had as lief have been myself alone.

ORLANDO: And so had I; but yet, for fashion sake, I thank you too for your society.

JAQUES: God be wi' you: let's meet as little as we can.

ORLANDO: I do desire we may be better strangers.

JAQUES: I pray you, mar no more trees with writing love-songs in their barks.

ORLANDO: I pray you, mar no moe[274] of my verses with reading them ill-favouredly.

JAQUES: Rosalind is your love's name?

ORLANDO: Yes, just.[275]

JAQUES: I do not like her name.

ORLANDO: There was no thought of pleasing you when she was christened.

JACQUES: What stature is she of?

ORLANDO: Just as high as my heart.

---

263 What was he wearing?   264 an enormous giant   265 motes   266 to solve a lover's problem
267 the oak tree   268 at full length   269 stop   270 prancing   271 equipped   272 refrain   273 put
274 more   275 exactly

JAQUES: You are full of pretty answers. Have you not been acquainted with goldsmiths' wives, and conned them out rings?[276]

ORLANDO: Not so; but I answer you right[277] painted cloth,[278] from whence you have studied your questions.

JAQUES: You have a nimble wit: I think 'twas made of Atalanta's heels. Will you sit down with me? and we two will rail against our mistress the world and all our misery.

ORLANDO: I will chide no breather[279] in the world but myself, against whom I know most faults.

JAQUES: The worst fault you have is to be in love.

ORLANDO: 'Tis a fault I will not change for your best virtue. I am weary of you.

JAQUES: By my troth, I was seeking for a fool when I found you.

ORLANDO: He is drowned in the brook: look but in, and you shall see him.

JAQUES: There I shall see mine own figure.

ORLANDO: Which I take to be either a fool or a cipher.

JAQUES: I'll tarry no longer with you: farewell, good Signior Love.

ORLANDO: I am glad of your departure; adieu, good Monsieur Melancholy. (*Exit* Jaques.)

ROSALIND: (*Aside to* Celia) I will speak to him like a saucy lackey[280] and under that habit play the knave with him. Do you hear, forester?

ORLANDO: Very well: what would you?

ROSALIND: I pray you, what is 't o'clock?

ORLANDO: You should ask me what time o'day: there's no clock in the forest.

ROSALIND: Then there is no true lover in the forest; else sighing every minute and groaning every hour would detect the lazy foot of Time as well as a clock.

ORLANDO: And why not the swift foot of Time? had not that been as proper?

ROSALIND: By no means, sir: Time travels in divers paces with divers[281] persons. I'll tell you who Time ambles withal, who Time trots withal, who Time gallops withal and who he stands still withal.

ORLANDO: I prithee, who doth he trot withal?

ROSALIND: Marry, he trots hard with a young maid between the contract of her marriage and the day it is solemnized: if the interim be but a se'nnight,[282] Time's pace is so hard that it seems the length of seven year.

ORLANDO: Who ambles Time withal?

ROSALIND: With a priest that lacks Latin and a rich man that hath not the gout, for the one sleeps easily because he cannot study and the other lives merrily because he feels no pain, the one lacking the burden of lean and wasteful learning, the other knowing no burden of heavy tedious penury; these Time ambles withal.

ORLANDO: Who doth he gallop withal?

ROSALIND: With a thief to the gallows, for though he go as softly[283] as foot can fall, he thinks himself too soon there.

ORLANDO: Who stays it still withal?

ROSALIND: With lawyers in the vacation; for they sleep between term and term and then they perceive not how Time moves.

ORLANDO: Where dwell you, pretty youth?

---

[276] Rings were often inscribed with short sentences or mottoes.   [277] true   [278] coarse cloth painted to look like tapestry   [279] living being   [280] servant   [281] different   [282] weak   [283] slowly

ROSALIND: With this shepherdess, my sister; here in the skirts of the forest, like fringe upon a petticoat.

ORLANDO: Are you native of this place?

ROSALIND: As the cony[284] that you see dwell where she is kindled.[285]

ORLANDO: Your accent is something finer than you could purchase[286] in so removed a dwelling.

ROSALIND: I have been told so of many: but indeed an old religious[287] uncle of mine taught me to speak, who was in his youth an inland man;[288] one that knew courtship too well, for there he fell in love. I have heard him read many lectures against it, and I thank God I am not a woman, to be touched with so many giddy offences as he hath generally taxed their whole sex withal.

ORLANDO: Can you remember any of the principal evils that he laid to the charge of women?

ROSALIND: There were none principal; they were all like one another as half-pence are, every one fault seeming monstrous till his fellowfault came to match it.

ORLANDO: I prithee, recount some of them.

ROSALIND: No, I will not cast away my physic but on those that are sick. There is a man haunts the forest, that abuses our young plants with carving 'Rosalind' on their barks; hangs odes upon hawthorns and elegies on brambles, all, forsooth, deifying the name of Rosalind: if I could meet that fancy-monger,[289] I would give him some good counsel, for he seems to have the quotidian[290] of love upon him.

ORLANDO: I am he that is so love-shaked: I pray you, tell me your remedy.

ROSALIND: There is none of my uncle's marks upon you: he taught me how to know a man in love; in which cage of rushes[291] I am sure you are not prisoner.

ORLANDO: What were his marks?

ROSALIND: A lean cheek, which you have not, a blue eye[292] and sunken, which you have not, an unquestionable[293] spirit, which you have not, a beard neglected, which you have not; but I pardon you for that, for simply your having in beard is a younger brother's revenue: then your hose should be ungartered, your bonnet unbanded,[294] your sleeve unbuttoned, your shoe untied and every thing about you demonstrating a careless desolation; but you are no such man; you are rather point-device[295] in your accoutrements as loving yourself than seeming the lover of any other.

ORLANDO: Fair youth, I would I could make thee believe I love.

ROSALIND: Me believe it! you may as soon make her that you love believe it; which, I warrant, she is apter to do than to confess she does: that is one of the points in the which women still[296] give the lie to their consciences. But, in good sooth, are you he that hangs the verses on the trees, wherein Rosalind is so admired?

ORLANDO: I swear to thee, youth, by the white hand of Rosalind, I am that he, that unfortunate he.

ROSALIND: But are you so much in love your rhymes speak?

ORLANDO: Neither rhyme nor reason can express how much.

ROSALIND: Love is merely a madness, and, I tell you, deserves as well a dark house and a whip as madmen do: and the reason why they are not so

[284] rabbit [285] brought forth young [286] acquire [287] hermit [288] city dweller [289] trader in love [290] fever recurring daily [291] reed cage for birds [292] an eye with dark circles [293] glum [294] hat without a band [295] faultless [296] always

punished and cured is, that the lunacy is so ordinary that the whippers are in love too. Yet I profess curing it by counsel.

ORLANDO: Did you ever cure any so?

ROSALIND: Yes, one, in this manner. He was to imagine me his love, his mistress; and I set him every day to woo me; at which time would I, being but a moonish[297] youth, grieve, be effeminate, changeable, longing and liking, proud, fantastical, apish, shallow, inconstant, full of tears, full of smiles, for every passion something and for no passion truly any thing, as boys and women are for the most part cattle of this colour; would now like him, now loathe him; then entertain him, then forswear[298] him; now weep for him, then spit at him; that I drave my suitor from his mad humour of love to a living humour of madness;[299] which was, to forswear the full stream of the world[300] and to live in a nook merely monastic.[301] And thus I cured him; and this way will I take upon me to wash your liver as clean as a sound sheep's heart, that there shall not be one spot of love in 't.

ORLANDO: I would not be cured, youth.

ROSALIND: I would cure you, if you would but call me Rosalind and come every day to my cote and woo me.

ORLANDO: Now, by the faith of my love, I will: tell me where it is.

ROSALIND: Go with me to it and I'll show it you: and by the way you shall tell me where in the forest you live. Will you go?

ORLANDO: With all my heart, good youth.

ROSALIND: Nay, you must call me Rosalind. Come, sister, will you go? (Exeunt.)

SCENE III. *The forest.*

(Enter Touchstone *and* Audrey; Jaques *behind.*)

TOUCHSTONE: Come apace,[302] good Audrey: I will fetch up your goats, Audrey. And how, Audrey? am I the man yet? doth my simple feature content you?

AUDREY: Your features! Lord warrant[303] us! what features?

TOUCHSTONE: I am here with thee and thy goats, as the most capricious poet, honest Ovid, was among the Goths.

JAQUES: (*Aside*) O knowledge ill-inhabited, worse than Jove in a thatched house!

TOUCHSTONE: When a man's verses cannot be understood, nor a man's good wit seconded with the forward child Understanding, it strikes a man more dead than a great reckoning in a little room. Truly, I would the gods had made thee poetical.

AUDREY: I do not know what 'poetical' is: is it honest in deed and word? is it a true thing?

TOUCHSTONE: No, truly; for the truest poetry is the most feigning;[304] and lovers are given to poetry, and what they swear in poetry may be said as lovers they do feign.

AUDREY: Do you wish then that the gods had made me poetical?

TOUCHSTONE: I do, truly; for thou swearest to me thou art honest:[305] now, if thou wert a poet, I might have some hope thou didst feign.

AUDREY: Would you not have me honest?

---

[297] changeable   [298] deny with an oath   [299] pass from the madness of love to real madness   [300] a full life   [301] an absolute monk   [302] quickly   [303] protect   [304] imaginative   [305] chaste

TOUCHSTONE: No, truly, unless thou wert hardfavoured;[306] for honesty coupled to beauty is to have honey a sauce to sugar.

JACQUES: (*Aside*) A material fool!

AUDREY: Well, I am not fair; and therefore I pray the gods make me honest.

TOUCHSTONE: Truly, and to cast away honesty upon a foul slut were to put good meat into an unclean dish.

AUDREY: I am not a slut, though I thank the gods I am foul.[307]

TOUCHSTONE: Well, praised the gods for thy foulness![308] sluttishness may come hereafter. But be it as it may be, I will marry thee, and to that end I have been with Sir Oliver Martext, the vicar of the next village, who hath promised to meet me in this place of the forest and to couple us.

JACQUES: (*Aside:*)I would fain see this meeting.

AUDREY: Well, the gods give us joy!

TOUCHSTONE: Amen. A man may, if he were of a fearful heart, stagger in this attempt; for here we have no temple but the wood, no assembly but horn-beasts. But what thought? Courage! As horns are odious, they are necessary.[309] It is said, 'many a man knows no end of his goods:' right; many a man has good horns, and knows no end of them. Well, that is the dowry of his wife; 'tis none of his own getting. Horns? Even so. Poor men alone? No, no; the noblest deer hath them as huge as the rascal.[310] Is the single man therefore blessed? No: as a walled town is more worthier than a village, so is the forehead of a married man more honourable than the bare brow of a bachelor; and by how much defence is better than no skill, by so much is a horn more previous than to want.[311] Here comes Sir Oliver.

(*Enter* Sir Oliver Martext.)

Sir Oliver Martext, you are well met: will you dispatch us here under this tree, or shall we go with you to your chapel?

SIR OLIVER: Is there none here to give the woman?

TOUCHSTONE: I will not take her on gift of any man.

SIR OLIVER: Truly, she must be given, or the marriage is not lawful.

JAQUES: (*Advancing*) Proceed, proceed: I'll give her.

TOUCHSTONE: Good even, good Master What-ye-call't: how do you, sir? You are very well met: God 'ild[312] you for your last company: I am very glad to see you: even a toy in hand here, sir: nay, pray be covered.[313]

JAQUES: Will you be married, motley?

TOUCHSTONE: As the ox hath his bow,[314] sir, the horse his curb and the falcon her bells, so man hath his desires; and as pigeons bill, so wedlock would be nibbling.[315]

JAQUES: And will you, being a man of your breeding, be married under a bush like a beggar? Get you to church, and have a good priest that can tell you what marriage is: this fellow will but join you together as they join wainscot;[316] then one of you will prove a shrunk panel and, like green timber, warp, warp.

TOUCHSTONE: (*Aside*) I am not in the mind[317] but I were better to be married of him than of another: for he is not like to marry me well; and not being well married, it will be a good excuse for me hereafter to leave my wife.

---

[306] homely   [307] ugly   [308] dirtiness   [309] unavoidable   [310] a young lean deer, out of season
[311] than to be without a horn   [312] God reward   [313] put on your hat   [314] yoke   [315] getting at a man
[316] wooden paneling   [317] I do not know

JAQUES: Go thou with me, and let me counsel thee.
TOUCHSTONE: Come, sweet Audrey:
We must be married, or we must live in bawdry.
Farewell, good Master Oliver: not,—
     O sweet Oliver,
     O brave Oliver,
Leave me not behind thee:
but,—
     Wind[318] away,
     Begone, I say,
I will not to wedding with thee.
(*Exeunt Jaques, Touchstone and Audrey.*)
SIRE OLIVER: 'Tis no matter: ne'er a fantastical knave of them all shall flout[319] me out of my calling. (*Exit.*)

SCENE IV. *The forest.*

    (*Enter* Rosalind *and* Celia.)

ROSALIND: Never talk to me; I will weep.
CELIA: Do, I prithee; but yet have the grace to consider that tears do not become a man.
ROSALIND: But have I not cause to weep?
CELIA: As good cause as one would desire; therefore weep.
ROSALIND: His very hair is of the dissembling colour.
CELIA: Something browner than Judas's: marry, his kisses are Judas's own children.
ROSALIND: I' faith, his hair is of a good colour.
CELIA: An excellent colour: your chestnut was ever the only colour.
ROSALIND: And his kissing is as full of sanctity as the touch of holy bread.
CELIA: He hath bought a pair of cast[320] lips of Diana:[321] a nun of winter's sisterhood kisses not more religiously; the very ice of chastity is in them.
ROSALIND: But why did he swear he would come this morning, and comes not?
CELIA: Nay, certainly, there is no truth in him.
ROSALIND: Do you think so?
CELIA: Yes; I think he is not a pick-purse nor a horse-stealer, but for his verity in love, I do think him as concave as a covered globlet or a worm-eaten nut.
ROSALIND: Not true in love?
CELIA: Yes, when he is in; but I think he is not in.
ROSALIND: You have heard him swear downright he was.
CELIA: 'Was' is not 'is:' besides, the oath of a lover is no stronger than the word of a tapster;[322] they are both the confirmer of false reckonings. He attends here in the forest on the duke your father.
ROSALIND: I met the duke yesterday and had much question[323] with him: he asked me of what parentage I was; I told him, of as good as he; so he laughed and let me go. But what[324] talk of fathers, when there is such a man as Orlando?
CELIA: O, that's a brave man! he writes brave verses, speaks brave words,

[318] Turn   [319] mock   [320] discarded   [321] goddess of chastity   [322] person who brings the drinks in a bar   [323] conversation   [324] why

swears brave oaths and breaks them bravely, quite traverse, athwart the heart of his lover; as a puisny[325] tilter, that spurs his horse but on one side, breaks his staff like a noble goose: but all's brave that youth mounts and folly guides. Who comes here?

(*Enter* Corin.)

CORIN: Mistress and master, you have oft inquired
After the shepherd that complain'd of love,
Who you saw sitting by me on the turf,
Praising the proud disdainful shepherdess
That was his mistress.
    CELIA: Well, and what of him?
    CORIN: If you will see a pageant[326] truly play'd,
Between the pale complexion of true love
And the red glow of scorn and proud disdain,
Go hence a little and I shall conduct you,
If you will mark it.
    ROSALIND: O, come, let us remove:
The sight of lovers feedeth those in love.
Bring us to this sight, and you shall say
I'll prove a busy actor in their play. (*Exeunt.*)

SCENE V. *Another part of the forest.*

(*Enter* Silvius *and* Phebe.)

SILVIUS: Sweet Phebe, do not scorn me; do not, Phebe;
Say that you love me not, but say not so
In bitterness. The common executioner,
Whose heart the accustom'd sight of death makes hard,
Falls not[327] the axe upon the humbled neck
But first begs pardon: will you sterner be
Than he that dies and lives by bloody drops?

(*Enter* Rosalind, Celia, *and* Corin, *behind.*)

PHEBE: I would not be thy executioner:
I fly thee, for I would not injure thee.
Thou tell'st me there is murder in mine eye:
'Tis pretty,[328] sure, and very probable,
That eyes, that are the frail'st and softest things,
Who shut their coward gates on atomies,
Should be call'd tyrants, butchers, murderers!
Now I do frown on thee with all my heart;
And if mine eyes can wound, now let them kill thee:
Now counterfeit to swoon; why now fall down;
Or if thou canst not, O, for shame, for shame,
Lie not, to say mine eyes are murderers!
Now show the wound mine eye hath made in thee:

---

[325] inexperienced   [326] play   [327] Lets fall not   [328] a pretty idea

Scratch thee but with a pin, and there remains
Some scar of it; lean but upon a rush,
The cicatrice[329] and capable impressure[330]
Thy palm some moment keeps; but now mine eyes,
Which I have darted at thee, hurt thee not,
Nor, I am sure, there is no force in eyes
That can do hurt.

    SILVIUS: O dear Phebe,
If ever,—as that ever may be near,—
You meet in some fresh cheek the power of fancy,[331]
Then shall you know the wounds invisible
That love's keen arrows make.

    PHEBE: But till that time
Come not thou near me: and when that time comes,
Afflict me with thy mocks, pity me not;
As till that time I shall not pity thee.

    ROSALIND: And why, I pray you? Who might be your mother,
That you insult, exult, and all at once,
Over the wretched? What though you have no beauty,—
As, by my faith, I see no more in you
Than without candle may go dark to bed—[332]
Must you be therefore proud and pitiless?
Why, what means this? Why do you look on me?
I see no more in you than in the ordinary
Of nature's sale-work.[333] Od's my little life,[334]
I think she means to tangle my eyes too!
No, faith, proud mistress, hope not after it:
'Tis not your inky brows, your black silk hair,[335]
Your bugle[336] eyeballs, nor your cheek of cream,
That can entame my spirits to your worship.
You foolish shepherd, wherefore do you follow her,
Like foggy south[337] puffing with wind and rain?
You are a thousand times a properer[338] man
Than she a woman: 'tis such fools as you
That makes the world full of ill-favour'd children:
'Tis not her glass, but you, that flatters her;
And out of you she sees herself more proper
Than any of her lineaments[339] can show her.
But, mistress, know yourself: down on your knees,
And thank heaven, fasting, for a good man's love:
For I must tell you friendly in your ear,
Sell when you can: you are not for all markets:
Cry the man mercy;[340] love him; take his offer:
Foul is most foul, being foul to be a scoffer.[341]
So take her to thee, shepherd: fare you well.

    PHEBE: Sweet youth, I pray you, chide a year together:
I had rather hear you chide than this man woo.

---

[329] scar [330] imprint retained [331] love [332] You're not so brilliant you could go to bed by your own illumination. [333] ordinary piece of goods [334] a mild oath [335] Black hair was not thought to be beautiful. [336] beady [337] winds from the south bringing fog, rain and illness [338] more handsome [339] features [340] Ask his pardon [341] You are ugly and even more so when you are abusive.

ROSALIND: He's fallen in love with your foulness and she'll fall in love with my anger. If it be so, as fast as she answers thee with frowning looks, I'll sauce her with bitter words. Why look you so upon me?

PHEBE: For no ill will I bear you.

ROSALIND: I pray you, do not fall in love with me,
For I am falser than vows made in wine:
Besides, I like you not. If you will know my house,
'Tis at the tuft of olives here hard by
Will you go, sister? Shepherd, ply[342] her hard.
Come, sister. Shepherdess, look on him better,
And be no proud: though all the world could see,
None could be so abused in sight as he.
Come, to our flock. (*Exeunt* Rosalind, Celia *and* Corin.)

PHEBE: Dead shepherd, now I find thy saw of might,
'Who ever loved that loved not a first sight?'

SILVIUS: Sweet Phebe,—

PHEBE: Ha, what say'st thou, Silvius?

SILVIUS: Sweet Phebe, pity me.

PHEBE: Why, I am sorry for thee, gentle Silvius.

SILVIUS: Wherever sorrow is, relief would be:
If you do sorrow at my grief in love,
By giving love your sorrow and my grief
Were both extermined.

PHEBE: Thou hast my love: is not that neighbourly?

SILVIUS: I would have you.

PHEBE: Why, that were covetousness.
Silvius, the time was that I hated thee,
And yet it is not that I bear thee love;
But since that thou canst talk of love so well,
Thy company, which erst[343] was irksome to me,
I will endure, and I'll employ thee too:
But do not look for further recompense
Than thine own gladness that thou are employ'd

SILVIUS: So holy and so perfect is my love,
And I in such a poverty of grace,[344]
That I shall think it a most plenteous crop
To glean the broken ears after the man
That the main harvest reaps: loose now and then
A scatter'd smile, and that I'll live upon.

PHEBE: Know'st thou the youth that spoke to me erewhile[345]

SILVIUS: Not very well, but I have met him oft;
And he hath bought the cottage and the bounds
That the old carlot[346] once was master of.

PHEBE: Think not I love him, though I ask for him;
'Tis but a peevish[347] boy; yet he talks well;
But what care I for words? yet words do well
When he that speaks them pleases those that hear.
It is a pretty youth: not very pretty:
But, sure, he's proud, and yet his pride becomes him:
He'll make a proper man: the best thing in him
Is his complexion; and faster than his tongue

---

[342] press [343] formerly [344] poor favor [345] just now [346] peasant [347] silly

Did make offence his eye did heal it up.
He is not very tall; yet for his years he's tall:
His leg is but so so; and yet 'tis well:
There was a pretty redness in his lip,
A little riper and more lusty red
Than that mix'd in his cheek; 'twas just the difference
Betwixt the constant[348] red and mingled[349] damask.
There be some women, Silvius, had they mark'd him
In parcels[350] as I did, would have gone near
To fall in love with him; but, for my part,
I love him not nor hate him not; and yet
I have more cause to hate him than to love him:
For what had he to do[351] to chide at me?
He said mine eyes were black and my hair black;
And, now I am remember'd,[352] scorn'd at me:
I marvel why I answer'd not again:
But that's all one; omittance is no quittance.[353]
I'll write to him a very taunting letter,
And thou shalt bear it: wilt thou, Silvius?
   SILVIUS: Phebe, with all my heart.
   PHEBE: I'll write it straight;[354]
The matter's in my head and in my heart:
I will be bitter with him and passing short.[355]
Go with me, Silvius. (*Exeunt.*)

ACT IV.

SCENE I. *The forest.*

   (*Enter* Rosalind, Celia, *and* Jaques.)

   JAQUES: I prithee, pretty youth, let me be better acquainted with thee.
   ROSALIND: They say you are a melancholy fellow.
   JAQUES: I am so; I do love it better than laughing.
   ROSALIND: Those that are in extremity of either are abominable fellows
and betray themselves to every modern[356] censure worse than drunkards.
   JAQUES: Why, 'tis good to be sad and say nothing.
   ROSALIND: Why then, 'tis good to be a post.
   JAQUES: I have neither the scholar's melancholy, which is emulation,[357]
nor the musician's, which is fantastical, nor the courtier's, which is proud,
nor the soldier's, which is ambitious, nor the lawyer's, which is politic,[358] nor
the lady's, which is nice,[359] nor the lover's, which is all these: but it is a
melancholy of mine own, compounded of many simples,[360] extracted from
many objects, and indeed the sundry contemplation of my travels, in which
my often rumination wraps me in a most humorous sadness.
   ROSALIND: A traveller! By my faith, you have great reason to be sad: I fear
you have sold your own lands to see other men's; then, to have seen much
and to have nothing, is to have rich eyes and poor hands.
   JAQUES: Yes, I have gained my experience.

---

[348] uniform   [349] striped   [350] In parts   [351] what business had he   [352] remember   [353] Just because
I let him off now doesn't mean he will escape altogether.   [354] now   [355] quite   [356] ordinary
[357] jealous rivalry   [358] crafty   [359] daintily refined   [360] ingredients

ROSALIND: And your experience makes you sad: I had rather have a fool to make me merry than experience to make me sad; and to travel for it too!

(*Enter* Orlando.)

ORLANDO: Good day and happiness, dear Rosalind!
JAQUES: Nay, then, God be wi' you, an you talk in blank verse. (*Exit.*)
ROSALIND: Farewell, Monsieur Traveller: look you lisp[361] and wear strange suits, disable[362] all the benefits of your own country, be out of love with your nativity and almost chide God for making you that countenance[363] you are, or I will scarce think you have swam in a gondola.[364] Why, how now, Orlando! where have you been all this while? You a lover! An you serve me such another trick, never come in my sight more.
ORLANDO: My fair Rosalind, I come within an hour of my promise.
ROSALIND: Break an hour's promise in love! He that will divide a minute into a thousand parts and break but a part of the thousandth part of a minute in the affairs of love, it may be said of him that Cupid hath clapped him o' the shoulder,[365] but I'll warrant him heartwhole.
ORLANDO: Pardon me, dear Rosalind.
ROSALIND: Nay, an you be so tardy, come no more in my sight: I had as lief be wooed of a snail.
ORLANDO: Of a snail?
ROSALIND: Ay, of a snail; for though he comes slowly, he carries his house on his head; a better jointure,[366] I think, than you make a woman: besides, he brings his destiny with him.
ORLANDO: What's that?
ROSALIND: Why, horns, which such as you are fain to be beholding to your wives for: but he comes armed in his fortune and prevents the slander of his wife.
ORLANDO: Virtue is no horn-maker; and my Rosalind is virtuous.
ROSALIND: And I am your Rosalind.
CELIA: It pleases him to call you so; but he hath a Rosalind of a better leer[367] than you.
ROSALIND: Come, woo me, woo me, for now I am in a holiday humour and like enough to consent. What would you say to me now, an I were your very very Rosalind?
ORLANDO: I would kiss before I spoke.
ROSALIND: Nay, you were better speak first, and when you were gravelled[368] for lack of matter, you might take occasion to kiss. Very good orators, when they are out, they will spit; and for lovers lacking—God warn[369] us!—matter, the cleanliest shift[370] is to kiss.
ORLANDO: How if the kiss be denied?
ROSALIND: Then she puts you to entreaty, and there begins new matter.
ORLANDO: Who would be out, being before his beloved mistress?
ROSALIND: Marry, that should you, if I were your mistress, or I should think my honesty ranker than my wit.
ORLANDO: What, of my suit?
ROSALIND: Not out of your apparel, and yet out of your suit. Am not I your Rosalind?

---

361 affect a foreign accent   362 make disparaging remarks about   363 face   364 been in Venice   365 arrested him   366 marriage settlement   367 look   368 at a standstill   369 defend   370 best way of getting around the difficulty

ORLANDO: I take some joy to say you are, because I would be talking of her.

ROSALIND: Well, in her person[371] I say I will not have you.

ORLANDO: Then in mine own person I die.

ROSALIND: No, faith, die by attorney.[372] The poor world is almost six thousand years old, and in all this time there was not any man died in his own person, videlicet, in a love-cause. Troilus had his brains dashed out with a Grecian club; yet he did what he could to die before, and he is one of the patterns of love. Leander, he would have lived many a fair year, though Hero had turned nun, if it had not been for a hot midsummer night; for, good youth, he went but forth to wash him in the Hellespont and being taken with the cramp was drowned: and the foolish chroniclers of that age found it was 'Hero of Sestos.' But these are all lies: men have died from time to time and worms have eaten them, but not for love.

ORLANDO: I would not have my right Rosalind of this mind, for, I protest, her frown might kill me.

ROSALIND: By this hand, it will not kill a fly. But come, now I will be your Rosalind in a more coming-on[373] disposition, and ask me what you will, I will grant it.

ORLANDO: Then love me, Rosalind.

ROSALIND: Yes, faith, will I, Fridays and Saturdays and all.

ORLANDO: And wilt thou have me?

ROSALIND: Ay, and twenty such.

ORLANDO: What sayest thou?

ROSALIND: Are you not good?

ORLANDO: I hope so.

ROSALIND: Why then, can one desire too much of a good thing? Come, sister, you shall be the priest and marry us. Give me your hand, Orlando. What do you say, sister?

ORLANDO: Pray thee, marry us.

CELIA: I cannot say the words.

ROSALIND: You must begin, 'Will you, Orlando—'

CELIA: Go to. Will you, Orlando, have to wife this Rosalind?

ORLANDO: I will.

ROSALIND: Ay, but when?

ORLANDO: Why now; as fast as she can marry us.

ROSALIND: Then you must say, 'I take thee, Rosalind, for wife.'

ORLANDO: I take thee, Rosalind, for wife.

ROSALIND: I might ask you for your commission,[374] but I do take thee, Orlando, for my husband: there's a girl goes before the priest; and certainly a woman's thought runs before her actions.

ORLANDO: So do all thoughts; they are winged.

ROSALIND: Now tell me how long you would have her after you have possessed her.

ORLANDO: For ever and a day.

ROSALIND: Say 'a day,' without the 'ever.' No, no, Orlando; men are April when they woo, December when they wed: maids are May when they are maids, but the sky changes when they are wives. I will be more jealous of thee than a Barbary cock-pigeon over his hen, more clamorous than a parrot against[375] rain, more new-fangled[376] than an ape, more giddy in my desires

---

[371] as her representative   [372] proxy   [373] encouraging   [374] authority   [375] before   [376] eager for novelties

than a monkey: I will weep for nothing, like Diana in the fountain,[377] and I will do that when you disposed to be merry; I will laugh like a hyen,[378] and that when thou art inclined to sleep.

ORLANDO: But will my Rosalind do so?

ROSALIND: By my life, she will do as I do.

ORLANDO: O, but she is wise.

ROSALIND: Or else she could not have the wit to do this: the wiser, the waywarder:[379] make the doors upon a woman's wit and it will out at the casement;[380] shut that and 'twill out at the key-hole; stop that, 'twill fly with the smoke out at the chimney.

ORLANDO: A man that had a wife with such a wit, he might say 'Wit, whither wilt?'

ROSALIND: Nay, you might keep that check[381] for it till you met your wife's wit going to your neighbour's bed.

ORLANDO: And what wit could wit have to excuse that?

ROSALIND: Marry, to say she came to seek you there. You shall never take her without her answer, unless you take her without her tongue. O, that woman that cannot make her fault her husband's occasion,[382] let her never nurse her child herself, for she will breed it like a fool!

ORLANDO: For these two hours, Rosalind, I will leave thee.

ROSALIND: Alas! dear love, I cannot lack thee two hours.

ORLANDO: I must attend the duke at dinner: by two o'clock I will be with thee again.

ROSALIND: Ay, go your ways, go your ways; I knew what you would prove: my friends told me as much, and I thought no less: that flattering tongue of yours won me: 'tis but one cast away, and so, come, death! Two o'clock is your hour?

ORLANDO: Ay, sweet Rosalind.

ROSALIND: By my troth,[383] and in good ernest, and so God mend me, and by all pretty oaths that are not dangerous, if you break one jot of your promise or come one minute behind your hour, I will think you the most pathetical break-promise and the most hollow lover and the most unworthy of her you call Rosalind that may be chosen out of the gross band of the unfaithful: therefore beware my censure and keep your promise.

ORLANDO: With no less religion[384] than if thou wert indeed my Rosalind: so adieu.

ROSALIND: Well, Time is the old justice that examines all such offenders, and let Time try: adieu. (*Exit* Orlando.)

CELIA: You have simply misused[385] our sex in your love-prate: we must have your doublet and hose plucked over your head, and show the world what the bird hath done to her own nest.[386]

ROSALIND: O coz, coz, coz, my pretty little coz, that thou didst know how many fathom deep I am in love! But it cannot be sounded: my affection hath an unknown bottom, like the bay of Portugal.

CELIA: Or rather, bottomless, that as fast as you pour affection in, it runs out.

ROSALIND: No, that same wicked bastard of Venus[387] that was begot of thought, conceived of spleen[388] and born of madness, that blind rascally boy that abuses every one's eyes because his own are out, let him be judge how

---

[377] the figure of Diana in a fountain [378] hyena [379] shut [380] window opening on hinges [381] rebuke [382] that can't blame her husband for her own faults [383] truth [384] fidelity [385] slandered [386] that the bird has fouled her own nest [387] Cupid [388] sudden anger

deep I am in love. I'll tell thee, Aliena, I cannot be out of the sight of Orlando:
I'll go find a shadow[389] and sigh till he come.
CELIA:　And I'll sleep. (*Exeunt.*)

SCENE II. *The forest.*

　　(*Enter* Jaques, Lords, *and* Foresters.)

JAQUES:　Which is he that killed the deer?
A LORD:　Sir, it was I.
JAQUES:　Let's present him to the duke, like a Roman conqueror; and it
would do well to set the deer's horns upon his head, for a branch of victory.
Have you no song, forester, for this purpose?
FORESTER:　Yes, sir.
JAQUES:　Sing it: 'tis no matter how it be in tune, so it make noise enough.

Song.

FORESTER:　What shall he have that kill'd the deer?
His leather skin and horns to wear.
　　Then sing him home;
　　(*The rest shall hear this burden.*)
Take thou no scorn[390] to wear the horn;
It was a crest ere thou wast born:
　　Thy father's father wore it,
　　And thy father bore it:
The horn, the horn, the lusty horn
Is not a thing to laugh to scorn. (*Exeunt.*)
SCENE III. *The forest.*

　　(*Enter* Rosalind *and* Celia.)

ROSALIND:　How say you now? Is it not past two o'clock? and here much
Orlando!
CELIA:　I warrant you, with pure love and troubled brain, he hath ta'en his
bow and arrows and is gone forth to sleep. Look, who comes here.

　　(*Enter* Silvius.)

SILVIUS:　My errand is to you, fair youth;
My gentle Phebe bid me give you this:
I know not the contents; but, as I guess
By the stern brow and waspish action
Which she did use as she was writing of it,
It bears an angry tenour:[391] pardon me;
I am but as a guiltless messenger.
ROSALIND:　Patience herself would startle at this letter
And play the swaggerer; bear this, bear all:
She says I am not fair, that I lack manners;
She calls me proud, and that she could not love me,

[389] shady place　[390] Don't be ashamed　[391] intention

Were man as rare as phoenix.[392] 'Od's my will!
Here love is not the hare that I do hunt:
Why writes she so to me? Well, shepherd, well,
This is a letter of your own device.

SILVIUS: No, I protest, I know not the contents:
Phebe did write it.

ROSALIND: Come, come, you are a fool
And turn'd[393] into the extremity of love.
I saw her hand: she has a leathern[394] hand,
A freestone-colour'd[395] hand: I verily did think
That her old gloves were on, but 'twas her hands:
She has a huswife's hand; but that's no matter:
I say she never did invent this letter;
This is a man's invention and his hand.

SILVIUS: Sure, it is hers.

ROSALIND: Why, 'tis a boisterous[396] and a cruel style,
A style for challengers; why, she defies me,
Like Turk to Christians: women's gentle brain
Could not drop forth such giant-rude invention,
Such Ethiope[397] words, blacker in their effect[398]
Than in their countenance. Will you hear the letter?

SILVIUS: So please you, for I never heard it yet;
Yet heard too much of Phebe's cruelty.

ROSALIND: She Phebes[399] me: mark how the tyrant writes (*Reads.*)
        Art thou god to shepherd turn'd,
        That a maiden's heart hath burn'd?
Can a woman rail thus?

SILVIUS: Call you this railing?

ROSALIND: (*Reads*)
        Why, thy godhead laid apart,[400]
        Warr'st thou with a woman's heart?
Did you ever hear such railing?
        Whiles the eye of man did woo me,
        That could do no vengeance to me.
Meaning me a beast.
        If the scorn of your bright eyne[401]
        Have power to raise such love in mine,
        Alack, in me what strange effect
        Would they work in mild aspect![402]
        Whiles you chid me, I did love;
        How then might your prayers move!
        He that brings this love to thee
        Little knows this love in me:
        And by him seal up thy mind;[403]
        Whether that thy youth and kind[404]
        Will the faithful offer take
        Of me and all that I can make;
        Or else by him my love deny,
        And then I'll study how to die.

---

[392] a bird that lived five hundred years and was reborn from its own ashes [393] brought
[394] workingman's hand [395] brown colored   [396] violent   [397] black   [398] intention   [399] treats me
cruelly [400] Why do you, a god, become a man [401] eyes [402] gentle looks [403] write your answer
and send it to him [404] nature

SILVIUS: Call you this chiding?
CELIA: Alas, poor shepherd!
ROSALIND: Do you pity him? no, he deserves no pity. Wilt thou love such a woman? What, to make thee an instrument and play false strains upon thee! not to be endured! Well, go your way to her, for I see love hath made thee a tame snake, and say this to her: that if she love me, I charge her to love thee; if she will not, I will never have her unless thou entreat for her. If you be a true lover, hence, and not a word; for here comes more company. (*Exit Silvius.*)

(*Enter* Oliver.)

OLIVER: Good morrow, fair ones: pray you, if you know,
Where in the purlieus[405] of this forest stands
A sheep-cote fenced about with olive trees?
CELIA: West of this place, down in the neighbour[406] bottom:
The rank of osiers[407] by the murmuring stream
Left on your right hand brings you to the place.
But at this hour the house doth keep itself;
There's none within.
OLIVER: If that an eye may profit by a tongue,
Then should I know you by description;
Such garments and such years: 'The boy is fair,
Of female favour,[408] and bestows himself
Like a ripe sister:[409] the woman low
And browner than her brother.' Are not you
The owner of the house I did enquire for?
CELIA: It is no boast, being ask'd, to say we are.
OLIVER: Orlando doth commend him to you both,
And to that youth he calls his Rosalind
He sends this bloody napkin.[410] Are you he?
ROSALIND: I am: what must we understand by this?
OLIVER: Some of my shame; if you will know of me
What man I am, and how, and why, and where
This hankercher was stain'd.
CELIA: I pray you, tell it.
Oliver: When last the young Orlando parted from you
He left a promise to return again
Within an hour, and pacing through the forest,
Chewing the food of sweet and bitter fancy,[411]
Lo, what befel! he threw his eye aside,
And mark what object did present itself:
Under an oak, whose boughs were moss'd with age
And high top bald with dry antiquity,
A wretched ragged man, o'ergrown with hair,
Lay sleeping on his back: about his neck
A green and gilded snake had wreathed itself,
Who with her head nimble in threats approach'd
The opening of his mouth; but suddenly,

---

[405] boundaries   [406] neighboring valley   [407] row of willows   [408] looks   [409] an older sister
[410] handerchief   [411] love

Seeing Orlando, it unlink'd itself,
And with indented[412] glides did slip away
Into a bush: under which bush's shade
A lioness, with udders all drawn dry,[413]
Lay couching, head on ground, with catlike watch,
When that the sleeping man should stir; for 'tis
The royal disposition of that beast
To prey on nothing that doth seem as dead:
This seen, Orlando did approach the man
And found it was his brother, his elder brother.
    CELIA: O, I have heard him speak of that same brother;
And he did render[414] him the most unnatural
That lived amongst men.
    OLIVER: And well he might so do,
For well I know he was unnatural.
    ROSALIND: But, to[415] Orlando: did he leave him there,
Food to the suck'd and hungry lioness?
    OLIVER: Twice did he turn his back and purposed so;
But kindness,[416] nobler ever than revenge,
And nature, stronger than his just occasion,[417]
Made him give battle to the lioness,
Who quickly fell before him: in which hurtling[418]
From miserable slumber I awaked.
    CELIA: Are you his brother?
    ROSALIND: Was't you he rescued?
    CELIA: Was't you that did so oft contrive to kill him?
    OLIVER: 'Twas I; but 'tis not I: I do not shame[419]
To tell you what I was, since my conversion
So sweetly tastes, being the thing I am.
    ROSALIND: But, for[420] the bloody napkin?
    OLIVER: By and by.
When from the first to last betwixt us two
Tears our recountments[421] had most kindly bathed,
As how I came into that desert place:—
In brief, he led me to the gentle duke,
Who gave me fresh array and entertainment,
Committing me unto my brother's love;
Who led me instantly unto his cave,
There stripp'd himself, and here upon his arm
The lioness had torn some flesh away,
Which all this while had bled; and now he fainted
And cried, in fainting, upon Rosalind.
Brief,[422] I recover'd him, bound up his wound;
And, after some small space, being strong at heart,
He sent me hither, stranger as I am,
To tell this story, that you might excuse
His broken promise, and to give this napkin
Dyed in his blood unto the shepherd youth
That he in sport doth call his Rosalind. (Rosalind *swoons*.)

---

[412] waving motions   [413] fierce with hunger   [414] describe   [415] in regard to   [416] natural affection
[417] chance for getting even   [418] clash of battle   [419] am not ashamed   [420] as regards   [421] accounts
of our adventures   [422] In brief

CELIA: Why, how now, Ganymede! sweet Ganymede!
OLIVER: Many will swoon when they do look on blood.
CELIA: There is more in it. Cousin Ganymede!
OLIVER: Look, he recovers.
ROSALIND: I would I were at home.
CELIA: We'll lead you thither.
I pray you, will you take him by the arm?
OLIVER: Be of good cheer, youth: you a man! you lack a man's heart.
ROSALIND: I do so, I confess it. Ah, sirrah, a body would think this was well counterfeited! I pray you, tell your brother how well I counterfeited. Heigh-ho!
OLIVER: This was not counterfeit: there is too great testimony in your complexion that it was a passion of ernest.
ROSALIND: Counterfeit, I assure you.
OLIVER: Well then, take a good heart and counterfeit to be a man.
ROSALIND: So I do: but, i' faith, I should have been a woman by right.
CELIA: Come, you look paler and paler: pray you, draw homewards. Good sir, go with us.
OLIVER: That will I, for I must bear answer back
How you excuse my brother, Rosalind.
ROSALIND: I shall devise something: but I pray you, commend my counterfeiting to him. Will you go? (*Exeunt.*)

ACT V.

SCENE I. *The forest.*

(*Enter* Touchstone *and* Audrey.)

TOUCHSTONE: We shall find a time, Audrey; patience, gentle Audrey.
AUDREY: Faith, the priest was good enough, for all the old gentleman's saying.
TOUCHSTONE: A most wicked Sir Oliver, Audrey, a most vile Martext. But, Audrey, there is a youth here in the forest lays claim to you.
AUDREY: Ay, I know who 'tis; he hath no interest in me in the world: here comes the man you mean.
TOUCHSTONE: It is meat and drink to me to see a clown:[423] by my troth, we that have good wits have much to answer for; we shall[424] be flouting,[425] we cannot hold.

(*Enter* William.)

WILLIAM: Good even, Audrey.
AUDREY: God ye good even,[426] William.
WILLIAM: And good even to you, sir.
TOUCHSTONE: Good even, gentle friend. Cover thy head, cover thy head; nay, prithee, be covered. How old are you, friend?
WILLIAM: Five and twenty, sir.
TOUCHSTONE: A ripe age. Is thy name William?
WILLIAM: William, sir.

---

[423] countryman   [424] must   [425] scoffing   [426] God give ye good evening

TOUCHSTONE: A fair name. Wast born i' the forest here?

WILLIAM: Ay, sir, I thank God.

TOUCHSTONE: 'Thank God;' a good answer. Art rich?

WILLIAM: Faith, sir, so so.

TOUCHSTONE: 'So so' is good, very good, very excellent good; and yet it is not; it is but so so. Art thou wise?

WILLIAM: Ay, sir, I have a pretty wit.

TOUCHSTONE: Why, thou sayest well. I do now remember a saying, 'The fool doth think he is wise, but the wise man knows himself to be a fool.' The heathen philosopher, when he had a desire to eat a grape, would open his lips when he put it into his houth; meaning thereby that grapes were made to eat and lips to open. You do love this maid?

WILLIAM: I do, sir.

TOUCHSTONE: Give me your hand. Art thou learned?

WILLIAM: No, sir.

TOUCHSTONE: Then learn this of me: to have, is to have; for it is a figure in rhetoric that drink, being poured out of a cup into a glass, by filling the one doth empty the other;[427] for all your writers do consent that ipse is he: now, and are not ipse,[428] for I am he.

WILLIAM: Which he, sir?

TOUCHSTONE: He, sir, that must marry this woman. Therefore, you clown, abandon,—which is in the vulgar[429] leave,—the society,—which in the boorish is company,—of this female,—which in the common is woman; which together is, abandon the society of this female, or, clown, thou perishest; or, to thy better understanding, diest; or, to wit, I kill thee, make thee away, translate thy life into death, thy liberty into bondage: I will deal in poison with thee, or in bastinado,[430] or in steel; I will bandy with thee in faction;[431] I will o'errun thee with policy;[432] I will kill thee a hundred and fifty ways: therefore tremble, and depart.

AUDREY: Do, good William.

WILLIAM: God rest you merry, sir. (*Exit.*)

(*Enter* Corin.)

CORIN: Our master and mistress seeks you; come, away, away!

TOUCHSTONE: Trip, Audrey! trip, Audrey! I attend, I attend. (*Exeunt.*)

SCENE II. *The forest.*

(*Enter* Orlando *and* Oliver.)

ORLANDO: Is't possible that on so little acquaintance you should like her? that but seeing you should love her? and loving woo? and, wooing, she should grant? and will you persever to enjoy her?

OLIVER: Neither call the giddiness[433] of it in question, the poverty of her, the small acquaintance, my sudden wooing, nor her sudden consenting; but say with me, I love *Aliena*; say with her that she loves me; consent with both that we may enjoy each other: it shall be to your good; for my father's house and all the revenue that was old Sir Rowland's will I estate[434] upon you, and here live and die a shepherd.

---

[427] William and Touchstone can't both have Audrey.   [428] himself   [429] common tongue   [430] a thrashing   [431] strive with you in contest   [432] overcome you by crafty means   [433] rashness   [434] bestow

ORLANDO: You have my consent. Let your wedding be to-morrow: thither will I invite the duke and all's contented followers. Go you and prepare Aliena; for look you, here comes my Rosalind.

(Enter Rosalind.)

ROSALIND: God save you, brother.
OLIVER: And you, fair sister. (*Exit.*)
ROSALIND: O, my dear Orlando, how it grieves me to see thee wear thy heart in a scarf!
ORLANDO: It is my arm.
ROSALIND: I thought thy heart had been wounded with the claws of a lion.
ORLANDO: Wounded it is, but with the eyes of a lady.
ROSALIND: Did your brother tell you how I counterfeited to swoon when he showed me your handercher?
ORLANDO: Ay, and greater wonders than that.
ROSALIND: O, I know where you are:[435] nay, 'tis true: there was never any thing so sudden but the fight of two rams and Caesar's thrasonical[436] brag of 'I camp, saw, and overcame:' for your brother and my sister no sooner met but they looked, no sooner looked but they loved, no sooner loved but they sighed, no sooner sighed but they asked one another the reason, no sooner knew the reason but they sought the remedy; and in these degrees have they made a pair of stairs to marriage which they will climb incontinent, or else be incontinent[437] before marriage: they are in the very wrath[438] of love and they will together; clubs cannot part them.
ORLANDO: They shall be married to-morrow, and I will bid the duke to the nuptial. But, O, how bitter a thing it is to look into happiness through another man's eyes! By so much the more shall I to-morrow be at the height of heart-heaviness, by how much I shall think my brother happy in having what he wishes for.
ROSALIND: Why then, to-morrow I cannot serve your turn for Rosalind?
ORLANDO: I can live no longer by thinking.[439]
ROSALIND: I will weary you then no longer with idle talking. Know of me then, for now I speak to some purpose, that I know you are a gentleman of good conceit:[440] I speak not this that you should bear a good opinion of my knowledge, insomuch I say I know you are; neither do I labour for a greater esteem than may in some little measure draw a belief from you, to do yourself good and not to grace me. Believe then, if you please, that I can do strange things: I have, since I was three year old, conversed with a magician, most profound in his art and yet not damnable.[441] If you do love Rosalind so near the heart as your gesture cries it out,[442] when your brother marries Aliena, shall you marry her: I know into what straits of fortune she is driven; and it is not impossible to me, if it appear not inconvenient to you, to set her before your eyes to-morrow human as she is and without any danger.
ORLANDO: Speakest thou in sober meanings?
ROSALIND: By my life, I do; which I tender dearly,[443] though I say I am a magician. Therefore, put you in your best array; bid your friends; for if you will be married to-morrow, you shall, and to Rosalind, if you will.

---

[435] what you mean   [436] boastful   [437] immediately   [438] passion   [439] pretense   [440] intelligence
[441] a practioner of black magic   [442] bearing proclaims   [443] value highly

(Enter Silvius *and* Phebe.*)*

Look, here comes a lover of mine and a lover of hers.

PHEBE: Youth, you have done me much ungentleness,
To show the letter that I writ to you.

ROSALIND: I care not if I have: it is my study[444]
To seem despiteful and ungentle to you:
You are there followed by a faithful shepherd;
Look upon him, love him; he worships you.

PHEBE: Good shepherd, tell this youth what 'tis to love.

SILVIUS: It is to be all made of sighs and tears;
And so am I for Phebe.

PHEBE: And I for Ganymede.

ORLANDO: And I for Rosalind.

ROSALIND: And I for no woman.

SILVIUS: It is to be all made of faith and service;
And so am I for Phebe.

PHEBE: And I for Ganymede.

ORLANDO: And I for Rosalind.

ROSALIND: And I for no woman.

SILVIUS: It is to be all made of fantasy,[445]
All made of passion and all made of wishes,
All adoration, duty, and observance,[446]
All humbleness, all patience and impatience,
öAll purity, all trial, all observance;
And so am I for Phebe.

PHEBE: And so am I for Ganymede.

ORLANDO: And so am I for Rosalind.

ROSALIND: And so am I for no woman.

PHEBE: If this be so, why blame you me to love[447] you?

SILVIUS: If this be so, why blame you me to love you?

ORLANDO: If this be so, why blame you me to love you?

ROSALIND: Who do you speak to, 'Why blame you me to love you?'

ORLANDO: To her that is not here, nor doth not hear.

ROSALIND: Pray you, no more of this; 'tis like the howling of Irish wolves
against the moon. *(To Silvius)* I will help you, if I can: *(To Phebe)* I would
love you, if I could. To-morrow meet me all together. *(To Phebe)* I will marry
you, if ever I marry woman, and I'll be married to-morrow: *(To Orlando)* I
will satisfy you, if ever I satisfied man, and you shall be married to-morrow:
(To Silvius) I will content you, if what pleases you contents you, and you
shall be married to-morrow. *(To Orlando)* As you love Rosalind, meet: *(To
Silvius)* as you love Phebe, meet: and as I love no woman, I'll meet. So fare
you well: I have left you commands.

SILVIUS: I'll not fail, if I live.

PHEBE: Nor I.

ORLANDO: Nor I. *(Exeunt.)*

SCENE III. *The forest.*

(Enter Touchstone *and* Audrey.*)*

---

[444] purpose   [445] imagination   [446] respect   [447] for loving

TOUCHSTONE: To-morrow is the joyful day, Audrey; to-morrow will we be married.

AUDREY: I do desire it with all my heart; and I hope it is no dishonest[448] desire to desire to be a woman of the world.[449] Here come two of the banished duke's pages.

(Enter two Pages.)

FIRST PAGE: Well met, honest gentleman.

TOUCHSTONE: By my troth, well met. Come, sit, sit, and a song.

SECOND PAGE: We are for you: sit i' the middle.

FIRST PAGE: Shall we clap into 't roundly,[450] without hawking or spitting or saying we are hoarse, which are the only prologues to a bad voice?

SECOND PAGE: I' faith, i' faith; and both in a tune,[451] like two gipsies on a horse.

Song.

It was a lover and his lass,
 With a hey, and a ho, and a hey nonino,
That o'er the green corn-field did pass
 In the spring time, the only pretty ring time,[452]
When birds do sing, hey ding a ding, ding:
Sweet lovers love the spring.
Between the acres of the rye,
 With a hey, and a ho, and a hey nonino,
These pretty country folks would lie,
 In spring time, &c.
This carol they began that hour,
 With a hey, and a ho, and a hey nonino,
How that a life was but a flower
 In spring time, &c.
And therefore take the present time,
 With a hey, and a ho, and a hey nonino;
For love is crowned with the prime[453]
 In spring time, &c.

TOUCHSTONE: Truly, young gentlemen, though there was no great matter[454] in the ditty, yet the note was very untuneable.[455]

FIRST PAGE: You are decieved, sir: we kept time, we lost not our time.

TOUCHSTONE: By my troth, yes; I count it but time lost to hear such a foolish song. God be wi' you; and God mend your voices! Come, Audrey.

(Exeunt.)

SCENE IV. *The forest.*

 (Enter Duke Senior, Amiens, Jaques,
 Orlando, Oliver, *and* Celia.)

DUKE SENIOR: Dost thou believe, Orlando, that the boy

---

[448] unchaste   [449] married woman   [450] begin at once with spirit   [451] in unison   [452] the time for weddings   [453] perfection   [454] meaning   [455] discordant

Can do all this that he hath promised?

ORLANDO: I sometimes do believe, and sometimes do not;
öAs those that fear they hope, and know they fear.

(Enter Rosalind, Silvius, *and* Phebe.*)*

ROSALIND: Patience once more, whiles our compact is urged:
You say, if I bring in your Rosalind,
You will bestow her on Orlando here?

DUKE SENIOR: That would I, had I kingdoms to give with her.

ROSALIND: And you say, you will have her, when I bring her?

ORLANDO: That would I, were I of all kingdoms king.

ROSALIND: You say, you'll marry me, if I be willing?

PHEBE: That will I, should I die the hour after.

ROSALIND: But if you do refuse to marry me,
You'll give yourself to this most faithful shepherd?

PHEBE: So is the bargain.

ROSALIND: You say, that you'll have Phebe, if she will?

SILVIUS: Though to have her and death were both one thing.

ROSALIND: I have promised to make all this matter even.[456]
Keep you your word, O duke, to give your daughter;
You yours, Orlando, to receive his daughter:
Keep your word, Phebe, that you'll marry me,
Or else refusing me, to wed this shepherd:
Keep your word, Silvius, that you'll marry her,
If she refuse me: and from hence I go,
To make these doubts all even. *(Exeunt* Rosalind *and* Celia.*)*

DUKE SENIOR: I do remember in this shepherd boy
Some lively[457] touches of my daughter's favour.[458]

ORLANDO: My lord, the first time that I ever saw him
Methought he was a brother to your daughter:
But, my good lord, this boy is forest-born,
And hath been tutor'd in the rudiments
Of many desperate[459] studies by his uncle,
Whom he reports to be a great magician,
Obscured in the circle of this forest.

(Enter Touchstone *and* Audrey.*)*

JAQUES: There is, sure, another flood toward,[460] and these couples are
coming to the ark. Here comes a pair of very strange beasts, which in all
tongues are called fools.

TOUCHSTONE: Salutation and greeting to you all!

JAQUES: Good my lord, bid him welcome: this is the motley-minded gentleman that I have so often met in the forest: he hath been a courtier, he
swears.

TOUCHSTONE: If any man doubt that, let him put me to my purgation.[461]
I have trod a measure;[462] I have flattered a lady; I have been politic[463] with
my friend, smooth with mine enemy; I have undone three tailors;[464] I have

---

[456] straighten out   [457] lifelike   [458] appearance   [459] dangerous   [460] approaching   [461] proof
[462] danced a formal dance   [463] crafty   [464] by not paying their bills

had four quarrels, and like[465] to have fought one.

JAQUES: And how was that ta'en up?[466]

TOUCHSTONE: Faith, we met, and found the quarrel was upon the seventh cause.

JAQUES: How seventh cause? Good my lord, like this fellow.

DUKE SENIOR: I like him very well.

TOUCHSTONE: God 'ild you, sir; I desire you of the like.[467] I press in here, sir, amongst the rest of the country copulatives, to swear and to forswear; according as marriage binds and blood[468] breaks: a poor virgin, sir, an ill-favoured thing, sir, but mine own; a poor humour of mine, sir, to take that that no man else will: rich honesty dwells like a miser, sir, in a poor house; as your pearl in your foul oyster.

DUKE SENIOR: By my faith, he is very swift and sententious.[469]

TOUCHSTONE: According to the fool's bolt,[470] sir, and such dulcet diseases.[471]

JAQUES: But, for the seventh cause; how did you find the quarrel on the seventh cause?

TOUCHSTONE: Upon a lie seven times removed:—bear your body more seeming,[472] Audrey:—as thus, sir. I did dislike the cut of a certain courtier's beard: he sent me word, if I said his beard was not cut well, he was in the mind[473] it was: this is called the Retort Courteous. If I sent him word again 'it was not well cut,' he would send me word, he cut it to please himself: this is called the Quip Modest. If again 'it was not well cut,' he disabled my judgment:[474] this is called the Reply Churlish. If again, 'it was not well cut,' he would answer, I spake not true: this is called the Reproof Valiant. If again 'it was not well cut,' he would say, I lied: this is called the Countercheck[475] Quarrelsome: and so to the Lie Circumstantial[476] and the Lie Direct.

JAQUES: And how oft did you say his beard was not well cut?

TOUCHSTONE: I durst go no further than the Lie Circumstantial, nor he durst not give me the Lie Direct; and so we measured swords[477] and parted.

JAQUES: Can you nominate in order now the degrees of the lie?

TOUCHSTONE: O sir, we quarrel in print, by the book; as you have books for good manners: I will name you the degrees. The first, the Retort Courteous; the second, the Quip Modest; the third, the Reply Churlish; the fourth, the Reproof Valiant; the fifth, the Countercheck Quarrelsome; the sixth, the Lie with Circumstance; the seventh, the Lie Direct. All these you may avoid but the Lie Direct; and you may avoid that too, with an If. I knew when seven justices could not take up[478] a quarrel, but when the parties were met themselves, one of them thought but of an If, as, 'If you said so, then I said so;' and they shook hands and swore brothers.[479] Your If is the only peace-maker; much virtue in If.

JAQUES: Is not this a rare fellow, my lord? he's as good at any thing and yet a fool.

DUKE SENIOR: He uses his folly like a stalkinghorse[480] and under the presentation of that he shoots his wit.

---

[465] been likely   [466] settled   [467] I wish the same to you   [468] passion   [469] full of pithy sayings   [470] refers to the proverb: a fool's bolt (arrow) is soon shot.   [471] pleasant failings   [472] becomingly   [473] of the opinion   [474] said my judgment was weak   [475] rebuff   [476] indirect   [477] preliminaries for a duel   [478] make up   [479] swore to be brothers   [480] a real or artificial horse used as cover by a hunter to approach game

(Enter Hymen, Rosalind, and Celia. Still[481] Music.)

HYMEN: Then is there mirth in heaven,
When earthly things made even
        Atone[482] together.
Good duke, receive thy daughter:
Hymen from heaven brought her,
        Yea, brought her hither,
That thou mightst join her hand with
        his
Whose heart within his bosom is.
ROSALIND: *(To duke)* To you I give myself, for I am yours.
(To Orlando) To you I give myself, for I am yours.
DUKE SENIOR: If there be truth in sight, you are my daughter.
ORLANDO: If there be truth in sight, you are my Rosalind.
PHEBE: If sight and shape be true,
When then, my love adieu!
ROSALIND: I'll have no father, if you be not he:
I'll have no husband, if you be not he:
Nor ne'er wed woman, if you be not she.
HYMEN: Peace, ho! I bar confusion:
'Tis I must make conclusion
        Of these most strange events:
Here's eight that must take hands
To join in Hymen's bands,
        If truth holds true contents.[483]
You and you no cross[484] shall part:
        You and you are heart in heart:
        You to his love must accord,[485]
        Or have a woman to[486] your lord:
You and you are sure[487] together,
As the winter to foul weather.
Whiles a wedlock-hymn we sing,
Feed yourselves with questioning;
That reason wonder may diminish,
How thus we met, and these things
        finish.

Song.

Wedding is great Juno's crown:
        O blessed bond of board and bed!
'Tis Hymen peoples every town;
        High[488] wedlock then be honoured:
Honour, high honour and renown,
To Hymen, god of every town!
DUKE SENIOR: O my dear niece, welcome thou art to me!
Even[489] daughter, welcome, in no less degree.
PHEBE: I will not eat my word, now thou art mine;
Thy faith my fancy to thee doth combine.

---

481 soft   482 agree   483 If truth is true   484 trouble   485 agree   486 for   487 closely united
488 solemn   489 As much my daughter as Rosalind

(Enter Jaques de Boys.)

JAQUES DE BOYS: Let me have audience for a word or two:
I am the second son of old Sir Rowland,
That bring these tidings to this fair assembly.
Duke Frederick, hearing how that every day
Men of greath worth resorted to this forest,
Address'd[490] a might power;[491] which were on foot,
In his own conduct,[492] purposely to take
His brother here and put him to the sword:
And to the skirts of this wild wood he came;
Where meeting with an old religious man,
After some question[493] with him, was converted
Both from his enterprise and from the world,
His crown bequeathing to his banish'd brother,
And all their lands restored to them again
That were with him exiled. This to be true,
I do engage[494] my life.
    DUKE SENIOR: Welcome, young man;
Thou offer'st fairly[495] to thy brothers' wedding:
To one his lands withheld, and to the other[496]
A land itself at large, a potent dukedom.
First, in this forest let us do those ends[497]
That here were well begun and well begot:
And after, every of this happy number
That have endured shrewd[498] days and nights with us
Shall share the good of our returned fortune,
According to the measure of their states.[499]
Meantime, forget this new-fall'n dignity
And fall into our rustic revelry.
Play, music! And you, brides and bridegrooms all,
With measure heap'd in joy, to the measures[500] fall.
    JAQUES: Sir, by your patience.[501] If I heard you rightly,
The duke hath put on a religious life[502]
And thrown into neglect the pompous court?
    JAQUES DE BOYS: He hath.
    JAQUES: To him will I: out of these convertites[503]
There is much matter[504] to be heard and learn'd.
(To Duke) You to your former honour I bequeath;
Your patience and your virtue well deserves it:
(To Orlando) You to a love that your true faith doth merit:
(To Oliver) You to your land and love and great allies:
(To Silvius) You to a long and well-deserved bed:
(To Touchstone) And you to wrangling; for thy loving voyage
Is but for two months victuall'd.[505] So, to your pleasures:
I am for other than for dancing measures.
    DUKE SENIOR: Stay, Jaques, stay.
    JAQUES: To see no pastime I: what you would have
I'll stay to know at your abandon'd cave. *(Exit.)*

490 prepared   491 army   492 Under his own command   493 conversation   494 pledge   495 contribute greatly   496 Orlando   497 accomplish those purposes   498 bitter   499 fortunes   500 dances 501 by your leave   502 ceremonious   503 converts   504 good sense   505 provisioned

DUKE SENIOR: Proceed, proceed: we will begin these rites,
As we do trust they'll end, in true delights. (*A dance.*)

Epilogue.

ROSALIND: It is not the fashion to see the lady the epilogue; but it is no more unhandsome[506] than to see the lord in the prologue. If it be true that good wine needs no bush,[507] 'tis true that a good play needs no epilogue; yet to good wine they do use good bushes, and good plays prove the better by the help of good epilogues. What a case am I in then, that am neither a good epilogue nor cannot insinuate[508] with you in the behalf of a good play! I am not furnished[509] like a beggar, therefore to beg will not become me: my way is to conjure[510] you; and I'll begin with the women. I charge you, O women, for the love you bear to men, to like as much of this play as please you: and I charge you, O men, for the love you bear to women—as I perceive by your simpering, none of you hates them—that between you and the women the play may please. If I were a woman[511] I would kiss as many of you as had beards that pleased me, complexions that liked[512] me and breaths that I defied[513] not: and, I am sure, as many as have good beards or good faces or sweet breaths will, for my kind offer, when I make curtsy, bid me farewell.[514] (*Exeunt.*)

---

[506] in bad taste [507] good wine needs no advertisement [508] ingratiate myself [509] dressed [510] win you over by magic [511] Boys played women's parts [512] pleased [513] disliked [514] applaud me

FOR DISCUSSION

1. Why is this play called a comedy? What are its humorous aspects?
2. Why does Rosalind continue to let Orlando think she is a boy?
3. Are the characters believable? Why or why not?
4. Why do you think Rosalind stayed with Celia after Duke Frederick took power?
5. Why does Oliver treat Orlando so badly?
6. Is the plot of *As You Like It* logical? Why or why not?
7. What part do fate and coincidence play in *As You Like It*?
8. Why is Touchstone called a fool? Is he one?
9. What is the theme of the play?
10. Would you like to see this play on the stage? Why or why not?
11. Why do you think Shakespeare has the two leading characters fall in love with each other so quickly?
12. Why is the character of Jaques included? Can you give a description of him? What does he say about life? Is he essential to the plot?
13. What is satire? What is satirized in this play?
14. Does the play have one main character? If so, who is it? What makes you think so?
15. Why do you think the play is called *As You Like It*?

IV

The Seventeenth and Eighteenth Centuries

English Theatre

At the beginning of the seventeenth century the theatre of England was little different from that of the Elizabethan era. Not only did public theatres continue to exist when James I assumed the throne in 1603, but all the acting companies came under royal patronage. Shakespeare's own company, for example, became the King's Men. The new king, however, was not content with visiting the public theatres and therefore established a court theatre, in which entertainments were presented on special occasions. These productions, called masques, employed elaborate staging methods similar to the Italian *intermezzi*. The designer of the settings, Inigo Jones, who was the court architect, introduced these staging methods to England after studying in Italy.

The masques, presented once a year at the court of James I and twice a year after Charles II assumed the throne in 1625, were costly spectacles, with allegorical stories honoring notable persons or occasions. The early masques were written by Ben Jonson, who viewed them as an opportunity to present fine poetry. However, the written word was always secondary to the spectacle of costumes, songs, dances, and scene design. In addition to the masques presented before the king, others were given at the Inns of Court.

During the first half of the seventeenth century, England was undergoing civil strife. The government was finally overthrown by the Puritans under Oliver Cromwell, and the king was tried and executed. Although the theatres were closed in 1642 and all theatrical entertainment forbidden, certain entertainments continued in inns and in the houses of noblemen. "Drolls," or comic excerpts from familiar plays, were given at fairs. Even masques were still sometimes presented. William D'Avenant, playwright, producer, and poet, got permission from Cromwell to put on an opera that would not offend the Puritans—*The Siege of Rhodes*. This was the first time music and drama were combined in operatic form in England, and the opera was presented in 1656 in a house owned by the Earl of Rutland.

Except for these isolated entertainments, England was without a theatre until 1660, when Charles II was restored to the throne. During the Restoration period, which lasted until 1702, the theatre underwent a number of major changes.

The first theatres were set up in tennis courts. Then Charles II opened two indoor theatres. The patents or permissions to operate them were issued to D'Avenant, who headed a company called the Duke's Men and to Thomas Killigrew, whose company was the King's Men. Just as in the Elizabethan era, the presentation of plays was strictly regulated by the government. All plays had to be licensed by a government censor, the Lord Chamberlain, who had the right to cut out any sections he disliked in any play.

The new theatres that were erected were similar to those of Italy. However, the Italian influence was secondary, in that they were patterned largely after the theatres in which the court masques had been presented. They had proscenium arches, and there were proscenium doors through which the actors could enter and exit. Two of these doors opened on each wall at the sides of the proscenium arch. There also was a large apron stage that projected into the audience, providing intimacy between audience and actors. This meant that the actors were forced to perform in front of the scenery. The audience now sat, rather than stood, in the pit, and in boxes and galleries as well as on the stage. The scenery was painted in perspective on wings and backdrops. By 1800 it began to depict specific locations and was not so generalized as during the Italian Renaissance.

During the Restoration period, actresses appeared for the first time on English stages, and by the mid-1660's were an accepted part of the theatre. One of earliest was Nell Gwyn, who had previously sold oranges on the streets of London. She began acting when she was fifteen and became such a favorite of Charles II that his dying words were, "Let not poor Nell starve." For a time, however, both men and women played female roles.

The eighteenth century ushered in the era of "actors' theatre." The actors became the most important part of any production, far surpassing the playwright in importance. The playwright now received no salary, nor did he share in the profits of a play. He was allowed only a benefit performance every third night of a play's run, at which time he was awarded all the gate receipts, minus expenses. Since plays were usually presented for only a few nights, the author was lucky if he was given even a second benefit. After the play's first run, the company owned it outright, but there were no copyright laws to protect the writer.

The social status of the actor was higher than previously. There are records of actresses marrying noblemen and of actors being buried in the prestigious Westminster Abbey. Despite this fact, the moral character of the performer was still questioned by a large percentage of the people. The best known actors of the time were Charles Macklin, James Quin, Colley Cibber, and Thomas Betterton.

The actors continued to play only certain types of roles and received their training through experience. The theatres still followed the repertory system, and once an actor was cast in a role, it was his property as long as he stayed with the company. A stage manager saw to the staging of the older plays, while the playwright directed any new plays he sold to the company. The acting style was much more exaggerated than it is today, but not as exaggerated or stylized as it had been previously.

The most important form of drama written and acted during the Restoration period was the comedy of manners, which satirized the social customs of the time. This type of play acknowledged that man is less than perfect, but that this is to be expected and nothing can be done to bring about a change in basic human nature. Most often the plays satirized either those persons who were self-deceived or those who tried to deceive others. The second most important dramatic form was heroic tragedy, which was written in rhymed couplets and dealt largely with the themes of love and honor.

Among the playwrights of the time was John Dryden, also a poet and essayist. His best known play, *All for Love,* was based on Shakespeare's *Antony and Cleopatra* but put into a neoclassic framework. He borrowed from other writers the plots for all of his tragedies; the comedies were his own.

The most notable playwright of the time was William Congreve. Considered an outstanding writer of English comedy, he developed the comedy of manners to a high style, particularly in *The Way of the World,* written in 1700. Intellectual in approach, it has a complicated plot, names descriptive of the type of characters, and deals with the intrigues of love.

By the end of the Restoration period, England was becoming industrialized and the middle class, enriched by the fruits of industrialism, began attending the theatre on a much wider scale. The drama was changing, and new playwrights, such as George Farquhar, were considered transition writers. Farquhar's work resembled the comedy of manners, but was more riotous than witty. This is evident in two of his plays, *The Recruiting Officer* (1706) and *The Beaux' Stratagem* (1707).

Queen Anne, who assumed the throne at the beginning of the eighteenth century, was not at all interested in art or the theatre. But the theatre went on, reflecting the changes in the social and economic structure of England. The emergence of the middle class as the main theatre audience led to romanticism and melodrama. The new audiences now wanted sensationalism in their plays, though at the same time they felt that plays should teach a moral lesson—for example, that only through hard work could one succeed. Thus, in many eighteenth-century plays, perseverance was rewarded, and dishonesty and laziness resulted in defeat. Interestingly enough, during this period Shakespeare became more popular in England than he had been during his own time.

One type of drama that was most prevalent at the time was sentimental comedy. This form, which seems much too exaggerated to be accepted by today's audiences, was characterized by false emotions and sentimentality over the misfortunes of others. The major characters bore all their misfortunes with a smile, and were always rewarded in the end. The plays were called comedies, not because they were funny but because they ended happily. The situations were often too bad to be believed, and the characters were too noble. The prevailing viewpoint was that man is basically good and has only to heed his inner conscience to remain good and reap his just rewards. Bourgeois tragedies were also popular. They were written in much the same style as the sentimental comedies, except that they ended unhappily when the major characters gave in to temptation. The playwright with the greatest influence on the writing of bourgeois tragedy was George Lillo, who lived from 1693 to 1739. His play *The London Merchant* first performed in 1731, shows how a good man is led astray through love of an undesirable woman. The play was performed on many occasions and influenced the writing of sentimental drama in France.

Other forms also developed during the eighteenth century. One was the burlesque farce, which made fun of the other dramas of the day. The master of this type of writing was the novelist Henry Fielding, who wrote *The Tragedy of Tragedies, or, the Life and Death of Tom Thumb the Great.* The pantomime was performed by John Rich was the most popular of all dramatic forms, featuring dances and mimicry to the accompaniment of music, not to mention both comic and serious scenes and elaborate scenery and effects. Another popular form was the ballad opera of which the best example is *The Beggar's Opera,* written in 1728 by John Gay. It not only burlesqued Italian opera but satirized the current political situation in England.

Among the major writers of plays during the eighteenth century was Oliver Goldsmith, who lived from 1730 to 1774 and also wrote novels and poems. His play *She Stoops to Conquer* was an attempt to return to comedy that was funny rather than merely sentimental. Goldsmith's dramatic works were based largely on the plays of Elizabethan writers. Another playwright was Richard Brinsley Sheridan, who wrote *The Rivals* and *The School for Scandal,* returning to comedy of manners.

Perhaps the most famous theatrical figure of the time was David Garrick (1717 to 1779). As manager of the Drury Lane Theatre, he was credited with introducing a natural style of acting to the English stage. He believed in closely supervised rehearsals in which he directed the actors. Before this time, there had been no directors who took complete charge. Garrick also brought the French set designer, Philippe Jacques de Loutherborg, to England to design three-dimensional settings. Moreover, Garrick insisted that the audience could no longer sit on the stage but must remain in the seating area of the theatre. Another of his innovations was that of concealing stage lighting from the audience.

In the seventeenth and eighteenth centuries, the English theatre underwent many changes, both in forms of drama and in staging. However, by the end of the eighteenth century, there was a definite movement toward realism in sets and staging. This move opened the way for the modern era of the theatre.

French Theatre

French theatre developed later than the theatre of England because of civil wars that divided the country from the 1560's to the 1620's. Various theatrical companies did play in Paris in the sixteenth century; and earlier, during the early part of the fifteenth century, religious plays had been presented.

The Confrérie de la Passion, organized in 1402, built a new theatre for such dramas in 1548, called the Hôtel de Bourgogne, but shortly after its construction religious plays were forbidden. The building was then rented to traveling companies and was in use until 1783. In about 1599, the Hôtel de Bourgogne was leased to the King's Players. The company was headed by France's first important theatre manager, Valleran LeComte, who was active until 1612. Thus, performances were not regularly presented until the early part of the seventeenth century. The most important early French playwright, who wrote for the King's Players, was Alexandre Hardy, who lived from 1572 to 1632 and is believed to have written more than five hundred plays. Most were tragicomedies characterized by continuous action. Although lacking in depth, Hardy's plays were immensely popular.

The staging differed from that in England in that the indoor stages resembled those advocated by Serlio. However, the medieval custom of simultaneous staging, with mansions and an unlocalized acting area, was followed, using the middle of the stage as the generalized area. Even in the Hôtel de Bourgogne, the stage was only about twenty-five feet wide, and simultaneous settings were used there until about 1640, when the Italian style of staging and scenery began to influence the French theatre.

After the civil strife ended in the 1620's, the new prime minister, Cardinal Richelieu, did much to establish a permanent form of theatre. Coming to power in 1625, he was concerned with the cultural image of his country and looked to Italy as the model for its improvement. As part of his effort to raise France's cultural level, in 1641 he built a theatre in his palace, the Palais Cardinal, which after his death became known as the Palais Royal. It was styled after Italian models and later became the home of the company led by France's most famous playwright, Molière. Previously, only the Hôtel de Bourgogne and another theatre, the Thâtre du Marais, had been operating in Paris. The latter had been constructed from a tennis court in 1634.

Cardinal Richelieu also established the French Academy in 1629. It was here that various playwrights gathered to write. They adhered to the rules of neoclassicism even more rigidly than had their counterparts in Italy. They thought that the aim of comedy should be to ridicule and the aim of tragedy should be to show the results of men's misdeeds and errors. These French playwrights were particularly concerned with the three classic unities and with purity of form. Drama, they also believed, had to have versimilitude, or the appearance of truth.

The two most important writers of the French academy were Pierre Corneille and Jean Racine. Corneille began writing in the late 1620's, and in 1636 wrote his most successful play, Le Cid. A tragicomedy, so called because it deals with a serious theme but ends happily, it was controversial in that it did not closely follow neoclassic dramatic principles. It was a misture of forms and did not adhere to the unities. Racine, who lived from 1639 to 1699, was the greatest writer of French classical tragedy. His most famous play, Phèdre, deals with the internal conflict of a single character, a woman who wanted to do right but was prevented from doing so by circumstances and emotions.

After Richelieu's death in 1642, Cardinal Mazarin of Italy became prime minister, and the French theatre was further influenced by Italian styles. The new prime minister was particularly partial to opera. After the Théâtre du Marais burned down in 1644 and was rebuilt, it was devoted to scenic spectacles and remained in use until 1673.

One of the greatest of all French playwrights was Jean-Batiste Poquelin, known as Molière, who lived from 1622 to 1673, and has often been called the Shakespeare of the French theatre. At the age of twenty-two, he joined an acting company which toured France and after returning to Paris in 1658 quickly established an excellent reputation. Louis XIV saw one of the performances and granted Molière the right to perform at a small theatre, the Petite Bourbon, and later at the Palais Royal. Many of the plays were written by Molière, who also was considered the best comic actor of his day.

The French acting companies during the seventeenth century were organized on the sharing plan. Women were admitted on an equal basis with men. Plays were accepted or rejected by a vote of the company. When a play was selected, the playwright was usually given a percentage of the gate receipts for a certain number of performances. After that, the company owned the play. Less commonly, plays were bought outright.

The playwright himself selected the cast for his plays and assisted with rehearsals. New members of a company learned their roles from the persons whom they were replacing. Actors would specialize either in comedy or in tragedy, men customarily playing old women's roles. Spectators sat on the stage, and because the stages were small anyway, there was little room for actors to move around. Usually a long play and a short one were presented on the same bill.

After Molière's death, the state of the French theatre declined. Corneille gave up writing in 1674, and Racine wrote no new plays for public presentation after 1677. Thus, the Golden Age of French drama came to a close. The only important French playwright of the eighteenth century was Voltaire, who lived from 1694 to 1778. He spent some time in England, and, upon returning to France, decided that French drama was too hampered by rules. He therefore tried such innovations as greater realism in acting and the portrayal of violence in plays. Like Garrick in England, he was responsible for moving the spectators off the stage and back into the auditorium.

Despite the fact that no French drama of merit was written during the eighteenth century, France was now recognized by the rest of Europe as the political and cultural center of Europe. The great plays that had been written during the seventeenth century became the models for other countries.

Nevertheless, several types of drama were popular in the eighteenth century. One was sentimental comedy, as written by Pierre Chausée. An important theatrical figure of the time was Denis Diderot, who advocated the writing of domestic tragedy. He was greatly concerned with audience reaction and felt that the more emotion was aroused in the spectators, the better the illusion of reality. He was in favor of naturalness of presentation, but believed the actor should not permit himself to feel anything in his role, conveying an emotion only by external signs. The playwright who followed most closely the style advocated by Diderot was Pierre-Augustine Beaumarchais, whose two best plays are *The Barber of Seville* (1775) and *The Marriage of Figaro* (1784).

Eighteenth-century France was also a period of actor supremacy. The most noted actress of the time was Adrienne Lecouvreur. Another famous performer was Joseph Talma, who startled audiences by wearing a Roman toga with his bare legs and arms showing. This faithfulness to history was unheard of at the time but did much to further exact costuming practices.

Although many important advances in drama were made in France and England during the seventeenth and eighteenth centuries, interesting theatrical activities were likewise occurring in other countries. In Italy the most popular dramatic form was still the opera and continued advances were being made in operatic staging and design. In Russia, the first public theatre was opened during the eighteenth century, but no good drama was written there until the nineteenth century. The countries of northern Europe also began to develop theatres and drama, but made no important progress. Theatre in America, too, began during the eighteenth century, but was really only a pale imitation of the English theatre. The first plays were performed by English actors, but all theatrical activity was suspended during the Revolutionary War.

German Theatre

More sweeping changes were occuring in the theatre of Germany than in the other countries of Europe. Until the beginning of the eighteenth century, Germany was a loose collection of small states. The country itself was generally poor, and its theatre consisted largely of performances by traveling companies and court productions, all of which featured unbelievable action and violence. Carolina Neuber, an actress who headed her own troupe beginning in 1727, did much to raise the level of acting and drama in Germany. She insisted on careful rehearsals, high personal morals, and the presentation of plays with higher literary standards than were common. Her work, with that of Johann Gottsched, is considered the turning point in the history of the German theatre: from that time on, drama was more respected.

During the eighteenth century there also was a trend toward romanticism as the government became centralized and a national awareness and pride began to emerge. A form of romanticism, the *Sturm und Drang* (storm and stress) movement was born, largely as a result of the writings of Johann Friedrich Schiller, who lived from 1759 to 1805 and is often considered Germany's greatest playwright. The movement was characterized by a reverence for Shakespeare, a return to nature, and a disregard for the dramatic unities as practiced in France. Romanticism emphasized freedom from the bounds of society, a clear division between good and evil, and a return to man's basic emotions. The play *The Robbers,* written by Schiller when he was nineteen years old, was largely responsible for the beginnings of German romanticism. Its story condemns the social laws of the day and advocates that men should turn away from the law in order to be free.

Another eighteenth-century German writer, Gotthold Ephraim Lessing (1729 to 1781), was one of the first playwrights to recognize the artistry of Shakespeare and to attack French neoclassicism, even though his plays followed the true classic model. He favored domestic tragedy and used a cause-effect structure in his plays. His *Nathan the Wise* (1779) deals with religious tolerance and is based on the theme that any religion is good which is concerned with humanitarianism.

Johann Wolfgang von Goethe (1749 to 1832) is best known for his play *Faust,* the first part of which was published in 1808. The play is considered the ultimate example of romanticism, although both Goethe and Schiller denied being romanticists. At any rate, by the end of the eighteenth century romanticism was well established in Germany. In some of the other European countries, the movement did not reach maturity until the nineteenth century.

PROJECTS

1. Discover as much as you can about the production of court masques in England.
2. Investigate the general history of England from 1600 to the Restoration period. How did the events of the time influence playwrights?
3. Find out about the production of the opera *The Siege of Rhodes*.
4. Prepare a report on two or three of the earliest English actresses. What kind of roles did they play? What was the social status of an actress at the time? How does it differ from the status of an actress today?
5. Investigate the life of a seventeenth-century English actor, such as Charles Macklin, James Quin, or Thomas Betterton.
6. Explore in depth David Garrick's contributions to the theatre.
7. Trace the general history of France during the seventeenth and eighteenth centuries. How was the history reflected in dramas of the time?
8. Report on German actors and actresses of the eighteenth century. How did their lives compare or contrast with the lives of English actors and actresses of the time?
9. Find out as much as you can about Denis Diderot's theories of drama.
10. Investigate the censorship of plays in England. How does it contrast with censorship today?

John Gay was best known as a political satirist.

Born in 1685 at Barnstable, Devonshire, where he attended grammar school, Gay was a versatile writer. He published four books of poems and two books of fables, which are considered the best in English fable literature, in addition to plays such as *The Wife of Bath* (1713), *The What D'ye Call It* (1715), and *The Captives* (1724). His best and best known play was *The Beggar's Opera*, first produced by John Rich at Lincoln's Inn Fields, a London theatre, in 1728.

The play is a ballad opera, the first of its kind. Gay's work and other ballad operas that followed were burlesque farces containing lyrics written to be sung to popular tunes of the time interspersed with dialogue.

The Beggar's Opera is both a burlesque of Italian opera, which was beginning to become popular in England around 1710, and a satire on the politics of the time. However, it is primarily as a comedy that the play has survived. Much of the humor comes from the fact that the characters are all, in one way or another, on the wrong side of the law. Yet they have a code of honor and a standard of ethics whereby they live—an idea that struck contemporary audiences as humorous. At that time (and perhaps also today) it seemed odd that criminals, persons who are not contributing to society, should have their own set of values from which they would not deviate. The characters in *The Beggar's Opera* are conscientious about their "work," because they believe that through hard work and ambition anyone can succeed. Gay's satire seems to suggest that criminals are no more wrong in their approach to life than are hard-working people whom one encounters everyday. The local groceryman and the shady Peachum, for instance, are both businessmen, but society openly approves of the one and condemns the other.

Although the characters are familiar types, they speak more cleverly, and at inappropriate moments burst into song. So it is easy to see that the play was primarily written just for fun and to entertain audiences. It still does, for *The Beggar's Opera* has been frequently produced since 1728. One of the most compelling adaptations is Bertolt Brecht's *The Threepenny Opera*, presented in 1928, with original music composed in the style of American jazz by Kurt Weill. (A continuously popular song from this version is "Mack the Knife.") In Brecht's satire there is bitterness as well as humor, and in his plot Macheath is an antisocial villain who victimizes Peachum.

In 1729, Gay wrote a sequel to *The Beggar's Opera* called *Polly*. Despite the fact that it was banned by the government for political reasons, it was published and widely read and was finally produced in 1777.

Gay also wrote the lyrics to many songs and the libretto for Handel's *Acis and Galatea*. His opera, *Achilles*, was first performed in London in 1733. However, his fame rests largely on *The Beggar's Opera*.

The Beggar's Opera

CHARACTERS

PEACHUM
LOCKIT
MACHEATH
FILCH
JEMMY TWITCHER
CROOK-FINGER'D JACK

WAT DREARY *Macheath's Gang*
ROBIN OF BAGSHOT
NIMMING NED
HARRY PADINGTON
MATT OF THE MINT
BEN BUDGE
BEGGAR

PLAYER

MRS. PEACHUM
POLLY PEACHUM
LUCY LOCKIT
DIANA TRAPES
MRS. COAXER
DOLLY TRULL *Women of the Town*

MRS. VIXEN
BETTY DOXY
JENNY DIVER
MRS. SLAMMEKIN
SUKY TAWDRY
MOLLY BRAZEN
CONSTABLES, DRAWER, TURNKEY, &C.

The Beggar's Opera

INTRODUCTION

(Beggar, Player)

BEGGAR: If Poverty be a Title to Poetry, I am sure No-body can dispute mine. I own myself of the Company of Beggars; and I make one at their Weekly Festivals at St. Giles. I have a small Yearly Salary for my Catches, and am welcome to a Dinner there whenever I please, which is more than most Poets can say.

PLAYER: As we live by the Muses, 'tis but Gratitude in us to encourage Poetical Merit where-ever we find it. The Muses, contrary to all other Ladies, pay no Distinction to Dress, and never partially mistake the Pertness of Embroidery for Wit, nor the Modesty of Want for Dulness. Be the Author who he will, we push his Play as far as it will go. So (though you are in Want) I wish you Success heartily.

BEGGAR: This Piece I own was originally writ for the celebrating the Marriage of James Chanter and Moll Lay, two most excellent Ballad-Singers. I have introduc'd the Similes that are in all your celebrated Operas: The Swallow, the Moth, the Bee, the Ship, the Flower, &c. Besides, I have a Prison Scene which the Ladies always reckon charmingly pathetick. As to the Parts, I have observ'd such a nice Impartiality to our two Ladies, that it is impossible for either of them to take Offence. I hope I may be forgiven, that I have not made my Opera throughout unnatural, like those in vogue; for I have no Recitative: Excepting this, as I have consented to have neither Prologue nor Epilogue, it must be allow'd an Opera in all its forms. The Piece indeed hath been heretofore frequently represented by our selves in our great Room at St. Giles's, so that I cannot too often acknowledge your Charity in bringing it now on the Stage.

PLAYER: But I see 'tis time for us to withdraw; the Actors are preparing to begin. Play away the Overture. (*Exeunt.*)

ACT I

SCENE I

(Peachum's House.)
Peachum sitting at a table with a large book of accounts before him

AIR

Through all the Employments of Life
Each Neighbour abuses his Brother;
Whore and Rogue they call Husband and Wife:
All Professions be-rogue one another.
The Priest calls the Lawyer a Cheat,
The Lawyer be-knaves the Divine;
And the Statesman, because he's so great,
Thinks his Trade as honest as mine.

A Lawyer is an honest Employment, so is mine. Like me too he acts in a double Capacity, both against Rogues and for 'em; for 'tis but fitting that we should protect and encourage Cheats, since we live by them.

SCENE II

PEACHUM, FILCH

FILCH: Sir, Black Moll hath sent word her Tryal comes on in the Afternoon, and she hopes you will order Matters so as to bring her off.

PEACHUM: Why, she may plead her Belly at worst; to my Knowledge she hath taken care of that Security. But as the Wench is very active and industrious, you may satisfy her that I'll soften the Evidence.

FILCH: Tom Gagg, Sir, is found guilty.

PEACHUM: A lazy Dog! When I took him the time before, I told him what he would come to if he did not mend his Hand. This is Death without Reprieve. I may venture to Book him. (*Writes.*) For Tom Gagg, forty Pounds. Let Betty Sly know that I'll save her from Transportation, for I can get more by her staying in England.

FILCH: Betty hath brought more Goods into our Lock to-year than any five of the Gang; and in truth, 'tis a pity to lose so good a Customer.

PEACHUM: If none of the Gang take her off, she may, in the common course of Business, live a Twelve-month longer. I love to let Women scape. A good Sportsman always lets the Hen Partridges fly, because the breed of the Game depends upon them. Besides, here the Law allows us no Reward; there is nothing to be got by the Death of Women—except our Wives.

FILCH: Without dispute, she is a fine Woman! 'Twas to her I was oblig'd for my Education, and (to say a bold Word) she hath train'd up more young Fellows to the Business than the Gaming-table.

PEACHUM: Truly, Filch, thy Observation is right. We and the Surgeons are more beholden to Women than all the Professions besides.

AIR

FILCH: *'Tis Woman that seduces all Mankind,*
By her we first were taught the wheedling Arts:
Her very Eyes can cheat; when most she's kind,
She tricks us of our Money with our Hearts.
For her, like Wolves by night we roam for Prey,
And practise ev'ry Fraud to bribe her Charms;
For Suits of Love, like Law, are won by Pay,
And Beauty must be fee'd into our Arms.

PEACHUM: But make haste to Newgate, Boy, and let my Friends know what I intend; for I love to make them easy one way or other.

FILCH: When a Gentleman is long kept in suspence, Penitence may break his Spirit ever after. Besides, Certainty gives a Man a good Air upon his Tryal, and makes him risque another without Fear or Scruple. But I'll away, for 'tis a Pleasure to be the Messenger of Comfort to Friends in Affliction.

SCENE III

PEACHUM

But 'tis now high time to look about me for a decent Execution against next Sessions. I hate a lazy Rogue, by whom one can get nothing 'til he is hang'd. A Register of the Gang, (*Reading.*) "Crook-finger'd Jack." A Year and a half in the Service; Let me see how much the Stock owes to his Industry; one, two, three, four, five Gold Watches, and seven Silver ones. A mighty clean-handed Fellow! Sixteen Snuff-boxes, five of them of true Gold. Six dozen of Handkerchiefs, four silver-hilted Swords, half a dozen of Shirts, three Tye-Perriwigs, and a Piece of Broad Cloth. Considering these are only the Fruits of his leisure Hours, I don't know a prettier Fellow, for no Man alive hath a more engaging Presence of Mind upon the Road. "Wat Dreary, alias Brown Will," an irregular Dog, who hath an underhand way of disposing of his Goods. I'll try him only for a Sessions or two longer upon his good Behaviour. "Harry Padington," a poor petty-larceny Rascal, without the least Genius; that Fellow, though he were to live these six Months, will never come to the Gallows with any Credit. "Slippery Sam;" he goes off the next Sessions, for the Villain hath the Impudence to have views of following his Trade as a Taylor, which he calls an honest Employment. "Mat of the Mint;" listed not above a Month ago, a promising sturdy Fellow, and diligent in his way; somewhat too bold and hasty, and may raise good Contributions on the Publick, if he does not cut himself short by Murder. "Tom Tipple" a guzzling soaking Sot, who is always too drunk to stand himself, or to make others stand. A Cart is absolutely necessary for him. "Robin of Bagshot, alias Gorgon, alias Bluff Bob, alias Carbuncle, alias Bob Booty."

SCENE IV

PEACHUM, MRS. PEACHUM

MRS. PEACHUM: What of Bob Booty, Husband? I hope nothing bad hath betided him. You know, my Dear, he's a favourite Customer of mine. 'Twas he made me a Present of this Ring.

PEACHUM: I have set his Name down in the Black-List, that's all, my Dear; he spends his Life among Women, and as soon as his Money is gone, one or other of the Ladies will hang him for the Reward, and there's forty Pound lost to us for-ever.

MRS. PEACHUM: You know, my Dear, I never meddle in matters of Death; I always leave those Affairs to you. Women indeed are bitter bad Judges in these cases, for they are so partial to the Brave that they think every Man handsome who is going to the Camp or the Gallows.

AIR

If any Wench Venus's Girdle wear,
Though she be never so ugly;
Lillys and Roses will quickly appear,
And her Face look wond'rous smuggly.
Beneath the left Ear so fit but a Cord,
(A Rope so charming a Zone is!)

> *The Youth in his Cart hath the Air of a Lord,*
> *And we cry, There dies an Adonis!*

But really, Husband, you should not be too hard-hearted, for you never had a finer, braver set of Men than at present. We have not had a Murder among them all, these seven Months. And truly, my Dear, that is a great Blessing.

PEACHUM: What a dickens is the Woman always a whimpring about Murder for? No Gentleman is ever look'd upon the worse for killing a Man in his own Defence; and if Business cannot be carried on without it, what would you have a Gentleman do?

MRS. PEACHUM: If I am in the wrong, my Dear, you must excuse me, for No-body can help the Frailty of an overscrupulous Conscience.

PEACHUM: Murder is as fashionable a Crime as a Man can be guilty of. How many fine Gentlemen have we in Newgate every Year, purely upon that Article! If they have wherewithal to persuade the Jury to bring it in Manslaughter, what are they the worse for it? So, my Dear, have done upon this Subject. Was Captain Macheath here this Morning, for the Bank-notes he left with you last Week?

MRS. PEACHUM: Yes, my Dear; and though the Bank hath stopt Payment, he was so cheerful and so agreeable! Sure there is not a finer Gentleman upon the Road than the Captain! If he comes from Bagshot at any reasonable Hour he hath promis'd to make one this Evening with Polly and me, and Bob Booty, at a Party of Quadrille. Pray, my Dear, is the Captain rich?

PEACHUM: The Captain keeps too good Company ever to grow rich. Marybone and the Chocolate-houses are his undoing. The Man that proposes to get Money by Play should have the Education of a fine Gentleman, and be train'd up to it from his Youth.

MRS. PEACHUM: Really, I am sorry upon Polly's Account the Captain hath not more Discretion. What business hath he to keep Company with Lords and Gentlemen? he should leave them to prey upon one another.

PEACHUM: Upon Polly's Account! What, a Plague, does the Woman mean? —Upon Polly's Account!

MRS. PEACHUM: Captain Macheath is very fond of the Girl.

PEACHUM: And what then?

MRS. PEACHUM: If I have any Skill in the Ways of Women, I am sure Polly thinks him a very pretty Man.

PEACHUM: And what then? You would not be so mad to have the Wench marry him! Gamesters and Highwaymen are generally very good to their Whores, but they are very Devils to their Wives.

MRS. PEACHUM: But if Polly should be in love, how should we help her, or how can she help herself? Poor Girl, I am in the utmost Concern about her.

AIR

> *If Love the Virgin's Heart invade,*
> *How, like a Moth, the simple Maid*
> *Still plays about the Flame!*
> *If soon she be not made a Wife,*
> *Her Honour's sing'd, and then for Life,*
> *She's—what I dare not name.*

PEACHUM: Look ye, Wife. A handsome Wench in our way of Business is as profitable as at the Bar of a Temple Coffee-House, who looks upon it as her livelihood to grant every Liberty but one. You see I would indulge the Girl as far as prudently we can. In any thing, but Marriage! After that, my Dear, how shall we be safe? Are we not then in her Husband's Power? For a Husband hath the absolute Power over all a Wife's Secrets but her own. If the Girl had the Discretion of a Court Lady, who can have a dozen young Fellows at her Ear without complying with one, I should not matter it; but Polly is Tinder, and a Spark will at once set her on a Flame. Married! If the Wench does not know her own Profit, sure she knows her own Pleasure better than to make her a Property! My Daughter to me should be, like a Court Lady to a Minister of State, a Key to the whole Gang. Married! If the Affair is not already done, I'll terrify her from it, by the Example of our Neighbours.

MRS. PEACHUM: May-hap, my Dear, you may injure the Girl. She loves to imitate the fine Ladies, and she may only allow the Captain Liberties in the View of Interest.

PEACHUM: But 'tis your Duty, my Dear, to warn the Girl against her Ruin, and to instruct her how to make the most of her Beauty. I'll go to her this moment, and sift her. In the mean time, Wife, rip out the Coronets and Marks of these dozen of Cambric Handkerchiefs, for I can dispose of them this Afternoon to a Chap in the City.

SCENE V

MRS. PEACHUM

Never was a Man more out of the way in an Argument than my Husband! Why must our Polly, forsooth, differ from her Sex, and love only her Husband? Any why must Polly's Marriage, contrary to all Observation, make her the less followed by other Men? All Men are Thieves in Love, and like a Woman the better for being another's Property.

AIR

A Maid is like the golden Oar,
Which hath Guineas intrinsical in't,
Whose Worth is never known, before
It is try'd and imprest in the Mint.

A Wife's like a Guinea in Gold,
Stampt with the Name of her Spouse;
Now here, now there; is bought, or is sold;
And is current in every House.

SCENE VI

MRS. PEACHUM, FILCH

MRS. PEACHUM: Come hither, Filch. I am as fond of this Child, as though my Mind misgave me he were my own. He hath as fine a Hand at picking a Pocket as a Woman, and is as nimble-finger'd as a Juggler. If an unlucky Session does not cut the Rope of thy Life, I pronounce, Boy, thou wilt be a great Man in History. Where was your Post last Night, my Boy?

FILCH: I ply'd at the Opera, Madam; and considering 'twas neither dark nor rainy, so that there was no great Hurry in getting Chairs and Coaches, made a tolerable hand on't. These seven Handkerchiefs, Madam.

MRS. PEACHUM: Colour'd ones, I see. They are of sure Sale from our Warehouse at Redress among the Seamen.

FILCH: And this Snuff-box.

MRS. PEACHUM: Set in Gold! A pretty Encouragement this to a young Beginner.

FILCH: I had a fair tug at a charming Gold Watch. Pox take the Taylors for making the Fobs so deep and narrow! It stuck by the way, and I was forc'd to make my Escape under a Coach. ReallY, Madam, I fear I shall be cut off in the Flower of my Youth, so that every now and then (since I was pumpt) I have thoughts of taking up and going to Sea.

MRS. PEACHUM: You should go to Hockley in the Hole, and to Marybone, Child, to learn Valour. These are the Schools that have bred so many brave Men. I thought, Boy, by this time, thou hadst lost Fear as well as Shame. Poor Lad! how little does he know as Yet of the Old-Bailey! For the first Fact I'll insure thee from being hang'd; and going to Sea, Filch, will come time enough upon a Sentence of Transportation. But now, since you have nothing better to do, ev'n go to your Book, and learn your Catechism; for really a Man makes but an ill Figure in the Ordinary's Paper, who cannot give a satisfactory Answer to his Questions. But, hark you, my Lad. Don't tell me a Lye; for you know I hate a Lyar. Do you know of any thing that hath past between Captain Macheath and our Polly?

FILCH: I beg you, Madam, don't ask me; for I must either tell a Lye to you or to Miss PollY; for I promis'd her I would not tell.

MRS. PEACHUM: But when the Honour of our Family is concern'd—

FILCH: I shall lead a sad Life with Miss Polly, if ever she come to know that I told you. Besides, I would not willingly forfeit my own Honour by betraying any body.

MRS. PEACHUM: Yonder comes my Husband and Polly. Come, Filch, you shall go with me into my own Room, and tell me the whole Story. I'll give thee a glass of a most delicious Cordial that I keep for my own drinking.

SCENE VII

PEACHUM, POLLY

POLLY: I know as well as any of the fine Ladies how to make the most of my self and of my Man too. A Woman knows how to be mercenary, though she hath never been in a Court or at an Assembly. We have it in our Natures, Papa. If I allow Captain Macheath some trifling Liberties, I have this Watch and other visible Marks of his Favour to show for it. A Girl who cannot grant some Things, and refuse what is most material, will make but a poor hand of her Beauty, and soon be thrown upon the Common.

AIR

Virgins are like the fair Flower in its Lustre,
Which in the Garden enamels the Ground;
Near it the Bees in Play flutter and cluster,
And gaudy Butterflies frolick around.
But, when once pluck'd, 'tis no longer alluring,
To Covent-Garden 'tis sent, (as yet sweet,)
There fades, and shrinks, and grows past all enduring,
Rots, stinks, and dies, and is trod under feet.

PEACHUM: You know, Polly, I am not against your toying and trifling with a Customer in the way of Business, or to get out a Secret, or so. But if I find out that you have play'd the fool and are married, you Jade you, I'll cut your Throat, Hussy. Now you know my Mind.

SCENE VIII
PEACHUM, POLLY, MRS. PEACHUM

AIR

Mrs. Peachum, *in a very great Passion*

Our Polly is a sad Slut! nor heeds what we taught her.
I wonder any Man alive will ever rear a Daughter!
For she must have both Hoods and Gowns, and Hoops to swell her
Pride.
With Scarfs and Stays, and Gloves and Lace; and she will have Men
beside;
And when she's drest with Care and Cost, all-tempting, fine and gay,
As Men should serve a Cowcumber, she flings herself away.
Our Polly is a sad Slut, &c.

You Baggage! you Hussy! you inconsiderate Jade! had you been hang'd, it would not have vex'd me, for that might have been your Misfortune; but to do such a mad thing by Choice! The Wench is married, Husband.

PEACHUM: Married! The Captain is a bold man, and will risque any thing for Money; to be sure he believes her a Fortune. Do you think your Mother and I should have liv'd comfortably so long together, if ever we had been married? Baggage!

MRS. PEACHUM: I knew she was always a proud Slut; and now the Wench hath play'd the Fool and married, because forsooth she would do like the Gentry. Can you support the expence of a Husband, Hussy, in gaming, drinking and whoring? have you Money enough to carry on the daily Quarrels of Man and Wife about who shall squander most? There are not many Husbands and Wifes, who can bear the Charges of plaguing one another in a handsome way. If you must be married, could you introduce no-body into our Family but a Highwayman? Why, thou foolish Jade, thou wilt be as ill-us'd, and as much neglected, as if thou hadst married a Lord!

PEACHUM: Let not your Anger, my Dear, break through the Rules of Decency, for the Captain looks upon himself in the Military Capacity, as a Gentleman by his Profession. Besides what he hath already, I know he is in a fair way of getting, or of dying; and both these ways, let me tell you, are most excellent Chances for a Wife. Tell me, Hussy, are you ruin'd or no?

MRS. PEACHUM: With Polly's Fortune, she might very well have gone off to a Person of Distinction. Yes, that you might, you pouting Slut!

PEACHUM: What, is the Wench dumb? Speak, or I'll make you plead by squeezing out an Answer from you. Are you really bound Wife to him, or are you only upon liking? (*Pinches her.*)

POLLY: Oh! (*Screaming.*)

MRS. PEACHUM: How the Mother is to be pitied who hath handsome Daughters! Locks, Bolts, Bars, and Lectures of Morality are nothing to them: They break through them all. They have as much Pleasure in cheating a Father and Mother, as in cheating at Cards.

PEACHUM: Why, Polly, I shall soon know if you are married, by Macheath's keeping from our House.

AIR

POLLY: *Can Love be controul'd by Advice?*
Will Cupid our Mothers obey?
Though my Heart were as frozen as Ice,
At his Flame 'twould have melted away.
When he kist me so closely he prest,
'Twas so sweet that I must have comply'd:
So I thought it both safest and best
To marry, for fear you should chide.

MRS. PEACHUM: Then all the Hopes of our Family are gone for ever and ever!

PEACHUM: And Macheath may hang his Father and Mother-in-Law, in hope to get into their Daughter's Fortune.

POLLY: I did not marry him (as 'tis the Fashion) cooly and deliberately for Honour or Money. But, I love him.

MRS. PEACHUM: Love him! worse and worse! I thought the Girl had been better bred. Oh Husband, Husband! her Folly makes me mad! my Head swims! I'm distracted! I can't support myself—Oh! (*Faints.*)

PEACHUM: See, Wench, to what a Condition you have reduc'd your poor Mother! a Glass of Cordial, this instant. How the poor Woman takes it to Heart!

(Polly *goes out, and returns with it.*)

Ah, Hussy, now this is the only Comfort your Mother has left!

POLLY: Give her another Glass, Sir; my Mama drinks double the Quantity whenever she is out of Order. This, you see, fetches her.

MRS. PEACHUM: The Girl shows such a Readiness, and so much Concern, that I could almost find in my Heart to forgive her.

AIR

O Polly, you might have toy'd and kist.
By keeping Men off, you keep them on.
POLLY: *But he so teaz'd me,*
   And he so pleas'd me,
What I did, you must have done.

MRS. PEACHUM: Not with a Highwayman.—You sorry Slut!

PEACHUM: A Word with you, Wife. 'Tis no new thing for a Wench to take a Man without consent of Parents. You know 'tis the Frailty of Woman, my Dear.

MRS. PEACHUM: Yes, indeed, the Sex is frail. But the first time a Woman is frail, she should be somewhat nice methinks, for then or never is the time to make her Fortune. After that, she hath nothing to do but to guard herself from being found out, and she may do what she pleases.

PEACHUM: Make your self a little easy; I have a Thought shall soon set all Matters again to rights. Why so melancholy, Polly since what is done cannot be undone, we must all endeavour to make the best of it.

MRS. PEACHUM: Well, Polly; as far as one Woman can forgive another, I forgive thee.—Your Father is too fond of you, Hussy.

POLLY: Then all my Sorrows are at an end.

MRS. PEACHUM: A mighty likely Speech in troth, for a Wench who is just married!

AIR

POLLY: *I, like a Ship in Storms, was tost;*
Yet afraid to put in to Land;
For seiz'd in the Port the Vessel's lost,
Whose Treasure is contreband.
The Waves are laid,
My Duty's paid.
O Joy beyond Expression!
This, safe a-shore,
I ask no more,
My All is in my Possession.

PEACHUM: I hear Customers in t'other Room; Go, talk with 'em, Polly; but come to us again, as soon as they are gone.—But, haerk ye, Child, if 'tis the Gentleman who was here Yesterday about the Repeating-Watch; say, you believe we can't get Intelligence of it, till to-morrow. For I lent it to Suky Straddle, to make a Figure with it to-night at a Tavern in Drury-Lane. If t'other Gentleman calls for the Silverhilted Sword; you know Beetle-brow'd Jemmy hath it on, and he doth not come from Tunbridge till Tuesday Night; so that it cannot be had till then.

SCENE IX

PEACHUM, MRS. PEACHUM

PEACHUM: Dear Wife, be a little pacified. Don't let your Passion run away with your Senses. Polly, I grant you, hath done a rash thing.

MRS. PEACHUM: If she had had only an Intrigue with the Fellow, why the very best Families have excus'd and huddled up a Frailty of that sort. 'Tis Marriage, Husband, that makes it a blemish.

PEACHUM: But Money, Wife, is the true Fuller's Earth for Reputations, there is not a Spot or a Stain but what it can take out. A rich Rogue now-a-days is fit Company for any Gentleman; and the World, my Dear, hath not such a Contempt for Roguery as you imagine. I tell you, Wife, I can make this Match turn to our Advantage.

MRS. PEACHUM: I am very sensible, Husband, that Captain Macheath is worth Money, but I am in doubt whether he hath not two or three Wives already, and then if he should dye in a Session or two, Polly's Dower would come into Dispute.

PEACHUM: That, indeed, is a Point which out to be consider'd.

Air

A Fox may steal your Hens, Sir,
A Whore your Health and Pence, Sir,
Your Daughter rob your Chest, Sir,
Your Wife may steal your Rest, Sir,
A Thief your Goods and Plate.
But this is all but picking;

With Rest, Pence, Chest and Chicken,
It ever was decreed, Sir,
If Lawyer's Hand is fee'd, Sir,
He steals your whole Estate.

The Lawyers are bitter Enemies to those in our Way. They don't care that any Body should get a Clandestine Livelihood but themselves.

SCENE X

MRS. PEACHUM, PEACHUM, POLLY

POLLY: 'Twas only Nimming Ned. He brought in a Damask Window-Curtain, a Hoop-Petticoat, a Pair of Silver Candlesticks, a Perriwig, and one Silk Stocking, from the Fire that happen'd last Night.

PEACHUM: There is not a Fellow that is cleverer in his way, and saves more Goods out of the Fire than Ned. But now, Polly, to your Affair; for Matters must not be left as they are. You are married then, it seems?

POLLY: Yes, Sir.

PEACHUM: And how do you propose to live, Child

POLLY: Like other Women, Sir, upon the Industry of my Husband.

MRS. PEACHUM: What, is the Wench turn'd Fool? A Highwayman's Wife, like a Soldier's, hath as little of his Pay, as of his Company.

PEACHUM: And had not you the common Views of a Gentlewoman in your Marriage, Polly?

POLLY: I don't know what you mean, Sir.

PEACHUM: Of a Jointure, and of being a Widow.

POLLY: But I love him, Sir: how then could I have Thoughts of parting with him

PEACHUM: Parting with him! Why, that is the whole Scheme and Intention of all Marriage Articles. The comfortable Estate of Widow-hood, is the only hope that keeps up a Wife's Spirits. Where is the Woman who would scruple to be a Wife, if she had it in her Power to be a widow whenever she pleas'd? If you have any Views of this sort, Polly, I shall think the Match not so very unreasonable.

POLLY: How I dread to hear your Advice! Yet I must beg you to explain yourself.

PEACHUM: Secure what he hath got, have him peach'd the next Sessions, and then at once you are made a rich Widow.

POLLY: What, murder the Man I love! The Blood runs cold at my Heart with the very Thought of it.

PEACHUM: Fye, Polly! What hath Murder to do in the Affair? Since the thing sooner or later must happen, I dare say, the Captain himself would like that we should get the Reward for his Death sooner than a Stranger. Why, Polly, the Captain knows, that as 'tis his Employment to rob, so 'tis ours to take Robbers; every Man in his Business. So that there is no Malice in the Case.

MRS. PEACHUM: Ay, Husband, now you have nick'd the Matter. To have him peach'd is the only thing could ever make me forgive her.

AIR

POLLY: *Oh, ponder well! be not severe;*
So save a wretched Wife!
For on the Rope that hangs my Dear
Depends poor Polly's Life.

MRS. PEACHUM: But your Duty to your Parents, Hussy, obliges you to
hang him. What would many a Wife give for such an Opportunity!
POLLY: What is a Jointure, what is Widow-hood to me? I know my Heart.
I cannot survive him.

AIR

The Turtle thus with plaintive crying,
Her Lover dying,
The Turtle thus with plaintive crying,
Laments her Dove.
Down she drops quite spent with sighing,
Pair'd in Death, as pair'd in Love.

Thus, Sir, it will happen to your poor Polly.
MRS. PEACHUM: What, is the Fool in love in earnest then? I hate thee for
being particular: Why, Wench, thou art a Shame to thy very Sex.
POLLY: But hear me, Mother.—If you ever lov'd—
MRS. PEACHUM: Those cursed Playbooks she reads have been her Ruin.
One Word more, Hussy, and I shall knock your Brains out, if you have any.
PEACHUM: Keep out of the way, Polly, for fear of Mischief, and consider
of what is propos'd to you.
MRS. PEACHUM: Away, Hussy. Hang your Husband, and be dutiful.

SCENE XI

MRS. PEACHUM, PEACHUM, POLLY *listning*

MRS. PEACHUM: The Thing, Husband, must and shall be done. For the sake
of Intelligence we must take other Measures, and have him peach'd the next
Session without her Consent. If she will not know her Duty, we know ours.
PEACHUM: But really, my Dear, it grieves one's Heart to take off a great
Man. When I consider his Personal Bravery, his fine Stratagem, how much
we have already got by him, and how much more we may get, methinks I
can't find in my Heart to have a Hand in his Death. I wish you could have
made Polly undertake it.
MRS. PEACHUM: But in a Case of Necessity—our own Lives are in danger.
PEACHUM: Then, indeed, we must comply with the Customs of the World,
and make Gratitude give way to Interest.—He shall be taken off.
MRS. PEACHUM: I'll undertake to manage Polly.
PEACHUM: And I'll prepare Matters for the Old-Baily.

SCENE XII

POLLY: Now I'm a Wretch, indeed.—Methinks I see him already in the
Cart, sweeter and more lovely than the Nosegay in his Hand!—I hear the
Crowd extolling his Resolution and Intrepidity!—What Vollies of Sighs are
sent from the Window of Holborn, that so comely a Youth should be brought
to disgrace!—I see him at the Tree! The whole Circle are in Tears!—even
Butchers weep!—Jack Ketch himself hesitates to perform his Duty, and
would be glad to lose his Fee, by Reprieve. What then will become of
Polly!—As yet I may inform him of their Design, and aid him in his Escape.
—I shall be so.—But then he flies, absents himself, and I bar myself from his
dear, dear Conversation! That too will distract me.—If he keep out of the

way, my Papa and Mama may in time relent, and we may be happy.—If he stays, he is hang'd and then he is lost for ever!—He intended to lye conceal'd in my Room, 'till the Dusk of the Evening: If they are abroad I'll this Instant let him out, lest some Accident should prevent him. (*Exit, and returns.*)

SCENE XIII

POLLY, MACHEATH

AIR

MACHEATH: *Pretty Polly, say,*
When I was away,
Did your Fancy never stray
To some newer Lover?
POLLY: *Without Disguise,*
Heaving Sighs,
Doating Eyes,
My constant Heart discover.
Fondly let me loll!
MACHEATH: *O pretty, pretty Poll.*

POLLY: And are *you* as fond as ever, my Dear?
MACHEATH: Suspect my Honour, my Courage, suspect any thing but my Love.—May my Pistols miss Fire, and my Mare slip her Shoulder while I am pursu'd, if I ever forsake thee!
POLLY: Nay, my Dear, I have no Reason to doubt you, for I find in the Romance you lent me, none of the great Heroes were ever false in Love.

AIR

MACHEATH: *My Heart was so free,*
It rov'd like the Bee,
'Till Polly my Passion requited;
I sipt each Flower,
I chang'd ev'ry Hour,
But here ev'ry Flower is United.

POLLY: Were you sentenc'd to Transportation, sure, my Dear, you could not leave me behind you—could you?
MACHEATH: Is there any Power, any Force that could tear me from thee? You might sooner tear a Pension out of the Hands of a Courtier, a Fee from a Lawyer, a pretty Woman from a Looking-glass, or any Woman from Quadrile.—But to tear me from thee is impossible!

AIR

Were I laid on Greenland's Coast
And in my Arms embrac'd my Lass;
Warm amidst eternal Frost,
Too Soon the Half Year's Night would pass.
POLLY: *Were I sold on Indian Soil,*
Soon as the burning Day was clos'd,
I could mock the sultry Toil,

When on my Charmer's Breast repos'd.
MACHEATH: *And I would love you all the Day,*
POLLY: *Every Night would kiss and play,*
MACHEATH: *If with me you'd fondly stray*
POLLY: *Over the Hills and far away.*

POLLY: Yes, I would go with thee. But oh!—how shall I speak it? I must be torn from thee. We must part.

Macheath: How! Part!

POLLY: We must, we must.—My papa and Mama are set against thy Life. They now, even now are in Search after thee. They are preparing Evidence against thee. Thy Life depends upon a Moment.

AIR

O what Pain it is to part!
Can I leave thee, can I leave thee?
O what Pain it is to part!
Can thy Polly ever leave thee?
But lest Death my Love should thwart,
And bring thee to the fatal Cart,
Thus I tear thee from my bleeding Heart!
Fly hence, and let me leave thee.

One Kiss and then—one Kiss—begone—farewell.

MACHEATH: My Hand, my Heart, my Dear, is so rivited to thine, that I cannot unloose my Hold.

POLLY: But my Papa may intercept thee, and then I should lose the very glimmering of Hope. A few Weeks, perhaps, may reconcile us all. Shall thy Polly hear from thee?

MACHEATH: Must I then go?

POLLY: And will not Absence change your Love?

MACHEATH: If you doubt it, let me stay—and be hang'd.

POLLY: O how I fear! how I tremble!—Go—but when Safety will give you leave, you will be sure to see me again; for 'till then Polly is wretched.

AIR

(Parting, and looking back at each other with fondness; he at one Door, she at the other.)

MACHEATH: *The Miser thus a Shilling sees,*
Which he's oblig'd to pay,
With Sighs resigns it by degrees,
And fears 'tis gone for aye.
POLLY: *The Boy, thus, when his Sparrow's flown,*
The Bird in Silence eyes;
But soon as out of Sight 'tis gone,
Whines, whimpers, sobs and cries.

ACT II

SCENE I. *A Tavern near Newgate*
Jemmy Twitcher, Crook-finger'd Jack, Wat Dreary, Robin of Bagshot,

Nimming Ned, Henry Padington, Matt of the Mint, Ben Budge, *and the rest of the* Gang, *at the Table, with Wine, Brandy and Tobacco.*

BEN: But pr'ythee, Matt, what is become of thy Brother Tom? I have not seen him since my Return from Transportation.

MATT: Poor Brother Tom had an Accident this time Twelvemonth, and so clever a made Fellow he was, that I could not save him from those fleaing Rasclas the Surgeons; and now, poor Man, he is among the Otamys at Surgeon's Hall.

BEN: So it seems, his Time was come.

JEMMY: But the present Time is ours, and no Body alive hath more. Why are the Laws levell'd at us? are we more dishonest than the rest of Mankind? What we win, Gentlemen, is our own by the Law of Arms, and the Right of Conquest.

JACK: Where shall we find such another Set of practical Philosophers, who to a Man are above the Fear of Death?

WAT: Sound Men, and true!

ROBIN: Of try'd Courage, and indefatigable Industry!

NED: Who is there here that would not dye for his Friend?

HARRY: Who is there here that would betray him for his Interest?

MATT: Show me a Gang of Courtiers that can say as much.

BEN: We are for a just Partition of the World, for every Man hath a Right to enjoy Life.

MATT: We retrench the Superfluities of Mankind. The World is avaritious, and I hate Avarice. A covetous fellow, like a Jackdaw, steals what he was never made to enjoy, for the sake of hiding it. These are the Robbers of Mankind, for Money was made for the Free-hearted and Generous, and where is the injury of taking from another, what he hath not the Heart to make use of?

JEMMY: Our several Stations for the Day are fixt. Good luck attend us all. Fill the Glasses.

AIR

MATT: *Fill ev'ry Glass, for Wine inspires us,*
And fires us
With Courage, Love and Joy.
Women and Wine should Life employ.
Is there ought else on Earth desirous?
CHORUS: *Fill ev'ry Glass, &c.*

SCENE II

(To them enter Macheath*)*

MACHEATH: Gentlemen, well met. My Heart hath been with you this Hour; but an unexpected Affair hath detain'd me. No Ceremony, I beg you.

MATT: We were just breaking up to go upon Duty. Am I to have the Honour of taking the Air with you, Sir, this Evening upon the Heath? I drink a Dram now and then with the Stage-Coachmen in the way of Friendship and Intelligence; and I know that about this Time there will be Passengers upon the Western Road, who are worth speaking with.

MACHEATH: I was to have been of that Party—but—

MATT: But what, Sir?

MACHEATH: Is there any man who suspects my Courage?

MATT: We have all been witnesses of it.

MACHEATH: My Honour and Truth to the Gang?

MATT: I'll be answerable for it.

MACHEATH: In the Division of our Booty, have I ever shown the least Marks of Avarice or Injustice?

MATT: By these Questions something seems to have ruffled you. Are any of us suspected?

MACHEATH: I have a fixt Confidence, Gentlemen, in you all, as Men of Honour, and as such I value and respect you. Peachum is a Man that is useful to us.

MATT: Is he about to play us any foul Play? I'll shoot him through the Head.

MACHEATH: I beg you, Gentlemen, act with Conduct and Discretion. A Pistol is your last resort.

MATT: He knows nothing of this Meeting.

MACHEATH: Business cannot go on without him. He is a Man who knows the World, and is a necessary Agent to us. We have had a slight Difference, and till it is accommodated I shall be oblig'd to keep out of his way. Any private Dispute of mine shall be of no ill consequence to my Friends. You must continue to act under his Direction, for the moment we break loose from him, our Gang is ruin'd.

MATT: As a Bawd to a Whore, I grant you, he is to us of great Convenience.

MACHEATH: Make him believe I have quitted the Gang, which I can never do but with Life. At our private Quarters I will continue to meet you. A Week or so will probably reconcile us.

MATT: Your Instructions shall be observ'd. 'Tis now high time for us to repair to our several Duties; so till the Evening at our Quarters in Moor-fields we bid you farewell.

MACHEATH: I shall wish my self with you. Success attend you. (*Sits down melancholy at the Table.*)

AIR

MATT: *Let us take the Road.*
Hark! I hear the sound of Coaches!
The hour of Attack approaches,
To your Arms, brave Boys, and load.
See the Ball I hold!
Let the Chymists toil like Asses,
Our fire their fire surpasses,
And turns all our Lead to Gold.

(*The Gang, rang'd in the Front of the Stage, load their Pistols, and stick them under their Girdles; then go off singing the first Part in Chorus.*)

SCENE III   MACHEATH, DRAWER

MACHEATH: What a Fool is a fond Wench! Polly is most confoundedly bit.—I love the Sex. And a Man who loves Money, might as well be contented with one Guinea, as I with one Woman. The Town perhaps hath been as much oblig'd to me, for recruiting it with free-hearted Ladies, as to any Recruiting Officer in the Army. If it were not for us and the other Gentlemen of the Sword, Drury-Lane would be uninhabited.

AIR

If the Heart of a Man is deprest with Cares,
The Mist is dispell'd when a Woman appears;
Like the Notes of a Fiddle, she sweetly, sweetly
Raises the Spirits, and charms our Ears.
Roses and Lillies her Cheeks disclose,
But her ripe Lips are more sweet than those.
Press her,
Caress her
With Blisses,
Her Kisses
Dissolve us in Pleasure, and soft Repose.

I must have Women. There is nothing unbends the Mind like them. Money is not so strong a Cordial for the Time. Drawer.

(Enter Drawer.)

Is the Porter gone for all the Ladies, according to my directions?

DRAWER: I expect him back every Minute. But you know, Sir, you sent him as far as Hockley in the Hole, for three of the Ladies, for one in Vinegar Yard, and for the rest of them somewhere about Lewkner's Lane. Sure some of them are below, for I hear the Barr Bell. As they come I will show them up. Coming, coming.

SCENE IV
    MACHEATH, MRS. COAXER, DOLLY TRULL, MRS. VIXEN, BETTY DOXY, JENNY
      DIVER, MRS. SLAMMEKIN, SUKY TAWDRY, and MOLLY BRAZEN.

MACHEATH: Dear Mrs. Coaxer, you are welcome. You look charmingly to-day. I hope you don't want the Repairs of Quality, and lay on Paint.—Dolly Trull! kiss me, you Slut; are you as amorous as ever, Hussy? You are always so taken up with stealing Hearts, that you don't allow your self Time to steal any thing else.—Ah Dolly, thou wilt ever be a Coquette!—Mrs. Vixen, I'm yours, I always lov'd a Woman of Wit and Spirit; they make charming Mistresses, but plaguy Wives.—Betty Doxy! Come hither, Hussy. Do you drink as hard as ever? You had better stick to good Wholesome Beer; for in troth, Betty, Strong-Waters will in time ruin your Constitution. You should leave those to your Betters.—What! and my pretty Jenny Diver too! As prim and demure as ever! There is not any Prude, though ever so high bred, hath a more sanctify'd Look, with a more mischievous Heart. Ah! thou art a dear artful Hypocrite.—Mrs. Slammekin! as careless and genteel as ever! all you fine Ladies, who know your own Beauty, affect an Undress.—But see, here's Suky Tawdry come to contradict what I was saying. Every thing she gets one way she lays out upon her Back. Why Suky, you must keep at least a dozen Tallymen. Molly Brazen! *(She kisses him.)* That's well done. I love a free-hearted Wench. Thou hast a most agreeable Assurance, Girl, and art as willing as a Turtle.—But hark! I hear musick. The Harper is at the Door.

If Musick be the Food of Love, play on. E'er you seat your selves, Ladies, what think you of a Dance? Come in.

(Enter Harper.)

Play the French Tune, that Mrs. Slammekin was so fond of.

(A Dance à la ronde in the French Manner; near the End of it this Song and Chorus.)

AIR

Youth's the Season made for Joys,
Love is then our Duty,
She alone who that employs,
Well deserves her Beauty.
Let's be gay,
While we may,
Beauty's a Flower, despis'd in decay.
Youth's the Season, &c.
Let us drink and sport to-day,
Ours is not to-morrow.
Love with Youth flies swift away,
Age is nought but Sorrow.
Dance and sing,
Time's on the Wing,
Life never knows the return of Spring.
CHORUS: Let us drink, &c.

MACHEATH: Now, pray Ladies, take your Places. Here Fellow (*Pays the Harper.*), Bid the Drawer bring us more Wine. (*Exit Harper.*) If any of the Ladies chuse Ginn, I hope they will be so free to call for it.

JENNY: You look as if you meant me. Wine is strong enough for me. Indeed, Sir, I never drink Strong-Waters, but when I have the Cholic.

MACHEATH: Just the Excuse of the fine Ladies! Why, a Lady of Quality is never without the Cholic. I hope, Mrs. Coaxer, you have had good Success of late in your Visits among the Mercers.

MRS. COAXER: We have so many Interlopers—Yet with Industry, one may still have a little Picking. I carried a silver flower'd Lute-string, and a Piece of black Padesoy to Mr. Peachum's Lock but last Week.

MRS. VIXEN: There's Molly Brazen hath the Ogle of a Rattle-Snake. She rivetted a Linnen-draper's Eye so fast upon her, that he was nick'd of three Pieces of Cambric before he could look off.

BRAZEN: Oh dear Madam!—But sure nothing can come up to your handling of Laces! And then you have such a sweet deluding Tongue! To cheat a Man is nothing; but the Woman must have fine Parts indeed who cheats a Woman!

MRS. VIXEN: Lace, Madam, lyes in a small Compass, and is of easy Conveyance. But you are apt, Madam, to think too well of your Friends.

MRS. COAXER: If any Woman hath more Art than another, to be sure, 'tis Jenny Diver. Though her Fellow be never so agreeable, she can pick his Pocket as cooly, as if Money were her only Pleasure. Now that is a Command of the Passions uncommon in a Woman!

JENNY: I never go to the Tavern with a Man, but in the View of Business. I have other Hours, and other sort of Men for my Pleasure. But had I your Address, Madam—

MACHEATH: Have done with your Compliments, Ladies; and drink about: You are not so fond of me, Jenny, as you use to be.

JENNY: 'Tis not convenient, Sir, to show my Fondness among so many Rivals. 'Tis your own Choice, and not the warmth of my Inclination that will determine you.

AIR

> Before the Barn-door crowing,
> The Cock by Hens attended,
> His Eyes around him throwing,
> Stands for a while suspended.
> Then One he singles from the Crew,
> And cheers the happy Hen;
> With how do you do, and how do you do,
> And how do you do again.

MACHEATH: Ah Jenny! thou art a dear Slut.

TRULL: Pray, Madam, were you ever in keeping?

TAWDRY: I hope, Madam, I ha'n been so long upon the Town, but I have met with some good Fortune as well as my Neighbours.

TRULL: Pardon me, Madam, I meant no harm by the Question; 'twas only in the way of Conversation.

TAWDRY: Indeed, Madam, if I had not been a Fool, I might have liv'd very handsomely with my last Friend. But upon his missing five Guineas, he turn'd me off. Now I never suspected he had counted them.

MRS. SLAMMEKIN: Who do you look upon, Madam, as your best sort of Keepers?

TRULL: That, Madam, is thereafter as they be.

MRS. SLAMMEKIN: I, Madam, was once kept by a Jew; and bating their Religion, to Women they are a good sort of People.

TAWDRY: Now for my part, I own I like and old Fellow: for we always make them pay for what they can't do.

MRS. VIXEN: A spruce Prentice, let me tell you, Ladies, is no ill thing, they bleed freely. I have sent at least two or three dozen of them in my time to the Plantations.

JENNY: But to be sure, Sir, with so much good Fortune as you have had upon the Road, you must be grown immensely rich.

MACHEATH: The Road, indeed, hath done me justice, but the Gaming-Table hath been my ruin.

AIR

> JENNY: The Gamesters and Lawyers are Jugglers alike,
> If they meddle your All is in danger.
> Like Gypsies, if once they can finger a Souse,
> Your Pockets they pick, and they pilfer your House,
> And give your Estate to a Stranger.

These are the Tools of a Man of Honour.

Cards and Dice are only fit for cowardly
Cheats, who prey upon their Friends.

(She takes up his Pistol. Tawdry takes up the other.)

TAWDRY: This, Sir, is fitter for your Hand. Besides your Loss of Money,
'tis a Loss to the Ladies. Gaming takes you off from Women. How fond could
I be of you! but before Company, 'tis ill bred.
MACHEATH: Wanton Hussies!
JENNY: I must and will have a Kiss to give my Wine a zest.
*(They take him about the Neck, and make Signs to Peachum and Consta-
bles, who rush in upon him.)*

SCENE V

(To them, Peachum and Constables)

PEACHUM: I seize you, Sir, as my Prisoner.
MACHEATH: Was this well done, Jenny —Women are Decoy Ducks; who
can trust them! Beasts, Jades, Jilts, Harpies, Furies, Whores!
PEACHUM: Your Case, Mr. Macheath, is not particular. The greatest Heroes
have been ruin'd by Women. But, to do them justice, I must own they are
a pretty sort of Creatures, if we could trust them. You must now, Sir, take
your leave of the Ladies, and if they have a Mind to make you a Visit, they
will be sure to find you at home. The Gentleman, Ladies, lodges in Newgate.
Constables, wait upon the Captain to his Lodgings.

AIR

MACHEATH: *At the Tree I shall suffer with pleasure,*
At the Tree I shall suffer with pleasure,
Let me go where I will,
In all kinds of Ill,

PEACHUM: Ladies, I'll take care the Reckoning shall be discharg'd.

I shall find no such Furies as these are.

(Exit Macheath, guarded with Peachum and Constables.)

SCENE VI

(The Women remain)

MRS. VIXEN: Look ye, Mrs. Jenny, though Mr. Peachum may have made
a private Bargain with you and Suky Tawdry for betraying the Captain, as
we were all assisting, we ought all to share alike.
MRS. COAXER: I think Mr. Peachum, after so long an acquaintance, might
have trusted me as well as Jenny Diver.
MRS. SLAMMEKIN: I am sure at least three Men of his hanging, and in a
Year's time too (if he did me justice) should be set down to my account.
TRULL: Mrs. Slammekin, that is not fair. For you know one of them was
taken in Bed with me.

JENNY: As far as a Bowl of Punch or a Treat, I believe Mrs. Suky will join
with me.—As for any thing else, Ladies, you cannot in conscince expect it.
MRS. SLAMMEKIN: Dear Madam—
TRULL: I would not for the World—
MRS. SLAMMEKIN: 'Tis impossible for me—
TRULL: As I hope to be sav'd, Madam—
MRS. SLAMMEKIN: Nay, then I must stay here all Night—
TRULL: Since you command me.

(*Exeunt with great Ceremony.*)

SCENE VII. *Newgate*

LOCKIT, TURNKEYS, MACHEATH, CONSTABLES

LOCKIT: Noble Captain, you are welcome. You have not been a Lodger of
mine this Year and half. You know the custom, Sir. Garnish, Captain, Gar-
nish. Hand me down those Fetters there.
MACHEATH: Those, Mr. Lockit, seem to be the heaviest of the whole sett.
With your leave, I should like the further pair better.
LOCKIT: Look ye, Captain, we know what is fittest for our Prisoners.
When a Gentleman uses me with Civility, I always do the best I can to please
him.—Hand them down I say.—We have them of all Prices, from one Guinea
to ten, and 'tis fitting every Gentleman should please himself.
MACHEATH: I understand you, Sir. (*Gives Money.*) The Fees here are so
many, and so exorbitant, that Few Fortunes can bear the Expense of getting
off handsomly, or of dying like a Gentleman.
LOCKIT: Those, I see, will fit the Captain better.—Take down the further
Pair. Do but examine them, Sir.—Never was better work.—How genteely
they are made!—They will fit as easy as a Glove, and the nicest Man in
England might not be asham'd to wear them. (*He puts on the Chains.*) If I
had the best Gentleman in the Land in my Custody I could not equip him
more handsomly. And so, Sir—I now leave you to your private Meditations.

SCENE VIII

MACHEATH

AIR

> Man may escape from Rope and Gun
> Nay, some have out-liv'd the Doctor's Pill;
> Who takes a Woman must be undone,
> That Basilisk is sure to kill.
> The Fly that sips Treacle is lost in the Sweets,
> So he that tastes Woman, Woman, Woman,
> He that tastes Woman, Ruin meets.

To what a woful plight have I brought my self! Here must I (all day long,
'till I am hang'd) be confin'd to hear the Reproaches of a Wench who lays
her Ruin at my Door.—I am in the Custody of her Father, and to be sure if
he knows of the matter, I shall have a fine time on't betwixt this and my
Execution.—But I promis'd the Wench Marriage.—What signifies a Promise
to a Woman? Does not Man in Marriage itself promise a hundred things that

he never means to perform? Do all we can, Women will believe us; for they look upon a Promise as an Excuse for following their own Inclinations.—But here comes Lucy, and I cannot get from her.—Wou'd I were deaf!

SCENE IX

MACHEATH, LUCY

LUCY: You base Man you,—how can you look me in the Face after what hath past between us?—See here, perfidious Wretch, how I am forc'd to bear about the load of Infamy you have laid upon me.—O Macheath! thou hast robb'd me of my Quiet—to see thee tortur'd would give me pleasure.

AIR

Thus when a good Huswife sees a Rat
In her Trap in the Morning taken,
With pleasure her Heart goes pit a pat,
In Revenge for her loss of Bacon.
Then she throws him
To the Dog or Cat,
To be worried, crush'd and shaken.

MACHEATH: Have you no Bowels, no Tenderness, my dear Lucy, to see a Husband in these Circumstances
LUCY: A Husband!
MACHEATH: In Ev'ry respect but the Form, and that, my Dear, may be said over us at any time.—Friends should not insist upon Ceremonies. From a Man of honour, his Word is as good as his Bond.
LUCY: 'Tis the pleasure of all you fine Men to insult the Women you have ruin'd.

AIR

How cruel are the Traytors,
Who lye and swear in jest,
To cheat unguarded Creatures
Of Virtue, Fame, and Rest!
Whoever steals a Shilling,
Through shame the Guilt conceals:
In Love the perjur'd Villain
With Boasts the Theft reveals.

MACHEATH: The very first opportunity, my Dear, (have but patience) you shall by my Wife in whatever manner you please.
LUCY: Insinuating Monster! And so you think I know nothing of the Affair of Miss Polly Peachum.—I could tear thy Eyes out!
MACHEATH: Sure Lucy, you can't be such a Fool as to be jealous of Polly!
LUCY: Are you not married to her, you Brute, you?
MACHEATH: Married! Very good. The Wench gives it out only to vex thee, and to ruin me in thy good Opinion. 'Tis true, I go to the House; I chat with the Girl, I kiss her, I say a thousand things to her (as all Gentlemen do) that mean nothing, to divert my self; and now the silly Jade hath set it about that I am married to her, to let me know what she would be at. Indeed, my dear

Lucy, these violent Passions may be of ill consequence to a Woman in your condition.

LUCY: Come, come, Captain, for all your Assurance, you know that Miss Polly hath put it out of your power to do me the Justice you promis'd me.

MACHEATH: A jealous Woman believes ev'ry thing her Passion suggests. To convince you of my Sincerity, if we can find the Ordinary. I shall have no scruples of making you my Wife, and I know the consequence of having two at a time.

LUCY: That you are only to be hang'd, and so get rid of them both.

MACHEATH: I am ready, my dear Lucy, to give you satisfaction—if you think there is any in Marriage.—What can a Man of Honour say more?

LUCY: So then it seems, you are not married to Miss Polly.

MACHEATH: You know, Lucy, the Girl is prodigiously conceited. No Man can say a civil thing to her, but (like other fine Ladies) her Vanity makes her think he's her own for ever and ever.

AIR

The first time at the Looking-glass
The Mother sets her Daughter,
The Image strikes the smiling Lass
With Self-love ever after.
Each time she looks, she, fonder grown,
Thinks ev'ry Charm grows stronger.
But alas, vain Maid, all Eyes but your own
Can see you are not younger.

When Women consider their own Beauties, they are all alike unreasonable in their demands; for they expect their Lovers should like them as long as they like themselves.

LUCY: Yonder is my Father—perhaps this way we may light upon the Ordinary, who shall try if you will be as good as your Word.—For I long to be made an honest Woman.

SCENE X

PEACHUM, LOCKIT with an Account-Book

LOCKIT: In this last Affair, Brother Peachum, we are agreed. You have consented to go halves in Macheath.

PEACHUM: We shall never fall out about an Execution.—But as to that Article, pray how stands our last Year's account?

LOCKIT: If you will run your Eye over it, you'll find 'tis fair and clearly stated.

PEACHUM: This long Arrear of the Government is very hard upon us! Can it be expected that we should hang our Acquaintance for nothing, when our Betters will hardly save theirs without being paid for it? Unless the People in employment pay better, I promise them for the future, I shall let other Rogues live besides their own.

LOCKIT: Perhaps, Brother, they are afraid these matters may be carried too far. We are treated too by them with Contempt, as if our Profession were not reputable.

PEACHUM: In one respect indeed, our Employment may be reckon'd dishonest, because, like Great Statesmen, we encourage those who betray their Friends.

LOCKIT: Such Language, Brother, any where else, might turn to your prejudice. Learn to be more guarded, I beg you.

AIR

When you censure the Age,
Be cautious and sage,
Lest the Courtiers offended should be:
If you mention Vice or Bribe,
'Tis so pat to all the Tribe;
Each crys—That was levell'd at me.

PEACHUM: Here's poor Ned Clincher's Name, I see. Sure, Brother Lockit, there was a little unfair proceeding in Ned's case: for he told me in the Condemn'd Hold, that for Value receiv'd you had promis'd him a Session or two longer without Molestation.

LOCKIT: Mr. Peachum—This is the first time my Honour was ever call'd in Question.

PEACHUM: Business is at an end—if once we act dishonourably.

LOCKIT: Who accuses me?

PEACHUM: You are warm, Brother.

LOCKIT: He that attacks my Honour, attacks my Livelyhood.—And this Usage—Sir—is not to be born.

PEACHUM: Since you provoke me to speak—I must tell you too, that Mrs. Coaxer charges you with defrauding her of her Information-Money, for the apprehending of curl-pated Hugh. Indeed, indeed, Brother, we must punctually pay our Spies, or we shall have no Information.

LOCKIT: Is this Language to me, Sirrah—who have sav'd you from the Gallows, Sirrah! (*Collaring each other.*)

PEACHUM: If I am hang'd, it shall be for ridding the World of an arrant Rascal.

LOCKIT: This Hand shall do the office of the Halter you deserve, and throttle you—you Dog!—

PEACHUM: Brother, Brother—We are both in the Wrong—We shall be both Losers in the Dispute—for you know we have it in our Power to hang each other. You should not be so passionate.

LOCKIT: Nor you so provoking.

PEACHUM: 'Tis our mutual Interest; 'tis for the Interest of the World we should agree. If I said any thing, Brother, to the Prejudice of your Character, I ask pardon.

LOCKIT: Brother Peachum—I can forgive as well as resent.—give me your Hand. Suspicion does not become a Friend.

PEACHUM: I only meant to give you occasion to justifie yourself: But I must now step home. for I expect the Gentleman about this Snuff-box, that Filch nimm'd two Nights ago in the Park. I appointed him at this hour.

SCENE XI

LOCKIT, LUCY

LOCKIT: Whence come you, Hussy?

LUCY: My Tears might answer that Question.

LOCKIT: You have then been whimpering and fondling, like a Spaniel, over the Fellow that hath abus'd you.

LUCY: One can't help Love; one can't cure it. 'Tis not in my Power to obey you, and hate him.

LOCKIT: Learn to bear your Husband's Death like a reasonable Woman. 'Tis not the fashion, now-a-days, so much as to affect Sorrow upon these Occasions. No Woman would ever marry, if she had not the Chance of Mortality for a Release. Act like a Woman of Spirit, Hussy, and thank your Father for what he is doing.

AIR

LUCY: *Is then his Fate decreed, Sir?*
Such a Man can I think of quitting?
When first we met, so moves me yet,
O see how my Heart is splitting!

LOCKIT: Look ye, Lucy—There is no saving him.—So, I think you must ev'n do like other Widows—Buy your self Weeds, and be cheerful.

AIR

You'll think e'er many Days ensue
This Sentence not severe;
I hang your Husband, Child, 'tis true,
But with him hang your Care.
Twang dang dillo dee.

Like a good Wife, go moan over your dying Husband. That, Child, is your Duty—Consider, Girl, you can't have the Man and the Money too—so make yourself as easy as you can, by getting all you can from him.

SCENE XII

LUCY, MACHEATH

LUCY: Though the Ordinary was out of the way to-day I hope, my Dear, you will, upon the first opportunity, quiet my Scruples—Oh Sir!—my Father's hard Heart is not to be soften'd, and I am in the utmost Despair.

MACHEATH: But if I could raise a small Sum—Would not twenty Guineas, think you, move him?—Of all the Arguments in the way of Business, the Perquisite is the most prevailing.—Your Father's Perquisites for the Escape of Prisoners must amount to a considerable Sum in the Year. Money well tim'd, and properly apply'd, will do any thing.

AIR

If you at an Office solicit your Due,
And would not have Matters neglected;
You must quicken the Clerk with the perquisite too,
To do what his Duty directed.
Or would you the Frowns of a Lady prevent,
She too has this palpable Failing
The Perquisite softens her into Consent;
That Reason with all is prevailing.

LUCY: What Love or Money can do shall be done: for all my Comfort depends upon your Safety.

SCENE XIII

LUCY, MACHEATH, POLLY

POLLY: Where is my dear Husband?—Was a Rope ever intended for this Neck!—O let me throw my Arms about it, and throttle thee with Love!— Why dost thou turn away from me?—'Tis thy Polly—'Tis thy Wife.

MACHEATH: Was ever such an unfortunate Rascal as I am!

LUCY: Was there ever such another Villain!

POLLY: O Macheath! was it for this we parted? Taken! Imprison'd! Try'd! Hang'd!—cruel Reflection! I'll stay with thee 'till Death—no Force shall tear thy dear Wife from thee now.—What means my Love?—Not one kind Word! not one kind Look! think what thy Polly suffers to see thee in this Condition.

AIR

Thus when the Swallow, seeking Prey,
Within the Sash is closely pent,
His Consort, with bemoaning Lay,
Without sits pining for th' Event.
Her chatt'ring Lovers all around her skim;
She heeds them not (poor Bird!), her Soul's with him.

MACHEATH: I must disown her. (*Aside.*) The Wench is distracted.

LUCY: Am I then bilk'd of my Virtue? Can I have no Reparation? Sure Men were born to lye, and Women to believe them! O Villain! Villain!

POLLY: Am I not thy Wife—Thy Neglect of me, thy Aversion to me too severely proves it.—Look on me.—Tell me, am I not thy Wife?

LUCY: Perfidious Wretch!

POLLY: Barbarous Husband!

LUCY: Hadst thou been hang'd five Months ago, I had been happy.

POLLY: And I too—If you had been kind to me 'till Death, it would not have vex'd me. And that's no very unreasonable Request, (though from a Wife) to a Man who hath not above seven or eight Days to live.

LUCY: Art thou then married to another? Hast thou two Wives, Monster?

MACHEATH: If Women's Tongues can cease for an Answer—hear me.

LUCY: I won't.—Flesh and Blood can't bear my Usage.

POLLY: Shall I not claim my own? Justice bids me speak.

AIR

MACHEATH: *How happy could I be with either,*
Were t'other dear Charmer away!
But while you thus teaze me together,
To neither a Word will I say;
But tol de rol, &c.

POLLY: Sure, my Dear, there ought to be some Preference shown to a Wife! At least she may claim the Appearance of it. He must be distracted with his Misfortunes, or he could not use me thus!

Lucy: O Villain, Villain! thou hast deceiv'd me—I could even inform against thee with Pleasure. Not a Prude wishes more heartily to have Facts against her intimate Acquaintance, than I now wish to have Facts against thee. I would have her Satisfaction, and they should all out.

AIR

POLLY: *I'm bubbled.*
LUCY: *. . . I'm bubbled.*
POLLY: *Oh how I am troubled!*

LUCY: *Bambouzled, and bit!*
POLLY: *. . . My Distresses are doubled.*
LUCY: *When you come to the Tree, should the Hangman refuse,*
These Fingers, with Pleasure, could fasten the Noose.

POLLY: *I'm bubbled, &c.*

MACHEATH: Be pacified, my dear Lucy—This is all a Fetch of Polly's, to make me desperate with you in case I get off. If I am hang'd, she would fain have the Credit of being thought my Widow—Really, Polly, this is no time for a Dispute of this sort; for whenever you are talking of Marriage, I am thinking of Hanging.
POLLY: And hast thou the Heart to persist in disowning me?
MACHEATH: And hast thou the Heart to persist in persuading me that I am married? Why Polly, dost thou seek to aggravate my Misfortunes?
LUCY: Really. Miss Peachum, you but expose yourself. Besides, 'tis barbarous in you to worry a Gentleman in his Circumstances.

AIR

POLLY: *Cease your Funning;*
Force or Cunning
Never shall my Heart trapan.
All these Sallies
Are but Malice
To seduce my constant Man.
'Tis most certain,
By their flirting
Women oft' have Envy shown;
Pleas'd, to ruin
Others wooing;
Never happy in their own!

POLLY: Decency, Madam, methinks might teach you to behave yourself with some Reserve with the Husband, while his Wife is present.
MACHEATH: But seriously, Polly, this is carrying the Joke a little too far.
LUCY: If you are determin'd, Madam, to raise a Distrubance in the Prison, I shall be oblig'd to send for the Turnkey to show you the Door. I am sorry, Madam, you force me to be so ill-bred.
POLLY: Give me leave to tell you, Madam: These forward Airs don't become you in the least, Madam. And my Duty, Madam, obliges me to stay with my Husband, Madam.

AIR

LUCY: *Why how now, Madam Flirt?*
If you thus must chatter;
And are for flinging Dirt,
Let's try for best can spatter;
Madam Flirt!
POLLY: *Why how now, saucy Jade;*
Sure the Wench is Tipsy!
How can you see me made (to him)
The Scoff of such a Gipsy?
Saucy Jade! (to her.)

SCENE XIV

LUCY, MACHEATH, POLLY, PEACHUM

PEACHUM: Where's my Wench? Ah Hussy! Hussy!—Come you home, you Slut; and when your Fellow is hang'd, hang youself, to make your Family some amends.

POLLY: Dear, dear Father, do not tear me from him—I must speak; I have more to say to him—Oh! twist thy Fetters about me, that he may not haul me from thee!

PEACHUM: Sure all Women are alike! If ever they commit the Folly, they are sure to commit another by exposing themselves—Away—Not a Word more—You are my Prisoner now, Hussy.

AIR

POLLY: *No Power on Earth can e'er divide,*
The Knot that Sacred Love hath ty'd.
When Parents draw against our Mind,
The True-love's Knot they faster bind.
Oh, oh ray, oh Amborah—oh, oh, &c.
(*Holding* Macheath, Peachum *pulling her.*)

SCENE XV

LUCY, MACHEATH

MACHEATH: I am naturally compassionate, Wife; so that I would not use the Wench as she deserv'd; which made you at first suspect there was something in what she said.

LUCY: Indeed, my Dear, I was strangely puzzled.

MACHEATH: If that had been the Case, her Father would never have brought me into this Circumstance—No, Lucy,—I had rather dye than be false to thee.

LUCY: How happy am I, if you say this from your Heart! For I love thee so, that I could sooner bear to see thee hang'd than in the Arms of another.

MACHEATH: But couldst thou bear to see me hang'd?

LUCY: O Macheath, I can never live to see that Day.

MACHEATH: You see, Lucy, in the Account of Love you are in my debt, and you must now be convinc'd that I rather chuse to die than be another's.— Make me, if possible, love thee more, and let me owe my Life to thee—If you refuse to assist me, Peachum and your Father will immediately put me beyond all means of Escape.

LUCY: My Father, I know, hath been drinking hard with the Prisoners: and I fancy he is now taking his Nap in his own Room—if I can procure the Keys, shall I go off with thee, my Dear?

MACHEATH: If we are together, 'twill be impossible to lye conceal'd. As soon as the Search begins to be a little cool, I will send to thee—'Till then my Heart is thy Prisoner.

LUCY: Come then, my dear Husband—owe thy Life to me—and though you love me not—be grateful—But that Polly runs in my Head strangely.

MACHEATH: A Moment of time may make us unhappy for-ever.

AIR

LUCY: *I like the Fox shall grieve,*
Whose Mate hath left her side,
Whom Hounds, from Morn to Eve,
Chase o'er the Country wide.
Where can my Lover hide?
Where cheat the weary Pack?
If Love be not his Guide,
He never will come back!

ACT III

SCENE I. *Newgate*

LOCKIT, LUCY

LOCKIT: To be sure, Wench, you must have been aiding and abetting to help him to this Escape.

LUCY: Sir, here hath been Peachum and his Daughter Polly, and to be sure they know the Ways of Newgate as well as if they had been born and bred in the Place all their Lives. Why must all your Suspicion light upon me?

LOCKIT: Lucy, Lucy, I will have none of these shuffling Answers.

LUCY: Well then—If I know any Thing of him I wish I may be burnt!

LOCKIT: Keep your Temper, Lucy, or I shall pronounce you guilty.

LUCY: Keep yours, Sir,—I do wish I may be burnt. I do—And what can I say more to convince you?

LOCKIT: Did he tip handsomely?—How much did he come down with? Come Hussy, don't cheat your Father; and I shall not be angry with you— Perhaps, you have made a better Bargain with him than I could have done— How much, my good Girl?

LUCY: You know, Sir, I am fond of him, and would have given Money to have kept him with me.

LOCKIT: Ah Lucy! thy Education might have put thee more upon thy Guard; for a Girl in the Bar of an Alehouse is always besieg'd.

LUCY: Dear Sir, mention not my Education—for 'twas to that I owe my Ruin.

AIR

When young at the Bar you first taught me to score,
And bid me be free of my Lips, and no more;
I was kiss'd by the Parson, the Squire, and the Sot.
When the Guest was departed, the Kiss was forgot.
But his Kiss was so sweet, and so closely he prest,
That I languish'd and pin'd till I granted the rest.

If you can forgive me, Sir, I will make a fair Confession, for to be sure he hath been a most barbarous Villain to me.

LOCKIT: And so you have let him escape, Hussy—Have you?

LUCY: When a Woman loves, a kind Look, a tender Word can persuade her to any thing—And I could ask no other Bribe.

LOCKIT: Thou wilt always be a vulgar Slut, Lucy.—If you would not be look'd upon as a Fool, you should never do any thing but upon the Foot of Interest. Those that act otherwise are their own Bubbles.

LUCY: But Love, Sir, is a Misfortune that may happen to the most discreet Woman, and in Love we are all Fools alike.—Notwithstanding all he swore, I am now fully convinc'd that Polly Peachum is actually his Wife.—Did I let him escape, (Fool that I was!) to go to her?—Polly will wheedle herself int his Money, and then Peachum will hang him, and cheat us both.

LOCKIT: So I am to be ruin'd, because forsooth, you must be in Love!—a very pretty Excuse!

LUCY: I could murder that impudent happy Strumpet:—I gave him his Life, and that Creature enjoys the Sweets of it.—Ungrateful Macheath!

AIR

My Love is all Madness and Folly,
Alone I lye,
Toss, tumble, and cry,
What a happy Creature is Polly!
Was e'er such a Wretch as I!
With Rage I redden like Scarlet,
That my dear inconstant Varlet,
Stark blind to my Charms,
Is lost in the Arms
Of that Jilt, that inveigling Harlot!
Stark blind to my Charms,
Is lost in the Arms
Of that Jilt, that inveigling Harlot!
This, this my Resentment alarms.

LOCKIT: And so, after all this Mischief, I must stay here to be entertain'd with your catterwauling, Mistress Puss!—Out of my sight, wanton Strumpet! you shall fast and mortify yourself into Reason, with now and then a little handsome Discipline to bring you to your Senses.—Go.

SCENE II   LOCKIT

Peachum then intends to outwit me in this Affair; but I'll be even with him—The Dog is leaky in his Liquor, so I'll ply him that way, get the Secret from him, and turn this Affair to my own Advantage.—Lions, Wolves, and Vulturs don't live together in Herds, Droves or Flocks.—Of all Animals of Prey, Man is the only sociable one. Every one of us preys upon his Neighbour, and yet we herd together.—Peachum is my Companion, my Friend—According to the Custom of the World, indeed, he may quote thousands of Precedents for cheating me—And shall not I make use of the Privilege of Friendship to make him a Return?

Air

Thus Gamesters united in Friendship are found,
Though they know that their Industry all is a Cheat;
They flock to their Prey at the Dice-Box's Sound,
And join to promote one another's Deceit.
But if by mishap
They fail of a Chap,
To keep in their Hands, they each other entrap.
Like Pikes, lank with Hunger, who miss of their Ends,
They bite their Companions, and prey on their Friends.

Now, Peachum, you and I, like honest Tradesmen, are to have a fair Tryal which of us two can over-reach the other.—Lucy.

(Enter Lucy.*)*

Are there any of Peachum's People now in the House?
LUCY: Filch, Sir, is drinking a Quartern of Strong-Waters in the next Room with Black Moll.
LOCKIT: Bid him come to me.

SCENE III

LOCKIT, FILCH

LOCKIT: Why, Boy, thou lookest as if thou wert half starv'd; like a shotten Herring.
FILCH: One had need have the Constitution of a Horse to go through the Business.—Since the favourite Child-getter was disabled by a Mis-hap, I have pick'd up a little Money by helping the Ladies to a Pregnancy against their being call'd down to Sentence.—But if a Man cannot get an honest Livelyhood any easier way, I am sure, 'tis what I can't undertake for another Session.
LOCKIT: Truly, if that great Man should tip off, 'twould be an irreparable Loss. The Vigour and Prowess of a Knight Errant never sav'd half the Ladies in Distress that he hath done.—But, Boy, can'st thou tell me where thy Master is to be found?
FILCH: At his Lock, Sir, at the Crooked Billet.
LOCKIT: Very well.—I have nothing more with you. (*Exit* Filch.) I'll go to him there, for I have many important Affairs to settle with him; and in the way of those Transactions, I'll artfully get into his Secret.—So that Macheath shall not remain a Day longer out of my Clutches.

SCENE IV

MACHEATH (*in a fine tarnish'd Coat,*) BEN BUDGE, MATT OF THE MINT

MACHEATH: I am sorry, Gentlemen, the Road was so barren of Money. When my Friends are in Difficulties, I am always glad that my Fortune can be serviceable to them. (*Gives them Money*) You see, Gentlemen, I am not a meer Court Friend, who professes every thing and will do nothing.

Air

The Modes of the Court so common are grown,
That a true Friend can hardly be met;

Friendship for Interest is but a Loan,
Which they let out for what they can get.
'Tis true, you find
Some Friends so kind,
Who will give you good Counsel themselves to defend.
In sorrowful Ditty,
They promise, they pity,
But shift you for Money, from Friend to Friend.

But we, Gentlemen, have still Honour enough to break through the Corruptions of the World.—And while I can serve you, you may command me.

BEN: It grieves my Heart that so generous a Man should be involv'd in such Difficulties, as oblige him to live with such ill Company, and herd with Gamesters.

MATT: See the Partiality of Mankind!—One Man may steal a Horse, better than another look over a Hedge—Of all Mechanics, of all servile Handy-crafts-men, a Gamester is the vilest. But yet, as many of the Quality are of the Profession, he is admitted amongst the politest Company. I wonder we are not more respected.

MACHEATH: There will be deep Play to-night at Marybone, and consequently Money may be pick'd up upon the Road. Meet me there, and I'll give you the Hint who is worth Setting.

MATT: The Fellow with a brown Coat with a narrow Gold Binding, I am told, is never without Money.

MACHEATH: What do you mean, Matt—Sure you will not think of meddling with him!—He's a good honest kind of a Fellow, and one of us.

BEN: To be sure, Sir, we will put our selves under your Direction.

MACHEATH: Have an Eye upon the Money-Lenders.—A Rouleau, or two, would prove a pretty sort of an Expedition. I hate Extortion.

MATT: Those Rouleaus are very pretty Things.—I hate your Bank Bills.—There is such a Hazard in putting them off.

MACHEATH: There is a certain Man of Distinction, who in his Time hath nick'd me out of a great deal of the Ready. He is in my Cash, Ben;—I'll point him out to you this Evening, and you shall draw upon him for the Debt.—The Company are met; I hear the Dice-box in the other Room. So, Gentlemen, your Servant. You'll meet me at Marybone.

SCENE V

(Peachum's *Lock: A Table with Wine, Brandy, Pipes and Tobacco)*

PEACHUM, LOCKIT

LOCKIT: The Coronation Account, Brother Peachum, is of so intricate a Nature, that I believe it will never be settled.

PEACHUM: It consists indeed of a great Variety of Articles.—It was worth to our People, in Fees of different Kinds, above ten Instalments.—This is part of the Account, Brother, that lies open before us.

LOCKIT: A Lady's Tail of rich Brocade—that, I see, is dispos'd of.

PEACHUM: To Mrs. Diana Trapes, the Tally-woman, and she will make a good Hand on't in Shoes and Slippers, to trick out young Ladies, upon their going into Keeping.—

LOCKIT: But I don't see any Article of the Jewels.

PEACHUM: Those are so well known, that they must be sent abroad—You'll find them enter'd under the Article of Exportation.—As for the Snuff-

Boxes, Watches, Swords, &c.—I thought it best to enter them under their several Heads.

LOCKIT: Seven and twenty Women's Pockets compleat; with the several things therein contain'd; all Seal'd, Number'd, and enter'd.

PEACHUM: But, Brother, it is impossible for us now to enter upon this Affair.—We should have the whole Day before us.—Besides, the Account of the last Half Year's Plate is in a Book by it self, which lies at the other Office.

LOCKIT: Bring us then more Liquor.—To-day shall be for Pleasure—To-morrow for Business.—Ah Brother, those Daughters of ours are two slippery Hussies—Keep a watchful Eye upon Polly, and Macheath in a Day or two shall be our own again.

AIR

LOCKIT: *What Gudgeons are we Men!*
Ev'ry Woman's easy Prey.
Though we have felt the Hook, agen
We bite and they betray.
The Bird that hath been trapt,
When he hears his calling Mate,
To her he flies, again he's clapt
Within the wiry Grate.

PEACHUM: But what signifies catching the Bird, if your Daughter Lucy will set open the Door of the Cage?

LOCKIT: If Men were answerable for the Follies and Frailties of their Wives and Daughters, no Friends could keep a good Correspondence together for two Days.—This is unkind of you, Brother; for among good Friends, what they say or do goes for nothing.

(Enter a Servant.*)*

SERVANT: Sir, here's Mrs. Diana Trapes wants to speak with you.

PEACHUM: Shall we admit her, Brother Lockit?

LOCKIT: By all means—She's a good Customer, and a fine-spoken Woman —And a Woman who drinks and talks so freely, will enliven the Conversation.

PEACHUM: Desire her to walk in. (*Exit* Servant.)

SCENE VI

PEACHUM, LOCKIT, MRS. TRAPES

PEACHUM: Dear Mrs. Dye, your Servant—One may know by your Kiss, that your Ginn is excellent.

MRS. TRAPES: I was always very curious in my Liquors.

LOCKIT: There is no perfum'd Breath like it—I have been long acquainted with the Flavour of those Lips—Han't I, Mrs. Dye?

MRS. TRAPES: Fill it up.—I take as large Draughts of Liquor, as I did of Love.—I hate a Flincher in either.

AIR

In the Days of my Youth I could bill like a Dove, fa, la, la, &c.
Like a Sparrow at all times was ready for Love, fa, la, la, &c.

The Life of all Mortals in Kissing should pass,
Lip to Lip while we're young—then the Lip to the Glass, fa, &c.

But now, Mr. Peachum, to our Business.—If you have Blacks of any kind, brought in of late, Mantoes—Velvet Scarfs—Petticoats—Let it be what it will—I am your Chap—for all my Ladies are very fond of Mourning.

PEACHUM: Why, look ye, Mrs. Dye—you deal so hard with us, that we can afford to give the Gentlemen, who venture their Lives for the Goods, little or nothing.

MRS. TRAPES: The hard Times oblige me to go very near in my Dealing.— To be sure, of late Years I have been a great Sufferer by the Parliament.— Three thousand Pounds would hardly make me amends.—The Act for destroying the Mint, was a severe Cut upon our Business—'Till then, if a Customer stept out of the way—we knew where to have her—No doubt you know Mrs. Coaxer—there's a Wench now ('till to-day) with a good Suit of Cloaths of mine upon her Back, and I could never set Eyes upon her for three Months together.—Since the Act too against Imprisonment for small Sums, my Loss there too hath been very considerable, and it must be so, when a Lady can borrow a handsome Petticoat, or a clean Gown, and I not have the least Hank upon her! And, o' my conscience, now-a-days most Ladies take a Delight in cheating, when they can do it with Safety.

PEACHUM: Madam, you had a handsome Gold Watch of us t'other Day for seven Guineas.—Considering we must have our Profit—To a Gentleman upon the Road, a Gold Watch will be scarce worth the taking.

MRS. TRAPES: Consider, Mr. Peachum, that Watch was remarkable, and not of very safe Sale.—If you have any black Velvet Scarfs—they are a handsome Winter-wear; and take with most Gentlemen who deal with my Customers.—'Tis I that put the Ladies upon a good Foot. 'Tis not Youth or Beauty that fixes their Price. The Gentlemen always pay according to their Dress, from half a Crown to two Guineas; and yet those Hussies make nothing of bilking of me.—Then, too, allowing for Accidents.—I have eleven fine Customers now down under the Surgeon's Hands,—what with Fees and other Expences, there are great Goings-out, and no Comings-in, and not a Farthing to pay for at least a Month's cloathing.—We run great Risques— great Risques indeed.

PEACHUM: As I remember, you said something just now of Mrs. Coaxer.

MRS. TRAPES: Yes, Sir.—To be sure I stript her of a Suit of my own Cloaths about two hours ago; and have left her as she should be, in her Shift, with a Lover of hers at my House. She call'd him up Stairs, as he was going to Marybone in a Hackney Coach.—And I hope, for her own sake and mine, she will perswade the Captain to redeem her, for the Captain is very generous to the Ladies.

LOCKIT: What Captain?

MRS. TRAPES: He thought I did not know him—An intimate Acquaintance of yours, Mr. Peachum—Only Captain Macheath—as fine as a Lord.

PEACHUM: To-morrow, dear Mrs. Dye, you shall set your own Price upon any of the Goods you like—We have at least half a dozen Velvet Scarfs, and all at your service. Will you give me leave to make you a Present of this Suit of Night-cloaths for your own wearing?—But are you sure it is Captain Macheath?

MRS. TRAPES: Though he thinks I have forgot him, no Body knows him better. I have taken a great deal of the Captain's Money in my Time at second-hand, for he always lov'd to have his Ladies well drest.

PEACHUM: Mr. Lockit and I have a little business with the Captain;—You understand me—and we will satisfye you for Mrs. Coaxer's Debt.

LOCKIT: Depend upon it—we will deal like Men of Honour.

MRS. TRAPES: I don't enquire after your Affairs—so whatever happens, I wash my Hands on't.—It hath always been my Maxim, that one Friend should assist another—But if you please—I'll take one of the Scarfs home with me. 'Tis always good to have something in Hand.

SCENE VII *Newgate*

LUCY

Jealousy, Rage, Love and Fear are at once tearing me to pieces. How I am weather-beaten and shatter'd with distresses!

AIR

I'm like a Skiff on the Ocean tost,
Now high, now low, with each Billow born,
With her Rudder broke, and her Anchor lost,
Deserted and all forlorn.
While thus I lye rolling and tossing all Night,
That Polly lyes sporting on Seas of Delight!
Revenge, Revenge, Revenge,
Shall appease my restless Sprite.

I have the Rats-bane ready.—I run no Risque; for I can lay her Death upon the Ginn, and so many dye of that naturally that I shall never be call'd in Question.—But say, I were to be hang'd—I never could be hang'd for any thing that would give me greater Comfort, than the poysoning that Slut.

(*Enter* Filch.)

FILCH: Madam, here's our Miss Polly come to wait upon you.

LUCY: Show her in.

SCENE VIII

LUCY, POLLY

LUCY: Dear Madam, your Servant.—I hope you will pardon my Passion, when I was so happy to see you last.—I was so overrun with the Spleen, that I was perfectly out of my self. And really when one hath the Spleen, every thing is to be excus'd by a Friend.

AIR

When a Wife's in her Pout
(As she's sometimes, no doubt;)
The good Husband as meek as a Lamb,
Her Vapours to still,
First grants her her Will,
And the quieting Draught is a Dram.
Poor Man! And the quieting Draught is a Dram.

—I wish all our Quarrels might have so comfortable a Reconciliation.

POLLY: I have no Excuse for my own Behaviour, Madam, but my Misfortunes.—And really, Madam, I suffer too upon your Account.

LUCY: But, Miss Polly—in the way of Friendship, will you give me leave to propose a Glass of Cordial to you?

POLLY: Strong-Waters are apt to give me the Head-ache—I hope, Madam, you will excuse me.

LUCY: Not the greatest Lady in the Land could have better in her Closet, for her own private drinking.—You seem mighty low in Spirits, my Dear.

POLLY: I am sorry, Madam, my Health will not allow me to accept of your Offer.—I should not have left you in the rude Manner I did when we met last, Madam, had not my Papa haul'd me away so unexpectedly—I was indeed somewhat provok'd, and perhaps might use some Expressions that were disrespectful.—But really, Madam, the Captain treated me with so much Contempt and Cruelty, that I deserv'd your Pity, rather than your Resentment.

LUCY: But since his Escape, no doubt all Matters are made up again.—Ah Polly! Polly! 'tis I am the unhappy Wife; and he loves you as if you were only his Mistress.

POLLY: Sure, Madam, you cannot think me so happy as to be the Object of your Jealousy.—A Man is always afraid of a Woman who loves him too well—so that I must expect to be neglected and avoided.

LUCY: Then our Cases, my dear Polly, are exactly alike. Both of us indeed have been too fond.

AIR

POLLY: *A Curse attends that Woman's Love,*
Who always would be pleasing.
LUCY: *The Pertness of the billing Dove,*
Like tickling, is but teazing.
POLLY: *What then in Love can Woman do?*
LUCY: *If we grow fond, they shun us.*
POLLY: *And when we fly them, they pursue.*
LUCY: *But leave us when they've won us.*

LUCY: Love is so very whimsical in both Sexes, that it is impossible to be lasting.—But my Heart is particular, and contradicts my own Observation.

POLLY: But really, Mistress Lucy, by his last Behaviour, I think I ought to envy you.—When I was forc'd from him, he did not shew the least Tenderness.—But perhaps, he hath a Heart not capable of it.

AIR

Among the Men, Coquets we find,
Who Court by turns all Woman-kind;
And we grant all their Hearts desir'd,
When they are flatter'd, and admir'd.

The Coquets of both Sexes are Self-lovers, and that is a Love no other whatever can dispossess. I fear, my dear Lucy, our Husband is one of those.

LUCY: Away with these melancholy Reflections,—indeed, my dear Polly, we are both of us a Cup too low.—Let me prevail upon you, to accept of my Offer.

AIR

Come, sweet Lass,
Let's banish Sorrow
'Till To-morrow;
Come, sweet Lass,
Let's take a chirping Glass.
Wine can clear
The Vapours of Despair;
And make us light as Air;
Then drink, and banish Care.

I can't bear, Child, to see you in such low Spirits.—And I must persuade you to what I know will do you good.—I shall now soon be even with the hypocritical Strumpet. (*Aside.*)

SCENE IX

POLLY

POLLY: All this wheedling of Lucy cannot be for nothing.—At this time too! when I know she hates me!—The Dissembling of a Woman is always the Fore-runner of Mischief.—By pouring strong-Waters down my Throat, she thinks to pump some Secrets out of me—I'll be upon my Guard, and won't taste a Drop of her Liquor, I'm resolv'd.

SCENE X

LUCY, *with Strong-Waters;* POLLY

LUCY: COME, MISS POLLY.
POLLY: Indeed, Child, you have given yourself trouble to no purpose.—You must, my Dear, excuse me.
LUCY: Really, Miss Polly, you are so squeamishly affected about taking a Cup of Strong-Waters as a Lady before Company. I vow, Polly, I shall take it monstrously ill if you refuse me.—Brandy and Men (though Women love them never so well) are always taken by us with some Reluctance—unless 'tis in private.
POLLY: I protest, Madam, it goes against me.—What do I see! Macheath again in Custody!—Now every glimm'ring of Happiness is lost. (*Drops the Glass of Liquor on the Ground.*)
LUCY: Since things are thus, I'm glad the Wench hath escap'd: for by this Event, 'tis plain, she was not happy enough to deserve to be poison'd. (*Aside.*)

SCENE XI

LOCKIT, MACHEATH, PEACHUM, LUCY, POLLY

LOCKIT: Set your Heart to rest, Captain.—You have neither the Chance of Love or Money for another Escape,—for you are order'd to be call'd down upon your Tryal immediately.
PEACHUM: Away, Hussies!—This is not a time for a Man to be hamper'd with his Wives.—You see, the Gentleman is in Chains already.
LUCY: O Husband, Husband, my heart long'd to see thee; but to see thee thus distracts me!
POLLY: Will not my dear Husband look upon his Polly? Why hadst thou not flown to me for Protection? with me thou hadst been safe.

AIR

POLLY: *Hither, dear Husband, turn your Eyes.*
LUCY: *Bestow one Glance to cheer me.*
POLLY: *Think with that Look thy Polly dyes.*
LUCY: *O shun me not—but hear me.*
POLLY: *'Tis Polly sues.*
LUCY: *. . . 'Tis Lucy speaks.*
POLLY: *Is thus true Love requited?*
LUCY: *My Heart is bursting.*
POLLY: *. . . Mine too breaks.*
LUCY: *Must I*
POLLY: *. . . Must I be slighted?*

MACHEATH: What would you have me say, Ladies —You see, this Affair will soon be at an end, without my disobliging either of you.
PEACHUM: But the settling this Point, Captain, might prevent a Law-suit between your two Widows.

AIR

MACHEATH: *Which way shall I turn me?—How can I decide?*
Wives, the Day of our Death, are as fond as a Bride.
One Wife is too much for most Husbands to hear,
But two at a time there's no Mortal can bear.
This way, and that way, and which way I will,
What would comfort the one, t'other Wife would take ill.

POLLY: But if his own Misfortunes have made him insensible to mine—A Father sure will be more compassionate.—Dear, dear Sir, sink the material Evidence, and bring him off at his Tryal—Polly upon her Knees begs it of you.

AIR

When my Hero in Court appears,
And stands arraign'd for his Life;
Then think of poor Polly's Tears;
For Ah! Poor Polly's his Wife.
Like the Sailor he holds up his Hand,
Distrest on the dashing Wave.
To die a dry Death at Land,
Is as bad as a watry Grave.
And alas, poor Polly!
Alack, and well-a-day!
Before I was in Love,
Oh! every Month was May.

LUCY: If Peachum's Heart is harden'd, sure you, Sir, will have more Compassion on a Daughter.—I know the Evidence is in your Power.—How then can you be a Tyrant to me?

(Kneeling.)

AIR

When he holds up his Hand arraign'd for his Life,
O think of your Daughter, and think I'm his Wife!
What are Cannons, or Bombs, or clashing of Swords?
For Death is more certain by Witnesses Words.
Then nail up their Lips; that dread Thunder allay;
And each Month of my Life will hereafter be May.

LOCKIT: Macheath's time is come, Lucy.—We know our own Affairs,
therefore let us have no more Whimpering or Whining.

PEACHUM: Set your Heart at rest, Polly.—Your Husband is to dye to-day.
—Therefore, if you are not already provided, 'tis high time to look about for
another. There's Comfort for you, you Slut.

LOCKIT: We are ready, Sir, to conduct you to the Old-Baily.

AIR

MACHEATH: *The Charge is prepar'd; The Lawyers are met,*
The Judges all rang'd (a terrible Show!)
I go, undismay'd.—For Death is a Debt,
A Debt on demand.—So, take what I owe.
Then farewell, my Love—Dear Charmers, adieu.
Contented I die—'Tis the better for you.
Here ends all Dispute the rest of our Lives.
For this way at once I please all my Wives.

Now, Gentlemen, I am ready to attend you.

SCENE XII

LUCY, POLLY, FILCH

POLLY: Follow them, Filch, to the Court. And when the Tryal is over,
bring me a particular Account of his Behaviour, and of every thing that
happen'd.—You'll find me here with Miss Lucy. (*Exit* Filch.) But why is all
this Musick?

LUCY: The Prisoners, whose Tryals are put off till next Session, are divert-
ing themselves.

POLLY: Sure there is nothing so charming as Musick! I'm fond of it to
distraction!—But alas!—now, all Mirth seems an Insult upon my Affliction.
—Let us retire, my dear Lucy, and indulge our Sorrows.—The noisy Crew,
you see, are coming upon us. (*Exeunt.*)

(*A Dance of Prisoners in Chains, &c.*)

SCENE XIII

(*The Condemn'd Hold*)

MACHEATH, *in a melancholy Posture*

AIR

O cruel, cruel, cruel Case!
Must I suffer this Disgrace?

AIR

Of all the Friends in time of Grief,
When threatning Death looks grimmer,
Not one so sure can bring Relief,
As this best Friend, a Brimmer. (Drinks.)

AIR

Since I must swing,—I scorn, I scorn to wince or whine. (Rises.)

AIR

But now again my Spirits sink;
I'll raise them high with Wine. (Drinks a Glass of Wine.)

AIR

But Valour the stronger grows,
The stronger Liquor we're drinking.
And how can we feel our Woes,
When we've lost the Trouble of Thinking? (Drinks.)

AIR

If thus—a Man can die
Much bolder with Brandy. (Pours out a Bumper of Brandy.)

AIR

So I drink off this Bumper.—And now I can stand the Test.
And my comrades shall see, that I die as brave as the Best. (Drinks.)

AIR

But can I leave my pretty Hussies,
Without one Tear, or tender Sigh?

AIR

Their Eyes, their Lips, their Busses
Recall my Love.—Ah, must I die?

AIR

Since laws were made for ev'ry Degree,
To curb Vice in others, as well as me,
I wonder we han't better Company,
Upon Tyburn Tree!
But Gold from Law can take out the Sting;
And if rich Men like us were to swing,
'Twould thin the Land, such Numbers to string
Upon Tyburn Tree!

JAILOR: Some Friends of yours, Captain, desire to be admitted.—I leave you together.

Scene XIV
MACHEATH, BEN BUDGE, MATT OF THE MINT

MACHEATH: For my having broke Prison, you see, Gentlemen, I am ordered immediate Execution.—The Sheriffs Officers, I believe, are now at the Door.—That Jemmy Twitcher should peach me, I own surpriz'd me!—'Tis a plain Proof that the World is all alike, and that even our Gang can no more trust one another than other People. Therefore, I beg you, Gentlemen, look well to yourselves, for in all probability you may live some Months longer.

MATT: We are heartily sorry, Captain, for your Misfortune.—But 'tis what we must all come to.

MACHEATH: Peachum and Lockit, you know, are infamous Scoundrels. Their Lives are as much in your Power, as yours are in theirs.—Remember your dying Friend!—'Tis my last Request.—Bring those Villains to the Gallows before you, and I am satisfied.

MATT: We'll do't.

JAILOR: Miss Polly and Miss Lucy intreat a Word with you.

MACHEATH: Gentlemen, Adieu.

Scene XV
LUCY, MACHEATH, POLLY

MACHEATH: My dear Lucy—My dear Polly—Whatsoever hath past between us is now at an end.—If you are fond of marrying again, the best advice I can give you, is to Ship yourselves off for the West-Indies, where you'll have a fair chance of getting a Husband a-piece; or by good Luck, two or three, as you like best.

POLLY: How can I support this Sight!

LUCY: There is nothing moves one so much as a great Man in Distress.

AIR

LUCY: *Would I might be hang'd!*
POLLY: *... And I would so too!*
LUCY: *To be hang'd with you.*
POLLY: *... My Dear, with you.*
MACHEATH: *O Leave me to Thought! I fear! I doubt!*
I tremble! I droop!—See, my Courage is out. (Turns to the empty Bottle.)
POLLY: *No token of Love?*

MACHEATH: ... *See, my Courage is out.* (Turns up the empty Pot.)
LUCY: *No token of Love?*
POLLY: ... *Adieu.*
LUCY: ... *Farewell.*
MACHEATH: *But hark! I hear the Toll of the Bell.*
CHORUS: *Tol de rol lo, &c.*

JAILOR: Four Women more, Captain, with a Child a-piece! See, here they come.

(Enter Women *and* Children.*)*

MACHEATH: What—four Wives more!—This is too much.— Here— tell the Sheriffs Officers I am ready. (*Exit* Macheath *guarded.*)

Scene XVI

(To them, Enter Player *and* Beggar*)*

PLAYER: But, honest Friend, I hope you don't intend that Macheath shall really be executed.
BEGGAR: Most certainly, Sir.—To make the Piece perfect, I was for doing strict poetical Justice.—Macheath is to be hang'd; and for the other Personages of the Drama, the Audience must have suppos'd they were all either hang'd or transported.
PLAYER: Why then, Friend, this is a down-right deep Tragedy. The Catastrophe is manisfestly wrong, for an Opera must end happily.
BEGGAR: Your Objection, Sir, is very just; and is easily remov'd. For you must allow that in this kind of Drama, 'tis no matter how absurdly things are brought about.—So—you Rabble there—run and cry a Reprieve—let the Prisoner be brought back to his Wives in Triumph.
PLAYER: All this we must do, to comply with the Taste of the Town.
BEGGAR: Through the whole Piece you may observe such a similitude of Manners in high and low Life, that it is difficult to determine whether (in the fashionable Vices) the fine Gentlemen imitate the Gentlemen of the Road, or the Gentlemen of the Road the fine Gentlemen.—Had the Play remain'd as I at first intended, it would have carried a most excellent Moral. 'Twould have shown that the lower Sort of People have their Vices in a degree as well as the Rich: And that they are punish'd for them.

Scene XVII

(To them, Macheath *with* Rabble, &c.*)*

MACHEATH: So, it seems, I am not left to my Choice, but must have a Wife at last.—Look ye, my Dears, we will have no Controversie now. Let us give this Day to Mirth, and I am sure she who thinks herself my Wife will testifie her Joy by a Dance.
ALL: Come, a Dance—a Dance.
MACHEATH: Ladies, I hope you will give me leave to present a Partner to each of you. And (if I may without Offence) for this time, I take Polly for mine.—And for Life, you Slut,—for we were really marry'd.—As for the rest—But at present keep your own Secret. (*To* Polly.)

A DANCE

AIR

Thus I stand like the Turk, with his Doxies around;
From all Sides their Glances his Passion confound;
For black, brown, and fair, his Inconstancy burns,
And the different Beauties subdue him by turns:
Each calls forth her Charms, to provoke his Desires:
Though willing to all, with but one he retires.
But think of this Maxim, and put off your Sorrow,
The Wretch of To-day, may be happy To-morrow.
CHORUS: But think of this Maxim, &c.

FOR DISCUSSION

1. Why is the play called *The Beggar's Opera?*
2. Why do the Beggar and the Player open and close the play?
3. Do you think the use of the songs in *The Beggar's Opera* is effective? Why or why not?
4. Is the play primarily a comedy, a commentary on society, or both? Discuss.
5. What is satire? Is this play a satire? If so, in what way? Discuss.
6. Do the characters seem like real people? Why or why not? Give specific examples to support your answer.
7. What qualities of ballad opera make it especially suited to comedy?
8. What are Mr. and Mrs. Peachum's attitude toward marriage? Polly's attitude? Macheath's? Yours?
9. Is there "honor among thieves" in this play?
10. Do you agree with Macheath when he says, "Money well tim'd and properly apply'd will do anything"?
11. Discuss the philosophy behind Locket's remark that "you should never do anything but upon the Foot of Interest."
12. What did you think of the ending? How do you think the play should have ended? Why?
13. Perhaps one moral in this play is that both the upper and the lower classes in society have their vices, but upper class are not punished for theirs while lower class are. Do you agree? Discuss.

Molière was the comic genius of France.

Jean-Baptiste Poquelin, who called himself Molière, was probably France's greatest actor-dramatist. The son of an upholsterer at the French court, he was born in 1622. Little is known of his early life other than that he saw a great number of plays and was said to have been good at mimicry. He attended a Jesuit school at Claremont, where he did well in his studies.

Molière trained for a legal career but instead of practicing law joined a small amateur theatrical company. The group, called the Illustre-Théâtre, was headed by Madeleine Béjart, the eldest member of a family of actors. Others in the company were friends of the family. Molière himself had little acting experience, but wanted to play tragic roles—for which, unfortunately, he was unsuited both physically and temperamentally. After a time, the company failed and Molière was imprisoned for debts.

In 1645, after his release from prison, Molière and other members of the acting company, who now no longer had a theatre, left Paris for a tour of the provinces of France. That tour lasted until 1658! Molière gained some recognition as an actor, began writing plays for the group, and soon was recognized as the company's leader. The plays he wrote were farces, similar in many respects to the performances given by *commedia dell' arte* troupes. The company is believed to have been sucessful, although there is no real proof that it was. The experience, however, provided background material for Molière's later plays.

Aided by friends, the company returned to Paris and became almost as popular as the troupe at the Hôtel de Bourgogne, who did only tragedy. Molière and his troupe presented comedy as well as tragedy. King Louis XIV, having seen the troupe perform, granted Molière permission to stay in Paris and share the Petite Bourbon, another theatre, with a *commedia dell' arte* company led by Tiberio Fiorelli. Molière paid rent to Fiorelli for the privilege of performing on three days a week, but Fiorelli reserved the best days for his troupe's performances. Beginning in 1661, Molière's company, now called the King's Men, was granted the right to play in the Palais Royal. The troupe continued to present some tragedies, but Molière's own plays became the most successful.

As a playwright, Molière is credited with introducing literary comedy to the French public in a form that combined farce and satire. His plots from many sources, including Greek, Roman, Italian, and Spanish plays. He created characters suited to the talents of available actors. Although they were based on the stock characters of Roman comedy and the *commedia dell' arte,* Molière gave them individual human characteristics.

Molière always played his own leading roles, and his plays often contained autobiographical elements. For instance, in *The School for Husbands,* an early satire, he borrowed from a variety of sources for the plot, but also ridiculed himself for his marriage at the age of forty to a girl less than half his age—Armande Béjart, the eighteen-year-old sister of Madeleine. *The*

Doctor in Spite of Himself is a light satire written when Molière was suffering from an incurable disease, now believed to have been tuberculosis. The play deals with hypochondria, as does his last play, *The Imaginary Invalid*, written in 1673. During a performance of this play, Molière became quite ill, and at the end, he left the stage, collapsed, and died. Because he was an actor he had never been admitted to the French Academy, nor could he be given a Christian burial.

The Miser is typical of Molière's plays in its reliance upon the *commedia dell' arte* for stock characters and comedy routines. The play contains many examples of slapstick humor and fantastic situations. Like Roman comedy, it relies often on mistaken motives and misunderstandings. Because the characters fail to communicate, they involve themselves in many unpleasant situations which they otherwise could have avoided. At the end they do not solve their own problems, but fate intervenes and solves them in much the same way that the gods intervened in some of the early Greek plays.

Despite what might be considered dramatic weaknesses in a modern play, *The Miser* still provides fun for audiences, and without a doubt was highly entertaining to those who saw it during the seventeenth century. The play also makes a serious statement in its ridicule of greed, suggesting that moderation is the best path for each of us to follow.

The Miser

CHARACTERS

HARPAGON, *father of Cléante and*
Élise, infatuated with Mariane.
CLÉANTE, *Harpagon's son,*
in love with Mariane.
ÉLISE, *Harpagon's daughter,*
in love with Valère.
VALÈRE, *Anselm's son,*
in love with Élise.

MARIANE, *Anselm's daughter,*
courted by
Harpagon but in love with
Cléante.

ANSELM, *father of*
Valère and Mariane.
FROSINE, *a woman of intrigue.*
SIMON, *a broker.*
JACQUES, *Harpagon's cook*
and coachman.
LA FLÈCHE, *Cléante's valet.*
DAME CLAUDE, *Harpagon's*
servant.

BRINDAVOINE, *Harpagon's*
lackey.

LA MERLUCHE, *Harpagon's*
lackey.
An OFFICER *and his* CLERK.

The place: Paris. A room in Harpagon's house. In the rear, a door leads to a garden.

The Miser

ACT I

(Enter Valère *and* Élise.*)*

VALERE: What is the matter, my dear Élise? Why so sad? And after the kind assurances you have given me of your faith? Alas! You sigh in the midst of my joy! Tell me, do you regret having made me happy? Do you repent the promise which my ardor has forced from you?

ÉLISE: No, Valère, I could not repent of anything that I have done for you. I feel enthralled by too pleasant a power, and I have not even the strength to wish that things were different. But, to tell you the truth, I am afraid of what may happen; and I am quite afraid of loving you a little more than I ought.

VALERE: Élise! what is there to fear in the affection you have for me?

ÉLISE: Alas! a hundred things: my father's anger, my family's reproaches, the world's censure; but most of all, Valère, a change in your heart and that criminal coldness with which those of your sex most often repay the too ardent professions of innocent love.

VALERE: Ah! do not wrong me by judging me according to others. Suspect me of anything. Élise, rather than of failing in my duty to you. I love you too much for that, and my love for you will last as long as I live.

ÉLISE: Ah! Valère, everyone makes the same speeches. All men are alike in their promises; it is only their actions which reveal their differences.

VALERE: Since actions alone show what we are, at least wait and judge my heart by mine. Do not search out faults in me that exist only in the unjust fears of a foolish foreboding. Do not kill me, I beg of you, with the sharp blows of outrageous suspicion. Give me time and I will convince you, by a thousand and one proofs, that my affections are sincere.

ÉLISE: Alas! how easily we are persuaded by those we love! Yes, Valère, I think your heart is incapable of deceiving me. I believe you really love me and will be faithful. I have not the slightest wish to doubt you; I confine my fears to dreading that others will blame me.

VALERE: But why this uneasiness?

ÉLISE: I should have nothing to fear if everyone saw you as I do, for I see in you enough to justify all I have done. My heart, for its defense, pleads your worth, and even Heaven has bound me to you with gratitude. Every hour I picture to myself the terrible disaster which brought us together; the wonderful generosity that made you risk your life to save mine from the fury

Reprinted by permission of the translators: Sylvan Barnet, Morton Berman, and William Burto.

of the waves; the tender care you took of me after rescuing me from the water; the unceasing attention of your ardent love which neither time nor difficulties have discouraged and which causes you to neglect both parents and country to remain in this place, your true rank disguised for my sake, reduced to wearing the livery of a servant in my father's house—in order to see me. All this has made a wonderful impression on me and is enough to justify to me the pledge I have consented to. But it is perhaps not enough to justify it to others, and I am not certain they share my feelings.

VALERE: Of all you have said of me, it is my love alone which gives me the right to merit anything from you. As for your scruples, your father himself has been only too careful to justify you before the world. His excessive avarice and the austere manner in which he lives with his children might authorize far stranger things. Forgive me, dear Élise, for talking this way in front of you, but you surely know that in this respect nothing good can be said of him. But if, as I hope, I can find my parents, we shall not have much difficulty winning him over. I impatiently await news of them, and if it is late in coming, I shall search it out myself.

ÉLISE: Oh! Valère, do not leave, I beg you. Think only of winning my father's confidence.

VALERE: You see how I go about it; the clever schemes I have had to put into practice in order to ingratiate myself into his service; what a mask of sympathy and of agreement I assume in order to please him; and what a role I daily play before him to gain his affection. I am making admirable progress. And I find that, in order to win men over, there is no better way than to seem to be of their inclinations, than to fall in with their maxims, flatter their faults, and applaud everything they do. There is no fear of overdoing flattery; the manner of fooling may be the most open—the shrewdest are always made the greatest dupes by flattery. There is nothing so impertinent or so ridiculous that they cannot be made to swallow, provided it is seasoned with praise. Sincerity suffers a little in this business. But when one has need of men, it is necessary to adjust oneself to them. Since there is no other way to win them over except by this means, it is not the fault of those who flatter, but of those who wish to be flattered.

ÉLISE: But why not also try to gain my brother's help, in case my maid decides to reveal our secret?

VALERE: I cannot manage both of them at once. The temperaments of father and son are so opposed that it would be hard to retain the confidence of both at the same time. But you could approach your brother and avail yourself of his friendship to get him to act in our interest. Here he comes now. I'll withdraw. Take this opportunity to speak with him. Don't reveal any more of our situation to him than you think proper. (*Exit* Valère.)

ÉLISE: I do not know if I shall have the courage to confide in him.

(*Enter* Cléante.)

CLEANTE: I am delighted to find you alone, Élise. I have been anxious to speak to you, to reveal a secret.

ÉLISE: Here I am, ready to listen, Cléante. What have you to tell me?

CLEANTE: Many things, Élise, but in a word: I'm in love.

ÉLISE: You're in love?

CLEANTE: Yes, I am in love. But, before going any further, I know that I am dependent on father, and that as his son I am subject to his wishes; that we ought never to make vows without the consent of those who gave us life;

that Heaven has made them masters of our affections; and that we are charged not to bestow them except by their counsel; that unaffected by foolish passion themselves, they are far less likely to be deceived than we and can see much better what is right for us. We should rather trust the light of their prudence than the blindness of our passion, for the eagerness of youth leads us most often toward troublesome precipices. I tell you all this, Élise, so you won't take the trouble of telling it to me. For, in a word, my passion will listen to nothing, and I beg you to forgo any remonstrances.

ÉLISE: Are you engaged to her whom you love?

CLEANTE: No, but I am resolved to be. And I ask you again not to attempt to dissuade me.

ÉLISE: Am I so strange a person, Cléante?

CLEANTE: No, dear sister, but you are not in love. You do not understand the sweet violence which tender love does to hearts, and I fear your prudence.

ÉLISE: Alas! let us not speak of my prudence, Cléante. There is no one who does not lack it at least once in his life; and if I opened my heart to you, perhaps I should appear in your eyes much less prudent than you.

CLEANTE: Ah! May Heaven grant that your heart, like mine—

ÉLISE: Let us first finish your difficulties. Tell me whom you love.

CLEANTE: A young girl who has been living nearby for a short time, and who seems created to inspire love in all who see her. Nature has fashioned nothing more lovable. I felt enthralled from the moment I saw her. Her name is Mariane and she lives under the protection of her mother, a good woman who is nearly always ill, and for whom this dear girl shows the greatest kindness imaginable. She waits upon her, sympathizes with her, and consoles her with a tenderness that would touch your soul. She has the most charming way in the world in whatever she does, and her every action shines with a thousand graces. Such attractive gentleness, such engaging goodness, such adorable modesty, such— Ah! Élise, if you could only see her.

ÉLISE: I see a great deal of her, Cléante, in what you tell me. And to understand what she is, it is enough for me that you love her.

CLEANTE: I have found out, secretly, that they are not very well off, and that, even though they live frugally, they have a difficult time making ends meet. Imagine, Élise, what joy it would be to be able to raise the fortune of the person one loves, discreetly to give some slight help to the modest needs of a virtuous family. Just think how miserable it makes me to find myself powerless, because of my father's avarice, to taste that pleasure, or to show the dear girl any evidence of my love.

ÉLISE: Yes, Cléante, I can see how grieved you must be.

CLEANTE: Ah! Élise, far more than you can imagine. Have you ever seen anything more cruel than this rigorous economy exercised over us, than this unheard-of-stinginess we are made to languish under? What good will wealth do us, if it comes only when we are no longer young enough to enjoy it; if even to maintain myself, I am forced on every side to run into debt; if you and I are reduced to obtaining daily help from tradesmen to keep decent clothes on our backs? So, I have wanted to talk with you, to ask you to help me sound father out about my present feelings. If he disapproves, I am resolved to go away with this dear girl, and enjoy whatever fortune Heaven may offer us. I am trying now to obtain money everywhere for this purpose; and if your difficulties resemble mine, Élise, if father insists on opposing our desires, we shall both leave him and free ourselves from the tyranny his unbearable avarice has so long imposed on us.

ÉLISE: It is certainly true that every day he gives us more and more reason to regret mother's death, and that—

CLEANTE: I hear his voice. Let us go somewhere else to finish our discussion. Later we will join forces and attack his hard heart. (*Exeunt* Clèante *and* Élise.)

(*Enter* Harpagon *and* La Flèche.)

HARPAGON: Get out of here immediately, and don't talk back! Go on, get out of my house! You master-crook! You gallows-bird!
LA FLECHE: (*aside*) I have never seen anyone so wicked as this accursed old scoundrel, and I believe, without a doubt, he is possessed of the devil.
HARPAGON: What are you muttering?
LA FLECHE: Why are you chasing me out of the house?
HARPAGON: It's just like you, you rogue, to ask for reasons. Be off before I beat you.
LA FLECHE: What have I done to you?
HARPAGON: Enough to make me want you to leave.
LA FLECHE: My master, your son, gave me orders to wait for him.
HARPAGON: Wait for him out in the street, not here in my house, planted as stiff as a post to watch what goes on and profit from everything. I won't have someone constantly near me, spying on my affairs, a traitor whose accursed eyes peer into everything I do, coveting everything I own, and ferreting in every corner to see if there is anything he can rob.
LA FLECHE: How the deuce could you be robbed of anything? Can a man be robbed who locks up everything and stands guard day and night?
HARPAGON: I will lock up everything I think fit, and stand guard as I please. (*To audience*) Doesn't he sound like a spy watching everything you do? I'm afraid that he suspects where my money is. (*To* La Flèche) Aren't you the kind of man who would go about spreading rumors that I have money hidden in my house?
LA FLECHE: You *have* money hidden in the house?
HARPAGON: No, you villain, I didn't say that! (*Aside*) I shall go mad. (*To* La Flèche) I am asking whether you wouldn't go around maliciously spreading tales that I do have some hidden?
LA FLECHE: Ah! what difference does it make to us whether you have any or not? It's all the same.
HARPAGON: Argue, will you! I'll knock your arguments about your ears. (*He raises his hand to give* La Flèche *a box on the ear.*) Once more—get out of here!
LA FLECHE: All right, I'm going.
HARPAGON: Wait! Are you taking anything of mine?
LA FLECHE: What could I take of yours?
HARPAGON: Come here, I'll see. Show me your hands.
LA FLECHE: There they are.
HARPAGON: The others.

Doubtless there was some stage business here, perhaps obscene, but it is lost.

LA FLECHE: The others?
HARPAGON: Yes.
LA FLECHE: There they are.
HARPAGON: Have you put anything down there? (*He points to* La Flèche's *breeches.*)
LA FLECHE: Look for yourself.
HARPAGON: (*kneeling, feels the bottoms of* La Flèche's *breeches*) These baggy breeches are just right for hiding stolen goods, and I wish people could be hanged for wearing them.

La Fleche: (*aside*) Ah! doesn't such a man as this deserve everything he fears! What joy I'd have in robbing him!
Harpagon: (*hearing "robbing," jumps up*) Eh?
La Fleche: What?
Harpagon: What did you say about robbing?
La Fleche: I said that you poke about everywhere to see if I'm robbing you.
Harpagon: That's just what I intend to do. (*He feels in* La Flèche's *pockets.*)
La Fleche: (*aside*) A plague on avarice and the avaricious.
Harpagon: What's that? What did you say?
La Fleche: What did I say?
Harpagon: Yes! What did you say about avarice and the avaricious?
La Fleche: I said, a plague on avarice and the avaricious.
Harpagon: Whom are you talking about?
La Fleche: About avaricious men.
Harpagon: And who are these avaricious men?
La Fleche: They are scoundrels and skinflints.
Harpagon: But whom do you mean by that?
La Fleche: What are *you* so upset about?
Harpagon: I'm upset about what I should be upset about.
La Fleche: Do you think I'm talking about you?
Harpagon: I think what I think. But tell me whom you were speaking to when you said that.
La Fleche: I was speaking to ... to my cap.
Harpagon: And I may knock your cap right off your head.
La Fleche: Would you stop me from cursing avaricious men?
Harpagon: No, but I'll stop you from chattering and being insolent. Keep quiet!
La Fleche: I didn't mention anyone's name.
Harpagon: If you talk any more, I'll give you a thrashing.
La Fleche: If the cap fits, wear it.
Harpagon: Will you hold your tongue?
La Fleche: Yes, in spite of myself.
Harpagon: Ah! Ah! (Harpagon *raises his cane to strike* La Flèche, *who wards off the blow by pointing to one of the pockets of his coat.*)
La Fleche: Look, here's another pocket. Are you satisfied?
Harpagon: Come, give it back to me without all this searching.
La Fleche: What?
Harpagon: What you've taken from me.
La Fleche: I've taken nothing at all from you.
Harpagon: Positively?
La Fleche: Positively.
Harpagon: Goodbye, and go to the devil.
La Fleche: (*aside*) That's a fine send-off.
Harpagon: Your conscience knows the truth, at least.
(*Exit* La Flèche.) That scoundrel of a valet really upsets me. I don't like to see that lame cur around at all. It's certainly no small worry guarding a large sum of money in the house. Happy is the man who has all his money well invested and keeps only what is necessary for his current expenses. It's hard to find a safe hiding place anywhere in the house. To my way of thinking, strong-boxes are suspect; I could never trust them. I see them as nothing but an open invitation to thieves; they are always the first thing pounced on. Still, I don't know whether it was wise to bury in the garden the ten thousand écus I was paid yesterday. Ten thousand gold écus is a pretty large sum to

have in one's house. . . . (Cléante *and* Elise, speaking in low voices, appear at the door to the garden but hesitate before entering.) Oh! Heavens! I have given myself away! My anxiety has undone me! I think I spoke aloud while thinking to myself. (*To* Cléante *and* Élise.) What do you want?

CLEANTE: Nothing, father.

HARPAGON: Have you been there long?

ÉLISE: We have just arrived.

HARPAGON: You heard—

CLEANTE: What, father?

HARPAGON: There—

ÉLISE: What?

HARPAGON: What I just said.

CLEANTE: No.

HARPAGON: Yes, you did, you did.

ÉLISE: I beg your pardon, but we didn't, father.

HARPAGON: I can see quite well that you heard something. The fact is I was talking to myself about how hard it is these days to find money, and I was saying how happy a man must be who has ten thousand écus about the house.

CLEANTE: We hesitated to come near for fear of interrupting you.

HARPAGON: I'm anxious to tell you what I said so that you won't get things mixed up and imagine I said it is *I* who have ten thousand écus.

CLEANTE: We don't mix into your affairs.

HARPAGON: Would to Heaven I had that much money . . . ten thousand écus!

CLEANTE: I do not believe—

HARPAGON: It would be a fortunate thing for me.

ÉLISE: These are things—

HARPAGON: I could use it.

CLEANTE: I think that—

HARPAGON: It would suit me exactly.

ÉLISE: You are—

HARPAGON: Then I wouldn't complain, as I do now, that times are hard.

CLEANTE: My God, father, you have no cause to complain. Everyone knows you are well off.

HARPAGON: What? I, well off? Whoever says that is a liar. Nothing is further from the truth. And those who spread such reports around are villains.

ÉLISE: Don't get angry.

HARPAGON: It's strange that my own children should betray me and become my enemies!

CLEANTE: Am I your enemy because I say you are well off?

HARPAGON: Yes! Such talk, and the expenses you run up, will, one of these days, cause somebody to come here and cut my throat, in hope that they will find me stuffed with gold.

CLEANTE: What great expenses have I run up?

HARPAGON: What? Can anything be more scandalous than the sumptuous apparel you parade around the city in? Yesterday I criticized your sister, but this is even worse. This cries aloud to Heaven for vengeance. From head to toe there is enough on your body to buy a good annuity. Son, I have told you twenty times that your ways greatly displease me. You outrageously give yourself the airs of a marquis, and to be able to go about dressed as you are, you must certainly be robbing me.

CLEANTE: What! How can I be robbing you?

HARPAGON: How do I know? Where, then, do you get the means to keep up your fashionable dress?

CLEANTE: I, father? I gamble, and, since I am very lucky, I put all the money I win on my back.

HARPAGON: That's badly done. If you are lucky at cards, you ought to profit by it and invest at good interest the money that you win, so that you'll have it on a rainy day. Without troubling about anything else, I'd really like to know what good are all those ribbons you are bedecked with from head to foot, and if a half-dozen laces are not enough to hold up your breeches. Is it really necessary to spend money on wigs when you can wear the hair of your own head, which costs nothing? I'll wager that your wigs and ribbons alone are worth at least twenty pistoles; and twenty pistoles bring in eighteen livres, six sous, and eight deniers a year, even at only eight per cent interest.

CLEANTE: You are right.

HARPAGON: Enough of this. Let's talk of something else. Eh? (Harpagon, seeing Cléante and Élise signalling to each other "You speak," "No, you speak," mutters in a low voice) I think they are signalling each other to steal my purse. (Aloud) What do those signs mean?

ÉLISE: Cléante and I are debating who shall speak first. Both of us have something to say to you.

HARPAGON: And I, too, have something to say to both of you.

CLEANTE: It is about marriage, father, that we wish to speak to you.

HARPAGON: And it is also about marriage that I wish to speak to you.

ÉLISE: Ah! father!

HARPAGON: Why this cry? Are you afraid, my daughter, of the word or the thing?

CLEANTE: Marriage, at least in the way you understand it, frightens both of us. We are afraid that our feelings may not agree with your choice.

HARPAGON: A little patience. Do not alarm yourselves. I know what is best for both of you; and neither of you will have cause to complain of anything that I intend to do. To begin at the beginning: tell me, have you ever seen a young person named Mariane, who lives not far from here?

CLEANTE: Yes, father.

HARPAGON: And you?

ÉLISE: I have heard of her.

HARPAGON: Well, my son, what do you think of this girl?

CLEANTE: A most charming person.

HARPAGON: Her looks?

CLEANTE: Very honest and full of intelligence.

HARPAGON: Her air and manner?

CLEANTE: Admirable, without a doubt.

HARPAGON: Don't you think that a girl like that is quite worthy of serious consideration?

CLEANTE: Yes, father.

HARPAGON: That she would make a desirable match?

CLEANTE: Very desirable.

HARPAGON: That she has all the appearances of making a good housewife?

CLEANTE: Without a doubt.

HARPAGON: And that a husband would be satisfied with her?

CLEANTE: Surely.

HARPAGON: But there is one little difficulty; I am afraid that she does not have as much money as one might expect.

CLEANTE: Ah! father, money should not be a consideration when it is a question of marrying a respectable person.

HARPAGON: Pardon me, pardon me! But there is this to be said: if one does not find all the wealth one wishes, one can try to make up for it in some other way.

CLEANTE: Quite so.

HARPAGON: Ah, I am so happy to find you agree with me, because her modest bearing and her gentleness have won my heart, and I am resolved to marry her, provided she has some means.

CLEANTE: What?

HARPAGON: What?

CLEANTE: You say you have resolved—

HARPAGON: To marry Mariane.

CLEANTE: Who, you, you?

HARPAGON: Yes, I, I, I. What do you mean by that?

CLEANTE: I suddenly feel dizzy. I must go (*Exit* Cléante.)

HARPAGON: Oh, that's nothing. Go into the kitchen immediately and drink a large glass of plain water. (*To* Élise) These are your effeminate dandies, who have no more strength than a chicken. That's what I have resolved to do, my daughter. As for your brother, I intend for him a certain widow that someone mentioned to me this morning. And for you, I am giving you to Signor Anselm.

ÉLISE: To Signor Anselm?

HARPAGON: Yes! A mature, prudent, wise man, who is not more than fifty, and who is said to have great wealth.

ÉLISE: (*She makes a curtsy.*) If you please, father, I do not want to marry.

HARPAGON: (*He imitates her curtsy.*) If *you* please, my little girl, my pet, I want you to marry.

ÉLISE: (*She makes another curtsy.*) I beg your pardon, father.

HARPAGON: (*He again imitates her curtsy.*) I beg *your* pardon, daughter.

ÉLISE: I am Signor Anselm's most humble servant, but (*making another curtsy*), with your permission, I will not marry him.

HARPAGON: I am *your* most humble servant, but (*imitating her curtsy*), with your permission, you *shall* marry him, and this very evening.

ÉLISE: This very evening?

HARPAGON: This very evening.

ÉLISE: That shall not be, father. (*She curtsies.*)

HARPAGON: That *shall* be, daughter. (*He curtsies.*)

ÉLISE: No!

HARPAGON: Yes!

ÉLISE: No, I tell you.

HARPAGON: Yes, I tell you.

ÉLISE: This is something you cannot force me to do.

HARPAGON: This is something I can force you to do.

ÉLISE: I would rather kill myself than marry such a husband.

HARPAGON: You will not kill yourself, and you will marry him. What impudence! Have you ever heard a daughter talk to her father like that?

ÉLISE: But have you ever heard of a father marrying off his daughter like that?

HARPAGON: Nothing can be said against such a match, and I'll wager that everyone will approve my choice.

ÉLISE: And I'll wager that it will not be approved by any reasonable person.

HARPAGON: (*seeing* Valère *approach*) Here is Valère. Are you willing to let him judge between us in this matter?

ÉLISE: I consent.

HARPAGON: Will you submit to his judgment?

ÉLISE: Yes, I will abide by his decision.

HARPAGON: Then it is agreed. (Valère *enters*.) Here, Valère. We have elected you to decide who is in the right, my daughter or I.

VALERE: You sir, without a doubt.

HARPAGON: You know, then, what we have been talking about?

VALERE: No, but you couldn't be wrong; you are reason itself.

HARPAGON: Tonight I wish to give her a husband as rich as he is wise, and the hussy tells me to my face that she scorns to take him. What do you say to that?

VALERE: What do I say to that?

HARPAGON: Yes.

VALERE: Ahem!

HARPAGON: What?

VALERE: I say that fundamentally I am of your opinion; and you cannot but be right. But I cannot say she is entirely wrong, and—

HARPAGON: What? Signor Anselm is a desirable match. He is a gentleman, noble, refined, poised, wise, and well off; furthermore, he has no children left from his first marriage. Could she meet anyone more desirable?

VALERE: That's true. But she might tell you that you were rushing matters a bit and that she ought at least to be allowed a little time to see if she could accommodate her feelings to—

HARPAGON: This is an opportunity which must be grasped by the forelock. I find in this match an advantage which I would not find elsewhere, for he promises to take her without a dowry.

VALERE: Without a dowry?

HARPAGON: Yes.

VALERE: Ah! Then I will say no more. Don't you see? Here is the absolutely conclusive reason; one must submit to it.

HARPAGON: For me it means a considerable saving.

VALERE: Certainly. There's no denying that. It's true that your daughter might suggest to you that marriage is a far more serious matter than most people believe; that it means being happy or unhappy all her life; and that a union which ought to last until death ought never to be made without the greatest precautions.

HARPAGON: But—without a dowry!

VALERE: You are right. That settles everything, of course. There are some people who might say to you that in such matters the feelings of the daughter ought, unquestionably, to be considered, and that this great difference in age, disposition, and sentiment might subject the marriage to most unfortunate accidents.

HARPAGON: Without a dowry!

VALERE: Ah! Everyone knows there's no reply to that. Who the deuce would argue the contrary? It isn't that there are not some fathers who would prefer to think more of their daughters' happiness than of the money they might have to give them; who would never sacrifice them for interest, and who would seek, above everything else, to secure for them in a marriage that gentle harmony which unfailingly produces honor, tranquility, and joy, and which—

HARPAGON: But—without a dowry!

VALERE: True. That shuts every mouth: without a dowry. How can one resist an argument like that?

HARPAGON: (*looking toward the garden*) What was that? I thought I heard a dog barking. (*Aside*) Is someone trying to find my money? (*To* Valère *and* Élise) Don't budge from here; I'll be right back. (*Exit*.)

ÉLISE: Are you joking, Valère, talking to him as you have done?

VALERE: I don't want to anger him, for then I shall better achieve my purpose. To oppose his wishes to his face is a sure way to spoil everything. There are certain natures which can be overcome only by indirect means; temperaments which are enemies of all resistance; restive minds, who rear at truth, who always stiffen against the straight path of reason. Only by leading them in an indirect way can you guide them where you want them to go. Pretend to consent to his wishes; you will better gain your ends, and—

ÉLISE: But this marriage, Valère.

VALERE: We will find some expedient to break it off.

ÉLISE: But they will discover the feint, if they call in doctors.

VALERE: Are you joking? What do doctors know? Come, come, as for them, you can have whatever sickness you please; they will find you reasons for having it and tell you where it came from.

(*Enter* Harpagon, *unseen*.)

HARPAGON: (*aside*) It was nothing, thank God.

VALERE: Our last resort could be flight, which will shelter us from everything. And if your love, fair Élise, is capable of such strength— (*He sees* Harpagon.) Yes, a girl ought to obey her father. She ought not to concern herself with what her husband is like. And when the powerful argument "without a dowry" is presented to her, she ought to be ready to accept all that is given her.

HARPAGON: Good! That was well spoken.

VALERE: Sir, I beg your pardon if I have been too forward in taking the liberty of speaking to her as I have.

HARPAGON: Why, I am delighted. I want you to assume absolute control over her. (*To* Élise, *who has moved to the back of the stage*) Yes, try running away. I give him the authority over you that God gave me, and I expect you to do everything he tells you.

VALERE: After that, just try to resist my remonstrances! Sir, I will follow her and continue the lessons I was giving her.

HARPAGON: Yes, you will oblige me greatly. By all means—

VALERE: It's a good idea to hold her in with a tight rein.

HARPAGON: That's right. You must—

VALERE: Do not trouble yourself. I know I shall get things right.

HARPAGON: Do, go on. I'm going for a stroll through the town, and I'll be back soon.

VALERE: Yes, money is more precious than anything else in the world, and you ought to thank God for the honest father He has given you. He knows what life is; when someone offers to take a daughter without a dowry, there's no need to look further. Everything is contained in that; "without a dowry" takes the place of beauty, youth, birth, honor, wisdom, and integrity. (*Exeunt* Valère *and* Élise.)

HARPAGON: Ah! Such a fine fellow. Spoken like an oracle. Happy the man who can have such a servant.

ACT II

(On stage: Cléante. *Enter* La Flèche.*)*

CLEANTE: Ah! you rogue! Where have you been hiding? Didn't I order you to—

LA FLECHE: Yes, sir! And I came here with every intention of waiting for you, but your father, the crudest man in the world chased me out of the house, in spite of myself, and I ran the risk of a beating.

CLEANTE: How is our affair going? Things are more pressing than ever. Since I last saw you, I have discovered that my father is my rival.

LA FLECHE: Your father is in love?

CLEANTE: Yes, and I had all the trouble in the world hiding from him how much this news pained me.

LA FLECHE: Mixing himself up with love! What the devil is he thinking of? Is he making a mockery of the world? Was love made for people built like him?

CLEANTE: This passion had to take hold of him as a result of my sins.

LA FLECHE: But why do you keep your love a secret from him?

CLEANTE: To make him less suspicious, and to keep the way open more easily so that I can, if necessary, prevent his marriage.—What answer did they give you?

LA FLECHE: Good Lord, sir, those who borrow are most unhappy. A man has to put up with strange things when, like you, he has to pass through the hands of the money-lenders.

CLEANTE: The matter cannot be managed?

LA FLECHE: Not quite. Our Master Simon, the broker, who was recommended to us as an active, zealous man, says he has worked furiously for you; and he swears that your appearance alone has won his heart.

CLEANTE: Will I get the fifteen thousand francs I asked for?

LA FLECHE: Yes, but with several little conditions attached, which you must accept, if you want things to go well.

CLEANTE: Did he let you speak to the man who is to lend the money?

LA FLECHE: Ah! It's not quite that simple. He takes even more care than you to remain unknown, for such dealings are much more mysterious than you realize. They would not even mention his name, and they are going to bring you face to face today in a house rented for the occasion, to learn, from your own lips, what your means are and who your family is. I have not the slightest doubt that the mere name of your father will make things easy.

CLEANTE: Especially as my mother is dead, and I cannot be deprived of her property.

LA FLECHE: Here are some of the conditions he himself dictated to our go-between, to be shown you before anything can be done. "Provided that the lender find all the securities satisfactory, and that the borrower be of age, and of a family whose estate is ample, solid, assured, clear, and free from all encumbrances, a valid and exact contract shall be drawn up in the presence of a notary, the most honest man available, who, on this account, shall be chosen by the lender, to whom it is of the utmost importance that the contract shall be properly executed."

CLEANTE: There's nothing to say against that.

LA FLECHE: "In order not to burden his conscience with any scruple, the lender proposes to charge no more than five and a half per cent interest."

CLEANTE: No more than five and a half per cent? Well, that's honest enough. There is no reason to complain about that.

LA FLECHE: That's true. "But, as the said lender does not have on hand the sum in question, and in order to please the borrower, he himself is compelled to borrow it from someone else at the rate of twenty per cent, it shall be agreed that the said first borrower shall pay this interest, without prejudice to the other, since it is only to oblige him that the said lender himself borrows the money."

CLEANTE: What the devil! What Jew, what Arab is this? That's more than twenty-five per cent.

LA FLECHE: Quite true. That's what I said. You had better look into it.

CLEANTE: What can I do? Since I need the money, I have to consent to everything.

LA FLECHE: That's what I said.

CLEANTE: Is there anything else?

LA FLECHE: Only one small condition. "Of the fifteen thousand francs asked, the lender can only pay out twelve thousand, and in place of the remaining one thousand écus, the borrower must take furniture, clothing, and jewels, according to the following memorandum, the said lender attaching to them, in good faith, the lowest price possible."

CLEANTE: What does that mean?

LA FLECHE: Listen to the memorandum. "First, one four-poster bed, with strips of Hungarian lace elegantly embroidered on olive-colored cloth, with six chairs and a counterpane to match; all in good condition and lined with iridescent red and blue silk. In addition, one canopy, of good, pale rose-colored Aumale serge, with silken tassels and fringes."

CLEANTE: What does he expect me to do with that?

LA FLECHE: Wait. "In addition, a set of tapestries showing the loves of Gombaut and Macaea. In addition, one large walnut table, with twelve columns or turned legs, which pulls out at either end, complete with six stools underneath."

CLEANTE: Good Heavens, what good is that to me!

LA FLECHE: Be patient. "In addition, three large muskets inlaid with mother-of-pearl, with three assorted rests. In addition, one brick furnace with two retorts and three receivers, very useful for those interested in distilling."

CLEANTE: This is infuriating.

LA FLECHE: Easy now. "In addition, a lute from Bologna with all its strings, or very nearly all. In addition, one gaming table, one checker board, with a game of goose, revived from the Greeks, quite fit for passing the time when one has nothing to do. In addition, one lizard skin, three and a half feet long, stuffed with straw, a pleasant curiosity to hang from the ceiling of a room. The total mentioned above, easily worth more than four thousand five hundred francs, is reduced to the value of one thousand écus at the discretion of the lender."

CLEANTE: May the plague choke the scoundrel and his discretion! Cut-throat that he is! Have you ever heard of such usury? Isn't he content with the outrageous interest he exacts, without wanting to make me take, for three thousand francs, all the old junk he's collected? I won't get two hundred écus for the lot. Nevertheless, I must give in, for he is in a position to make me accept anything, and so the villain has me, with a knife at my throat.

LA FLECHE: Sir, if I may say so, I see you on the same broad road that Panurge travelled to his ruin, taking money in advance, buying dear, selling cheap, and eating your wheat while it's still in the blade.

CLEANTE: What would you have me do? This is what young men are reduced to by the cursed avarice of their fathers. And yet people are astonished when sons wish that their fathers would die.

LA FLECHE: I must confess that yours would arouse the most placid man in the world against his stinginess. I have, thank God, no strong desire for the gallows, and among my colleagues, whom I see mixed up in many petty schemes, I am clever enough to keep out of scrapes, and to drop out prudently from any gallantries that smell even slightly of the gallows. But, to tell you the truth, your father's actions would tempt *me* to rob him; and I believe that if I did I would be performing a good deed.

CLEANTE: Give me the memorandum a moment; I want to look it over again.

(Enter Simon and Harpagon.)

SIMON: Yes, sir, he is a young man in need of money. His affairs force him to find some, and he will agree to everything you demand.

HARPAGON: But are you certain, Simon, that I run no risk? Do you know the name, the fortune, and the family of the client you represent?

SIMON: No, I cannot really tell you anything definite; it was only by chance that he was recommended to me. But he will explain everything to you himself; and his servant has assured me that you will be satisfied when you meet him. All I can tell you is that his family is very rich, that his mother is dead, and that he will guarantee, if you wish, that his father will die before eight months are over.

HARPAGON: Well, that's something. Charity, Simon, requires us to please people, when we can.

SIMON: Quite so.

LA FLECHE: *(low to* Cléante) What does this mean? Simon's talking to your father!

CLEANTE: *(low to* La Flèche) Can anyone have told him who I am? Have you betrayed me?

SIMON: *(seeing* Cléante *and* La Flèche) Aha! you certainly are in a hurry! Who told you this was the house? *(To* Harpagon) It was not I, sir, in any event, who revealed your name and residence. But, in my opinion, there's no great harm done. They are discreet fellows, and you can discuss things together here.

HARPAGON: What do you mean?

SIMON: *(pointing to* CLÉANTE) This gentleman is the one I have mentioned to you, the person who wants to borrow the fifteen thousand francs.

HARPAGON: What! rogue! It is you who abandon yourself to such sinful excesses?

CLEANTE: What! father! It is you who deal in such shameful actions?

HARPAGON: It is you who want to ruin yourself by such detestable borrowing?

CLEANTE: It is you who seek to enrich yourself by such criminal usury?

HARPAGON: How dare you, after this, appear before me?

CLEANTE: How dare you, after this, show yourself to the world?

HARPAGON: Tell me, have you no shame at all, to indulge in such debauchery? to throw yourself into such horrible expenses? to squander shamelessly the wealth your parents have amassed for you by the sweat of their brows?

CLEANTE: Do you not blush at dishonoring your rank by this trade you carry on? sacrificing glory and reputation to the insatiable desire of heaping up gold upon gold, and outdoing by your rate of interest the most infamous schemes ever invented by the most notorious usurers?

HARPAGON: Get out of my sight, you villain, get out of my sight!

CLEANTE: Who is the greater criminal in your opinion: the man who buys money he needs, or the man who steals money he does not need?

HARPAGON: Get out of here, I tell you; you make my blood boil. (*Exeunt* Cléante, La Flèche, *and* Simon.) I am not sorry this has happened; it is a warning to me to keep a stricter eye than ever on all his actions.

(Enter Frosine.)

FROSINE: Sir—

HARPAGON: Just a moment. I'll be right back to talk to you. (*Aside*) It's time to take a little look at my money. (*Exit.*)

(Enter La Flèche.)

LA FLECHE: (*without seeing* Frosine) The whole thing is most amusing. Somewhere he certainly must have a large storehouse of junk, for we couldn't recognize anything from here in that inventory list.

FROSINE: Ah! it's you, my good La Flèche! How do you happen to be here?

LA FLECHE: Aha! it's you, Frosine! What are *you* doing here?

FROSINE: What I do everywhere else: play the go-between in affairs, make myself useful to people, and profit as best I can from the little talent I possess. In this world, you know, you have to live by your wits. Heaven has not endowed people like me with any resources other than intrigue and cleverness.

LA FLECHE: Have you some business with the master of the house?

FROSINE: Yes, I am negotiating a trifling matter for him, for which I hope to be compensated.

LA FLECHE: By him? Aha! you will be very clever indeed if you get anything from him. I warn you that around here money is very scarce.

FROSINE: There are certain services that have a wonderful effect.

LA FLECHE: I am your humble servant, but you don't know Monsieur Harpagon yet. Monsieur Harpagon is of all humans the least human, of all mortals the hardest and tightest. There is not one single service that can rouse his gratitude to the point of making him put his hand into his purse. Praise, esteem, kind words, and friendship, as much as you like. But money, out of the question! Nothing is drier and more withered than his favors and caresses, and "give" is a word for which he has such an aversion that he never says "I give you" but "I lend you good day."

FROSINE: Heavens! But I know the art of drawing men out; I have the secret for opening up their tenderness to me, for tickling their hearts, for finding their sensitive spots.

LA FLECHE: No use here! I defy you to soften the man in question when it comes to money. In that matter he is a Turk, but he out-Turks a Turk to the despair of everyone. You could be dying and he wouldn't lift a finger. In a word, he loves money more than reputation, than honor, than virtue, and the mere sight of anyone asking for money sends him into convulsions. It's a mortal wound. It pierces his heart. It rips out his entrails. And if—He's coming back! I must be off! (*Exit.*)

(Enter Harpagon.)

HARPAGON: (*aside, low*) All's well. (*To* Frosine) Well now! What is it, Frosine?

FROSINE: Ah! My, how well you look! You are the very picture of health!
HARPAGON: Who? I?
FROSINE: I've never seen your complexion so fresh and sparkling.
HARPAGON: Really?
FROSINE: Really. You've never in your life looked so young as you do now.
I see men of twenty-five who are older than you.
HARPAGON: Nevertheless, Frosine, I'm over sixty.
FROSINE: Well, what is sixty? A mere trifle! It's the flower of one's age, and
you are now entering upon the prime of manhood.
HARPAGON: That's true. But twenty years younger wouldn't do me any
harm.
FROSINE: You're joking! You don't need them. You're the type that will
live to be a hundred.
HARPAGON: Do you think so?
FROSINE: Certainly. You show every sign of it. Hold still a moment! Oh!
most certainly, there between your eyes—a sign of long life.
HARPAGON: Do you really know what you're talking about?
FROSINE: Without a doubt. Let me see your hand. My goodness! What a
life line!
HARPAGON: Where?
FROSINE: Don't you see how far that line goes?
HARPAGON: Well! But what does it mean?
FROSINE: Upon my word! I said a hundred, but you'll survive one hundred
and twenty!
HARPAGON: Is it possible?
FROSINE: They'll have to club you to death, I tell you. You'll bury your
children and your children's children.
HARPAGON: So much the better!—But how is our little business going
along?
FROSINE: Need you ask? Has anyone ever seen me start anything I didn't
finish? I have a marvellous talent, especially for matchmaking. There aren't
two people in the world that I couldn't join in a short time. I believe, if I took
it into my head, that I could marry the Grand Turk to the Republic of Venice.
Of course, there weren't any such great difficulties in your case. As I have
business in their house, I have often spoken to both of them about you, and
I have told the mother about the future you've been planning for Mariane,
since you saw her pass by in the street and take the air at her window.
HARPAGON: What answer did—
FROSINE: She received the proposition with pleasure. And when I told her
you greatly desired that her daughter be present this evening at the signing
of the marriage contract here at your house, she consented willingly, and
even entrusted her daughter to me for that purpose.
HARPAGON: I have to give a supper for Signor Anselm, Frosine, and I
should like her to be present.
FROSINE: You are quite right. After dinner she has to pay your daughter
a visit; then she plans to go to the fair, and will return here for supper.
HARPAGON: Very well. They can go together in my coach, which I shall
lend them.
FROSINE: That will suit her exactly.
HARPAGON: But, Frosine, have you talked to the mother about the money
she can give her daughter? Have you told her that she ought to help a little,
if only slightly; that she should make some attempt; that she should bleed
herself for an occasion such as this? For, after all, a man does not marry a
girl unless she brings along something.

FROSINE: What? This girl will bring you twelve thousand francs a year.

HARPAGON: Twelve thousand francs a year?

FROSINE: Yes. First of all: she has been brought up and nourished on a very sparing diet. She is a girl accustomed to live on salads, milk, cheese, and apples; and, consequently, she does not need elaborate meals, or exquisite broths, or barley syrups all the time, nor all the rest of the delicacies other women need. And they are no slight matter, for year after year they mount up to three thousand francs to least. Besides this, she cares only for what is simple in dress, and does not like gorgeous clothes, expensive jewels, or sumptuous furniture, to which her contemporaries are so much addicted. This saving is worth more than four thousand franc a year. Furthermore, she has a positive loathing for cards, a taste not common in women today. I know of one in our neighborhood who has lost twenty thousand francs at cards this year! But let us figure it at a quarter of that. Five thousand francs a year for cards, four thousand francs for clothes and jewels, make nine thousand francs. And three thousand francs which we set aside for food. Doesn't that make your twelve thousand francs a year all accounted for?

HARPAGON: Yes, that's not bad. But your figures have no reality.

FROSINE: I beg your pardon. Isn't perfect sobriety a real asset in marriage? Or her inheritance of a great love for simplicity in dress? Or the acquisition of a deep well of hatred for gambling?

HARPAGON: It's mockery to make up her dowry with the expenses that she *won't* run up. I give no receipt for something I don't actually get. I have to put my hands on something.

FROSINE: Great Heavens! you'll put your hands on enough. And they did mention to me some property they own in a foreign country of which you will become the master.

HARPAGON: I'll have to see it. But, Frosine, there is something else that upsets me. The girl is young, as you know, and the young generally like only those of their own age, and seek only their company. I'm afraid that a man of my age won't be to her liking, and that can only produce in my house certain little vexations which wouldn't please me.

FROSINE: Ah! how little you know her! This was one other characteristic that I was going to tell you about. She has a frightful aversion to all young men, and only likes old ones.

HARPAGON: She?

FROSINE: Yes, she. I wish you had heard her on that subject. She cannot bear the sight of a young man. But she says that nothing delights her more than the sight of a handsome old man with a majestic beard. The older they are, the more charming they are for her, and I warn you not to make yourself appear younger than you are. She likes a man to be at least sixty. Not four months ago, on the point of getting married, she promptly broke off the match, when she found out that her lover was only fifty-six and didn't need glasses to sign the marriage contract.

HARPAGON: Just for that?

FROSINE: Yes! She said that she wasn't satisfied with a man of only fifty-six, and, above all, she likes noses with spectacles on them.

HARPAGON: Really, this is something quite new!

FROSINE: It goes even further than I have told you. There are a few pictures and engravings in her room. But what do you think they are? Adonis? Cephalus? Paris? Apollo? Not at all! Fine portraits of Saturn, of King Priam, of old Nestor, and of good father Anchises on his son's shoulders.

HARPAGON: That *is* admirable! I should never have thought it. And my mind is eased to learn she has that attitude. In fact, if I had been a woman, I wouldn't have liked young men either.

FROSINE: I quite believe it. Love young men! What are they but worthless trash! They are mere puppies, show-offs that make you envy their complexions. I'd really like to know who likes them!

HARPAGON: As for me, I don't understand it either. I don't know how some women can like them so much.

FROSINE: One has to be an utter fool to find youth charming! Is that common sense? Are they men, these young fops? Can one really be attached to such animals?

HARPAGON: That's what I say day after day: with their effeminate voices, and their three little wisps of beard turned up like cat's whiskers, their straw-colored wigs, their baggy pants, and their fancy waistcoats.

FROSINE: They make a fine comparison next to a man like you. (*To the audience*) Here is a man. There's something here that satisfies the eye. This is the way a man should be made, and dressed, to inspire love.

HARPAGON: You find me attractive?

FROSINE: What? Ah! you are stunning, and your portrait ought to be painted. Turn around a bit, if you please. Nothing could be better. Let me see you walk. (*To the audience*) Here is a body that is trim, free, and easy in its motions, as it should be, without a trace of any physical weakness.

HARPAGON: Nothing much is the matter with me, thank God. (*He coughs.*) That's only my catarrh, which bothers me occasionally.

FROSINE: That's nothing. Your catarrh is not unbecoming, since you cough with such grace.

HARPAGON: Tell me something. Hasn't Mariane ever seen me yet? Hasn't she ever noticed me in passing?

FROSINE: No, but we have often talked about you. I've sketched a portrait of your person and I've not failed to extol your merits and the advantage it would be to her to have a husband such as you.

HARPAGON: You have done well and I thank you for it.

FROSINE: I have, sir, a small favor to ask of you. There's a lawsuit I am about to lose for want of a little money; and you could easily enable me to win this lawsuit if you would show me some kindness. (Harpagon *frowns.*) You would not believe how pleased she will be to see you. (Harpagon *smiles.*) Ah! how you will please her. How admirable an effect on her your old-fashioned ruff will have. But above all, she will be charmed by your breeches, attached to your doublet with laces; that will make her mad for you. And a laced-up lover will be a marvellous treat for her.

HARPAGON: Really! I am delighted to hear you say so.

FROSINE: To tell the truth, sir, this lawsuit is of the greatest consequence to me. I shall be ruined if I lose it. Some slight aid would set right my affairs. (Harpagon *frowns.*) I wish you could see her rapture when I talk to her of you. (Harpagon *smiles again.*) Her eyes shone with joy at the recitation of your qualities. In fact, I have made her extremely impatient to see this marriage completed.

HARPAGON: You have given me great pleasure, Frosine, and I assure you, I am deeply indebted to you.

FROSINE: I beg you, sir, to give me the slight help I ask for. (Harpagon *frowns again.*) It will set me back on my feet, and I shall be eternally obligated to you.

HARPAGON: Goodbye! I am going to finish my letters.

FROSINE: I assure you, sir, you could never assist me in a greater need.

HARPAGON: I will give orders for my carriage to be ready to drive you to the fair.

FROSINE: I would not trouble you, if I were not forced by necessity.

HARPAGON: And I'll take care that we dine early so that you won't get sick.

FROSINE: Do not refuse me the favor I beg of you. You would not believe, sir, the pleasure that—

HARPAGON: I am going. There! Someone is calling me. Until later. (*Exit.*)

FROSINE: May a fever burn you up! Thieving dog! The devil take you! The skinflint has fended off all my attacks. But I mustn't drop the business now. In any case, there's the other party; I'm sure to be well rewarded there.

ACT III

(*On stage:* Harpagon, Cléante, Élise, Valère, Dame Claude, Jacques, Brindavoine, *and* La Merluche.)

HARPAGON: All right! come here, all of you! I want to give you orders for the rest of the day, and assign each of you to your tasks! Come, Dame Claude, I'll begin with you. (*She approaches, carrying a broom.*) Good, you carry your arms along with you. To you I assign the task of cleaning the entire house; but above all take care not to rub the furniture too hard, or you'll wear it out. In addition you're assigned to look after the bottles during supper; and if any are lost, or if anything is broken, I shall hold you responsible and deduct it from your wages.

JACQUES: (*aside*) A shrewd punishment.

HARPAGON: (*to* Dame Claude) Go. (*Exit* Dame Claude.) You, Brindavoine, and you, La Merluche, I put in charge of rinsing the glasses, and serving the drinks, but only when someone is thirsty. And don't be like those impertinent lackeys who deliberately encourage people to drink when they had no intention at all of doing so. Wait until they have asked you more than once, and always remember to keep plenty of water at hand.

JACQUES: (*aside*) Yes, undiluted wine goes to the head.

LA MERLUCHE: Shall we serve without aprons, sir?

HARPAGON: Yes, when you see the guests coming, but be careful not to soil your clothes.

BRINDAVOINE: But, sir you know that one of the lapels of my doublet is covered with a large stain of lamp-oil.

LA MERLUCHE: And I, sir, have a large hole in the back of my breeches, and, begging your pardon, people can see my—

HARPAGON: That's enough! Keep that side discreetly to the wall and always show people your front only. (Harpagon *holds his hat in front of his doublet to show* Brindavoine *how to hide the oil-stain.*) And you must always hold your cap like this when you serve. (*Exeunt* La Merluche *and* Brindavoine.) As for you, my daughter, you must keep an eye on what is cleared away from the table and take care that nothing is wasted. That's a daughter's proper work. But meanwhile, prepare yourself to receive my fiancée, who is coming to visit you and to take you to the fair. Did you hear what I said?

ÉLISE: Yes, father.

HARPAGON: And you, my son, the dandy, whose latest escapade I have been kind enough to pardon, be careful not to make sour faces at her.

CLEANTE: I, father, a sour face? Why should I?

HARPAGON: My God, we all know the attitude of children when their fathers remarry and how they look upon what is called a stepmother. But, if you want me to forget your last prank I recommend above all that you receive this lady pleasantly and give her the best welcome you possibly can.

CLEANTE: To tell you the truth, father, I can't promise you I'll be very glad she is to become my stepmother. I would be lying if I were to tell you so. But as for welcoming her and receiving her pleasantly, I promise to obey you to the letter.

HARPAGON: Take care you do that, at least.

CLEANTE: You'll see that you will have no cause for complaint.

HARPAGON: That will be wise. (*Exeunt* Cléante *and* Élise.) Valère, help me with this. Ho there, Jacques! Come here! I have kept you for the last.

JACQUES: Do you wish to speak to your coachman, sir, or to your cook, for I am both?

HARPAGON: To both of you.

JACQUES: But to which one first?

HARPAGON: The cook.

JACQUES: One moment, then, if you please. (*He takes off his coachman's livery and appears dressed as a cook.*)

HARPAGON: What the deuce does this ceremony mean?

JACQUES: I am at your service, sir.

HARPAGON: Jacques, I am committed to give a supper tonight.

JACQUES: (*aside*) What a miracle!

HARPAGON: Tell me, can you serve us something good?

JACQUES: Yes, if you give me plenty of money.

HARPAGON: What the devil! Always money! It seems they have nothing else to say than money, money, money. Always talking of money. Money is their best friend.

VALERE: I have never heard a more impertinent answer than that. What kind of miracle is it to be able to provide a fine feast with plenty of money? That's the easiest thing in the world to do; any poor fool could do as much. But it's the work of a clever man to arrange good fare with little money.

JACQUES: Good fare with little money?

VALERE: Yes.

JACQUES: Upon my word, Monsieur Steward, you would oblige us if you'd let us in on your secret and take my place as cook. You interfere with so much that you might as well be the factotum.

HARPAGON: Hold your tongue! What shall we need?

JACQUES: There's your steward who will provide you with fine dishes for little money.

HARPAGON: Stop that! I want you to answer me.

JACQUES: How many will there be?

HARPAGON: We will be eight or ten; but you need only provide for eight. When there's enough for eight, there's plenty for ten.

VALERE: Of course.

JACQUES: Very well. We will need four good soups, and five dishes. Soups, entrées—

HARPAGON: What the devil! that's enough to feed an entire city.

JACQUES: Roast—

HARPAGON: (*putting his hand over Jacques's mouth*) Ah, spendthrift, you are eating up all my money!

JACQUES: Side dishes—

HARPAGON: (*again putting his hand over Jacques's mouth*) More?

VALERE: Do you want to make everyone burst? Has our master invited people here to murder them by overeating? Go and read the manual of health, and ask a doctor if there's anything more harmful to a man than eating to excess.

HARPAGON: He's right.

VALERE: You must learn, Jacques, you and your kind, that an overladen table is a cut-throat; that to prove yourself a friend of those you invite, frugality must reign over the meals you serve; and, following the sayings of the ancients, "One should eat to live, and not live to eat."

HARPAGON: Ah! that is well said! Come here; I want to embrace you for those words. That is the most beautiful sentence I've ever heard in my life. "One should live to eat, and not eat to li—' ' No, that's not it. How did you say it?

VALERE: "One should eat to live, and not live to eat."

HARPAGON: (to Jacques) Yes! Do you hear that? (To Valère) Who is the great man who said that?

VALERE: I don't remember his name offhand.

HARPAGON: Don't forget to write those words down for me: I shall have them engraved in gold letters above the mantel-piece of my dining room.

VALERE: I shall not forget. And as for your supper, just leave it to me. I'll arrange everything as it should be.

HARPAGON: Do so.

JACQUES: So much the better; there will be less trouble for me.

HARPAGON: We should have those things people don't eat much of, and which will fill them up quickly—a rather fatty mutton stew, with a meat pie well stuffed with chestnuts.

VALERE: Leave everything to me.

HARPAGON: Now, Jacques, my coach must be cleaned.

JACQUES: Just a moment. This concerns the coachman. (Exit, and reappears in coachman's livery.) You were saying . . .?

HARPAGON: That my coach must be cleaned, and my horses made ready to drive to the fair. . . .

JACQUES: Your horses, sir? My goodness, they are not in a fit state to walk. I won't tell you that they can't get up from their straw; the poor beasts have none at all—so that would be a lie. But you make them observe such strict fasts that they are no more than ideas or ghosts—mere shadows of horses.

HARPAGON: Why should they be sick? They never do anything.

JACQUES: And because they do nothing, sir, is that any reason why they shouldn't eat? It would be much better for them, poor beasts, if they worked a lot and were fed accordingly. It breaks my heart to see them so emaciated, for I have such affection for my horses that when I see them suffering, it's as if I myself were suffering. Everyday I feed them food out of my own mouth. It's a very hard nature, sir, that feels no pity for a fellow creature.

HARPAGON: It won't be too hard work for them to go as far as the fair.

JACQUES: No sir, I haven't the heart to drive them, and my conscience would bother me if I gave them a lash of the whip, the state they're in. How can you expect them to draw a carriage when they can't drag themselves?

VALERE: Sir, I will ask our neighbor Picard if he will drive them. Besides, we shall need him to help us prepare the supper.

JACQUES: Very well. I'd much rather they died under someone else's hands than mine.

VALERE: Jacques is becoming an arguer.

JACQUES: Monsieur Steward is becoming a busybody.

HARPAGON: Enough!

JACQUES: Sir, I cannot endure flatterers. I see what he is doing. His perpetual surveillance over the bread, wine, wood, salt, and candles has no other end than to inch up to you, to win your favor. It makes me mad, and it grieves me to hear what people are saying about you every day. For I do have a real affection for you, in spite of myself, and after my horses, you are the person I like most.

HARPAGON: Might I know, Jacques, what people are saying about me?

JACQUES: Yes, sir, if I could be sure it wouldn't make you angry.

HARPAGON: No, not in the least.

JACQUES: Begging your pardon, I know only too well I shall make you angry.

HARPAGON: Not at all. On the contrary, it will give me pleasure. I shall be most glad to learn what they say about me.

JACQUES: Since you wish it, sir, I will tell you frankly that everyone everywhere laughs at you. On all sides, they make a hundred jokes about you. And nothing pleases them more than to pull you to pieces and to tell endless stories of your stinginess. One person says you have special almanacs printed, in which you double the ember days and vigils, in order to profit from the fasts you make your household keep. Another says you always have a quarrel ready with your servants when it's time to give New Year's gifts or when one of them is leaving, so that you can find an excuse for not giving them something. This one tells the story that you once brought a lawsuit against a neighbor's cat for having eaten the remains of a leg of mutton. That one says you were caught one night stealing the hay from your own horses, and that your coachman—the one who preceded me—gave you I don't know how many blows with his stick in the dark, about which you never said a word. Shall I go on? We can't go anywhere without hearing you pulled inside out. You are the joke and laughingstock of the whole world. And they never talk of you except by the name of miser, skinflint, villain, or usurer.

HARPAGON (beating him):   You're an idiot, a scoundrel, a rascal, and an impudent knave.

JACQUES: Oh! Oh! didn't I predict it? You wouldn't believe me. I warned you that I'd make you angry if I told you the truth.

HARPAGON: That will teach you how to talk. (Exit.)

VALERE: (laughing) From what I can see, Jacques, your frankness has paid off rather badly.

JACQUES: By God! Monsieur Newcomer—who thinks he's a man of importance—it's none of your business. Laugh at your own beatings, when you get them, and don't come laughing at mine.

VALERE: Ah! Jacques, don't be angry, I beg of you.

JACQUES: (aside) He's backing down. I'll bully him, and if he's fool enough to be afraid of me, I'll thrash him a bit. (To Valère) Do you know, Monsieur Laugher, that I never laugh? And that if you arouse my anger, I'll make you laugh out of the other side of your mouth? (Jacques pushes Valère to the back of the stage, threatening him.)

VALERE: Gently, now!

JACQUES: What do you mean gently? I don't want to be gentle.

VALERE: Pray—

JACQUES: You're an impudent fellow.

VALERE: My dear Monsieur Jacques!

JACQUES: There's no "my dear Monsieur Jacques" for a nobody like you. If I had a club, I'd beat the importance out of you.

VALERE: What! a club? (Valère picks up a stick and makes Jacques retreat.)

JACQUES: Er, I didn't mean that.

VALERE: Do you know, Monsieur Fool, that I'm just the man to give you a good beating?

JACQUES: I don't doubt it.

VALERE: And that, for all your soups, you're nothing at all but a pot-washing cook?
JACQUES: I know it.
VALERE: And that you don't know me yet?
JACQUES: Pardon me.
VALERE: You'll thrash me, you said?
JACQUES: I was only joking.
VALERE: I don't care at all for your jokes. (*He thrashes him with the stick.*) Learn what a poor joker you are. (*Exit.*)
JACQUES: A plague on sincerity. It's a bad business. I give it up from now on, and I'll no longer tell the truth. My master, at least, has some right to beat me, but as for this steward, I'll get revenge on him if I can.

(*Enter* Frosine *and* Mariane.)

FROSINE: Jacques, do you know if your master is at home?
JACQUES: Yes, indeed, he is. I know only too well.
FROSINE: Tell him, if you please, that we are here. (*Exit* Jacques.)
MARIANE: Ah, Frosine, what a strange position I am in. And, if I may speak out my thoughts, how I dread this meeting.
FROSINE: But why? What makes you uneasy?
MARIANE: Alas! Need you ask me? Can you not imagine the fears of a girl about to see the rack on which she is to be bound?
FROSINE: I see well enough that Harpagon is not the rack you'd willingly embrace for a pleasant death, and I can tell from your face that you are thinking again of the fair young man you spoke to me about.
MARIANE: Yes. I do not wish to deny that, Frosine. The respectful visits he has paid us have, I admit, made some impression on my heart.
FROSINE: But have you found out who he is?
MARIANE: No, I do not know who he is, but I know he is made to be loved; that, if things were up to me, I would have him rather than any other man, and that he contributes not a little to my vision of horrible torment in the arms of the man chosen for me.
FROSINE: Oh, Lord, all these fair young men are agreeable, and play their roles quite well; but most of them are poor as church-mice. It's best for you to take an old husband who can give you material comfort. I admit that the senses aren't fully satisfied by the course I advise, and that there are several petty revulsions to overcome with such a husband. But that won't last, and his death, I assure you, will soon put you in a position to take a more agreeable husband, who will make things all right.
MARIANE: Oh, my goodness, Frosine, it is a strange business where, to be happy, one must wish and wait for the death of someone. And death does not always come to suit our plans.
FROSINE: Are you jesting? You are marrying him only on the condition that he will soon make you a widow; that ought to be one of the articles in the marriage contract. It would be most impertinent of him not to die within three months.—Here he comes in person.
MARIANE: Oh. Frosine, what a figure!

(*Enter* Harpagon.)

HARPAGON: Do not be offended, my pretty one, if I come to you wearing spectacles. I know that your charms strike the unaided eye—that they are visible in themselves—and that spectacles are not necessary in order to see them. But after all, it is with lenses that one observes the stars, and I claim and guarantee that you are a star, the most beautiful star in the world of stars. Frosine, she makes no reply, and displays, I think, no joy in seeing me.

FROSINE: Because she is still taken by surprise. Furthermore, girls are ashamed to display immediately what their hearts feel.

HARPAGON: You are right. (*To* Mariane) Here, my little one, is my daughter, who comes to welcome you.

(*Enter* Élise.)

MARIANE: I have delayed my visit too long, Madam.

ÉLISE: *You* have done, Madam, what *I* ought to have done. I ought to have come first to you.

HARPAGON: You can see how tall she is; but weeds always flourish.

MARIANE: (*whispering to* Frosine) What a horrid man!

HARPAGON: What is the lovely creature saying?

FROSINE: That she finds you admirable.

HARPAGON: You do me too great an honor, adorable darling.

MARIANE: (*aside*) What a beast!

HARPAGON: I am most obliged to you for these sentiments.

MARIANE: (*aside*) I cannot bear any more.

(*Enter* Cléante.)

HARPAGON: Here is my son, who also comes to pay you his respects.

MARIANE: (*looks at* Cléante *and whispers to* Frosine) Ah, Frosine, what a coincidence! It is the very young man I told you of.

FROSINE: (*to* Mariane) What odd luck!

HARPAGON: I see you are astonished to see me with such grown-up children. But I shall soon be rid of both them.

CLEANTE: Madam, to tell the truth, I certainly did not expect this encounter. My father surprised me not a little when he recently told me of the plans he had made.

MARIANE: I may say the same. This is an unforeseen meeting which surprises me as well as you; I was not at all prepared for such an occurrence.

CLEANTE: Madam, it is true that my father could not make a better choice, and the honor of seeing you gives me heartfelt joy. But, for all that, I cannot assure you that I rejoice in the plan to make you my stepmother. That congratulation, I confess, is beyond me. It is a title, if you please, that I do not wish for you. This greeting will seem brutal to some eyes, but I am confident that you will be one to take it as it was intended. This is a marriage, Madam, which you can well imagine I have an aversion to. You cannot be ignorant, knowing who I am, how it conflicts with my interests. And you will allow me to tell you, with my father's permission, that if matters depended on me, this marriage would not take place.

HARPAGON: This is a most impertinent congratulation! What a fine admission to make to her!

MARIANE: And I, in reply, must say the same to you. If you have an aversion to seeing me your stepmother, I feel no less at seeing you my stepson. Do not think, I beg you, it is I who sought to cause you this uneasiness. I would be most disturbed to cause you any displeasure. And, if I am not forced to it by despotic power, I give you my word that I will not consent to a marriage which grieves you.

HARPAGON: She's right. A foolish compliment deserves an answer of the same sort. I beg your pardon, my fair lady, for my son's impertinence. He's a young fool who has not yet learned the consequences of the words he speaks.

MARIANE: I assure you that what he has told me is not at all offensive. On the contrary, he pleased me by thus explaining his real feelings. I like such an open avowal as his, and if he had spoken otherwise, I should think less of him.

HARPAGON: It is too good of you to wish thus to excuse his faults. Time will make him wiser, and you will see that he will change his sentiments.

CLEANTE: No, father, I am incapable of changing them, and I urgently beg Madam to believe me.

HARPAGON: What madness! He's worse than ever.

CLEANTE: Would you want me to betray my heart?

HARPAGON: Again? Let's change the conversation.

CLEANTE: Well, since you wish me to speak in a different manner, allow me, Madam, to put myself in my father's place and to tell you that in all the world I have seen nothing so charming as you. I can conceive of nothing equal to the happiness of pleasing you, and the title of your husband is a glory, a felicity which I would prefer to the fates of the greatest princes of the earth. Yes, Madam, the happiness of possessing you is, in my eyes, the most beautiful of fortunes. All my ambition is directed to that. There is nothing that I am incapable of in order to make so precious a conquest, and the most insuperable obstacles—

HARPAGON: Easy, son, if you please.

CLEANTE: I am complimenting Madam on your behalf.

HARPAGON: My God, I have a tongue to talk for myself, and I don't need any intermediary like you. Come, bring some chairs.

FROSINE: No. It would be best to go to the fair now, so that we can return sooner and have the remaining time for conversation.

HARPAGON: Have the horses hitched to the carriage.—I beg you, fair lady, to excuse me for not having thought to offer you some refreshment before leaving.

CLEANTE: I have provided for some, father, and have ordered some bowls of China oranges, candied lemons, and preserves, which I have sent for in you name.

HARPAGON: (*in a low voice, to* Valère) Valère!

VALERE (*to* Harpagon):   He's out of his mind.

CLEANTE: Father, do you think this is not enough? Madam will have the kindness to forgive it, I trust.

MARIANE: It was quite unnecessary.

CLEANTE: (*as Harpagon offers his hand to lead* Mariane *to the carriage*) Madam, have you ever seen a diamond more brilliant than the one on my father's finger?

MARIANE: It sparkles brightly, indeed.

CLEANTE: (*taking the ring from his father's finger and placing it on* Mariane's) You must see it close up.

MARIANE: It is most handsome, indeed, and full of fire.

CLEANTE: (*placing himself before* Mariane, *who wishes to return the ring*) No, no, Madam, it is on too beautiful a hand. It is a gift which my father gives you.

HARPAGON: I?

CLEANTE: Father, isn't it true that you wish Madam to keep it for your love's sake?

HARPAGON: (*aside, to his son*) What?
CLEANTE: A charming request. He indicates to me that I should make you accept it.
MARIANE: But I do not wish—
CLEANTE: Are you jesting? He does not wish to take it back.
HARPAGON: (*aside*) I'm furious!
MARIANE: It would be—
CLEANTE: (*still preventing* Mariane *from returning the ring*) No, I tell you, you will offend him.
MARIANE: For pity's sake—
CLEANTE: Not at all.
HARPAGON: (*aside*) May the plague—
CLEANTE: See how shocked he is by your refusal?
HARPAGON: (*low, to his son*) Ah, traitor!
CLEANTE: You see how he is driven to despair.
HARPAGON: (*low, threatening his son*) Scoundrel!
CLEANTE: Madam, you are making my father angry with me.
HARPAGON: (*low, continues to threaten* Cléante) You rogue!
CLEANTE: You will make him ill. Pray, Madam, do not resist any further.
FROSINE: My God, what a fuss! Keep the ring, since Monsieur wishes you to.
MARIANE: In order not to anger you, I shall keep it for now, and I will take some other opportunity to return it to you.

(*Enter* Brindavoine.)

BRINDAVOINE: Sir, there is a man who wishes to speak to you.
HARPAGON: Tell him I'm busy; tell him to come back some other time.
BRINDAVOINE: He says he brings you some money.
HARPAGON: (*to* Mariane) I shall return immediately.
LA MERLUCHE: (*running in, knock,* Harpagon *over*) Sir—
HARPAGON: Oh, I'm killed!
CLEANTE: What is it, father? Have you hurt yourself?
HARPAGON: This traitor must have been bribed by my debtors to break my neck.
VALERE: (*to* Harpagon) It's nothing.
LA MERLUCHE: Sir, I beg your pardon; I meant well in hurrying.
HARPAGON: Well, what are you here for, you wretch?
LA MERLUCHE: To tell you your two horses are shoeless.
HARPAGON: Have them taken to the blacksmith immediately.
CLEANTE: While we're waiting to have them shod, father, I will do the honors of your house for you, and show Madam to the garden, where the refreshments shall be brought.

(*Exeunt all but* Harpagon *and* Valère.)

HARPAGON: Valère, keep you eye on them, and take care, please, to save as much as you can to return to the shop.
VALERE: (*leaving*) I understand. (*Exit.*)
HARPAGON: (*alone*) Impertinent son! Have you set out to ruin me?

ACT IV

(Enter Cléante, Mariane, Élise, *and* Frosine.*)*

CLEANTE: Let us go in here; we shall be safer. There are no suspicious people around, and we can talk freely.

ÉLISE: Yes, Madam, my brother has confided to me the love he feels for you. I know the grief and the unpleasantness such obstacles can cause, and, I assure you, I am deeply sympathetic to your difficulties.

MARIANE: It is a pleasant consolation when someone like you sympathizes with one's problems. And I beg you, Madam, always to preserve your generous affection for me—an affection so capable of softening the cruelties of fate.

FROSINE: On my word, you are both unlucky people, not to have told me of the situtation sooner. I would undoubtedly have warded off this mishap and not brought things as far as they are now.

CLEANTE: How could we help it? My evil destiny has willed this. But, fair Mariane, what have you resolved to do?

MARIANE: Alas! Can I resolve to do anything? Dependent as I am, can I do more than wish?

CLEANTE: Can I find no other encouragement within your heart but simple wishes? No tender pity? No helpful goodwill? No lively affection?

MARIANE: What can I say to you? Put yourself in my place and see what I might do. Advise me, command me yourself! I will place myself in your hands; I think you are too fair-minded a person to demand from me more than what honor and decency permit.

CLEANTE: Alas! To what am I reduced when you bind me with the vexing sentiments of rigorous honor and scrupulous decency!

MARIANE: But what would you have me do? Even if I could disregard many of the restrictions which bind my sex, I must have some consideration for my mother. She brought me up most tenderly, and I could never make up my mind to cause her pain. You do something with her; deal with her; do your utmost to win her sympathy. I give you permission to do and say what you will; and if nothing is lacking except my approval, I am willing to avow to her all that I feel for you.

CLEANTE: Frosine, dear Frosine, won't you help us?

FROSINE: Good Lord, need you ask? I want to, with all my heart. My nature, you know, is pretty human. Heaven didn't give me a heart of iron, and I am only too well disposed to render little services to people decently and honestly in love. But what can we do about this situation?

CLEANTE: Give it a little thought. I beg you.

MARIANE: Show us some way out.

ÉLISE: Find some means to undo what you have done.

FROSINE: That's quite difficult. (*To* Mariane) As for your mother, she's not unreasonable; perhaps we could win her over and induce her to give the son the gift she plans to give the father. (*To* Cléante) But the real trouble here is—that your father is your father.

CLEANTE: Too true!

FROSINE: (*to* Mariane) I mean that he will be spiteful if he's rejected, and he will not be willing, later, to consent to the marriage. The best thing would be for the rejection to come from himself and for you to attempt in some way to make him disgusted with you.

CLEANTE: You're right.

FROSINE: Yes, I'm right, I know that well enough. That's the only way, but how the deuce can we find the means.—Wait! Suppose we found a woman, somewhat along in years, and who had my talent, who acted well enough to counterfeit a lady of quality, with the help of a hastily collected entourage, and some bizarre name of a marchioness or viscountess, say from Lower Brittany. I've enough skill to make your father think her rich, with a hundred thousand écus in cash as well as great houses, and so madly in love with him and so determined to be his wife, that she would give all her wealth for a marriage contract. I've not the slightest doubt that he'd lend an ear to the proposition, for, though he loves you well, I know he loves money a little more. And, dazzled by this bait, when he once consents to your wishes, it won't matter much if later he is disabused when he wants to see more precisely our marchioness' property.

CLEANTE: Excellently planned!

FROSINE: Leave it to me. I've just thought of a friend of mine who'll suit our purpose exactly.

CLEANTE: Frosine, you can be sure of my gratitude if you succeed. But, charming Mariane, let us begin, I beg you, by winning over your mother; it will be something to break off this marriage. I beg you to make every possible effort. Use over her all the power which her affection for you gives you; display, without reserve, the eloquent graces, the all-powerful charms which Heaven placed in your eyes and on your lips. And I beg of you, overlook none of those soft words, those gentle prayers, those sweet caresses to which, I am sure, nothing can be refused.

MARIANE: I shall do all I can; I will overlook nothing.

(Enter Harpagon, *unseen.)*

HARPAGON: *(aside)* What! My son kissing the hand of his intended step-mother, and his intended stepmother not objecting very strongly! Can there be something behind all this?

ÉLISE: Here comes father!

HARPAGON: The carriage is ready. You can leave as soon as you like.

CLEANTE: Since you are not going, father, I will accompany them.

HARPAGON: No, you stay here. They will be all right by themselves, and I need you.

(Exeunt Mariane, Élise, *and* Frosine.)

Well, now, putting aside the question of a stepmother, what do you think of the lady?

CLEANTE: What do I think of her?

HARPAGON: Yes! Of her manner, her figure, her beauty, her mind?

CLEANTE: So-so.

HARPAGON: Be more precise.

CLEANTE: To speak frankly, I have not found her to be what I expected. Her manner is that of an out-and-out coquette, her figure rather awkward, her beauty very mediocre, and her mind most ordinary. Don't think, father, that this is said to disgust you with her, for, stepmother for stepmother, I like this one as well as another.

HARPAGON: But just now you were telling her—

CLEANTE: I was saying sweet nothings in your name, but only to please you.

HARPAGON: Then you don't feel any inclination for her?

CLEANTE: I? None at all!

HARPAGON: That's too bad, for it spoils a plan that had occurred to me. Seeing her here, I reflected on my age, and I thought that people might talk about my marrying so young a girl. This consideration made me drop the idea, but, as I have asked for her hand and have given her my word, I would have given her to you if you hadn't shown your aversion.

CLEANTE: To me?

HARPAGON: To you.

CLEANTE: In marriage?

HARPAGON: In marriage.

CLEANTE: Listen: it's true that she isn't much to my taste, but to please you, father, I will resign myself to marrying her, if you wish.

HARPAGON: I? I am more reasonable than you think; I will not force your inclinations.

CLEANTE: Pardon me; I will make this effort out of affection for you.

HARPAGON: No, no: a marriage can't be happy if the heart isn't in it.

CLEANTE: Perhaps it will be, later, father; they say that love is often the fruit of marriage.

HARPAGON: The man ought to risk nothing in such a situation; grievous consequences may follow which I don't want to be responsible for. If you had felt a liking for her, fine; I would have had her marry you instead of me; but, that not being the case, I'll follow my original plan and marry her myself.

CLEANTE: Look, father. Since things have come to this, I must disclose our secret. The truth is that I have loved her since the day I first saw her taking a walk. My plan, until just recently, was to ask your permission to make her my wife, and only your declaration of your feelings and my fear of displeasing you restrained me.

HARPAGON: Have you paid her any visits?

CLEANTE: Yes, father.

HARPAGON: Often?

CLEANTE: Enough, considering how little time there has been.

HARPAGON: Have you been well received?

CLEANTE: Very well, but without her knowing who I was. That is why Mariane was so surprised just now.

HARPAGON: Have you declared your love and your intention to marry her?

CLEANTE: Certainly, and I've even made some overtures to her mother about it.

HARPAGON: Did she listen to your proposal for her daughter?

CLEANTE: Yes, most civilly.

HARPAGON: And does the daughter return your love?

CLEANTE: If I can believe appearances, father, I think she has some affection for me.

HARPAGON: (softly, aside) I am delighted to have learned this secret; it's just what I wanted to know. (Aloud) Now, my son, do you know what you have to do? You must think, if you please, of getting rid of your love, of ceasing to pursue a lady I intend for myself, and of marrying shortly the one I have decided on for you.

CLEANTE: So, father, this is how you trick me! Very well. Since it's come to this, I declare to you that I will never give up my love for Mariane, that there is no extremity from which I will shrink to prevent your triumph, and that if you have the mother's consent on your behalf, I shall have other resources, perhaps, which will fight on mine.

HARPAGON: What, you rogue! You dare to hunt my game?

CLEANTE: It's you who are hunting mine; I was there first.

HARPAGON: Am I not your father? Don't you owe me respect?

CLEANTE: This is not a matter where children are obliged to defer to their parents; love is no respecter of persons.

HARPAGON: I'll make you respect me with a good stick.

CLEANTE: All your threats will accomplish nothing.

HARPAGON: You shall renounce Mariane.

CLEANTE: I will do nothing of the sort.

HARPAGON: (*calling out*) Quick, give me a stick.

JACQUES: (*entering*) Ah, ah, gentlemen, what's all this? What can you be thinking of?

CLEANTE: I couldn't care less.

JACQUES: (*to* Cléante) Ah, sir, gently.

HARPAGON: To talk so impudently to me!

JACQUES: (*to* Harpagon) Ah, sir, for Heaven's sake.

CLEANTE: I won't yield an inch.

JACQUES: (*to* Cléante) What! This to your father?

HARPAGON: Let me get at him.

JACQUES: (*to* Harpagon) What! This to your son? You're not dealing with me, you know.

HARPAGON: Jacques, I'll make you the judge in this affair, to prove I'm right.

JACQUES: I'm agreeable. (*To* Cléante) Stand away a little, please.

HARPAGON: I love a girl whom I want to marry—and this rogue has the insolence to love her, too—and despite my orders, he wants to marry her.

JACQUES: Ah! He is wrong.

HARPAGON: Isn't it frightful for a son to wish to compete with his father? Shouldn't he, out of respect, refrain from meddling with my intentions?

JACQUES: You are right. Let me speak to him while you stay here. (*He goes to* Cléante *at the other end of the stage.*)

CLEANTE: Well, all right, if he wants to appoint you as judge, I won't hold back. I don't care who the judge is, and I am willing to refer our differences to you, Jacques.

JACQUES: I am honored.

CLEANTE: I love a young lady who returns my affection and who tenderly accepts the offer of my love. But my father decides to come along and interfere in our love by making her an offer himself.

JACQUES: He's certainly wrong.

CLEANTE: Shouldn't he be ashamed, at his age, to think of marrying? Does it still become him to be amorous? Shouldn't he leave that to younger people?

JACQUES: You're right. He's joking. Let me have a word with him. (*He goes back to* Harpagon.) Well, your son isn't as difficult as you think, and he will be reasonable. He says that he knows the respect he owes you, that he was only carried away by momentary passion, and that he will not refuse to submit to your wishes, provided that you will treat him better than you now do, and will give him someone in marriage with whom he will be content.

HARPAGON: Ah! In that case, Jacques, tell him that he can expect everything of me, and that, except for Mariane, I give him freedom to choose whomever he wishes.

JACQUES: Let me handle it. (*He goes to* Cléante.) Well, your father isn't so unreasonable as you make out. He explained that your violence angered him; that he objects only to your behavior, and that he is quite willing to agree to what you wish, provided you behave gently and show him the deference, the respect, and the submission a son owes a father.

CLEANTE: Ah! Jacques, you may assure him that if he will give me Mariane, he will always find me the most submissive of men, and I shall never do anything against his wishes.

JACQUES: (*to* Harpagon) Everything's arranged. He agrees to what you say.

HARPAGON: Then things will go excellently.

JACQUES: (*to* Cléante) Everything's arranged. He is satisfied with your promise.

CLEANTE: Heaven be praised!

JACQUES: Gentlemen, you have only to talk together. You are in agreement now; you were about to quarrel simply for want of understanding each other.

CLEANTE: Good Jacques, I am indebted to you for the rest of my life.

JACQUES: It is nothing, sir.

HARPAGON: You have pleased me, Jacques, and you deserve a reward. (Harpagon *reaches into his pocket;* Jacques *extends his hand, but* Harpagon *only pulls out a handkerchief.*) Go, now, I'll keep it in mind, I assure you.

JACQUES: Your servant, sir. (*Exit.*)

CLEANTE: I ask your pardon, father, for the anger I've shown.

HARPAGON: It's nothing.

CLEANTE: I assure you that I am filled with regret.

HARPAGON: And I, I am filled with joy to see you so reasonable.

CLEANTE: How generous of you to forget my fault so quickly!

HARPAGON: A father easily forgets his children's faults when they return to their duty.

CLEANTE: Ah, then you harbor no resentment for all my outrageous behavior?

HARPAGON: You force me not to, by the submission and respect which you show.

CLEANTE: Father, I promise you that to my death I will preserve the memory of your kindness.

HARPAGON: And as for me, I promise that there is nothing which you shall not obtain from me.

CLEANTE: Oh, father, I ask no more of you; you have given me enough in giving me Mariane.

HARPAGON: What?

CLEANTE: I say, father, that I am quite content, and that you give me everything when you give me Mariane.

HARPAGON: Who's talking about giving you Mariane?

CLEANTE: You, father.

HARPAGON: Me?

CLEANTE: Certainly.

HARPAGON: What! *You* are the one who promised to renounce her!

CLEANTE: Me? Renounce her?

HARPAGON: Yes!

CLEANTE: Not at all!

HARPAGON: Then you haven't given up your claim to her?

CLEANTE: On the contrary, I hold to it now more than ever.

HARPAGON: What! Again, you scoundrel?

CLEANTE: Nothing can change me!

HARPAGON: Let me at you, you wretch!

CLEANTE: Do whatever you please.

HARPAGON: I forbid you from ever coming into my sight.

CLEANTE: Fine.

HARPAGON: I disown you.

CLEANTE: Disown me.

HARPAGON: I renounce you as my son.

CLEANTE: So be it.

HARPAGON: I disinherit you.

CLEANTE: Whatever you please.

HARPAGON: (*rushing out*) I give you my curse. (*Exit.*)

CLEANTE: (*shouting after him*) I don't want any of your gifts.

LA FLECHE: (*entering from the garden with a money box in his hand*) Ah! sir, I've found you just in the nick of time. Follow me, quickly!

CLEANTE: What's the matter?

LA FLECHE: Follow me, I say. Everything's all right.

CLEANTE: How do you mean?

LA FLECHE: Here's your answer. (*Shows him a money box.*)

CLEANTE: What?

LA FLECHE: I've kept my eye on this all day.

CLEANTE: What is it?

LA FLECHE: Your father's money—which I've got hold of.

CLEANTE: How did you get it?

LA FLECHE: You'll hear everything. Let's get away—I hear him calling. (*Exeunt.*)

HARPAGON: (*enters from the garden hatless and shouting*) Thieves. thieves! Assassins! Murderers! Justice, merciful Heaven! I am lost, I am killed! They've cut my throat, they've stolen my money! Who can it be? What has become of him? Where is he? Where is he hiding? What shall I do to find him? Where shall I run? Where shall I not run? Is he there? Is he here? (*Seeing his own shadow on the wall.*) Who is that? Stop! (*Seizing his own arm.*) Give me back my money, villain! Ah! It's me. My mind's in a turmoil and I don't know where I am, who I am, or what I'm doing. Alas! My poor money, my poor money, my dear friend, they have deprived me of you. And with you taken away from me, I have lost my support, my consolation, my joy; all is over for me, and I have nothing further to do on earth. Without you, life is impossible. All is over, I can bear no more, I am dying, I am dead, I am buried. Will no one revive me by returning my dear money or by telling me who took it? Eh? (*To someone in the audience*) What are you saying? There's no one. Whoever did this must have been watching for exactly the right moment, and he chose just the time when I was speaking to that treacherous son of mine. I must go out! I must find the police and have the whole household examined: servants, valets, son, daughter—and myself, too. What a mob! Everyone I look at is suspect, and they all look like thieves. Eh? What are they talking about over there? Of the man who robbed me? What's that noise up there? Is the thief there? For Heaven's sake, if anyone knows anything about the thief, I implore him to tell me. Isn't he hiding down there among you? They are all looking up at me and beginning to laugh. You'll see, doubtless, that they all had a share in the theft. Come, quickly, police, provosts, judges, thumbscrews and racks, gibbets and executioners. I'll have everybody hanged—and if I don't get back my money, I'll hang myself afterwards.

ACT V

(*Enter* Harpagon, *an* Officer, *and his* Clerk.)

OFFICER: (*calmly*) Let me handle it. I know my business, thank Heaven.

Today isn't the first time I've dealt with robbery. I wish I had a bag of a thousand francs for every person I've had hanged.

HARPAGON: (*excitedly*) Every magistrate is involved in this affair; and if they don't get my money back, I'll demand justice of Justice itself.

OFFICER: We shall take all the necessary steps. There was, you said, in the box . . . ?

HARPAGON: Exactly ten thousand écus!

OFFICER: Ten thousand écus?

HARPAGON: Ten thousand écus.

OFFICER: A considerable theft.

HARPAGON: No torture is too great for such an enormous crime; and if it goes unpunished, the most sacred things are no longer safe.

OFFICER: What denominations was this sum in?

HARPAGON: In good louis d'or and solid pistoles.

OFFICER: Whom do you suspect of the theft?

HARPAGON: Everyone. I want you to arrest the whole city and the suburbs.

OFFICER: Take my word for it, we must not frighten anybody, but must try to get the evidence quietly so that later we can rigorously act to recover the money stolen from you.

JACQUES: (*enters at the far end of the stage, speaking over his shoulder*) I'll be back soon. Meanwhile, have them slit his throat, scorch his feet, put him in boiling water, and hang him from the ceiling.

HARPAGON: Who? The man who robbed me?

JACQUES: I'm talking about the suckling pig your steward has just sent in for supper, and I want to prepare it for you in my own special way.

HARPAGON: That's not the problem; here is a gentleman to whom you must talk about another matter.

OFFICER: Don't be alarmed. I'm not the man to accuse you unfairly, and matters will be handled gently.

JACQUES: Is the gentleman a dinner guest?

OFFICER: You must hide nothing from your master, my friend.

JACQUES: Good Lord, sir, I'll show all I know, and serve you the best I can.

HARPAGON: That's not the problem.

JACQUES: If I don't give you as sumptuous a dinner as I'd like to, it's your steward's fault, who clipped my wings with the scissors of his economy.

HARPAGON: Wretch, it concerns something other than supper; I want you to give me some information about the money someone has stolen from me.

JACQUES: Someone has taken your money?

HARPAGON: Yes, scoundrel. And I'll have you hanged if you don't give it back.

OFFICER: Heavens, don't abuse him. I see by his face that he's an honest man and that without being jailed he will tell you what you want to know. Yes, my friend, if you tell us, no harm will come to you, and your master will reward you appropriately. Today someone stole his money, and you must know something about the affair.

JACQUES: (*aside*) Here's just what I need to be revenged on the steward: ever since he came into the house he's been favored; they listen only to his advice. And I won't forget the beating I got.

HARPAGON: What are you mumbling?

OFFICER: Let him alone. He's getting ready to do as you wish. I told you he was an honest man.

JACQUES: Sir, if you want the truth, I think that your steward is responsible.

HARPAGON: Valère?

JACQUES: Yes.

HARPAGON: He, who seemed so faithful?

JACQUES: The very same! I think he's the one who robbed you.

HARPAGON: On what grounds do you think so?

JACQUES: On what grounds?

HARPAGON: Yes.

JACQUES: I think so on the grounds . . . that I think so.

OFFICER: But it is necessary to cite what evidence you have.

HARPAGON: Have you seen him prowling around the place where I put my money?

JACQUES: Yes, indeed. Where was your money?

HARPAGON: In the garden.

JACQUES: Exactly. I saw him prowling around in the garden. What was the money in?

HARPAGON: In a money box.

JACQUES: That's it. I saw him with a money box.

HARPAGON: What was this money box like? I'll soon see if it is mine.

JACQUES: What was it like?

HARPAGON: Yes!

JACQUES: It was like . . . it was like a money box.

OFFICER: Naturally, that's understood. But describe it a little, so we can visualize it.

JACQUES: It is a large money box.

HARPAGON: The one they stole from me is small.

JACQUES: Yes! it *is* small, if you consider its size. But I call it large considering its contents.

OFFICER: What color is it?

JACQUES: What color?

OFFICER: Yes.

JACQUES: Its color is . . . well, a certain color. Can't you help me express it?

HARPAGON: Ah!

JACQUES: Isn't it red?

HARPAGON: No, gray.

JACQUES: Ah, yes, grayish red; that's what I meant.

HARPAGON: There's no doubt about it. That's absolutely it. Write, sir, write down his testimony. Heavens! Whom can I trust from now on? One can no longer swear to anything. After this I could believe that I would rob myself.

JACQUES: Sir, here he comes. Be sure not to tell him that it was I who revealed this to you.

(*Enter* Valère.)

HARPAGON: Come here! Come and confess the blackest deed, the most horrible crime ever committed.

VALERE: What do you mean, sir?

HARPAGON: What, traitor! You do not blush for your crime?

VALERE: What crime are you talking about?

HARPAGON: What crime am I talking about: Infamous wretch! As though you don't know what I mean. You seek to cover up in vain. The deed is revealed; I have just learned all. Ah! To abuse my kindness like this and to get yourself into my house expressly to betray me, to play such a trick on me!

VALERE: Sir, since everything has been revealed to you, I will not sidestep or deny the matter.

JACQUES: (aside) Aha! Could I have unconsciously guessed right?

VALERE: I planned to speak to you, and I wanted to wait for a favorable moment, but since this is the way things are, I implore you not to be angry, and to listen to my motives.

HARPAGON: And what fine motives can you give me, infamous thief?

VALERE: Ah, sir, I do not deserve these names. True, I have committed an offense against you, but, after all, the fault is pardonable.

HARPAGON: What? Pardonable? A sneak attack, a murder like that?

VALERE: For Heaven's sake, don't get angry. When you have heard me out, you will see that the harm isn't as great as you make it.

HARPAGON: The harm isn't as great as I make it! What! My blood! My vitals! Villain!

VALERE: Sir, your blood has not fallen into evil hands. I am of a rank not to wrong it, and there is nothing in all this that I cannot fully repair.

HARPAGON: That is fully my intention; you must restore to me what you have robbed me of.

VALERE: Sir, your honor will be fully satisfied.

HARPAGON: There is no question of honor involved. But tell me, who drove you to such a deed?

VALERE: Ah, you have to ask me that?

HARPAGON: I most certainly do.

VALERE: A god who is his own excuse for all that he makes us do: Love.

HARPAGON: Love?

VALERE: Yes.

HARPAGON: A fine love, a fine love, indeed. Love of my louis d'or.

VALERE: No, sir your wealth did not tempt me at all; that does not dazzle me, and I insist that I care nothing for all your property, provided vou let me keep what I have.

HARPAGON: By the devil, I'll do no such thing! I will not let you keep it. What insolence to want to keep what he has stolen!

VALERE: You call it stealing?

HARPAGON: Yes, I call it stealing. A treasure like that!

VALERE: It is indeed a treasure, and doubtless the most precious you have; but it is not losing it to let me have it. On my knees I ask for this treasure full of charms. And, indeed, you must award it to me.

HARPAGON: I'll do nothing of the sort. Why talk like this?

VALERE: We have pledged our mutual faith; we have sworn never to be parted.

HARPAGON: The pledge is admirable, and the promise amusing.

VALERE: Yes, we are bound to one another, forever.

HARPAGON: I'll prevent that, I guarantee you.

VALERE: Nothing but death can separate us.

HARPAGON: You are devilishly set on my money.

VALERE: Sir, I have already told you that your money did not drive me to do what I have done. My heart was not at all moved by the motives you think; a more noble goal inspired my resolution.

HARPAGON: Next you'll see that it is from Christian charity that he wants my money. But I'll take care of that; and the law, you outrageous scoundrel, will give me justice.

VALERE: Do what you please, and I shall readily suffer all the violence you like; but I beg you to believe, at least, that if harm has been done, I alone am to blame, and that your daughter is in no way guilty.

HARPAGON: I'm sure of that! It would certainly be strange if my daughter were involved in this crime. But I want to regain my property and I want you to confess where you've carried my treasure off to.

VALERE: I? I haven't carried your treasure out of the house.

HARPAGON: (aside) Ah, my dear money box. (Aloud) Not left my house?

VALERE: No, sir.

HARPAGON: Ah! Tell me now, you haven't tampered . . . ?

VALERE: I? Tamper? Ah, you wrong us. I burn with a wholly pure and respectful ardor.

HARPAGON: (aside) Burn for my money box?

VALERE: I would rather die than express any offensive thought. Your treasure is too wise and too modest for that.

HARPAGON: (aside) My money box too modest!

VALERE: All my desires are limited to the pleasures of gazing, and nothing criminal has profaned the passion those beautiful eyes have inspired in me.

HARPAGON: (aside) My money box's beautiful eyes? He talks like a lover about his mistress.

VALERE: Sir, Dame Claude knows the whole truth, and she can testify—

HARPAGON: What? My servant is an accomplice?

VALERE: Yes, sir, she was a witness to our engagement, and after seeing the purity of my love, she helped me persuade your daughter to give me her pledge and to accept mine.

HARPAGON: (aside) Ah! Does the fear of justice make him rave? (To Valère.) Why do you bring in this nonsense about my daughter?

VALERE: Sir, I say that I have labored greatly to persuade her modesty to accept my love.

HARPAGON: Whose modesty?

VALERE: Your daughter's. And only yesterday she consented to sign a marriage agreement.

HARPAGON: My daughter signed a promise of marriage?

VALERE: Yes, sir, just as I signed one to her.

HARPAGON: Heavens! Another disgrace!

JACQUES: (to the Officer) Write, sir, write it down.

HARPAGON: More trouble! Further agony! (To the Officer) Come, sir, do your duty and arraign him as a thief and a seducer.

VALERE: These are names which do not apply to me; and when you all know who I am—

(Enter Élise, Mariane, and Frosine.)

HARPAGON: (to Élise) Ah! Shameless daughter, daughter unworthy of a father like me! This is how you put into practice the lessons I taught you. You let yourself fall in love with an infamous thief, and you pledge yourself to him without my consent. But both of you will see what a mistake you have made. Four solid walls will answer for your conduct; (to Valère) and a solid gibbet will satisfy me for your audacity.

VALERE: It will not be your rage which will judge this affair; at least the law will give me a hearing before condemning me.

HARPAGON: I was wrong to say a gibbet; you will be broken alive on the rack.

ÉLISE: (kneeling before her father) Oh, father, show some human feelings, I beg you, and do not push matters with all the violence of paternal power. Do not yield to the first impulses of your rage, but give yourself time to consider what you will do. Take the trouble to know better who he is who angers you. He is quite different from what your eyes judge, and you will find it less strange that I have given myself to him when you know that without him you would not have me now. Yes, father, he is the man who saved me from the great danger I encountered in the ocean, and to whom you owe the life of this very daughter who—

HARPAGON: All this is nothing, and it would have been better for me if he had let you drown, than do what he has done.

ÉLISE: Father, I implore you by your paternal love to—

HARPAGON: No, no. I don't want to hear anything. The law must do its duty.

JACQUES: (aside) You'll pay me for the beating I got.

FROSINE: (aside) What a strange situation.

(Enter Signor Anselm.)

ANSELM: What is this, Signor Harpagon? I see you are quite upset.

HARPAGON: Ah, Signor Anselm, you see here the most unfortunate of men. A lot of trouble and disorder has come up about the contract you have come to sign. They have murdered my fortune, they have murdered my honor; and there is the traitor, the wretch who has violated the most sacred rights, who sneaked into my house disguised as a servant in order to steal my money and seduce my daughter.

VALERE: Who is even thinking about the money which you are making such a fuss over?

HARPAGON: Yes, they have exchanged promises of marriage. This affront concerns you, Signor Anselm; it is you who should retaliate with the law, and it is you who should undergo the legal expenses to get revenge for his insolence.

ANSELM: It is not my intention to marry anyone by force or to claim a heart which has given itself elsewhere. But, as for your interests, I am ready to defend them as my own.

HARPAGON: Monsieur, here is a worthy officer, who neglects, he told me, none of the functions of his office. (To the Officer) Indict him, sir, as necessary, and make the charges very criminal.

VALERE: I do not see what crime can be made out of my love for your daughter, nor to what punishment I can be condemned for our marriage engagement. When you know who I am—

HARPAGON: I scorn all these stories. Nowadays society is full of fake noblemen, impostors who take advantage of their obscurity to cloak themselves insolently in the first illustrious name that pops into their heads.

VALERE: I would have you know that I have too noble a heart to deck myself out in something not my own, and that all Naples can bear witness to my birth.

ANSELM: One moment, please. Be careful of what you say. You risk more than you realize, for you speak before a man who knows all Naples, and who can easily see through any tale you make up.

VALERE: (putting on his hat with dignity) I am not a man who has anything to fear. If Naples is well known to you, you know who was Don Thomas d'Alburcy.

ANSELM: I know him indeed; and few men have known him better than I.

HARPAGON: What do I care about Don Thomas or Don Anyone! (*Seeing two candles burning,* Harpagon *blows one out.*)

ANSELM: For Heaven's sake, let him speak. Let us see what he means.

VALERE: I mean that it is to him that I owe my birth.

ANSELM: Him?

VALERE: Yes.

ANSELM: Come, you are jesting. Get some other story which you can use better, and do not try to save yourself by such an imposture.

VALERE: Learn to speak more civilly. It is not an imposture, and I claim nothing which I cannot easily prove.

ANSELM: What? Do you dare to call yourself the son of Don Thomas d'Alburcy?

VALERE: Yes, I dare, and I am ready to maintain this truth against anyone.

ANSELM: His audacity is fantastic. Learn, to your confusion, that at least sixteen years ago the man of whom you speak perished at sea with his children and his wife while trying to save their lives from the cruel persecutions which accompanied the uprising in Naples, persecutions which caused the exile of several noble families.

VALERE: Yes, but learn to *your* confusion, that his son, seven years old, together with a servant, was saved from the shipwreck by a Spanish vessel, and it is this rescued son who speaks to you now. Learn, too, that the captain of the vessel, touched by my misfortune, took pity on me and brought me up as his own son; and that soldiering has been my profession ever since I could bear arms; and that I have recently learned that my father is not dead, as I had always believed; that, as I was passing through this city to find him, a heaven-sent accident allowed me to see the charming Élise; that this sight made me a slave of her beauty, and that the power of my love and the severity of her father made me decide to introduce myself into his house, and to send someone else in search of my parents.

ANSELM: What proofs—beyond your words—have you to assure us that this is not a fable constructed on a truth?

VALERE: The Spanish captain; a ruby seal which was my father's; an agate bracelet which my mother had put on my arm; old Pedro, the servant who was saved with me in the wreck.

MARIANE: Alas! I can vouch for your words; this is no imposture. All that you say proves clearly to me that you are my brother.

VALERE: You, my sister?

MARIANE: Yes, my heart was stirred the moment you began to speak. Our mother, who will be overjoyed to see you, has told me a thousand times of our family's misfortunes. Heaven did not let us perish either in that sad shipwreck, but it saved our lives only at the cost of our liberty, for pirates picked up my mother and me from the wreckage of our vessel. After ten years of slavery a happy accident gave us our freedom, and we returned to Naples, where we found all our property sold and no news about my father. We went on to Genoa, where my mother recovered some little scraps of a dissipated family inheritance. And from there, fleeing the barbarous injustice of her relatives, we came here, where she is now scarcely able to go on living.

ANSELM: Oh, Heaven, how great is the evidence of your power! And how plainly you show that you alone perform miracles. Embrace me, my children, and unite your joys with those of your father.

VALERE: You are our father?

MARIANE: It is you for whom my mother has wept so many years?

ANSELM: Yes, my daughter, yes, my son, I am Don Thomas d'Alburcy, whom Heaven rescued from the sea with all the money I had with me, and who, believing you all dead for over sixteen years, after a long journey prepared to seek the consolation of a new family with a gentle and prudent girl. The insecurities which I experienced in Naples made me renounce it for ever, and, having found means to sell what I owned there, I settled here under the name of Anselm, endeavoring to forget the sorrows of this other name which caused me so much grief.

HARPAGON: Is this your son?

ANSELM: Yes.

HARPAGON: Then I hold you responsible for payment of the ten thousand écus he has stolen.

ANSELM: He? Robbed you?

HARPAGON: Yes, indeed.

VALERE: Who told you so?

HARPAGON: Jacques.

VALERE: (to Jacques) It's you who says so?

JACQUES: You can see that I say nothing.

HARPAGON: Yes. Here is the officer who took down the deposition.

VALERE: Can you believe me capable of so base an action?

HARPAGON: Capable or not capable, I want my money back.

(Enter Cléante.)

CLEANTE: Don't be troubled, father, and don't accuse anyone. I have learned something about your money, and I have come to tell you that if you let me wed Mariane, your money will be returned.

HARPAGON: Where is it?

CLEANTE: Don't worry about it. It is in a place I can vouch for. Everything depends on me. It is for you to tell me what you decide; and you can choose either to give me Mariane or to lose your money box.

HARPAGON: Nothing has been taken out of it?

CLEANTE: Not a thing. Make up your mind whether to accept this marriage and join your consent with that of her mother, who allows her to choose between the two of us.

MARIANE: But you do not know that this consent is not enough, and that Heaven has restored to me my brother (pointing to Valère) and also (pointing to Anselm) my father from whom you must get consent.

ANSELM: My children, Heaven did not restore me to you that I should thwart your desires. Monsieur Harpagon, you surely realize that a young girl's choice will fall on the son rather than on the father. Come, do not make people say what need not be heard; consent, as I do, to this double marriage.

HARPAGON: I must see my money box before I can decide.

CLEANTE: You will see it safe and sound.

HARPAGON: I have no money to give my children for their marriage.

ANSELM: Well, I have enough for all. Don't worry about that.

HARPAGON: Will you pledge to pay the expenses for the marriages of these two?

ANSELM: Yes, I pledge it. Are you satisfied?

HARPAGON: Yes, provided that you give me a new suit of clothes for the wedding.

ANSELM: Agreed! Come, let us rejoice in the happiness this day has brought us.

OFFICER: One moment, gentlemen, one moment. Easy, if you please. Who is going to pay me for these depositions?

HARPAGON: We have nothing to do with your depositions.

OFFICER: Oh, but I don't intend to have drawn them up for nothing.

HARPAGON: (*pointing to* Jacques) For your payment, here is a man whom I give you to hang.

JACQUES: Ah, what can one do? They beat me for telling the truth, and they want to hang me for telling a lie.

ANSELM: Monsieur Harpagon, you must forgive him his hoax.

HARPAGON: Then will you pay the officer?

ANSELM: So be it. Come, let us go quickly to share our joy with your mother.

HARPAGON: And I, to see my darling money box.

FOR DISCUSSION

1. What problems are presented at the beginning of the play? Can you tell how each of these is resolved?
2. Do you think the situation, the characters, or the lines contributed most to your enjoyment of the play? Why?
3. If you were introduced to Valère, would you like him? Why or why not? What character do you like best? Least? Why?
4. Do the characters seem like real people to you? If so, which ones? Why? Which ones do not seem to be real people? Why?
5. Which character in the play is the most laughable? Why?
6. Do you think that this play would be fun to see on the stage or on television today? Why or why not? Whom would you like to see play the leading roles?
7. Can you tell anything about how the author views life by reading this play? Why do you suppose he wrote *The Miser?*
8. Does *The Miser* have a theme? What would you say it is?
9. What situations in the play are contrived? Why do you suppose they are?
10. What role does coincidence play in *The Miser?*
11. *Commedia dell'arte* is discussed in the preceding chapter. What influences of this form are seen in *The Miser?*
12. Harpagon is based on the stock character of the Miser, which began to appear in plays during the classical period. Does he have any qualities which make him seem like a real human being?
13. Why does Harpagon allow himself to be flattered by Frosine?
14. Molière uses certain comic devices to provide humor in *The Miser.* What are these devices? In which scenes is each used?
15. *The Miser* relies much on misunderstandings. How could these misunderstandings have been avoided?
16. Do you ever feel sorry for Harpagon when people try to take advantage of him? Why or why not?

SUPPLEMENTARY READING

Pierre Augustin Beaumarchais   *The Barber of Seville*
William Congreve   *The Way of the World*
Pierre Corneille   *Le Cid*
John Dryden   *All for Love*
George Farquhar   *The Beaux' Stratagem*
Johann Wolfgang von Goethe   *Faust, Part One*
Oliver Goldsmith   *She Stoops to Conquor*
Gotthold Lessing   *Minna von Barnhelm*
Molière   *Tartuffe; The Imaginary Invalid*
Jean Racine   *Phaedra*
Richard Brinsley Sheridan   *The School for Scandal*

V

The Nineteenth and Twentieth Centuries

Although the storm and stress movement developed in Germany, many of the concepts of romanticism had already appeared in England. In fact, it was easier for romanticism to gain a foothold there because neoclassicism had never been as widely adopted by English writers. The lure of romanticism showed that there was a growing distrust of reason and a growing conviction that one had only to follow his instincts to know and do what was right. Hence man could discover truth by examining nature.

The subject matter of nineteenth-century romantic plays often dealt with man's need to be free from the restraining forces of society, but actually, although the concepts of romanticism were developed largely in England, there were few such plays in that country. The most successful romantic playwright was James Sheridan Knowles, who lived from 1784 to 1862. His *Virginius* was written in 1820, *The Hunchback* in 1832.

Romanticism was receding in both England and Germany before it was even accepted in France. It finally became established through the writings of Victor Hugo, notably his play *Hernani,* which was produced in 1830.

Melodrama, which developed during the period when romantic drama was being presented, became highly popular during the nineteenth century. These plays were simple and suspenseful in plot, with a strong emotional appeal. Their themes were characterized by a strict division between good and evil: good was always rewarded and evil punished. Episodic in structure, they included scenes of comic relief and invariably ended happily. The name "melodrama," which today means a play full of action and almost unbearable suspense, goes back to the time when musical accompaniments were used to heighten the changes in mood and pace. The first two major European writers of melodrama were August Kotzebue of Germany and Guilbert de Pixerécourt of France.

In America, the most popular and most often produced nineteenth-century play was a melodrama—*Uncle Tom's Cabin,* based on the Harriet Beecher Stowe novel. There were several dramatized versions, but the most successful was an adaptation by George Aikin, which ran for more than two hundred performances at New York's National Theatre. Until the early part of the twentieth century, touring companies presented "Uncle Tom" shows up to five or more times a year in many U.S. communities.

Throughout the Western world, the theatre increased in popularity during the nineteenth century. Everybody went to the theatre, and the theatre had something for everybody. Many new theatres were erected so as to offer specialized types of entertainment, which ranged from variety and burlesque to serious dramas.

Settings were now built for individual plays, and they had to be historically accurate, following the trend which began in Germany just after the turn of the century. In England, Charles Kemble's production of Shakespeare's *King John* in 1823 was the first play in which the costuming was historically accurate. It was followed in 1824 by a production of *Henry IV, Part I,* which was scenically accurate. By mid-century, nearly every production reflected the backgrounds and costumes of its period.

Until the 1830's, in both Europe and America, the most popular type of acting troupe was the repertory company. After that, however, the star system developed rapidly. This meant that as soon as an actor gained some prominence he began traveling to various communities with his company. Many cities found it difficult to keep a good resident troupe. In America this system was aided by the rapid expansion of the railroads. Even so, the star system gradually was replaced by "combination companies" which traveled for an entire season presenting only a single play. The beginning of the twentieth century saw the end of repertory. Almost all actors were hired only for specific roles in specific plays.

An outgrowth of these changes was the Theatrical Syndicate that came into prominence in America. The Syndicate was formed in 1896 in order to book touring shows in various communities. However, it demanded that local theatre owners work exclusively with the Syndicate, and because it handled most of the major touring companies, theatre managers were afraid to try to run a season independently. Those who did usually found that the Syndicate would buy rival theatres and put the local managers out of business. The Syndicate's monopoly on theatrical booking was not broken until 1915.

In England, acting was becoming a socially accepted profession. Henry Irving was the first actor to be knighted. Irving, who lived from 1838 to 1905, was renowned for his presentations of romantic plays and melodramas. Among other actors and actresses of the time were John Philip Kemble, his sister, Mrs. Sarah Siddons, and Ellen Terry, who often acted with Irving.

The playwrights of the nineteenth century were now protected by copyright laws which prevented their works from being pirated. At first the laws were inadequate, in that they protected a writer only within the boundaries of his own country. By the beginning of the twentieth century, however, international copyright laws were in effect.

New dramatic forms slowly replaced the old. Following romanticism and melodrama came realism, which was a revolt against the ideals of romanticism. Actually, the movement came about as a result of oppressive political and economic conditions. Playwrights who favored realism felt that Western society was unacceptable and must be changed. But in order to bring about such change, they must reveal the facts about social evils and injustices. They emphasized the importance of what could be observed through the senses. Only through such observations could the real truth be learned. Playwrights who presented them in a dramatic way believed that if the audiences did not like what they saw on the stage, they would be impelled to change the social conditions, rather than simply attacking the playwright.

The development of the realistic movement, which began in France around 1850, was aided by technical advances that made for more believable settings. The box set, developed by 1840, was in general use by the end of the century. This type of setting showed the actual interior walls of a building, within which the actors could move around. The audience was privileged to view the play through an imaginary fourth wall between the stage and the auditorium. Now, too, was a trend toward making stage floors flat rather than raking them for purposes of perspective.

Other technical advances contributed to realism in the theatre. By 1840 most theatres had gas, which allowed stage settings to be lighted to any desired intensity. By 1880 electricity was in general use and lighting could be even better controlled. To facilitate quick changes of scene, elevator stages and revolving stages were used, as were wagons on which entire sets would be rolled on and off the stage.

Realistic dramas had been seen at times before the beginning of the nineteenth century, but did not gain popularity until Eugène Scribe (1791 to 1861) began writing such plays. Critics called his work, and that of his followers, "well-made plays." In such a play, a cause or problem is introduced early, and the effects of the problem are progressively explored. Not only does the well-made play have a plot, which builds to a climax, but (as developed by Scribe) a clear exposition of background material which lays the groundwork for everything that occurs. There is much suspense, and logical but unexpected reversals in the action. The play has a logical ending.

One of the most popular early authors of the well-made play was Alexandre Dumas, fils, who lived from 1824 to 1895. His best known play is *The Lady of the Camellias,* based on his novel of the same name, but known simply as *Camille.* The play, written in 1849, was romantic in style but also moved toward realism, in that it dealt with a social problem and attempted to teach a moral lesson. As everyone who has seen the opera *La Traviata* knows, the major character is a prostitute.

A play of this type, which attempted to teach a moral lesson, came to be called a "thesis play," a specific type of the well-made play. Most of the nineteenth-century thesis plays are now somewhat dated because the current problems which they pointed up no longer exist.

The man who brought the thesis play to its highest development was the

Norwegian playwright Henrik Ibsen, who lived from 1828 to 1906. Although he began writing in 1850, his early plays were romantic. Not until the 1870's did he shift to a realistic vein and deal with socially significant themes. More than any other playwright of his time, he established realism and naturalism as an integral part of drama; in fact, many critics have called him the father of modern drama.

Naturalism was what carried realistic drama to its ultimate end. As first developed by the novelist Émile Zola, naturalism meant that the writer should constantly seek the truth through objectivity—that is, his own ideas must not be allowed to intrude upon the facts presented in his writing. Thus, the playwright must be only a recorder of events, not an interpreter. He should select the beginning and ending of his drama at random. Any attempt to concoct a plot would result in a distortion of the truth, since life itself has no real beginnings or endings. This form of writing, called the "slice of life" technique, insists that the dramatist should try to reproduce actual life on the stage. There should be no concessions to the audience. Indeed, in some naturalistic productions the actors made no attempt to project their voices. In line with contemporary controversies about human heredity and environment, the settings of plays had to depict the characters' environment accurately in every detail. There were cases of the actual complete furnishings of apartments being transported to a stage, and one case where real sides of beef were hung in a staged butcher shop.

Such naturalism, however, defeats itself, because a play, no matter how realistic, is written ahead of time and the actors are performing gestures and speaking lines they have already memorized. Therefore the presentation is not life, but art. Nineteenth-century naturalism also was greatly criticized for depicting in great detail the seamiest sides of life. Despite this fact, Zola's ideas quickly spread over Europe and influenced writers and producers everywhere.

In England, the most important playwright of the late nineteenth and early twentieth century was George Bernard Shaw, whose witty plays emphasize social themes and have believable characters. In his plays, all comedies, he preached his own social beliefs, and many of them, such as *Saint Joan, Misalliance, Androcles and the Lion,* and *Arms and the Man* are often presented today. Shaw lived a long life, from 1856 to 1950.

Other important English playwrights of the time were W. S. Gilbert (1836 to 1911) and Arthur Sullivan (1842 to 1900). Through their operettas satirizing the upper classes, they hoped to bring about changes in the social structure of their country. Among their best known works are *H.M.S. Pinafore, The Mikado,* and *The Pirates of Penzance.* Another satirist of the time was Oscar Wilde. He lived from 1856 to 1900, and among his many works are his novel *The Picture of Dorian Gray* and his play *The Importance of Being Earnest.* He, too, was a witty and entertaining writer who satirized the prudery of his day.

Close by in Ireland, Sean O'Casey was writing satiric tragedies and became known as the playwright of the Irish slums. O'Casey (1880 to 1964) is best known for *Juno and the Paycock* and *The Plough and the Stars.* Ireland's greatest dramatist, however, was John Millington Synge who, on the recommendation of William Butler Yeats, spent several years observing the Irish peasants. As a result of his observations, he wrote six plays that are considered the best among any written in Ireland.

In Russia, Anton Chekhov (1860 to 1904) wrote many fine plays—among them *Uncle Vanya* and *The Cherry Orchard*—based on contemporary Russian life and presenting sympathetic characters who are defeated by circumstances. Another noted Russian playwright, Maxim Gorky, lived from 1868 to 1936. His play, *The Lower Depths,* deals with derelicts living in a basement. At the same time in America, David Belasco (1854 to 1931) was giving naturalistic productions of melodramatic plays. That is, their settings were detailed and true to life, but the plots were sentimental and contrived.

The trend toward a style of drama that would be strongly representative of life—a trend that began in the mid-nineteenth century and continued into the mid-twentieth—had its effect on the productions themselves. There was a need for more careful rehearsals and a more thorough coordination of all the elements of a production. Thus, the director gradually began to become the most important figure of the theatre.

In a small duchy, now Turingia, Germany, the Duke of Saxe-Meiningen (1826 to 1914) developed the concept of ensemble acting, in which no one actor is more important than any other and the effect of the total production is more important than any of its parts. The Duke believed that the director should be the dominant artist in the theatre, with complete authority over his actors. In France, André Antoine (1858 to 1943) organized the Free Theatre, which produced all types of plays but was largely concerned with naturalism. He believed that the actors' environment determined their movements, and even went so far as to bring in people off the streets to act in his plays, so they would appear natural. Back in Germany, Otto Brahm (1856 to 1912) established the German Free Theatre and gave a hearing, at least, to plays forbidden by the censor. In Russia, Constantin Stanislavsky (1863 to 1938) developed a system of acting based on true human emotions and experiences—a psychological realism that required each actor to feel and understand his role.

Today's theatre has once more become eclectic; that is, it is a combination of many forms. The eclectic approach was given impetus by the work of the famed director Max Reinhardt (1873 to 1943). He believed each play required a different style of presentation and that the director must control the style. Reinhardt, perhaps more than anyone else, made various movements in the theatre acceptable to audiences. Another person who used a variety of styles was Vsevolod Meyerhold of Russia (1874 to 1942), who favored a return to such forms as the *commedia dell'arte,* Japanese drama, and Greek theatre. To Meyerhold the actors were no more important than any other elements of a production.

Many new forms of staging and directing were widely accepted in Europe before they gained a foothold in America. Most important in bringing the new European stagecraft to America were Robert Edmond Jones (1887 to 1954) and Lee Simonson (1888 to 1967). The new stagecraft was first presented to American audiences by little theatre groups such as the Provincetown Players, which produced many of Eugene O'Neill's plays, and the Group Theatre, which worked with the playwright Clifford Odets and directors Elia Kazan and Harold Clurman. Indeed, the Group Theatre was responsible for developing the talents of many performers who later became America's foremost actors.

Another form that developed along with realism and naturalism was symbolism, which began in France and usually took its subject matter from the past. The symbolists did not believe in realistic scenery but in backgrounds which gave a general impression of the mood of the play. The outstanding symbolist playwright, Maurice Maeterlinck, lived from 1862 to 1949.

Although not of the symbolist school, Adolphe Appia, an Italian Swiss (1862 to 1928) and Edward Gordon Craig, the English producer, actor, and stage designer (1872 to 1966), dealt largely with creating an environment that was fitting for each play. Working independently of each other, they laid the foundations upon which much of modern theatrical practice was built. Craig's settings were designed to capture the feeling of a work without representing an actual place. Appia emphasized the role of light in creating unity for his productions.

Expressionism was another important trend in playwriting. The entire drama is presented through the eyes of a central character, so that the audience views reality as he does. Expressionist writers, at the opposite extreme from the realists, feel that the way to truth is through an understanding of man's soul. One of the best known expressionist playwrights was August Strindberg (1849 to 1912), the first important Swedish playwright. He began writing in a realistic vein, but his later plays, such as *The Ghost Sonata* (1907), were actually forerunners of the new movement. Another early expressionist playwright was Georg Kaiser, a German (1878 to 1945). One of his best plays is *From Morn to Midnight,* written in 1918. Several important American playwrights, including Eugene O'Neill (1888–1953), wrote expressionistic plays. O'Neill, however, experimented successfully with a variety of styles.

Another dramatic form was developed by Bertolt Brecht, whose *Threepenny Opera,* as we know, was an adaptation of John Gay's *Beggar's Opera.* In what is called "epic theatre" or "the theatre of alienation," Brecht set himself the goal of "making strange." This meant that, as a writer and a director, Brecht did not want the audience simply to identify with his characters but instead to grasp the larger problems presented. Two of Brecht's plays that achieve this "making strange" are *Mother Courage* (1937) and *The Good Woman of Setzuan* first produced in 1943.

Still another important new form was Absurdist drama, which asserts that nothing is good or bad as such; only what man himself attributes to something can make it either moral or immoral. Truth is to be found in disorder and chaos, because everything is equally illogical. Among the forerunners of Absurdism were the French writers Jean-Paul Sartre and Albert Camus. Later Absurdist playwrights were Samuel Beckett, who wrote *Waiting for Godot* in 1952, and Eugene Ionesco, whose first play, *The Bald Soprano,* was written in 1950.

Amid such a diversity of dramatic forms, the eclectic approach became a necessity. The distinctions between forms became blurred in the course of time. Even realism is modified in the plays of Tennessee Williams, who combines realism with symbolism in *The Glass Menagerie,* written in 1945. Another plawright who modifies realism is Arthur Miller, whose *Death of a Salesman* (1949) some critics consider the best American play yet written. Another of America's foremost contemporary playwrights is Edward Albee, author of *Who's Afraid of Virginia Woolf?,* produced in 1962.

Many of America's contemporary playwrights are recognized worldwide, although theatre in America has only recently become a powerful force. It began to come into its own in the early part of the century, with the writings of such dramatists as Eugene O'Neill and Maxwell Anderson. Its forerunners were several specific but diverse types of entertainment. The minstrel show, with its jokes and songs and variety; the circus, which developed on a larger scale than in Europe; the showboat, which provided entertainment for isolated communities; and variety shows and vaudeville—all played an important part in the growth of the American theatre.

The most purely American form to emerge, however, was the "musical," which uses material from many sources. Unlike the opera or operettas of Europe, it is a unique combination of dialogue, dancing, music, singing, and acting. The great George Gershwin and his brother Ira, Jerome Kern, Richard Rodgers and Oscar Hammerstein helped to launch musicals whose songs are still sung to this day.

Recent trends in modern American theatre have led to many plays that do not follow a plot-line but only present a certain viewpoint or depict an aspect of life. Off-Broadway and off-off-Broadway theatres have been open to a wide range of experimentation in form and style. Many effective experiments in the modern drama are taking place in college and university theatres—such plays as *Sticks and Bones,* which deals with a returning Vietnam veteran. Even the musical theatre has undergone changes in its attempts to identify with the audience and at times to involve the spectators in its productions. For example, two modern musicals that depart from the established style are *Hair* and *Jesus Christ, Superstar.* The latter is an attempt to make religion relevant, as is a musical play which was presented off-Broadway in 1974, *Hosea.* It is based on the biblical story of Hosea but was done first as improvisation, with no recorded speeches, and, second, in the language of modern young people. The play is performed by a cast whose ages range from fourteen to twenty-eight, most of them high school and college students who originally performed the play in churches.

Despite all this experimentation, Broadway plays at present tend to stay with the more established dramatic forms. During recent years, revivals of older plays have been highly successful—for example, the New York production of O'Neill's *A Moon for the Misbegotten.* This move toward revival of earlier forms seems to suggest that audiences are tiring of experimentation and that a change is imminent. All major changes in the theatre come about as a revolt against prior forms. The modern theatre is in revolution, but as yet has developed no entirely new, popular form.

PROJECTS

1. Investigate the specific conditions that led to the rise of either romanticism or realism in Europe and America.
2. Write and present a short scene in the style of a nineteenth-century melodrama.
3. Report on the touring "combination companies" in America. How did they differ from touring companies elsewhere?
4. Investigate Henry Irving's life and contributions to the theatre.
5. Who was Sarah Siddons? Find out as much as you can about her.
6. Trace the history of the colonial theatre in America. What were the major themes of plays in the colonies?
7. Investigate the methods of staging plays in England and America during the nineteenth century.
8. Write a short "slice of life" scene and present it to the class.
9. Explore the staging theories of Adolphe Appia or Edward Gordon Craig.
10. Make a report on the history of the Group Theatre.
11. Investigate Stanislavsky's theories of acting. How are his theories regarded today?
12. Write a scene in the style of an Absurdist play.
13. Find out more about André Antoine's Free Theatre.
14. Investigate the "new stagecraft" movement in America.

15. Trace the history of musical theatre in America. What happened to it once moving pictures became popular? How has the musical theatre changed? What has contributed to change in the musical theatre?
16. Do you think the theatre is dying? Why or why not?
17. Attend a play and write a review of it. What historical influences did you see in the play? Did it fit into a specific style? What innovations in staging or acting did you notice?

Ibsen is called the father of modern drama.

Born in 1826, he was the son of wealthy parents. When he was eight years old, however, they lost their money, and his early years were spent in poverty. When he was fifteen, he was apprenticed to a pharmacist in Grimstad, a small town in southern Norway. While there, he read many books, began composing poetry, and first thought of making a career of writing.

His first play, *Catilina*, was written in 1850—a romantic melodrama with historical subject matter. He then wrote *The Warrior's Barrow*, which was produced in the city of Christiania (Oslo), although his first play had been refused production. Next, he wrote a verse prologue for the opening of the National Theatre in Bergen. As a result, he was asked to become assistant to the theatre's director and founder, Ole Bull, a famous violinist. The trustees of the theatre gave Ibsen money to study theatres in Denmark and Germany on the condition that he serve as stage manager at the Bergen theatres for five years. His contract also stated that he was to write one play a year for the theatre. His first was *Saint John's Night*.

In 1862, Ibsen became artistic director of the Norwegian Theatre in Christiania. His play, *The Pretenders*, was produced there in 1863, and in the same year he was awarded a government fellowship which allowed him to visit Italy and Germany. Then, after the production of his next play, *Brand*, in 1865, he received a state pension on the basis of his work. He spent much of the remainder of his life abroad.

Ibsen was Norway's first important dramatist. Although a great deal of his early writing was based on Norwegian legends, his entire dramatic work can be divided into three periods. The first, his romantic period, lasted from 1850, with his first play, to 1873, with the writing of *Emperor and Galilean.* In the second period, from 1877 to 1890, Ibsen wrote realistic drama. In the third period, from 1888 to 1899, his work was largely composed of symbolist dramas. While Ibsen is often remembered best for his realistic plays, the dramas of all three periods are uniformly high in quality. Furthermore, he had the capacity to combine his styles—realism with romanticism in his early plays, and symbolism with realism in the later ones.

One of his early works, *Peer Gynt*, written in 1867, combines romanticism with social criticism, perhaps indicating the later switch to social problem plays. His first realistic social-problem play was *The Pillars of Society*, in which he attacked unscrupulous shipbuilders and the shaky foundations of social respectability. *A Doll's House* caused heated controversy about his treatment of women's rights, especially the end of the play when Nora leaves her husband. Ibsen was even persuaded to write an alternate ending, which was sometimes used, in which Nora remains at home for the sake of her children. *Ghosts* (1881) presents a central character who should have left home but did not. The play shows the effects of venereal disease on a family.

In his later plays, beginning with *Rosmersholm* (1886), Ibsen moved away from social problems to concentrate upon personal relationships. However, throughout his writing he continued to deal with the conflict of personal integrity versus duty to others.

Among Ibsen's dramatic reforms was a discontinuation of the use of soliloquies and asides. He also provided a thorough exposition of prior events and circumstances woven into the story, thus building a framework in which everything was both logical and interesting. Each scene led directly into the one that followed, showing a cause-and-effect relationship. The dialogue, sets, costumes, and movements were all chosen to contribute to the overall effect. Finally, each character was an individual affected by his heredity and his environment.

Because of his innovations and the development of his plays, Ibsen has been called the father of modern drama and has influenced playwrights the world over. His work is profound and full of personal conviction; it shows thought and introspection; and above all it is enduring.

An Enemy of the People is the story of one man's courage in facing a selfish majority, each member of whom is afraid to be an individual because of group pressure. Ibsen himself held certain views which no doubt influenced his work. Perhaps because of the way Ghosts had been received, he said that the "intellectual soil" of Norway should be cleansed and the swamps drained. Only then could there be proper conditions for the advancement of artistic endeavors. He also expressed the opinion that the only man who is right is the one who pushes ahead and looks to the future. Such a man has to be in the minority, but not the stagnant minority. Ibsen said that he himself would always be a few years ahead of the majority in his thinking.

An Enemy of the People appeals to our sensibilities as do Ibsen's other plays. Ibsen injects his own attitudes and feelings into the play and bases his characters on real people. There is a naturalness to both situation and dialogue. The story is believable and realistic, but still endowed with idealism, which is particularly apparent in Doctor Stockmann's speech to the people. Various elements are woven together to make a significant statement and a great drama.

An Enemy of the People

CHARACTERS

DOCTOR THOMAS
    STOCKMANN,
    medical officer of the Baths.

MRS. STOCKMANN, *his wife.*

PETRA, *their daughter, a teacher.*

EILIF   *their sons, thirteen and*

MORTEN   *ten years old*
    respectively.

PETER STOCKMANN, *the*
    doctor's elder brother,
    Burgomaster and chief of police,
    chairman of the Baths
    Committee, etc.

MORTEN KIIL, *master tanner,*
    Mrs. Stockmann's
    adoptive-father.

HOVSTAD, *editor of the*
    "People's Messenger."

BILLING, *on the staff of the paper.*

HORSTER, *a ship's captain.*

ASLAKSEN, *a printer.*

Participants in a meeting of citizens: all sorts and conditions of men, some women, and a band of schoolboys.

The action passes in a town on the South Coast of Norway.

An Enemy of the People

PLAY IN FIVE ACTS

ACT FIRST

Evening. Dr. Stockmann's sitting-room; simply but neatly decorated and furnished. In the wall to the right are two doors, the further one leading to the hall, the nearer one to the Doctor's study. In the opposite wall, facing the hall door, a door leading to the other rooms of the house. Against the middle of this wall stands the stove; further forward a sofa with a mirror above it, and in front of it an oval table with a cover. On the table a lighted lamp, with a shade. In the back wall an open door leading to the dining-room, in which is seen a supper-table, with a lamp on it.

Billing is seated at the supper-table, with a napkin under his chin. Mrs. Stockmann is standing by the table and placing before him a dish with a large joint of roast beef. The other seats round the table are empty; the table is in disorder, as after a meal.

MRS. STOCKMANN: If you come an hour late, Mr. Billing, you must put up with a cold supper.

BILLING: (*Eating*) It is excellent—really first rate.

MRS. STOCKMANN: You know how Stockmann insists on regular meal-hours—

BILLING: Oh, I don't mind at all. I almost think I enjoy my supper more when I can sit down to it like this, alone and undisturbed.

MRS. STOCKMANN: Oh, well, if you enjoy it—(*Listening in the direction of the hall.*) I believe this is Mr. Hovstad coming too.

BILLING: Very likely.

(*Burgomaster Stockmann enters, wearing an overcoat and an official gold-laced cap, and carrying a stick.*)

BURGOMASTER: Good evening, sister-in-law.

MRS. STOCKMANN: (*Coming forward into the sitting-room.*) Oh, good evening; it is you? It is good of you to look in.

BURGOMASTER: I was just passing, and so—(*Looks toward the drawing-room.*) Ah, I see you have company.

MRS. STOCKMANN: (*Rather embarrased.*) Oh no, not at all; it's the merest chance. (*Hurridly.*) Won't you sit down and have a little supper?

BURGOMASTER: I? No, thank you. Good gracious! hot meat in the evening! That wouldn't suit my digestion.

MRS. STOCKMANN: Oh, for once in a way—

BURGOMASTER: No, no,—much obliged to you. I stick to tea and bread and butter. It's more wholesome in the long run—and rather more economical, too.

MRS. STOCKMANN: (*Smiling.*) You mustn't think Thomas and I are mere spendthrifts, either.

BURGOMASTER: You are not, sister-in-law; far be it from me to say that. (*Pointing to the Doctor's study.*) Is he not at home?

MRS. STOCKMANN: No, he has gone for a little turn after supper—with the boys.

BURGOMASTER: I wonder if that is a good thing to do? (*Listening.*) There he is, no doubt.

MRS. STOCKMANN: No, that is not he. (*A knock.*) Come in!

(Hovstad *enters from the hall.*)

MRS. STOCKMANN: Ah, it's Mr. Hovstad—

HOVSTAD: You must excuse me; I was detained at the printer's. Good evening, Burgomaster.

BURGOMASTER: (*Bowing rather stiffly.*) Mr. Hovstad? You come on business, I presume?

HOVSTAD: Partly. About an article for the paper.

BURGOMASTER: So I supposed. I hear my brother is an extremely prolific contributor to the *People's Messenger.*

HOVSTAD: Yes, when he wants to unburden his mind on one thing or another, he gives the *Messenger* the benefit.

MRS. STOCKMANN: (*To* Hovstad.) But will you not—? (*Points to the dining-room.*)

BURGOMASTER: Well, well, I am far from blaming him for writing for the class of readers he finds most in sympathy with him. And, personally, I have no reason to bear your paper any ill-will, Mr. Hovstad.

HOVSTAD: No, I should think not.

BURGOMASTER: One may say, on the whole, that a fine spirit of mutual tolerance prevails in our town—an excellent public spirit. And that is because we have a great common interest to hold us together—an interest in which all right-minded citizens are equally concerned—

HOVSTAD: Yes—the Baths.

BURGOMASTER: Just so. We have our magnificent new Baths. Mark my words! The whole life of the town will centre around the Baths, Mr. Hovstad. There can be no doubt of it!

MRS. STOCKMANN: That is just what Thomas says.

BRUGOMASTER: How marvellously the place has developed, even in this couple of years! Money has come into circulation, and brought life and movement with it. Houses and ground-rents rise in value every day.

HOVSTAD: And there are fewer people out of work.

BURGOMASTER: That is true. There is a gratifying diminution in the burden imposed on the well-to-do classes by the poor-rates; and they will be still further lightened if only we have a really good summer this year—a rush of visitors—plenty of invalids, to give the Baths a reputation.

HOVSTAD: I hear there is every prospect of that.

BURGOMASTER: Things look most promising. Inquiries about apartments and so forth keep on pouring in.

HOVSTAD: Then the Doctor's paper will come in very opportunely.

BURGOMASTER: Has he been writing again?

HOVSTAD: This is a thing he wrote in the winter; enlarging on the virtues of the Baths, and on the excellent sanitary conditions of the town. But at that time I held it over.

BURGOMASTER: Ah—I suppose there was something not quite judicious about it?

HOVSTAD: Not at all. But I thought it better to keep it till the spring, when people are beginning to look about them, and think of their summer quarters—

BURGOMASTER: You were right, quite right, Mr. Hovstad.

MRS. STOCKMANN: Yes, Thomas is really indefatigable where the Baths are concerned.

BURGOMASTER: It is his duty as one of the staff.

HOVSTAD: And of course he was really their creator.

BURGOMASTER: Was he? Indeed! I gather that certain persons are of that opinion. But I should have thought that I, too, had a modest share in that undertaking.

MRS. STOCKMANN: Yes, that is what Thomas is always saying.

HOVSTAD: No one dreams of denying it, Burgomaster. You set the thing going, and put it on a practical basis; everybody knows that. I only meant that the original idea was the doctor's.

BURGOMASTER: Yes, my brother has certainly had ideas enough in his time—worse luck! But when it comes to realising them, Mr. Hovstad, we want men of another stamp. I should have thought that in this house at any rate—

MRS. STOCKMANN: Why, my dear brother-in-law—

HOVSTAD: Burgomaster, how can you—?

MRS. STOCKMANN: Do go in and have some supper, Mr. Hovstad; my husband is sure to be home directly.

HOVSTAD: Thanks; just a mouthful, perhaps. (*He goes into the dining-room.*)

BURGOMASTER: (*Speaking in a low voice.*) It is extraordinary how people who spring direct from the peasant class never can get over their want of tact.

MRS. STOCKMANN: But why should you care? Surely you and Thomas can share the honour, like brothers.

BURGOMASTER: Yes, one would suppose so; but it seems a share of the honour is not enough for some persons.

MRS. STOCKMANN: What nonsense! You and Thomas always get on so well together. (*Listening.*) There, I think I hear him. (*Goes and opens the door to the hall.*)

DR. STOCKMANN: (*Laughing and talking loudly, without.*) Here's another visitor for you, Katrina. Isn't it capital, eh? Come in, Captain Horster. Hang your coat on that peg. What! you don't wear an overcoat? Fancy, Katrina, I caught him in the street, and I could hardly get him to come in.

CAPTAIN HORSTER: (*Enters and bows to Mrs. Stockmann.*)

DR. STOCKMANN: (*In the doorway.*) In with you, boys. They're famishing again! Come along, Captain Horster; you must try our roast beef—

(He forces Horster *into the dining-room.* Eilif *and* Morten *follow them.)*

MRS. STOCKMANN: But, Thomas, don't you see—
DR. STOCKMANN: (*Turning round in the doorway.*) Oh, is that you, Peter! (*Goes up to him and holds out his hand.*) Now this is really capital.
BURGOMASTER: Unfortunately, I have only a moment to spare—
DR. STOCKMANN: Nonsense! We shall have some toddy in a minute. You're not forgetting the toddy, Katrina?
MRS. STOCKMANN: Of course not; the water's boiling. (*She goes into the dining-room.*)
BURGOMASTER: Toddy too—!
DR. STOCKMANN: Yes; sit down, and let's make ourselves comfortable.
BURGOMASTER: Thanks; I never join in drinking parties.
DR. STOCKMANN: But this isn't a party.
BURGOMASTER: I don't know what else— (*Looks towards the dining-room.*) It's extraordinary how they can get through all that food.
DR. STOCKMANN: (*Rubbing his hands.*) Yes, doesn't it do one good to see young people eat? Always hungry! That's as it should be. They need good, solid meat to put stamina into them! It is they that have got to whip up the ferment of the future, Peter.
BURGOMASTER: May I ask what there is to be "whipped up" as you call it?
DR. STOCKMANN: You'll have to ask the young people that—when the time comes. We shan't see it, of course. Two old fogies like you and me—
BURGOMASTER: Come, come! Surely that is a very extraordinary expression to use—
DR. STOCKMANN: Oh, you mustn't mind my nonsense, Peter. I'm in such glorious spirits, you see. I feel so unspeakably happy in the midst of all this growing, germinating life. Isn't it a marvellous time we live in! It seems as though a whole new world were springing up around us.
BURGOMASTER: Do you really think so?
DR. STOCKMANN: Of course, you can't see it as clearly as I do. You have passed your life in the midst of it all; and that deadens the impression. But I who had to vegetate all those years in that little hole in the north, hardly ever seeing a soul that could speak a stimulating word to me—all this affects me as if I had suddenly dropped into the heart of some teeming metropolis.
BURGOMASTER: Well, metropolis—
DR. STOCKMANN: Oh, I know well enough that things are on a small scale here, compared with many other places. But there's life here—there's promise —there's an infinity of things to work and strive for; and that is the main point. (*Calling.*) Katrina, haven't there been any letters?
MRS. STOCKMANN: (*In the dining-room.*) No, none at all.
DR. STOCKMANN: And then a good income, Peter! That's a thing one learns to appreciate when one has lived on starvation wages—
BURGOMASTER: Good heavens—!
DR. STOCKMANN: Oh yes, I can tell you we often had hard times of it up there. And now we can live like princes! To-day, for example, we had roast beef for dinner; and we've had some of it for supper too. Won't you have some? Come along—just look at it, at any rate—
BURGOMASTER: No, no; certainly not—
DR. STOCKMANN: Well then, look here—do you see we've bought a table-cover?
BURGOMASTER: Yes, so I observed.
DR. STOCKMANN: And a lamp-shade, too. Do you see? Katrina has been

saving up for them. They make the room look comfortable, don't they? Come over here. No, no, no, not there. So—yes! Now you see how it concentrates the light—. I really think it has quite an artistic effect. Eh?

BURGOMASTER: Yes, when one can afford such luxuries—

DR. STOCKMAN: Oh, I can afford it now. Katrina says I make almost as much as we spend.

BURGOMASTER: Ah—almost!

DR. STOCKMANN: Besides, a man of science must live in some style. Why, I believe a mere sheriff spends much more a year than I do.

BURGOMASTER: Yes, I should think so! A member of the superior magistracy—

DR. STOCKMANN: Well then, even a common shipowner! A man of that sort will get through many times as much—

BURGOMASTER: That is natural, in your relative positions.

DR. STOCKMANN: And after all, Peter, I really don't squander any money. But I can't deny myself the delight of having people about me. I must have them. After living so long out of the world, I find it a necessity of life to have bright, cheerful, freedom-loving, hard-working young fellows around me— and that's what they are, all of them, that are sitting there eating so heartily. I wish you knew more of Hovstad—

BURGOMASTER: Ah, that reminds me—Hovstad was telling me that he is going to publish another article of yours.

DR. STOCKMAN: An article of mine?

BURGOMASTER: Yes, about the Baths. An article you wrote last winter.

DR. STOCKMAN: Oh, that one! But I don't want that to appear for the present.

BURGOMASTER: Why not? It seems to me this is the very time for it.

DR. STOCKMANN: Very likely—under ordinary circumstances—(*Crosses the room.*)

BURGOMASTER: (*Following him with his eyes.*) And what is unusual in the circumstances now?

DR. STOCKMAN: (*Standing still.*) The fact is, Peter, I really cannot tell you just now; not this evening, at all events. There may prove to be a great deal that is unusual in the circumstances. On the other hand, there may be nothing at all. Very likely it's only my fancy.

BURGOMASTER: Upon my word, you are very enigmatical. Is there anything in the wind? Anything I am to be kept in the dark about? I should think, as Chairman of the Bath Committee—

DR. STOCKMANN: And I should think that I—Well, well, don't let us get our backs up, Peter.

BURGOMASTER: God forbid! I am not in the habit of "getting my back up," as you express it. But I must absolutely insist that all arrangements shall be made and carried out in a businesslike manner, and through the properly constituted authorities. I cannot be a party to crooked or underhand courses.

DR. STOCKMANN: Have *I* ever been given to crooked or underhand courses?

BURGOMASTER: At any rate you have an ingrained propensity to taking your own course. And that, in a well-ordered community, is almost as inadmissible. The individual must subordinate himself to society, or, more precisely, to the authorities whose business it is to watch over the welfare of society.

DR. STOCKMANN: Maybe. But what the devil has that to do with me?

BURGOMASTER: Why this is the very thing, my dear Thomas, that it seems you will never learn. But take care; you will have to pay for it—sooner or later. Now I have warned you. Good-bye.

DR. STOCKMANN: Are you stark mad? You're on a totally wrong track—
BURGOMASTER: I am not often on the wrong track. Moreover, I must pro-
test against— (*Bowing towards dining-room.*) Good-bye, sister-in-law;
good-day to you, gentlemen. (*He goes.*)
MRS. STOCKMANN: (*Entering the sitting-room.*) Has he gone?
DR. STOCKMANN: Yes, and in a fine temper, too.
MRS. STOCKMANN: Why, my dear Thomas, what have you been doing to
him now?
DR. STOCKMANN: Nothing at all. He can't possibly expect me to account
to him for everything—before the time comes.
MRS. STOCKMANN: What have you to account to him for?
DR. STOCKMANN: H'm;—never mind about that, Katrina.—It's very odd
the postman doesn't come.

(Hovstad, Billing *and* Horster *have risen from table and come forward
into the sitting-room.* Eilif *and* Morten *presently follow.*)

BILLING: (*Stretching himself.*) Ah! Strike me dead if one doesn't feel a new
man after such a meal.
HOVSTAD: The Burgomaster didn't seem in the best of tempers this eve-
ning.
DR. STOCKMANN: That's his stomach. He has a very poor digestion.
HOVSTAD: I fancy it's the staff of the *Messenger* he finds it hardest to
stomach.
MRS. STOCKMANN: I thought you got on well enough with him.
HOVSTAD: Oh, yes; but it's only a sort of armistice between us.
BILLING: That's it. That word sums up the situation.
DR. STOCKMANN: We must remember that Peter is a lonely bachelor, poor
devil! He has no home to be happy in; only business, business. And then all
that cursed weak tea he goes and pours down his throat! Now then, chairs
round the table, boys! Katrina, shan't we have the toddy now?
MRS. STOCKMANN: (*Going towards the dining-room.*) I am just getting it.
DR. STOCKMANN: And you, Captain Horster, sit beside me on the sofa. So
rare a guest as you—. Sit down, gentlemen, sit down.

(*The men sit round the table;* Mrs. Stockmann *brings in a tray with
kettle, glasses, decanters, etc.*)

MRS. STOCKMANN: Here you have it: here's arrak, and this is rum, and this
cognac. Now, help yourself.
DR. STOCKMANN: (*Taking a glass.*) So we will. (*While the toddy is being
mixed*) And now out with the cigars. Eilif, I think you know where the box
is. And Morten, you may fetch my pipe. (*The boys go into the room on the
right.*) I have a suspicion that Eilif sneaks a cigar now and then, but I pretend
not to notice. (*Calls.*) And my smoking-cap, Morten! Katrina, can't you tell
him where I left it. Ah, he's got it. (*The boys bring in the things.*) Now,
friends, help yourselves. I stick to my pipe, you know;—this one has been
on many a stormy journey with me, up there in the north. (*They clink
glasses.*) Your health! Ah, I can tell you it's better fun to sit cosily here, safe
from wind and weather.
MRS. STOCKMANN: (*Who sits knitting.*) Do you sail soon, Captain Horster?
HORSTER: I hope to be ready for a start by next week.
MRS. STOCKMANN: And you're going to America?
HORSTER: Yes, that's the intention.

BILLING: But then you'll miss the election of the new Town Council.

HORSTER: Is there to be an election again?

BILLING: Didn't you know?

HORSTER: No, I don't trouble myself about those things.

BILLING: But I suppose you take an interest in public affairs?

HORSTER: No, I don't understand anything about them.

BILLING: All the same, one ought at least to vote.

HORSTER: Even those who don't understand anything about it?

BILLING: Understand? Why, what do you mean by that? Society is like a ship: every man must put his hand to the helm.

HORSTER: That may be all right on shore; but at sea it wouldn't do at all.

HOVSTAD: It's remarkable how little sailors care about public affairs as a rule.

BILLING: Most extraordinary.

DR. STOCKMANN: Sailors are like birds of passage; they are at home both in the south and in the north. So it behoves the rest of us to be all the more energetic, Mr. Hovstad. Will there be anything of public interest in the *People's Messenger* tomorrow?

HOVSTAD: Nothing of local interest. But the day after to-morrow I think of printing your article—

DR. STOCKMANN: Oh confound it, that article! No, you'll have to hold it over.

HOVSTAD: Really? We happen to have plenty of space, and I should say this was the very time for it—

DR. STOCKMANN: Yes, yes, you may be right; but must hold it over all the same. I shall explain to you by-and-by.

(Petra, *wearing a hat and cloak, and with a number of exercise-books under her arm, enters from the hall.*)

PETRA: Good evening.

DR. STOCKMANN: Good evening, Petra. Is that you? (*General greetings.* Petra *puts her cloak, hat, and books on a chair by the door.*)

PETRA: Here you all are, enjoying yourselves, while I've been out slaving.

DR. STOCKMANN: Well then, you come and enjoy yourself too.

BILLING: May I mix you a little—?

PETRA: (*Coming towards the table.*) Thank you, I'd rather help myself— you always make-it too strong. By the way, father, I have a letter for you. (*Goes to the chair where her things are lying.*)

DR. STOCKMANN: A letter! From whom?

PETRA: (*Searching in the pocket of her cloak.*) I got it from the postman just as I was going out—

DR. STOCKMANN: (*Rising and going towards her.*) And you only bring it me now?

PETRA: I really hadn't time to run up again. Here it is.

DR. STOCKMANN: (*Seizing the letter.*) Let me see, let me see, child. (*Reads the address.*) Yes; this is it—!

MRS. STOCKMANN: Is it the one you have been so anxious about, Thomas?

DR. STOCKMANN: Yes it is. I must go at once. Where shall I find a light, Katrina? Is there no lamp in my study again!

MRS. STOCKMANN: Yes—the lamp is lighted. It's on the writing-table.

DR. STOCKMANN: Good, good. Excuse me one moment— (*He goes into the room on the right.*)

PETRA: What can it be, mother?

MRS. STOCKMANN: I don't know. For the last few days he has been continually on the look-out for the postman.

BILLING: Probably a country patient—

PETRA: Poor father! He'll soon have far too much to do. (*Mixes her toddy.*) Ah, this will taste good!

HOVSTAD: Have you been teaching in the night school as well to-day?

PETRA: (*Sipping from her glass.*) Two hours.

BILLING: And four hours in the morning at the institute—

PETRA: (*Sitting down by the table.*) Five hours.

MRS. STOCKMANN: And I see you have exercises to correct this evening.

PETRA: Yes, a heap of them.

HORSTER: It seems to me you have plenty to do, too.

PETRA: Yes, but I like it. You feel so delightfully tired after it.

BILLING: Do you like that?

PETRA: Yes, for then you sleep so well.

MORTEN: I say, Petra, you must be a great sinner.

PETRA: A sinner?

MORTEN: Yes, if you work so hard. Mr. Rörlund I says work is a punishment for our sins.

EILIF: (*Contemptuously.*) Bosh! What a silly you are, to believe such stuff as that.

MRS. STOCKMANN: Come come, Eilif.

BILLING: (*Laughing.*) Capital, capital!

HOVSTAD: Should you not like to work so hard, Morten?

MORTEN: No, I shouldn't.

HOVSTAD: Then what will you do with yourself in the world?

MORTEN: I should like to be a Viking.

EILIF: But then you'd have to be a heathen.

MORTEN: Well, so I would.

BILLING: There I agree with you, Morten! I say just the same thing.

See *Pillars of Society*.

MRS. STOCKMANN: (*Making a sign to him*) No, no, Mr. Billing, I'm sure you don't.

BILLING: Strike me dead but I do, though. I am a heathen, and I'm proud of it. You'll see we shall all be heathens soon.

MORTEN: And shall we be able to do anything we like then?

BILLING: Well, you see, Morten—

MRS. STOCKMANN: Now run away, boys; I'm sure you have lessons to prepare for to-morrow.

EILIF: You might let me stay just a little longer—

MRS. STOCKMANN: No, you must go too. Be off, both of you.

(*The boys say good-night and go into the room on the left.*)

HOVSTAD: Do you really think it can hurt the boys to hear these things?

MRS. STOCKMANN: Well, I don't know; I don't like it.

PETRA: Really, mother, I think you are quite wrong there.

MRS. STOCKMANN: Perhaps. But I don't like it—not here, at home.

PETRA: There's no end of hypocrisy both at home and at school. At home you must hold your tongue, and at school you have to stand up and tell lies to the children.

HORSTER: Have you to tell lies?

PETRA: Yes; do you think we don't have to tell them many and many a thing we don't believe ourselves?

BILLING: Ah, that's too true.

PETRA: If only I could afford it, I should start a school myself, and things should be very different there.

BILLING: Oh, afford it—!

HORSTER: If you really think of doing that, Miss Stockmann, I shall be delighted to let you have a room at my place. You know my father's old house is nearly empty; there's a great big dining-room on the ground floor—

PETRA: (*Laughing.*) Oh, thank you very much—but I'm afraid it won't come to anything.

HOVSTAD: No, I fancy Miss Petra is more likely to go over to journalism. By the way, have you had time to look into the English novel you promised to translate for us?

PETRA: Not yet. But you shall have it in good time.

(Dr. Stockmann *enters from his room, with the letter open in his hand.*)

DR. STOCKMANN: (*Flourishing the letter.*) Here's news, I can tell you, that will waken up the town!

BILLING: News?

MRS. STOCKMANN: What news?

DR. STOCKMAN: A great discovery, Katrina!

HOVSTAD: Indeed?

MRS. STOCKMANN: Made by you?

DR. STOCKMANN: Precisely—by me! (*Walks up and down.*) Now let them go on accusing me of fads and crack-brained notions. But they won't dare to! Ha-ha! I tell you they won't dare!

PETRA: Do tell us what it is, father.

DR. STOCKMANN: Well, well, give me time, and you shall hear all about it. If only I had Peter here now! This just shows how we men can go about forming judgments like the blindest moles—

HOVSTAD: What do you mean, doctor?

DR. STOCKMANN: (*Stopping beside the table.*) Isn't it the general opinion that our town is a healthy place?

HOVSTAD: Of course.

DR. STOCKMANN: A quite exceptionally healthy place, indeed—a place to be warmly recommended, both to invalids and people in health.

MRS. STOCKMANN: My dear Thomas—

DR. STOCKMANN: And assuredly we haven't failed to recommend and be-laud it. I've sung its praises again and again, both in the *Messenger* and in pamphlets—

HOVSTAD: Well, what then?

DR. STOCKMANN: These Baths, that we have called the pulse of the town, its vital nerve, and—and the devil knows what else—

BILLING: "Our city's palpitating heart," I once ventured to call them in a convivial moment—

DR. STOCKMANN: Yes, I daresay. Well—do you know what they really are, these mighty, magnificent, belauded Baths, that have cost so much money—do you know what they are?

HOVSTAD: No, what are they?

MRS. STOCKMANN: Do tell us.

DR. STOCKMANN: Simply a pestiferous hole, carrying or spreading infec-
tious disease.

PETRA: The Baths, father?

MRS. STOCKMANN: (*At the same time.*) Our Baths!

HOVSTAD: (*Also at the same time.*) But, Doctor—!

BILLING: Oh, its incredible!

DR. STOCKMANN: I tell you the whole place is a poisonous whited-sepul-
chre; noxious in the highest degree! All that filth up there in the Mill Dale—
the stuff that smells so horribly—taints the water in the feedpipes of the
Pump-Room; and the same accursed poisonous refuse oozes out by the
beach—

HOVSTAD: Where the sea-baths are?

DR. STOCKMANN: Exactly.

HOVSTAD: But how are you so sure of all this, Doctor?

DR. STOCKMANN: I've investigated the whole thing as conscientiously as
possible. I've long had my suspicions about it. Last year we had some extraordinary cases of illness among the patients—both typhoid and gastric
attacks—

MRS. STOCKMANN: Yes, I remember.

DR. STOCKMANN: We thought at the time that the visitors had brought the
infection with them; but afterwards—last winter—I began to question that.
So I set about testing the water as well as I could.

MRS. STOCKMANN: It was that you were working so hard at!

DR. STOCKMANN: Yes, you may well say I've worked, Katrina. But here,
you know, I hadn't the necessary scientific appliances; so I sent samples both
of our drinking water and of our sea-water to the University, for exact
analysis by a chemist.

HOVSTAD: And you have received his report?

DR. STOCKMANN: (*Showing letter.*) Here it is! And it proves beyond dispute the presence of putrefying organic matter in the water—millions of
infusoria. It's absolutely pernicious to health, whether used internally or
externally.

MRS. STOCKMANN: What a blessing you found it out in time.

DR. STOCKMANN: Yes, you may well say that.

HOVSTAD: And what do you intend to do now, Doctor?

DR. STOCKMANN: Why, to set things right, of course.

HOVSTAD: You think it can be done, then?

DR. STOCKMAN: It must be done. Else the whole Baths are useless, ruined.
But there's no fear. I am quite clear as to what is required.

MRS. STOCKMANN: But, my dear Thomas, why should you have made such
a secret of all this?

DR. STOCKMANN: Would you have had me rush all over the town and
chatter about it, before I was quite certain? No, thank you; I'm not so mad
as that.

PETRA: But to us at home—

DR. STOCKMANN: I couldn't say a word to a living soul. But to-morrow you
may look in at the Badger's—

MRS. STOCKMANN: Oh, Thomas!

DR. STOCKMANN: Well, well, at your grandfather's. The old fellow will be
astonished! He thinks I'm not quite right in my head—yes, and plenty of
others think the same, I've noticed. But now these good people shall see—
yes, they shall see now! (*Walks up and down rubbing his hands.*) What a
stir there will be in the town, Katrina! Just think of it! All the water pipes
will have to be relaid.

HOVSTAD: (*Rising.*) All the water pipes—?

DR. STOCKMANN: Why, of course. The intake is too low down; it must be moved much higher up.

PETRA: So you were right, after all?

DR. STOCKMANN: Yes, do you remember, Petra? I wrote against it when they were beginning the works. But no one would listen to me then. Now, you may be sure, I shall give them my full broadside—for of course I've prepared a statement for the Directors; it has been lying ready a whole week; I've only been waiting for this report. (*Points to letter.*) But now they shall have it at once. (*Goes into his room and returns with a MS. in his hand.*) See! Four closely-written sheets! And I'll enclose the report. A newspaper, Katrina! Get me something to wrap them up in. There—that's it. Give it to—to —(*Stamps.*)—what the devil's her name? Give it to the girl, I mean, and tell her to take it at once to the Burgomaster.

(Mrs. Stockmann *goes out with the packet through the dining-room.*)

PETRA: What do you think Uncle Peter will say, father?

DR. STOCKMANN: What should he say? He can't possibly be otherwise than pleased that so important a fact has been brought to light.

HOVSTAD: I suppose you will let me put a short announcement of your discovery in the *Messenger.*

DR. STOCKMANN: Yes, I shall be much obliged if you will.

HOVSTAD: It is highly desirable that the public should know about it as soon as possible.

DR. STOCKMANN: Yes, certainly.

MRS. STOCKMANN: (*Returning*) She's gone with it.

BILLING: Strike me dead if you won't be the first man in the town, Doctor!

DR. STOCKMANN: (*Walks up and down in high glee.*) Oh, nonsense! After all, I have done no more than my duty. I've been a lucky treasure-hunter, that's all. But all the same—

BILLING: Hovstad, don't you think the town ought to get up a torchlight procession in honour of Dr. Stockmann?

HOVSTAD: I shall certainly propose it.

BILLING: And I'll talk it over with Aslaksen.

DR. STOCKMANN: No, my dear friends; let all such claptrap alone. I won't hear of anything of the sort. And if the Directors should want to raise my salary, I won't accept it. I tell you, Katrina, I will not accept it.

MRS. STOCKMANN: You are quite right, Thomas.

PETRA: (*Raising her glass.*) Your health, father!

HOVSTAD *and* BILLING: Your health, your health, Doctor!

HORSTER: (*Clinking glasses with the* Doctor) I hope you may have nothing but joy of your discovery.

DR. STOCKMANN: Thanks, thanks, my dear friends! I can't tell you how happy I am—! Oh, what a blessing it is to feel that you have deserved well of your native town and your fellow citizens. Hurrah, Katrina!

(He puts both his arms round her neck, and whirls her round with him. Mrs. Stockmann *screams and struggles. A burst of laughter, applause, and cheers for the* Doctor. *The boys thrust their heads in at the door.*)

ACT SECOND

The Doctor's *sitting-room. The dining-room door is closed. Morning.*

MRS. STOCKMANN: (*Enters from the dining-room with a sealed letter in her hand, goes to the foremost door on the right, and peeps in.*) Are you there, Thomas?

DR. STOCKMANN: (*Within*) Yes, I have just come in. (*Enters.*) What is it?

MRS. STOCKMANN: A letter from your brother. (*Hands it to him.*)

DR. STOCKMANN: Aha, let us see. (*Opens the envelope and reads.*) "The MS. sent me is returned herewith—" (*Reads on, mumbling to himself.*) H'm—

MRS. STOCKMANN: Well, what does he say?

DR. STOCKMANN: (*Putting the paper in his pocket.*) Nothing; only that he'll come up himself about midday.

MRS. STOCKMANN: Then be sure you remember to stay at home.

DR. STOCKMANN: Oh, I can easily manage that; I've finished my morning's visits.

MRS. STOCKMANN: I am very curious to know how he takes it.

DR. STOCKMANN: You'll see he won't be over-pleased that it is I that have made the discovery, and not he himself.

MRS. STOCKMANN: Ah, that's just what I'm afraid of.

DR. STOCKMANN: Of course at bottom he'll be glad. But still— Peter is damnably unwilling that any one but himself should do anything for the good of the town.

MRS. STOCKMANN: Do you know, Thomas, I think you might stretch a point, and share the honour with him. Couldn't it appear that it was he that put you on the track—?

DR. STOCKMANN: By all means, for aught I care. If only I can get things put straight—

(*Old* Morten Kiil *puts his head in at the hall door, and asks slyly*)

MORTEN KIIL: Is it—is it true?

MRS. STOCKMANN: (*Going towards him.*) Father—is that you?

DR. STOCKMANN: Hallo, father-in-law! Good morning, good morning.

MRS. STOCKMANN: Do come in.

MORTEN KIIL: Yes, if it's true; if not, I'm off again.

DR. STOCKMANN: If what is true?

MORTEN KIIL: This crazy business about the water-works. Now, is it true?

DR. STOCKMANN: Of course it is. But how came you to hear of it?

MORTEN KIIL: (*Coming in.*) Petra looked in on her way to the school—

DR. STOCKMANN: Oh, did she?

MORTEN KIIL: Ay ay—and she told me—. I thought she was only making game of me; but that's not like Petra either.

DR. STOCKMANN: No, indeed; how could you think so?

MORTEN KIIL: Oh, you can never be sure of anybody. You may be made a fool of before you know where you are. So it is true, after all?

DR. STOCKMANN: Most certainly it is. Do sit down, father-in-law. (*Forces him down on the sofa.*) Now isn't it a real blessing for the town—?

MORTEN KIIL: (*Suppressing his laughter.*) A blessing for the town?

DR. STOCKMANN: Yes, that I made this discovery in time—

MORTEN KIIL: (*As before.*) Ay, ay, ay!—Well, I could never have believed that you would play monkey-tricks with your very own brother.

DR. STOCKMANN: Monkey-tricks!

MRS. STOCKMANN: Why, father dear—

MORTEN KIIL: (*Resting his hands and chin on the top of his stick and blinking slyly at the* Doctor.) What was it again? Wasn't it that some animals had got into the water-pipes?

DR. STOCKMANN: Yes; infusorial animals.

MORTEN KIIL: And any number of these animals had got in, Petra said— whole swarms of them.

DR. STOCKMANN: Certainly; hundreds of thousands.

MORTEN KIIL: But no one can see them—isn't that it?

DR. STOCKMANN: Quite right; no one can see them.

MORTEN KIIL: (*With a quiet, chuckling laugh.*) I'll be damned if that isn't the best thing I've heard of you yet.

DR. STOCKMANN: What do you mean?

MORTEN KIIL: But you'll never in this world make the Burgomaster take in anything of the sort.

DR. STOCKMANN: Well, that we shall see.

MORTEN KIIL: Do you really think he'll be so crazy?

DR. STOCKMANN: I hope the whole town will be so crazy.

MORTEN KIIL: The whole town! Well, I don't say but it may. But it serves them right; it'll teach them a lesson. They wanted to be so much cleverer than we old fellows. They hounded me out of the Town Council. Yes; I tell you they hounded me out like a dog, that they did. But now it's their turn. Just you keep up the game with them, Stockmann.

DR. STOCKMANN: Yes, but, father-in-law—

MORTEN KIIL: Keep it up, I say. (*Rising.*) If you can make the Burgomaster and his gang eat humble pie, I'll give a hundred crowns straight away to the poor.

DR. STOCKMANN: Come, that's good of you.

MORTEN KIIL: Of course I've little enough to throw away; but if you can manage that, I shall certainly remember the poor at Christmas-time, to the tune of fifty crowns.

(Hovstad *enters from hall.*)

HOVSTAD: Good morning! (*Pausing.*) Oh! I beg your pardon—

DR. STOCKMANN: Not at all. Come in, come in.

MORTEN KIIL: (*Chuckling again.*) He! Is he in it too?

HOVSTAD: What do you mean?

DR. STOCKMANN: Yes, of course he is.

MORTEN KIIL: I might have known it! It's to go into the papers. Ah, you're the one, Stockmann! Do you two lay your heads together; I'm off.

DR. STOCKMANN: Oh no; don't go yet, father-in-law.

MORTEN KIIL: No, I'm off now. Play them all the monkey-tricks you can think of. Deuce take me but you shan't lose by it.

(He goes, Mrs. Stockmann *accompanying him.*)

DR. STOCKMANN: (*Laughing*) What do you think—? The old fellow doesn't believe a word of all this about the water-works.

HOVSTAD: Was that what he—?

DR. STOCKMANN: Yes; that was what we were talking about. And I daresay you have come on the same business?

HOVSTAD: Yes. Have you a moment to spare, Doctor?

DR. STOCKMANN: As many as you like, my dear fellow.

HOVSTAD: Have you heard anything from the Burgomaster?

DR. STOCKMANN: Not yet. He'll be here presently.

HOVSTAD: I have been thinking the matter over since last evening.

DR. STOCKMANN: Well?

HOVSTAD: To you, as a doctor and a man of science, this business of the water-works appears an isolated affair. I daresay it hasn't occurred to you that a good many other things are bound up with it?

DR. STOCKMANN: Indeed! In what way? Let us sit down, my dear fellow.— No; there, on the sofa.

(Hovstad *sits on sofa: the* Doctor *in an easy-chair on the other side of the table.)*

DR. STOCKMANN: Well, so you think—?

HOVSTAD: You said yesterday that the water is polluted by impurities in the soil.

DR. STOCKMANN: Yes, undoubtedly; the mischief comes from that poisonous swamp up in the Mill Dale.

HOVSTAD: Excuse me, Doctor, but I think it comes from a very different swamp.

DR. STOCKMANN: What swamp may that be?

HOVSTAD: The swamp in which our whole municipal life is rotting.

DR. STOCKMANN: The devil, Mr. Hovstad! What notion is this you've got hold of?

HOVSTAD: All the affairs of the town have gradually drifted into the hands of a pack of bureaucrats—

DR. STOCKMANN: Come now, they're not all bureaucrats.

HOVSTAD: No; but those who are not are the friends and adherents of those who are. We are entirely under the thumb of a ring of wealthy men, men of old family and position in the town.

DR. STOCKMANN: Yes, but they are also men of ability and insight.

HOVSTAD: Did they show ability and insight when they laid the water-pipes where they are?

DR. STOCKMANN: No; that, of course, was a piece of stupidity. But that will be set right now.

HOVSTAD: Do you think it will go so smoothly?

DR. STOCKMANN: Well, smoothly or not, it will have to be done.

HOVSTAD: Yes, if the press exerts its influence.

DR. STOCKMANN: Not at all necessary, my dear fellow; I am sure my brother—

HOVSTAD: Excuse me, Doctor, but I must tell you that I think of taking the matter up.

DR. STOCKMANN: In the paper?

HOVSTAD: Yes. When I took over the *People's Messenger,* I was determined to break up the ring of obstinate old blockheads who held everything in their hands.

DR. STOCKMANN: But you told me yourself what came of it. You nearly ruined the paper.

HOVSTAD: Yes, at that time we had to draw in our horns, that's true enough. The whole Bath scheme might have fallen through if these men had been sent about their business. But now the Baths are an accomplished fact, and we can get on without these august personages.

DR. STOCKMANN: Get on without them, yes; but still we owe them a great deal.

HOVSTAD: The debt shall be duly acknowledged. But a journalist of my democratic tendencies cannot let such an opportunity slip through his fingers. We must explode the tradition of official infallibility. That rubbish must be got rid of, like every other superstition.

DR. STOCKMANN: There I am with you with all my heart, Mr. Hovstad. If it's a superstition, away with it!

HOVSTAD: I should be sorry to attack the Burgomaster, as he is your brother. But I know you think with me—the truth before all other considerations.

DR. STOCKMANN: Why, of course (*Vehemently.*) But still—! but still—!

HOVSTAD: You mustn't think ill of me. I am neither more self-interested nor more ambitious than other men.

DR. STOCKMANN: Why, my dear fellow—who says you are?

HOVSTAD: I come of humble folk, as you know; and I have had ample opportunities of seeing what the lower classes really require. And that is to have a share in the direction of public affairs, Doctor. That is what develops ability and knowledge and self-respect—

DR. STOCKMANN: I understand that perfectly.

HOVSTAD: Yes; and I think a journalist incurs a heavy responsibility if he lets slip a chance of helping to emancipate the downtrodden masses. I know well enough that our oligarchy will denounce me as an agitator, and so forth; but what do I care? If only my conscience is clear, I—

DR. STOCKMANN: Just so, just so, my dear Mr. Hovstad. But still—deuce take it—! (*A knock at the door.*) Come in!

(Aslaksen, *the printer, appears at the door leading to the hall. He is humbly but respectably dressed in black, wears a white necktie, slightly crumpled, and has a silk hat and gloves in his hand.*)

ASLAKSEN: (*Bowing.*) I beg pardon, Doctor, for making so bold—

DR. STOCKMANN: (*Rising.*) Hallo! If it isn't Mr. Aslaksen!

ASLAKSEN: Yes, it's me, Doctor.

HOVSTAD: (*Rising.*) Is it me you want, Aslaksen?

ASLAKSEN: No, not at all. I didn't know you were here. No, it's the Doctor himself—

DR. STOCKMANN: Well, what can I do for you?

ASLAKSEN: Is it true, what Mr. Billing tells me, that you're going to get us a better set of water-works?

DR. STOCKMANN: Yes, for the Baths.

ASLAKSEN: Of course, of course. Then I just looked in to say that I'll back up the movement with all my might.

HOVSTAD: (*To the* Doctor.) You see!

DR. STOCKMANN: I'm sure I thank you heartily; but—

ASLAKSEN: You may find it no such bad thing to have us small middle-class men at your back. We form what you may call a compact majority in the town—when we really make up our minds, that's to say. And it's always well to have the majority with you, Doctor.

DR. STOCKMANN: No doubt, no doubt; but I can't conceive that any special measures will be necessary in this case. I should think in so clear and straight-forward a matter—

ASLAKSEN: Yes, but all the same, it can do no harm. I know the local authorities very well—the powers that be are not over ready to adopt suggestions from outsiders. So I think it wouldn't be amiss if we made some sort of a demonstration.

HOVSTAD: Precisely my opinion.

DR. STOCKMANN: A demonstration, you say? But in what way would you demonstrate?

ASLAKSEN: Of course with great moderation, Doctor, I always insist upon moderation; for moderation is a citizen's first virtue—at least that's my way of thinking.

DR. STOCKMANN: We all know that, Mr. Aslaksen.

ASLAKSEN: Yes, I think my moderation is generally recognized. And this affair of the water-works is very important for us small middle-class men. The Baths bid fair to become, as you might say, a little gold-mine for the town. We shall all have to live by the Baths, especially we house-owners. So we want to support the Baths all we can; and as I am Chairman of the House-owners' Association—

DR. STOCKMANN: Well—?

ASLAKSEN: And as I'm an active worker for the Temperance Society—of course you know, Doctor, that I'm a temperance man?

DR. STOCKMANN: To be sure, to be sure.

ASLAKSEN: Well, you'll understand that I come in contact with a great many people. And as I'm known to be a prudent and law-abiding citizen, as you yourself remarked, Doctor, I have a certain influence in the town, and hold some power in my hands—though I say it that shouldn't.

DR. STOCKMANN: I know that very well, Mr. Aslaksen.

ASLAKSEN: Well then, you see—it would be easy for me to get up an address, if it came to a pinch.

DR. STOCKMANN: An address?

ASLAKSEN: Yes, a kind of vote of thanks to you, from the citizens of the town, for your action in a matter of such general concern. Of course it will have to be drawn up with all fitting moderation, so as to give no offence to the authorities and parties in power. But so long as we're careful about that, no one can take it ill, I should think.

HOVSTAD: Well, even if they didn't particularly like it—

ASLAKSEN: No no no; no offence to the powers that be, Mr. Hovstad. No opposition to people that can take it out of us again so easily. I've had enough of that in my time; no good ever comes of it. But no one can object to the free but temperate expression of a citizen's opinion.

DR. STOCKMANN: (Shaking his hand.) I can't tell you, my dear Mr. Aslaksen, how heartily it delights me to find so much support among my fellow townsmen. I'm so happy—so happy! Come, you'll have a glass of sherry? Eh?

ASLAKSEN: No, thank you; I never touch spirituous liquors.

DR. STOCKMANN: Well, then, a glass of beer—what do you say to that?

ASLAKSEN: Thanks, not that either, Doctor. I never take anything so early in the day. And now I'll be off round the town, and talk to some of the house-owners, and prepare public opinion.

DR. STOCKMANN: It's extremely kind of you, Mr. Aslaksen; but I really cannot get it into my head that all these preparations are necessary. The affair seems to me so simple and self-evident.

ASLAKSEN: The authorities always move slowly, Doctor—God forbid I should blame them for it—

HOVSTAD: We'll stir them up in the paper to-morrow, Aslaksen.

ASLAKSEN: No violence, Mr. Hovstad. Proceed with moderation, or you'll do nothing with them. Take my advice; I've picked up experience in the school of life.—And now I'll say good morning, Doctor. You know now that at least you have us small middle-class men behind you, solid as a wall. You have the compact majority on your side, Doctor.

DR. STOCKMANN: Many thanks, my dear Mr. Aslaksen. (*Holds out his hand.*) Good-bye, good-bye.

ASLAKSEN: Are you coming to the office, Mr. Hovstad?

HOVSTAD: I shall come on presently. I have still one or two things to arrange.

ASLAKSEN: Very well.

(*Bows and goes.* Dr. Stockmann *accompanies him into the hall.*)

HOVSTAD: (*As the* Doctor *re-enters.*) Well, what do you say to that, Doctor? Don't you think it is high time we should give all this weak-kneed, half-hearted cowardice a good shaking up?

DR. STOCKMANN: Are you speaking of Aslaksen?

HOVSTAD: Yes, I am. He's a decent enough fellow, but he's one of those who are sunk in the swamp. And most people here are just like him; they are for ever wavering and wobbling from side to side; what with scruples and misgivings, they never dare advance a step.

DR. STOCKMANN: Yes, but Aslaksen seems to me thoroughly well-intentioned.

HOVSTAD: There is one thing I value more than good intentions, and that is an attitude of manly self-reliance.

DR. STOCKMANN: There I am quite with you.

HOVSTAD: So I am going to seize this opportunity, and try whether I can't for once put a little grit into their good intentions. The worship of authority must be rooted up in this town. This gross, inexcusable blunder of the waterworks must be brought home clearly to every voter.

DR. STOCKMANN: Very well. If you think it's for the good of the community, so be it; but not till I have spoken to my brother.

HOVSTAD: At all events, I shall be writing my leader in the meantime. And if the Burgomaster won't take the matter up—

DR. STOCKMANN: But how can you conceive his refusing?

HOVSTAD: Oh, it's not inconceivable. And then—

DR. STOCKMANN: Well then, I promise you—; look here—in that case you may print my paper—put it in just as it is.

HOVSTAD: May I? Is that a promise?

DR. STOCKMANN: (*Handing him the manuscript-*) There it is; take it with you. You may as well read it in any case; you can't return it to me afterwards.

HOVSTAD: Very good; I shall do so. And now, good-bye, Doctor.

DR. STOCKMANN: Good-bye, good-bye. You'll see it will all go smoothly, Mr. Hovstad—as smoothly as possible.

HOVSTAD: H'm—we shall see. (*Bows and goes out through the hall.*)

DR. STOCKMANN: (*Going to the dining-room door and looking in.*) Katrina! Hallo! are you back, Petra?

PETRA: (*Entering.*) Yes, I've just got back from school.

MRS. STOCKMANN: (*Entering.*) Hasn't he been here yet?

DR. STOCKMANN: Peter? No; but I have been having a long talk with Hovstad. He's quite enthusiastic about my discovery. It turns out to be much wider import than I thought at first. So he has placed his paper at my disposal, if I should require it.

MRS. STOCKMANN: Do you think you will?

DR. STOCKMANN: Not I! But at the same time, one cannot but be proud to know that the enlightened, independent press is on one's side. And what do you think? I have had a visit from the Chairman of the House-owners' Association too.

MRS. STOCKMANN: Really? What did he want?

DR. STOCKMANN: To assure me of his support. They will all stand by me at a pinch. Katrina, do you know what I have behind me?

MRS. STOCKMANN: Behind you? No. What have you behind you?

DR. STOCKMANN: The compact majority!

MRS. STOCKMANN: Oh! Is that good for you, Thomas?

DR. STOCKMANN: Yes, indeed; I should think it was good. (*Rubbing his hands as he walks up and down.*) Great God! what a delight it is to feel oneself in such brotherly unison with one's fellow townsmen?

PETRA: And to do so much that's good and useful, father!

DR. STOCKMANN: And all for one's native town, too!

MRS. STOCKMANN: There's the bell.

DR. STOCKMANN: That must be he. (*Knock at the door.*) Come in!

(Enter Burgomaster Stockmann *from the hall.)*

BURGOMASTER: Good morning.

DR. STOCKMANN: I'm glad to see you, Peter.

MRS. STOCKMANN: Good morning, brother-in-law. How are you?

BURGOMASTER: Oh, thanks, so-so. (*To the* doctor.) Yesterday evening, after office hours, I received from you a dissertation upon the state of the water at the Baths.

DR. STOCKMANN: Yes. Have you read it?

BURGOMASTER: I have.

DR. STOCKMANN: And what do you think of the affair?

BURGOMASTER: H'm—(*with a sidelong glance.*)

MRS. STOCKMANN: Come, Petra. (*She and* Petra *go into the room on the left.*)

BURGOMASTER: (*After a pause.*) Was it necessary to make all these investigations behind my back?

DR. STOCKMANN: Yes, till I was absolutely certain, I—

BURGOMASTER: And are you absolutely certain now?

DR. STOCKMANN: My paper must surely have convinced you of that.

BURGOMASTER: Is it your intention to submit this statement to the Board of Directors, as a sort of official document?

DR. STOCKMANN: Of course. Something must be done in the matter, and that promptly.

BURGOMASTER: As usual, you use very strong expressions in your statement. Amongst other things, you say that what we offer our visitors is a slow poison.

DR. STOCKMANN: Why, Peter, what else can it be called? Only think— poisoned water both internally and externally! And that to poor invalids who come to us in all confidence, and pay us handsomely to cure them!

BURGOMASTER: And then you announce as your conclusion that we must build a sewer to carry off the alleged impurities from the Mill Dale, and must re-lay all the water-pipes.

DR. STOCKMANN: Can you suggest any other plan?—I know of none.

BURGOMASTER: I found a pretext for looking in at the town engineer's this morning, and—in a half-jesting way—I mentioned these alterations as things we might possibly have to consider, at some future time.

DR. STOCKMANN: At some future time!

BURGOMASTER: Of course he smiled at what he thought my extravagance. Have you taken the trouble to think what your proposed alterations would cost? From what the engineer said, I gathered that the expenses would probably mount up to several hundred thousand crowns.

DR. STOCKMANN: So much as that?

BURGOMASTER: Yes. But that is not the worst. The work would take at least two years.

DR. STOCKMANN: Two years! Do you mean to say two whole years?

BURGOMASTER: At least. And what are we to do with the Baths in the meanwhile? Are we to close them? We should have no alternative. Do you think any one would come here, if it got abroad that the water was pestilential?

DR. STOCKMANN: But, Peter, that's precisely what it is.

BURGOMASTER: And all this now, just now, when the Baths are doing so well! Neigbouring towns, too, are not without their claims to rank as health-resorts. Do you think they would not at once set to work to divert the full stream of visitors to themselves? Undoubtedly they would; and we should be left stranded. We should probably have to give up the whole costly undertaking; and so you would have ruined your native town.

DR. STOCKMANN: I—ruined—!

BURGOMASTER: It is only through the Baths that the town has any future worth speaking of. You surely know that as well as I do.

DR. STOCKMANN: Then what do you think should be done?

BURGOMASTER: I have not succeeded in convincing myself that the condition of the water at the Baths is as serious as your statement represents.

DR. STOCKMANN: I tell you it's if anything worse—or will be in the summer, when the hot weather sets in.

BURGOMASTER: I repeat that I believe you exaggerate greatly. A competent physician should know what measures to take—he should be able to obviate deleterious influences, and to counteract them in case they should make themselves unmistakably felt.

DR. STOCKMANN: Indeed—? And then—?

BURGOMASTER: The existing water-works are, once for all, a fact, and must naturally be treated as such. But when the time comes, the Directors will probably not be indisposed to consider whether it may not be possible, without unreasonable pecuniary sacrifices, to introduce certain improvements.

DR. STOCKMANN: And do you imagine I could ever be a party to such dishonesty?

BURGOMASTER: Dishonesty?

DR. STOCKMANN: Yes, it would be dishonesty—a fraud, a lie, an absolute crime against the public, against society as a whole!

BURGOMASTER: I have not, as I before remarked, been able to convince myself that there is really any such imminent danger.

DR. STOCKMANN: You have! You must have! I know that my demonstration is absolutely clear and convincing. And you understand it perfectly, Peter, only you won't admit it. It was you who insisted that both the Bath-buildings and the water-works should be placed where they now are; and it's that—it's that damned blunder that you won't confess. Pshaw! Do you think I don't see through you?

BURGOMASTER: And even if it were so? If I do watch over my reputation with a certain anxiety, I do it for the good of the town. Without moral authority I cannot guide and direct affairs in the way I consider most conducive to the general welfare. Therefore—and on various other grounds—it is of great moment to me that your statement should not be submitted to the Board of Directors. It must be kept back, for the good of the community. Later on I will bring up the matter for discussion, and we will do the best we can, quietly; but not a word, not a whisper, of this unfortunate business must come to the public ears.

DR. STOCKMANN: But it can't be prevented now, my dear Peter.

BURGOMASTER: It must and shall be prevented.

DR. STOCKMANN: It can't be, I tell you; far too many people know about it already.

BURGOMASTER: Know about it! Who? Surely not those fellows on the *People's Messenger*—?

DR. STOCKMANN: Oh yes; they know. The liberal, independent press will take good care that you do your duty.

BURGOMASTER: (*After a short pause.*)You are an amazingly reckless man, Thomas. Have you not reflected what the consequences of this may be to yourself?

DR. STOCKMANN: Consequences?—Consequences to me?

BURGOMASTER: Yes—to you and yours.

DR. STOCKMANN: What the devil do you mean?

BURGOMASTER: I believe I have always shown myself ready and willing to lend you a helping hand.

DR. STOCKMANN: Yes, you have, and I thank you for it.

BURGOMASTER: I ask for no thanks. Indeed, I was in some measure forced to act as I did—for my own sake. I always hoped I should be able to keep you a little in check, if I helped to improve your pecuniary position.

DR. STOCKMANN: What! So it was only for your own sake—!

BURGOMASTER: In a measure, I say. It is painful for a man in an official position, when his nearest relative goes and compromises himself time after time.

DR. STOCKMANN: And you think I do that?

BURGOMASTER: Yes, unfortunately, you do, without knowing it. Yours is a turbulent, unruly, rebellious spirit. And then you have an unhappy propensity for rushing into print upon every possible and impossible occasion. You no sooner hit upon an idea than you must needs write a newspaper article or a whole pamphlet about it.

DR. STOCKMANN: Isn't it a citizen's duty, when he has conceived a new idea, to communicate it to the public!

BURGOMASTER: Oh, the public has no need for new ideas. The public gets on best with the good old recognised ideas it has already.

DR. STOCKMANN: You say that right out!

BURGOMASTER: Yes, I must speak frankly to you for once. Hitherto I have tried to avoid it, for I know how irritable you are; but now I must tell you the truth, Thomas. You have no conception how much you injure yourself by your officiousness. You complain of the authorities, ay, of the Government itself—you cry them down and maintain that you have been slighted, persecuted. But what else can you expect, with your impossible disposition?

DR. STOCKMANN: Oh, indeed! So I am impossible, am I?

BURGOMASTER: Yes, Thomas, you are an impossible man to work with. I know that from experience. You have no consideration for any one or any thing; you seem quite to forget that you have me to thank for your position as medical officer of the Baths—

DR. STOCKMANN: It was mine by right! Mine, and no one else's! I was the first to discover the town's capabilities as a watering place; I saw them, and, at that time, I alone. For years I fought single-handed for this idea of mine; I wrote and wrote—

BURGOMASTER: No doubt; but then the right time had not come. Of course, in that out-of-the-world corner, you could not judge of that. As soon as the propitious moment arrived, I—and others—took the matter in hand—

DR. STOCKMANN: Yes, and you went and bungled the whole of my glorious plan. Oh, we see now what a set of wiseacres you were!

BURGOMASTER: All *I* can see is that you are again seeking an outlet for your pugnacity. You want to make an onslaught on your superiors—that is an old habit of yours. You cannot endure any authority over you; you look askance at any one who holds a higher post than your own; you regard him as a personal enemy—and then you care nothing what kind of weapon you use against him. But now I have shown you how much is at stake for the town, and consequently for me too. And therefore I warn you, Thomas, that I am inexorable in the demand I am about to make of you!

DR. STOCKMANN: What demand?

BURGOMASTER: As you have not had the sense to refrain from chattering to outsiders about this delicate business, which should have been kept an official secret, of course it cannot now be hushed up. All sorts of rumours will get abroad, and evil-disposed persons will invent all sorts of additions to them. It will therefore be necessary for you publicly to contradict these remours.

DR. STOCKMANN: I! How? I don't understand you?

BURGOMASTER: We expect that, after further investigation, you will come to the conclusion that the affair is not nearly so serious or pressing as you had at first imagined.

DR. STOCKMANN: Aha! So you expect that?

BURGOMASTER: Furthermore, we expect you to express your confidence that the Board of Directors will thoroughly and conscientiously carry out all measures for the remedying of any possible defects.

DR. STOCKMANN: Yes, but that you'll never be able to do, so long as you go on tinkering and patching. I tell you that, Peter; and it's my deepest, sincerest conviction—

BURGOMASTER: As an official, you have no right to hold any individual conviction.

DR. STOCKMANN: (*Starting.*) No right to—?

BURGOMASTER: As an official, I say. In your private capacity, of course, it is another matter. But as a subordinate official of the Baths, you have no right to express any conviction at issue with that of your superiors.

DR. STOCKMANN: This is too much! I, a doctor, a man of science, have no right to—!

BURGOMASTER: The matter in question is not a purely scientific one; it is a complex affair; it has both a technical and an economic side.

DR. STOCKMANN: What the devil do I care what it is! I will be free to speak my mind upon any subject under the sun!

BURGOMASTER: As you please—so long as it does not concern the Baths. With them we forbid you to meddle.

DR. STOCKMANN: (*Shouts.*) You forbid—! You! A set of—

BURGOMASTER: I forbid it—*I*, your chief; and when I issue an order, you have simply to obey.

DR. STOCKMANN: (*Controlling himself.*) Upon my word, Peter, if you weren't my brother—

PETRA: (*Tears open the door.*) Father, you shan't submit to this!

MRS. STOCKMANN: (*Following her.*) Petra, Petra!

BURGOMASTER: Ah! So we have been listening!

MRS. STOCKMANN: The partition is so thin, we couldn't help—

PETRA: I stood and listened on purpose.

BURGOMASTER: Well, on the whole, I am not sorry—

DR. STOCKMANN: (*Coming nearer to him.*) You spoke to me of forbidding and obeying—

BURGOMASTER: You have forced me to adopt that tone.

DR. STOCKMANN: And am I to give myself the lie, in a public declaration?

BURGOMASTER: We consider it absolutely necessary that you should issue a statement in the terms indicated.

DR. STOCKMANN: And if I do not obey?

BURGOMASTER: Then we shall ourselves put forth a statement to reassure the public.

DR. STOCKMANN: Well and good; then I shall write against you. I shall stick to my point and prove that *I* am right, and you wrong. And what will you do then?

BURGOMASTER: Then I shall be unable to prevent your dismissal.

DR. STOCKMANN: What—!

PETRA: Father! Dismissal!

MRS. STOCKMANN: Dismissal!

BURGOMASTER: Your dismissal from the Baths. I shall be compelled to move that notice be given you at once, and that you have henceforth no connection whatever with the Baths.

DR. STOCKMANN: You would dare to do that!

BURGOMASTER: It is you who are playing the daring game.

PETRA: Uncle, this is a shameful way to treat a man like father!

MRS. STOCKMANN: Do be quiet, Petra!

BURGOMASTER: (*Looking at* Petra.) Aha! We have opinions of our own already, eh? To be sure, to be sure! (*To Mrs. Stockmann.*) Sister-in-law, you are presumably the most rational member of this household. Use all your influence with your husband; try to make him realise what all this will involve both for his family—

DR. STOCKMANN: My family concerns myself alone!

BURGOMASTER: —both for his family, I say, and for the town he lives in.

DR. STOCKMANN: It is I that have the real good of the town at heart! I want to lay bare the evils that, sooner or later, must come to light. Ah! You shall be whether I love my native town.

BURGOMASTER: You, who, in your blind obstinacy, want to cut off the town's chief source of prosperity!

DR. STOCKMANN: That source is poisoned, man! Are you mad? We live by trafficking in filth and corruption! The whole of our flourishing social life is rooted in a lie!

BURGOMASTER: Idle fancies—or worse. The man who scatters broadcast such offensive insinuations against his native place must be an enemy of society.

DR. STOCKMANN: (*Going towards him.*) You dare to—

MRS. STOCKMANN: (*Throwing herself between them.*) Thomas!

PETRA: (*Seizing her father's arm.*) Keep calm, father!

BURGOMASTER: I will not expose myself to violence. You have had your warning now. Reflect upon what is due to yourself and to your family. Good-bye. (*He goes.*)

DR. STOCKMANN: (*Walking up and down.*) And I must put up with such treatment! In my own house, Katrina! What do you say to that!

MRS. STOCKMAN: Indeed, it's a shame and a disgrace, Thomas—

PETRA: Oh, if I could only get hold of uncle—!

DR. STOCKMANN: It's my own fault—I ought to have stood up against them long ago—to have shown my teeth—and used them too!—And to be called an enemy of society! Me! I won't bear it; by Heaven, I won't!

MRS. STOCKMANN: But my dear Thomas, after all, your brother has the power—

DR. STOCKMANN: Yes, but I have the right.

MRS. STOCKMANN: Ah yes, right, right! What good does it do to have the right, if you haven't any might?

PETRA: Oh, mother—how can you talk so?

DR. STOCKMANN: What! No good, in a free community, to have right on your side? What an absurd idea, Katrina! And besides—haven't I the free and independent press before me—and the compact majority at my back? That is might enough, I should think!

MRS. STOCKMANN: Why, good heavens, Thomas! you're surely not thinking of—?

DR. STOCKMANN: What am I not thinking of?

MRS. STOCKMANN: —of setting yourself up against your brother, I mean.

DR. STOCKMANN: What the devil would you have me do, if not stick to what is right and true?

PETRA: Yes, that's what I should like to know?

MRS. STOCKMANN: But it will be of no earthly use. If they won't, they won't.

DR. STOCKMANN: Ho-ho Katrina! just wait a while, and you shall see whether I can fight my battles to the end.

MRS. STOCKMANN: Yes, to the end of getting your dismissal; that is what will happen.

DR. STOCKMANN: Well then, I shall at any rate have done my duty towards the public, towards society—I who am called an enemy of society!

MRS. STOCKMANN: But towards your family, Thomas? Towards us at home? Do you think that is doing your duty towards those who are dependent on you?

PETRA: Oh, mother, don't always think first of us.

MRS. STOCKMANN: Yes, it's easy for you to talk; you can stand alone if need be.—But remember the boys, Thomas; and think a little of yourself too, and of me—

DR. STOCKMANN: You're surely out of your senses, Katrina! If I were to be such a pitiful coward as to knuckle under to this Peter and his confounded crew—should I ever have another happy hour in all my life?

MRS. STOCKMANN: I don't know about that; but God preserve us from the happiness we shall all of us have if you persist in defying them. There you will be again, with nothing to live on, with no regular income. I should have thought we had had enough of that in the old days. Remember them, Thomas; think of what it all means.

DR. STOCKMANN: (*Struggling with himself and clenching his hands.*) And this is what these jacks-in-office can bring upon a free and honest man! Isn't it revolting, Katrina?

MRS. STOCKMANN: Yes, no doubt they are treating you shamefully. But God knows there's plenty of injustice one must just submit to in this world. —Here are the boys, Thomas. Look at them! What is to become of them? Oh no, no! you can never have the heart—

(Eilif *and* Morten, *with school-books, have meanwhile entered.*)

DR. STOCKMANN: The boys—! (*With a sudden access of firmness and deci-sion.*) Never, though the whole earth should crumble, will I bow my neck beneath the yoke. (*Goes towards his room.*)

MRS. STOCKMANN: (*Following him.*) Thomas—what are you going to do?

DR. STOCKMANN: (*At the door.*) I must have the right to look my boys in the face when they have grown into free men. (*Goes into his room.*)

MRS. STOCKMANN: (*Bursts into tears.*) Ah, God help us all!

PETRA: Father is true to the core. He will never give in!

(*The boys ask wonderingly what it all means;* Petra *signs to them to be quiet.*)

ACT THIRD

The Editor's Room of the "People's Messenger" in the background, to the left, an entrance-door; to the right another door, with glass panes, through which can be seen the composing-room. A door in the right-hand wall. In the middle of the room a large table covered with papers, newspapers, and books. In front, on the left, a window, and by it a desk with a high stool. A couple of arm-chairs beside the table; some other chairs along the walls. The room is dingy and cheerless, the furniture shabby, the arm-chairs dirty and torn. In the composing-room are seen a few compositors at work; further back, a hand-press in operation.
Hovstad *is seated at the desk, writing. Presently* Billing *enters from the right, with the Doctor's manuscript in his hand.*

BILLING: Well, I must say—!

HOVSTAD: (*Writing.*) Have you read it through?

BILLING: (*Laying the MS. on the desk.*) Yes, I should think I had.

HOVSTAD: Don't you think the Doctor comes out strong?

BILLING: Strong! Why, strike me dead if he isn't crushing! Every word falls like a—well, like a sledge-hammer.

HOVSTAD: Yes, but these fellows won't collapse at the first blow.

BILLING: True enough; but we'll keep on hammering away, blow after blow, till the whole officialdom comes crashing down. As I sat in there reading that article, I seemed to hear the revolution thundering afar.

HOVSTAD: (*Turning around.*) Hush! Don't let Aslaksen hear that.

BILLING: (*In a lower voice.*) Aslaksen's a white-livered, cowardly fellow, without a spark of manhood in him. But this time you'll surely carry your point? Eh? You'll print the Doctor's paper?

HOVSTAD: Yes, if only the Burgomaster doesn't give in—

BILLING: That would be deuced annoying.

HOVSTAD: Well, whatever happens, fortunately we can turn the situation to account. If the Burgomaster won't agree to the Doctor's proposal, he'll have all the small middle-class down upon him—all the Houseowners' As-sociation, and the rest of them. And if he does agree to it, he'll fall out with the whole crew of big shareholders in the Baths, who have hitherto been his main support—

BILLING: Yes, of course; for no doubt they'll have to fork out a lot of money—

HOVSTAD: You may take your oath of that. And then, don't you see, when the ring is broken up, we'll din it into the public day by day that the

Burgomaster is incompetent in every respect, and that all responsible positions in the town, the whole municipal government in short, must be entrusted to men of liberal ideas.

BILLING: Strike me dead if that isn't the square truth! I see it—I see it: we are on the eve of a revolution! (*A knock at the door.*)

HOVSTAD: Hush! (*Calls.*) Come in!

(Dr. Stockmann *enters from the back, left.*)

HOVSTAD: (*Going towards him.*) Ah, here is the Doctor. Well?

DR. STOCKMANN: Print away, Mr. Hovstad!

HOVSTAD: So it has come to that?

BILLING: Hurrah!

DR. STOCKMANN: Print away, I tell you. To be sure it has come to that. Since they will have it so, they must. War is declared, Mr. Billing!

BILLING: War to the knife, say I! War to the death, Doctor!

DR. STOCKMANN: This article is only the beginning. I have four or five others sketched out in my head already. But where do you keep Aslaksen?

BILLING: (*Calling into the printing-room.*) Aslaksen! just come here a moment.

HOVSTAD: Four or five more articles, eh? On the same subject?

DR. STOCKMANN: Oh no—not at all, my dear fellow. No; they will deal with quite different matters. But they're all of a piece with the water-works and sewer question. One thing leads to another. It's just like beginning to pick at an old house, don't you know?

BILLING: Strike me dead, but that's true! You feel you can't leave off till you've pulled the whole lumberheap to pieces.

ASLAKSEN: (*Enters from the printing-room.*) Pulled to pieces! Surely the Doctor isn't thinking of pulling the Baths to pieces?

HOVSTAD: Not at all. Don't be alarmed.

DR. STOCKMANN: No, we were talking of something quite different. Well, what do you think of my article, Mr. Hovstad?

HOVSTAD: I think it's simply a masterpiece—

DR. STOCKMANN: Yes, isn't it? I'm glad you think so—very glad.

HOVSTAD: It's so clear and to the point. One doesn't in the least need to be a specialist to understand the gist of it. I am certain every intelligent man will be on your side.

ASLAKSEN: And all the prudent ones too, I hope?

BILLING: Both the prudent and imprudent—in fact, almost the whole town.

ASLAKSEN: Then I suppose we may venture to print it.

DR. STOCKMANN: I should think so!

HOVSTAD: It shall go in to-morrow.

DR. STOCKMANN: Yes, plague take it, not a day must be lost. Look here, Mr. Aslaksen, this is what I wanted to ask you: won't you take personal charge of the article?

ASLAKSEN: Certainly I will.

DR. STOCKMANN: Be as careful as if it were gold. No printers' errors; every word is important. I shall look in again presently; perhaps you'll be able to let me see a proof.—Ah! I can't tell you how I long to have the thing in print—to see it launched—

BILLING: Yes, like a thunderbolt!

DR. STOCKMANN: —and submitted to the judgment of every intelligent citizen. Oh, you have no idea what I have had to put up with to-day. I've been threatened with all sorts of things. I was to be robbed of my clearest rights as a human being—

BILLING: What! Your rights as a human being!

DR. STOCKMANN: —I was to humble myself, and eat the dust; I was to set my personal interests above my deepest, holiest convictions—

BILLING: Strike me dead, but that's too outrageous.

HOVSTAD: Oh, what can you expect from that quarter?

DR. STOCKMANN: But they shall find they were mistaken in me, they shall learn that in black and white, I promise them! I shall throw myself into the breach every day in the *Messenger,* bombard them with one explosive article after another—

ASLAKSEN: Yes, but look here—

BILLING: Hurrah! It's war! War!

DR. STOCKMANN: I shall smite them to the earth, I shall crush them, I shall level their entrenchments to the ground in the eyes of all right-thinking men! That's what I shall do!

ASLAKSEN: But above all things be temperate, Doctor; bombard with moderation—

BILLING: Not at all, not at all! Don't spare the dynamite!

DR. STOCKMANN: (*Going on imperturbably.*) For now it's no mere question of water-works and sewers, you see. No, the whole community must be purged, disinfected—

BILLING: There sounds the word of salvation.

DR. STOCKMANN: All the old bunglers must be sent packing, you understand. And that in every possible department! Such endless vistas have opened out before me to day. I am not quite clear about everything yet, but I shall see my way presently. It's young and vigorous standard-bearers we must look for, my friends; we must have new captains at all the outposts.

BILLING: Hear, hear!

DR. STOCKMANN: And if only we hold together, it will go so smoothly, so smoothly! The whole revolution will glide off the stocks just like a ship. Don't you think so?

HOVSTAD: For my part, I believe we have now every prospect of placing our municipal affairs in the right hands.

ASLAKSEN: And if only we proceed with moderation, I really don't think there can be any danger.

DR. STOCKMANN: Who the devil cares whether there's danger or not! What I do, I do in the name of truth and for conscience' sake.

HOVSTAD: You are a man to be backed up; Doctor.

ASLAKSEN: Yes, there's no doubt the Doctor is a true friend to the town; he's what I call a friend of society.

BILLING: Strike me dead if Dr. Stockmann isn't a Friend of the People, Aslaksen!

ASLAKSEN: I have no doubt the House-owners' Association will soon adopt that expression.

DR. STOCKMANN: (*Shaking their hands, deeply moved.*) Thanks, thanks, my dear, faithful friends; it does me good to hear you. My respected brother called me something very different. Never mind! Trust me to pay him back with interest! But I must be off now to see a poor devil of a patient. I shall look in again, though. Be sure you look after the article, Mr. Aslaksen; and, whatever you do, don't leave out any of my notes of exclamation! Rather put in a few more! Well, good-bye for the present, good-bye, good-bye.

(Mutual salutations while they accompany him to the door. He goes out.)

HOVSTAD: He will be invaluable to us.

ASLAKSEN: Yes, so long as he confines himself to this matter of the Baths. But if he goes further, it will scarcely be advisable to follow him.

HOVSTAD: H'm—that entirely depends on—

BILLING: You're always so confoundedly timid, Aslaksen.

ASLAKSEN: Timid? Yes, when it's a question of attacking local authorities, I am timid, Mr. Billing; I have learnt caution in the school of experience, let me tell you. But start me on the higher politics, confront me with the Government itself, and then see if I'm timid.

BILLING: No, you're not; but that's just where your inconsistency comes in.

ASLAKSEN: The fact is, I am keenly alive to my responsibilities. If you attack the Government, you at least do society no harm; for the men attacked don't care a straw, you see—they stay where they are all the same. But local authorities can be turned out; and then we might get some incompetent set into power, to the irreparable injury both of house-owners and other people.

HOVSTAD: But the education of citizens by self-government—do you never think of that?

ASLAKSEN: When a man has solid interests to protect, he can't think of everything, Mr. Hovstad.

HOVSTAD: Then I hope I may never have solid interests to protect.

BILLING: Hear, hear!

ASLAKSEN: *(Smiling.)* H'm! *(Points to the desk.)* Governor Stensgard sat in that editorial chair before you.

BILLING: *(Spitting.)* Pooh! A turncoat like that!

HOVSTAD: I am no weathercock—and never will be.

ASLAKSEN: A politician should never be too sure of anything on earth, Mr. Hovstad. And as for you, Mr. Billing, you ought to take in a reef or two, I should say, now that you are applying for the secretaryship to the Town Council.

BILLING: I—!

HOVSTAD: Is that so, Billing?

BILLING: Well, yes—but, deuce take it, you understand, I'm only doing it to spite their high-mightinesses.

ASLAKSEN: Well, that has nothing to do with me. But if I am to be accused of cowardice and inconsistency, I should just like to point out this: My political record is open to every one. I have not changed at all, except in becoming more moderate. My heart still belongs to the people; but I don't deny that my reason inclines somewhat towards the authorities—the local ones, I mean. *(Goes into the printing-room.)*

BILLING: Don't you think we should try to get rid of him, Hovstad?

HOVSTAD: Do you know of any one else that will pay for our paper and printing?

BILLING: What a confounded nuisance it is to have no capital!

HOVSTAD: *(Sitting down by the desk.)* Yes, if we only had that—

BILLING: Suppose you applied to Dr. Stockmann?

HOVSTAD: *(Turning over his papers.)* What would be the good? He hasn't a rap.

BILLING: No; but he has a good man behind him—old Morten Kiil—"The Badger," as they call him.

HOVSTAD: *(Writing.)* Are you so sure he has money?

BILLING: Yes, strike me dead if he hasn't! And part of it must certainly go to Stockmann's family. He's bound to provide for—for the children at any rate.

HOVSTAD: (*Half turning.*) Are you counting on that?

BILLING: Counting? How should I be counting on it?

HOVSTAD: Best not! And that secretaryship you shouldn't count on either; for I can assure you you won't get it.

BILLING: Do you think I don't know that? A refusal is the very thing I want. Such a rebuff fires the spirit of opposition in you, gives you a fresh supply of gall, as it were; and that's just what you need in a god-forsaken hole like this, where anything really stimulating so seldom happens.

HOVSTAD: (*Writing.*) Yes, yes.

BILLING: Well—they shall soon hear from me!—Now I'll go and write the appeal to the House-owners' Association. (*Goes into the room on the right.*)

HOVSTAD: (*Sits at his desk, biting his penholder, and says slowly:*) H'm— so that's the way of it.—(*A knock at the door.*) Come in.

(Petra *enters from the back, left.*)

HOVSTAD: (*Rising.*) What! Is it you? Here?

PETRA: Yes; please excuse me—

HOVSTAD: (*Offering her an arm-chair.*) Won't you sit down?

PETRA: No, thanks; I must go again directly.

HOVSTAD: Perhaps you bring a message from your father—?

PETRA: No, I have come on my own account. (*Takes a book from the pocket of her cloak.*) Here is that English story.

HOVSTAD: Why have you brought it back?

PETRA: Because I won't translate it.

HOVSTAD: But you promised—

PETRA: Yes; but then I hadn't read it. I suppose you have not read it either?

HOVSTAD: No; you know I can't read English; but—

PETRA: Exactly; and that's why I wanted to tell you that you must find something else. (*Putting the book on the table.*) This will never do for the *Messenger.*

HOVSTAD: Why not?

PETRA: Because it flies in the face of all your convictions.

HOVSTAD: Well, for that matter—

PETRA: You don't understand me. It makes out that a supernatural power looks after the so-called good people in this world, and turns everything to their advantage at last; while all the so-called bad people are punished.

HOVSTAD: Yes, but that's all right. That's the very thing the public like.

PETRA: And would you supply the public with such stuff? You don't believe a word of it yourself. You know well enough that things do not really happen like that.

HOVSTAD: Of course not; but an editor can't always do as he likes. He has often to humour people's fancies in minor matters. After all, politics is the chief thing in life—at any rate for a newspaper; and if I want the people to follow me along the path of emancipation and progress, I mustn't scare them away. If they find a moral story like this down in the cellar, they are all the more ready to take in what we tell them above—they feel themselves safer.

PETRA: For shame! You're not such a hypocrite as to set traps like that for your readers. You're not a spider.

HOVSTAD: (*Smiling.*) Thanks for your good opinion. It's true that the idea is Billing's, not mine.

PETRA: Mr. Billing's!

HOVSTAD: Yes, at least he was talking in that strain the other day. It was Billing that was so anxious to get the story into the paper; I don't even know the book.

PETRA: But how can Mr. Billing, with his advanced views—

HOVSTAD: Well, Billing is many-sided. He's applying for the secretary-ship to the Town Council, I hear.

PETRA: I don't believe that, Mr. Hovstad. How could he descend to such a thing?

HOVSTAD: That you must ask him.

PETRA: I could never have thought it of Billing!

HOVSTAD: (*Looking more closely at her.*) No? Is it such a surprise to you?

PETRA: Yes. And yet—perhaps not. Oh, I don't know—

HOVSTAD: We journalists are not worth much, Miss Petra.

PETRA: Do you really say that?

HOVSTAD: I think so, now and then.

PETRA: Yes, in the little every-day squabbles—that I can understand. But now that you have taken up a great cause—

HOVSTAD: You mean this affair of your father's?

PETRA: Of course. I should think you must feel yourself worth more than the general run of people now.

HOVSTAD: Yes, to-day I do feel something of the sort.

PETRA: Yes, surely you must. Oh, it's a glorious career you have chosen! To be the pioneer of unrecognised truths and new and daring ways of thought!—even, if that were all, to stand forth fearlessly in support of an injured man—

HOVSTAD: Especially when the injured man is—I hardly know how to put it—

PETRA: You mean when he is so upright and true?

HOVSTAD: (*In a low voice.*) I mean—especially when he is your father.

PETRA: (*Suddenly taken aback.*) That?

HOVSTAD: Yes, Petra—Miss Petra.

PETRA: So that is your chief thought, is it? Not the cause itself? Not the truth? Not father's great, warm heart?

HOVSTAD: Oh, that too, of course.

PETRA: No, thank you; you said too much that time, Mr. Hovstad. Now I shall never trust you again, in anything.

HOVSTAD: Can you be so hard on me because it's mainly for your sake—?

PETRA: What I blame you for is that you have not acted straightforwardly towards father. You have talked to him as if you cared only for the truth and the good of the community. You have trifled with both father and me. You are not the man you pretended to be. And that I will never forgive you—never.

HOVSTAD: You shouldn't say that so bitterly, Miss Petra—least of all now.

PETRA: Why not now?

HOVSTAD: Because your father cannot do without my help.

PETRA: (*Measuring him from head to foot.*) So you are capable of that, too? Oh, shame!

HOVSTAD: No, no. I spoke without thinking. You mustn't believe that of me.

PETRA: I know what to believe. Good-bye.

(Aslaksen enters from printing-room, hurriedly and mysteriously.)

ASLAKSEN: What do you think, Mr. Hovstad—*(Seeing* Petra.) Ow, that's awkward—
PETRA: Well, there is the book. You must give it to some one else. *(Going towards the main door.)*
HOVSTAD: *(Following her.)* But, Miss Petra—
PETRA: Good-bye. *(She goes.)*
ASLAKSEN: I say, Mr. Hovstad!
HOVSTAD: Well well; what is it?
ASLAKSEN: The Burgomaster's out there, in the printing-office.
HOVSTAD: The Burgomaster?
ASLAKSEN: Yes. He wants to speak to you; he came in by the back way— he didn't want to be seen, you understand.
HOVSTAD: What can be the meaning of this? Stop, I'll go myself—

(Goes towards the printing-room, opens the door, bows and invites the Burgomaster to enter.)

HOVSTAD: Keep a look-out, Aslaksen, that no one—
ASLAKSEN: I understand. *(Goes into the printing-room.)*
BURGOMASTER: You didn't expect to see me here, Mr. Hovstad.
HOVSTAD: No, I cannot say that I did.
BURGOMASTER: *(Looking about him.)* You are very comfortably installed here—capital quarters.
HOVSTAD: Oh—
BURGOMASTER: And here have I come, without with your leave or by your leave, to take up your time—
HOVSTAD: You are very welcome, Burgomaster; I am at your service. Let me take your cap and stick. *(He does so, and puts them on a chair.)* And won't you be seated?
BURGOMASTER: *(Sitting down by the table.)* Thanks. (Hovstad *also sits by the table.)* I have been much—very much worried to-day, Mr. Hovstad.
HOVSTAD: Really? Well, I suppose with all your various duties, Burgomaster—
BURGOMASTER: It is the Doctor that has been causing me annoyance to-day.
HOVSTAD: Indeed! The Doctor?
BURGOMASTER: He has written a sort of memorandum to the Directors about some alleged shortcomings in the Baths.
HOVSTAD: Has he really?
BURGOMASTER: Yes; hasn't he told you? I thought he said—
HOVSTAD: Oh yes, by-the-bye, he did mention something—
ASLAKSEN: *(From the printing-office.)* I've just come for the manuscript—
HOVSTAD: *(In a tone of vexation.)* Oh!—there it is on the desk.
ASLAKSEN: *(Finding it.)* All right.
BURGOMASTER: Why, that is the very thing—
ASLAKSEN: Yes, this is the Doctor's article, Burgomaster.
HOVSTAD: Oh, is that what you were speaking of?
BURGOMASTER: Precisely. What do you think of it?
HOVSTAD: I have no technical knowledge of the matter, and I've only glanced through it.
BURGOMASTER: And yet you are going to print it!

HOVSTAD: I can't very well refuse a signed communication—

ASLAKSEN: I have nothing to do with the editing of the paper, Burgomaster—

BURGOMASTER: Of course not.

ASLAKSEN: I merely print what is placed in my hands.

BURGOMASTER: Quite right, quite right.

ASLAKSEN: So I must—(*Goes towards the printing-room.*)

BURGOMASTER: No, stop a moment, Mr. Aslaksen. With your permission, Mr. Hovstad—

HOVSTAD: By all means, Burgomaster.

BURGOMASTER: You are a discreet and thoughtful man, Mr. Aslaksen.

ASLAKSEN: I am glad you think so, Burgomaster.

BURGOMASTER: And a man of very wide influence.

ASLAKSEN: Well—chiefly among the lower middle-class.

BURGOMASTER: The small taxpayers form the majority—here as everywhere.

ASLAKSEN: That's very true.

BURGOMASTER: And I have no doubt that you know the general feeling among them. Am I right?

ASLAKSEN: Yes, I think I may say that I do, Burgomaster.

BURGOMASTER: Well—since our townsfolk of the poorer class appear to be so heroically eager to make sacrifices—

ASLAKSEN: How so?

HOVSTAD: Sacrifices?

BURGOMASTER: It is a pleasing evidence of public spirit—a most pleasing evidence. I admit it is more than I should quite have expected. But, of course, you know public feeling better than I do.

ASLAKSEN: Yes but, Burgomaster—

BURGOMASTER: And assuredly it is no small sacrifice the town will have to make.

HOVSTAD: The town?

ASLAKSEN: But I don't understand—. It's the Baths—

BURGOMASTER: At a rough provisional estimate, the alterations the Doctor thinks desirable will come to two or three hundred thousand crowns.

ASLAKSEN: That's a lot of money; but—

BURGOMASTER: Of course we shall be obliged to raise a municipal loan.

HOVSTAD: (*Rising.*) You surely can't mean that the town—?

ASLAKSEN: Would you come upon the rates? Upon the scanty savings of the lower middle-class?

BURGOMASTER: Why, my dear Mr. Aslaksen, where else are the funds to come from?

ASLAKSEN: The proprietors of the Baths must see to that.

BURGOMASTER: The proprietors are not in a position to go to any further expense.

ASLAKSEN: Are you quite sure of that, Burgomaster?

BURGOMASTER: I have positive information. So if these extensive alterations are called for, the town itself will have to bear the cost.

ASLAKSEN: Oh, plague take it all—I beg your pardon!—but this is quite another matter, Mr. Hovstad.

HOVSTAD: Yes, it certainly is.

BURGOMASTER: The worst of it is, that we shall be obliged to close the establishment for a couple of years.

HOVSTAD: To close it? Completely?

ASLAKSEN: For two years!

BURGOMASTER: Yes, the work will require that time—at least.

ASLAKSEN: But, damn it all! we can't stand that, Burgomaster. What are we house-owners to live on in the meantime?

BURGOMASTER: It's extremely difficult to say, Mr. Aslaksen. But what would you have us do? Do you think a single visitor will come here if we go about making them fancy that the water is poisoned, that the place is pestilential, that the whole town—

ASLAKSEN: And it's all nothing but fancy?

BURGOMASTER: With the best will in the world, I have failed to convince myself that it is anything else.

ASLAKSEN: In that case it's simply inexcusable of Dr. Stockmann—I beg your pardon, Burgomaster, but—

BURGOMASTER: I'm sorry to say you are only speaking the truth, Mr. Aslaksen. Unfortunately, my brother has always been noted for his rashness.

ASLAKSEN: And yet you want to back him up in this, Mr Hovstad!

HOVSTAD: But who could possibly imagine that—?

BURGOMASTER: I have drawn up a short statement of the facts, as they appear from a sober-minded standpoint; and I have intimated that any drawbacks that may possibly exist can no doubt be remedied by measures compatible with the finances of the Baths.

HOVSTAD: Have you the article with you, Burgomaster?

BURGOMASTER: (*Feeling in his pockets.*) Yes; I brought it with me, in case you—

ASLAKSEN: (*Quickly.*) Plague take it, there he is!

BURGOMASTER: Who? My brother?

HOVSTAD: Where? where?

ASLAKSEN: He's coming through the composing-room.

BURGOMASTER: Most unfortunate! I don't want to meet him here, and yet there are several things I want to talk to you about.

HOVSTAD: (*Pointing to the door on the right.*) Go in there for a moment.

BURGOMASTER: But—?

HOVSTAD: You'll find nobody but Billing there.

ASLAKSEN: Quick, quick, Burgomaster; he's just coming.

BURGOMASTER: Very well, then. But try to get rid of him quickly.

(*He goes out by the door on the right, which* Aslaksen *opens, and closes behind him.*)

HOVSTAD: Pretend to be busy, Aslaksen.

(*He sits down and writes.* Aslaksen *turns over a heap of newspapers on a chair, right.*)

DR. STOCKMANN: (*Entering from the composing-room.*) Here I am, back again. (*Puts down his hat and stick.*)

HOVSTAD: (*Writing.*) Already, Doctor? Make haste with what we were speaking of, Aslaksen. We've no time to lose to-day.

DR. STOCKMANN: (*To Aslaksen.*) No proof yet, I hear.

ASLAKSEN: (*Without turning round.*) No; how could you expect it?

DR. STOCKMANN: Of course not; but you understand my impatience. I can have no rest or peace until I see the thing in print.

HOVSTAD: H'm; it will take a good while yet. Don't you think so, Aslaksen?

ASLAKSEN: I'm afraid it will.

DR. STOCKMANN: All right, all right, my good friend; then I shall look in again. I'll look in twice if necessary. With so much at stake—the welfare of the whole town—one mustn't grudge a little trouble. (*Is on the point of going but stops and comes back.*) Oh, by the way—there's one other thing I must speak to you about.

HOVSTAD: Excuse me; wouldn't some other time—?

DR. STOCKMANN: I can tell you in two words. You see it's this: when people read my article in the paper to-morrow, and find I have spent the whole winter working quietly for the good of the town—

HOVSTAD: Yes but, Doctor—

DR. STOCKMANN: I know what you're going to say. You don't think it was a bit more than my duty—my simple duty as a citizen. Of course I know that, as well as you do. But you see, my fellow townsmen—good Lord! the poor souls think so much of me—

ASLAKSEN: Yes, the townspeople have hitherto thought very highly of you, Doctor.

DR. STOCKMANN: That's exactly why I'm afraid that—. What I wanted to say was this: when all this comes to them—especially to the poorer classes—as a summons to take the affairs of the town into their own hands for the future—

HOVSTAD: (*Rising.*) H'm, Doctor, I won't conceal from you—

DR. STOCKMANN: Aha! I thought there was something brewing! But I won't hear of it. If they are getting up anything of that sort—

HOVSTAD: Of what sort?

DR. STOCKMANN: Well, anything of any sort—a procession with banners, or a banquet, or a subscription for a testimonial, or whatever it may be—you must give me your solemn promise to put a stop to it. And you too, Mr. Aslaksen; do you hear?

HOVSTAD: Excuse me, Doctor; we may as well tell you the whole truth first as last—

(Mrs. Stockmann *enters from the back, left.*)

MRS. STOCKMANN: (*Seeing the* Doctor.) Ah! just as I thought.

HOVSTAD: (*Going towards her.*) Mrs. Stockmann, too?

DR. STOCKMANN: What the devil do you want here, Katrina?

MRS. STOCKMANN: You know very well what I want.

HOVSTAD: Won't you sit down? Or perhaps—

MRS. STOCKMANN: Thanks, please don't trouble. And you must forgive my following my husband here; remember, I am the mother of three children.

DR. STOCKMANN: Stuff and nonsense! We all know that well enough.

MRS. STOCKMANN: Well, it doesn't look as if you thought very much about your wife and children to-day, or you wouldn't be so ready to plunge us all into ruin.

DR. STOCKMANN: Are you quite mad, Katrina! Has a man with a wife and children no right to proclaim the truth? Has he no right to be an active and useful citizen? Has he no right to do his duty by the town he lives in?

MRS. STOCKMANN: Everything in moderation, Thomas!

ASLAKSEN: That's just what I say. Moderation in everything.

MRS. STOCKMANN: You are doing us a great wrong, Mr. Hovstad, in enticing my husband away from house and home, and befooling him in this way.

HOVSTAD: I am not befooling any one—

DR. STOCKMANN: Befooling! Do you think I should let myself be befooled?

MRS. STOCKMANN: Yes, that's just what you do. I know very well that you are the cleverest man in the town; but you're very easily made a fool of, Thomas. (*To* Hovstad.) Remember that he loses his post at the Baths if you print what he has written—

ASLAKSEN: What!

HOVSTAD: Well now, really, Doctor—

DR. STOCKMANN: (*Laughing.*) Ha ha! just let them try—! No no, my dear, they'll think twice about that. I have the compact majority behind me, you see!

MRS. STOCKMANN: That's just the misfortune, that you should have such a horrid thing behind you.

DR. STOCKMANN: Nonsense, Katrina;—you go home and look after your house, and let me take care of society. How can you be in such a fright when you see me so confident and happy? (*Rubbing his hands and walking up and down.*) Truth and the People must win the day; and you may be perfectly sure of that. Oh! I can see all our free-souled citizens standing shoulder to shoulder like a conquering army—! (*Stopping by a chair.*) Why, what the devil is that?

ASLAKSEN: (*Looking at it.*) Oh Lord!

HOVSTAD: (*The same.*) H'm—

DR. STOCKMANN: Why, here's the top-knot of authority!

(*He takes the* Burgomaster's *official cap carefully between the tips of his fingers and holds it up.*)

MRS. STOCKMANN: The Burgomaster's cap!

DR. STOCKMANN: And here's the staff of office, too! But how in the devil's name did they—?

HOVSTAD: Well then—

DR. STOCKMANN: Ah, I understand! He has been here to talk you over. Ha, ha! He reckoned without his host that time! And when he caught sight of me in the printing-room—(*Bursts out laughing*)—he took to his heels, eh, Mr. Aslaksen?

ASLAKSEN: (*Hurriedly.*) Exactly; he took to his heels, Doctor.

DR. STOCKMANN: Made off without his stick and—. No, that won't do! Peter never left anything behind him. But where the devil have you stowed him? Ah—in here, of course. Now you shall see, Katrina.

MRS. STOCKMANN: Thomas—I implore you—!

ASLAKSEN: Take care, Doctor!

(*Dr.* Stockmann *has put on the* Burgomaster's *cap and grasped his stick; he now goes up to the door, throws it open, and makes a military salute.*)

(*The* Burgomaster *enters, red with anger. Behind him comes* Billing.)

BURGOMASTER: What is the meaning of these antics?

DR. STOCKMANN: Respect, my good Peter! Now, it's I that am in power in this town. (*He struts up and down.*)

MRS. STOCKMANN: (*Almost in tears.*) Oh, Thomas!

BURGOMASTER: (*Following him.*) Give me my cap and stick!

DR. STOCKMANN: (*As before.*) You may be Chief of Police, but I am Burgomaster. I am master of the whole town I tell you!

BURGOMASTER: Put down my cap, I say. Remember it is an official cap, as by law prescribed!

DR. STOCKMANN: Pshaw! Do you think the awakening lion of the democracy will let itself be scared by a gold-laced cap? There's to be a revolution in the town to-morrow, let me tell you. You threatened me with dismissal; but now *I* dismiss you—dismiss you from all your offices of trust—. You think I can't do it?—Oh, yes, I can! I have the irresistible forces of society on my side. Hovstad and Billing will thunder in the *People's Messenger,* and Aslaksen will take the field at the head of the House-owners' Association—

ASLAKSEN: No, Doctor, I shall not.

DR. STOCKMANN: Why, of course you will—

BURGOMASTER: Aha! Perhaps Mr. Hovstad would like to join the agitation after all?

HOVSTAD: No, Burgomaster.

ASLAKSEN: No, Mr. Hovstad isn't such a fool as to ruin both himself and the paper for the sake of a delusion.

DR. STOCKMANN: (*Looking about him.*) What does all this mean?

HOVSTAD: You have presented your case in a false light, Doctor; therefore I am unable to give you my support.

BILLING: And after what the Burgomaster has been so kind as to explain to me, I—

DR. STOCKMANN: In a false light! Well, I am responsible for that. Just you print my article, and I promise you I shall prove it up to the hilt.

HOVSTAD: I shall not print it. I cannot, and will not, and dare not print it.

DR. STOCKMANN: You dare not? What nonsense is this? You are editor; and I suppose it's the editor that controls a paper.

ASLAKSEN: No, it's the subscribers, Doctor.

BURGOMASTER: Fortunately.

ASLAKSEN: It's public opinion, the enlightened majority, the house-owners and all the rest. It's they who control a paper.

DR. STOCKMANN: (*Calmly.*) And all these powers I have against me?

ASLAKSEN: Yes, you have. It would mean absolute ruin for the town if your article were inserted.

DR. STOCKMANN: So that is the way of it!

BURGOMASTER: My hat and stick!

(Dr. Stockmann *takes off the cap and lays it on the table along with the stick.*)

BURGOMASTER: (*Taking them both.*) Your term of office has come to an untimely end.

DR. STOCKMANN: This end is not yet. (*To* Hovstad.) So you are quite determined not to print my article in the *Messenger?*

HOVSTAD: Quite; for the sake of your family, if for no other reason.

MRS. STOCKMANN: Oh, be kind enough to leave his family out of the question, Mr. Hovstad.

BURGOMASTER: (*Takes a manuscript from his pocket.*) When this appears, the public will be in possession of all necessary information; it is an authentic statement. I place it in your hands.

HOVSTAD: (*Taking the MS.*) Good. It shall appear in due course.

DR. STOCKMANN: And not mine! You imagine you can kill me and the truth by a conspiracy of silence! But it won't be so easy as you think. Mr. Aslaksen, will you be good enough to print my article at once, as a pamphlet? I'll pay for it myself, and be my own publisher. I'll have four hundred copies—no, five—six hundred.

ASLAKSEN: No. If you offered me its weight in gold, I dare not lend my press to such a purpose, Doctor. I daren't fly in the face of public opinion. You won't get it printed anywhere in the whole town.

DR. STOCKMANN: Then give it me back.

HOVSTAD: (*Handing him the MS.*) By all means.

DR. STOCKMANN: (*Taking up his hat and cane.*) It shall be made public all the same. I shall read it at a great mass meeting; all my fellow citizens shall hear the voice of truth!

BURGOMASTER: Not a single society in the town would let you their hall for such a purpose.

ASLAKSEN: Not one, I'm quite certain.

BILLING: No, strike me dead if they would!

MRS. STOCKMANN: That would be too disgraceful! Why do they turn against you like this, every one of them?

DR. STOCKMANN: (*Irritated.*) I'll tell you why. It's because in this town all the men are old women—like you. They all think of nothing but their families, not of the general good.

MRS. STOCKMANN: (*Taking his arm.*) Then I'll show them that an—an old woman can be a man for once in a way. For now I'll stand by you, Thomas.

DR. STOCKMANN: Bravely said, Katrina! I swear by my soul and conscience the truth shall out! If they won't let me a hall, I'll hire a drum and march through the town with it; and I'll read my paper at every street corner.

BURGOMASTER: You can scarcely be such a raving lunatic as that?

DR. STOCKMANN: I am.

ASLAKSEN: You would not get a single man in the whole town to go with you.

BILLING: No, strike me dead if you would!

MRS. STOCKMANN: Don't give in, Thomas, I'll ask the boys to go with you.

DR. STOCKMANN: That's a splendid idea!

MRS. STOCKMANN: Morten will be delighted; and Eilif will go too, I dare-say.

DR. STOCKMANN: Yes, and so will Petra! And you yourself, Katrina!

MRS. STOCKMANN: No, no, not I. But I'll stand at the window and watch you—that I will.

DR. STOCKMANN: (*Throwing his arms about her and kissing her.*) Thank you for that! Now, my good sirs, we're ready for the fight! Now we shall see whether your despicable tactics can stop the mouth of the patriot who wants to purge society!

(*He and his wife go out together by the door in the back, left.*)

BURGOMASTER: (*Shaking his head dubiously.*) Now he has turned her head too!

ACT FOURTH

A large old-fashioned room in CAPTAIN HORSTER'S *house. An open folding-door in the background leads to an anteroom. In the wall on the left are three windows. About the middle of the opposite wall is a platform, and on it a*

small table, two candles, a water-bottle and glass, and a bell. For the rest, the room is lighted by sconces placed between the windows. In front, on the left, is a table with a candle on it, and by it a chair. In front, to the right, a door, and near it a few chairs.
Large assemblage of all classes of townsfolk. In the crowd are a few women and schoolboys. More and more people gradually stream in from the back until the room is quite full.

FIRST CITIZEN: (*To another standing near him.*) So you're here too, Lamstad?

SECOND CITIZEN: I never miss a public meeting.

A BYSTANDER: I suppose you've brought your whistle?

SECOND CITIZEN: Of course I have; haven't you?

THIRD CITIZEN: I should think so. And Skipper Evensen said he'd bring a thumping big horn.

SECOND CITIZEN: He's a good 'un, is Evensen! (*Laughter in the group.*)

A FOURTH CITIZEN: (*Joining them.*) I say, what's it all about? What's going on here to-night?

SECOND CITIZEN: Why, it's Dr. Stockmann that's going to lecture against the Burgomaster.

FOURTH CITIZEN;   But the Burgomaster's his brother.

FIRST CITIZEN: That makes no difference. Dr. Stockmann's not afraid of him.

THIRD CITIZEN: But he's all wrong; the *People's Messenger* says so.

SECOND CITIZEN: Yes, he must be wrong this time; for neither the House-owners' Association nor the Citizens' Club would let him have a hall.

FIRST CITIZEN: They wouldn't even lend him the hall at the Baths.

SECOND CITIZEN: No, you may be sure they wouldn't.

A MAN: (*In another group.*) Now, who's the one to follow in this business, eh?

ANOTHER MAN: (*In the same group.*) Just keep your eye on Aslaksen, and do as he does.

BILLING: (*With a portfolio under his arm, makes his way through the crowd.*) Excuse me, gentlemen. Will you allow me to pass? I'm here to report for the *People's Messenger*. Many thanks. (*Sits by the table on the left.*)

A WORKING-MAN: Who's he?

ANOTHER WORKING-MAN: Don't you know him? It's that fellow Billing, that writes for Aslaksen's paper.

(Captain Horster *enters by the door in front on the right, escorting* Mrs. Stockmann *and* Petra. Eilif *and* Morten *follow them.*)

HORSTER: This is where I thought you might sit; you can so easily slip out is anything should happen.

MRS. STOCKMANN: Do you think there will be any disturbance?

HORSTER: One can never tell—with such a crowd. But there's no occasion for anxiety.

MRS. STOCKMANN: (*Sitting down.*) How kind it was of you to offer Stockmann this room.

HORSTER: Since no one else would, I—

PETRA: (*Who has also seated herself.*) And it was brave too, Captain Horster.

HORSTER: Oh, I don't see where the bravery comes in.

(Hovstad *and* Aslaksen *enter at the same moment, but make their way through the crowd separately.*)

ASLAKSEN: (*Going up to* Horster.) Hasn't the Doctor come yet?
HORSTER: He's waiting in there. (*A movement at the door in the background.*)
HOVSTAD: (*To* Billing.) There's the Burgomaster! Look!
BILLING: Yes, strike me dead if he hasn't put in an appearance after all!

(Burgomaster Stockmann *makes his way blandly through the meeting, bowing politely to both sides, and takes his stand by the wall on the left. Soon afterwards,* Dr. Stockmann *enters by the door on the right. He wears a black frock-coat and white necktie. Faint applause, met by a subdued hissing. Then silence.*)

DR. STOCKMANN: (*In a low tone.*) How do you feel, Katrina?
MRS. STOCKMANN: Quite comfortable, thank you. (*In a low voice.*) Now do keep your temper, Thomas.
DR. STOCKMANN: Oh, I shall keep myself well in hand. (*Looks at his watch, ascends the platform, and bows.*) It's a quarter past the hour, so I shall begin—(*Takes out his MS.*)
ASLAKSEN: But surely a chairman must be elected first.
DR. STOCKMANN: No, that's not at all necessary.
SEVERAL GENTLEMEN: (*Shouting.*) Yes, yes.
BURGOMASTER: I should certainly say that a chairman ought to be elected.
DR. STOCKMANN: But I've called this meeting to give a lecture, Peter!
BURGOMASTER: Dr. Stockmann's lecture may possibly lead to differences of opinion.
SEVERAL VOICES IN THE CROWD: A chairman! A chairman!
HOVSTAD: The general voice of the meeting seems to be for a chairman!
DR. STOCKMANN: (*Controlling himself.*) Very well then; let the meeting have its way.
ASLAKSEN: Will not the Burgomaster take the chair?
THREE GENTLEMEN: (*Clapping.*) Bravo! Bravo!
BURGOMASTER: For reasons you will easily understand, I must decline. But, fortunately, we have among us one whom I think we can all accept. I allude to the president of the House-owners' Association, Mr. Aslaksen.
MANY VOICES: Yes, yes! Bravo Aslaksen! Hurrah for Aslaksen! (Dr. Stockmann *takes his MS. and descends from the platform.*)
ASLAKSEN: Since my fellow citizens repose this trust in me, I cannot refuse —(*Applause and cheers.* Aslaksen *ascends the platform.*)
BILLING: (*Writing.*) So—"Mr. Aslaksen was elected by acclamation—"
ASLAKSEN: And now, as I have been called to the chair, I take the liberty of saying a few brief words. I am a quiet, peace-loving man; I am in favour of discreet moderation, and of—and of moderate discretion. Every one who knows me, knows that.
MANY VOICES: Yes, yes, Aslaksen!
ASLAKSEN: I have learnt in the school of life and of experience that moderation is the virtue in which the individual citizen finds his best advantage—
BURGOMASTER: Hear, hear!
ASLAKSEN: —and it is discretion and moderation, too, that best serve the community. I could therefore suggest to our respected fellow citizen, who has called this meeting, that he should endeavour to keep within the bounds of moderation.

A Man: (*By the door.*) Three cheers for the Temperance Society!

A Voice: Go to the devil!

Voices: Hush! hush!

Aslaksen: No interruptions, gentlemen!—Does any one wish to offer any observations?

Burgomaster: Mr. Chairman!

Aslaksen: Burgomaster Stockmann will address the meeting.

Burgomaster: On account of my close relationship—of which you are probably aware—to the present medical officer of the Baths, I should have preferred not to speak here this evening. But my position as chairman of the Baths, and my care for the vital interests of this town, force me to move a resolution. I may doubtless assume that not a single citizen here present thinks it desirable that untrustworthy and exaggerated statements should get abroad as to the sanitary condition of the Baths and of our town.

Many Voices: No, no, no! Certainly not! We protest!

Burgomaster: I therefore beg to move, "That this meeting declines to hear the proposed lecture or speech on the subject by the medical officer of the Baths."

Dr. Stockmann: (*Flaring up.*) Declines to hear—! What do you mean?

Mrs. Stockmann: (*Coughing.*) H'm! h'm!

Dr. Stockmann: (*Controlling himself.*) So I am not to be heard?

Burgomaster: In my statement in the *People's Messenger* I have made the public acquainted with the essential facts, so that all well-disposed citizens can easily form their own judgment. From that statement it will be seen that the medical officer's proposal—besides amounting to a vote of censure upon the leading men of the town—at bottom only means saddling the ratepayers with an unnecessary outlay of at least a hundred thousand crowns. (*Sounds of protest and some hissing.*)

Aslaksen: (*Ringing the bell.*) Order, gentlemen! I must beg leave to support the Burgomaster's resolution. I quite agree with him that there is something beneath the surface of the Doctor's agitation. In all his talk about the Baths, it is really a revolution he is aiming at; he wants to effect a redistribution of power. No one doubt the excellence of Dr. Stockmann's intentions—of course there cannot be two opinions as to that. I, too, am in favour of self-government by the people, if only it doesn't cost the ratepayers too much. But in this case it would do so; and therefore I'll be hanged if—excuse me—in short, I cannot go with Dr. Stockmann upon this occasion. You can buy even gold too dear; that's my opinion. (*Loud applause on all sides.*)

Hovstad: I, too feel bound to explain my attitude. Dr. Stockmann's agitation seemed at first to find favour in several quarters, and I supported it as impartially as I could. But it presently appeared that we had been misled by a false representation of the facts—

Dr. Stockmann: False—!

Hovstad: Well then, an untrustworthy representation. This the Burgomaster's report has proved. I trust no one here present doubts my liberal principles; the attitude of the *Messenger* on all great political questions is well known to you all. But I have learned from men of judgment and experience that in purely local matters a paper must observe a certain amount of caution.

Aslaksen: I entirely agree with the speaker.

Hovstad: And in the matter under discussion it is quite evident that Dr. Stockmann has public opinion against him. But, gentlemen, what is an editor's clearest and most imperative duty? Is it not to work in harmony with his readers? Has he not in some sort received a tacit mandate to further assiduously and unweariedly the interests of his constituents? Or am I mistaken in this?

MANY VOICES: No, no, no! Hovstad is right!

HOVSTAD: It has cost me a bitter struggle to break with a man in whose house I have of late been a frequent guest—with a man who, up to this day, has enjoyed the unqualified goodwill of his fellow citizens—with a man whose only, or, at any rate, whose chief fault is that he consults his heart rather than his head.

A FEW SCATTERED VOICES: That's true! Hurrah for Dr. Stockmann!

HOVSTAD: But my duty towards the community has constrained me to break with him. Then, too, there is another consideration that impels me to oppose him, and, if possible, to block the ill omened path upon which he is entering: consideration for his family—

DR. STOCKMANN: Keep to the water-works and sewers!

HOVSTAD: —consideration for his wife and his unprotected children.

MORTEN: Is that us, mother?

MRS. STOCKMANN: Hush!

ASLAKSEN: I will now put the Burgomaster's resolution to the vote.

DR. STOCKMANN: You need not. I have no intention of saying anything this evening of all the filth at the Baths. No! You shall hear something quite different.

BURGOMASTER: (Half aloud.) What next, I wonder?

A DRUNKEN MAN: (At the main entrance.) I'm a ratepayer, so I've a right to my opinion! And it's my full, firm, incomprehensible opinion that—

SEVERAL VOICES: Silence up there!

OTHERS: He's drunk! Turn him out! (The drunken man is turned out.)

DR. STOCKMANN: Can I speak?

ASLAKSEN: (Ringing the bell.) Dr. Stockmann will address the meeting.

DR. STOCKMANN: A few days ago, I should have liked to see any one venture upon such an attempt to gag me as has been made here to-night! I would have fought like a lion for my sacred rights! But now I care little enough; for now I have more important things to speak of.

(The people crowd closer round him. Morten Kiil comes in sight among the bystanders.)

DR. STOCKMANM: (Continuing.) I have been pondering a great many things during these last days—thinking such a multitude of thoughts, that at last my head was positively in a whirl—

BURGOMASTER: (Coughing.) H'm—!

DR. STOCKMANN: But presently things seemed to straighten themselves out, and I saw them clearly in all their bearings. That is why I stand here this evening. I am about to make great revelations, my fellow citizens! I am going to announce to you a far-reaching discovery, beside which the trifling fact that our water-works are poisoned, and that our health-resort is built on pestilential ground, sinks into insignificance.

MANY VOICES: (Shouting.) Don't speak about the Baths! We won't listen to that! No more of that!

DR. STOCKMANN: I have said I would speak of the great discovery I have made within the last few days—the discovery that all our sources of spiritual life are poisoned, and that our whole society rests upon a pestilential basis of falsehood.

SEVERAL VOICES: (In astonishment and half aloud.) What's he saying?

BURGOMASTER: Such an insinuation—!

ASLAKSEN: (*With his hand on the bell.*) I must call upon the speaker to moderate his expressions.

DR. STOCKMANN: I have loved my native town as dearly as any man can love the home of his childhood. I was young when I left our town, and distance, homesickness and memory threw, as it were, a glamour over the place and its people. (*Some applause and cries of approval.*)

DR. STOCKMANN: Then for years I was imprisoned in a horrible hole, far away in the north. As I went about among the people scattered here and there over the stony wilderness, it seemed to me, many a time, that it would have been better for these poor famished creatures to have had a cattle-doctor to attend them, instead of a man like me. (*Murmurs in the room.*)

BILLING: (*Laying down his pen.*) Strike me dead if I've ever heard—!

HOVSTAD: What an insult to an estimable peasantry!

DR. STOCKMANN: Wait a moment!—I don't think any one can reproach me with forgetting my native town up there. I sat brooding like an eider duck and what I hatched was—the plan of the Baths. (*Applause and expressions of dissent.*)

DR. STOCKMANN: And when, at last, fate ordered things so happily that I could come home again—then, fellow citizens, it seemed to me that I hadn't another desire in the world. Yes, one desire I had: an eager, constant, burning desire to be of service to my birthplace, and to its people.

BURGOMASTER: (*Gazing into vacancy.*) A strange method to select—

DR. STOCKMANN: So I went about revelling in my happy illusions. But yesterday morning—no, it was really two nights ago—my mind's eyes were opened wide, and the first thing I saw was the colossal stupidity of the authorities— (*Noise, cries, and laughter.* Mrs. Stockmann *coughs repeatedly.*)

BURGOMASTER: Mr. Chairman!

ASLAKSEN: (*Ringing his bell.*) In virtue of my position—!

DR. STOCKMANN: It's petty to catch me up on a word, Mr. Aslaksen! I only mean that I became alive to the extraordinary muddle our leading men had been guilty of, down at the Baths. I cannot for the life of me abide leading men—I've seen enough of them in my time. They are like goats in a young plantation: they do harm at every point; they block the path of a free man wherever he turns—and I should be glad if we could exterminate them like other noxious animals—(*Uproar in the room.*)

BURGOMASTER: Mr. Chairman, are such expressions permissible?

ASLAKSEN: (*With his hand on the bell.*) Dr. Stockmann—

DR. STOCKMANN: I can't conceive how it is that I have only now seen through these gentry; for haven't I had a magnificent example before my eyes here every day—my brother Peter—slow of understanding, tenacious in prejudice— (*Laughter, noise, and whistling.* Mrs. Stockmann *coughs.* Aslaksen *rings violently.*)

THE DRUNKEN MAN: (*Who has come in again.*) Is it me you're alluding to? Sure enough, my name's Petersen; but devil take me if—

ANGRY VOICES: Out with that drunken man! Turn him out! (*The man is again turned out.*)

BURGOMASTER: Who is that person?

A BYSTANDER: I don't know him, Burgomaster.

ANOTHER: He doesn't belong to the town.

A THIRD: I believe he's a timber-dealer from— (*The rest is inaudible.*)

ASLAKSEN: The man was evidently intoxicated.—Continue, Dr. Stockmann; but pray endeavour to be moderate.

DR. STOCKMANN: Well, fellow citizens, I shall say no more about our leading men. If any one imagines, from what I have just said, that it's these gentlemen I want to make short work of to-night, he is mistaken—altogether mistaken. For I cherish the comfortable conviction that these laggards, these relics of a decaying order of thought, are diligently cutting their own throats. They need no doctor to hasten their end. And it is not people of that sort that constitute the real danger to society; it is not they who are most active in poisoning the sources of our spiritual life and making a plague-spot of the ground beneath our feet; it is not they who are the most dangerous enemies of truth and freedom in our society.

CRIES FROM ALL SIDES: Who, then? Who is it? Name, name!

DR. STOCKMANN: Yes, you may be sure I shall name them! For this is the great discovery I made yesterday: (*In a louder tone.*) The most dangerous foe to truth and freedom in our midst is the compact majority. Yes, it's the confounded, compact, liberal majority—that, and nothing else! There, I've told you.

(*Immense disturbance in the room. Most of the audience are shouting, stamping, and whistling. Several elderly gentlemen exchange furtive glances and seem to be enjoying the scene.* Mrs. Stockmann *rises in alarm.* Eilif *and* Morten *advance threateningly towards the schoolboys, who are making noises.* Aslaksen *rings the bell and calls for order.* Hovstad *and* Billing *both speak, but nothing can be heard. At last quiet is restored.*)

ASLAKSEN: I must request the speaker to withdraw his ill considered expressions.

DR. STOCKMANN: Never, Mr. Aslaksen! For it's this very majority that robs me of my freedom, and wants to forbid me to speak the truth.

HOVSTAD: The majority always has right on its side.

BILLING: Yes, and truth too, strike me dead!

DR. STOCKMANN: The majority never has right on its side. Never I say! That is one of the social lies that a free, thinking man is bound to rebel against. Who make up the majority in any given country? Is it the wise men or the fools? I think we must agree that the fools are in a terrible, overwhelming majority, all the wide world over. But how in the devil's name can it ever be right for the fools to rule over the wise men? (*Uproar and yells.*)

DR. STOCKMANN: Yes, yes, you can shout me down, but you cannot gainsay me. The majority has might—unhappily—but right it has not. It is I, and the few, the individuals, that are in the right. The minority is always right. (*Renewed uproar.*)

HOVSTAD: Ha ha! Dr. Stockmann has turned aristocrat since the day before yesterday!

DR. STOCKMANN: I have said that I have no words to waste on the little, narrow-chested, short-winded crew that lie in our wake. Pulsating life has nothing more to do with them. I am speaking of the few, the individuals among us, who have made all the new, germinating truths their own. These men stand, as it were, at the outposts, so far in the van that the compact majority has not yet reached them—and there they fight for truths that are too lately born into the world's consciousness to have won over the majority.

HOVSTAD: So the Doctor's a revolutionist now!

DR. STOCKMANN: Yes, by Heaven, I am, Mr. Hovstad! I am going to revolt against the lie that truth belongs exclusively to the majority. What sort of truths do the majority rally round? Truths so stricken in years that they are sinking into decrepitude. When a truth is so old as that, gentlemen, it's in a fair way to become a lie. (*Laughter and jeers.*)

DR. STOCKMANN: Yes, yes, you may believe me or not, as you please; but truths are by no means the wiry Methusalehs some people think them. A normally-constituted truth lives—let us say—as a rule, seventeen or eighteen years; at the outside twenty; very seldom more. And truths so patriarchal as that are always shockingly emaciated; yet it's not till then that the majority takes them up and recommends them to society as wholesome food. I can assure you there's not much nutriment in that sort of fare; you may take my word as a doctor for that. All these majority-truths are like last year's salt pork; they're like rancid, mouldy ham, producing all the moral scurvy that devastates society.

ASLAKSEN: It seems to me that the honourable speaker is wandering rather far from the subject.

BURGOMASTER: I beg to endorse the Chairman's remark.

DR. STOCKMANN: Why you're surely mad, Peter! I'm keeping as closely to my text as I possibly can; for my text is precisely this—that the masses, the majority, this devil's own compact majority—it's that, I say, that's poisoning the sources of our spiritual life, and making a plague-spot of the ground beneath our feet.

HOVSTAD: And you make this charge against the great, independent majority, just because they have the sense to accept only certain and acknowledged truths?

DR. STOCKMANN: Ah, my dear Mr. Hovstad, don't talk about certain truths! The truths acknowledged by the masses, the multitude, were certain truths to the vanguard in our grandfathers' days. We, the vanguard of to-day, don't acknowledge them any longer; and I don't believe there exists any other certain truth but this—that no society can live a healthy life upon truths so old and marrowless.

HOVSTAD: But instead of all this vague talk, suppose you were to give us some specimens of these old marrowless truths that we are living upon. (*Approval from several quarters.*)

DR. STOCKMANN: Oh, I could give you no end of samples from the rubbish-heap; but, for the present, I shall keep to one acknowledged truth, which is a hideous lie at bottom, but which Mr. Hovstad, and the *Messenger*, and all adherents of the *Messenger*, live on all the same.

HOVSTAD: And that is—?

DR. STOCKMANN: That is the doctrine you have inherited from your forefathers, and go on thoughtlessly proclaiming far and wide—the doctrine that the multitude, the vulgar herd, the masses, are the pith of the people—that they are the people—that the common man, the ignorant, undeveloped member of society, has the same right to sanction and to condemn, to counsel and to govern, as the intellectually distinguished few.

BILLING: Well, now, strike me dead—!

HOVSTAD: (*Shouting at the same time.*) Citizens, please note this!

ANGRY VOICES: Ho-ho! Aren't we the people? Is it only the grand folks that are to govern?

A WORKING MAN: Out with the fellow that talks like that!

OTHERS: Turn him out!

A CITIZEN: (*Shouting.*) Blow your horn, Evensen.

(*The deep notes of a horn are heard; whistling, and terrific noise in the room.*)

DR. STOCKMANN: *(When the noise has somewhat subsided.)* Now do be reasonable! Can't you bear even for once in a way to hear the voice of truth? I don't ask you all to agree with me on the instant. But I certainly should have expected Mr. Hovstad to back me up, as soon as he had collected himself a bit. Mr. Hovstad sets up to be a freethinker—

SEVERAL VOICES: *(Subdued and wondering.)* Freethinker, did he say? What? Mr. Hovstad a freethinker?

HOVSTAD: *(Shouting.)* Prove it, Dr. Stockmann. When have I said so in print?

DR. STOCKMANN: *(Reflecting.)* No, upon my soul, you're right there; you've never had the frankness to do that. Well, well, I won't put you on the rack, Mr. Hovstad. Let me be the freethinker then. And now I'll make it clear to you all, and on scientific grounds too, that the *Messenger* is leading you shamefully by the nose, when it tells you that you, the masses, the crowd, are the true pith of the people. I tell you that's only a newspaper lie. The masses are nothing but the raw material that must be fashioned into a People. *(Murmurs, laughter and disturbance in the room.)*

DR. STOCKMANN: Is it not so with all other living creatures? What a difference between a cultivated and an uncultivated breed of animals! Just look at a common barn-door hen. What meat do you get from such a skinny carcas? Not much, I can tell you! And what sort of eggs does she lay? A decent crow or raven can lay nearly as good. Then take a cultivated Spanish or Japanese hen, or take a fine pheasant or turkey—ah! then you'll see the difference! And now look at the dog, our near relation. Think first of an ordinary vulgar cur—I mean one of those wretched, ragged, plebeian mongrels that haunt the gutters, and soil the sidewalks. Then place such a mongrel by the side of a poodle-dog, descended through many generations from an aristocratic stock, who have lived on delicate food, and heard harmonious voices and music. Do you think the brain of the poodle isn't very differently developed from that of the mongrel? Yes, you may be sure it is! It's well-bred poodle-pups like this that jugglers train to perform the most marvellous tricks. A common peasant-cur could never learn anything of the sort—not if he tried till doomsday. *(Noise and laughter are heard all round.)*

A CITIZEN: *(Shouting.)* Do you want to make dogs of us now?

ANOTHER MAN: We're not animals, Doctor!

DR. STOCKMANN: Yes, on my soul, but we are animals, my good sir! We're one and all of us animals, whether we like it or not. But truly there are few enough aristocratic animals among us. Oh, there's a terrible difference between poodle-men and mongrel-men! And the ridiculous part of it is, that Mr. Hovstad quite agrees with me so long as it's four-leged animals we're talking of—

HOVSTAD: Oh, beasts are only beasts.

DR. STOCKMANN: Well and good—but no sooner do I apply the law to two-legged animals, than Mr. Hovstad stops short; then he daren't hold his own opinions, or think out his own thoughts; then he turns the whole principle upside down, and proclaims in the *People's Messenger* that the barn-door hen and the gutter mongrel are precisely the finest specimens in the menagerie. But that's always the way, so long as the commonness still lingers in your system, and you haven't worked your way up to spiritual distinction.

HOVSTAD: I make no pretence to any sort of distinction. I come of simple peasant folk, and I am proud that my root should lie deep down among the common people, who are here being insulted.

WORKMEN: Hurrah for Hovstad. Hurrah! hurrah!

DR. STOCKMANN: The sort of common people I am speaking of are not found among the lower classes alone; they crawl and swarm all around us—up to the very summits of society. Just look at your own smug, respectable Burgomaster! Why, my brother Peter belongs as clearly to the common people as any man that walks on two legs— (*Laughter and hisses.*)

BURGOMASTER: I protest against such personalities.

DR. STOCKMANN: (*Imperturbably.*)—and that not because, like myself, he's descended from a good-for-nothing old pirate from Pomerania, to thereabouts—for that's our ancestry—

BURGOMASTER: An absurd tradition! Utterly groundless.

DR. STOCKMANN: —but he is so because he thinks the thoughts and holds the opinions of his official superiors. Men who do that, belong, intellectually-speaking, to the common people; and that is why my distinguished brother Peter is at bottom so undistinguished,—and consequently so illiberal.

BURGOMASTER: Mr. Chairman—!

HOVSTAD: So that the distinguished people in this country are the Liberals? That's quite a new light on the subject. (*Laughter.*)

DR. STOCKMANN: Yes, that is part of my new discovery. And this, too, follow that liberality of thought is almost precisely the same thing as morality. Therefore I say it's absolutely unpardonable of the *Messenger* to proclaim, day out, day in, the false doctrine that it's the masses, the multitude, the compact majority, that monopolise liberality and morality,—and that vice and corruption and all sorts of spiritual uncleanness ooze out of culture, as all that filth oozes down to the Baths from the Mill Dale tan-works! (*Noise and interruptions.*)

DR. STOCKMANN: (*Goes on imperturbably, smiling in his eagerness.*) And yet this same *Messenger* can preach about elevating the masses and the multitude to a higher level of well-being! Why, deuce take it, if the *Messenger's* own doctrine holds good, the elevation of the masses would simply mean hurling them straight to perdition! But, happily, the notion that culture demoralises is nothing but an old traditional lie. No it's stupidity, poverty, the ugliness of life, that do the devil's work! In a house that isn't aired and swept every day—my wife maintains that the floors ought to be scrubbed too, but perhaps that is going too far;—well,—in such a house, I say, within two or three years, people lose the power of thinking or acting morally. Lack of oxygen enervates the conscience. And there seems to be precious little oxygen in many and many a house in this town, since the whole compact majority is unscrupulous enough to want to found its future upon a quagmire of lies and fraud.

ASLAKSEN: I cannot allow so gross an insult to be levelled against a whole community.

A GENTLEMAN: I move that the Chairman order the speaker to sit down.

EAGER VOICES: Yes, yes! That's right! Sit down! Sit down!

DR. STOCKMANN: (*Flaring up.*) Then I shall proclaim the truth at every street corner! I shall write to newspapers in other towns! The whole country shall know how matters stand here!

HOVSTAD: It almost seems as if the Doctor's object were to ruin the town.

DR. STOCKMANN: Yes, so well do I love my native town that I would rather ruin it than see it flourishing upon a lie.

ASLAKSEN: That's plain speaking.

(*Noise and whistling.* Mrs. Stockmann *coughs in vain; the* Doctor *no longer heeds her.*)

HOVSTAD: (*Shouting amid the tumult.*) The man who would ruin a whole community must be an enemy to his fellow citizens!

DR. STOCKMANN: (*With growing excitement.*) What does it matter if a lying community is ruined! Let it be levelled to the ground, say I! All men who live upon a lie ought to be exterminated like vermin! You'll end by poisoning the whole country; you'll bring it to such a pass that the whole country will deserve to perish. And if ever it comes to that, I shall say, from the bottom of my heart: Perish the country! Perish all its people!

A MAN: (*In the crowd.*) Why, he talks like a regular enemy of the people!

BILLING: Strike me dead but there spoke the people's voice!

THE WHOLE ASSEMBLY: (*Shouting.*) Yes! yes! yes! He's an enemy of the people! He hates his country! He hates the whole people!

ASLAKSEN: Both as a citizen of this town and as a human being, I am deeply shocked at what it has been my lot to hear to-night. Dr. Stockmann has unmasked himself in a manner I should never have dreamt of. I must reluctantly subscribe to the opinion just expressed by some estimable citizens; and I think we ought to formulate this opinion in a resolution. I therefore beg to move, "That this meeting declares the medical officer of the Baths, Dr. Thomas Stockmann, to be an enemy of the people."

(*Thunders of applause and cheers. Many form a circle round the* Doctor *and hoot at him.* Mrs. Stockmann *and* Petra *have risen.* Morten *and* Eilif *fight the other school-boys, who have also been hooting. Some grown-up persons separate them.*)

DR. STOCKMANN: (*To the people hooting.*) Ah, fools that you are! I tell you that—

ASLAKSEN: (*Ringing.*) The Doctor is out of order in speaking. A formal vote must be taken; but out of consideration for personal feelings, it will be taken in writing and without names. Have you any blank paper, Mr. Billing?

BILLING: Here's both blue and white paper—

ASLAKSEN: Capital; that will save time. Cut it up into slips. That's it. (*To the meeting.*) Blue means no, white means aye. I myself will go round and collect the votes.

(*The* Burgomaster *leaves the room.* Aslaksen *and a few others go round with pieces of paper in hats.*)

A GENTLEMAN: (*To* Hovstad.) What can be the matter with the Doctor? What does it all mean?

HOVSTAD: Why, you know what a hare-brained creature he is.

ANOTHER GENTLEMAN: (*To* Billing.) I say, you're often at his house. Have you ever noticed if the fellow drinks?

BILLING: Strike me dead if I know what to say. The toddy's always on the table when any one looks in.

A THIRD GENTLEMAN: No, I should rather say he went off his head at times.

FIRST GENTLEMAN: I wonder if there's madness in the family?

BILLING: I shouldn't be surprised.

A FOURTH GENTLEMAN: No, it's pure malice. He wants to be revenged for something or other.

BILLING: He was certainly talking about a rise in his salary the other day; but he didn't get it.

ALL THE GENTLEMEN: (*Together.*) Aha! That explains everything.

THE DRUNKEN MAN: (*In the crowd.*) I want a blue one, I do! And I'll have a white one too.

SEVERAL PEOPLE: There's the tipsy man again! Turn him out.

MORTEN KIIL: (*Approaching the* Doctor.) Well, Stockmann, you see now what such monkey-tricks lead to?

DR. STOCKMANN: I have done my duty.

MORTEN KIIL: What was that you said about the Mill Dale tanneries?

DR. STOCKMANN: You heard what I said—that all the filth comes from them.

MORTEN KIIL: From my tannery as well?

DR. STOCKMANN: I'm sorry to say yours is the worst of all.

MORTEN KIIL: Are you going to put that in the papers, too?

DR. STOCKMANN: I can't gloze anything over.

MORTEN KIIL: This may cost you dear, Stockmann! (*He goes out.*)

A FAT GENTLEMAN: (*Goes up to* Horster, *without bowing to the ladies.*) Well, Captain, so you lend your house to enemies of the people.

HORSTER: I suppose I can do as I please with my own property, Sir.

THE GENTLEMAN: Then of course you can have no objection if I follow your example?

HORSTER: What do you mean, Sir?

THE GENTLEMAN: You shall hear from me to-morrow. (*Turns away and goes out.*)

PETRA: Wasn't that the owner of your ship, Captain Horster?

HORSTER: Yes, that was Mr. Vik.

ASLAKSEN: (*With the voting papers in his hands, ascends the platform and rings.*) Gentlemen! I have now to announce the result of the vote. All the voters, with one exception—

A YOUNG GENTLEMAN: That's the tipsy man!

ASLAKSEN: With the exception of one intoxicated person, this meeting of citizens unanimously declares the medical officer of the Baths, Dr. Thomas Stockmann, to be an enemy of the people. (*Cheers and applause.*) Three cheers for our fine old municipality! (*Cheers.*) Three cheers for our able and energetic Burgomaster, who has so loyally set family prejudice aside! (*Cheers.*) The meeting is dissolved. (*He descends.*)

BILLING: Three cheers for the Chairman!

ALL: Hurrah for Aslaksen.

DR. STOCKMANN: My hat and coat, Petra. Captain, have you room for passengers to the new world?

HORSTER: For you and yours, Doctor, we'll make room.

DR. STOCKMANN: (*While* Petra *helps him to put on his coat.*) Good! Come Katrina, come boys! (*He gives his wife his arm.*)

MRS. STOCKMANN: (*In a low voice.*) Thomas, dear, let us go out by the back way.

DR. STOCKMANN: No back ways, Katrina. (*In a loud voice.*) You shall hear from the enemy of the people, before he shakes the dust from his feet! I am not so forbearing as a certain person; I don't say: I forgive you, for you know not what you do.

ASLAKSEN: (*Shouts.*) That is a blasphemous comparison, Dr. Stockmann!

BILLING: Strike me—! This is more than a serious man can stand!

A COARSE VOICE: And he threatens us into the bargain!

ANGRY CRIES: Let's smash his windows! Duck him in the hord!

A MAN: (*In the crowd.*) Blow your horn, Evensen! Blow man, blow!

(Horn-blowing, whistling, and wild shouting. The Doctor, with his family, goes toward the door. Horster clears the way for them.)

ALL: (*Yelling after them as they go out.*) Enemy of the people! Enemy of the people! Enemy of the people!

BILLING: Strike me dead if I'd care to drink toddy at Stockmann's to-night!

(The people throng towards the door; the shouting is taken up by others outside; from the street are heard cries of "Enemy of the people! Enemy of the people!")

ACT FIFTH

DR. STOCKMANN's *Study. Bookshelves and glass cases with various collections along the walls. In the back, a door leading to the hall; in front, on the left, a door to the sitting-room. In the wall to the right are two windows, all the panes of which are smashed. In the middle of the room is the* DOCTOR's *writing-table, covered with books and papers. The room is in disorder. It is forenoon.*

DR. STOCKMANN, *in dressing-gown, slippers, and skull-cap, is bending down and raking with an umbrella under one of the cabinets; at last he rakes out a stone.*

DR. STOCKMANN: (*Speaking through the sitting-room doorway.*) Katrina, I've found another!

MRS. STOCKMANN: (*In the sitting-room.*) Oh, I'm sure you'll find plenty more.

DR. STOCKMANN: (*Placing the stone on a pile of others on the table.*) I shall keep these stones as sacred relics. Eilif and Morten shall see them every day, and when I die they shall be heirlooms. (*Raking under the bookcase.*) Hasn't —what the devil is her name?—the girl—hasn't she been for the glazier yet?

MRS. STOCKMANN: (*Coming in.*) Yes, but he said he didn't know whether he would be able to come to-day.

DR. STOCKMANN: I believe, if the truth were told, he daren't come.

MRS. STOCKMANN: Well, Randina, too, had an idea he was afraid to come because of the neighbours. (*Speaks through the sitting-room doorway.*) What is it, Randina?—Very well. (*Goes out, and returns immediately.*) Here is a letter for you, Thomas.

DR. STOCKMANN: Let me see. (*Opens the letter and reads.*) Aha!

MRS. STOCKMANN: Who is it from?

DR. STOCKMANN: From the landlord. He gives us notice.

MRS. STOCKMANN: Is it possible? he is such a nice man—

DR. STOCKMANN: (*Looking at the letter.*) He daren't do otherwise, he says. He is very unwilling to do it; but he daren't do otherwise—on account of his fellow citizens—out of respect for public opinion—is in a dependent position —doesn't dare to offend certain influential men—

MRS. STOCKMANN: There, you see, Thomas.

DR. STOCKMANN: Yes, yes, I see well enough; they are all cowards, every one of them, in this town; no one dares do anything for fear of all the rest. (*Throws the letter on the table.*) But it's all the same to us, Katrina. We will shape our course for the new world, and then—

MRS. STOCKMANN: But are you sure this idea of going abroad is altogether wise, Thomas?

DR. STOCKMANN: Would you have me stay here, where they have pilloried me as an enemy of the people, branded me, smashed my windows! And look here, Katrina, they've torn a hole in my black trousers, too.

MRS. STOCKMANN: Oh dear; and these are the best you have!

DR. STOCKMANN: A man should never put on his best trousers when he goes out to battle for freedom and truth. Well, I don't care so much about the trousers, them you can always patch up for me. But that the mob, the rabble, should dare to attack me as if they were my equals—that is what I can't, for the life of me, stomach

MRS. STOCKMANN: Yes, they have behaved abominably to you here, Thomas; but is that any reason for leaving the country altogether?

DR. STOCKMANN: Do you think the plebeians aren't just as insolent in other towns? Oh yes, they are, my dear; it's six of one and half a dozen of the other. Well, never mind; let the curs yelp; that's not the worst; the worst is that every one, all over the country, is the slave of his party. Not that I suppose—very likely it's no better in the free West either; the compact majority, and enlightened public opinion, and all the other devil's trash is rampant there too. But you see the conditions are larger there than here; they may kill you, but they don't slow-torture you; they don't screw up a free soul in a vice, as they do at home here. And then, if need be, you can keep out of it all. (*Walks up and down.*) If I only knew of any primeval forest, or a little South Sea island to be sold cheap—

MRS. STOCKMANN: Yes, but the boys, Thomas.

DR. STOCKMANN: (*Comes to a standstill.*) What an extraordinary woman you are, Katrina! Would you rather have the boys grow up in such a society as ours? Why, you could see for yourself yesterday evening that one half of the population is stark mad, and if the other half hasn't lost its wits, that's only because they are brute beasts who haven't any wits to lose.

MRS. STOCKMANN: But really, my dear Thomas, you do say such imprudent things.

DR. STOCKMANN: What! Isn't it the truth that I tell them? Don't they turn all ideas upside down? Don't they stir up right and wrong into one hotchpotch? Don't they call lies everything that I know to be the truth? But the maddest thing of all is to see crowds of grown men, calling themselves Liberals, go about persuading themselves and others that they are friends of freedom! Did you ever hear anything like it, Katrina?

MRS. STOCKMANN: Yes, yes, no doubt. But—

(Petra *enters from the sitting-room.*)

MRS. STOCKMANN: Back from school already?

PETRA: Yes; I have been dismissed.

MRS. STOCKMANN: Dismissed?

DR. STOCKMANN: You too!

PETRA: Mrs. Busk gave me notice, and so I thought it best to leave there and then.

DR. STOCKMANN: You did perfectly right!

MRS. STOCKMANN: Who could have thought Mrs. Busk was such a bad woman!

PETRA: Oh mother, Mrs. Busk isn't bad at all; I saw clearly how sorry she was. But she dared not do otherwise, she said; and so I am dismissed.

DR. STOCKMANN: (*Laughing and rubbing his hands.*) She dared not do otherwise—just like the rest! Oh, it's delicious.

MRS. STOCKMANN: Oh well, after that frightful scene last night—

PETRA: It wasn't only that. What do you think, father—?

DR. STOCKMANN: Well?

PETRA: Mrs. Busk showed me no fewer than three letters she had received this morning—

DR. STOCKMANN: Anonymous, of course?

PETRA: Yes.

DR. STOCKMANN: They never dare give their names, Katrina!

PETRA: And two of them stated that a gentleman who is often at our house said at the club last night that I held extremely advanced opinions upon various things—

DR. STOCKMANN: Of course you didn't deny it.

PETRA: Of course not. You know Mrs. Busk herself is pretty advanced in her opinions when we're alone together; but now that this has come out about me, she dared not keep me on.

MRS. STOCKMANN: Some one that is often at our house, too. There, you see, Thomas, what comes of all your hospitality.

DR. STOCKMANN: We won't live any longer in such a pig-sty! Pack up as quickly as you can, Katrina; let's get away—the sooner the better.

MRS. STOCKMANN: Hush! I think there is some one in the passage. See who it is, Petra.

PETRA: (*Opening the door.*) Oh, is it you, Captain Horster? Please come in.

HORSTER: (*From the hall.*) Good morning. I thought I might just look in and ask how you are.

DR. STOCKMANN: (*Shaking his hand.*) Thanks; that's very good of you.

MRS. STOCKMANN: And thank you for helping us through the crowd last night, Captain Horster.

PETRA: How did you ever get home again?

HORSTER: Oh, that was all right. I am tolerably able-bodied, you know; and these fellows' bark is worse than their bite.

DR. STOCKMANN: Yes, isn't it extraordinary, this piggish cowardice? Come here, and let me show you something! Look, here are all the stones they threw in at us. Only look at them? Upon my soul there aren't more than two decent-sized lumps in the whole heap; the rest are nothing but pebbles— mere gravel. They stood down there, and yelled, and swore they'd half kill me;—but as for really doing it—no, there's mighty little fear of that in this town!

HORSTER: You may thank your stars for that this time, Doctor.

DR. STOCKMANN: So I do, of course. But it's depressing all the same; for if ever it should come to a serious national struggle, you may be sure public opinion would be for taking to its heels, and the compact majority would scamper for their lives like a flock of sheep, Captain Horster. That is what's so melancholy to think of; it grieves me to the heart.—But deuce take it—it's foolish of me to feel anything of the sort! They have called me an enemy of the people; well then, let me be an enemy of the people!

MRS. STOCKMANN: That you'll never be, Thomas.

DR. STOCKMANN: You'd better not take your oath of it, Katrina. A bad name may act like a pin-scratch in the lung. And that confounded word—I can't get rid of it; it has sunk deep into my heart; and there it lies gnawing and sucking like an acid. And no magnesia can cure me.

PETRA: Pooh; you should only laugh at them, father.

HORSTER: People will think differently yet, Doctor.

MRS. STOCKMANN: Yes, Thomas, that's as certain as that you are standing here.

Dr. Stockmann: Yes, perhaps, when it is too late. Well, as they make their bed so they must lie! Let them go on wallowing here in their pig-sty, and learn to repent having driven a patriot into exile. When do you sail, Captain Horster?

Horster: Well—that's really what I came to speak to you about—

Dr. Stockmann: What? Anything wrong with the ship?

Horster: No; but the fact is, I shan't be sailing in her.

Petra: Surely you have not been dismissed?

Horster: (Smiling.) Yes, I have.

Petra: You too!

Mrs. Stockmann: There, you see, Thomas.

Dr. Stockmann: And for the truth's sake! Oh, if I could possibly have imagined such a thing—

Horster: You mustn't be troubled about this; I shall soon find a berth with some other company, elsewhere.

Dr. Stockmann: And this is that man Vik! A wealthy man, independent of every one! Faugh!

Horster: Oh, for that matter, he's a very well-meaning man. He said himself he would gladly have kept me on if only he dared—

Dr. Stockmann: But he didn't dare? Of course not!

Horster: It's not so easy, he said, when you belong to a party—

Dr. Stockmann: My gentleman has hit it there! A party is like a sausage-machine; it grinds all the brains together in one mash; and that's why we see nothing but porridge-heads and pulp-heads all around!

Mrs. Stockmann: Now really, Thomas!

Petra: (To Horster.) If only you hadn't seen us home, perhaps it would not have come to this.

Horster: I don't regret it.

Petra: (Gives him her hand.) Thank you for that!

Horster: (To Dr. Stockmann.) And then, too, I wanted to tell you this: if you are really determined to go abroad, I've thought of another way—

Dr. Stockmann: That's good—if only we can get off quickly—

Mrs. Stockmann: Hush! Isn't that a knock?

Petra: I believe it is uncle.

Dr. Stockmann: Aha! (Calls.) Come in!

Mrs. Stockmann: My dear Thomas, now do promise me—

(The Burgomaster enters from the hall.)

Burgomaster: (In the doorway.) Oh, you are engaged. Then I'd better—

Dr. Stockmann: No no; come in.

Burgomaster: But I wanted to speak to you alone.

Mrs. Stockmann: We can go into the sitting-room.

Horster: And I shall look in again presently.

Dr. Stockmann: No no; go with the ladies, Captain Horster; I must hear more about—

Horster: All right, then I'll wait.

(He follows Mrs. Stockmann and Petra into the sitting-room. The Burgomaster says nothing, but casts glances at the windows.)

Dr. Stockmann: I daresay you find it rather draughty here to-day? Put on your cap.

BURGOMASTER: Thanks, if I may. (*Does so.*) I fancy I caught cold yesterday evening. I stood there shivering—

DR. STOCKMANN: Really. O my soul, now, I found it quite warm enough.

BURGOMASTER: I regret that it was not in my power to prevent these nocturnal excesses.

DR. STOCKMANN: Have you anything else in particular to say to me?

BURGOMASTER: (*Producing a large letter.*) I have this document for you from the Directors of the Baths.

DR. STOCKMANN: My dismissal?

BURGOMASTER: Yes; dated from to-day. (*Places the letter on the table.*) We are very sorry—but frankly, we dared not do otherwise, on account of public opinion.

DR. STOCKMANN: (*Smiling.*) Dared not? I've heard that phrase already to-day.

BURGOMASTER: I beg you to realise your position clearly. For the future, you cannot count upon any sort of practice in the town.

DR. STOCKMANN: Devil take the practice! But how can you be so sure of that?

BURGOMASTER: The House-owners' Association is sending round a circular from house to house, in which all well-disposed citizens are called upon not to employ you; and I dare swear that not a single head of a family will venture to refuse his signature; he simply dare not.

DR. STOCKMANN: Well well; I don't doubt that. But what then?

BURGOMASTER: If I might advise, I would suggest that you should leave the town for a time—

DR. STOCKMANN: Yes, I've had some such idea in my mind already.

BURGOMASTER: Good. And when you have had six months or so for mature deliberation, if you could make up your mind to acknowledge your error, with a few words of regret—

DR. STOCKMANN: I might perhaps be reinstated, you think?

BURGOMASTER: Perhaps it's not quite out of the question.

DR. STOCKMANN: Yes, but how about public opinion? You daren't, on account of public opinion.

BURGOMASTER: Opinion is extremely variable. And, to speak candidly, it is of the greatest importance for us to have such an admission under your own hand.

DR. STOCKMANN: Yes, I daresay is would be mightily convenient for you! But you remember what I've said to you before about such foxes' tricks!

BURGOMASTER: At that time your position was infinitely more favourable; at that time you thought you had the whole town at your back—

DR. STOCKMANN: Yes, and now I have the whole town on my back— (*Flaring up.*) But no—not if I had the devil and his dam on my back—! Never—never, I tell you!

BURGOMASTER: The father of a family has no right to act as you are doing. You have no right to do it, Thomas.

DR. STOCKMANN: I have no right! There's only one thing in the world that a free man has no right to do; and do you know what that is?

BURGOMASTER: No.

DR. STOCKMANN: Of course not; but *I* will tell you. A free man has no right to wallow in filth like a cur; he has no right to act so that he ought to spit in his own face!

BURGOMASTER: That sounds extremely plausible; and if there were not another explanation of your obstinacy—but we all know there is—

DR. STOCKMANN: What do you mean by that?

BURGOMASTER: You understand well enough. But as your brother, and as a man who knows the world, I warn you not to build too confidently upon prospects and expectations that may very likely come to nothing.

DR. STOCKMANN: Why, what on earth are you driving at?

BURGOMASTER: Do you really want me to believe that you are ignorant of the terms of old Morten Kiil's will?

DR. STOCKMANN: I know that the little he has is to go to a home for old and needy artizans. But what has that got to do with me?

BURGOMASTER: To begin with, "the little he has" is no trifle. Morten Kiil is a tolerably wealthy man.

DR. STOCKMANN: I have never had the least notion of that!

BURGOMASTER: H'm—really? Then I suppose you have no notion that a not inconsiderable part of his fortune is to go to your children, you and your wife having a life-interest in it. Has he not told you that?

DR. STOCKMANN: No, I'll be hanged if he has! On the contrary, he has done nothing but grumble about being so preposterously over-taxed. But are you really sure of this, Peter?

BURGOMASTER: I have it from a thoroughly trustworthy source.

DR. STOCKMANN: Why, good heavens, then Katrina's provided for—and the children too! Oh, I must tell her—(Calls.) Katrina, Katrina!

BURGOMASTER: (Holding him back.) Hush! don't say anything about it yet.

MRS. STOCKMANN: (Opening the door.) What is it?

DR. STOCKMANN: Nothing my dear; go in again.

(Mrs. Stockmann *closes the door.*)

DR. STOCKMANN: (Pacing up and down.) Provided for! Only think—all of them provided for! And for life! After all, it's a grand thing to feel yourself secure!

BURGOMASTER: Yes, but that is just what you are not. Morten Kiil can revoke his will any day or hour he chooses.

DR. STOCKMANN: But he won't, my good Peter. The Badger is only too delighted to see me fall foul of you and your wiseacre friends.

BURGOMASTER: (Starts and looks searchingly at him.) Aha! That throws a new light on the good many things.

DR. STOCKMANN: What things?

BURGOMASTER: So the whole affair has been a carefully-concocted intrigue. Your recklessly violent onslaught—in the name of truth—upon the leading men of the town—

DR. STOCKMANN: Well, what of it?

BURGOMASTER: It was nothing but a preconcerted requital for that vindictive old Morten Kiil's will.

DR. STOCKMANN: (Almost speechless.) Peter—you are the most abominable plebeian I have ever known in all my born days.

BURGOMASTER: All is over between us. Your dismissal is irrevocable—for now we have a weapon against you. (He goes out.)

DR. STOCKMANN: Shame! shame! shame! (Calls.) Katrina! The floor must be scrubbed after him! Tell her to come here with a pail—what's her name? confound it—the girl with the smudge on her nose—

MRS. STOCKMANN: (In the sitting-room doorway.) Hush, hush Thomas!

PETRA: (Also in the doorway.) Father, here's grandfather; he wants to know if he can speak to you alone.

DR. STOCKMANN: Yes, of course he can. (By the door.) Come in, father-in-law.

(Morten Kiil enters. Dr. Stockmann *closes the door behind him.)*

Dr. Stockmann: Well, what is it? Sit down.
Morten Kiil: I won't sit down. *(Looking about him.)* It looks cheerful here to-day, Stockmann.
Dr. Stockmann: Yes, don't you think so?
Morten Kiil: Sure enough. And you've plenty of fresh air too; you've got your fill of that oxygen you were talking about yesterday. You must have a rare good conscience to-day, I should think.
Dr. Stockmann: Yes, I have.
Morten Kiil: So I should suppose. *(Tapping himself on the breast.)* But do you know what *I* have got here?
Dr. Stockmann: A good conscience too, I hope.
Morten Kiil: Pooh! No! Something far better than that.

(Takes out a large pocket-book, opens it, and shows Stockmann *a bundle of papers.)*

Dr. Stockmann: *(Looking at him in astonishment.)* Shares in the Baths!
Morten Kiil: They weren't difficult to get to-day.
Dr. Stockmann: And you've gone and bought these up—?
Morten Kiil: All I had the money to pay for.
Dr. Stockmann: Why, my dear sir,—just when things are in such a desperate way at the Baths—
Morten Kiil: If you behave like a reasonable being, you can soon set the Baths all right again.
Dr. Stockmann: Well, you can see for yourself I'm doing all I can. But the people of this town are mad!
Morten Kiil: You said yesterday that the worst filth came from my tannery. Now, if that's true, then my grandfather, and my father before me, and I myself, have for ever so many years been poisoning the town with filth, like three destroying angels. Do you think I'm going to sit quiet under such a reproach?
Dr. Stockmann: Unfortunately, you can't help it.
Morten Kiil: No, thank you. I hold fast to my good name. I've heard that people call me "the Badger." A badger's a sort of a pig, I know; but I'm determined to give them the lie. I will live and die a clean man.
Dr. Stockmann: And how will you manage that?
Morten Kiil: You shall make me clean, Stockmann.
Dr. Stockmann: I!
Morten Kiil: Do you know what money I've used to buy these shares with? No, you can't know; but now I'll tell you. It's the money Katrina and Petra and the boys are to have after my death. For, you see, I've laid by something after all.
Dr. Stockmann: *(Flaring up.)* And you've taken Katrina's money and done this with it!
Morten Kiil: Yes; the whole of it is invested in the Baths now. And now I want to see if you're really so stark, staring mad after all, Stockmann. If you go on making out that these beasts and other abominations dribble down from my tannery, it'll be just as if you were to flay broad stripes of Katrina's skin—and Petra's too, and the boys. No decent father would ever do that— unless he were a madman.

DR. STOCKMANN: (*Walking up and down*) Yes, but I am a madman; I am a madman!

MORTEN KIIL: You surely can't be so raving, ramping mad where your wife and children are concerned.

DR. STOCKMANN: (*Stopping in front of him.*) Why couldn't you have spoken to me before you went and bought all that rubbish?

MORTEN KIIL: What's done can't be undone.

DR. STOCKMANN: (*Walking restlessly about.*) If only I weren't so certain about the affair—! But I am absolutely convinced that I'm right.

MORTEN KIIL: (*Weighing the pocket book in his hand.*) If you stick to this lunacy, these aren't worth much. (*Puts the book into his pocket.*)

DR. STOCKMANN: But, deuce take it! surely science ought to be able to hit upon some antidote, some sort of prophylactic—

MORTEN KIIL: Do you mean something to kill the beasts?

DR. STOCKMANN: Yes, or at least to make them harmless.

MORTEN KIIL: Couldn't you try ratsbane?

DR. STOCKMANN: Oh, nonsense, nonsense!—But since every one declares it's nothing but fancy, why fancy let it be! Let them have it their own way! Haven't the ignorant, narrow-hearted curs reviled me as an enemy of the people?—and weren't they on the point of tearing the clothes off my back?

MORTEN KIIL: And they've smashed all your windows for you too!

DR. STOCKMANN: Yes, and then there's one's duty to one's family! I must talk that over with Katrina; such things are more in her line.

MORTEN KIIL: That's right! You just follow the advice of a sensible woman.

DR. STOCKMANN: (*Turning upon him angrily.*) How could you act so preposterously! Risking Katrina's money, and putting me to this torture! When I look at you, I seem to see the devil himself—!

MORTEN KIIL: Then I'd better be off. But I must hear from you, yes, or no, by two o'clock. If it's no, all the shares go to the Hospital, and that this very day.

DR. STOCKMANN: And what will Katrina get?

MORTEN KIIL: Not a rap.

(*The door leading to the hall opens. Hovstad and Aslaksen are seen outside it.*)

MORTEN KIIL: Hullo! look at these two.

DR. STOCKMANN: (*Staring at them.*) What! Do you actually venture to come here?

HOVSTAD: Why, to be sure we do.

ASLAKSEN: You see, we've something to discuss with you.

MORTEN KIIL: (*Whispers.*) Yes or no—by two o'clock.

ASLAKSEN: (*With a glance at Hovstad.*) Aha!

DR. STOCKMANN: Well, what do you want with me? Be brief.

HOVSTAD: I can quite understand that you resent our attitude at the meeting yesterday—

DR. STOCKMANN: Your attitude, you say? Yes, it was a pretty attitude! I call it the attitude of cowards—of old women— Shame upon you!

HOVSTAD: Call it what you will; but we could not act otherwise.

DR. STOCKMANN: You dared not, I suppose? Isn't that so?

HOVSTAD: Yes, if you like to put it so.

ASLAKSEN: But why didn't you just say a word to us beforehand? The merest hint to Mr. Hovstad or to me—

DR. STOCKMANN: A hint? What about?

ASLAKSEN: About what was really behind it all.

DR. STOCKMANN: I don't in the least understand you?

ASLAKSEN: (Nods confidentially.) Oh yes, you do, Dr. Stockmann.

HOVSTAD: It's no good making a mystery of it any longer.

DR. STOCKMANN: (Looking from one to the other.) Why, what in the devil's name—?

ASLAKSEN: May I ask—isn't your father-in-law going about the town buying up all the Bath stock?

DR. STOCKMANN: Yes, he has been buying Bath stock to-day but—

ASLAKSEN: It would have been more prudent to let somebody else do that—some one not so closely connected with you.

HOVSTAD: And then you ought not to have appeared in the matter under your own name. No one need have known that the attack on the Baths came from you. You should have taken me into your counsel, Dr. Stockmann.

DR. STOCKMANN: (Stares straight in front of him; a light seems to break in upon him, and he says as though thunderstruck.) Is this possible? Can such things be?

ASLAKSEN: (Smiling.) It's plain enough that they can. But they ought to be managed delicately, you understand.

HOVSTAD: And there ought to be more people in it; for the responsibility always falls more lightly when there are several to share it.

DR. STOCKMANN: (Calmly.)In one word, gentlemen—what is it you want?

ASLAKSEN: Mr. Hovstad can best—

HOVSTAD: No, you explain, Aslaksen.

ASLAKSEN: Well, it's this: now that we know how the matter really stands, we believe we can venture to place the People's Messenger at your disposal.

DR. STOCKMANN: You can venture to now, eh? But how about public opinion? Aren't you afraid of bringing down a storm upon us?

HOVSTAD: We must manage to ride out the storm.

ASLAKSEN: And you must be ready to put about quickly, Doctor. As soon as your attack has done its work—

DR. STOCKMANN: As soon as my father-in-law and I have bought up the shares at a discount, you mean?

HOVSTAD: I presume it is mainly on scientific grounds that you want to take the management of the Baths into your own hands.

DR. STOCKMANN: Of course; it was on scientific grounds that I got the old Badger to stand in with me. And then we'll tinker up the water-Works a little, and potter about a bit down at the beach, without its costing the town sixpence. That ought to do the business Eh?

HOVSTAD: I think so—if you have the Messenger to back you up.

ASLAKSEN: In a free community the press is a power, Doctor.

DR. STOCKMANN: Yes, indeed; and so is public opinion. And you, Mr. Aslaksen—I suppose you will answer for the House-owners' Association?

ASLAKSEN: Both for the House-owners' Association and the Temperance Society. You may make your mind easy.

DR. STOCKMANN: But, gentlemen—really I'm quite ashamed to mention such a thing—but—what return—?

HOVSTAD: Of course, we should prefer to give you our support for nothing. But the Messenger is not very firmly established; it's not getting on as it ought to; and I should be very sorry to have to stop the paper just now, when there's so much to be done in general politics.

DR. STOCKMANN: Naturally; that would be very hard for a friend of the people like you. (*Flaring up.*) But I—I am an enemy of the people! (*Striding about the room.*) Where's my stick? Where the devil is my stick?

HOVSTAD: What do you mean?

ASLAKSEN: Surely you wouldn't—

DR. STOCKMANN: (*Standing still.*) And suppose I don't give you a single farthing out of all my shares? You must remember we rich folk don't like parting with our money.

HOVSTAD: And you must remember that this business of the shares can be represented in two ways.

DR. STOCKMANN: Yes, you are the man for that; if I don't come to the rescue of the *Messenger*, you'll manage to put a vile complexion on the affair; you'll hunt me down, I suppose—bait me—try to throttle me as a dog throttles a hare!

HOVSTAD: That's a law of nature—every animal fights for its own subsistence.

ASLAKSEN: And must take its food where it can find it, you know.

DR. STOCKMANN: Then see if you can't find some out in the gutter; (*Striding about the room.*) for now, by heaven! we shall see which is the strongest animal of us three. (*Finds his umbrella and brandishes it.*) Now, look here—!

HOVSTAD: You surely don't mean to assault us!

ASLAKSEN: I say, be careful with that umbrella!

DR. STOCKMANN: Out at the window with you, Mr. Hovstad!

HOVSTAD: (*By the hall door.*) *Are you utterly crazy?*

DR. STOCKMANN: Out at the window, Mr. Aslaksen! Jump I tell you! Be quick about it!

ASLAKSEN: (*Running round the writing-table.*) Moderation, Doctor; I'm not at all strong; I can't stand much— (*Screams.*) Help! help!

(Mrs. Stockmann, Petra, *and* Horster *enter from sitting-room.*)

MRS. STOCKMANN: Good heavens, Thomas! what can be the matter?

DR. STOCKMANN: (*Brandishing the umbrella.*) Jump, I tell you! Out into the gutter!

HOVSTAD: An unprovoked assault! I call you to witness, Captain Horster. (*Rushes off through the hall.*)

ASLAKSEN: (*Bewildered.*) If one only knew the local situation—! (*He slinks out by the sitting-room door.*)

MRS. STOCKMANN: (*Holding back the* Doctor.) Now, do restrain yourself, Thomas!

DR. STOCKMANN: (*Throwing down the umbrella.*) I'll be hanged if they haven't got off after all.

MRS. STOCKMANN: Why, what can they have wanted with you?

DR. STOCKMANN: I'll tell you afterwards; I have other things to think of now. (*Goes to the table and writes on a visiting-card.*) Look here, Katrina: what's written here?

MRS. STOCKMANN: Three big Noes; what does that mean?

DR. STOCKMANN: That I'll tell you afterwards, too. (*Handing the card.*) There, Petra; let smudgy face run to the Badger's with this as fast as she can. Be quick! (Petra *goes out through the hall with the card.*)

DR. STOCKMANN: Well, if I haven't had visits to-day from all the emissaries of the devil! But now I'll sharpen my pen against them till it becomes a goad; I'll dip it in gall and venom; I'll hurl my inkstand straight at their skulls.

MRS. STOCKMANN: You forget we are going away, Thomas.

(Petra returns.)

DR. STOCKMANN: Well?

PETRA: She has gone.

DR. STOCKMANN: Good. Going away, do you say? No, I'll be damned if we do; we stay where we are, Katrina!

PETRA: Stay!

MRS. STOCKMANN: Here in the town?

DR. STOCKMANN: Yes, here; the field of battle is here; here the fight must be fought; here I will conquer! As soon as my trousers are mended, I shall go out into the town and look for a house; we must have a roof over our heads for the winter.

HORSTER: That you can have in my house.

DR. STOCKMANN: Can I?

HORSTER: Yes, there's no difficulty about that. I have room enough, and I'm hardly ever at home myself.

MRS. STOCKMANN: Oh, how kind of you, Captain Horster.

PETRA: Thank you!

DR. STOCKMANN: *(Shaking his hand.)* Thanks, thanks! So that is off my mind. And this very day I shall set to work in earnest. Oh, there's no end of work to be done here, Katrina! It's a good thing I shall have all my time at my disposal now; for you must know I've had notice from the Baths—

MRS. STOCKMANN: *(Sighing.)* Oh, yes, I was expecting that.

DR. STOCKMANN: —And now they want to take away my practice as well. But let them! The poor I shall keep anyhow—those that can't pay; and, good Lord! it's they that need me most. But by heaven! I'll make them listen to me; I'll preach to them in season and out of season, as the saying goes.

MRS. STOCKMANN: My dear Thomas, I should have thought you had learnt what good preaching does.

DR. STOCKMANN: You really are absurd, Katrina. Am I to let myself be beaten off the field by public opinion, and the compact majority, and all that sort of devilry? No, thank you! Besides, my point is so simple, so clear and straightforward. I only want to drive it into the heads of these curs that the Liberals are the craftiest foes free men have to face; that party-programmes wring the neck of all young and living truths; that considerations of expediency turn justice and morality upside down, until life here becomes simply unlivable. Come, Captain Horster, don't you think I shall be able to make the people understand that?

HORSTER: Maybe; I don't know about these things myself.

DR. STOCKMANN: Well, you see-this is the way of it! It's the party-leaders that must be exterminated. For a party-leader is just like a wolf, you see—like a ravening wolf; he must devour a certain number of small animals a year, if he's to exist at all. Just look at Hovstad and Aslaksen! How many small animals they polish off—or at least mangle and maim, so that they're fit for nothing else but to be house-owners and subscribers to the *People's Messenger!* *(Sits on the edge of the table.)* Just come here, Katrina—see how bravely the sun shines to-day! And how the blessed fresh spring air blows in upon me!

MRS. STOCKMANN: Yes, if only we could live on sunshine and spring air, Thomas.

DR. STOCKMANN: Well, you'll have to pinch and save to eke them out—
and then we shall get on all right. That's what troubles me least. No, what
does trouble me is that I don't see any man free enough and high-minded
enough to dare to take up my work after me.

PETRA: Oh, don't think about that, father; you have time enough before
you.—Why, see, there are the boys already.

(Eilif and Morten *enter from the sitting-room.*)

MRS. STOCKMANN: Have you a holiday to-day?

MORTEN: No; but we had a fight with the other fellows in play-time—

EILIF: That's not true; it was the other fellows that fought us.

MORTEN: Yes, and then Mr. Rörlund said we had better stop at home for
a few days.

DR. STOCKMANN: (*Snapping his fingers and springing down from the table.*) Now I have it! Now I have it, on my soul! You shall never set foot in
school again!

THE BOYS: Never go to school!

MRS. STOCKMANN: Why, Thomas—

DR. STOCKMANN: Never, I say! I shall teach you myself—that's to say, I
won't teach you any mortal thing—

MORTEN: Hurrah!

DR. STOCKMANN: —but I shall help you to grow into free, high-minded
men.—Look here, you'll have to help me, Petra.

PETRA: Yes, father, you may be sure I will.

DR. STOCKMANN: And we'll have our school in the room where they have
reviled me as an enemy of the people. But we must have more pupils. I must
have at least a dozen boys to begin with.

MRS. STOCKMANN: You'll never get them in this town.

DR. STOCKMANN: We shall see. (*To the boys.*) Don't you know any street
urchins—any regular ragamuffins—?

MORTEN: Yes, father, I know lots!

DR. STOCKMANN: That's all right; bring me a few of them. I shall experiment with the street-curs for once in a way; there are sometimes excellent
heads amongst them.

MORTEN: But what are we to do when we've grown into free and high-
minded men?

DR. STOCKMANN: Drive all the wolves out to the far west, boys!

(Eilif *looks rather doubtful;* Morten *jumps about shouting "Hurrah!")*

MRS. STOCKMANN: If only the wolves don't drive you out, Thomas.

DR. STOCKMANN: Are you quite mad, Katrina! Drive me out! Now that I
am the strongest man in the town?

MRS. STOCKMANN: The strongest—now?

DR. STOCKMANN: Yes, I venture to say this; that now I am one of the
strongest men in the whole world.

MORTEN: I say, what fun!

DR. STOCKMANN: (*In a subdued voice.*) Hush; you mustn't speak about it
yet; but I have made a great discovery.

MRS. STOCKMANN: What, another?

Dr. Stockmann: Yes, of course! (*Gathers them about him, and speaks confidentially.*) This is what I have discovered, you see: the strongest man in the world is he who stands most alone.

Mrs. Stockmann: (*Shakes her head, smiling.*) Ah, Thomas dear—!

Petra: (*Grasping his hands cheerily.*) Father!

FOR DISCUSSION

1. For what reason does Dr. Stockmann insist that the truth about the baths be made public? What are his motives? Do you agree with him or not? Why?
2. Why does the Burgomaster want to keep the truth a secret? What reason does he give? Is he justified in taking this position?
3. Can you draw any parallels between the situation in this play and situations in today's world?
4. What position does Aslaksen take? What do you think of him as a person for acting as he did?
5. According to Hovstad, what is the chief purpose of a newspaper? Do you agree?
6. Does Dr. Stockmann believe that the majority is always right? Do you agree with him?
7. Compare Dr. Stockmann's views to those of the Burgomaster concerning the role of the individual in society. What do you believe it should be?
8. When Dr. Stockmann speaks of "common" people, what does he mean? According to him, what makes people "common"?
9. Do you think that Mrs. Stockmann plays an important role in this play? Why or why not? What about Petra? The two sons? Discuss.
10. What is the theme of the play?
11. Who is the real "enemy of the people"?
12. How closely does An Enemy of the People follow the structure of a "well-made play"?
13. This play is usually considered realistic. Why? Does it contain elements of any other style, such as romanticism?
14. When do you first suspect that Dr. Stockmann's discovery will cause problems?
15. If you were to write a sixth act to this play, what would happen to Dr. Stockmann and his family?
16. How do Dr. Stockmann's, Mrs. Stockmann's, and Petra's attitudes toward life differ? Consider such things as their religious, political, and sociological views.

Oscar Wilde wrote drawing-room comedy.

He was born in Dublin in 1854 of socially prominent parents. After attending Oxford, where he was a distinguished student of the classics, he traveled in Italy and Greece. Upon returning to London, he published a book of poetry and a play, *Vera*, which was later produced in the United States but was unsuccessful. His second play, a blank-verse tragedy, *The Duchess of Padua*, was produced in New York in 1891. Wilde also wrote novels, stories, and poetry. Supported largely by his wife's fortune, he gained notoriety for his extravagance.

Wilde's best plays were comedies. The first, *Lady Windermere's Fan*, written in 1892, was followed by *An Ideal Husband* and *The Importance of Being Earnest*. The latter, produced in 1895 at the St. James Theatre in London, was highly successful but was withdrawn from production when Wilde was sentenced to prison for immoral behavior. He spent two years in prison and after his release went to Paris. His health began to fail, and on November 30, 1900, he died.

Wilde was a master of what is called drawing-room comedy. His plays satirize British society, of which he was very critical, in light and witty dialogue. Particularly humorous is his repartee in which moral standards and general beliefs are inverted. Note, for example (in *The Importance of Being Earnest*) how, when Jack tells Lady Bracknell that he smokes, she replies that smoking is good, since a man needs an occupation! On the other hand, Wilde has been criticized for three things: his characters lack depth, his plots are not well developed, and his situations too contrived.

Wilde himself never doubted his talent as a playwright and felt that style, not sincerity, was important. His most successful play, *The Importance of Being Earnest*, is a farce in which two-dimensional characters and contrivances in the plot add to the overall effect, rather than detracting from it. The play shows Wilde's writing at its height. It is literate and polished, but full of absurdities. The characters are not believable, but this makes them more humorous. The dialogue is flippant and effective.

Victorian England, with its stuffy attitudes and strict code of ethics, gave Wilde something to react against. *The Importance of Being Earnest* is most entertaining when it pokes fun at Victorian "earnestness" carried to extremes. It was probably the most successful comedy of the nineteenth century. It has had many professional revivals and continues to be a favorite of amateur groups. A musical version, *Earnest in Love*, was presented in 1959.

The Importance of Being Earnest

A TRIVIAL COMEDY FOR SERIOUS PEOPLE

CHARACTERS

JOHN WORTHING, J.P.
ALGERNON MONCRIEFF
REV. CANON CHASUBLE, D.D.
MERRIMAN, *butler*
LANE, *manservant*

LADY BRACKNELL
HON. GWENDOLEN FAIRFAX
CECILY CARDEW
MISS PRISM, *governess*

The Importance of Being Earnest

ACT I

(*Morning-room in Algernon's flat in Half-Moon Street. The room is luxuriously and artistically furnished. The sound of a piano is heard in the adjoining room.*
Lane *is arranging afternoon tea on the table, and after the music has ceased,* Algernon *enters.*)

ALGERNON: Did you hear what I was playing, Lane?

LANE: I didn't think it polite to listen, sir.

ALGERNON: I'm sorry for that, for your sake. I don't play accurately—any one can play accurately—but I play with wonderful expression. As far as the piano is concerned, sentiment is my forte. I keep science for Life.

LANE: Yes, sir.

ALGERNON: And, speaking of the science of Life, have you got the cucumber sandwiches cut for Lady Bracknell?

LANE: Yes, sir. (*Hands them on a salver.*)

ALGERNON: (*Inspects them, takes two, and sits down on the sofa.*) Oh! . . . by the way, Lane, I see from your book that on Thursday night, when Lord Shoreman and Mr. Worthing were dining with me, eight bottles of champagne are entered as having been consumed.

LANE: Yes, sir; eight bottles and a pint.

ALGERNON: Why is it that at a bachlor's establishment the servants invariably drink the champagne? I ask merely for information.

LANE: I attribute it to the superior quality of the wine, sir. I have often observed that in married households the champagne is rarely of a first-rate brand.

ALGERNON: Good heavens! Is marriage so demoralizing as that?

LANE: I believe it *is* a very pleasant state, sir. I have had very little experience of it myself up to the present. I have only been married once. That was in consequence of a misunderstanding between myself and a young person.

ALGERNON: (*Languidly*) I don't know that I am much interested in your family life, Lane.

LANE: No, sir; it is not a very interesting subject. I never think of it myself.

ALGERNON: Very natural, I am sure. That will do, Lane, thank you.

LANE: Thank you, sir.

(Lane *goes out.*)

ALGERNON: Lane's views on marriage seem somewhat lax. Really, if the lower orders don't set us a good example, what on earth is the use of them? They seem, as a class, to have absolutely no sense of moral responsibility.

(Enter Lane.)

LANE: Mr. Ernest Worthing.

(Enter Jack. Lane goes out.)

ALGERNON: How are you, my dear Ernest? What brings you up to town?

JACK: Oh, pleasure, pleasure! What else should bring one anywhere? Eating as usual, I see, Algy!

ALGERNON: *(stiffly)* I believe it is customary in good society to take some slight refreshment at five o'clock. Where have you been since last Thursday?

JACK: *(sitting down on the sofa)* In the country.

ALGERNON: What on earth do you do there?

JACK: *(pulling off his gloves)* When one is in town one amuses oneself. When one is in the country one amuses other people. It is excessively boring.

ALGERNON: And who are the people you amuse?

JACK: *(airily)* Oh, neighbours, neighbours.

ALGERNON: Got nice neighbours in your part of Shropshire?

JACK: Perfectly horrid! Never speak to one of them.

ALGERNON: How immensely you must amuse them! *(Goes over and takes sandwich.)* By the way, Shropshire is your county, is it not?

JACK: Eh? Shropshire? Yes, of course. Hallo! Why all these cups? Why cucumber sandwiches? Why such reckless extravagance in one so young? Who is coming to tea?

ALGERNON: Oh! merely Aunt Augusta and Gwendolen.

JACK: How perfectly delightful!

ALGERNON: Yes, that is all very well; but I am afraid Aunt Augusta won't quite approve of your being here.

JACK: May I ask why?

ALGERNON: My dear fellow, the way you flirt with Gwendolen is perfectly disgraceful. It is almost as bad as the way Gwendolen flirts with you.

JACK: I am in love with Gwendolen. I have come up to town expressly to propose to her.

ALGERNON: I thought you had come up for pleasure? ... I call that business.

JACK: How utterly unromantic you are!

ALGERNON: I really don't see anything romantic in proposing. It is very romantic to be in love. But there is nothing romantic about a definite proposal. Why, one may be accepted. One usually is, I believe. Then the excitement is all over. The very essence of romance is uncertainty. If ever I get married, I'll certainly try to forget the fact.

JACK: I have no doubt about that, dear Algy. The Divorce Court was specially invented for people whose memories are so curiously constituted.

ALGERNON: Oh! there is no use speculating on that subject. Divorces are made in Heaven—(Jack *puts out his hand to take a sandwich.* Algernon *at once interferes.*) Please don't touch the cucumber sandwiches. They are ordered specially for Aunt Augusta. *(Takes one and eats it.)*

JACK: Well, you have been eating them all the time.

ALGERNON: That is quite a different matter. She is my aunt. *(Takes plate from below.*) Have some bread and butter. The bread and butter is for Gwendolen. Gwendolen is devoted to bread and butter.

JACK: (*advancing to table and helping himself*) And very good bread and butter it is too.

ALGERNON: Well, my dear fellow, you need not eat as if you were going to eat it all. You behave as if you were married to her already. You are not married to her already, and I don't think you ever will be.

JACK: Why on earth do you say that?

ALGERNON: Well, in the first place, girls never marry the men they flirt with. Girls don't think it right.

JACK: Oh, that is nonsense!

ALGERNON: It isn't. It is a great truth. It accounts for the extraordinary number of bachelors that one sees all over the place. In the second place, I don't give my consent.

JACK: Your consent!

ALGERNON: My dear fellow, Gwendolen is my first cousin. And before I allow you to marry her, you will have to clear up the whole question of Cecily. (*Rings bell.*)

JACK: Cecily! What on earth do you mean? What do you mean, Algy, by Cecily! I don't know any one of the name of Cecily.

(*Enter* Lane.)

ALGERNON: Bring me that cigarette case Mr. Worthing left in the smoking-room the last time he dined here.

LANE: Yes, sir.

(Lane *goes out.*)

JACK: Do you mean to say you have had my cigarette case all this time? I wish to goodness you had let me know. I have been writing frantic letters to Scotland Yard about it. I was very nearly offering a large reward.

ALGERNON: Well, I wish you would offer one. I happen to be more than usually hard up.

JACK: There is no good offering a large reward now that the thing is found.

(*Enter* Lane *with the cigarette case on a salver.* Algernon *takes it at once.* Lane *goes out.*)

ALGERNON: I think that is rather mean of you, Ernest, I must say. (*Opens case and examines it.*) However, it makes no matter, for, now that I look at the inscription inside, I find that the thing isn't yours after all.

JACK: Of course it's mine. (*Moving to him.*) You have seen me with it a hundred times, and you have no right whatsoever to read what is written inside. It is a very ungentlemanly thing to read a private cigarette case.

ALGERNON: Oh! it is absurd to have a hard and fast rule about what one should read and what one shouldn't. More than half of modern culture depends on what one shouldn't read.

JACK: I am quite aware of the fact, and I don't propose to discuss modern culture. It isn't the sort of thing one should talk of in private. I simply want my cigarette case back.

ALGERNON: Yes; but this isn't your cigarette case. This cigarette case is a present from someone of the name of Cecily, and you said you didn't know anyone of that name.

JACK: Well, if you want to know, Cecily happens to be my aunt.

ALGERNON: Your aunt!

JACK: Yes. Charming old lady she is, too. Lives at Tunbridge Wells. Just give it back to me, Algy.

ALGERNON: (*retreating to back of sofa*) But why does she call herself little Cecily if she is your aunt and lives at Tunbridge Wells. (*Reading.*) "From little Cecily with her fondest love."

JACK: (*moving to sofa and kneeling upon it*) My dear fellow, what on earth is there in that? Some aunts are tall, some aunts are not tall. That is a matter that surely an aunt may be allowed to decide for herself. You seem to think that every aunt should be exactly like your aunt! That is absurd. For Heaven's sake give me back my cigarette case. (*Follows* Algernon *round the room.*)

ALGERNON: Yes. But why does your aunt call you her uncle? "From little Cecily, with her fondest love to her dear Uncle Jack." There is no objection, I admit, to an aunt being a small aunt, but why an aunt, no matter what her size may be, should call her own nephew her uncle, I can't quite make out. Besides, your name isn't Jack at all; it is Ernest.

JACK: It isn't Ernest; it's Jack.

ALGERNON: You have always told me it was Ernest. I have introduced you to every one as Ernest. You answer to the name of Ernest. You look as if your name was Ernest. You are the most earnest-looking person I ever saw in my life. It is perfectly absurd your saying that your name isn't Ernest. It's on your cards. Here is one of them (*taking it from case*). "Mr. Ernest Worthing, B.4, The Albany." I'll keep this as a proof that your name is Ernest if ever you attempt to deny it to me, or to Gwendolen, or to any one else. (*Puts the card in his pocket.*)

JACK: Well, my name is Ernest in town and Jack in the country, and the cigarette case was given to me in the country.

ALGERNON: Yes, but that does not account for the fact that your small Aunt Cecily, who lives at Tunbridge Wells, calls you her dear uncle. Come, old boy, you had much better have the thing out at once.

JACK: My dear Algy, you talk exactly as if you were a dentist. It is very vulgar to talk like a dentist when one isn't a dentist. It produces a false impression.

ALGERNON: Well, that is exactly what dentists always do. Now, go on! Tell me the whole thing. I may mention that I have always suspected you of being a confirmed and secret Bunburyist; and I am quite sure of it now.

JACK: Bunburyist? What on earth do you mean by a Bunburyist?

ALGERNON: I'll reveal to you the meaning of that incomparable expression as soon as you are kind enough to inform me why you are Ernest in town and Jack in the country.

JACK: Well, produce my cigarette case first.

ALGERNON: Here it is. (*Hands cigarette case.*) Now produce your explanation, and pray make it improbable. (*Sits on sofa.*)

JACK: My dear fellow, there is nothing improbable about my explanation at all. In fact it's perfectly ordinary. Old Mr. Thomas Cardew, who adopted me when I was a little boy, made me in his will guardian to his granddaughter, Miss Cecily Cardew. Cecily, who addresses me as her uncle from motives of respect that you could not possibly appreciate, lives at my place in the country under the charge of her admirable governess, Miss Prism.

ALGERNON: Where is that place in the country, by the way?

JACK: That is nothing to you, dear boy. You are not going to be invited. . . .
I may tell you candidly that the place is not in Shropshire.

ALGERNON: I suspected that, my dear fellow! I have Bunburyed all over
Shropshire on two separate occasions. Now, go on. Why are you Ernest in
town and Jack in the country?

JACK: My dear Algy, I don't know whether you will be able to understand
my real motives. You are hardly serious enough. When one is placed in the
position of guardian, one has to adopt a very high moral tone on all subjects.
It's one's duty to do so. And as a high moral tone can hardly be said to
conduce very much to one's health or one's happiness, in order to get up to
town I have always pretended to have a younger brother of the name of
Ernest, who lives in the Albany, and gets into the most dreadful scrapes.
That, my dear Algy, is the whole truth pure and simple.

ALGERNON: The truth is rarely pure and never simple. Modern life would
be very tedious if it were either, and modern literature a complete impossibil-
ity!

JACK: That wouldn't be at all a bad thing.

ALGERNON: Literary criticism is not your forte, my dear fellow. Don't try
it. You should leave that to people who haven't been at a University. They
do it so well in the daily papers. What you really are is a Bunburyist. I was
quite right in saying you were a Bunburyist. You are one of the most advanced Bunburyists I know.

JACK: What on earth do you mean?

ALGERNON: You have invented a very useful younger brother called Ernest, in order that you may be able to come up to town as often as you like.
I have invented an invaluable permanent invalid called Bunbury, in order
that I may be able to go down into the country whenever I choose. Bunbury
is perfectly invaluable. If it wasn't for Bunbury's extraordinary bad health,
for instance, I wouldn't be able to dine with you at Willis's to-night, for I
have been really engaged to Aunt Augusta for more than a week.

JACK: I haven't asked you to dine with me anywhere to-night.

ALGERNON: I know. You are absurdly careless about sending out invitations. It is very foolish of you. Nothing annoys people so much as not
receiving invitations.

JACK: You had much better dine with your Aunt Augusta.

ALGERNON: I haven't the smallest intention of doing anything of the kind.
To begin with, I dined there on Monday, and once a week is quite enough
to dine with one's own relations. In the second place, whenever I do dine
there I am always treated as a member of the family, and sent down with
either no woman at all, or two. In the third place, I know perfectly well whom
she will place me next to, to-night. She will place me next Mary Farquhar,
who always flirts with her own husband across the dinner-table. That is not
very pleasant. Indeed, it is not even decent . . . and that sort of thing is
enormously on the increase. The amount of women in London who flirt with
their own husbands is perfectly scandalous. It looks so bad. It is simply
washing one's clean linen in public. Besides, now that I know you to be a
confirmed Bunburyist I naturally want to talk to you about Bunburying. I
want to tell you the rules.

JACK: I'm not a Bunburyist at all. If Gwendolen accepts me, I am going
to kill my brother, indeed I think I'll kill him in any case. Cecily is a little
too much interested in him. It is rather a bore. So I am going to get rid of
Ernest. And I strongly advise you to do the same with Mr. . . . with your
invalid friend who has the absurd name.

ALGERNON: Nothing will induce me to part with Bunbury, and if you ever get married, which seems to me extremely problematic, you will be very glad to know Bunbury. A man who marries without knowing Bunbury has a very tedious time of it.

JACK: That is nonsense. If I marry a charming girl like Gwendolen, and she is the only girl I ever saw in my life that I would marry, I certainly won't want to know Bunbury.

ALGERNON: Then your wife will. You don't seem to realize, that in married life three is company and two is none.

JACK (*sententiously*):   That, my dear young friend, is the theory that the corrupt French Drama has been propounding for the last fifty years.

ALGERNON: Yes; and that the happy English home has proved in half the time.

JACK: For heaven's sake, don't try to be cynical. It's perfectly easy to be cynical.

ALGERNON: My dear fellow, it isn't easy to be anything nowadays. There's such a lot of beastly competition about. (*The sound of an electric bell is heard.*) Ah! that must be Aunt Augusta. Only relatives, or creditors, ever ring in that Wagnerian manner. Now, if I get her out of the way for ten minutes, so that you can have an opportunity for proposing to Gwendolen, may I dine with you to-night at Willis's?

JACK: I suppose so, if you want to.

ALGERNON: Yes, but you must be serious about it. I hate people who are not serious about meals. It is so shallow of them.

(*Enter* Lane.)

LANE: Lady Bracknell and Miss Fairfax.

(Algernon *goes forward to meet them. Enter* Lady Bracknell *and* Gwendolen.)

LADY BRACKNELL: Good afternoon, dear Algernon, I hope you are behaving well.

ALGERNON: I'm feeling very well, Aunt Augusta.

LADY BRACKNELL: That's not quite the same thing. In fact the two things rarely go together. (*Sees* Jack *and bows to him with icy coldness.*)

ALGERNON: (*to* Gwendolen) Dear me, you are smart!

GWENDOLEN: I am always smart! Am I not, Mr. Worthing?

JACK: You're quite perfect, Miss Fairfax.

GWENDOLEN: Oh! I hope I am not that. It would leave no room for developments, and I intend to develop in many directions. (Gwendolen *and* Jack *sit down together in the corner.*)

LADY BRACKNELL: I'm sorry if we are a little late, Algernon, but I was obliged to call on dear Lady Harbury. I hadn't been there since her poor husband's death. I never saw a woman so altered; she looks quite twenty years younger. And now I'll have a cup of tea and one of those nice cucumber sandwiches you promised me.

ALGERNON: Certainly, Aunt Augusta. (*Goes over to teatable.*)

LADY BRACKNELL: Won't you come and sit here, Gwendolen?

GWENDOLEN: Thanks, mamma, I'm quite comfortable where I am.

ALGERNON: (*picking up empty plate in horror*) Good heavens! Lane! Why are there no cucumber sandwiches? I ordered them specially.

LANE: (*gravely*) There were no cucumbers in the market this morning, sir. I went down twice.

ALGERNON: No cucumbers!

LANE: No, sir. Not even for ready money.

ALGERNON: That will do, Lane, thank you.

LANE: Thank you, sir. (*Goes out.*)

ALGERNON: I am greatly distressed, Aunt Augusta, about there being no cucumbers, not even for ready money.

LADY BRACKNELL: It really makes no matter, Algernon. I had some crumpets with Lady Harbury, who seems to me to be living entirely for pleasure now.

ALGERNON: I hear her hair has turned quite gold from grief.

LADY BRACKNELL: It certainly has changed its colour. From what cause I, of course, cannot say. (Algernon *crosses and hands tea.*) Thank you. I've quite a treat for you tonight, Algernon. I am going to send you down with Mary Farquhar. She is such a nice woman, and so attentive to her husband. It's delightful to watch them.

ALGERNON: I am afraid, Aunt Augusta, I shall have to give up the pleasure of dining with you to-night after all.

LADY BRACKNELL: (*frowning*) I hope not, Algernon. It would put my table completely out. Your uncle would have to dine upstairs. Fortunately he is accustomed to that.

ALGERNON: It is a great bore, and, I need hardly say, a terrible disappointment to me, but the fact is I have just had a telegram to say that my poor friend Bunbury is very ill again. (*Exchanges glances with* Jack.) They seem to think I should be with him.

LADY BRACKNELL: It is very strange. This Mr. Bunbury seems to suffer from curiously bad health.

ALGERNON: Yes; poor Bunbury is a dreadful invalid.

LADY BRACKNELL: Well, I must say, Algernon, that I think it is high time that Mr. Bunbury made up his mind whether he was going to live or to die. This shilly-shallying with the question is absurd. Nor do I in any way approve of the modern sympathy with invalids. I consider it morbid. Illness of any kind is hardly a thing to be encouraged in others. Health is the primary duty of life. I am always telling that to your poor uncle, but he never seems to take much notice . . . as far as any improvement in his ailments goes. I should be much obliged if you would ask Mr. Bunbury, from me, to be kind enough not to have a relapse on Saturday, for I rely on you to arrange my music for me. It is my last reception, and one wants something that will encourage conversation, particularly at the end of the season when every one has practically said whatever they had to say, which, in most cases, was probably not much.

ALGERNON: I'll speak to Bunbury, Aunt Augusta, if he is still conscious, and I think I can promise you he'll be all right by Saturday. Of course the music is a great difficulty. You see, if one plays good music, people don't listen, and if one plays bad music, people don't talk. But I'll run over the programme I've drawn out, if you will kindly come into the next room for a moment.

LADY BRACKNELL: Thank you, Algernon. It is very thoughtful of you. (*Rising, and following* Algernon.) I'm sure the programme will be delightful, after a few expurgations. French songs I cannot possibly allow. People always seem to think that they are improper, and either look shocked, which is vulgar, or laugh, which is worse. But German sounds a thoroughly respectable language, and, indeed I believe is so. Gwendolen, you will accompany me.

GWENDOLEN: Certainly, Mamma.

(Lady Bracknell *and* Algernon *go into the music-room;* Gwendolen *remains behind.)*

JACK: Charming day it has been, Miss Fairfax.

GWENDOLEN: Pray don't talk to me about the weather, Mr. Worthing. Whenever people talk to me about the weather, I always feel quite certain that they mean something else. And that makes me so nervous.

JACK: I do mean something else.

GWENDOLEN: I thought so. In fact, I am never wrong.

JACK: And I would like to be allowed to take advantage of Lady Bracknell's temporary absence. . . .

GWENDOLEN: I would certainly advise you to do so. Mamma has a way of coming back suddenly into a room that I have often had to speak to her about.

JACK: (*nervously*) Miss Fairfax, ever since I met you I have admired you more than any girl . . . I have ever met since . . . I met you.

GWENDOLEN: Yes, I am quite aware of the fact. And I often wish that in public, at any rate, you had been more demonstrative. For me you have always had an irresistible fascination. Even before I met you I was far from indifferent to you. (Jack *looks at her in amazement.*) We live, as I hope you know, Mr. Worthing, in an age of ideals. The fact is constantly mentioned in the more expensive monthly magazines, and has reached the provincial pulpits, I am told; and my ideal has always been to love some one of the name of Ernest. There is something in that name that inspires absolute confidence. The moment Algernon first mentioned to me that he had a friend called Ernest, I knew I was destined to love you.

JACK: You really love me, Gwendolen?

GWENDOLEN: Passionately!

JACK: Darling! You don't know how happy you've made me.

GWENDOLEN: My own Ernest!

JACK: But you don't really mean to say that you couldn't love me if my name wasn't Ernest?

GWENDOLEN: But your name is Ernest.

JACK: Yes, I know it is. But supposing it was something else? Do you mean to say you couldn't love me then?

GWENDOLEN: (*glibly*) Ah! that is clearly a metaphysical speculation, and like most metaphysical speculations has very little reference at all to the actual facts of real life, as we know them.

JACK: Personally, darling, to speak quite candidly, I don't much care about the name of Ernest. . . . I don't think the name suits me at all.

GWENDOLEN: It suits you perfectly. It is a divine name. It has a music of its own. It produces vibrations.

JACK: Well, really, Gwendolen, I must say that I think there are lots of other much nicer names. I think Jack, for instance, a charming name.

GWENDOLEN: Jack? . . . No, there is very little music in the name Jack, if any at all, indeed. It does not thrill. It produces absolutely no vibrations. . . . I have known several Jacks, and they all, without exception, were more than usually plain. Besides, Jack is a notorious domesticity for John! And I pity any woman who is married to a man called John. She would probably never be allowed to know the entrancing pleasure of a single moment's solitude. The only really safe name is Ernest.

JACK: Gwendolen, I must get christened at once—I mean we must get married at once. There is no time to be lost.

GWENDOLEN: Married, Mr. Worthing?

JACK: (astounded) Well . . . surely. You know that I love you, and you led me to believe, Miss Fairfax, that you were not absolutely indifferent to me.

GWENDOLEN: I adore you. But you haven't proposed to me yet. Nothing has been said at all about marriage. The subject has not even been touched on.

JACK: Well . . . may I propose to you now?

GWENDOLEN: I think it would be an admirable opportunity. And to spare you any possible disappointment, Mr. Worthing, I think it only fair to tell you quite frankly beforehand that I am fully determined to accept you.

JACK: Gwendolen!

GWENDOLEN: Yes, Mr. Worthing, what have you got to say to me?

JACK: You know what I have got to say to you.

GWENDOLEN: Yes, but you don't say it.

JACK: Gwendolen, will you marry me? (Goes on his knees.)

GWENDOLEN: Of course I will, darling. How long you have been about it! I am afraid you have had very little experience in how to propose.

JACK: My own one, I have never loved any one in the world but you.

GWENDOLEN: Yes, but men often propose for practice. I know my brother Gerald does. All my girl-friends tell me so. What wonderfully blue eyes you have, Ernest! They are quite, quite blue. I hope you will always look at me just like that, especially when there are other people present.

(Enter Lady Bracknell.)

LADY BRACKNELL: Mr. Worthing! Rise sir, from this semirecumbent posture. It is most indecorous.

GWENDOLEN: Mamma! (He tries to rise; she restrains him.) I must beg you to retire. This is no place for you. Besides, Mr. Worthing has not quite finished yet.

LADY BRACKNELL: Finished what, may I ask?

GWENDOLEN: I am engaged to Mr. Worthing, mamma. (They rise together.)

LADY BRACKNELL: Pardon me, you are not engaged to any one. When you do become engaged to some one, I, or your father, should his health permit him, will inform you of the fact. An engagement should come on a young girl as a surprise, pleasant or unpleasant, as the case may be. It is hardly a matter that she could be allowed to arrange for herself. . . . And now I have a few questions to put to you, Mr. Worthing. While I am making these inquiries, you, Gwendolen, will wait for me below in the carriage.

GWENDOLEN: (reproachfully) Mamma!

LADY BRACKNELL: In the carriage, Gwendolen! (Gwendolen goes to the door. She and Jack blow kisses to each other behind Lady Bracknell's back. Lady Bracknell looks vaguely about as if she could not understand what the noise was. Finally turns round) Gwendolen, the carriage!

GWENDOLEN: Yes, mamma. (Goes out, looking back at Jack.)

LADY BRACKNELL: (sitting down) You can take a seat, Mr. Worthing.

(Looks in her pocket for note-book and pencil.)

JACK: Thank you, Lady Bracknell, I prefer standing.

LADY BRACKNELL: (pencil and note-book in hand) I feel bound to tell you that you are not down on my list of eligible young men, although I have the same list as the dear Duchess of Bolton has. We work together, in fact. However, I am quite ready to enter your name, should your answers be what a really affectionate mother requires. Do you smoke?

JACK: Well, yes, I must admit I smoke.

LADY BRACKNELL: I am glad to hear it. A man should always have an occupation of some kind. There are far too many idle men in London as it is. How old are you?

JACK: Twenty-nine.

LADY BRACKNELL: A very good age to be married at. I have always been of opinion that a man who desires to get married should know either everything or nothing. Which do you know?

JACK: (after some hesitation) I know nothing, Lady Bracknell.

LADY BRACKNELL: I am pleased to hear it. I do not approve of anything that tampers with natural ignorance. Ignorance is like a delicate exotic fruit; touch it and the bloom is gone. The whole theory of modern education is radically unsound. Fortunately in England, at any rate, education produces no effect whatsoever. If it did, it would prove a serious danger to the upper classes, and probably lead to acts of violence in Grosvenor Square. What is your income?

JACK: Between seven and eight thousand a year.

LADY BRACKNELL: (makes a note in her book) In land, or in investments?

JACK: In investments, chiefly.

LADY BRACKNELL: That is satisfactory. What between the duties expected of one during one's lifetime, and the duties exacted from one after one's death, land has ceased to be either a profit or a pleasure. It gives one position, and prevents one from keeping it up. That's all that can be said about land.

JACK: I have a country house with some land, of course, attached to it, about fifteen hundred acres, I believe; but I don't depend on that for my real income. In fact, as far as I can make out, the poachers are the only people who make anything out of it.

LADY BRACKNELL: A country house! How many bedrooms? Well, that point can be cleared up afterwards. You have a town house, I hope? A girl with a simple, unspoiled nature, like Gwendolen, could hardly be expected to reside in the country.

JACK: Well, I own a house in Belgrave Square, but it is let by the year to Lady Bloxham. Of course, I can get it back whenever I like, at six months' notice.

LADY BRACKNELL: Lady Bloxham? I don't know her.

JACK: Oh, she goes about very little. She is a lady considerably advanced in years.

LADY BRACKNELL: Ah, nowadays that is no guarantee of respectability of character. What number in Belgrave Square?

JACK: 149.

LADY BRACKNELL: (shaking her head) The unfashionable side. I thought there was something. However, that could easily be altered.

JACK: Do you mean the fashion, or the side?

LADY BRACKNELL: (sternly) Both, if necessary, I presume. What are your politics?

JACK: Well, I am afraid I really have none. I am a Liberal Unionist.

LADY BRACKNELL: Oh, they count as Tories. They dine with us. Or come in the evening, at any rate. Now to minor matters. Are your parents living?

JACK: I have lost both my parents.

LADY BRACKNELL: To lose one parent, Mr. Worthing, may be regarded as a misfortune; to lose both looks like carelessness. Who was your father? He was evidently a man of some wealth. Was he born in what the Radical papers call the purple of commerce, or did he rise from the ranks of the aristocracy?

JACK: I am afraid I really don't know. The fact is, Lady Bracknell, I said I had lost my parents. It would be nearer the truth to say that my parents seem to have lost me. . . . I don't actually know who I am by birth. I was . . . well, I was found.

LADY BRACKNELL: Found!

JACK: The late Mr. Thomas Cardew, an old gentleman of a very charitable and kindly disposition, found me, and gave me the name of Worthing, because he happened to have a first-class ticket for Worthing in his pocket at the time. Worthing is a place in Sussex. It is a seaside resort.

LADY BRACKNELL: Where did the charitable gentleman who had a first-class ticket for this seaside resort find you?

JACK: (gravely) In a hand-bag.

LADY BRACKNELL: A hand-bag?

JACK: (very seriously) Yes, Lady Bracknell. I was in a hand-bag—a somewhat large, black leather hand-bag, with handles to it—an ordinary hand-bag in fact.

LADY BRACKNELL: In what locality did this Mr. James, or Thomas, Cardew come across this ordinary hand-bag?

JACK: In the cloak-room at Victoria Station. It was given to him in mistake for his own.

LADY BRACKNELL: The cloak-room at Victoria Station?

JACK: Yes. The Brighton line.

LADY BRACKNELL: The line is immaterial. Mr. Worthing, I confess I feel somewhat bewildered by what you have just told me. To be born, or at any rate bred, in a hand-bag, whether it had handles or not, seems to me to display a contempt for the ordinary decencies of family life that reminds one of the worst excesses of the French Revolution. And I presume you know what that unfortunate movement led to? As for the particular locality in which the hand-bag was found, a cloak-room at a railway station might serve to conceal a social indiscretion—has probably, indeed, been used for that purpose before now—but it could hardly be regarded as an assured basis for a recognized position in good society.

JACK: May I ask you then what you would advise me to do? I need hardly say I would do anything in the world to ensure Gwendolen's happiness.

LADY BRACKNELL: I would strongly advise you, Mr. Worthing, to try and acquire some relations as soon as possible, and to make a definite effort to produce at any rate one parent, of either sex, before the season is quite over.

JACK: Well, I don't see how I could possibly manage to do that. I can produce the hand-bag at any moment. It is in my dressing-room at home. I really think that should satisfy you, Lady Bracknell.

LADY BRACKNELL: Me, sir! What has it to do with me? You can hardly imagine that I and Lord Bracknell would dream of allowing our only daughter—a girl brought up with the utmost care—to marry into a cloak-room, and form an alliance with a parcel. Good morning, Mr. Worthing!

(Lady Bracknell *sweeps out in majestic indignation.*)

JACK: Good morning! (Algernon, *from the other room, strikes up the Wedding March.* Jack *looks perfectly furious, and goes to the door.*) For goodness' sake don't play that ghastly tune, Algy! How idiotic you are!

(The music stops and Algernon *enters cheerily.)*

ALGERNON: Didn't it go off all right, old boy? You don't mean to say Gwendolen refused you? I know it is a way she has. She is always refusing people. I think it is most ill-natured of her.

JACK: Oh, Gwendolen is as right as a trivet. As far as she is concerned, we are engaged. Her mother is perfectly unbearable. Never met such a Gorgon. . . . I don't really know what a Gorgon is like, but I am quite sure that Lady Bracknell is one. In any case, she is a monster, without being a myth, which is rather unfair. . . . I beg your pardon, Algy, I suppose I shouldn't talk about your own aunt in that way before you.

ALGERNON: My dear boy, I love hearing my relations abused. It is the only thing that makes me put up with them all. Relations are simply a tedious pack of people, who haven't got the remotest knowledge of how to live, nor the smallest instinct about when to die.

JACK: Oh, that is nonsense!

ALGERNON: It isn't!

JACK: Well, I won't argue about the matter. You always want to argue about things.

ALGERNON: That is exactly what things were originally made for.

JACK: Upon my word, if I thought that, I'd shoot myself. . . . *(A pause.)* You don't think there is any chance of Gwendolen becoming like her mother in about a hundred and fifty years, do you, Algy?

ALGERNON: All women become like their mothers. That is their tragedy. No man does. That's his.

JACK: Is that clever?

ALGERNON: It is perfectly phrased! and quite as true as any observation in civilized life should be.

JACK: I am sick to death of cleverness. Everybody is clever nowadays. You can't go anywhere without meeting clever people. The thing has become an absolute public nuisance. I wish to goodness we had a few fools left.

ALGERNON: We have.

JACK: I should extremely like to meet them. What do they talk about?

ALGERNON: The fools? Oh! about the clever people, of course.

JACK: What fools.

ALGERNON: By the way, did you tell Gwendolen the truth about your being Ernest in town, and Jack in the country?

JACK: *(in a very patronizing manner)* My dear fellow, the truth isn't quite the sort of thing one tells to a nice, sweet, refined girl. What extraordinary ideas you have about the way to behave to a woman!

ALGERNON: The only way to behave to a woman is to make love to her, if she is pretty, and to someone else, if she is plain.

JACK: Oh, that is nonsense.

ALGERNON: What about your brother? What about the profligate Ernest?

JACK: Oh, before the end of the week I shall have got rid of him. I'll say he died in Paris of apoplexy. Lots of people die of apoplexy, quite suddenly, don't they?

ALGERNON: Yes, but it's hereditary, my dear fellow. It's a sort of thing that runs in families. You had much better say a severe chill.

JACK: You are sure a severe chill isn't hereditary, or anything of that kind?

ALGERNON: Of course it isn't!

JACK: Very well, then. My poor brother Ernest is carried off suddenly, in Paris, by a severe chill. That gets rid of him.

ALGERNON: But I thought you said that . . . Miss Cardew was a little too much interested in your poor brother Ernest? Won't she feel his loss a good deal?

JACK: Oh, that is all right. Cecily is not a silly romantic girl, I am glad to say. She has got a capital appetite, goes long walks, and pays no attention at all to her lessons.

ALGERNON: I would rather like to see Cecily.

JACK: I will take very good care you never do. She is excessively pretty, and she is only just eighteen.

ALGERNON: Have you told Gwendolen yet that you have an excessively pretty ward who is only just eighteen?

JACK: Oh! one doesn't blurt these things out to people. Cecily and Gwendolen are perfectly certain to be extremely great friends. I'll bet you anything you like that half an hour after they have met, they will be calling each other sister.

ALGERNON: Women only do that when they have called each other a lot of other things first. Now, my dear boy, if we want to get a good table at Willis's, we really must go and dress. Do you know it is nearly seven?

JACK: (irritably) Oh! it always is nearly seven.

ALGERNON: Well, I'm hungry.

JACK: I never knew you when you weren't. . . .

ALGERNON: What shall we do after dinner? Go to a theatre?

JACK: Oh, no! I loathe listening.

ALGERNON: Well, let us go to the Club?

JACK: Oh, no! I hate talking.

ALGERNON: Well, we might trot round to the Empire at ten?

JACK: Oh, no! I can't bear looking at things. It is so silly.

ALGERNON: Well, what shall we do?

JACK: Nothing!

ALGERNON: It is awfully hard work doing nothing. However, I don't mind hard work where there is no definite object of any kind.

(Enter Lane.)

LANE: Miss Fairfax.

(Enter Gwendolen. Lane goes out.)

ALGERNON: Gwendolen, upon my word!

GWENDOLEN: Algy, kindly turn your back. I have something very particular to say to Mr. Worthing.

ALGERNON: Really, Gwendolen, I don't think I can allow this at all.

GWENDOLEN: Algy, you always adopt a strictly immoral attitude towards life. You are not quite old enough to do that. (Algernon retires to the fireplace.)

JACK: My own darling!

GWENDOLEN: Ernest, we may never be married. From the expression on mamma's face I fear we never shall. Few parents nowadays pay any regard to what their children say to them. The old-fashioned respect for the young is fast dying out. Whatever influence I ever had over mamma, I lost at the age of three. But although she may prevent us from becoming man and wife, and I may marry someone else, and marry often, nothing that she can possibly do can alter my eternal devotion to you.

JACK: Dear Gwendolen!

GWENDOLEN: The story of your romantic origin, as related to me by mamma, with unpleasing comments, has naturally stirred the deeper fibres of my nature. Your Christian name has an irresistible fascination. The simplicity of your character makes you exquisitely incomprehensible to me. Your town address at the Albany I have. What is your address in the country?

JACK: The Manor House, Woolton, Hertfordshire.

(Algernon, *who has been carefully listening, smiles to himself, and writes the address on his shirt-cuff. Then picks up the Railway Guide.*)

GWENDOLEN: There is a good postal service, I suppose? It may be necessary to do something desperate. That of course will require serious consideration. I will communicate with you daily.

JACK: My own one!

GWENDOLEN: How long do you remain in town?

JACK: Till Monday.

GWENDOLEN: Good! Algy, you may turn round now.

ALGERNON: Thanks, I've turned round already.

GWENDOLEN: You may also ring the bell.

JACK: You will let me see you to your carriage, my own darling?

GWENDOLEN: Certainly.

JACK: (*to* Lane, *who now enters*) I will see Miss Fairfax out.

LANE: Yes, sir. (Jack *and* Gwendolen *go off.*)

(Lane *presents several letters on a salver to* Algernon. *It is to be surmised that they are bills, as* Algernon, *after looking at the envelopes, tears them up.*)

ALGERNON: A glass of sherry, Lane.

LANE: Yes, sir.

ALGERNON: To-morrow, Lane, I'm going Bunburying.

LANE: Yes, sir.

ALGERNON: I shall probably not be back till Monday. You can put up my dress clothes, my smoking jacket, and all the Bunbury suits . . .

LANE: Yes, sir. (*Handing sherry.*)

ALGERNON: I hope to-morrow will be a fine day, Lane.

LANE: It never is, sir.

ALGERNON: Lane, you're a perfect pessimist.

LANE: I do my best to give satisfaction, sir.

(*Enter* Jack. Lane *goes off.*)

JACK: There's a sensible, intellectual girl! the only girl I ever cared for in my life. (Algernon *is laughing immoderately.*) What on earth are you so amused at?

ALGERNON: Oh, I'm a little anxious about poor Bunbury, that is all.

JACK: If you don't take care, your friend Bunbury will get you into a serious scrape some day.

ALGERNON: I love scrapes. They are the only things that are never serious.

JACK: Oh, that's nonsense, Algy. You never talk anything but nonsense.

ALGERNON: Nobody ever does.

(Jack looks indignantly at him, and leaves the room. Algernon lights a cigarette, reads his shirt-cuff, and smiles.)

ACT II

(Garden at the Manor House. A flight of grey stone steps leads up to the house. The garden, an old-fashioned one, full of roses. Time of year, July. Basket chairs, and a table covered with books, are set under a large yew-tree.)

(Miss Prism discovered seated at the table. Cecily is at the back, watering flowers.)

MISS PRISM: *(calling)* Cecily, Cecily! Surely such a utilitarian occupation as the watering of flowers is rather Moulton's duty than yours? Especially at a moment when intellectual pleasures await you. Your German grammar is on the table. Pray open it at page fifteen. We will repeat yesterday's lesson.

CECILY: *(coming over very slowly)* But I don't like German. It isn't at all a becoming language. I know perfectly well that I look quite plain after my German lesson.

MISS PRISM: Child, you know how anxious your guardian is that you should improve yourself in every way. He laid particular stress on your German, as he was leaving for town yesterday. Indeed, he always lays stress on your German when he is leaving for town.

CECILY: Dear Uncle Jack is so very serious! Sometimes he is so serious that I think he cannot be quite well.

MISS PRISM: *(drawing herself up)* Your guardian enjoys the best of health, and his gravity of demeanour is especially to be commended in one so comparatively young as he is. I know no one who has a higher sense of duty and responsibility.

CECILY: I suppose that is why he often looks a little bored when we three are together.

MISS PRISM: Cecily! I am surprised at you. Mr. Worthing has many troubles in his life. Idle merriment and triviality would be out of place in his conversation. You must remember his constant anxiety about that unfortunate young man his brother.

CECILY: I wish Uncle Jack would allow that unfortunate young man, his brother, to come down here sometimes. We might have a good influence over him, Miss Prism. I am sure you certainly would. You know German, and geology, and things of that kind influence a man very much. *(Cecily begins to write in her diary.)*

MISS PRISM: *(shaking her head)* I do not think that even I could produce any effect on a character that according to his own brother's admission is irretrievably weak and vacillating. Indeed I am not sure that I would desire to reclaim him. I am not in favour of this modern mania for turning bad people into good people at a moment's notice. As a man sows so let him reap. You must put away your diary, Cecily. I really don't see why you should keep a diary at all.

CECILY: I keep a diary in order to enter the wonderful secrets of my life. If I didn't write them down, I should probably forget all about them.

MISS PRISM: Memory, my dear Cecily, is the diary that we all carry about with us.

CECILY: Yes, but it usually chronicles the things that have never happened, and couldn't possibly have happened. I believe that Memory is responsible for nearly all the three-volume novels that Mudie sends us.

MISS PRISM: Do not speak slightingly of the three-volume novel, Cecily. I wrote one myself in earlier days.

CECILY: Did you really, Miss Prism? How wonderfully clever you are! I hope it did not end happily? I don't like novels that end happily. They depress me so much.

MISS PRISM: The good ended happily, and the bad unhappily. That is what Fiction means.

CECILY: I suppose so. But it seems very unfair. And was your novel ever published?

MISS PRISM: Alas! no. The manuscript unfortunately was abandoned. (*Cecily starts.*) I used the word in the sense of lost or mislaid. To your work, child, these speculations are profitless.

CECILY: (*smiling*) But I see dear Dr. Chasuble coming up through the garden.

MISS PRISM: (*rising and advancing*) Dr. Chasuble! This is indeed a pleasure.

(Enter Canon Chasuble.)

CHASUBLE: And how are we this morning? Miss Prism, you are, I trust, well?

CECILY: Miss Prism has just been complaining of a slight headache. I think it would do her so much good to have a short stroll with you in the Park, Dr. Chasuble.

MISS PRISM: Cecily, I have not mentioned anything about a headache.

CECILY: No, dear Miss Prism, I know that, but I felt instinctively that you had a headache. Indeed I was thinking about that, and not about my German lesson, when the Rector came in.

CHASUBLE: I hope, Cecily, you are not inattentive.

CECILY: Oh, I am afraid I am.

CHASUBLE: That is strange. Were I fortunate enough to be Miss Prism's pupil, I would hang upon her lips. (*Miss Prism glares.*) I spoke metaphorically.—My metaphor was drawn from bees. Ahem! Mr. Worthing, I suppose, has not returned from town yet?

MISS PRISM: We do not expect him till Monday afternoon.

CHASUBLE: Ah yes, he usually likes to spend his Sunday in London. He is not one of those whose sole aim is enjoyment, as, by all accounts, that unfortunate young man his brother seems to be. But I must not disturb Egeria and her pupil any longer.

MISS PRISM: Egeria? My name is Laetitia, Doctor.

CHASUBLE: (*bowing*) A classical allusion merely, drawn from the Pagan authors. I shall see you both no doubt at Evensong?

MISS PRISM: I think, dear Doctor, I will have a stroll with you. I find I have a headache after all, and a walk might do it good.

CHASUBLE: With pleasure, Miss Prism, with pleasure. We might go as far as the schools and back.

MISS PRISM: That would be delightful. Cecily, you will read your Political Economy in my absence. The chapter on the Fall of the Rupee you may omit. It is somewhat too sensational. Even these metallic problems have their melodramatic side.

(Goes down the garden with Dr. Chasuble.*)*

CECILY: *(picks up books and throws them back on table)* Horrid Political Economy! Horrid Geography! Horrid, horrid German!

(Enter Merriman *with a card on a salver.)*

MERRIMAN: Mr. Ernest Worthing has just driven over from the station. He has brought his luggage with him.
CECILY: *(takes the card and reads it)* "Mr. Ernest Worthing, B.4, The Albany, W." Uncle Jack's brother! Did you tell him Mr. Worthing was in town?
MERRIMAN: Yes, Miss. He seemed very much disappointed. I mentioned that you and Miss Prism were in the garden. He said he was anxious to speak to you privately for a moment.
CECILY: Ask Mr. Ernest Worthing to come here. I suppose you had better talk to the housekeeper about a room for him.
MERRIMAN: Yes, Miss. (Merriman *goes off.)*
CECILY: I have never met any really wicked person before. I feel rather frightened. I am so afraid he will look just like every one else.

(Enter Algernon, *very gay and debonnair.)*

He does!
ALGERNON: *(raising his hat)* You are my little cousin Cecily, I'm sure.
CECILY: You are under some strange mistake. I am not little. In fact, I believe I am more usually tall for my age. (Algernon *is rather taken aback.)* But I am your cousin Cecily. You, I see from your card, are Uncle Jack's brother, my cousin Ernest, my wicked cousin Ernest.
ALGERNON: Oh! I am not really wicked at all, Cousin Cecily. You mustn't think that I am wicked.
CECILY: If you are not, then you have certainly been deceiving us all in a very inexcusable manner. I hope you have not been leading a double life, pretending to be wicked and being really good all the time. That would be hypocrisy.
ALGERNON: *(looks at her in amazement)* Oh! Of course I have been rather reckless.
CECILY: I am glad to hear it.
ALGERNON: In fact, now you mention the subject, I have been very bad in my own small way.
CECILY: I don't think you should be so proud of that, though I am sure it must have been very pleasant.
ALGERNON: It is much pleasanter being here with you.
CECILY: I can't understand how you are here at all. Uncle Jack won't be back till Monday afternoon.
ALGERNON: That is a great disappointment. I am obliged to go up by the first train on Monday morning. I have a business appointment that I am anxious . . . to miss!
CECILY: Couldn't you miss it anywhere but in London?
ALGERNON: No: the appointment is in London.
CECILY: Well, I know, of course, how important it is not to keep a business engagement, if one wants to retain any sense of the beauty of life, but still I think you had better wait till Uncle Jack arrives. I know he wants to speak to you about your emigrating.
ALGERNON: About my what?

CECILY: Your emigrating. He has gone up to buy your outfit.

ALGERNON: I certainly wouldn't let Jack buy my outfit. He has no taste in neckties at all.

CECILY: I don't think you will require neckties. Uncle Jack is sending you to Australia.

ALGERNON: Australia! I'd sooner die.

CECILY: Well, he said at dinner on Wednesday night, that you would have to choose between this world, the next world, and Australia.

ALGERNON: Oh, well! The accounts I have received of Australia and the next world are not particularly encouraging. This world is good enough for me, Cousin Cecily.

CECILY: Yes, but are you good enough for it?

ALGERNON: I'm afraid I'm not that. That is why I want you to reform me. You might make that your mission, if you don't mind, cousin Cecily.

CECILY: I'm afraid I've no time, this afternoon.

ALGERNON: Well, would you mind my reforming myself this afternoon?

CECILY: It is rather Quixotic of you. But I think you should try.

ALGERNON: I will. I feel better already.

CECILY: You are looking a little worse.

ALGERNON: That is because I am hungry.

CECILY: How thoughtless of me. I should have remembered that when one is going to lead an entirely new life, one requires regular and wholesome meals. Won't you come in?

ALGERNON: Thank you. Might I have a buttonhole first? I never have any appetite unless I have a buttonhole first.

CECILY: A Maréchal Niel? (*Picks up scissors.*)

ALGERNON: No, I'd sooner have a pink rose.

CECILY: Why? (*Cuts a flower.*)

ALGERNON: Because you are like a pink rose, Cousin Cecily.

CECILY: I don't think it can be right for you to talk to me like that. Miss Prism never says such things to me.

ALGERNON: Then Miss Prism is a short-sighted old lady. (Cecily *puts the rose in his buttonhole.*) You are the prettiest girl I ever saw.

CECILY: Miss Prism says that all good looks are a snare.

ALGERNON: They are a snare that every sensible man would like to be caught in.

CECILY: Oh, I don't think I would care to catch a sensible man. I shouldn't know what to talk to him about.

(*They pass into the house.* Miss Prism *and* Dr. Chasuble *return.*)

MISS PRISM: You are too much alone, dear Dr. Chasuble. You should get married. A misanthrope I can understand—a womanthrope, never!

CHASUBLE: (*with a scholar's shudder*) Believe me, I do not deserve so neologistic a phrase. The precept as well as the practice of the Primitive Church was distinctly against matrimony.

MISS PRISM: (*sententiously*) That is obviously the reason why the Primitive Church has not lasted up to the present day. And you do not seem to realize, dear Doctor, that by persistently remaining single, a man converts himself into a permanent public temptation. Men should be more careful; this very celibacy leads weaker vessels astray.

CHASUBLE: But is a man not equally attractive when married?

MISS PRISM: No married man is ever attractive except to his wife.

CHASUBLE: And often, I've been told, not even to her.

MISS PRISM: That depends on the intellectual sympathies of the woman. Maturity can always be depended on. Ripeness can be trusted. Young women are green. (Dr. Chasuble *starts*.) I spoke horticulturally. My metaphor was drawn from fruits. But where is Cecily?

CHASUBLE: Perhaps she followed us to the schools.

(Enter Jack *slowly from the back of the garden. He is dressed in the deepest mourning, with crepe hatband and black gloves.*)

MISS PRISM: Mr. Worthing!

CHASUBLE: Mr. Worthing?

MISS PRISM: This is indeed a surprise. We did not look for you till Monday afternoon.

JACK: (*shakes* Miss Prism's *hand in a tragic manner*) I have returned sooner than I expected. Dr. Chasuble, I hope you are well?

CHASUBLE: Dear Mr. Worthing, I trust this garb of woe does not betoken some terrible calamity?

JACK: My brother.

MISS PRISM: More shameful debts and extravagance?

CHASUBLE: Still leading his life of pleasure?

JACK: (*shaking his head*) Dead!

CHASUBLE: Your brother Ernest dead?

JACK: Quite dead.

MISS PRISM: What a lesson for him! I trust he will profit by it.

CHASUBLE: Mr. Worthing, I offer you my sincere condolence. You have at least the consolation of knowing that you were always the most generous and forgiving of brothers.

JACK: Poor Ernest! He had many faults, but it is a sad, sad blow.

CHASUBLE: Very sad indeed. Were you with him at the end?

JACK: No. He died abroad; in Paris, in fact. I had a telegram last night from the manager of the Grand Hotel.

CHASUBLE: Was the cause of death mentioned?

JACK: A severe chill, it seems.

MISS PRISM: As a man sows, so shall he reap.

CHASUBLE: (*raising his hand*) Charity, dear Miss Prism, charity! None of us are perfect. I myself am peculiarly susceptible to draughts. Will the interment take place here?

JACK: No. He seems to have expressed a desire to be buried in Paris.

CHASUBLE: In Paris! (*Shakes his head.*) I fear that hardly points to any very serious state of mind at the last. You would no doubt wish me to make some slight allusion to this tragic domestic affliction next Sunday. (Jack *presses his hand convulsively.*) My sermon on the meaning of the manna in the wilderness can be adapted to almost any occasion, joyful, or, as in the present case, distressing. (*All sigh.*) I have preached it at harvest celebrations, christenings, confirmations, on days of humiliation and festal days. The last time I delivered it was in the Cathedral, as a charity sermon on behalf of the Society for the Prevention of Discontent among the Upper Orders. The Bishop, who was present, was much struck by some of the analogies I drew.

JACK: Ah! that reminds me, you mentioned christenings I think, Dr. Chasuble? I suppose you know how to christen all right? (Dr. Chasuble *looks astounded.*) I mean, of course, you are continually christening, aren't you?

MISS PRISM: It is, I regret to say, one of the Rector's most constant duties in this parish. I have often spoken to the poorer classes on the subject. But they don't seem to know what thrift is.

CHASUBLE: But is there any particular infant in whom you are interested, Mr. Worthing? Your brother was, I believe, unmarried, was he not?

JACK: Oh, yes.

MISS PRISM: (*bitterly*) People who live entirely for pleasure usually are.

JACK: But it is not for any child, dear Doctor. I am very fond of children. No! the fact is, I would like to be christened myself, this afternoon, if you have nothing better to do.

CHASUBLE: But surely, Mr. Worthing, you have been christened already?

JACK: I don't remember anything about it.

CHASUBLE: But have you any grave doubts on the subject?

JACK: I certainly intend to have. Of course I dont know if the thing would bother you in any way, or if you think I am a little too old now.

CHASUBLE: Not at all. The sprinkling, and, indeed, the immersion of adults is a perfectly canonical practice.

JACK: Immersion!

CHASUBLE: You need have no apprehensions. Sprinkling is all that is necessary, or indeed I think advisable. Our weather is so changeable. At what hour would you wish the ceremony performed?

JACK: Oh, I might trot round about five if that would suit you.

CHASUBLE: Perfectly, perfectly! In fact I have two similar ceremonies to perform at that time. A case of twins that occurred recently in one of the outlying cottages on your own estate. Poor Jenkins the carter, a most hard-working man.

JACK: Oh! I don't see much fun in being christened along with other babies. It would be childish. Would half-past five do?

CHASUBLE: Admirably! Admirably! (*Takes out watch.*) And now, dear Mr. Worthing, I will not intrude any longer into a house of sorrow. I would merely beg you not to be too much bowed down by grief. What seem to us bitter trials are often blessings in disguise.

MISS PRISM: This seems to me a blessing of an extremely obvious kind.

(*Enter* Cecily *from the house.*)

CECILY: Uncle Jack! Oh, I am pleased to see you back. But what horrid clothes you have got on. Do go and change them.

MISS PRISM: Cecily!

CHASUBLE: My child! my child! (Cecily *goes towards* Jack; *he kisses her brow in a melancholy manner.*)

CECILY: What is the matter, Uncle Jack? Do look happy! You look as if you had toothache, and I have got such a surprise for you. Who do you think is in the dining-room? Your brother!

JACK: Who?

CECILY: Your brother Ernest. He arrived about half an hour ago.

JACK: What nonsense! I haven't got a brother.

CECILY: Oh, don't say that. However badly he may have behaved to you in the past he is still your brother. You couldn't be so heartless as to disown him. I'll tell him to come out. And you will shake hands with him, won't you, Uncle Jack? (*Runs back into the house.*)

CHASUBLE: These are very joyful tidings.

MISS PRISM: After we had all been resigned to his loss, his sudden return seems to me peculiarly distressing.

JACK: My brother is in the dining-room? I don't know what it all means. I think it is perfectly absurd.

(Enter Algernon and Cecily hand in hand. They come slowly up to Jack.)

JACK: Good heavens! (Motions Algernon away.)

ALGERNON: Brother John, I have come down from town to tell you that I am very sorry for all the trouble I have given you, and that I intend to lead a better life in the future. (Jack glares at him and does not take his hand.)

CECILY: Uncle Jack, you are not going to refuse your own brother's hand?

JACK: Nothing will induce me to take his hand. I think his coming down here disgraceful. He knows perfectly well why.

CECILY: Uncle Jack, do be nice. There is some good in everyone. Ernest has just been telling me about his poor invalid friend Mr. Bunbury whom he goes to visit so often. And surely there must be much good in one who is kind to an invalid, and leaves the pleasures of London to sit by a bed of pain.

JACK: Oh! he has been talking about Bunbury, has he?

CECILY: Yes, he has told me all about poor Mr. Bunbury, and his terrible state of health.

JACK: Bunbury! Well, I won't have him talk to you about Bunbury or about anything else. It is enough to drive one perfectly frantic.

ALGERNON: Of course I admit that the faults were all on my side. But I must say that I think that Brother John's coldness to me is peculiarly painful. I expected a more enthusiastic welcome, especially considering it is the first time I have come here.

CECILY: Uncle Jack, if you don't shake hands with Ernest I will never forgive you.

JACK: Never forgive me?

CECILY: Never, never, never!

JACK: Well, this is the last time I shall ever do it. (Shakes hands with Algernon and glares.)

CHASUBLE: It's pleasant, is it not, to see so perfect a reconciliation? I think we might leave the two brothers together.

MISS PRISM: Cecily, you will come with us.

CECILY: Certainly, Miss Prism. My little task of reconciliation is over.

CHASUBLE: You have done a beautiful action to-day, dear child.

MISS PRISM: We must not be premature in our judgements.

CECILY: I feel very happy. (They all go off except Jack and Algernon.)

JACK: You young scoundrel, Algy, you must get out of this place as soon as possible. I don't allow any Bunburying here.

(Enter Merriman.)

MERRIMAN: I have put Mr. Ernest's things in the room next to yours, sir. I suppose that is all right?

JACK: What?

MERRIMAN: Mr. Ernest's luggage, sir. I have unpacked it and put it in the room next to your own.

JACK: His luggage?

MERRIMAN: Yes, sir. Three portmanteaus, a dressing-case, two hat-boxes, and a large luncheon-basket.

ALGERNON: I am afraid I can't stay more than a week this time.

JACK: Merriman, order the dog-cart at once. Mr. Ernest has been suddenly called back to town.

MERRIMAN: Yes, sir. (*Goes back into the house.*)

ALGERNON: What a fearful liar you are, Jack. I have not been called back to town at all.

JACK: Yes, you have.

ALGERNON: I haven't heard any one call me.

JACK: Your duty as a gentleman calls you back.

ALGERNON: My duty as a gentleman has never interfered with my pleasures in the smallest degree.

JACK: I can quite understand that.

ALGERNON: Well, Cecily is a darling.

JACK: You are not to talk of Miss Cardew like that. I don't like it.

ALGERNON: Well, I don't like your clothes. You look perfectly ridiculous in them. Why on earth don't you go up and change? It is perfectly childish to be in deep mourning for a man who is actually staying for a whole week with you in your house as a guest. I call it grotesque.

JACK: You are certainly not staying with me for a whole week as a guest or anything else. You have got to leave . . . by the four-five train.

ALGERNON: I certainly won't leave you so long as you are in mourning. It would be most unfriendly. If I were in mourning you would stay with me, I suppose. I should think it very unkind if you didn't.

JACK: Well, will you go if I change my clothes?

ALGERNON: Yes, if you are not too long. I never saw anybody take so long to dress, and with such little result.

JACK: Well, at any rate, that is better than being always over-dressed as you are.

ALGERNON: If I am occasionally a little over-dressed, I make up for it by being always immensely over-educated.

JACK: Your vanity is ridiculous, your conduct an outrage, and your presence in my garden utterly absurd. However, you have got to catch the four-five, and I hope you will have a pleasant journey back to town. This Bunburying, as you call it, has not been a great success for you.

(*Goes into the house.*)

ALGERNON: I think it has been a great success. I'm in love with Cecily, and that is everything.

(*Enter Cecily at the back of the garden. She picks up the can and begins to water the flowers.*)

But I must see her before I go, and make arrangements for another Bunbury. Ah, there she is.

CECILY: Oh, I merely came back to water the roses. I thought you were with Uncle Jack.

ALGERNON: He's gone to order the dog-cart for me.

CECILY: Oh, is he going to take you for a nice drive?

ALGERNON: He's going to send me away.

CECILY: Then have we got to part?

ALGERNON: I am afraid so. It's a very painful parting.

CECILY: It is always painful to part from people whom one has known for a very brief space of time. The absence of old friends one can endure with equanimity. But even a momentary separation from any one to whom one has just been introduced is almost unbearable.

ALGERNON: Thank you.

(Enter Merriman.)

MERRIMAN: The dog-cart is at the door, sir.

(Algernon looks appealingly at Cecily.)

CECILY: It can wait, Merriman . . . for . . . five minutes.

MERRIMAN: Yes, miss.

(Exit Merriman.)

ALGERNON: I hope, Cecily, I shall not offend you if I state quite frankly and openly that you seem to me to be in every way the visible personification of absolute perfection.

CECILY: I think your frankness does you great credit, Ernest. If you will allow me, I will copy your remarks into my diary. *(Goes over to table and begins writing in diary.)*

ALGERNON: Do you really keep a diary? I'd give anything to look at it. May I?

CECILY: Oh no. *(Puts her hand over it.)* You see, it is simply a very young girl's record of her own thoughts and impressions, and consequently meant for publication. When it appears in volume form I hope you will order a copy. But pray, Ernest, don't stop. I delight in taking down from dictation. I have reached "absolute perfection." You can go on. I am quite ready for more.

ALGERNON: *(somewhat taken aback)* Ahem! Ahem!

CECILY: Oh, don't cough, Ernest. When one is dictating one should speak fluently and not cough. Besides, I don't know how to spell a cough. *(Writes as Algernon speaks.)*

ALGERNON: *(speaking very rapidly)* Cecily, ever since I first looked upon your wonderful and incomparable beauty, I have dared to love you wildly, passionately, devotedly, hopelessly.

CECILY: I don't think that you should tell me that you love me wildly, passionately, devotedly, hopelessly. Hopelessly doesn't seem to make much sense, does it?

ALGERNON: Cecily.

(Enter Merriman.)

MERRIMAN: The dog-cart is waiting, sir.

ALGERNON: Tell it to come round next week, at the same hour.

MERRIMAN: *(looks at Cecily, who makes no sign)* Yes, sir.

(Merriman retires.)

CECILY: Uncle Jack would be very much annoyed if he knew you were staying on till next week, at the same hour.

ALGERNON: Oh, I don't care about Jack. I don't care for anybody in the whole world but you. I love you, Cecily. You will marry me, won't you?

CECILY: You silly boy! Of course. Why, we have been engaged for the last three months.

ALGERNON: For the last three months?

CECILY: Yes, it will be exactly three months on Thursday.

ALGERNON: But how did we become engaged?

CECILY: Well, ever since dear Uncle Jack first confessed to us that he had a younger brother who was very wicked and bad, you of course have formed the chief topic of conversation between myself and Miss Prism. And of course a man who is much talked about is always very attractive. One feels there must be something in him, after all. I daresay it was foolish of me, but I fell in love with you, Ernest.

ALGERNON: Darling. And when was the engagement actually settled?

CECILY: On the 14th of February last. Worn out by your entire ignorance of my existence, I determined to end the matter one way or the other, and after a long struggle with myself I accepted you under this dear old tree here. The next day I bought this little ring in your name, and this is the little bangle with the true lovers' knot I promised you always to wear.

ALGERNON: Did I give you this? It's very pretty, isn't it?

CECILY: Yes, you've wonderfully good taste, Ernest. It's the excuse I've always given for your leading such a bad life. And this is the box in which I keep all your dear letters. (*Kneels at table, opens box, and produces letters tied up with blue ribbon.*)

ALGERNON: My letters! But, my own sweet Cecily, I have never written you any letters.

CECILY: You need hardly remind me of that, Ernest. I remember only too well that I was forced to write your letters for you. I wrote always three times a week, and sometimes oftener.

ALGERNON: Oh, do let me read them, Cecily?

CECILY: Oh, I couldn't possibly. They would make you far too conceited. (*Replaces box.*) The three you wrote me after I had broken off the engagement are so beautiful, and so badly spelled, that even now I can hardly read them without crying a little.

ALGERNON: But was our engagement ever broken off?

CECILY: Of course it was. On the 22nd of last March. You can see the entry if you like. (*Shows diary.*) "To-day I broke off my engagement with Ernest. I feel it is better to do so. The weather still continues charming."

ALGERNON: But why on earth did you break it off? What had I done? I had done nothing at all. Cecily, I am very much hurt indeed to hear you broke it off. Particularly when the weather was so charming.

CECILY: It would hardly have been a really serious engagement if it hadn't been broken off at least once. But I forgave you before the week was out.

ALGERNON: (*crossing to her, and kneeling*) What a perfect angel you are, Cecily.

CECILY: You dear romantic boy. (*He kisses her, she puts her fingers through his hair*). I hope your hair curls naturally, does it?

ALGERNON: Yes, darling, with a little help from others.

CECILY: I am so glad.

ALGERNON: You'll never break off our engagement again, Cecily?

CECILY: I don't think I could break it off now that I have actually met you. Besides, of course, there is the question of your name.

ALGERNON: Yes, of course. (*Nervously.*)

CECILY: You must not laugh at me, darling, but it had always been a girlish dream of mine to love some one whose name was Ernest. (Algernon *rises*, Cecily *also*.) There is something in that name that seems to inspire absolute confidence. I pity any poor married woman whose husband is not called Ernest.

ALGERNON: But, my dear child, do you mean to say you could not love me if I had some other name?

CECILY: But what name?

ALGERNON: Oh, any name you like—Algernon—for instance . . .

CECILY: But I don't like the name of Algernon.

ALGERNON: Well, my own dear, sweet, loving little darling, I really can't see why you should object to the name of Algernon. It is not at all a bad name. In fact, it is rather an aristocratic name. Half of the chaps who get into the Bankruptcy Court are called Algernon. But seriously, Cecily . . . (*moving to her*) if my name was Algy, couldn't you love me?

CECILY: (*rising*) I might respect you, Ernest, I might admire your character, but I fear that I should not be able to give you my undivided attention.

ALGERNON: Ahem! Cecily! (*Picking up hat.*) Your Rector here is, I suppose, thoroughly experienced in the practice of all the rites and ceremonials of the Church?

CECILY: Oh, yes. Dr. Chasuble is a most learned man. He has never written a single book, so you can imagine how much he knows.

ALGERNON: I must see him at once on a most important christening—I mean on most important business.

CECILY: Oh!

ALGERNON: I shan't be away more than half an hour.

CECILY: Considering that we have been engaged since February the 14th, and that I only met you to-day for the first time, I think it is rather hard that you should leave me for so long a period as half an hour. Couldn't you make it twenty minutes?

ALGERNON: I'll be back in no time. (*Kisses her and rushes down the garden.*)

CECILY: What an impetuous boy he is! I like his hair so much. I must enter his proposal in my diary.

(*Enter* Merriman.)

MERRIMAN: A Miss Fairfax just called to see Mr. Worthing. On very important business, Miss Fairfax states.

CECILY: Isn't Mr. Worthing in his library?

MERRIMAN: Mr. Worthing went over in the direction of the Rectory some time ago.

CECILY: Pray ask the lady to come out here; Mr. Worthing is sure to be back soon. And you can bring tea.

MERRIMAN: Yes, Miss.

(*Goes out.*)

CECILY: Miss Fairfax! I suppose one of the many good elderly women who are associated with Uncle Jack in some of his philanthropic work in London. I don't quite like women who are interested in philanthropic work. I think it is so forward of them.

(*Enter* Merriman.)

MERRIMAN: Miss Fairfax.

(*Enter* Gwendolen. *Exit* Merriman.)

CECILY: (*Advancing to meet her*) Pray let me introduce myself to you. My name is Cecily Cardew.

GWENDOLEN: Cecily Cardew? (*Moving to her and shaking hands.*) What
a very sweet name! Something tells me that we are going to be great friends.
I like you already more than I can say. My first impressions of people are
never wrong.

CECILY: How nice of you to like me so much after we have known each
other such a comparatively short time. Pray sit down.

GWENDOLEN: (*still standing up*) I may call you Cecily, may I not?

CECILY: With pleasure!

GWENDOLEN: And you will always call me Gwendolen, won't you?

CECILY: If you wish.

GWENDOLEN: Then that is all quite settled, is it not?

CECILY: I hope so. (*A pause. They both sit down together.*)

GWENDOLEN: Perhaps this might be a favourable opportunity for my men-
tioning who I am. My father is Lord Bracknell. You have never heard of papa,
I suppose?

CECILY: I don't think so.

GWENDOLEN: Outside the family circle, papa, I am glad to say, is entirely
unknown. I think that is quite as it should be. The home seems to me to be
the proper sphere for the man. And certainly once a man begins to neglect
his domestic duties he becomes painfully effeminate, does he not? And I
don't like that. It makes men so very attractive. Cecily, mamma, whose views
on education are remarkably strict, has brought me up to be extremely
shortsighted; it is part of her system; so do you mind my looking at you
through my glasses?

CECILY: Oh! not at all, Gwendolen. I am very fond of being looked at.

GWENDOLEN: (*after examining* Cecily *carefully through a lorgnette*) You
are here on a short visit, I suppose.

CECILY: Oh no! I live here.

GWENDOLEN: (*severely*) Really? Your mother, no doubt, or some female
relative of advanced years, resides here also?

CECILY: Oh no! I have no mother, nor, in fact, any relations.

GWENDOLEN: Indeed?

CECILY: My dear guardian, with the assistance of Miss Prism, has the
arduous task of looking after me.

GWENDOLEN: Your guardian?

CECILY: Yes, I am Mr. Worthing's ward.

GWENDOLEN: Oh! It is strange he never mentioned to me that he had a
ward. How secretive of him! He grows more interesting hourly. I am not sure,
however, that the news inspires me with feelings of unmixed delight. (*Rising
and going to her.*) I am very fond of you, Cecily: I have liked you ever since
I met you! But I am bound to state that now that I know that you are Mr.
Worthing's ward, I cannot help expressing a wish you were—well, just a little
older than you seem to be—and not quite so very alluring in appearance. In
fact, if I may speak candidly—

CECILY: Pray do! I think that whenever one has anything unpleasant to
say, one should always be quite candid.

GWENDOLEN: Well, to speak with perfect candour, Cecily, I wish that you
were fully forty-two, and more than usually plain for your age. Ernest has
a strong upright nature. He is the very soul of truth and honour. Disloyalty
would be as impossible to him as deception. But even men of the noblest
possible moral character are extremely susceptible to the influence of the
physical charms of others. Modern, no less than Ancient History, supplies
us with many most painful examples of what I refer to. If it were not so,
indeed, History would be quite unreadable.

CECILY: I beg your pardon, Gwendolen, did you say Ernest?

GWENDOLEN: Yes.

CECILY: Oh, but it is not Mr. Ernest Worthing who is my guardian. It is his brother—his elder brother.

GWENDOLEN: (*sitting down again*) Ernest never mentioned to me that he had a brother.

CECILY: I am sorry to say they have not been on good terms for a long time.

GWENDOLEN: Ah! that accounts for it. And now that I think of it I have never heard any man mention his brother. The subject seems distasteful to most men. Cecily, you have lifted a load from my mind. I was growing almost anxious. It would have been terrible if any cloud had come across a friendship like ours, would it not? Of course you are quite, quite sure that it is not Mr. Ernest Worthing who is your guardian?

CECILY: Quite sure. (*A pause.*) In fact, I am going to be his.

GWENDOLEN: (*inquiringly*) I beg your pardon?

CECILY: (*rather shy and confidingly*) Dearest Gwendolen, there is no reason why I should make a secret of it to you. Our little country newspaper is sure to chronicle the fact next week. Mr. Ernest Worthing and I are engaged to be married.

GWENDOLEN: (*quite politely, rising*) My darling Cecily, I think there must be some slight error. Mr. Ernest Worthing is engaged to me. The announcement will appear in the *Morning Post* on Saturday at the latest.

CECILY: (*very politely, rising*) I am afraid you must be under some misconception. Ernest proposed to me exactly ten minutes ago. (*Shows diary.*)

GWENDOLEN: (*examines diary through her lorgnette carefully*) It is very curious, for he asked me to be his wife yesterday afternoon at 5:30. If you would care to verify the incident, pray do so. (*Produces diary of her own.*) I never travel without my diary. One should always have something sensational to read in the train. I am so sorry, dear Cecily, if it is any disappointment to you, but I am afraid I have the prior claim.

CECILY: It would distress me more than I can tell you, dear Gwendolen, if it caused you any mental or physical anguish, but I feel bound to point out that since Ernest proposed to you he clearly has changed his mind.

GWENDOLEN: (*Meditatively*) If the poor fellow has been entrapped into any foolish promise I shall consider it my duty to rescue him at once, and with a firm hand.

CECILY: (*thoughtfully and sadly*) Whatever unfortunate entanglement my dear boy may have got into, I will never reproach him with it after we are married.

GWENDOLEN: Do you allude to me, Miss Cardew, as an entanglement? You are presumptuous. On an occasion of this kind it becomes more than a moral duty to speak one's mind. It becomes a pleasure.

CECILY: Do you suggest, Miss Fairfax, that I entrapped Ernest into an engagement? How dare you? This is no time for wearing the shallow mask of manners. When I see a spade I call it a spade.

GWENDOLEN: (*satirically*) I am glad to say that I have never seen a spade. It is obvious that our social sphere have been widely different.

(*Enter Merriman, followed by the footman. He carries a salver, table cloth, and plate stand. Cecily is about to retort. The presence of the servants exercises a restraining influence, under which both girls chafe.*)

MERRIMAN: Shall I lay tea here as usual, Miss?

CECILY: (*sternly, in a clam voice*) Yes, as usual. (Merriman *begins to clear table and lay cloth. A long pause.* Cecily *and* Gwendolen *glare at each other.*)

GWENDOLEN: Are there many interesting walks in the vicinity, Miss Cardew?

CECILY: Oh! yes! a great many. From the top of one of the hills quite close one can see five counties.

GWENDOLEN: Five counties! I don't think I should like that; I hate crowds.

CECILY: (*sweetly*) I suppose that is why you live in town? (Gwendolen *bites her lip, and beats her foot nervously with her parasol.*)

GWENDOLEN: (*looking round*) Quite a well-kept garden this is, Miss Cardew.

CECILY: So glad you like it, Miss Fairfax.

GWENDOLEN: I had no idea there were any flowers in the country.

CECILY: Oh, flowers are as common here, Miss Fairfax, as people are in London.

GWENDOLEN: Personally I cannot understand how anybody manages to exist in the country, if anybody who is anybody does. The country always bores me to death.

CECILY: Ah! This is what the newspapers call agricultural depression, is it not? I believe the aristocracy are suffering very much from it just at present. It is almost an epidemic amongst them, I have been told. May I offer you some tea, Miss Fairfax?

GWENDOLEN: (*with elaborate politeness*) Thank you. (*Aside.*) Detestable girl! But I require tea!

CECILY: (*sweetly*) Sugar?

GWENDOLEN: (*superciliously*) No, thank you. Sugar is not fashionable any more. (Cecily *looks angrily at her, takes up the tongs and puts four lumps of sugar into the cup.*)

CECILY: (*severely*) Cake or bread and butter?

GWENDOLEN: (*in a bored manner*) Bread and butter, please. Cake is rarely seen at the best houses nowadays.

CECILY: (*cuts a very large slice of cake and puts it on the tray*) Hand that to Miss Fairfax.

(Merriman *does so, and goes out with footman.* Gwendolen *drinks the tea and makes a grimace. Puts down cup at once, reaches out her hand to the bread and butter, looks at it, and finds it is cake. Rises in indignation.*)

GWENDOLEN: You have filled my tea with lumps of sugar, and though I asked most distinctly for bread and butter, you have given me cake. I am known for the gentleness of my disposition, and the extraordinary sweetness of my nature, but I warn you, Miss Cardew, you may go too far.

CECILY: (*rising*) To save my poor, innocent, trusting boy from the machinations of any other girl there are no lengths to which I would not go.

GWENDOLEN: From the moment I saw you I distrusted you. I felt that you were false and deceitful. I am never deceived in such matters. My first impressions of people are invariably right.

CECILY: It seems to me, Miss Fairfax, that I am trespassing on your valuable time. No doubt you have many other calls of a similar character to make in the neighbourhood.

(Enter Jack.*)*

GWENDOLEN: *(catching sight of him)* Ernest! My own Ernest!

JACK: Gwendolen! Darling! *(Offers to kiss her.)*

GWENDOLEN: *(drawing back)* A moment! May I ask if you are engaged to be married to this young lady? *(Points to* Cecily.*)*

JACK: *(laughing)* To dear little Cecily! Of course not! What could have put such an idea into your pretty little head?

GWENDOLEN: Thank you. You may! *(Offers her cheek.)*

CECILY: *(very sweetly)* I knew there must be some misunderstanding, Miss Fairfax. The gentleman whose arm is at present round your waist is my dear guardian, Mr. John Worthing.

GWENDOLEN: I beg your pardon?

CECILY: This is Uncle Jack.

GWENDOLEN: *(receding)* Jack! Oh!

(Enter Algernon.)

CECILY: Here is Ernest.

ALGERNON: *(goes straight over to* Cecily *without noticing anyone else)* My own love! *(Offers to kiss her.)*

CECILY: *(drawing back)* A moment, Ernest! May I ask you—are you engaged to be married to this young lady?

ALGERNON: *(looking round)* To what young lady? Good heavens! Gwendolen!

CECILY: Yes: to good heavens, Gwendolen, I mean to Gwendolen.

ALGERNON: *(laughing)* Of course not! What could have put such an idea into your pretty little head?

CECILY: Thank you. *(Presenting her cheek to be kissed.)* You may. (*Algernon kisses her.)*

GWENDOLEN: I felt there was some slight error, Miss Cardew. The gentleman who is now embracing you is my cousin, Mr. Algernon Moncrieff.

CECILY: *(breaking away from Algernon)* Algernon Moncrieff! Oh! (*The two girls move towards each other and put their arms round each other's waists as if for protection.)*

CECILY: Are you called Algernon?

ALGERNON: I cannot deny it.

CECILY: Oh!

GWENDOLEN: Is your name really John?

JACK: *(standing rather proudly)* I could deny it if I liked. I could deny anything if I liked. But my name certainly is John. It has been John for years.

CECILY: *(to* Gwendolen) A gross deception has been practised on both of us.

GWENDOLEN: My poor wounded Cecily!

CECILY: My sweet wronged Gwendolen!

GWENDOLEN: *(slowly and seriously)* You will call me sister, will you not? *(They embrace. Jack and Algernon groan and walk up and down.)*

CECILY: *(rather brightly)* There is just one question I would like to be allowed to ask my guardian.

GWENDOLEN: An admirable idea! Mr. Worthing, there is just one question I would like to be permitted to put to you. Where is your brother Ernest? We are both engaged to be married to your brother Ernest, so it is a matter of some importance to us to know where your brother Ernest is at present.

JACK: (*slowly and hesitatingly*) Gwendolen—Cecily—it is very painful for me to be forced to speak the truth. It is the first time in my life that I have ever been reduced to such a painful position, and I am really quite inexperienced in doing anything of the kind. However, I will tell you quite frankly that I have no brother Ernest. I have no brother at all. I never had a brother in my life, and I certainly have not the smallest intention of ever having one in the future.

CECILY: (*surprised*) No brother at all?

JACK: (*cheerily*) None!

GWENDOLEN: (*severely*) Had you never a brother of any kind?

JACK: (*pleasantly*) Never. Not even of any kind.

GWENDOLEN: I am afraid it is quite clear, Cecily, that neither of us is engaged to be married to anyone.

CECILY: It is not a very pleasant position for a young girl suddenly to find herself in. Is it?

GWENDOLEN: Let us go into the house. They will hardly venture to come after us there.

CECILY: No, men are so cowardly, aren't they?

(They retire into the house with scornful looks.)

JACK: This ghastly state of things is what you call Bunburying, I suppose?

ALGERNON: Yes, and a perfectly wonderful Bunbury it is. The most wonderful Bunbury I have ever had in my life.

JACK: Well, you've no right whatsoever to Bunbury here.

ALGERNON: That is absurd. One has a right to Bunbury anywhere one chooses. Every serious Bunburyist knows that.

JACK: Serious Bunburyist? Good heavens!

ALGERNON: Well, one must be serious about something, if one wants to have any amusement in life. I happen to be serious about Bunburying. What on earth you are serious about I haven't got the remotest idea. About everything, I should fancy. You have such an absolutely trivial nature.

JACK: Well, the only small satisfaction I have in the whole of this wretched business is that your friend Bunbury is quite exploded. You won't be able to run down to the country quite so often as you used to do, dear Algy. And a very good thing too.

ALGERNON: Your brother is a little off colour, isn't he, dear Jack? You won't be able to disappear to London quite so frequently as your wicked custom was. And not a bad thing either.

JACK: As for your conduct towards Miss Cardew, I must say that your taking in a sweet, simple, innocent girl like that is quite inexcusable. To say nothing of the fact that she is my ward.

ALGERNON: I can see no possible defence at all for your deceiving a brilliant, clever, thoroughly experienced young lady like Miss Fairfax. To say nothing of the fact that she is my cousin.

JACK: I wanted to be engaged to Gwendolen, that is all. I love her.

ALGERNON: Well, I simply wanted to be engaged to Cecily. I adore her.

JACK: There is certainly no chance of your marrying Miss Cardew.

ALGERNON: I don't think there is much likelihood, Jack, of you and Miss Fairfax being united.

JACK: Well, that is no business of yours.

ALGERNON: If it was my business, I wouldn't talk about it. (*Begins to eat muffins.*) It is very vulgar to talk about one's business. Only people like stockbrokers do that, and then merely at dinner parties.

 JACK: How you can sit there, calmly eating muffins when we are in this horrible trouble, I can't make out. You seem to me to be perfectly heartless.

ALGERNON: Well, I can't eat muffins in an agitated manner. The butter would probably get on my cuffs. One should always eat muffins quite calmly. It is the only way to eat them.

JACK: I say it's perfectly heartless your eating muffins at all, under the circumstances.

ALGERNON: When I am in trouble, eating is the only thing that consoles me. Indeed, when I am in really great trouble, as any one who knows me intimately will tell you, I refuse everything except food and drink. At the present moment I am eating muffins because I am unhappy. Besides, I am particularly fond of muffins. (*Rising.*)

JACK: (*rising*) Well, there is no reason why you should eat them all in that greedy way. (*Takes muffins from Algernon.*)

ALGERNON: (*offering tea-cake*) I wish you would have tea-cake instead. I don't like tea-cake.

JACK: Good heavens! I suppose a man may eat his own muffins in his own garden.

ALGERNON: But you have just said it was perfectly heartless to eat muffins.

JACK: I said it was perfectly heartless of you, under the circumstances. That is a very different thing.

ALGERNON: That may be. But the muffins are the same. (*He seizes the muffin-dish from* Jack.)

JACK: Algy, I wish to goodness you would go.

ALGERNON: You can't possibly ask me to go without having some dinner. It's absurd. I never go without my dinner. No one ever does, except vegetarians and people like that. Besides I have just made arrangements with Dr. Chasuble to be christened at a quarter to six under the name of Ernest.

JACK: My dear fellow, the sooner you give up that nonsense the better. I made arrangements this morning with Dr. Chasuble to be christened myself at 5:30, and I naturally will take the name of Ernest. Gwendolen would wish it. We can't both be christened Ernest. It's absurd. Besides, I have a perfect right to be christened if I like. There is no evidence at all that I have ever been christened by anybody. I should think it extremely probable I never was, and so does Dr. Chasuble. It is entirely different in your case. You have been christened already.

ALGERNON: Yes, but I have not been christened for years.

JACK: Yes, but you have been christened. That is the important thing.

ALGERNON: Quite so. So I know my constitution can stand it. If you are not quite sure about your ever having been christened, I must say I think it rather dangerous your venturing on it now. It might make you very unwell. You can hardly have forgotten that someone very closely connected with you was very nearly carried off this week in Paris by a severe chill.

JACK: Yes, but you said yourself that a severe chill was not hereditary.

ALGERNON: It usen't to be, I know—but I daresay it is now. Science is always making wonderful improvements in things.

JACK: (*picking up the muffin-dish*) Oh, that is nonsense; you are always talking nonsense.

ALGERNON: Jack, you are at the muffins again! I wish you wouldn't. There are only two left. (*Takes them.*) I told you I was particularly fond of muffins.

JACK: But I hate tea-cake.

ALGERNON: Why on earth then do you allow tea-cake to be served up for your guests? What ideas you have of hospitality!

JACK: Algernon! I have already told you to go. I don't want you here. Why don't you go!

ALGERNON: I haven't quite finished my tea yet! and there is still one muffin left. (Jack *groans, and sinks into a chair.* Algernon *still continues eating.*)

ACT III

(*Morning-room at the Manor House.* Gwendolen *and* Cecily *are at the window, looking out into the garden.*)

GWENDOLEN: The fact that they did not follow us at once into the house, as any one else would have done, seems to me to show that they have some sense of shame left.

CECILY: They have been eating muffins. That looks like repentance.

GWENDOLEN: (*after a pause*) They don't seem to notice us at all. Couldn't you cough?

CECILY: But I haven't got a cough.

GWENDOLEN: They're looking at us. What effrontery!

CECILY: They're approaching. That's very forward of them.

GWENDOLEN: Let us preserve a dignified silence.

CECILY: Certainly. It's the only thing to do now.

(*Enter* Jack *followed by* Algernon. *They whistle some dreadful popular air from a British Opera.*)

GWENDOLEN: This dignified silence seems to produce an unpleasant effect.

CECILY: A most distasteful one.

GWENDOLEN: But we will not be the first to speak.

CECILY: Certainly not.

GWENDOLEN: Mr. Worthing, I have something very particular to ask you. Much depends on your reply.

CECILY: Gwendolen, your common sense is invaluable. Mr. Moncrieff, kindly answer me the following question. Why did you pretend to be my guardian's brother?

ALGERNON: In order that I might have an opportunity of meeting you.

CECILY: (*to* Gwendolen) That certainly seems a satisfactory explanation, does it not?

GWENDOLEN: Yes, dear, if you can believe him.

CECILY: I don't. But that does not affect the wonderful beauty of his answer.

GWENDOLEN: True. In matters of grave importance, style, not sincerity, is the vital thing. Mr. Worthing, what explanation can you offer to me for pretending to have a brother? Was it in order that you might have an opportunity of coming up to town to see me as often as possible?

JACK: Can you doubt it, Miss Fairfax?

GWENDOLEN: I have the gravest doubts upon the subject. But I intend to crush them. This is not the moment for German scepticism. (*Moving to* Cecily.) Their explanations appear to be quite satisfactory, especially Mr. Worthing's. That seems to me to have the stamp of truth upon it.

CECILY: I am more than content with what Mr. Moncrieff said. His voice alone inspires one with absolute credulity.

GWENDOLEN: Then you think we should forgive them?

CECILY: Yes. I mean no.

GWENDOLEN: True! I had forgotten. There are principles at stake that one cannot surrender. Which of us should tell them? The task is not a pleasant one.

CECILY: Could we not both speak at the same time?

GWENDOLEN: An excellent idea! I nearly always speak at the same time as other people. Will you take the time from me?

CECILY: Certainly. (Gwendolen *beats time with uplifted finger.*)

GWENDOLEN AND CECILY: (*speaking together*) Your Christian names are still an insuperable barrier. That is all!

JACK AND ALGERNON: (*speaking together*) Our Christian names! Is that all? But we are going to be christened this afternoon.

GWENDOLEN: (*to* Jack) For my sake you are prepared to do this terrible thing?

JACK: I am.

CECILY: (*to* Algernon) To please me you are ready to face this fearful ordeal?

ALGERNON: I am!

GWENDOLEN: How absurd to talk of the equality of the sexes! Where questions of self-sacrifice are concerned, men are infinitely beyond us.

JACK: We are. (*Clasps hands with* Algernon.)

CECILY: They have moments of physical courage of which we women know absolutely nothing.

GWENDOLEN: (*to* Jack) Darling!

ALGERNON: (*to* Cecily) Darling! (*They fall into each other's arms.*)

(*Enter* Merriman. *When he enters he coughs loudly, seeing the situation.*)

MERRIMAN: Ahem! Ahem! Lady Bracknell.

JACK: Good heavens!

(*Enter* Lady Bracknell. *The couples separate in alarm. Exit* Merriman.)

LADY BRACKNELL: Gwendolen! What does this mean?

GWENDOLEN: Merely that I am engaged to be married to Mr. Worthing, mamma.

LADY BRACKNELL: Come here. Sit down. Sit down immediately. Hesitation of any kind is a sign of mental decay in the young, of physical weakness in the old. (*Turns to* Jack.) Apprised, sir, of my daughter's sudden flight by her trusty maid, whose confidence I purchased by means of a small coin, I followed her at once by a luggage train. Her unhappy father is, I am glad to say, under the impression that she is attending a more than usually lengthy lecture by the University Extension Scheme on the Influence of a permanent income on Thought. I do not propose to undeceive him. Indeed I have never undeceived him on any question. I would consider it wrong. But of course, you will clearly understand that all communication between yourself and my daughter must cease immediately from this moment. On this point, as indeed on all points, I am firm.

JACK: I am engaged to be married to Gwendolen, Lady Bracknell!

LADY BRACKNELL: You are nothing of the kind, sir. And now as regards Algernon! ... Algernon!

ALGERNON: Yes, Aunt Augusta.

LADY BRACKNELL: May I ask if it is in this house that your invalid friend Mr. Bunbury resides?

ALGERNON: (*stammering*) Oh! No! Bunbury doesn't live here. Bunbury is somehwere else at present. In fact, Bunbury is dead.

LADY BRACKNELL: Dead! When did Mr. Bunbury die? His death must have been extremely sudden.

ALGERNON: (*airily*) Oh! I killed Bunbury this afternoon. I mean poor Bunbury died this afternoon.

LADY BRACKNELL: What did he die of?

ALGERNON: Bunbury? O, he was quite exploded.

LADY BRACKNELL: Exploded! Was he the victim of a revolutionary outrage? I was not aware that Mr. Bunbury was interested in social legislation. If so, he is well punished for his morbidity.

ALGERNON: My dear Aunt Augusta, I mean he was found out! The doctors found out that Bunbury could not live, that is what I mean—so Bunbury died.

LADY BRACKNELL: He seems to have had great confidence in the opinion of his physicians. I am glad, however, that he made up his mind at the last to some definite course of action, and acted under proper medical advice. And now that we have finally got rid of this Mr. Bunbury, may I ask, Mr. Worthing, who is that young person whose hand my nephew Algernon is now holding in what seems to me a peculiarly unnecessary manner?

JACK: That lady is Miss Cecily Cardew, my ward. (Lady Bracknell *bows coldly to* Cecily.)

ALGERNON: I am engaged to be married to Cecily, Aunt Augusta.

LADY BRACKNELL: I beg your pardon?

CECILY: Mr. Moncrieff and I are engaged to be married, Lady Bracknell.

LADY BRACKNELL: (*with a shiver, crossing to the sofa and sitting down*) I do not know whether there is anything peculiarly exciting in the air of this particular part of Hertfordshire, but the number of engagements that go on seems to me considerably above the proper average that statistics have laid down for our guidance. I think some preliminary inquiry on my part would not be out of place. Mr. Worthing, is Miss Cardew at all connected with any of the larger railway stations in London? I merely desire information. Until yesterday I had no idea that there were any families or persons whose origin was a Terminus. (Jack *looks perfectly furious, but restrains himself.*)

JACK: (*in a cold, clear voice*) Miss Cardew is the granddaughter of the late Mr. Thomas Cardew of 149 Belgrave Square, S.W.; Gervase Park, Dorking, Surrey; and the Sporran, Fifeshire, N.B.

LADY BRACKNELL: That sounds not unsatisfactory. Three addresses always inspire confidence, even in tradesmen. But what proof have I of their authenticity?

JACK: I have carefully preserved the Court Guides of the period. They are open to your inspection, Lady Bracknell.

LADY BRACKNELL: (*grimly*) I have known strange errors in that publication.

JACK: Miss Cardew's family solicitors are Messrs. Markby, Markby, and Markby.

LADY BRACKNELL: Markby, Markby, and Markby? A firm of the very highest position in their profession. Indeed I am told that one of the Mr. Markbys is occasionally to be seen at dinner parties. So far I am satisfied.

JACK: (*very irritably*) How extremely kind of you, Lady Bracknell! I have also in my possession, you will be pleased to hear, certificates of Miss Cardew's birth, baptism, whooping cough, registration, vaccination, confirmation, and the measles; both the German and the English variety.

LADY BRACKNELL: Ah! A life crowded with incident, I see; though perhaps somewhat too exciting for a young girl. I am not myself in favour of premature experiences. (*Rises, looks at her watch.*) Gwendolen! the time approaches for our departure. We have not a moment to lose. As a matter of form, Mr. Worthing, I had better ask you if Miss Cardew has any little fortune?

JACK: Oh! about a hundred and thirty thousand pounds in the Funds. That is all. Good-bye, Lady Bracknell. So pleased to have seen you.

LADY BRACKNELL: (*sitting down again*) A moment, Mr. Worthing. A hundred and thirty thousand pounds! And in the Funds! Miss Cardew seems to me a most attractive young lady, now that I look at her. Few girls of the present day have any really solid qualities, any of the qualities that last, and improve with time. We live, I regret to say, in an age of surfaces. (*To Cecily.*) Come over here, dear. (Cecily *goes across.*) Pretty child! your dress is sadly simple, and your hair seems almost as Nature might have left it. But we can soon alter all that. A thoroughly experienced French maid produces a really marvellous result in a very brief space of time. I remember recommending one to young Lady Lancing, and after three months her own husband did not know her.

JACK: And after six months nobody knew her.

LADY BRACKNELL: (*glares at Jack for a few moments. Then bends, with a practised smile, to Cecily*) Kindly turn round, sweet child. (Cecily *turns completely round.*) No, the side view is what I want. (Cecily *presents her profile.*) Yes, quite as I expected. There are distinct social possibilities in your profile. The two weak points in our age are its want of principle and its want of profile. The chin a little higher, dear. Style largely depends on the way the chin is worn. They are worn very high, just at present. Algernon!

ALGERNON: Yes, Aunt Augusta!

LADY BRACKNELL: There are distinct social possibilities in Miss Cardew's profile.

ALGERNON: Cecily is the sweetest, dearest, prettiest girl in the whole world. And I don't care twopence about social possibilities.

LADY BRACKNELL: Never speak disrespectfully of Society, Algernon. Only people who can't get into it do that. (*To Cecily.*) Dear child, of course you know that Algernon has nothing but his debts to depend upon. But I do not approve of mercenary marriages. When I married Lord Bracknell I had no fortune of any kind. But I never dreamed for a moment of allowing that to stand in my way. Well, I suppose I must give my consent.

ALGERNON: Thank you, Aunt Augusta.

LADY BRACKNELL: Cecily, you may kiss me!

CECILY: (*kisses her*) Thank you, Lady Bracknell.

LADY BRACKNELL: You may also address me as Aunt Augusta for the future.

CECILY: Thank you, Aunt Augusta.

LADY BRACKNELL: The marriage, I think, had better take place quite soon.

ALGERNON: Thank you, Aunt Augusta.

CECILY: Thank you, Aunt Augusta.

LADY BRACKNELL: To speak frankly, I am not in favour of long engagements. They give people the opportunity of finding out each other's character before marriage, which I think is never advisable.

JACK: I beg your pardon for interrupting you, Lady Bracknell, but this engagement is quite out of the question. I am Miss Cardew's guardian, and she cannot marry without my consent until she comes of age. That consent I absolutely decline to give.

LADY BRACKNELL: Upon what grounds, my I ask? Algernon is an extremely, I may almost say an ostentatiously, eligible young man. He has nothing, but he looks everything. What more can one desire?

JACK: It pains me very much to have to speak frankly to you, Lady Bracknell, about your nephew, but the fact is that I do not approve at all of his moral character. I suspect him of being untruthful. (Algernon *and* Cecily *look at him in indignant amazement.*)

LADY BRACKNELL: Untruthful! My nephew Algernon? Impossible! He is an Oxonian.

JACK: I fear there can be no possible doubt about the matter. This afternoon during my temporary absence in London on an important question of romance, he obtained admission to my house by means of the false pretence of being my brother. Under an assumed name he drank, I've just been informed by my butler, an entire pint bottle of my Perrier-Jouet, Brut, '89; wine I was specially reserving for myself. Continuing his disgraceful deception, he succeeded in the course of the afternoon in alienating the affections of my only ward. He subsequently stayed to tea, and devoured every single muffin. And what makes his conduct all the more heartless is, that he was perfectly well aware from the first that I have no brother, that I never had a brother, and that I don't intend to have a brother, not even of any kind. I distinctly told him so myself yesterday afternoon.

LADY BRACKNELL: Ahem! Mr. Worthing, after careful consideration I have decided entirely to overlook my nephew's conduct to you.

JACK: That is very generous of you, Lady Bracknell. My own decision, however, is unalterable. I decline to give my consent.

LADY BRACKNELL: (*to* Cecily) Come here, sweet child. (Cecily *goes over.*) How old are you, dear?

CECILY: Well, I am really only eighteen, but I always admit to twenty when I go to evening parties.

LADY BRACKNELL: You are perfectly right in making some slight alteration. Indeed, no woman should ever be quite accurate about her age. It looks so calculating. . . . (*In a meditative manner.*) Eighteen, but admitting to twenty at evening parties. Well, it will not be very long before you are of age and free from the restraints of tutelage. So I don't think your guardian's consent is, after all, a matter of any importance.

JACK: Pray excuse me, Lady Bracknell, for interrupting you again, but it is only fair to tell you that according to the terms of her grandfather's will Miss Cardew does not come legally of age till she is thirty-five.

LADY BRACKNELL: That does not seem to me to be a grave objection. Thirty-five is a very attractive age. London society is full of women of the very highest birth who have, of their own free choice, remained thirty-five for years. Lady Dumbleton is an instance in point. To my own knowledge she has been thirty-five ever since she arrived at the age of forty, which was many years ago now. I see no reason why our dear Cecily should not be even still more attractive at the age you mention than she is at present. There will be a large accumulation of property.

CECILY: Algy, could you wait for me till I was thirty-five?

ALGERNON: Of course I could, Cecily. You know I could.

CECILY: Yes, I felt it instinctively, but I couldn't wait all that time. I hate waiting even five minutes for anybody. It always makes me rather cross. I am not punctual myself, I know, but I do like punctuality in others, and waiting, even to be married, is quite out of the question.

ALGERNON: Then what is to be done, Cecily?

CECILY: I don't know, Mr. Moncrieff.

LADY BRACKNELL: My dear Mr. Worthing, as Miss Cardew states positively that she cannot wait till she is thirty-five—a remark which I am bound to say seems to me to show a somewhat impatient nature—I would beg of you to reconsider your decision.

JACK: But my dear Lady Bracknell, the matter is entirely in your own hands. The moment you consent to my marriage with Gwendolen, I will most gladly allow your nephew to form an alliance with my ward.

LADY BRACKNELL: (*rising and drawing herself up*) You must be quite aware that what you propose is out of the question.

JACK: Then a passionate celibacy is all that any of us can look forward to.

LADY BRACKNELL: That is not the destiny I propose for Gwendolen. Algernon, of course, can choose for himself. (*Pulls out her watch.*) Come, dear (Gwendolen *rises*), we have already missed five, if not six, trains. To miss any more might expose us to comment on the platform.

(*Enter* Dr. Chasuble.)

CHASUBLE: Everything is quite ready for the chirstenings.

LADY BRACKNELL: The chirstenings, sir! Is not that somewhat premature?

CHASUBLE: (*looking rather puzzled, and pointing to* Jack *and* Algernon) Both these gentlemen have expressed a desire for immediate baptism.

LADY BRACKNELL: At their age? The idea is grotesque and irreligious! Algernon, I forbid you to be baptized. I will not hear of such excesses. Lord Bracknell would be highly displeased if he learned that that was the way in which you wasted your time and money.

CHASUBLE: Am I to understand then that there are to be no christenings at all this afternoon?

JACK: I don't think that, as things are now, it would be of much practical value to either of us, Dr. Chasuble.

CHASUBLE: I am grieved to hear such sentiments from you, Mr. Worthing. They savour of the heretical views of the Anabaptists, views that I have completely refuted in four of my unpublished sermons. However, as your present mood seems to be one peculiarly secular, I will return to the church at once. Indeed, I have just been informed by the pew-opener that for the last hour and a half Miss Prism has been waiting for me in the vestry.

LADY BRACKNELL: (*starting*) Miss Prism! Did I hear you mention a Miss Prism?

CHASUBLE: Yes, Lady Bracknell. I am on my way to join her.

LADY BRACKNELL: Pray allow me to detain you for a moment. This matter may prove to be one of vital importance to Lord Bracknell and myself. Is this Miss Prism a female of repellent aspect, remotely connected with education?

CHASUBLE: (*somewhat indignantly*) She is the most cultivated of ladies, and the very picture of respectability.

LADY BRACKNELL: It is obviously the same person. May I ask what position she holds in your household?

CHASUBLE: (*severely*) I am a celibate, madam.

JACK: (*interposing*) Miss Prism, Lady Bracknell, has been for the last three years Miss Cardew's esteemed governess and valued companion.

LADY BRACKNELL: In spite of what I hear of her, I must see her at once. Let her be sent for.

CHASUBLE: (*looking off*) She approaches; she is nigh.

(*Enter* Miss Prism *hurriedly.*)

MISS PRISM: I was told you expected me in the vestry, dear Canon. I have been waiting for you there for an hour and three-quarters. (*Catches sight of* Lady Bracknell, *who has fixed her with a stony glare.* Miss Prism *grows pale and quails. She looks anxiously round as if desirous to escape.*)

LADY BRACKNELL: (*in a severe, judicial voice*) Prism! (Miss Prism *bows her head in shame.*) Come here, Prism! (Miss Prism *approaches in a humble manner.*) Prism! Where is that baby? (*General consternation. The Canon starts back in horror.* Algernon *and* Jack *pretend to be anxious to shield* Cecily *and* Gwendolen *from hearing the details of a terrible public scandal.*) Twenty-eight years ago, Prism, you left Lord Bracknell's house, Number 104, Upper Grosvenor Square, in charge of a perambulator that contained a baby of the male sex. You never returned. A few weeks later, through the elaborate investigations of the Metropolitan police, the perambulator was discovered at midnight standing by itself in a remote corner of Bayswater. It contained the manuscript of a three-volume novel of more than usually revolting sentimentality. (Miss Prism *starts in involuntary indignation.*) But the baby was not there. (*Every one looks at* Miss Prism.) Prism! Where is that baby? (*A pause.*)

MISS PRISM: Lady Bracknell, I admit with shame that I do not know. I only wish I did. The plain facts of the case are these. On the morning of the day you mention, a day that is for ever branded on my memory, I prepared as usual to take the baby out in its perambulator. I had also with me a somewhat old, but capacious hand-bag in which I had intended to place the manuscript of a work of fiction that I had written during my few unoccupied hours. In a moment of mental abstraction, for which I can never forgive myself, I deposited the manuscript in the bassinette and placed the baby in the hand-bag.

JACK: (*who has been listening attentively*) But where did you deposit the hand-bag?

MISS PRISM: Do not ask me, Mr. Worthing.

JACK: Miss Prism, this is a matter of no small importance to me. I insist on knowing where you deposited the hand-bag that contained that infant.

MISS PRISM: I left it in the cloak-room of one of the larger railway stations in London.

JACK: What railway station?

MISS PRISM: (*quite crushed*) Victoria. The Brighton line. (*Sinks into a chair.*)

JACK: I must retire to my room for a moment. Gwendolen, wait here for me.

GWENDOLEN: If you are not too long, I will wait here for you all my life. (*Exit* Jack *in great excitement.*)

CHASUBLE: What do you think this means, Lady Bracknell?

LADY BRACKNELL: I dare not even suspect, Dr. Chasuble. I need hardly tell you that in families of high position strange coincidences are not supposed to occur. They are hardly considered the thing.

(*Noises heard overhead as if some one was throwing trunks about. Every one looks up.*)

CECILY: Uncle Jack seems strangely agitated.

CHASUBLE: Your guardian has a very emotional nature.

LADY BRACHNELL: This noise is extremely unpleasant. It sounds as if he was having an argument. I dislike arguments of any kind. They are always vulgar, and often convincing.

CHASUBLE: (looking up) It has stopped now. (The noise is redoubled.)

LADY BRACKNELL: I wish he would arrive at some conclusion.

GWENDOLEN: This suspense is terrible. I hope it will last.

(Enter Jack with a hand-bag of black leather in his hand.)

JACK: (rushing over to Miss Prism) Is this the hand-bag, Miss Prism? Examine it carefully before you speak. The happiness of more than one life depends on your answer.

MISS PRISM: (calmly) It seems to be mine. Yes, here is the injury it received through the upsetting of a Gower Street omnibus in younger and happier days. Here is the stain on the lining caused by the explosion of a temperance beverage, an incident that occurred at Leamington. And here, on the lock, are my initials. I had forgotten that in an extravagant mood I had had them placed there. The bag is undoubtedly mine. I am delighted to have it so unexpectedly restored to me. It has been a great inconvenience being without it all these years.

JACK: (in a pathetic voice) Miss Prism, more is restored to you than this hand-bag. I was the baby you placed in it.

MISS PRISM: (amazed.) You?

JACK: (embracing her) Yes . . . mother!

MISS PRISM: (recoiling in indignant astonishment) Mr. Worthing. I am unmarried!

JACK: Unmarried! I do not deny that is a serious blow. But after all, who has the right to cast a stone against one who has suffered? Cannot repentance wipe out an act of folly? Why should there be one law for men, and another for women? Mother, I forgive you. (Tries to embrace her again.)

MISS PRISM: (still more indignant) Mr. Worthing, there is some error. (Pointing to Lady Bracknell.) There is the lady who can tell you who you really are.

JACK: (after a pause) Lady Bracknell, I hate to seem inquisitive, but would you kindly inform me who I am?

LADY BRACKNELL: I am afraid that the news I have to give you will not altogether please you. You are the son of my poor sister, Mrs. Moncrieff, and consequently Algernon's elder brother.

JACK: Algy's elder brother! Then I have a brother after all. I knew I had a brother! I always said I had a brother! Cecily—how could you have ever doubted that I had a brother? (Seizes hold of Algernon.) Dr. Chasuble, my unfortunate brother. Miss Prism, my unfortunate brother. Gwendolen, my unfortunate brother. Algy, you young scoundrel, you will have to treat me with more respect in the future. You have never behaved to me like a brother in all your life.

ALGERNON: Well, not till to-day, old boy, I admit. I did my best, however, though I was out of practice.

(Shakes hands.)

GWENDOLEN: (to Jack) My own! But what own are you? What is your Christian name, now that you have become some one else?

JACK: Good heavens! . . . I had quite forgotten that point. Your decision on the subject of my name is irrevocable, I suppose?

GWENDOLEN: I never change, except in my affections.

CECILY: What a noble nature you have, Gwendolen!

JACK: Then the question had better be cleared up at once. Aunt Augusta, a moment. At the time when Miss Prism left me in the hand-bag, had I been christened already?

LADY BRACKNELL: Every luxury that money could buy, including christening, had been lavished on you by your fond and doting parents.

JACK: Then I was christened! That is settled. Now, what name was I given? Let me know the worst.

LADY BRACKNELL: Being the eldest son you were naturally chirstened after your father.

JACK: (*irritably*) Yes, but what was my father's Christian name?

LADY BRACKNELL: (*meditatively*) I cannot at the present moment recall what the General's Christian name was. But I have no doubt he had one. He was eccentric, I admit. But only in later years. And that was the result of the Indian climate, and marriage, and indigestion, and other things of that kind.

JACK: Algy! Can't you recollect what our father's Christian name was?

ALGERNON: My dear boy, we were never even on speaking terms. He died before I was a year old.

JACK: His name would appear in the Army Lists of the period, I suppose, Aunt Augusta?

LADY BRACKNELL: The General was essentially a man of peace, except in his domestic life. But I have no doubt his name would appear in any military directory.

JACK: The Army Lists of the last forty years are here. These delightful records should have been my constant study. (*Rushes to bookcase and tears the books out.*) M. Generals . . . Mallam, Maxbohm, Magley—what ghastly names they have—Markby, Migsby, Mobbs, Moncrieff! Lieutenant 1840, Captain, Lieutenant-Colonel, Colonel, General 1869, Christian names, Ernest John. (*Puts book very quietly down and speaks quite clamly.*) I always told you, Gwendolen, my name was Ernest, didn't I? Well, it is Ernest after all. I mean it naturally is Ernest.

LADY BRACKNELL: Yes, I remember now that the General was called Ernest. I knew I had some particular reason for disliking the name.

GWENDOLEN: Ernest! My own Ernest! I felt from the first that you could have no other name!

JACK: Gwendolen, it is a terrible thing for a man to find out suddenly that all his life he has been speaking nothing but the truth. Can you forgive me?

GWENDOLEN: I can. For I feel that you are sure to change.

JACK: My own one!

CHASUBLE: (*to* Miss Prism) Laetitia! (*Embraces her.*)

MISS PRISM: (*enthusiastically*) Frederick! At last!

ALGERNON: Cecily! (*Embraces her.*) At last!

JACK: Gwendolen! (*Embraces her.*) At last!

LADY BRACKNELL: My nephew, you seem to be displaying signs of triviality.

JACK: On the contrary, Aunt Augusta, I've now realized for the first time in my life the vital Importance of Being Earnest.

TABLEAU

FOR DISCUSSION

1. Are the characters in *The Importance of Being Earnest* believable? Why or why not?
2. Does the play have a theme? What is it?
3. What devices does Oscar Wilde use to make the dialogue humorous?
4. What is the significance of the title?
5. What does the author have to say about social standing? Through what characters does he convey his views?
6. Is this, in your opinion, a good play? Discuss.
7. Compare the comic devices used in this play with those used in Molière's *The Miser*.
8. Do you think coincidence is skillfully handled in the unraveling of the plot?
9. What contributes most to the humor of the play—the plot, the dialogue, or the characters? Why?
10. Do you think the situation in the play is logical? Why or why not?
11. What sort of married lives do you think the two couples in the play will have? Give your reasons.

J. M. Synge wrote simple, powerful plays.

He was born near Dublin, Ireland, in 1871. After graduating from Trinity College in 1892, he went to continental Europe for six years, spending most of his time in Paris. There he became a book reviewer and also met the Irish poet and playwright William Butler Yeats. Yeats urged him to return to Ireland to develop his talent as a writer. Synge took the advice, and in 1899 settled in the western section of Ireland where he studied the lives of the peasant people. Their way of life and speech patterns gave him the material he needed in order to write. He became steeped in their ways, and his experiences with them led him to become Ireland's first major playwright.

Synge's writing, to a certain degree, was a reaction against what he felt were "seedy" problems presented by such playwrights as Ibsen. Although Synge believed in a back-to-nature kind of romanticism, he was not totally absorbed in the beauty around him. He saw the poor people's struggle against the forces of nature and embodied it in his plays. Thus his writing is unique —highly poetic but realistic in the problems it presents.

Synge wrote six plays. His first, *In the Shadow of the Glen* (1903), deals with an unhappy peasant girl whose husband drives her out of her home. It was in this play that he began portrayals of the Irish character. *Riders to the Sea,* (1904), was followed by a comedy, *The Well of the Saints,* in 1905, then by *The Tinker's Wedding,* another comedy of which the date of completion is uncertain; and *The Playboy of the Western World,* a comedy written in 1907, *Deidre of the Sorrows,* his last play, was never finished. Synge died in 1909 at the age of thirty-eight.

The Playboy of the Western World and *Riders to the Sea* are Synge's best plays. The latter has been praised for its simplicity and its intensity. Through the utmost condensation, it eliminates all but what is necessary to the folding of its tragedy. The story clearly shows Synge's feelings for the common people of Ireland, but it's structure is strongly controlled. The dialogue is alive, yet poetic. Although the viewer does not personally witness the tragedy, he strongly identifies with Maurya while she waits for the men. The play is intensely dramatic yet never deviates from its purpose of showing man's struggle against nature. *Riders to the Sea* has often been called the best modern one-act play.

Riders to the Sea

CHARACTERS

MAURYA, *an old woman*
BARTLEY, *her son*
CATHLEEN, *her daughter*

NORA, *a younger daughter*
MEN AND WOMEN

Riders to the Sea

An Island off the west of Ireland.
Cottage kitchen, with nets, oil-skins, spinning-wheel, some new boards
standing by the wall, etc. Cathleen, a girl of about twenty, finishes kneading
cake, and puts it down on the pot-oven by the fire; then wipes her hands,
and begins to spin at the wheel. Nora, a young girl, puts her head in at the
door.

NORA: (*In a low voice*) Where is she?

CATHLEEN: She's lying down, God help her, and may be sleeping, if she's
able.

(Nora *comes in softly, and takes a bundle from under her shawl.*)

CATHLEEN: (*Spinning the wheel rapidly*) What is it you have?

NORA: The young priest is after bringing them. It's a shirt and a plain
stocking were got off a drowned man in Donegal.

(Cathleen *stops her wheel with a sudden movement, and leans out to*
listen.)

NORA: We're to find out if it's Michael's they are, some time herself will
be down looking by the sea.

CATHLEEN: How would they be Michael's, Nora? How would he go the
length of that way to the Far North?

NORA: The young priest says he's known the like of it. "If it's Michael's
they are," says he, "you can tell herself he's got a clean burial by the grace
of God, and if they're not his, let no one say a word about them, for she'll
be getting her death," says he, "with crying and lamenting."

(*The door which* Nora *half closed is blown open by a gust of wind.*)

CATHLEEN: (*Looking out anxiously*) Did you ask him would he stop Bartley going this day with the horses to the Galway fair?

NORA: "I won't stop him," says he, "but let you not be afraid. Herself
does be saying prayers half through the night, and the Almighty God won't
leave her destitute," says he, "with no son living."

CATHLEEN: Is the sea bad by the white rocks, Nora?

NORA: Middling bad, God help us. There's a great roaring in the west, and
it's worse it'll be getting when the tide's turned to the wind. (*She goes over*
to the table with the bundle.) Shall I open it now?

CATHLEEN: Maybe she'd wake up on us, and come in before we'd done. (*Coming to the table*) It's a long time we'll be, and the two of us crying.

NORA: (*Goes to the inner door and listens*) She's moving about on the bed. She'll be coming in a minute.

CATHLEEN: Give me the ladder, and I'll put them up in the turf-loft, the way she won't know of them at all, and maybe when the tide turns she'll be going down to see would he be floating from the east.

(*They put the ladder against the gable of the chimney; Cathleen goes up a few steps and hides the bundle in the turf-loft. Maurya comes from the inner room.*)

MAURYA: (*Looking up at Cathleen and speaking querulously*) Isn't it turf enough you have for this day and evening?

CATHLEEN: There's a cake baking at the fire for a short space (*Throwing down the turf*) and Bartley will want it when the tide turns if he goes to Connemara.

(Nora *picks up the turf and puts it round the pot-oven.*)

MAURYA: (*Sitting down on a stool at the fire*) He won't go this day with the wind rising from the south and west. He won't go this day, for the young priest will stop him surely.

NORA: He'll not stop him, Mother, and I heard Eamon Simon and Stephen Pheety and Colum Shawn saying he would go.

MAURYA: Where is he itself?

NORA: He went down to see would there be another boat sailing in the week, and I'm thinking it won't be long till he's here now, for the tide's turning at the green head, and the hooker's[1] tacking from the east.

CATHLEEN: I hear some one passing the big stones.

NORA: (*Looking out*) He's coming now, and he in a hurry.

BARTLEY: (*Comes in and looks round the room; speaking sadly and quietly*) Where is the bit of new rope, Cathleen, was bought in Connemara?

CATHLEEN: (*Coming down*) Give it to him, Nora; it's on a nail by the white boards. I hung it up this morning, for the pig with the black feet was eating it.

NORA: (*Giving him a rope*) Is that it, Bartley?

MAURYA: You'd do right to leave that rope, Bartley, hanging by the boards. (Bartley *takes the rope.*) It will be wanting in this place, I'm telling you, if Michael is washed up tomorrow morning, or the next morning, or any morning in the week, for it's a deep grave we'll make him by the grace of God.

BARTLEY: (*Beginning to work with the rope*) I've no halter the way I can ride down on the mare, and I must go now quickly. This is the one boat going for two weeks or beyond it, and the fair will be a good fair for horses I heard them saying below.

MAURYA: It's a hard thing they'll be saying below if the body is washed up and there's no man in it to make the coffin, and I after giving a big price for the finest white boards you'd find in Connemara. (*She looks round at the boards.*)

BARTLEY: How would it be washed up, and we after looking each day for

---

[1] A single-masted fishing boat.

nine days, and a strong wind blowing a while back from the west and south?

MAURYA: If it wasn't found itself, that wind is raising the sea, and there was a star up against the moon, and it rising in the night. If it was a hundred horses, or a thousand horses you had itself, what is the price of a thousand horses against a son where there is one son only?

BARTLEY: (*Working at the halter, to* Cathleen) Let you go down each day, and see the sheep aren't jumping in on the rye, and if the jobber comes you can sell the pig with the black feet if there is a good price going.

MAURYA: How would the like of her get a good price for a pig?

BARTLEY: (*To* Cathleen) If the west wind holds with the last bit of the moon let you and Nora get up weed enough for another cock[2] for the kelp. It's hard set we'll be from this day with no one in it but one man to work.

MAURYA: It's hard set we'll be surely the day you're drownd'd with the rest. What way will I live and the girls with me, and I an old woman looking for the grave?

(Bartley *lays down the halter, takes off his old coat, and puts on a newer one of the same flannel.*)

BARTLEY: (*To* Nora) Is she coming to the pier?

NORA: (*Looking out*) She's passing the green head and letting fall her sails.

BARTLEY: (*Getting his purse and tobacco*) I'll have half an hour to go down, and you'll see me coming again in two days, or in three days, or maybe in four days if the wind is bad.

MAURYA: (*Turning round to the fire, and putting her shawl over her head*) Isn't it a hard and cruel man won't hear a word from an old woman, and she holding him from the sea?

CATHLEEN: It's the life of a young man to be going on the sea, and who would listen to an old woman with one thing and she saying it over?

BARTLEY: (*Taking the halter*) I must go now quickly. I'll ride down on the red mare, and the gray pony'll run behind me. . . . The blessing of God on you. (He goes out.)

MAURYA: (*Crying out as he is in the door*) He's gone now, God spare us, and we'll not see him again. He's gone now, and when the black night is falling I'll have no son left me in the world.

CATHLEEN: Why wouldn't you give him your blessing and he looking round in the door? Isn't it sorrow enough is on every one in this house without your sending him out with an unlucky word behind him, and a hard word in his ear?

(Maurya *takes up the tongs and begins raking the fire aimlessly without looking round.*)

NORA: (*Turning toward her*) You're taking away the turf from the cake.

CATHLEEN: (*Crying out*) The Son of God forgive us, Nora, we're after forgetting his bit of bread. (*She comes over to the fire.*)

NORA: And it's destroyed he'll be going till dark night, and he after eating nothing since the sun went up.

CATHLEEN: (*Turning the cake out of the oven*) It's destroyed he'll be, surely. There's no sense left on any person in a house where an old woman will be talking forever.

---

[2] A stack for burning seaweed into the ashes (kelp) useful as fertilizer.

(Maurya *sways herself on her stool.*)

CATHLEEN: (*Cutting off some of the bread and rolling it in a cloth; to* Maurya) Let you go down now to the spring well and give him this and he passing. You'll see him then and the dark word will be broken, and you can say "God speed you," the way he'll be easy in his mind.
MAURYA: (*Taking the bread*) Will I be in it as soon as himself?
CATHLEEN: If you go now quickly.
MAURYA: (*Standing up unsteadily*) It's hard set I am to walk.
CATHLEEN (*Looking at her anxiously*) Give her the stick, Nora, or maybe she'll slip on the big stones.
NORA: What stick?
CATHLEEN: The stick Michael brought from Connemara.
MAURYA: (*Taking a stick Nora gives her*) In the big world the old people do be leaving things after them for their sons and children, but in this place it is the young men do be leaving things behind for them that do be old.

(*She goes out slowly. Nora goes over to the ladder.*)

CATHLEEN: Wait, Nora, maybe she'd turn back quickly. She's that sorry, God help her, you wouldn't know the thing she'd do.
NORA: Is she gone round by the bush?
CATHLEEN: (*Looking out*) She's gone now. Throw it down quickly, for the Lord knows when she'll be out of it again.
NORA: (*Getting the bundle from the loft*) The young priest said he'd be passing tomorrow, and we might go down and speak to him below if it's Michael's they are surely.
CATHLEEN: (*Taking the bundle*) Did he say what way they were found?
NORA: (*Coming down*) "There were two men," says he, "and they rowing round with poteen[3] before the cocks crowed, and the oar of one of them caught the body, and they passing the black cliffs of the north."
CATHLEEN: (*Trying to open the bundle*) Give me a knife, Nora, the string's perished with the salt water, and there's a black knot on it you wouldn't loosen in a week.
NORA: (*Giving her a knife*) I've heard tell it was a long way to Donegal.
CATHLEEN: (*Cutting the string*) It is surely. There was a man in here a while ago—the man sold us that knife—and he said if you set off walking from the rocks beyond, it would be seven days you'd be in Donegal.
NORA: And what time would a man take, and he floating?

(Cathleen *opens the bundle and takes out a bit of a stocking. They look at them eagerly.*)

CATHLEEN: (*In a low voice*) The Lord spare us, Nora! isn't it a queer hard thing to say if it's his they are surely?
NORA: I'll get his shirt off the hook the way we can put the one flannel on the other. (*She looks through some clothes hanging in the corner.*) It's not with them, Cathleen, and where will it be?

---

[3] A strong whiskey illegally brewed and sold.

CATHLEEN: I'm thinking Bartley put it on him in the morning, for his own shirt was heavy with the salt in it. (*Pointing to the corner*) There's a bit of a sleeve was of the same stuff. Give me that and it will do.

(*Nora brings it to her and they compare the flannel.*)

CATHLEEN: It's the same stuff, Nora; but if it is itself aren't there great rolls of it in the shops of Galway, and isn't it many another man may have a shirt of it as well as Michael himself?

NORA: (*Who has taken up the stocking and counted the stitches, crying out*) It's Michael, Cathleen, it's Michael; God spare his soul, and what will herself say when she hears this story, and Bartley on the sea?

CATHLEEN: (*Taking the stocking*) It's a plain stocking.

NORA: It's the second one of the third pair I knitted, and I put up three-score stitches, and I dropped four of them.

CATHLEEN: (*Counts the stitches*) It's that number is in it. (*Crying out*) Ah, Nora, isn't it a bitter thing to think of him floating that way to the Far North, and no one to keen him but the black hags that do be flying on the sea?

NORA: (*Swinging herself round, and throwing out her arms on the clothes*) And isn't it a pitiful thing when there is nothing left of a man who was a great rower and fisher, but a bit of an old shirt and a plain stocking?

CATHLEEN: (*After an instant*) Tell me is herself coming, Nora? I hear a little sound on the path.

NORA: (*Looking out*) She is, Cathleen. She's coming up to the door.

CATHLEEN: Put these things away before she'll come in. Maybe it's easier she'll be after giving her blessing to Bartley, and we won't let on we've heard anything the time he's on the sea.

NORA: (*Helping Cathleen to close the bundle*) We'll put them here in the corner.

(*They put them into a howle in the chimney corner. Cathleen goes back to the spinning-wheel.*)

NORA: Will she see it was crying I was?

CATHLEEN: Keep your back to the door the way the light'll not be on you.

(*Nora sits down at the chimney corner, with her back to the door. Maurya comes in very slowly, without looking at the girls, and goes over to her stool at the other side of the fire. The cloth with the bread is still in her hand. The girls look at each other, and Nora points to the bundle of bread.*)

CATHLEEN: (*After spinning for a moment*) You didn't give him his bit of bread? (*Maurya begins to keen softly, without turning round.*)

CATHLEEN: Did you see him riding down?

(*Maurya goes on keening.*)

CATHLEEN (*A little impatiently*): God forgive you; isn't it a better thing to raise your voice and tell what you seen, than to be making lamentation for a thing that's done? Did you see Bartley, I'm saying to you.

MAURYA: (*With a weak voice*) My heart's broken from this day.

CATHLEEN: (*As before*) Did you see Bartley?

MAURYA: I seen the fearfulest thing.

CATHLEEN: (*Leaves her wheel and looks out*) God forgive you; he's riding the mare now over the green head, and the gray pony behind him.

MAURYA: (*Starts, so that her shawl falls back from her head and shows her white tossed hair. With a frightened voice*) The gray pony behind him.

CATHLEEN: (*Coming to the fire*) What is it ails you, at all?

MAURYA: (*Speaking very slowly*) I've seen the fearfulest thing any person has seen, since the day Bride Dara seen the dead man with a child in his arms.

CATHLEEN AND NORA: Uah.

(*They crouch down in front of the old woman at the fire.*)

NORA: Tell us what it is you seen.

MAURYA: I went down to the spring well, and I stood there saying a prayer to myself. Then Bartley came along, and he riding on the red mare with the gray pony behind him. (*She puts her hands, as if to hide something from her eyes.*) The Son of God spare us, Nora!

CATHLEEN: What is it you seen?

MAURYA: I seen Michael himself.

CATHLEEN: (*Speaking softly*) You did not, Mother; it wasn't Michael you seen, for his body is after being found in the Far North, and he's got a clean burial by the grace of God.

MAURYA: (*A little defiantly*) I'm after seeing him this day, and he riding and galloping. Bartley came first on the red mare; and I tried to say, "God speed you," but something choked the words in my throat. He went by quickly; and "the blessing of God on you," says he, and I could say nothing. I looked up then, and I crying, at the gray pony, and there was Michael upon it—with fine clothes on him, and new shoes on his feet.

CATHLEEN: (*Begins to keen*) It's destroyed we are from this day. It's destroyed, surely.

NORA: Didn't the young priest say the Almighty God wouldn't leave her destitute with no son living?

MAURYA: (*In a low voice, but clearly*) It's little the like of him knows of the sea. . . . Bartley will be lost now, and let you call in Eamon and make me a good coffin out of the white boards, for I won't live after them. I've had a husband, and a husband's father, and six sons in this house—six fine men, though it was a hard birth I had with every one of them and they coming to the world—and some of them were found and some of them were not found, but they're gone now the lot of them. . . . There were Stephen, and Shawn, were lost in the great wind, and found after in the Bay of Gregory of the Golden Mouth, and carried up the two of them on the one plank, and in by that door.

(*She pauses for a moment, the girls start as if they heard something through the door that is half open behind them.*)

NORA: (*In a whisper*) Did you hear that, Cathleen? Did you hear a noise in the northeast?

CATHLEEN: (*In a whisper*) There's some one after crying out by the seashore.

MAURYA (*Continues without hearing anything*) There was Sheamus and his father, and his own father again, were lost in a dark night, and not a stick or sign was seen of them when the sun went up. There was Patch after was drowned out of a curagh that turned over. I was sitting here with Bartley, and he a baby, lying on my two knees, and I seen two women, and three women, and four women coming in, and they crossing themselves, and not saying a word. I looked out then, and there were men coming after them, and they holding a thing in the half of a red sail, and water dripping out of it—it was a dry day, Nora—and leaving a track to the door.

(She pauses again with her hand stretched out toward the door. It opens softly and old women begin to come in, crossing themselves on the threshold, and kneeling down in front of the stage with red petticoats over their heads.)

MAURYA: *(Half in a dream, to* Cathleen) Is it Patch or Michael, or what is it at all?

CATHLEEN: Michael is after being found in the Far North, and when he is found there how could he be here in this place?

MAURYA: There does be a power of young men floating round in the sea, and what way would they know if it was Michael they had, or another man like him, for when a man is nine days in the sea, and the wind blowing, it's hard set his own mother would be to say what man was it.

CATHLEEN: It's Michael, God spare him, for they're after sending us a bit of his clothes from the Far North.

(She reaches out and hands Maurya *the clothes that belonged to Michael.* Maurya *stands up slowly, and takes them in her hands.* Nora *looks out.)*

NORA: They're carrying a thing among them and there's water dripping out of it and leaving a track by the big stones.

CATHLEEN: *(In a whisper to the women who have come in)* Is it Bartley it is?

ONE OF THE WOMEN: It is surely, God rest his soul.

(Two younger women come in and pull out the table. Then men carry in the body of Bartley, *laid on a plank, with a bit of a sail over it, and lay it on the table.)*

CATHLEEN: *(To the women, as they are doing so)* What way was he drowned?

ONE OF THE WOMEN: The gray pony knocked him into the sea, and he was washed out where there is a great surf on the white rocks.

(Maurya has gone over and knelt down at the head of the table. The women are keening softly and swaying themselves with a slow movement. Cathleen *and* Nora *kneel at the other end of the table. The men kneel near the door.)*

MAURYA: *(Raising her head and speaking as if she did not see the people around her)* They're all gone now, and there isn't anything more the sea can do to me. . . . I'll have no call now to be up crying and praying when the wind breaks from the south, and you can hear the surf is in the east, and the surf is in the west, making a great stir with the two noises, and they hitting one on the other. I'll have no call now to be going down and getting Holy Water in the dark nights after Samhain,[4] and I won't care what way the sea is when the other woman will be keening. (*To* Nora) Give me the Holy Water, Nora, there's a small sup still on the dresser.

(Nora *gives it to her.*)

MAURYA: (*Drops Michael's clothes across Bartley's feet, and sprinkles the Holy Water over him*) It isn't that I haven't prayed for you, Bartley, to the Almighty God. It isn't that I haven't said prayers in the dark night till you wouldn't know what I'd be saying; but it's a great rest I'll have now, and it's time surely. It's a great rest I'll have now, and great sleeping in the long nights after Samhain, if it's only a bit of wet flour we do have to eat, and maybe a fish that would be stinking.

(*She kneels down again, crossing herself, and saying prayers under her breath.*)

CATHLEEN: (To an old man) Maybe yourself and Eamon would make a coffin when the sun rises. We have fine white boards herself bought, God help her, thinking Michael would be found, and I have a new cake you can eat while you'll be working.
THE OLD MAN: (*Looking at the boards*) Are there nails with them?
CATHLEEN: There are not, Colum; we didn't think of the nails.
ANOTHER MAN: It's a great wonder she wouldn't think of the nails, and all the coffins she's seen made already.
CATHLEEN: It's getting old she is, and broken.

(Maurya *stands up again very slowly and spreads out the pieces of Michael's clothes beside the body, sprinkling them with the last of the Holy Water.*)

NORA: (*In a whisper to* Cathleen) She's quiet now and easy; but the day Michael was drowned you could hear her crying out from this to the spring well. It's fonder she was of Michael, and would any one have thought that?
CATHLEEN: (*Slowly and clearly*) An old woman will be soon tired with anything she will do, and isn't it nine days herself is after crying and keening, and making great sorrow in the house?
MAURYA: (*Puts the empty cup mouth downwards on the table, and lays her hands together on Bartley's feet*) They're all together this time, and the end is come. May the Almighty God have mercy on Bartley's soul, and on Michael's soul, and on the souls of Sheamus and Patch, and Stephen and Shawn; (*Bending her head*) and may He have mercy on my soul, Nora, and on the soul of every one is left living in the world.

(*She pauses, and the keen rises a little more loudly from the women, then sinks away.*)

MAURYA: (*Continuing*) Michael has a clean burial in the Far North, by the grace of the Almighty God. Bartley will have a fine coffin out of the white

---

[4] The equivalent of Allhallows. If falls on November 1 and marks the beginning of winter; it is celebrated with harvest rites and a Feast of the Dead.

boards, and a deep grave surely. What more can we want than that? No man at all can be living forever, and we must be satisfied.

(She kneels down again and the curtain falls slowly.)

FOR DISCUSSION

1. Is there conflict in the play? If so, between whom or what?
2. What do you think is the theme of the play?
3. Does the play have a plot? How is the situation developed?
4. What feelings do you have while reading this play? What contributes the most to these feelings?
5. Is this play realistic? Is it romantic? Is it poetic? Discuss.
6. What part does fate play in this tragedy?
7. If you were staging this play, what would your setting be like? Your sound effects? Your costumes?
8. Is the play, in your opinion, effectively written? Why or why not?
9. Do you like this play? Why or why not?
10. Does the tight structure of the story add to or detract from its effectiveness?
11. Why do you think Synge wrote *Riders to the Sea?*

Eugene O'Neill was a daring playwright.

Born in a Broadway hotel on October 16, 1888 in New York City, he was the son of a well-known actor, James O'Neill. He attended a variety of Catholic schools while his father toured with his acting company. O'Neill later was expelled from Princeton University and spent the next year prospecting for gold in the Honduras. Becoming ill with malarial fever, he was forced to return home and afterward toured with his father's company. He served as a seaman for several years and worked for American companies in Argentina. Later he became a reporter and columnist in Connecticut, but ill health caused him to enter a tuberculosis sanitorium.

In 1914, O'Neill enrolled in George Pierce Baker's playwriting workshop at Harvard, where he began his long career as a dramatist. In 1916, he became affiliated with the Provincetown Players, which gave summer performances in Cape Cod and winter performances in Greenwich Village. The group was one of the most important in the little theatre movement that was beginning to spread through America. These theatrical groups were formed to produce plays for the sake of art rather than for making money. While O'Neill worked with the Provincetown Players as an actor he also submitted plays to the organization. His *Bound East for Cardiff* was presented during the summer of 1916, the first of many of his one-acts produced by the group. Progressing to full-length plays, he won acclaim as one of America's foremost playwrights. He died in 1953.

O'Neill was primarily responsible for the worldwide recognition given to American drama in the 1920's. An extremely prolific writer, he received a Nobel Prize for Literature in 1936 and Pulitzer prizes in 1920, 1922, and 1928. Boldly experimenting with both style and theatrical technique, he wrote highly individualized plays that show an uncommon theatrical know-how. Because of his constant experimentation, O'Neill's plays ranged from critical and commercial successes to absolute failures. Several, such as *Desire Under the Elms* and *Anna Christie,* are largely realistic, while others, like *The Great God Brown* and *Strange Interlude,* are largely expressionistic. He also wrote romantic plays such as *Marco Millions.* However, his dramas are really a mixture of styles. Those about the sea are realistic in content and dialogue but have poetic elements. Even *Anna Christie,* which is the epitome of realism as written during that time, ends romantically. *The Emperor Jones* and *All God's Chillun Got Wings* deal with social problems in their treatment of the struggles of the black man in America. His experiments with technique included the use of masks in *The Great God Brown,* asides and soliloquies in the long play *Strange Interlude,* and a chorus in *Lazarus Laughed.*

O'Neill's plays are very subjective and so personal that he even requested that some of them not be produced until after his death. *A Long Day's Journey into Night,* for example, was written in 1941, but was not published until 1956. It deals with his father's failure to become a truly outstanding actor, his mother's involvement with heroin, his brother's alcoholism, and his own bouts with tuberculosis. Many of O'Neill's plays have been given successful professional productions since the playwright's death.

The Hairy Ape, first presented by the Provincetown Players on March 9, 1922, shows what could happen if the rules of the universe were changed so that our worst fears would become reality. The central character, Yank, is called an ape and begins to doubt his humanness. The doubt becomes reality when he is refused acceptance in New York City. He finally goes to a zoo to claim kinship with an ape, but discovers he does not belong there either. The play is similar in many ways to the work of European expressionists and is highly symbolic in its subject matter and content. Yank is the symbol of man, who has emerged from an animal state but has failed to progress spiritually. Since he can go neither forward nor backward, the struggle in the play is between Yank and himself or his destiny. Alienated from society, Yank makes the ultimate discovery that he does not belong in the world either as a man or as a worker. Despite the symbolism and expressionism in the play, much of the dialogue is realistic. Like many of O'Neill's plays, The Hairy Ape is a blending of a variety of styles.

The Hairy Ape

CHARACTERS

ROBERT SMITH, "YANK"
PADDY
LONG
MILDRED DOUGLAS
HER AUNT

SECOND ENGINEER
A GUARD
A SECRETARY OF AN
ORGANIZATION
STOKERS, LADIES, GENTLEMEN,
ETC.

SCENES

I. *The firemen's forecastle of an ocean liner—an hour after sailing from New York.*
II. *Section of promenade deck, two days out—morning.*
III. *The stockade. A few minutes later.*
IV. *Same as Scene I. Half an hour later.*
V. *Fifth Avenue, New York. Three weeks later.*
VI. *An island near the city. The next night.*
VII. *In the city. About a month later.*
VIII. *In the city. Twilight of the next day.*
   Time—Modern.

The Hairy Ape

SCENE I: *The firemen's forecastle of a transatlantic liner an hour after sailing from New York for the voyage across. Tiers of narrow, steel bunks, three deep, on all sides. An entrance in rear. Benches on the floor before the bunks. The room is crowded with men, shouting, cursing, laughing, singing—a confused, inchoate uproar swelling into a sort of unity, a meaning—the bewildered, furious, baffled defiance of a beast in a cage. Nearly all the men are drunk. Many bottles are passed from hand to hand. All are dressed in dungaree pants, heavy ugly shoes. Some wear singlets, but the majority are stripped to the waist.*

The treatment of this scene, or of any other scene in the play, should by no means be naturalistic. The effect sought after is a cramped space in the bowels of a ship, imprisoned by white steel. The lines of bunks, the uprights supporting them, cross each other like the steel framework of a cage. The ceiling crushes down upon the men's heads. They cannot stand upright. This accentuates the natural stooping posture which shoveling coal and the result-ant over-development of back and shoulder muscles have given them. The men themselves should resemble those pictures in which the appearance of Neanderthal Man is guessed at. All are hairy-chested, with long arms of tremendous power, and low, receding brows above their small, fierce, resent-ful eyes. All the civilized white races are represented, but except for the slight differentiation in color of hair, skin, eyes, all these men are alike.

The curtain rises on a tumult of sound. Yank is seated in the foreground. He seems broader, fiercer, more truculent, more powerful, more sure of him-self than the rest. They respect his superior strength—the grudging respect of fear. Then, too, he represents to them a self-expression, the very last word in what they are, their most highly developed individual.

VOICES: Gif me trink dere, you!
'Ave a wet!
Salute!
Gesundheit!
Skoal!
Drunk as a lord, God stiffen you!
Here's how!
Luck!
Pass back that bottle, damn you!
Pourin' it down his neck!

Ho, Groggy! Where the devil have you been?
La Touraine.
I hit him smash in yaw, py Gott!
Jenkins—the First—he's a rotten swine—
And the coppers nabbed him—and I run—
I like peer better. It don't pig head gif you.
A slut, I'm sayin'! She robbed me aslape—
To hell with 'em all!
You're a bloody liar!
Say dot again! (*Commotion. Two men about to fight are pulled apart.*)
No scrappin' now!
Tonight—
See who's the best man!
Bloody Dutchman!
Tonight on the for'ard square.
I'll bet on Dutchy.
He packa da wallop, I tella you!
Shut up, Wop!
No fightin', maties. We're all chums, ain't we?

   (*A voice starts bawling a song.*)
"Beer, beer, glorious beer!
Fill yourselves right up to here."

   YANK: (*For the first time seeming to take notice of the uproar about him, turns around threateningly—in a tone of contemptuous authority.*) Choke off dat noise! Where d'yuh get dat beer stuff? Beer, hell! Beer's for goils—and Dutchmen. Me for somep'n wit a kick to it! Gimme a drink, one of youse guys.

   (*Several bottles are eagerly offered. He takes a tremendous gulp at one of them; then, keeping the bottle in his hand, glares belligerently at the* Owner, *who hastens to acquiesce in this robbery by saying:*)

All righto, Yank. Keep it and have another.

   (*Yank contemptuously turns his back on the crowd again. For a second there is an embarrassed silence. Then:*)

   VOICES: We must be passing the Hook.
She's beginning to roll to it.
Six days in hell—and then Southampton.
Py Yesus, I vish somepody take my first vatch for me!
Gittin' seasick, Square-head?
Drink up and forget it!
What's in your bottle?
Gin.
Dot's nigger trink.
Absinthe? It's doped. You'll go off your chump, Froggy!
Cochon!
Whiskey, that's the ticket!
Where's Paddy?
Going asleep.
Sing us that whiskey song, Paddy.

(They all turn to an old, wizened Irishman *who is dozing, very drunk, on the benches forward. His face is extremely monkey-like with all the sad, patient pathos of that animal in his small eyes)*

Singa da song, Caruso Pat!
He's getting old. The drink is too much for him.
He's too drunk.

PADDY: *(Blinking about him, starts to his feet resentfully, swaying, holding on to the edge of a bunk)* I'm never too drunk to sing. 'Tis only when I'm dead to the world I'd be wishful to sing at all. *(With a sort of sad contempt)* "Whiskey Johnny," ye want? A chanty, ye want? Now that's a queer wish from the ugly like of you, God help you. But no matther. *(He starts to sing in a thin, nasal, doleful tone)*
Oh, whiskey is the life of man!
   Whiskey! O Johnny! *(They all join in on this)*
Oh, whiskey is the life of man!
   Whiskey for my Johnny! *(Again chorus)*
Oh, whiskey drove my old man mad!
   Whiskey! O Johnny!
Oh, whiskey drove my old man mad!
   Whiskey for my Johnny!

YANK: *(Again turning around scornfully)* Aw hell! Nix on dat old sailing ship stuff! All dat bull's dead, see? And you're dead, too, yuh damned old Harp, on'y yuh don't know it. Take it easy, see? Give us a rest. Nix on de loud noise. *(With a cynical grin)* Can't youse see I'm tryin' to t'ink?

ALL: *(Repeating the word after him, as one, with the same cynical amused mockery)* Think!

(The chorused word has a brazen metallic quality as if their throats were phonograph horns. It is followed by a general uproar of hard, barking laughter)

VOICES: Don't be cracking your head wit ut. Yank.
You gat headache, py yingo!
One thing about it—it rhymes with drink!
Ha, ha, ha!
Drink, don't think!
Drink, don't think!
Drink, don't think!

(A whole chorus of voices has taken up this refrain, stamping on the floor, pounding on the benches with fists)

YANK: *(Taking a gulp from his bottle—good-naturedly)* Aw right. Can de noise. I got yuh de foist time.

(The uproar subsides. A very drunken sentimental Tenor *begins to sing)*

   "Far away in Canada,
      Far across the sea,
   There's a lass who fondly waits
      Making a home for me—"
YANK: *(Fiercely contemptuous)* Shut up, yuh lousy boob! Where d'yuh

get dat tripe? Home? Home, hell! I'll make a home for yuh! I'll knock yuh
dead. Home! T'hell wit home! Where d'yuh get dat tripe? Dis is home, see?
What d'yuh want wit home? (*Proudly*) I runned away from mine when I was
a kid. On'y too glad to beat it, dat was me. Home was lickings for me, dat's
all. But yuh can bet your shoit no one ain't never licked me since! Wanter
try it, any of youse? Huh! I guess not. (*In a more placated but still contemptuous tone*) Goils waitin' for yuh, huh? Aw, hell! Dat's all tripe. Dey don't
wait for no one. Dey'd double-cross yuh for a nickel. Dey're all tarts, get me?
Treat 'em rough, dat's me. To hell wit 'em. Tarts, dat's what, de whole bunch
of 'em.

LONG: (*Very drunk, jumps on a bench excitedly, gesticulating with a
bottle in his hand*) Listen 'ere, Comrades! Yank 'ere, is right. 'E says this 'ere
stinkin' ship is our 'ome. And 'e says as 'ome is 'ell. And 'e's right! This is
'ell. We lives in 'ell, Comrades—and right enough we'll die in it. (*Raging*)
And who's ter blame, I arsks yer. We ain't. We wasn't born this rotten way.
All men is born free and ekal. That's in the bleedin' Bible, maties. But what
d'they care for the Bible—them lazy, bloated swine what travels first cabin?
Them's the ones. They dragged us down 'til we're on'y wage slaves in the
bowels of a bloody ship, sweatin', burnin' up, eatin' coal dust! Hit's them's
ter blame—the damned Capitalist clarss!

(*There had been a gradual murmur of contemptuous resentment rising
among the* Men *until now he is interrupted by a storm of cat-calls, hisses,
boos, hard laughter*)

VOICES: Turn it off!
Shut up!
Sit down!
Closa da face!
Tamn fool! (*Etc.*)

YANK: (*Standing up and glaring at* Long) Sit down before I knock yuh
down! (Long *makes haste to efface himself.* Yank *goes on contemptuously*)
De Bible, huh? De Cap'tlist class, huh? Aw, nix on dat Salvation Army-
Socialist bull. Git a soapbox! Hire a hall! Come and be saved, huh? Jerk us
to Jesus, huh? Aw g'wan! I've listened to lots of guys like you, see? Yuh're
all wrong. Wanter know what I t'ink? Yuh ain't no good for no one. Yuh're
de bunk. Yuh ain't got no noive, get me? Yuh're yellow, dat's what. Yellow,
dat's you. Say! What's dem slobs in de foist cabin got to do wit us? We're
better men dan dey are, ain't we? Sure! One of us guys could clean up de
whole mob wit one mit. Put one of 'em down here for one watch in de
stokehole, what'd happen? Dey'd carry him off on a stretcher. Dem boids
don't amount to nothin'. Dey're just baggage. Who makes dis old tub run?
Ain't it us guys? Well den, we belong, don't we? We belong and dey don't.
Dat's all. (*A loud chorus of approval.* Yank *goes on.*) As for dis bein' hell—
aw nuts! Yuh lost your noive, dat's what. Dis is a man's job, bet me? It
belongs. It runs dis tub. No stiffs need apply. But yuh're a stiff, see? Yuh're
yellow, dat's you.

VOICES: (*With a great hard pride in them*) Righto!
A man's job!
Talk is cheap, Long.
He never could hold up his end.
Divil take him!
Yank's right. We make it go.

Py Gott, Yank say right ting!
We don't need no one cryin' over us.
Makin' speeches.
Throw him out!
Yellow!
Chuck him overboard!
I'll break his jaw for him!

(*They crowd around* Long *threateningly*)

YANK: (*Half good-natured again—contemptuously*) Aw, take it easy.
Leave him alone. He ain't woith a punch. Drink up. Here's how, whoever
owns dis.

(*He takes a long swallow from his bottle. All drink with him. In a flash
all is hilarious amiability again, back-slapping, loud talk, etc.*)

PADDY: (*Who has been sitting in a blinking, melancholy daze—suddenly
cries out in a voice full of old sorrow*) We belong to this, you're saying? We
make the ship to go, you're saying? Yerra then, that Almighty God have pity
on us! (*His voice runs into the wail of a keen; he rocks back and forth on his
bench. The men stare at him, startled and impressed in spite of themselves*)
Oh, to be back in the fine days of my youth, ochone! Oh, there was fine
beautiful ships them days—clippers wid tall masts touching the sky—fine
strong men in them—men that was sons of the sea as if 'twas the mother that
bore them. Oh, the clean skins of them, and the clear eyes, the straight backs
and full chests of them! Brave men they was, and bold men surely! We'd be
sailing out, bound down round the Horn maybe. We'd be making sail in the
dawn, with a fair breeze, singing a chanty song wid no care to it. And astern
the land would be sinking low and dying out, but we'd give it no heed but
a laugh, and never a look behind. For the day that was, was enough, for we
was free men—and I'm thinking 'tis only slaves do be giving heed to the day
that's gone or the day to come—until they're old like me. (*With a sort of
religious exaltation*) Oh, to be scudding south again wid the power of the
Trade Winds driving her on steady through the nights and the days! Full sail
on her! Nights and days! Nights when the foam of the wake would be
flaming wid fire, when the sky'd be blazing and winking wid stars. Or the
full of the moon maybe. Then you'd see her driving through the gray night,
her sails stretching aloft all silver and white, not a sound on the deck, the
lot of us dreaming dreams, till you'd believe 'twas no real ship at all you was
on but a ghost ship like the *Flying Dutchman* they says does be roaming the
seas forevermore widout touching a port. And there was the days, too. A
warm sun on the clean decks. Sun warming the blood of you, and wind over
the miles of shiny green ocean like strong drink to your lungs. Work—aye,
hard work—but who'd mind that at all? Sure, you worked under the sky and
'twas work wid skill and daring to it. And wid the day done, in the dog
watch, smoking me pipe at ease, the lookout would be raising land maybe,
and we'd see the mountains of South Americy wid the red fire of the setting
sun painting their white tops and the clouds floating by them! (*His tone of
exaltation ceases. He goes on mournfully*) Yerra, what's the use of talking?
'Tis a dead man's whisper. (*To* Yank *resentfully*) 'Twas them days a ship was
part of the sea, and a man was part of a ship, and the sea joined all together
and made it one. (*Scornfully*) Is it one wid this you'd be, Yank—black smoke

from the funnels smudging the sea, smudging the decks—the bloody engines
pounding and throbbing and shaking—wid divil a sight of sun or a breath
of clean air—choking our lungs wid coal dust—breaking our backs and hearts
in the hell of the stokehole—feeding the bloody furnace—feeding our lives
along wid the coal, I'm thinking—caged in by steel from a sight of the sky
like bloody apes in the zoo! (*With a harsh laugh*) Ho-ho, divil mend you!
Is it to belong to that you're wishing? Is it a flesh and blood wheel of the
engines you'd be?

YANK: (*Who has been listening with a contemptuous sneer, barks out the
answer*) Sure ting! Dat's me. What about it?

PADDY: (*As if to himself—with great sorrow:*) Me time is past due. That
a great wave wid sun in the heart of it may sweep me over the side sometime
I'd be dreaming of the days that's gone!

YANK: Aw, yuh crazy Mick! (*He springs to his feet and advances on*
Paddy *threateningly—then stops, fighting some queer struggle within himself—lets his hands fall to his sides—contemptuously:*) Aw, take it easy.
Yuh're aw right, at dat. Yuh're bugs, dat's all—nutty as a cuckoo. All dat tripe
yuh been pullin'—Aw, dat's all right. On'y it's dead, get me? Yuh don't
belong no more, see. Yuh don't get de stuff. Yuh're too old. (*Disgustedly*)
But aw say, come up for air onct in a while, can't yuh? See what's happened
since yuh croaked. (*He suddenly bursts forth vehemently, growing more and
more excited*) Say! Sure! Sure I meant it! What de hell—Say, lemme talk!
Hey! Hey, you old Harp! Hey, youse guys! Say, listen to me—wait a moment
—I gotter talk, see? I belong and he don't. He's dead but I'm livin'. Listen
to me! Sure I'm part of de engines! Why de hell not! Dey move, don't they?
Dey're speed, ain't dey? Dey smash trou, don't dey? Twenty-five knots a
hour! Dat's goin' some! Dat's new stuff! Dat belongs! But him, he's too old.
He gets dizzy. Say, listen. All dat crazy tripe about nights and days; all dat
crazy tripe about stars and moons; all dat crazy tripe about suns and winds,
fresh air and de rest of it—Aw hell, dat's all a dope dream! Hittin' de pipe
of de past, dat's what he's doin'. He's old and don't belong no more. But me,
I'm young! I'm in de pink! I move wit it! It, get me! I mean de ting dat's de
guts of all dis. It ploughs trou all de tripe he's been sayin'. It blows dat up!
It knocks dat dead! It slams dat offen de face of de oith! It, get me! De engines
and de coal and de smoke and all de rest of it! He can't breathe and swallow
coal dust, but I kin, see? Dat's fresh air for me! Dat's food for me! I'm new,
get me? Hell in de stokehole? Sure! It takes a man to work in hell. Hell, sure,
dat's my fav'rite climate. I eat it up! I git fat on it! It's me makes it hot! It's
me makes it roar! It's me makes it move! Sure, on'y for me everything stops.
It all goes dead, get me? De noise and smoke and all de engines movin' de
woild, dey stop. Dere ain't nothin' no more! Dat's what I'm sayin'. Everyting
else dat makes de woild move, somep'n makes it move. It can't move witout
somep'n else, see? Den yuh get down to me. I'm at de bottom, get me! Dere
ain't nothin' foither. I'm de end! I'm de start! I start somep'n and de woild
moves! It—dat's me!—de new dat's moiderin' de old! I'm de ting in coal dat
makes it boin; I'm steam and oil for de engines; I'm de ting in noise dat makes
yuh hear it; I'm smoke and express trains and steamers and factory whistles;
I'm de ting in gold dat makes it money! And I'm what makes iron into steel!
Steel, dat stands for de whole ting! And I'm steel—steel—steel! I'm de muscles in steel, de punch behind it! (*As he says this he pounds with his fist
against the steel bunks. All the* Men, *roused to a pitch of frenzied self-
glorification by his speech, do likewise. There is a deafening metallic roar,
through which* Yank's *voice can be heard bellowing:*) Slaves, hell! We run
de whole woiks. All de rich guys dat tink dey're somep'n, dey ain't nothin'!

Dey don't belong. But us guys, we're in de move, we're at de bottom, de whole ting is us! (Paddy *from the start of* Yank's *speech has been taking one gulp after another from his bottle, at first frightenedly, as if he were afraid to listen, then desperately, as if to drown his senses, but finally has achieved complete indifferent, even amused, drunkeness.* Yank *sees his lips moving. He quells the uproar with a shout*) Hey, youse guys, take it easy! Wait a moment! De nutty Harp is saying somep'n.

PADDY: (*Is heard now—throws his head back with a mocking burst of laughter*) Ho-ho-ho-ho-ho—

YANK: (*Drawing back his fist, with a snarl*) Aw! Look out who yuh're givin' the bark!

PADDY: (*Begins to sing the "Miller of Dee" with enormous good nature*)
    "I care for nobody, no, not I,
    And nobody cares for me."

YANK: (*Good-natured himself in a flash, interrupts* Paddy *with a slap on the bare back like a report*) Dat's de stuff! Now yuh're gettin' wise to somep'n. Care for nobody, dat's de dope! To hell wit 'em all! And nix on nobody else carin'. I kin care for myself, get me! (*Eight bells sound, muffled, vibrating through the steel walls as if some enormous brazen gong were imbedded in the heart of the ship. All the men jump up mechanically, file through the door silently, close upon each other's heels in what is very like a prisoners' lock-step.* Yank *slaps* Paddy *on the back*) Our watch, yuh old Harp! (*Mockingly*) Come on down in hell. Eat up de coal dust. Drink in de heat. It's it, see! Act like yuh liked it, yuh better—or croak yuhself.

PADDY: (*With jovial defiance*) To the divil wid it! I'll not report this watch. Let thim log me and be damned. I'm no slave the like of you. I'll be settin' here at me ease, and drinking, and thinking, and dreaming dreams.

YANK: (*Contemptuously*) Tinkin' and dreamin', what'll that get yuh? What's tinkin' got to do wit it? We move, don't we? Speed, ain't it? Fog, dat's all you stand for. But we drive trou dat, don't we? We split dat up and smash trou—twenty-five knots a hour! (*Turns his back on* Paddy *scornfully*) Aw, yuh make me sick! Yuh don't belong!

(*He strides out the door in rear.* Paddy *hums to himself, blinking drowsily.*)

CURTAIN

SCENE II: *Two days out. A section of the promenade deck.* Mildred Douglas *and her* Aunt *are discovered reclining in deck chairs. The former is a girl of twenty, slender, delicate, with a pale, pretty face marred by a self-conscious expression of disdainful superiority. She looks fretful, nervous, and discontented, bored by her own anemia. Her* Aunt *is a pompous and proud—and fat—old lady. She is a type even to the point of a double chin and lorgnettes. She is dressed pretentiously, as if afraid her face alone would never indicate her position in life.* Mildred *is dressed all in white.*

The impression to be conveyed by this scene is one of the beautiful, vivid life of the sea all about—sunshine on the deck in a great flood, the fresh sea wind blowing across it. In the midst of this, these two incongruous, artificial figures, inert and disharmonious, the elder like a gray lump of dough touched up with rouge, the younger looking as if the vitality of her stock had been sapped before she was conceived, so that she is the expression not of its life energy but merely of the artificialities that energy had won for itself in the spending.

MILDRED: (*Looking up with affected dreaminess*) How the black smoke swirls back against the sky! Is it not beautiful?

AUNT: (*Without looking up*) I dislike smoke of any kind.

MILDRED: My great-grandmother smoked a pipe—a clay pipe.

AUNT: (*Ruffling*) Vulgar!

MILDRED: She was too distant a relative to be vulgar. Time mellows pipes.

AUNT: (*Pretending boredom but irritated*) Did the sociology you took up at college teach you that—to play the ghoul on every possible occasion, excavating old bones? Why not let your great-grandmother rest in her grave?

MILDRED: (*Dreamily*) With her pipe beside her—puffing in Paradise.

AUNT: (*With spite*) Yes, you are a natural born ghoul. You are even getting to look like one, my dear.

MILDRED: (*In a passionless tone*) I detest you, Aunt. (*Looking at her critically*) Do you know what you remind me of? Of a cold pork pudding against a background of linoleum tablecloth in the kitchen of a—but the possibilities are wearisome. (*She closes her eyes*)

AUNT: (*With a bitter laugh*) Merci for your candor. But since I am and must be your chaperon—in appearance, at least—let us patch up some sort of armed truce. For my part you are quite free to indulge any pose of eccentricity that beguiles you—as long as you observe the amenities—

MILDRED: (*Drawling*) The inanities?

AUNT: (*Going on as if she hadn't heard*) After exhausting the morbid thrills of social service work on New York's East Side—how they must have hated you, by the way, the poor that you made so much poorer in their own eyes!—you are now bent on making your slumming international. Well, I hope Whitechapel will provide the needed nerve tonic. Do not ask me to chaperon you there, however. I told your father I would not. I loathe deformity. We will hire an army of detectives and you may investigate everything—they allow you to see.

MILDRED: (*Protesting with a trace of genuine earnestness*) Please do not mock at my attempts to discover how the other half lives. Give me credit for some sort of groping sincerity in that at least. I would like to help them. I would like to be some use in the world. Is it my fault I don't know how? I would like to be sincere, to touch life somewhere. (*With weary bitterness*) But I'm afraid I have neither the vitality nor integrity. All that was burnt out in our stock before I was born. Grandfather's blast furnaces, flaming to the sky, melting steel, making millions—then father keeping those home fires burning, making more millions—and little me at the tail-end of it all. I'm a waste product in the Bessemer process—like the millions. Or rather, I inherit the acquired trait of the by-product, wealth, but none of the energy, none of the strength of the steel that made it. I am sired by gold and dammed by it, as they say at the race track—damned in more ways than one. (*She laughs mirthlessly*)

AUNT: (*Unimpressed—superciliously*) You seem to be going in for sincerity today. It isn't becoming to you, really—except as an obvious pose. Be as artificial as you are, I advise. There's a sort of sincerity in that, you know. And, after all, you must confess you like that better.

MILDRED: (*Again affected and bored*) Yes, I suppose I do. Pardon me for my outburst. When a leopard complains of its spots, it must sound rather grotesque. (*In a mocking tone*) Purr, little leopard. Purr, scratch, tear, kill, gorge yourself and be happy—only stay in the jungle where your spots are camouflage. In a cage they make you conspicuous.

AUNT: I don't know what you are talking about.

MILDRED: It would be rude to talk about anything to you. Let's just talk.

(*She looks at her wrist watch.*) Well, thank goodness, it's about time for them to come for me. That ought to give me a new thrill, Aunt.

AUNT: (*Affectedly troubled*) You don't mean to say you're really going? The dirt—the heat must be frightful—

MILDRED: Grandfather started as a puddler. I should have inherited an immunity to heat that would make a salamander shiver. It will be fun to put it to the test.

AUNT: But don't you have to have the captain's—or someone's—permission to visit the stokehole?

MILDRED: (*With a triumphant smile*) I have it—both his and the chief engineer's. Oh, they didn't want to at first, in spite of my social service credentials. They didn't seem a bit anxious that I should investigate how the other half lives and works on a ship. So I had to tell them that my father, the president of Nazareth Steel, chairman of the board of directors of this line, had told me it would be all right.

AUNT: He didn't.

MILDRED: How naïve age makes one! But I said he did, Aunt. I even said he had given me a letter to them—which I had lost. And they were afraid to take the chance that I might be lying. (*Excitedly*) So it's ho! for the stokehole. The second engineer is to escort me. (*Looking at her watch again*) It's time. And here he comes, I think.

(*The* Second Engineer *enters. He is a husky, fine-looking man of thirty-five or so. He stops before the two and tips his cap, visibly embarrassed and ill-at-ease.*)

SECOND ENGINEER: Miss Douglas?

MILDRED: Yes. (*Throwing off her rugs and getting to her feet*) Are we all ready to start?

SECOND ENGINEER: In just a second, ma'am. I'm waiting for the Fourth. He's coming along.

MILDRED: (*With a scornful smile*) You don't care to shoulder this responsibility alone, is that it?

SECOND ENGINEER: (*Forcing a smile*) Two are better than one. (*Disturbed by her eyes, glances out to sea—blurts out:*) A fine day we're having.

MILDRED: Is it?

SECOND ENGINEER: A nice warm breeze—

MILDRED: It feels cold to me.

SECOND ENGINEER: But it's hot enough in the sun—

MILDRED: Not hot enough for me. I don't like Nature. I was never athletic.

SECOND ENGINEER: (*Forcing a smile*) Well, you'll find it hot enough where you're going.

MILDRED: Do you mean hell?

SECOND ENGINEER: (*Flabbergasted, decides to laugh*) Ho-ho! No, I mean the stokehole.

MILDRED: My grandfather was a puddler. He played with boiling steel.

SECOND ENGINEER: (*All at sea—uneasily*) Is that so? Hum, you'll excuse me, ma'am, but are you intending to wear that dress?

MILDRED: Why not?

SECOND ENGINEER: You'll likely rub against oil and dirt. It can't be helped.

MILDRED: It doesn't matter. I have lots of white dresses.

SECOND ENGINEER: I have an old coat you might throw over—

MILDRED: I have fifty dresses like this. I will throw this one into the sea when I come back. That ought to wash it clean, don't you think?

SECOND ENGINEER: (*Doggedly*) There's ladders to climb down that are none too clean—and dark alleyways—

MILDRED: I will wear this very dress and none other.

SECOND ENGINEER: No offense meant. It's none of my business. I was only warning you—

MILDRED: Warning? That sounds thrilling.

SECOND ENGINEER: (*Looking down the deck—with a sigh of relief*) There's the Fourth now. He's waiting for us. If you'll come—

MILDRED: Go on. I'll follow you. (*He goes. Mildred turns a mocking smile on her* Aunt) An oaf—but a handsome, virile oaf.

AUNT: (*Scornfully*) Poser!

MILDRED: Take care. He said there were dark alleyways—

AUNT: (*In the same tone*) Poser!

MILDRED: (*Biting her lips angrily*) You are right. But would that my millions were not so anemically chaste!

AUNT: Yes, for a fresh pose I have no doubt you would drag the name of Douglas in the gutter!

MILDRED: From which it sprang. Good-by, Aunt. Don't pray too hard that I may fall into the fiery furnace.

AUNT: Poser!

MILDRED: (*Viciously*) Old hag!

(*She slaps her* Aunt *insultingly across the face and walks off, laughing gaily*)

AUNT: (*Screams after her:*) I said poser!

CURTAIN

SCENE III: *The stokehole. In the rear, the dimly outlined bulks of the furnaces and boilers. High overhead one hanging electric bulb sheds just enough light through the murky air laden with coal dust to pile up masses of shadows everywhere. A line of men, stripped to the waist, is before the furnace doors. They bend over, looking neither to right nor left, handling their shovels as if they were part of their bodies, with a strange, awkward, swinging rhythm. They use the shovels to throw open the furnace doors. Then from these fiery round holes in the black a flood of terrific light and heat pours full upon the men who are outlined in silhouette in the crouching, inhuman attitudes of chained gorillas. The men shovel with a rhythmic motion, swinging as on a pivot from the coal which lies in heaps on the floor behind to hurl it into the flaming mouths before them. There is a tumult of noise—the brazen clang of the furnace doors as they are flung open or slammed shut, the grating, teeth-gritting grind of steel against steel, and of crunching coal. This clash of sounds stuns one's ears with its rending dissonance. But there is order in it, rhythm, a mechanically regulated recurrence, a tempo. And rising above all making the air hum with the quiver of liberated energy, the roar of leaping flames in the furnaces, the monotonous throbbing beat of the engines.*

As the curtain rises, the furnace doors are shut. The Men *are taking a breathing spell. One or two are arranging the coal behind them, pulling it into more accessible heaps. The others can be dimly made out leaning on their shovels in relaxed attitudes of exhaustion.*

PADDY: (*From somewhere in the line—plaintively*) Yerra, will this divil's own watch nivir end? Me back is broke. I'm destroyed entirely.

YANK: (*From the center of the line—with exuberant scorn*) Aw, yuh make me sick! Lie down and croak, why don't yuh? Always beefin', dat's you! Say, dis is a cinch! Dis was made for me! It's my meat, get me! (*A whistle is blown—a thin, shrill note from somewhere overhead in the darkness. Yank curses without resentment*) Dere's de damn engineer crackin' de whip. He tinks we're loafin'.

PADDY: (*Vindictively*) God stiffen him!

YANK: (*In an exultant tone of command*) Come on, youse guys! Git into de game! She's gittin' hungry! Pile some grub in her. Trow it into her belly! Come on now, all of youse! Open her up!

(*At this last all the* Men, *who have followed his movements of getting into position, throw open their furnace doors with a deafening clang. The fiery light floods over their shoulders as they bend round for the coal. Rivulets of sooty sweat have traced maps on their backs. The enlarged muscles form bunches of high light and shadow*)

YANK: (*Chanting a count as he shovels without seeming effort*) One-two-three—(*His voice rising exultantly in the joy of battle*) Dat's de stuff! Let her have it! All togedder now! Sling it into her! Let her ride! Shoot de piece now! Call de toin on her! Drive her into it! Feel her move! Watch her smoke! Speed, dat's her middle name! Give her coal, youse guys! Coal, dat's her booze! Drink it up, baby! Let's see yuh sprint! Dig in and gain a lap! Dere she go-o-es.

(*This last in the chanting formula of the gallery gods at the six-day bike race. He slams his furnace door shut. The others do likewise with as much unison as their wearied bodies will permit. The effect is of one fiery eye after another being blotted out with a series of accompanying bangs*)

PADDY: (*Groaning*) Me back is broke. I'm bate out—bate—

(*There is a pause. Then the inexorable whistle sounds again from the dim regions above the electric light. There is a growl of cursing rage from all sides*)

YANK: (*Shaking his fist upward—contemptuously*) Take it easy dere, you! Who d'yuh tink's runnin' dis game, me or you? When I get ready, we move. Not before! When I git ready, get me!

VOICES: (*Approvingly*) That's the stuff! Yank tal him, py golly!
Yank ain't affeerd.
Goot poy, Yank!
Give him hell!
Tell 'im 'e's a bloody swine!
Bloody slave-driver!

YANK: (*Contemptuously*) He ain't got no noive. He's yellow, get me? All de engineers is yellow. Dey got streaks a mile wide. Aw, to hell wit him! Let's move, youse guys. We had a rest. Come on, she needs it! Give her pep! It ain't for him. Him and his whistle, dey don't belong. But we belong, see! We gotter feed de baby! Come on!

(He turns and flings his furnace door open. They all follow his lead. At this instant the Second and Fourth Engineers enter from the darkness on the left with Mildred *between them. She starts, turns paler, her pose is crumbling, she shivers with fright in spite of the blazing heat, but forces herself to leave the* Engineers *and take a few steps nearer the men. She is right behind* Yank. *All this happens quickly while the men have their backs turned)*

YANK: Come on, youse guys!

(He is turning to get coal when the whistle sounds again in a peremptory, irritating note. This drives Yank *into a sudden fury. While the other* Men *have turned full around and stopped dumbfounded by the spectacle of* Mildred *standing there in her white dress,* Yank *does not turn far enough to see her. Besides, his head is thrown back, he blinks upward through the murk trying to find the owner of the whistle, he brandishes his shovel murderously over his head in one hand, pounding on his chest, gorilla-like, with the other, shouting)*

YANK: Toin off dat whistle! Come down outa dere, yuh yellow, brass-buttoned, Belfast bum, yuh! Come down and I'll knock yer brains out! Yuh lousy, stinkin', yellow mut of a Catholic-moiderin' bastard! Come down and I'll moider yuh! Pullin' dat whistle on me, huh? I'll show yuh! I'll crash yer skull in! I'll drive yer teet' down yer troat! I'll slam yer nose trou de back of yer head! I'll cut yer guts out for a nickel, yuh lousy boob, yuh dirty, crummy, muck-eatin' son of a—

(Suddenly he becomes conscious of all the other Men *staring at something directly behind his back. He whirls defensively with a snarling, murderous growl, crouching to spring, his lips drawn back over his teeth, his small eyes gleaming ferociously. He sees* Mildred, *like a white apparition in the full light from the open furnace doors. He glares into her eyes, turned to stone. As for her, during his speech she has listened, paralyzed with horror, terror, her whole personality crushed, beaten in, collapsed, by the terrific impact of this unknown, abysmal brutality, naked and shameless. As she looks at his gorilla face, as his eyes bore into hers, she utters a low, choking cry and shrinks away from him, putting both hands up before her eyes to shut out the sight of his face, to protect her own. This startles* Yank *to a reaction. His mouth falls open, his eyes grow bewildered)*

MILDRED: *(About to faint—to the* Engineers, *who now have her one by each arm—whimperingly)* Take me away! Oh, the filthy beast!

(She faints. They carry her quickly back, disappearing in the darkness at the left, rear. An iron door clangs shut. Rage and bewildered fury rush back on Yank. *He feels himself insulted in some unknown fashion in the very heart of his pride. He roars)*

YANK: God damn yuh!

(And hurls his shovel after them at the door which has just closed. It hits the steel bulkhead with a clang and falls clattering on the steel floor. From overhead the whistle sounds again in a long, angry, insistent command)

CURTAIN

SCENE IV: *The firemen's forecastle.* Yank's *watch has just come off duty and* had dinner. *Their faces and bodies shine from a soap and water scrubbing but around their eyes, where a hasty dousing does not touch, the coal dust sticks like black make-up, giving them a queer, sinister expression.*

Yank *has not washed either face or body. He stands out in contrast to them, a blackened, brooding figure. He is seated forward on a bench in the exact attitude of Rodin's "The Thinker." The others, most of them smoking pipes, are staring at* Yank *half-apprehensively, as if fearing an outburst; half-amusedly, as if they saw a joke somewhere that tickled them.*

VOICES: He ain't ate nothin'.
Py golly, a fallar gat to gat grub in him.
Divil a lie.
Yank feeda da fire, no feeda da face.
Ha-ha.
He ain't even washed hisself.
He's forgot.
Hey, Yank, you forgot to wash.
   YANK: (*Sullenly*) Forgot nothin'! To hell wit washin'.
   VOICES: It'll stick to you.
It'll get under your skin.
Give yer the bleedin' itch, that's wot.
It makes spots on you—like a leopard.
Like a piebald nigger, you mean.
Better wash up, Yank.
You sleep better.
Wash up, Yank.
Wash up! Wash up!
   YANK: (*Resentfully*) Aw say, youse guys. Lemme alone. Can't youse see I'm tryin' to tink?
   ALL: (*Repeating the word after him, as one, with cynical mockery*) Think!

(*The word has a brazen, metallic quality as if their throats were phonograph horns. It is followed by a chorus of hard, barking laughter*)

   YANK: (*Springing to his feet and glaring at them belligerently*) Yes, tink! Tink, dat's what I said! What about it?

(*They are silent, puzzled by his sudden resentment at what used to be one of his jokes.* Yank *sits down again in the same attitude of "The Thinker"*)

   VOICES: Leave him alone.
He's got a grouch on.
Why wouldn't he?
   PADDY: (*With a wink at the others*) Sure I know what's the matter. 'Tis aisy to see. He's fallen in love, I'm telling you.
   ALL: (*Repeating the word after him, as one, with cynical mockery*) Love!

(*The word has a brazen metallic quality as if their throats were phonograph horns. It is followed by a chorus of hard, barking laughter*)

YANK: (*With a contemptuous snort*) Love, hell! Hate, dat's what. I've fallen in hate, get me?

PADDY: (*Philosophically*) 'Twould take a wise man to tell one from the other. (*With a bitter, ironical scorn, increasing as he goes on*) But I'm telling you it's love that's in it. Sure what else but love for us poor bastes in the stokehole would be bringing a fine lady, dressed like a white quane, down a mile of ladders and steps to be havin' a look at us?

(*A growl of anger goes up from all sides*)

LONG: (*Jumping on a bench—hectically*) Hinsultin' us! Hinsultin' us, the bloody cow! And them bloody engineers! What right 'as they got to be exhibitin' us 's if we was bleedin' monkeys in a menagerie? Did we sign for hinsults to our dignity as 'onest workers? Is that in the ship's articles? You kin bloody well bet it ain't! But I knows why they done it. I arsked a deck steward 'oo she was and 'e told me. 'Er old man's a bleedin' millionaire, a bloody Capitalist! 'E's got enuf bloody gold to sink this bleedin' ship! 'E makes arf the bloody steel in the world! 'E owns this bloody boat! And you and me, Comrades, we're 'is slaves! And the skipper and mates and engineers, they're 'is slaves! And she's 'is bloody daughter and we're all 'er slaves, too! And she gives 'er orders as 'ow she wants to see the bloody animals below decks and down they takes 'er!

(*There is a roar of rage from all sides*)

YANK: (*Blinking at him bewilderedly*) Say! Wait a moment! Is all dat straight goods?

LONG: Straight as string! The bleedin' steward as waits on 'em, 'e told me about 'er. And what're we goin' ter do, I arsks yer? 'Ave we got ter swaller 'er hinsults like dogs? It ain't in the ship's articles. I tell yer we got a case. We kin go to law—

YANK: (*With abysmal contempt*) Hell! Law!

ALL: (*Repeating the word after him, as one, with cynical mockery*) Law!

(*The word has a brazen metallic quality as if their throats were phonograph horns. It is followed by a chorus of hard, barking laughter*)

LONG: (*Feeling the ground slipping from under his feet—desperately*) As voters and citizens we kin force the bloody governments—

YANK: (*With abysmal contempt*) Hell! Governments!

All: (*Repeating the word after him, as one, with cynical mockery*) Governments!

(*The word has a brazen metallic quality as if their throats were phonograph horns. It is followed by a chorus of hard, barking laughter*)

LONG: (*Hysterically*) We're free and equal in the sight of God—

YANK: (*With abysmal contempt*) Hell! God!

ALL: (*Repeating the word after him, as one, with cynical mockery*) God!

(*The word has a brazen metallic quality as if their throats were phonograph horns. It is followed by a chorus of hard, barking laughter*)

YANK: (*Witheringly*) Aw, join de Salvation Army!
ALL: Sit down! Shut up! Damn fool! Sea-lawyer!

(*Long slinks back out of sight*)

PADDY: (*Continuing the trend of his thoughts as if he had never been interrupted—bitterly*) And there she was standing behind us, and the Second pointing at us like a man you'd hear in a circus would be saying: In this cage is a queerer kind of baboon than ever you'd find in darkest Africy. We roast them in their own sweat—and be damned if you won't hear some of thim saying they like it! (*He glances scornfully at* Yank)
YANK: (*With a bewildered uncertain growl*) Aw!
PADDY: And there was Yank roarin' curses and turning round wid his shovel to brain her—and she looked at him, and him at her—
YANK: (*Slowly*) She was all white. I tought she was a ghost. Sure.
PADDY: (*With heavy, biting sarcasm*) 'Twas love at first sight, divil a doubt of it! If you'd seen the endearin' look on her pale mug when she shriveled away with her hands over her eyes to shut out the sight of him! Sure, 'twas as if she'd seen a great hairy ape escaped from the Zoo!
YANK: (*Stung—with a growl of rage*) Aw!
PADDY: And the loving way Yank heaved his shovel at the skull of her, only she was out the door! (*A grin breaking over his face*) 'Twas touching, I'm telling you! It put the touch of home, swate home in the stokehole.

(*There is a roar of laughter from all*)

YANK: (*Glaring at* Paddy *menacingly*) Aw, choke dat off, see!
Paddy: (*Not heeding him—to the others*) And her grabbin' at the Second's arm for protection. (*With a grotesque imitation of a woman's voice*) Kiss me, Engineer dear, for it's dark down here and me old man's in Wall Street making money; Hug me tight, darlin', for I'm afeerd in the dark and me mother's on deck makin' eyes at the skipper!

(*Another roar of laughter*)

YANK: (*Threateningly*) Say! What yuh tryin' to do, kid me, yuh old Harp?
PADDY: Divil a bit! Ain't I wishin' myself you'd brained her?
YANK: (*Fiercely*) I'll brain her! I'll brain her yet, wait 'n' see! (*Coming over to* Paddy—*slowly*) Say, is dat what she called me—a hairy ape?
PADDY: She looked it at you if she didn't say the word itself.
YANK: (*Grinning horribly*) Hairy ape, huh? Sure! Dat's de way she looked at me, aw right. Hairy ape! So dat's me, huh! (*Bursting into rage—as if she were still in front of him*) Yuh skinny tart! Yuh white-faced bum, yuh! I'll show yuh who's a ape! (*Turning to the others, bewilderment seizing him again*) Say, youse guys. I was bawlin' him out for pullin' de whistle on us. You heard me. And den I seen youse lookin' at somep'n and I tought he'd sneaked down to come up in back of me, and I hopped round to knock him dead wit de shovel. And dere she was wit de light on her! Christ, yuh coulda pushed me over wit a finger! I was scared, get me? Sure! I tought she was a ghost, see? She was all in white like dey wrap around stiffs. You seen her. Kin yuh blame me? She didn't belong, dat's what. And den when I come to and seen it was a real skoit and seen de way she was lookin' at me—like Paddy said—Christ, I was sore, get me? I don't stand for dat stuff from

nobody. And I flung de shovel—on'y she'd beat it. (*Furiously*) I wished it'd banged her! I wished it'd knocked her block off!

LONG: And be 'anged for murder or 'lectrocuted? She ain't bleedin' well worth it.

YANK: I don't give a damn what! I'd be square wit her, wouldn't I? Tink I wanter let her put somep'n over on me? Tink I'm goin' to let her git away wit dat stuff! Yuh don't know me! No one ain't never put nothin' over on me and got away wit it, see!—not dat kind of stuff—no guy and no skoit neither! I'll fix her! Maybe she'll come down again—

VOICE: No chance, Yank. You scared her out of a year's growth.

YANK: I scared her? Why de hell should I scare her? Who de hell is she? Ain't she de same as me? Hairy ape, huh? (*With his old confident bravado*) I'll show her I'm better'n her, if she on'y knew it. I belong and she don't, see! I move and she's dead! Twenty-five knots a hour, dat's me! Dat carries her but I make dat. She's on'y baggage. Sure! (*Again bewilderedly*) But, Christ, she was funny lookin'! Did yuh pipe her hands? White and skinny. Yuh could see de bones through 'em. And her mush, dat was dead white, too. And her eyes, dey was like dey'd seen a ghost. Me, dat was! Sure! Hairy ape! Ghost, huh? Look at dat arm! (*He extends his right arm, swelling out the great muscles*) I coulda took her wit dat, wit just my little finger even, and broke her in two. (*Again bewilderedly*) Say, who is dat skoit, huh? What is she? What's she come from? Who made her? Who give her de noive to look at me like dat? Dis ting's got my goat right. I don't get her. She's new to me. What does a skoit like her mean, huh? She don't belong, get me! I can't see her. (*With growing anger*) But one ting I'm wise to, aw right, aw right! Youse all kin bet your shoits I'll git even wit her. I'll show her if she tinks she— She grinds de organ and I'm on de string, huh? I'll fix her! Let her come down again and I'll fling her in de furnace! She'll move den! She won't shiver at nothin', den! Speed, dat'll be her! She'll belong den! (*He grins horribly*)

PADDY: She'll never come. She's had her bellyfull, I'm telling you. She'll be in bed now, I'm thinking, wid ten doctors and nurses feedin' her salts to clean the fear out of her.

YANK: (*Enraged*) Yuh tink I made her sick too, do yuh? Just lookin' at me, huh? Hairy ape, huh? (*In a frenzy of rage*) I'll fix her! I'll tell her where to git off! She'll git down on her knees and take it back or I'll bust de face offen her! (*Shaking one fist upward and beating on his chest with the other*) I'll find yuh! I'm comin', d'yuh hear? I'll fix yuh, God damn yuh! (*He makes a rush for the door*)

VOICES: Stop him!

He'll get shot!
He'll murder her!
Trip him up!
Hold him!
He's gone crazy!
Gott, he's strong!
Hold him down!
Look for a kick!
Pin his arms!

(*They have all piled on him and, after a fierce struggle, by sheer weight of numbers have borne him to the floor just inside the door*)

PADDY: (*Who has remained detached*) Kape him down till he's cooled off. (*Scornfully*) Yerra, Yank, you're a great fool. Is it payin' attention at all you are to the like of the skinny sow widout one drop of rale blood in her?

YANK: (*Frenziedly, from the bottom of the heap*) She done me doit! She done me doit, didn't she! I'll git square wit her! I'll get her some way! Git offen me, youse guys! Lemme up! I'll show her who's a ape!

CURTAIN

SCENE V: *Three weeks later. A corner of Fifth Avenue in the Fifties on a fine Sunday morning. A general atmosphere of clean, well-tidied, wide street; a flood of mellow, tempered sunshine; gentle, genteel breezes. In the rear, the show windows of two shops, a jewelry establishment on the corner, a furrier's next to it. Here the adornments of extreme wealth are tantalizingly displayed. The jeweler's window is gaudy with glittering diamonds, emeralds, rubies, pearls, etc., fashioned in ornate tiaras, crowns, necklaces, collars, etc. From each piece hangs an enormous tag from which a dollar sign and numerals in intermittent electric lights wink out the incredible prices. The same in the furrier's. Rich furs of all varieties hang there bathed in a downpour of artificial light. The general effect is of a background of magnificence cheapened and made grotesque by commercialism, a background in tawdry disharmony with the clear light and sunshine on the street itself.*

Up the side street Yank and Long come swaggering. Long is dressed in shore clothes, wears a black Windsor tie, cloth cap. Yank is in his dirty dungarees. A fireman's cap with black peak is cocked defiantly on the side of his head. He has not shaved for days and around his fierce, resentful eyes—as around those of Long to a lesser degree—the black smudge of coal dust still sticks like make-up. They hesitate and stand together at the corner, swaggering, looking about them with a forced, defiant contempt.

LONG: (*Indicating it all with an oratorical gesture*) Well, 'ere we are. Fif' Avenoo. This 'ere's their bleedin' private lane, as yer might say. (*Bitterly*) We're trespassers 'ere. Proletarians keep orf the grass!

YANK: (*Dully*) I don't see no grass, yuh boob. (*Staring at the sidewalk*) Clean, ain't it? Yuh could eat a fried egg offen it. The white wings got some job sweepin' dis up. (*Looking up and down the avenue—surlily*) Where's all de white-collar stiffs yuh said was here—and de skoits—her kind?

LONG: In church, blarst 'em! Arskin' Jesus to give 'em more money.

YANK: Choich, huh? I useter go to choich onct—sure—when I was a kid. Me old man and woman, dey made me. Dey never went demselves, dough. Always got too big a head on Sunday mornin', dat was dem. (*With a grin*) Dey was scrappers for fair, bot' of dem. On Satiday nights when dey bot' got a skinful dey could put up a bout oughter been staged at de Garden. When dey got trough dere wasn't a chair or table wit a leg under it. Or else dey bot' jumped on me for somep'n. Dat was where I loined to take punishment. (*With a grin and a swagger*) I'm a chip offen de old block, get me!

LONG: Did yer old man follow the sea?

YANK: Naw. Worked along shore. I runned away when me old lady croaked wit de tremens. I helped at truckin' and in de market. Den I shipped in de stokehole. Sure. Dat belongs. De rest was nothin'. (*Looking around him*) I ain't never seen dis before. De Brooklyn waterfront, dat was where I was dragged up. (*Taking a deep breath*) Dis ain't so bad at dat, huh?

LONG: Not bad? Well, we pays for it wiv our bloody sweat, if yer wants to know!

YANK: (*With sudden angry disgust*) Aw, hell! I don't see no one, see—

like her. All dis gives me a pain. It don't belong. Say, ain't dere a back room around dis dump? Let's go shoot a ball. All dis is too clean and quiet and dolled-up, get me? It gives me a pain.

LONG: Wait and yer'll bloody well see-

YANK: I don't wait for no one. I keep on de move. Say, what yuh drag me up here for, anyway? Tryin' to kid me, yuh simp, yuh?

LONG: Yer wants to get back at 'er, don't yer? That's what yer been sayin' every bloomin' hour since she hinsulted yer.

YANK: (Vehemently) Sure ting I do! Didn't I try to get even wit her in Southampton? Didn't I sneak on de deck and wait for her by de gangplank? I was goin' to spit in her pale mug, see! Sure, right in her pop-eyes! Dat woulda made me even, see! But no chanct. Dere was a whole army of plain-clothes bulls around. Dey spotted me and gimme de bum's rush. I never seen her. But I'll git square wit her yet, you watch! (Furiously) De lousy tart! She tinks she kin get away wit moider—but not wit me! I'll fix her! I'll tink of a way!

LONG: (As disgusted as he dares to be) Ain't that why I brought yer up 'ere—to show yer? Yer been lookin' at this 'ere 'ole affair wrong. Yer been actin' an' talkin' 's if it was all a bleedin' personal matter between yer and that bloody cow. I wants to convince yer she was on'y a representative of 'er clarss. I wants to awaken yer bloody clarss consciousness. Then yer'll see it's 'er clarss ye've got to fight, not 'er alone. There's a 'ole mob of 'em like 'er, Gawd blind 'em!

YANK: (Spitting on his hands—belligerently) De more de merrier when I gits started. Bring on de gang!

LONG: Yer'll see 'em in arf a mo', when that church lets out. (He turns and sees the window display in the two stores for the first time) Blimey! Look at that, will yer? (They both walk back and stand looking in the jeweler's. Long flies into a fury) Just look at this 'ere bloomin' mess! Just look at it! Look at the bleedin' prices on 'em—more'n our 'ole bloody stokehole makes in ten voyages sweatin' in 'ell! And they—'er and 'er bloody clarss—buys 'em for toys to dangle on 'em! One of these 'ere would buy scoff for a starvin' family for a year!

YANK: Aw, cut de sob stuff! T' hell wit de starvin' family! Yuh'll be passin' de hat to me next. (With naïve admiration) Say, dem tings is pretty, huh? Bet yuh dey'd hock for a piece of change aw right. (Then turning away, bored) But, aw hell, what good are dey? Let her have 'em. Dey don't belong no more'n she does. (With a gesture of sweeping the jeweler's into oblivion) All dat don't count, get me?

LONG: (Who has moved to the furrier's—indignantly) And I s'pose this 'ere don't count neither—skins of poor, 'armless animals slaughtered so as 'er and 'ers can keep their bleedin' noses warm!

YANK: (Who has been staring at something inside—with queer excitement) Take a slant at dat! Give it de once-over! Monkey fur—two t'ousand bucks! (Bewilderedly) Is dat straight goods—monkey fur? What de hell—?

LONG: (Bitterly) It's straight enuf. (With grim humor) They wouldn't bloody well pay that for a 'airy ape's skin—no, nor for the 'ole livin' ape with all 'is 'ead, and body, and soul thrown in!

YANK: (Clenching his fists, his face growing pale with rage as if the skin in the window were a personal insult) Trowin' it up in my face! Christ! I'll fix her!

LONG: (Excitedly) Church is out. 'Ere they come, the bleedin' swine. (After a glance at Yank's lowering face—uneasily) Easy goes, Comrade. Keep yer bloomin' temper. Remember force defeats itself. It ain't our weapon. We must impress our demands through peaceful means—the votes of the on-marching proletarians of the bloody world!

YANK: (*With abysmal contempt*) Votes, hell! Votes is a joke, see? Votes for women! Let dem do it!

LONG: (*Still more uneasily*) Calm, now. Treat 'em wiv the proper contempt. Observe the bleedin' parasites but 'old yer 'orses.

YANK: (*Angrily*) Git away from me! Yuh're yellow, dat's what. Force, dat's me! De punch, dat's me every time, see!

(*The* Crowd *from church enter from the right, sauntering slowly and affectedly, their heads held stiffly up, looking neither to right nor left, talking in toneless, simpering voices. The* Women *are rouged, calcimined, dyed, overdressed to the nth degree. The* Men *are in Prince Alberts, high hats, spats, canes, etc. A procession of gaudy marionettes, yet with something of the relentless horror of Frankensteins in their detached, mechanical unawareness*)

VOICES: Dear Doctor Caiaphas! He is so sincere! What was the sermon? I dozed off.

About the radicals, my dear —and the false doctrines that are being preached.

We must organize a hundred per cent American bazaar.

And let everyone contribute one one-hundredth per cent of their income tax.

What an original idea!

We can devote the proceeds to rehabilitating the veil of the temple.

But that has been done so many times.

YANK: (*Glaring from one to the other of them—with an insulting snort of scorn*) Huh! Huh!

(*Without seeming to see him, they make wide detours to avoid the spot where he stands in the middle of the sidewalk*)

LONG: (*Frightenedly*) Keep yer bloomin' mouth shut, I tells yer.

YANK: (*Viciously*) G'wan! Tell it to Sweeney! (*He swaggers away and deliberately lurches into a tophatted* Gentleman, *then glares at him pugnaciously*) Say, who d'yuh tink yuh're bumpin'? Tink yuh own de oith?

GENTLEMAN: (*Coldly and affectedly*) I beg your pardon. (*He has not looked at* Yank *and passes on without a glance, leaving him bewildered*)

LONG: (*Rushing up and grabbing* Yank's *arm*) 'Ere! Come away! This wasn't what I meant. Yer'll 'ave the bloody coppers down on us.

YANK: (*Savagely—giving him a push that sends him sprawling*) G'wan!

LONG: (*Picks himself up—hysterically*) I'll pop orf then. This ain't what I meant. And whatever 'appens, yer can't blame me. (*He slinks off left*)

YANK: T' hell wit youse! (*He approaches a* Lady—*with a vicious grin and a smirking wink*) Hello, Kiddo. How's every little ting? Got anything on for tonight? I know an old boiler down to de docks we kin crawl into. (*The* Lady *stalks by without a look, without a change of pace.* Yank *turns to others— insultingly*) Holy smokes, what a mug! Go hide yuhself before de horses shy at yuh. Gee, pipe de heinie on dat one! Say, youse, yuh look like de stoin of a ferryboat. Paint and powder! All dolled up to kill! Yuh look like stiffs laid out for de boneyard! Aw, g'wan, de lot of youse! Yuh give me de eyeache. Yuh don't belong, get me? Look at me, why don't youse dare? I belong, dat's me! (*Pointing to a sky-scraper across the street which is in process of construction—with bravado*) See dat building goin' up dere? See de steel work?

Steel, dat's me! Youse guys live on it and tink yuh're somep'n. But I'm *in* it, see! I'm de hoistin' engine dat makes it go up! I'm it—de inside and bottom of it! Sure! I'm steel and steam and smoke and de rest of it! It moves—speed—twenty-five stories up—and me at de top and bottom—movin'! Youse simps don't move. Yuh're on'y dolls I winds up to see 'm spin. Yuh're de garbage, get me—de leavins—de ashes we dump over de side! Now, what 'a' yuh gotta say? (*But as they seem neither to see nor hear him, he flies into a fury*) Bums! Pigs! Tarts! Bitches! (*He turns in a rage on the* Men, *bumping viciously into them but not jarring them the least bit. Rather it is he who recoils after each collision. He keeps growling*) Git off de oith! G'wan, yuh bum! Look where yuh're goin', can't yuh! Git outa here! Fight, why don't yuh? Put up yer mits! Don't be a dog! Fight or I'll knock yuh dead! (*But, without seeming to see him, they all answer with mechanical affected politeness:*) I beg your pardon.

(*Then, at a cry from one of the* Women, *they all scurry to the furrier's window*)

THE WOMAN: (*Ecstatically, with a gasp of delight*) Monkey fur! (*The whole crowd of* Men *and* Women *chorus after her in the same tone of affected delight*) Monkey fur!
YANK: (*With a jerk of his head back on his shoulders, as if he had received a punch full in the face—raging*) I see yuh, all in white! I see yuh, yuh white-faced tart, yuh! Hairy ape, huh? I'll hairy ape yuh!

(*He bends down and grips at the street curbing as if to pluck it out and hurl it. Foiled in this, snarling with passion, he leaps to the lamppost on the corner and tries to pull it up for a club. Just at that moment a bus is heard rumbling up. A fat, high-hatted, spatted* Gentleman *runs out from the side street. He calls out plaintively:*)

GENTLEMAN: Bus! Bus! Stop there! (*And runs full tilt into the bending, straining* Yank, *who is bowled off his balance*)
YANK: (*Seeing a fight—with a roar of joy as he springs to his feet*) At last! Bus, huh? I'll bust yuh! (*He lets drive a terrific swing, his fist landing full on the fat* Gentleman's *face. But the* Gentleman *stands unmoved as if nothing had happened*)
GENTLEMAN: I beg your pardon. (*Then irritably*) You have made me lose my bus. (*He claps his hands and begins to scream:*) Officer! Officer!

(*Many police whistles shrill out on the instant and a whole platoon of* Policemen *rush in on* Yank *from all sides. He tries to fight but is clubbed to the pavement and fallen upon. The* Crowd *at the window have not moved or noticed this disturbance. The clanging gong of the patrol wagon approaches with a clamoring din*)

CURTAIN

SCENE VI: *Night of the following day. A row of cells in the prison on Blackwell's Island. The cells extend back diagonally from right front to left rear. They do not stop, but disappear in the dark background as if they ran on, numberless, into infinity. One electric bulb from the low ceiling of the narrow corridor sheds its light through the heavy steel bars of the cell at the extreme front and reveals part of the interior.*

Yank *can be seen within, crouched on the edge of his cot in the attitude of Rodin's "The Thinker." His face is spotted with black and blue bruises. A blood-stained bandage is wrapped around his head.*

Yank: (*Suddenly starting as if awakening from a dream, reaches out and shakes the bars—aloud to himself, wonderingly*) Steel. Dis is de Zoo, huh?

(*A burst of hard, barking laughter comes from the unseen* Occupants *of the cells, runs back down the tier, and abruptly ceases*)

Voices: (*Mockingly*) The Zoo? That's a new name for this coop—a damn good name!
Steel, eh? You said a mouthful. This is the old iron house.
Who is that boob talkin'?
He's the bloke they brung in out of his head. The bulls had beat him up fierce.
Yank: (*Dully*) I musta been dreamin'. I tought I was in a cage at de Zoo—but de apes don't talk, do dey?
Voices: (*With mocking laughter*) You're in a cage aw right.
A coop!
A pen!
A sty!
A kennel!

(*Hard laughter—a pause*)

Say, guy! Who are you? No, never mind lying. What are you?
Yes, tell us your sad story. What's your game?
What did they jug yuh for?
Yank: (*Dully*) I was a fireman—stokin' on de liners. (*Then with sudden rage, rattling his cell bars*) I'm a hairy ape, get me? And I'll bust youse all in de jaw if yuh don't lay off kiddin' me.
Voices: Huh! You're a hard boiled duck, ain't youse?
When you spit, it bounces!

(*Laughter*)

Aw, can it. He's a regular guy. Ain't you?
What did he say he was—a ape?
Yank: (*Defiantly*) Sure ting! Ain't dat what youse all are—apes?

(*A silence. Then a furious rattling of bars from down the corridor*)

A Voice: (*Thick with rage*) I'll show yuh who's a ape, yuh bum!
Voices: Ssshh! Nix!
Can de noise!
Piano!
You'll have the guard down on us!
Yank: (*Scornfully*) De guard? Yuh mean de keeper, don't yuh?

(Angry exclamations from all the cells)

VOICE: (*Placatingly*) Aw, don't pay no attention to him. He's off his nut from the beatin'-up he got. Say, you guy! We're waitin' to hear what they landed you for—or ain't yuh tellin'?

YANK: Sure, I'll tell youse. Sure! Why de hell not? On'y—youse won't get me. Nobody gets me but me, see? I started to tell de Judge and all he says was: "Toity days to tink it over." Tink it over! Christ, dat's all I been doin' for weeks! (*After a pause*) I was tryin' to git even with someone, see?—someone dat done me doit.

VOICES: (*Cynically*) De old stuff, I bet. Your goil, huh?
Give yuh the double-cross, huh?
That's them every time!
Did yuh beat up de odder guy?

YANK: (*Disgustedly*) Aw, yuh're all wrong! Sure dere was a skoit in it—but not what youse mean, not dat ole tripe. Dis was a new kind of skoit. She was dolled up all in white—in de stokehole. I tought she was a ghost. Sure.

(A pause)

VOICES: (*Whispering*) Gee, he's still nutty.
Let him rave. It's fun listenin'.

YANK: (*Unheeding—groping in his thoughts*) Her hands—dey was skinny and white like dey wasn't real but painted on somep'n. Dere was a million miles from me to her—twenty-five knots a hour. She was like some dead ting de cat brung in. Sure, dat's what. She didn't belong. She belonged in de window of a toy store, or on de top of a garbage can, see! Sure! (*He breaks out angrily*) But would yuh believe it, she had de noive to do me doit. She lamped me like she was seein' somep'n broke loose from de menagerie. Christ, yuh'd oughter seen her eyes! (*He rattles the bars of his cell furiously*) But I'll get back at her yet, you watch! And if I can't find her I'll take it out on de gang she runs wit. I'm wise to where dey hangs out now. I'll show her who belongs! I'll show her who's in de move and who ain't. You watch my smoke!

VOICES: (*Serious and joking*) Dat's de talkin'!
Take her for all she's got!
What was this dame, anyway? Who was she, eh?

YANK: I dunno. First cabin stiff. Her old man's a millionaire, dey says—name of Douglas.

VOICES: Douglas? That's the president of the Steel Trust, I bet.
Sure. I seen his mug in de papers.
He's filthy with dough.

VOICE: Hey, feller, take a tip from me. If you want to get back at that dame, you better join the Wobblies. You'll get some action then.

YANK: Wobblies? What de hell's dat?

VOICE: Ain't you ever heard of the I. W. W.?

YANK: Naw. What is it?

VOICE: A gang of blokes—a tough gang. I been readin' about 'em today in the paper. The guard give me the *Sunday Times*. There's a long spiel about 'em. It's from a speech made in the Senate by a guy named Senator Queen. (*He is in the cell next to* Yank's. *There is a rustling of paper*) Wait'll I see if I got light enough and I'll read you. Listen. (*He reads:*) "There is a menace existing in this country today which threatens the vitals of our fair Republic —as foul a menace against the very life-blood of the American Eagle as was the foul conspiracy of Catiline against the eagles of ancient Rome!"

VOICE: (*Disgustedly*) Aw, hell! Tell him to salt de tail of dat eagle!

VOICE: (*Reading*) "I refer to that devil's brew of rascals, jailbirds, murderers and cutthroats who libel all honest working men by calling themselves the Industrial Workers of the World; but in the light of their nefarious plots, I call them the Industrious *Wreckers* of the World!"

YANK: (*With vengeful satisfaction*) Wreckers, dat's de right dope! Dat belongs! Me for dem!

VOICE: Ssshh! (*Reading*) "This fiendish organization is a foul ulcer on the fair body of our Democracy—"

VOICE: Democracy, hell! Give him the boid, fellers—the raspberry! (*They do*)

VOICE: Ssshh! (*Reading*) "Like Cato I say to this Senate, the I. W. W. must be destroyed! For they represent an ever-present dagger pointed at the heart of the greatest nation the world has ever known, where all men are born free and equal, with equal opportunities to all, where the Founding Fathers have guaranteed to each one happiness, where Truth, Honor, Liberty, Justice, and the Brotherhood of Man are a religion absorbed with one's mother milk, taught at our father's knee, sealed, signed, and stamped in the glorious Constitution of these United States!"

(*A perfect storm of hisses, catcalls, boos, and hard laughter*)

VOICES: (*Scornfully*) Hurrah for de Fort' of July!
Pass de hat!
Liberty!
Justice!
Honor!
Opportunity!
Brotherhood!

ALL: (*With abysmal scorn*) Aw, hell!

VOICE: Give the Queen Senator guy the bark! All togedder now—one—two—three—

(*A terrific chorus of barking and yapping*)

GUARD: (*From a distance*) Quiet there, youse—or I'll git the hose.

(*The noise subsides*)

YANK: (*With growling rage*) I'd like to catch dat senator guy alone for a second. I'd loin him some trute!

VOICE: Ssshh! Here's where he gits down to cases on the Wobblies. (*Reads:*) "They plot with fire in one hand and dynamite in the other. They stop not before murder to gain their ends, nor at the outraging of defenseless womanhood. They would tear down society, put the lowest scum in the seats of the mighty, turn Almighty God's revealed plan for the world topsy-turvy, and make of our sweet and lovely civilization a shambles, a desolation where man, God's masterpiece, would soon degenerate back to the ape!"

VOICE: (*To* Yank) Hey, you guy. There's your ape stuff again.

YANK: (*With a growl of fury*) I got him. So dey blow up tings, do they? Dey turn tings round, do dey? Hey, lend me dat paper, will yuh?

VOICE: Sure. Give it to him. On'y keep it to yourself, see? We don't wanter listen to no more of that slop.

VOICE: Here you are. Hide it under your mattress.

YANK: (*Reaching out*) Tanks. I can't read much but I kin manage. (*He sits, the paper in the hand at his side, in the attitude of Rodin's "The Thinker." A pause. Several snores from down the corridor. Suddenly Yank jumps to his feet with a furious groan as if some appalling thought had crashed on him—bewilderedly*) Sure—her old man—president of de Steel Trust—makes half de steel in de world—steel—where I thought I belonged— drivin' trou—movin'—in dat—to make *her*—and cage me in for her to spit on! Christ! (*He shakes the bars of his cell door till the whole tier trembles. Irritated, protesting exclamations from those awakened or trying to get to sleep*) He made dis—dis cage! Steel! *It* don't belong, dat's what! Cages, cells, locks, bolts, bars—dat's what it means!—holdin' me down with him at de top! But I'll drive trou! Fire, dat melts it! I'll be fire—under de heap—fire dat never goes out—hot-as hell—breakin' out in de night—

(*While he has been saying this last he has shaken his cell door to a clanging accompaniment. As he comes to the "breakin' out" he seizes one bar with both hands and, putting his two feet up against the others so that his position is parallel to the floor like a monkey's, he gives a great wrench backwards. The bar bends like a licorice stick under his tremendous strength. Just at this moment the* Prison Guard *rushes in, dragging a hose behind him*)

GUARD: (*Angrily*) I'll loin youse bums to wake me up! (*Sees* Yank) Hello, it's you, huh? Got the D. Ts., hey? Well, I'll cure 'em. I'll drown your snakes for yuh! (*Noticing the bar*) Hell, look at dat bar bended! On'y a bug is strong enough for dat!

YANK: (*Glaring at him*) Or a hairy ape, yuh big yellow bum! Look out! Here I come! (*He grabs another bar*)

GUARD: (*Scared now—yelling off left*) Toin de hose on, Ben!—full pressure! And call de others—and a straitjacket!

(*The curtain is falling. As it hides* Yank *from view, there is a splattering smash as the stream of water hits the steel of* Yank's *cell*)

CURTAIN

SCENE VII: *Nearly a month later. An I. W. W. local near the waterfront, showing the interior of a front room on the ground floor, and the street outside. Moonlight on the narrow street, buildings massed in black shadow. The interior of the room, which is general assembly room, office, and reading room, resembles some dingy settlement boys' club. A desk and high stool are in one corner. A table with paper, stacks of pamphlets, chairs about it, is at center. The whole is decidedly cheap, banal, commonplace, and unmysterious as a room could well be.*

The Secretary *is perched on the stool making entries in a large ledger. An eye shade casts his face into shadows. Eight or ten* Men, Longshoremen, Iron Workers, *and the like, are grouped about the table. Two are playing checkers. One is writing a letter. Most of them are smoking pipes. A big signboard is on the wall at the rear, "Industrial Workers in the World—Local No. 57."* Yank *comes down the street outside. He is dressed as in Scene Five. He moves cautiously, mysteriously. He comes to a point opposite the door; tiptoes softly up to it, listens, is impressed by the silence within, knocks carefully,*

*as if he were guessing at the password to some secret rite. Listens. No answer.
Knocks again a bit louder. No answer. Knocks impatiently, much louder.*

SECRETARY: (*Turning around on his stool*) What the hell is that—someone knocking? (*Shouts*) Come in, why don't you?

(*All the* Men *in the room look up.* Yank *opens the door slowly, gingerly,
as if afraid of an ambush. He looks around for the secret doors, mystery, is
taken aback by the commonplaceness of the room and the* Men *in it, thinks
he may have gotten in the wrong place, then sees the signboard on the wall
and is reassured*)

YANK: (*Blurts out*) Hello.
MEN: (*Reservedly*) Hello.
YANK: (*More easily*) I tought I'd bumped into de wrong dump.
SECRETARY: (*Scrutinizing him carefully*) Maybe you have. Are you a
member?
YANK: Naw, not yet. Dat's what I come for—to join.
SECRETARY: That's easy. What's your job—longshore?
YANK: Naw. Fireman—stoker on de liners.
SECRETARY: (*With satisfaction*) Welcome to our city. Glad to know you
people are waking up at last. We haven't got many members in your line.
YANK: Naw. Dey're all dead to de woild.
SECRETARY: Well, you can help to wake 'em. What's your name? I'll make
out your card.
YANK: (*Confused*) Name? Lemme tink.
SECRETARY: (*Sharply*) Don't you know your own name?
YANK: Sure; but I been just Yank for so long—Bob, dat's it—Bob Smith.
SECRETARY: (*Writing*) Robert Smith. (*Fills out the rest of card*) Here you
are. Cost you half a dollar.
YANK: Is dat all—four bits? Dat's easy.

(*Gives the* Secretary *the money*)

SECRETARY: (*Throwing it in drawer*) Thanks. Well, make yourself at
home. No introductions needed. There's literature on the table. Take some
of those pamphlets with you to distribute aboard ship. They may bring
results. Sow the seed, only go about it right. Don't get caught and fired. We
got plenty out of work. What we need is men who can hold their jobs—and
work for us at the same time.
YANK: Sure. (*But he still stands, embarrassed and uneasy*)
SECRETARY: (*Looking at him—curiously*) What did you knock for? Think
we had a coon in uniform to open doors?
YANK: Naw. I tought it was locked—and dat yuh'd wanter give me the
once-over trou a peephole or somep'n to see if I was right.
SECRETARY: (*Alert and suspicious but with an easy laugh*) Think we were
running a crap game? That door is never locked. What put that in your nut?
YANK: (*With a knowing grin, convinced that this is all camouflage, a part
of the secrecy*) Dis burg is full of bulls, ain't it?
SECRETARY: (*Sharply*) What have the cops got to do with us? We're break-
ing no laws.
YANK: (*With a knowing wink*) Sure. Youse wouldn't for woilds. Sure.
I'm wise to dat.
SECRETARY: You seem to be wise to a lot of stuff none of us knows about.

YANK: (*With another wink*) Aw, dat's aw right, see? (*Then made a bit resentful by the suspicious glances from all sides*) Aw, can it! Youse needn't put me trou de toid degree. Can't youse see I belong? Sure! I'm reg'lar. I'll stick, get me? I'll shoot de woiks for youse. Dat's why I wanted to join in.

SECRETARY: (*Breezily, feeling him out*) That's the right spirit. Only are you sure you understand what you've joined? It's all plain and above board; still, some guys get a wrong slant on us. (*Sharply*) What's your notion of the purpose of the I. W. W.?

YANK: Aw, I know all about it.

SECRETARY: (*Sarcastically*) Well, give us some of your valuable information.

YANK: (*Cunningly*) I know enough not to speak outa my toin. (*Then resentfully again*) Aw, say! I'm reg'lar. I'm wise to de game. I know yuh got to watch your step wit a stranger. For all youse know, I might be a plain-clothes dick, or somep'n, dat's what yuh're thinkin', huh? Aw, forget it! I belong, see? Ask any guy down to de docks if I don't.

SECRETARY: Who said you didn't?

YANK: After I'm 'nitiated, I'll show yuh.

SECRETARY: (*Astounded*) Initiated? There's no initiation.

YANK: (*Disappointed*) Ain't there no password—no grip nor nothin'?

SECRETARY: What'd you think this is—the Elks—or the Black Hand?

YANK: De Elks, hell! De Black Hand, dey're a lot of yellow backstickin' Ginees. Naw. Dis is a man's gang, ain't it?

SECRETARY: You said it! That's why we stand on two feet in the open. We got no secrets.

YANK: (*Surprised but admiringly*) Yuh mean to say yuh always run wide open—like dis?

SECRETARY: Exactly.

YANK: Den yuh sure got your noive wit youse!

SECRETARY: (*Sharply*) Just what was it made you want to join us? Come out with that straight.

YANK: Yuh call me? Well, I got noive, too! Here's my hand. Yuh wanter blow tings up, don't yuh? Well, dat's me! I belong!

SECRETARY: (*With pretended carelessness*) You mean change the unequal conditions of society by legitimate direct action—or with dynamite?

YANK: *Dynamite!* Blow it offen de oith—steel—all de cages—all de factories, steamers, buildings, jails—de Steel Trust and all dat makes it go.

SECRETARY: So—that's your idea, eh? And did you have any special job in that line you wanted to propose to us? (*He makes a sign to the* Men, *who get up cautiously one by one and group behind* Yank)

YANK: (*Boldly*) Sure, I'll come out wit it. I'll show youse I'm one of de gang. Dere's dat millionaire guy, Douglas—

SECRETARY: President of the Steel Trust, you mean? Do you want to assassinate him?

YANK: Naw, dat don't get yuh nothin'. I mean blow up de factory, de woiks, where he makes de steel. Dat's what I'm after—to blow up de steel, knock all de steel in de woild up to de moon. Dat'll fix tings! (*Eagerly, with a touch of bravado*) I'll do it by me lonesome! I'll show yuh! Tell me where his woiks is, how to git there, all de dope. Gimme de stuff, de old butter—and watch me do de rest! Watch de smoke and see it move! I don't give a damn if dey nab me—long as it's done! I'll soive life for it—and give 'em de laugh! (*Half to himself*) And I'll write her a letter and tell her de hairy ape done it. Dat'll square tings.

SECRETARY: (*Stepping away from* Yank) Very interesting.

(He gives a signal. The Men, *huskies all, throw themselves on* Yank *and before he knows it they have his legs and arms pinioned. But he is too flabbergasted to make a struggle, anyway. They feel him over for weapons)*

MAN: No gat, no knife. Shall we give him what's what and put the boots to him?

SECRETARY: No. He isn't worth the trouble we'd get into. He's too stupid. *(He comes closer and laughs mockingly in* Yank's *face)* Ho-ho! By God, this is the biggest joke they've put up on us yet. Hey, you Joke! Who sent you—Burns or Pinkerton? No, by God, you're such a bonehead I'll bet you're in the Secret Service! Well, you dirty spy, you rotten agent provocateur, you can go back and tell whatever skunk is paying you blood-money for betraying your brothers that he's wasting his coin. You couldn't catch a cold. And tell him that all he'll ever get on us, or ever has got, is just his own sneaking plots that he's framed up to put us in jail. We are what our manifesto says we are, neither more nor less—and we'll give him a copy of that any time he calls. And as for you— *(He glares scornfully at* Yank, *who is sunk in an oblivious stupor)* Oh, hell, what's the use of talking? You're a brainless ape.

YANK: *(Aroused by the word to fierce but futile struggles)* What's dat, yuh Sheeny bum, yuh!

SECRETARY: Throw him out, boys.

(In spite of his struggles, this is done with gusto and éclat. Propelled by several parting kicks, Yank *lands sprawling in the middle of the narrow cobbled street. With a growl he starts to get up and storm the closed door, but stops bewildered by the confusion in his brain, pathetically impotent. He sits there, brooding, in as near to the attitude of Rodin's "Thinker" as he can get in his position)*

YANK: *(Bitterly)* So dem boids don't tink I belong, neider. Aw, to hell wit 'em! Dey're in de wrong pew—de same old bull—soapboxes and Salvation Army—no guts! Cut out an hour offen de job a day and make me happy! Gimme a dollar more a day and make me happy! Tree squares a day, and cauliflowers in de front yard—ekal rights—a woman and kids—a lousy vote —and I'm all fixed for Jesus, huh? Aw, hell! What does dat get yuh? Dis ting's in your inside, but it ain't your belly. Feedin' your face—sinkers and coffee—dat don't touch it. It's way down—at de bottom. Yuh can't grab it, and yuh can't stop it. It moves, and everything moves. It stops and de whole woild stops. Dat's me now—I don't tick, see?—I'm a busted Ingersoll, dat's what. Steel was me, and I owned de woild. Now I ain't steel, and de woild owns me. Aw, hell! I can't see—it's all dark, get me? It's all wrong! *(He turns a bitter mocking face up like an ape gibbering at the moon)* Say, youse up dere, Man in de Moon, yuh look so wise, gimme de answer, huh? Slip me de inside dope, de information right from de stable—where do I get off at, huh?

A POLICEMAN: *(Who has come up the street in time to hear this last—with grim humor)* You'll get off at the station, you boob, if you don't get up out of that and keep movin'.

YANK: *(Looking up at him—with a hard, bitter laugh)* Sure! Lock me up! Put me in a cage! Dat's de on'y answer yuh know. G'wan, lock me up!

POLICEMAN: What you been doin'?

YANK: Enuf to gimme life for! I was born, see? Sure, dat's de charge. Write it in de blotter. I was born, get me?

POLICEMAN: (*Jocosely*) God pity your old woman! (*Then matter-of-fact*) But I've no time for kidding. You're soused. I'd run you in but it's too long a walk to the station. Come on now, get up, or I'll fan your ears with this club. Beat it now! (*He hauls* Yank *to his feet*)

YANK: (*In a vague mocking tone*) Say, where do I go from here?

POLICEMAN: (Giving him a push—with a grin, indifferently) Go to hell.

CURTAIN

SCENE VIII: *Twilight of the next day. The monkey house at the Zoo. One spot of clear gray light falls on the front of one cage so that the interior can be seen. The other cages are vague, shrouded in shadow from which chatterings pitched in a conversational tone can be heard. On the one cage a sign from which the word "gorilla" stands out. The gigantic* Animal *himself is seen squatting on his haunches on a bench in much the same attitude as Rodin's "Thinker."*

Yank *enters from the left. Immediately a chorus of angry chattering and screeching breaks out. The* Gorilla *turns his eyes but makes no sound or move.*

YANK: (*With a hard, bitter laugh*) Welcome to your city, huh? Hail, hail, de gang's all here! (*At the sound of his voice the chattering dies away into an attentive silence. Yank walks up to the Gorilla's cage and, leaning over the railing, stares in at its occupant, who stares back at him, silent and motionless. There is a pause of dead stillness. Then Yank begins to talk in a friendly confidential tone, half-mockingly, but with a deep undercurrent of sympathy*) Say, yuh're some hard-lookin' guy, ain't yuh? I seen lots of tough nuts dat de gang called gorillas, but yuh're de foist real one I ever seen. Some chest yuh got, and shoulders, and dem arms and mits! I bet yuh got a punch in eider fist dat'd knock 'em all silly (*This with genuine admiration. The* Gorilla, *as if he understood, stands upright, swelling out his chest and pounding on it with his fist.* Yank *grins sympathetically*) Sure, I get yuh. Yuh challenge de whole woild, huh? Yuh got what I was sayin' even if yuh muffed de woids. (*Then bitterness creeping in*) And why wouldn't yuh get me? Ain't we both members of de same club—de Hairy Apes? (*They stare at each other—a pause—then* Yank *goes on slowly and bitterly*) So yuh're what she seen when she looked at me, de white-faced tart! I was you to her, get me? On'y outa de cage— broke out—free to moider her, see? Sure! Dat's what she tought. She wasn't wise dat I was in a cage, too—worser'n yours— sure—a damn sight—'cause you got some chanct to bust loose—but me— (*He grows confused*) Aw, hell! It's wrong, ain't it? (*A pause*) I s'pose yuh wanter know what I'm doin' here, huh? I been warmin' a bench down to de Battery—ever since last night. Sure. I seen de sun come up. Dat was pretty, too—all red and pink and green. I was lookin' at de skyscrapers—steel—and all de ships comin' in, sailin' out, all over de oith—and dey was steel, too. De sun was warm, dey wasn't no clouds, and dere was a breeze blowin'. Sure, it was great stuff. I got it aw right—what Paddy said about dat bein' de right dope—on'y I couldn't get *in* it, see? I couldn't belong in dat. It was over my head, and I kept tinkin'—and den I beat it up here to see what youse was like. And I waited till dey was all gone to git yuh alone. Say, how d'yuh feel sittin' in dat pen all de time, havin' to stand for 'em comin' and starin' at yuh—de white-faced, skinny tarts and de boobs what marry 'em—makin' fun of yuh, laughin' at yuh, gittin' scared of yuh—damn 'em! (*He pounds on the rail with his fist. The Gorilla rattles the bars of his cage and snarls. All the other monkeys set up an angry chattering in the darkness.* Yank *goes on excitedly*) Sure! Dat's de way it hits me, too. On'y yuh're lucky, see! Yuh don't belong wit 'em and yuh know it. But me, I belong wit 'em—but I don't, see? Dey don't belong wit me, dat's what. Get me? Tinkin' is hard— (*He passes one hand across his forehead with a painful gesture. The Gorilla growls impatiently.* Yank *goes on gropingly*) It's dis way, what I'm drivin' at. Youse can sit and dope dream in de past, green woods, de jungle, and de rest of it. Den yuh belong and dey don't. Den yuh kin laugh at 'em, see? Yuh're de champ of de woild. But me—I ain't got no past to tink in, nor nothin' dat's comin', on'y what's now—and dat don't belong. Sure, you're de best off! Yuh can't tink, can yuh? Yuh can't talk neider. But I kin make a bluff at talkin' and tinkin'—a'most git away wit it—a'most!—and dat's where de joker comes in. (*He laughs*) I ain't on oith and I ain't in heaven, get me? I'm in de middle tryin' to separate 'em, takin' all de woist punches from bot' of 'em. Maybe dat's what dey call hell, huh? But you, yuh're at de bottom. You belong! Sure! Yuh're de on'y one in de woild dat does, yuh lucky stiff! (*The* Gorilla *growls proudly*) And dat's why dey gotter put yuh in a cage, see? (*The* Glorilla *roars angrily*) Sure! Yuh get me. It beats it when you try to tink it or talk it—it's way down—deep—behind—you 'n' me we feel it. Sure! Bot' members of dis club! (*He laughs—then in a savage tone*) What de hell! T'hell wit it! A little action, dat's our meat! Dat belongs! Knock 'em down and keep bustin' 'em till dey croaks yuh wit a gat—wit steel! Sure! Are yuh game? Dey've looked at youse, ain't dey—in a cage? Wanter git even? Wanter wind up like a sport 'stead of croakin' slow in dere? (*The* Gorilla *roars an emphatic affirmative.* Yank *goes on with a sort of furious exaltation*) Sure! Yuh're reg'lar. Yuh'll stick to de finish! Me 'n' you, huh?— bot' members of this club! We'll put up one last star bout dat'll knock 'em offen deir seats! Dey'll have to make de cages stronger after we're trou! (*The* Gorilla *is straining at his bars, growling, hopping from one foot to the other.* Yank *takes a jimmy from under his coat and forces the lock on the cage door. He throws this open*) Pardon from de governor! Step out and shake hands! I'll take yuh for a walk down Fif' Avenoo. We'll knock 'em offen de oith and croak wit de band playin'. Come on, Brother. (*The* Gorilla *scrambles gingerly out of his cage. Goes to* Yank *and stands looking at him.* Yank *keeps his mocking tone—holds out his hand*) Shake—de secret grip of our order. (*Something, the tone of mockery, perhaps, suddenly enrages the Animal. With a spring he wraps his huge arms around* Yank *in a murderous hug. There is a crackling snap of crushed ribs—a gasping cry, still mocking, from* Yank) Hey, I didn't say kiss me! (*The* Gorilla *lets the crushed body slip to the floor; stands over it uncertainly, considering; then picks it up, throws it in the cage, shuts the door, and shuffles off menacingly into the darkness at left. A great uproar of frightened chattering and whimpering comes from the other cages. Then* Yank *moves, groaning, opening his eyes, and there is silence. He mutters painfully*) Say—dey oughter match him—wit Zybszko. He got me, aw right. I'm trou. Even him didn't tink I belonged. (*Then, with sudden passionate despair*) Christ, where do I get off at? Where do I fit in? (*Checking himself as suddenly*) Aw, what de hell! No squawkin', see! No quittin', get me! Croak wit your boots on! (*He grabs hold of the bars of the cage and hauls himself painfully to his feet—looks around him bewilderedly —forces a mocking laugh*) In de cage, huh? (*In the strident tones of a circus*

barker) Ladies and gents, step forward and take a slant at de one and only—
(*His voice weakening*)—one and original—Hairy Ape from de wilds of—

(He slips in a heap on the floor and dies. The monkeys set up a chatter-ing, whimpering wail. And, perhaps, the Hairy Ape at last belongs)

CURTAIN

FOR DISCUSSION

1. In what way is Yank a symbol of man and of the worker?
2. What are Yank's views on life? How do they differ from Paddy's? From Long's? From Mildred's?
3. How does Yank judge the worth of a man?
4. Why does Yank become upset over Mildred's appearance? Is this justified?
5. Why are people not affected when Yank bumps into them in New York City?
6. What is Mildred's motive in wanting to tour the ship? Why does her aunt object?
7. What is Yank's mental state? What contributed to it?
8. In what way is Yank influenced by the other characters in the play?
9. What is the significance of Yank's trying to think?
10. Do you like Yank? Why or why not?
11. Why does Yank say he belongs and Paddy and the "rich guys" don't? Why does Yank later feel he does not belong?
12. What elements of the play are realistic? Symbolic? Expressionistic? Romantic?
13. What is the significance of Yank's shaking hands with the gorilla?
14. Is the gorilla's crushing of Yank a satisfactory conclusion to the play? Why or why not?
15. What is the theme of *The Hairy Ape?*

Tennessee Williams gave new life to theatre.

Thomas Lanier (Tennessee) Williams was born on March 26, 1911, in Columbus, Mississippi. His grandfather was an Episcopalian minister and his father a traveling shoe salesman, who was often away from home. His mother may have provided the basis for the character of Amanda in *The Glass Menagerie*. Williams had a sister, Rose, who was slightly lame and tended to withdraw from the world, finally becoming a recluse. She was the person upon whom the character of Laura, in the same play, was based.

As a child, Williams himself suffered from a series of illnesses. When he was about twelve, his family moved to St. Louis, where Williams first decided he wanted to be a writer. He began with short stories, one of which was published in 1928 in *Weird Tales*. He attended the University of Missouri, but was forced to leave because of financial difficulties. Later, his grandparents helped him to return to college, and he finally received a degree from the University of Iowa.

While in school and for a time afterward, Williams held a variety of jobs. His first plays, three one-acts, were produced while he was a student at Washington University in St. Louis. Then he went to New York, where his first successful plays were a series of one-acts which won him a prize from the Group Theatre. His first full-length play, *Battle of the Angels*, was produced in Boston in 1940 by the Theatre Guild but was unsuccessful. An altered version, entitled *Orpheus Descending*, was produced in New York in 1957.

Williams' second full-length play was *The Glass Menagerie*, which opened in Chicago in 1944. This was the turning point of his career, since the play was popular with audiences and critics alike. Brought to New York, it ran for more than 550 performances. His next play, *A Streetcar Named Desire*, produced in 1947, won him both a Pulitzer Prize and the New York Drama Critics Circle Award. A later play, *Cat on a Hot Tin Roof*, written in 1955, was also awarded a Pulitzer Prize.

Williams has written both prose and poetry, but his outstanding work has been his plays. The best of these are realistic, although his form of realism is original and employs the use of nonrealistic devices. He has the ability to create highly dramatic dialogue and believable characters. Most of the characters are Southerners, but exhibit traits that have meaning for audiences everywhere. Most often they are sad, lonely people, facing a fleeting youth and the absence of love. Often they become ensnared in situations involving brutality, violence, or sex. However, there is a tenderness and gentleness in Williams' treatment of them. Many times they are persons who have trouble adjusting to the present and long to return to a safer, happier past.

Despite realistic dialogue and characterizations, Williams uses such nonrealistic devices as fragmentary settings. However, the fragments of the interiors and exteriors that are shown are themselves detailed and realistic. His plays have symbolic titles and also use symbols in the text, like the unicorn in *The Glass Menagerie*. Williams is concerned with the psychological makeup of his characters, and the main conflict is often between the spiritual and materialistic sides of human nature.

Realism and nonrealistic elements are combined in *The Glass Menagerie*. Williams calls it a "memory play," since it is presented through the eyes of Tom Wingfield, who is looking back upon his youth with his mother and sister. Thus, the format is unrealistic because the action occurs in the past, not the present. Even so, it is realistic action. Screen projections were not used in the original production and have rarely been used in subsequent productions.

The four characters in *The Glass Menagerie* are trapped. Amanda is trapped in the present but longs to return to the past. Laura is trapped by extreme shyness and a physical handicap. Tom is trapped by his family and circumstances. He manages to escape physically but, like Amanda, is still held by the past. Even the gentleman caller, Jim, is trapped by his own inadequacies and his inability to get ahead, though he has dreams of doing so. The characters are all victims of things they cannot control.

Throughout the play Williams presents many-faceted individuals, whose various traits are strongly depicted. The audience feels a compassion for the characters and shares their frustration.

Williams' dramatic technique is eclecticism at its best. He has a strong sense of theatre and of what will hold an audience's attention. He has been criticized for some of the degradation in his plays and for the fact that he has written nothing truly significant during the past several years. However, he is in large part responsible for bringing new life to the American theatre after World War II.

The Glass Menagerie

CHARACTERS

AMANDA WINGFIELD, *the mother.* A little woman of great but confused vitality clinging frantically to another time and place. Her characterization must be carefully created, not copied from type. She is not paranoiac, but her life is paranoia. There is much to admire in Amanda, and as much to love and pity as there is to laugh at. Certainly she has endurance and a kind of heroism, and though her foolishness makes her unwittingly cruel at times, there is tenderness in her slight person.

LAURA WINGFIELD, *her daughter.* Amanda, having failed to establish contact with reality, continues to live vitally in her illusions, but Laura's situation is even graver. A childhood illness has left her crippled, one leg slightly shorter than the other, and held in a brace. This defect need not be more than suggested on the stage. Stemming from this, Laura's separation increases till she is like a piece of her own glass collection, too exquisitely fragile to move from the shelf.

TOM WINGFIELD, *her son.* And the narrator of the play. A poet with a job in a warehouse. His nature is not remorseless, but to escape from a trap he has to act without pity.

JIM O'CONNOR, *the gentleman caller.* A nice, ordinary, young man.

SCENE *An Alley in St. Louis.*

PART I *Preparation for a Gentleman Caller*

PART II *The Gentleman Calls*

TIME *Now and the Past.*

418

The Glass Menagerie

Scene One: *The Wingfield apartment is in the rear of the building, one of those vast hive-like conglomerations of cellular living-units that flower as warty growths in overcrowded urban centers of lower middle-class population and are symptomatic of the impulse of this largest and fundamentally enslaved section of American society to avoid fluidity and differentiation and to exist and function as one interfused mass of automatism.*

The apartment faces an alley and is entered by a fire escape, a structure whose name is a touch of accidental poetic truth, for all of these huge buildings are always burning with the slow and implacable fires of human desperation. The fire escape is included in the set—that is, the landing of it and steps descending from it.

The scene is memory and is therefore nonrealistic. Memory takes a lot of poetic license. It omits some details; others are exaggerated, according to the emotional value of the articles it touches, for memory is seated predominantly in the heart. The interior is therefore rather dim and poetic.

At the rise of the curtain, the audience is faced with the dark, grim rear wall of the Wingfield tenement. This building, which runs parallel to the footlights, is flanked on both sides by dark narrow alleys which run into murky canyons of tangled clotheslines, garbage cans, and the sinister latticework of neighboring fire escapes. It is up and down these side alleys that exterior entrances and exits are made, during the play. At the end of Tom's opening commentary, the dark tenement wall slowly reveals (by means of a transparency) the interior of the ground floor Wingfield apartment.

Downstage is the living room, which also serves as a sleeping room for Laura, the sofa unfolding to make her bed. Upstage, center, and divided by a wide arch or second proscenium with transparent faded portieres (or second curtain), is the dining room. In an old-fashioned what-not in the living room are seen scores of transparent glass animals. A blown-up photograph of the father hangs on the wall of the living room, facing the audience, to the left of the archway. It is the face of a very handsome young man in a doughboy's First World War cap. He is gallantly smiling, ineluctably smiling, as if to say, "I will be smiling forever."

The audience hears and sees the opening scene in the dining room through both the transparent fourth wall of the building and the transparent gauze portieres of the dining-room arch. It is during this revealing scene that the fourth wall slowly ascends, out of sight. This transparent exterior wall is not brought down again until the very end of the play, during Tom's *final speech.*

The narrator is an undisguised convention of the play. He takes whatever license with dramatic convention is convenient to his purposes.

Tom *enters dressed as a merchant sailor from alley, stage left, and strolls across the front of the stage to the fire escape. There he stops and lights a cigarette. He addresses the audience.*

TOM: Yes, I have tricks in my pocket, I have things up my sleeve. But I am the opposite of a stage magician. He gives you illusion that has the appearance of truth. I give you truth in the pleasant disguise of illusion.

To begin with, I turn back time. I reverse it to that quaint period, the thirties, when the huge middle class of America was matriculating in a school for the blind. Their eyes had failed them, or they had failed their eyes, and so they were having their fingers pressed forcibly down on the fiery Braille alphabet of a dissolving economy.

In Spain there was revolution. Here there was only shouting and confusion.

In Spain there was Guernica. Here there were disturbances of labor, sometimes pretty violent, in otherwise peaceful cities such as Chicago, Cleveland, Saint Louis . . .

This is the social background of the play.

(*Music*)

The play is memory.

Being a memory play, it is dimly lighted, it is sentimental, it is not realistic.

In memory everything seems to happen to music. That explains the fiddle in the wings.

I am the narrator of the play, and also a character in it.

The other characters are my mother, Amanda, my sister, Laura, and a gentleman caller who appears in the final scenes.

He is the most realistic character in the play, being an emissary from a world of reality that we were somehow set apart from.

But since I have a poet's weakness for symbols, I am using this character also as a symbol; he is the long delayed but always expected something that we live for.

There is a fifth character in the play who doesn't appear except in this larger-than-life-size photograph over the mantel.

This is our father who left us a long time ago.

He was a telephone man who fell in love with long distances; he gave up his job with the telephone company and skipped the light fantastic out of town . . .

The last we heard of him was a picture post-card from Mazatlan, on the Pacific coast of Mexico, containing a message of two words—

"Hello—Good-bye!" and no address.

I think the rest of the play will explain itself. . . .

(*Amanda's voice becomes audible through the portieres*)

(*Legend on screen: "Où sont les neiges"*)[1]

(*He divides the portieres and enters the upstage area*)

(*Amanda and Laura are seated at a drop-leaf table. Eating is indicated by gestures without food or utensils. Amanda faces the audience,* Tom *and*

[1] "Where are the snows (of yesteryear)?" part of the refrain of François Villon's "Ballade of Dead Ladies."

Laura *are seated in profile. The interior has lit up softly and through the scrim we see* Amanda *and* Laura *seated at the table in the upstage area)*

AMANDA: (*Calling*) Tom?
TOM: Yes, Mother.
AMANDA: We can't say grace until you come to the table!
TOM: Coming, Mother. (*He bows slightly and withdraws, reappearing a few moments later in his place at the table*)
AMANDA: (*To her son*) Honey, don't *push* with your *fingers*. If you have to push with something, the thing to push with is a crust of bread. And chew—chew! Animals have sections in their stomachs which enable them to digest food without mastication, but human beings are supposed to chew their food before they swallow it down. Eat food leisurely, son, and really enjoy it. A well-cooked meal has lots of delicate flavors that have to be held in the mouth for appreciation. So chew your food and give your salivary glands a chance to function!

(Tom *deliberately lays his imaginary fork down and pushes his chair back from the table*)

TOM: I haven't enjoyed one bite of this dinner because of your constant directions on how to eat it. It's you that make me rush through meals with your hawk-like attention to every bite I take. Sickening—spoils my appetite —all this discussion of—animals' secretion—salivary glands—mastication!
AMANDA: (*Lightly*) Temperament like a Metropolitan star! (*He rises and crosses downstage*) You're not excused from the table.
TOM: I'm getting a cigarette.
AMANDA: You smoke too much.

(Laura *rises*)

LAURA: I'll bring in the blanc mange.

(*He remains standing with his cigarette by the portieres during the following*)

AMANDA: (*Rising*) No, sister, no, sister—you be the lady this time and I'll be the darky.
LAURA: I'm already up.
AMANDA: Resume your seat, little sister—I want you to stay fresh and pretty—for gentlemen callers!
LAURA: I'm not expecting any gentlemen callers.
AMANDA: (*Crossing out to kitchenette. Airily*) Sometimes they come when they are least expected! Why, I remember one Sunday afternoon in Blue Mountain—(*Enters kitchenette*)
TOM: I know what's coming!
LAURA: Yes. But let her tell it.
TOM: Again?
LAURA: She loves to tell it.

(Amanda *returns with bowl of dessert*)

AMANDA: One Sunday afternoon in Blue Mountain—your mother received—*seventeen!*—gentlemen callers! Why, sometimes there weren't chairs enough to accommodate them all. We had to send the nigger over to bring the folding chairs from the parish house.

TOM: (*Remaining at portieres*) How did you entertain those gentlemen callers?

AMANDA: I understood the art of conversation!

TOM: I bet you could talk.

AMANDA: Girls in those days *knew* how to talk, I can tell you.

TOM: Yes?

(*Image: Amanda as a girl on a porch, greeting callers*)

AMANDA: They knew how to entertain their gentlemen callers. It wasn't enough for a girl to be possessed of a pretty face and a graceful figure— although I wasn't slighted in either respect. She also needed to have a nimble wit and a tongue to meet all occasions.

TOM: What did you talk about?

AMANDA: Things of importance going on in the world! Never anything coarse, or common or vulgar. (*She addresses* Tom *as though he were seated in the vacant chair at the table though he remains by portieres. He plays this scene as though he held the book*) My callers were gentlemen—all! Among my callers were some of the most prominent young planters of the Mississippi Delta—planters and sons of planters!

(Tom *motions for music and a spot of light on* Amanda)
(*Her eyes lift, her face glows, her voice becomes rich and elegiac*)
(*Screen legend: "Où sont les neiges"*)

There was young Champ Laughlin, who later became vice-president of the Delta Planters Bank.

Hadley Stevenson who was drowned in Moon Lake and left his widow one hundred and fifty thousand in Government bonds.

There were the Cutrere brothers, Wesley and Bates. Bates was one of my bright particular beaux! He got in a quarrel with that wild Wainwright boy. They shot it out on the floor of Moon Lake Casino. Bates was shot through the stomach. Died in the ambulance on his way to Memphis. His widow was also well-provided for, came into eight or ten thousand acres, that's all. She married him on the rebound—never loved her—carried my picture on him the night he died!

And there was that boy that every girl in the Delta had set her cap for! That beautiful, brilliant young Fitzhugh boy from Greene County!

TOM: What did he leave his widow?

AMANDA: He never married! Gracious, you talk as though all of my old admirers had turned up their toes to the daisies!

TOM: Isn't this the first you've mentioned that still survives?

AMANDA: That Fitzhugh boy went North and made a fortune—came to be known as the Wolf of Wall Street! He had the Midas touch, whatever he touched turned to gold!

And I could have been Mrs. Duncan J. Fitzhugh, mind you! But—I picked your *father*!

LAURA: (*Rising*) Mother, let me clear the table.

AMANDA: No, dear, you go in front and study your typewriter chart. Or practice your shorthand a little. Stay fresh and pretty!—It's almost time for our gentlemen callers to start arriving. (*She flounces girlishly toward the kitchenette*) How many do you suppose we're going to entertain this afternoon?

(Tom *throws down the paper and jumps up with a groan*)

LAURA: (*Alone in the dining room*) I don't believe we're going to receive any, Mother.
AMANDA: (*Reappearing, airily*) What? No one—not one? You must be joking! (Laura *nervously echoes her laugh. She slips in a fugitive manner through the half-open portieres and draws them gently behind her. A shaft of very clear light is thrown on her face against the faded tapestry of the curtains. Music: "The glass menagerie" under faintly. Lightly*) Not one gentleman caller? It can't be true! There must be a flood, there must have been a tornado!
LAURA: It isn't a flood, it's not a tornado, Mother. I'm just not popular like you were in Blue Mountain. . . . (Tom *utters another groan. Laura glances at him with a faint, apologetic smile. Her voice catching a little*) Mother's afraid I'm going to be an old maid.

(*The Scene Dims Out with "Glass Menagerie" Music*)

SCENE TWO: *"Laura, Haven't You Ever Liked Some Boy?"*
On the dark stage the screen is lighted with the image of blue roses.
Gradually Laura's figure becomes apparent and the screen goes out.
The music subsides.
Laura is seated in the delicate ivory chair at the small clawfoot table.
She wears a dress of soft violet material for a kimono—her hair tied back from her forehead with a ribbon.
She is washing and polishing her collection of glass.
Amanda appears on the fire-escape steps. At the sound of her ascent, Laura catches her breath, thrusts the bowl of ornaments away and seats herself stiffly before the diagram of the typewriter keyboard as though it held her spellbound.
Something has happened to Amanda. It is written in her face as she climbs to the landing: a look that is grim and hopeless and a little absurd.
She has on one of those cheap or imitation velvety-looking cloth coats with imitation fur collar. Her hat is five or six years old, one of those dreadful cloche hats that were worn in the late twenties and she is clasping an enormous black patent-leather pocketbook with nickel clasps and initials. This is her full-dress outfit, the one she usually wears to the D.A.R.
Before entering she looks through the door.
She purses her lips, opens her eyes very wide, rolls them upward and shakes her head.
Then she slowly lets herself in the door. Seeing her mother's expression Laura touches her lips with a nervous gesture.
LAURA: Hello, Mother., I was—(She *makes a nervous gesture toward the chart on the wall. Amanda leans against the shut door and stares at Laura with a martyred look*)
AMANDA: Deception? Deception? (She *slowly removes her hat and gloves, continuing the sweet suffering stare. She lets the hat and gloves fall on the floor—a bit of acting*)
LAURA: (*Shakily*) How was the D.A.R. meeting? (Amanda *slowly opens her purse and removes a dainty white handkerchief which she shakes out*

delicately and delicately touches to her lips and nostrils) Didn't you go to the D.A.R. meeting, Mother?

AMANDA: (*Faintly, almost inaudibly*)—No—No. (*Then more forcibly*) I did not have the strength—to go to the D.A.R. In fact, I did not have the courage! I wanted to find a hole in the ground and hide myself in it forever! (*She crosses slowly to the wall and removes the diagram of the typewriter keyboard. She holds it in front of her for a second, staring at it sweetly and sorrowfully—then bites her lips and tears it in two pieces*)

LAURA: (*Faintly*) Why did you do that, Mother? (*Amanda repeats the same procedure with the chart of the Gregg Alphabet*) Why are you—

AMANDA: Why? Why? How old are you, Laura?

LAURA: Mother, you know my age.

AMANDA: I thought that you were an adult; it seems that I was mistaken. (*She crosses slowly to the sofa and sinks down and stares at* Laura)

LAURA: Please don't stare at me, Mother, (*Amanda closes her eyes and lowers her head. Count ten*)

AMANDA: What are we going to do, what is going to become of us, what is the future? (*Count ten*)

LAURA: Has something happened, Mother? (*Amanda draws a long breath and takes out the handkerchief again. Dabbing process*) Mother, has—something happened?

AMANDA: I'll be all right in a minute, I'm just bewildered—(*Count five*)—by life. . . .

LAURA: Mother, I wish that you would tell me what's happened!

AMANDA: As you know, I was supposed to be inducted into my office at the D.A.R. this afternoon. (IMAGE: A SWARM OF TYPEWRITERS) But I stopped off at Rubicam's Business College to speak to your teachers about your having a cold and ask them what progress they thought you were making down there.

LAURA: Oh. . . .

AMANDA: I went to the typing instructor and introduced myself as your mother. She didn't know who you were. Wingfield, she said. We don't have any such student enrolled at the school!

I assured her she did, that you had been going to classes since early in January.

"I wonder," she said, "if you could be talking about that terribly shy little girl who dropped out of school after only a few days' attendance?"

"No," I said, "Laura, my daughter, has been going to school every day for the past six weeks!"

"Excuse me," she said. She took the attendance book out and there was your name, unmistakably printed, and all the dates you were absent until they decided that you had dropped out of school.

I still said, "No, there must have been some mistake! There must have been some mix-up in the records!"

And she said, "No—I remember her perfectly now. Her hands shook so that she couldn't hit the right keys! The first time we gave a speed-test, she broke down completely—was sick at the stomach and almost had to be carried into the wash-room! After that morning she never showed up any more. We phoned the house but never got any answer"—while I was working at Famous and Barr, I suppose, demonstrating those—Oh!

I felt so weak I could barely keep on my feet!

I had to sit down while they got me a glass of water!

Fifty dollars' tuition, all of our plans—my hopes and ambitions for you—just gone up the spout, just gone up the spout like that.

(Laura *draws a long breath and gets awkwardly to her feet. She crosses to the victrola and winds it up*)

What are you doing?
LAURA: Oh! (*She releases the handle and returns to her seat*)
AMANDA: Laura, where have you been going when you've gone out pretending that you were going to business college?
LAURA: I've just been going out walking.
AMANDA: That's not true.
LAURA: It is. I just went walking.
AMANDA: Walking? Walking? In winter? Deliberately courting pneumonia in that light coat? Where did you walk to, Laura?
LAURA: All sorts of places—mostly in the park.
AMANDA: Even after you'd started catching that cold?
LAURA: It was the lesser of two evils, Mother. (*Image: Winter scene in park*) I couldn't go back up. I—threw up—on the floor!
AMANDA: From half past seven till after five every day you mean to tell me you walked around in the park, because you wanted to make me think that you were still going to Rubicam's Business College?
LAURA: It wasn't as bad as it sounds. I went inside places to get warmed up.
AMANDA: Inside where?
LAURA: I went in the art museum and the bird-houses at the Zoo. I visited the penguins every day! Sometimes I did without lunch and went to the movies. Lately I've been spending most of my afternoons in the Jewel-box, that big glass house where they raise the tropical flowers.
AMANDA: You did all this to deceive me, just for deception? (*Laura looks down*) Why?
LAURA: Mother, when you're disappointed, you get that awful suffering look on your face, like the picture of Jesus' mother in the museum!
AMANDA: Hush!
LAURA: I couldn't face it.

(*Pause. A whisper of strings*)
(*Legend: "The crust of humility"*)

AMANDA: (*Hopelessly fingering the huge pocketbook*) So what are we going to do the rest of our lives? Stay home and watch the parades go by? Amuse ourselves with the glass menagerie, darling? Eternally play those worn-out phonograph records your father left as a painful reminder of him?
We won't have a business career—we've given that up because it gave us nervous indigestion! (*Laughs wearily*) What is there left but dependency all our lives? I know so well what becomes of unmarried women who aren't prepared to occupy a position. I've seen such pitiful cases in the South— barely tolerated spinsters living upon the grudging patronage of sister's husband or brother's wife!—stuck away in some little mouse-trap of a room —encouraged by one in-law to visit another—little birdlike women without any nest—eating the crust of humility all their life!
Is that the future that we've mapped out for ourselves?
I swear it's the only alternative I can think of!
It isn't a very pleasant alternative, is it?
Of course—some girls *do marry.*

(*Laura twists her hands nervously*)

Haven't you ever liked some boy?
LAURA: Yes. I liked one once. (*Rises*) I came across his picture a while ago.
AMANDA: (*With some interest*) He gave you his picture?
LAURA: No, it's in the year-book.
AMANDA: (*Disappointed*) Oh—a high-school boy.

(*Screen image:* Jim *as high-school hero bearing a silver cup*)

LAURA: Yes. His name was Jim. (Laura *lifts the heavy annual from the
claw-foot table*) Here he is in *The Pirates of Penzance*.
AMANDA: (*Absently*) The what?
LAURA: The operetta the senior class put on. He had a wonderful voice
and we sat across the aisle from each other Mondays, Wednesdays, and
Fridays in the Aud. Here he is with the silver cup for debating! See his grin?
AMANDA: (*Absently*) He must have had a jolly disposition.
LAURA: He used to call me—Blue Roses.

(*Image: Blue roses*)

AMANDA: Why did he call you such a name as that?
LAURA: When I had that attack of pleurosis—he asked me what was the
matter when I came back. I said pleurosis—he thought that I said Blue Roses!
So that's what he always called me after that. Whenever he saw me, he'd
holler, "Hello, Blue Roses!" I didn't care for the girl that he went out with.
Emily Meisenbach. Emily was the best-dressed girl at Soldan. She never
struck me, though, as being sincere.... It says in the Personal Section—
they're engaged. That's—six years ago! They must be married by now.
AMANDA: Girls that aren't cut out for business careers usually wind up
married to some nice man. (*Gets up with a spark of revival*) Sister, that's
what you'll do!

(*Laura utters a startled, doubtful laugh. She reaches quickly for a piece
of glass*)

LAURA: But, Mother—
AMANDA: Yes? (*Crossing to photograph*)
LAURA: (*In a tone of frightened apology*) I'm— crippled!

(*Image: Screen*)

AMANDA: Nonsense! Laura, I've told you never, never to use that word.
Why, you're not crippled, you just have a little defect—hardly noticeable,
even! When people have some slight disadvantage like that, they cultivate
other things to make up for it—develop charm—and vivacity—and—*charm!*
That's all you have to do! (*She turns again to the photograph*) One thing
your father had *plenty of*—was *charm!*

(Tom *motions to the fiddle in the wings*)
(*The Scene Fades Out with Music*)

SCENE THREE: *Legend on screen: "After the fiasco—" Tom speaks from the fire-escape landing.*

TOM: After the fiasco at Rubicam's Business College, the idea of getting a gentleman caller for Laura began to play a more and more important part in Mother's calculations.

It became an obsession. Like some archetype of the universal unconscious, the image of the gentleman caller haunted our small apartment. . . .

(*Image: Young man at door with flowers*)

An evening at home rarely passed without some allusion to this image, this specter, this hope. . . .

Even when he wasn't mentioned, his presence hung in Mother's preoccupied look and in my sister's frightened, apologetic manner—hung like a sentence passed upon the Wingfields!

Mother was a woman of action as well as words.

She began to take logical steps in the planned direction.

Late that winter and in the early spring—realizing that extra money would be needed to properly feather the nest and plume the bird—she conducted a vigorous campaign on the telephone, roping in subscribers to one of those magazines for matrons called *The Homemaker's Companion,* the type of journal that features the serialized sublimations of ladies of letters who think in terms of delicate cuplike breasts, slim, tapering waists, rich, creamy thighs, eyes like wood-smoke in autumn, fingers that soothe and caress like strains of music, bodies as powerful as Etruscan sculpture.

(*Screen image: Glamor magazine cover*)
(*Amanda enters with phone on long extension cord. She is spotted in the dim stage*)

AMANDA: Ida Scott? This is Amanda Wingfield! We *missed* you at the D.A.R. last Monday!

I said to myself: She's probably suffering with that sinus condition! How is that sinus condition?

Horrors! Heaven have mercy!—You're a Christian martyr, yes, that's what you are, a Christian martyr!

Well, I just now happened to notice that your subscription to the *Companion's* about to expire! Yes, it expires with the next issue, honey!—just when that wonderful new serial by Bessie Mae Hopper is getting off to such an exciting start. Oh, honey, it's something that you can't miss! You remember how *Gone With the Wind* took everbody by storm? You simply couldn't go out if you hadn't read it. All everybody *talked* was Scarlett O'Hara. Well, this is a book that critics already compare to *Gone With the Wind.* It's the *Gone With the Wind* of the post-World War generation!—What?—Burning? —Oh, honey, don't let them burn, go take a look in the oven and I'll hold the wire! Heavens—I think she's hung up!

DIM OUT

(*Legend on screen: "You think I'm in love with continental shoemakers?"*)
(*Before the stage is lighted, the violent voices of Tom and Amanda are heard*)

(They are quarreling behind the portieres. In front of them stands Laura *with clenched hands and panicky expression)*
(A clear pool of light on her figure throughout this scene)

TOM: What in Christ's name am I—
AMANDA: *(Shrilly)* Don't you use that—
TOM: Supposed to do!
AMANDA: Expression! Not in my—
TOM: Ohhh!
AMANDA: Presence! Have you gone out of your senses?
TOM: I have, that's true, *driven* out!
AMANDA: What is the matter with you, you—big—big—*idiot!*
TOM: Look!—I've got *no thing,* no single thing—
AMANDA: Lower your voice!
TOM: In my life here that I can call my *own!* Everything is—
AMANDA: Stop that shouting!
TOM: Yesterday you confiscated my books! You had the nerve to—
AMANDA: I took that horrible novel back to the library—yes! That hideous book by that insane Mr. Lawrence. (Tom *laughs wildly*) I cannot control the output of diseased minds or people who cater to them—(Tom *laughs still more wildly*) BUT I WON'T ALLOW SUCH FILTH BROUGHT INTO MY HOUSE! No, no, no, no, no!
TOM: House, house! Who pays rent on it, who makes a slave of himself to—
AMANDA: *(Fairly screeching)* Don't you DARE to—
TOM: No, no, *I* mustn't say things! *I've* got to just—
AMANDA: Let me tell you—
TOM: I don't want to hear any more! (*He tears the portieres open. The upstage area is lit with a turgid smoky red glow*)

(Amanda's hair is in metal curlers and she wears a very old bathrobe, much too large for her slight figure, a relic of the faithless Mr. Wingfield)
(An upright typewriter and a wild disarray of manuscripts is on the drop-leaf table. The quarrel was probably precipitated by Amanda's interruption of his creative labor. A chair lying overthrown on the floor)
(Their gesticulating shadows are cast on the ceiling by the fiery glow)

AMANDA: You *will* hear more, you—
TOM: No, I won't hear more, I'm going out!
AMANDA: You come right back in—
TOM: Out, out, out! Because I'm—
AMANDA: Come back here, Tom Wingfield! I'm not through talking to you!
TOM: Oh, go—
LAURA: *(Desperately)*—Tom!
AMANDA: You're going to listen, and no more insolence from you! I'm at the end of my patience!

(He comes back toward her)

TOM: What do you think I'm at? Aren't I supposed to have any patience to reach the end of, Mother? I know, I know. It seems unimportant to you, what I'm *doing*—what I *want* to do—having a little *difference* between them! You don't think that—

AMANDA: I think you've been doing things that you're ashamed of. That's why you act like this. I don't believe that you go every night to the movies. Nobody goes to the movies night after night. Nobody in their right minds goes to the movies as often as you pretend to. People don't go to the movies at nearly midnight, and movies don't let out at two A.M. Come in stumbling. Muttering to yourself like a maniac! You get three hours' sleep and then go to work. Oh, I can picture the way you're doing down there. Moping, doping, because you're in no condition.

TOM: (*Wildly*) No, I'm in no condition!

AMANDA: What right have you got to jeopardize your job? Jeopardize the security of us all? How do you think we'd manage if you were—

TOM: Listen! You think I'm crazy *about the warehouse?* (*He bends fiercely toward her slight figure*) You think I'm in love with the Continental Shoemakers? You think I want to spend fifty-five *years* down there in that—*celotex interior!* with—*fluorescent*—*tubes!* Look! I'd rather somebody picked up a crowbar and battered out my brains—than go back mornings! I *go!* Every time you come in yelling that God damn *"Rise and Shine!" "Rise and Shine!"* I say to myself, "How *lucky dead* people are!" But I get up. I *go!* For sixty-five dollars a month I give up all that I dream of doing and being *ever!* And you say self—*self's* all I ever think of. Why, listen, if self is what I thought of, Mother, I'd be where he is—GONE! (*Pointing to father's picture*) As far as the system of transportation reaches! (*He starts past her. She grabs his arm*) Don't grab at me, Mother!

AMANDA: Where are you going?

TOM: I'm going to the *movies!*

AMANDA: I don't believe that lie!

TOM: (*Crouching toward her, overtowering her tiny figure. She backs away, gasping*) I'm going to opium dens! Yes, opium dens, dens of vice and criminals' hang-outs, Mother. I've joined the Hogan gang, I'm a hired assassin, I carry a tommy-gun in a violin case! I run a string of cat-houses in the Valley! They call me Killer, Killer Wingfield, I'm leading a double-life, a simple, honest warehouse worker by day, by night a dynamic *czar* of the *underworld, Mother,* I go to gambling casinos, I spin away fortunes on the roulette table! I wear a patch over one eye and a false mustache, sometimes I put on green whiskers. On those occasions they call me—*El Diablo!* Oh, I could tell you things to make you sleepless! My enemies plan to dynamite this place. They're going to blow us all sky-high some night! I'll be glad, very happy, and so will you! You'll go up, up on a broomstick, over Blue Mountain with seventeen gentlemen callers! You ugly—babbling old—*witch.* . . . (*He goes through a series of violent, clumsy movements, seizing his overcoat, lunging to the door, pulling it fiercely open. The women watch him, aghast. His arm catches in the sleeve of the coat as he struggles to pull it on. For a moment he is pinioned by the bulky garment. With an outraged groan he tears the coat off again, splitting the shoulder of it, and hurls it across the room. It strikes against the shelf of Laura's glass collection, there is a tinkle of shattering glass. Laura cries out as if wounded*)

(*Music. Legend: "The glass menagerie"*)

LAURA: (*Shrilly*) My glass!—menagerie. . . . (*She covers her face and turns away*)

(But Amanda *is still stunned and stupefied by the "ugly witch" so that she barely notices this occurrence. Now she recovers her speech)*

AMANDA: *(In an awful voice)* I won't speak to you—until you apologize! *(She crosses through portieres and draws them together behind her. Tom is left with* Laura. Laura *clings weakly to the mantel with her face averted. Tom stares at her stupidly for a moment. Then he crosses to shelf. Drops awkwardly on his knees to collect the fallen glass, glancing at* Laura *as if he would speak but couldn't)*

("The Glass Menagerie" steals in as the Scene Dims Out)

SCENE FOUR: *The interior is dark. Faint light in the alley.*
   A deep-voiced bell in a church is tolling the hour of five as the scene commences.
   Tom *appears at the top of the alley. After each solemn boom of the bell in the tower, he shakes a little noise-maker or rattle as if to express the tiny spasm of man in contrast to the sustained power and dignity of the Almighty. This and the unsteadiness of his advance make it evident that he has been drinking.*
   As he climbs the few steps to the fire-escape landing light steals up inside.
Laura *appears in night-dress, observing* Tom's *empty bed in the front room.*
   Tom *fishes in his pockets for door key, removing a motley assortment of articles in the search, including a perfect shower of movie-ticket stubs and an empty bottle. At last he finds the key, but just as he is about to insert it, it slips from his fingers. He strikes a match and crouches below the door.*
   TOM: *(Bitterly)* One crack—and it falls through
   *(*Laura *opens the door)*
   LAURA: Tom, Tom, what are you doing?
   TOM: Looking for a door key.
   LAURA: Where have you been all this time?
   TOM: I have been to the movies.
   LAURA: All this time at the movies?
   TOM: There was a very long program. There was a Garbo picture and a Mickey Mouse and a travelogue and a newsreel and a preview of coming attractions. And there was an organ solo and a collection for the milk-fund—simultaneously—which ended up in a terrible fight between a fat lady and an usher!
   LAURA: *(Innocently)* Did you have to stay through everything?
   TOM: Of course! And, oh, I forgot! There was a big stage show! The headliner on this stage show was Malvolio the Magician. He performed wonderful tricks, many of them, such as pouring water back and forth between pitchers. First it turned to wine and then it turned to beer and then it turned to whiskey. I know it was whiskey it finally turned into because he needed somebody to come up out of the audience to help him, and I came up—both shows! It was Kentucky Straight Bourbon. A very generous fellow, he gave souvenirs. *(He pulls from his back pocket a shimmering rainbow-colored scarf)* He gave me this. This is his magic scarf. You can have it, Laura. You wave it over a canary cage and you get a bowl of goldfish. You wave it over the gold-fish bowl and they fly away canaries. . . . But the wonderfullest trick of all was the coffin trick. We nailed him into a coffin and he got out of the coffin without removing one nail. *(He has come inside)* There is a trick that would come in handy for me—get me out of this 2 by

4 situation! (*Flops onto bed and starts removing shoes*)

LAURA: Tom—Shhh!

TOM: What're you shushing me for?

LAURA: You'll wake up Mother.

TOM: Goody, goody! Pay 'er back for all those "Rise an Shines." (*Lies down, groaning*) You know it don't take much intelligence to get yourself into a nailed-up coffin, Laura. But who in hell ever got himself out of one without removing one nail?

(*As if in answer, the father's grinning photograph lights up*) and SCENE DIMS OUT

(*Immediately following: The church bell is heard striking six. At the sixth stroke the alarm clock goes off in Amanda's room, and after a few moments we hear her calling: "Rise and Shine! Rise and Shine! Laura, go tell your brother to rise and shine!"*)

TOM: (*Sitting up slowly*) I'll rise—but I won't shine.

(*The light increases*)

AMANDA: Laura, tell your brother his coffee is ready.

(*Laura slips into front room*)

LAURA: Tom!—It's nearly seven. Don't make Mother nervous. (*He stares at her stupidly. Beseechingly*) Tom, speak to Mother this morning. Make up with her, apologize, speak to her!

TOM: She won't to me. It's her that started not speaking.

LAURA: If you just say you're sorry she'll start speaking.

TOM: Her not speaking—is that such a tragedy?

LAURA: Please—please!

AMANDA: (*Calling from kitchenette*) Laura, are you going to do what I asked you to do, or do I have to get dressed and go out myself?

LAURA: Going, going—soon as I get on my coat! (*She pulls on a shapeless felt hat with nervous, jerky movement, pleadingly glancing at* Tom. *Rushes awkwardly for coat. The coat is one of* Amanda's, *inaccurately made-over, the sleeves too short for* Laura) Butter and what else?

AMANDA: (*Entering upstage*) Just butter. Tell them to charge it.

LAURA: Mother, they make such faces when I do that.

AMANDA: Sticks and stones can break our bones, but the expression on Mr. Garfinkel's face won't harm us! Tell your brother his coffee is getting cold.

LAURA: (*At door*) Do what I asked you, will you, will you, Tom?

(*He looks sullenly away*)

AMANDA: Laura, go now or just don't go at all!

LAURA: (*Rushing out*) Going—going! (*A second later she cries out.* Tom springs up and crosses to door. Amanda rushes anxiously in. Tom opens the door)

TOM: Laura?

LAURA: I'm all right. I slipped, but I'm all right.

AMANDA: (*Peering anxiously after her*) If anyone breaks a leg on those fire-escape steps, the landlord ought to be sued for every cent he possesses! (*She shuts door. Remembers she isn't speaking and returns to other room*)

(*As* Tom *enters listlessly for his coffee, she turns her back to him and stands rigidly facing the window on the gloomy gray vault of the areaway. Its light on her face with its aged but childish features is cruelly sharp, satirical as a Daumier print*)
(*Music under: "Ave Maria"*)
(Tom *glances sheepishly but sullenly at her averted figure and slumps at the table. The coffee is scalding hot; he sips it and gasps and spits it back in the cup. At his gasp,* Amanda *catches her breath and half turns. Then catches herself and turns back to window*)
(Tom *blows on his coffee, glancing sidewise at his mother. She clears her throat.* Tom *clears his. He starts to rise. Sinks back down again, scratches his head, clears his throat again.* Amanda *coughs.* Tom *raises his cup in both hands to blow on it, his eyes staring over the rim of it at his mother for several moments. Then he slowly sets the cup down and awkwardly and hesitantly rises from the chair*)

Tom: (*Hoarsely*) Mother. I—I apologize, Mother. (Amanda *draws a quick, shuddering breath. Her face works grotesquely. She breaks into child-like tears*) I'm sorry for what I said, for everything that I said, I didn't mean it.

Amanda: (*Sobbingly*) My devotion has made me a witch and so I make myself hateful to my children!

Tom: *No, you don't.*

Amanda: I worry so much, don't sleep, it makes me nervous!

Tom: (*Gently*) I understand that.

Amanda: I've had to put up a solitary battle all these years. But you're my right-hand bower! Don't fall down, don't fail!

Tom: (*Gently*) I try, Mother.

Amanda: (*With great enthusiasm*) Try and you will succeed! (*The notion makes her breathless*) Why, you—you're just *full* of natural endowments! Both my children—they're *unusual* children! Don't you think I know it? I'm so—*proud!* Happy and—feel I've—so much to be thankful for but—Promise me one thing, Son!

Tom: What, Mother?

Amanda: Promise, Son, you'll—never be a drunkard!

Tom: (*Turns to her grinning*) I will never be a drunkard, Mother.

Amanda: That's what frightened me so, that you'd be drinking! Eat a bowl of Purina!

Tom: Just coffee, Mother.

Amanda: Shredded wheat biscuit?

Tom: No. No, Mother, just coffee.

Amanda: You can't put in a day's work on an empty stomach. You've got ten minutes—don't gulp! Drinking too-hot liquids makes cancer of the stomach. . . . Put cream in.

Tom: No, thank you.

Amanda: To cool it.

Tom: No! No, thank you, I want it black.

Amanda: I know, but it's not good for you. We have to do all that we can to build ourselves up. In these trying times we live in, all that we have to cling to is—each other. . . . That's why it's so important to—Tom, I—I sent out your sister so I could discuss something with you. If you hadn't spoken I would have spoken to you. (*Sits down*)

TOM: (*Gently*) What is it, Mother, that you want to discuss?

AMANDA: *Laura!*

(Tom *puts his cup down slowly*)
(*Legend on screen: "Laura"*)
(*Music: "The glass menagerie"*)

TOM: —Oh—Laura . . .

AMANDA: (*Touching his sleeve*) You know how Laura is. So quiet but—still water runs deep! She notices things and I think she—broods about them. (Tom *looks up*) A few days ago I came in and she was crying.

TOM: What about?

AMANDA: You.

TOM: Me?

AMANDA: She has an idea that you're not happy here.

TOM: What gave her that idea?

AMANDA: What gives her any idea? However, you do act strangely. I—I'm not criticizing, understand *that!* I know your ambitions do not lie in the warehouse, that like everybody in the whole wide world—you've had to—make sacrifices, but—Tom—Tom—life's not easy, it calls for—Spartan endurance! There's so many things in my heart that I cannot describe to you! I've never told you but I—*loved* your father. . . .

TOM: (*Gently*) I know that, Mother.

AMANDA: And you—when I see you taking after his ways! Staying out late—and—well, you *had* been drinking the night you were in that—terrifying condition! Laura says that you hate the apartment and that you go out nights to get away from it! Is that true, Tom?

TOM: No. You say there's so much in your heart that you can't describe to me. That's true of me, too. There's so much in my heart that I can't describe to *you!* So let's respect each other's—

AMANDA: But, why—*why*, Tom—are you always so *restless?* Where do you go to, nights?

TOM: I—go to the movies.

AMANDA: Why do you go to the movies so much, Tom?

TOM: I go to the movies because—I like adventure. Adventure is something I don't have much of at work, so I go to the movies.

AMANDA: But, Tom, you go to the movies *entirely* too *much!*

TOM: I like a lot of adventure.

(Amanda *looks baffled, then hurt. As the familiar inquisition resumes he becomes hard and impatient again. Amanda* slips back into her querulous attitude toward him)
(*Image on screen: Sailing vessel with Jolly Roger*)

AMANDA: Most young men find adventure in their careers.

TOM: Then most young men are not employed in a warehouse.

AMANDA: The world is full of young men employed in warehouses and offices and factories.

TOM: Do all of them find adventure in their careers?

AMANDA: They do or they do without it! Not everybody has a craze for adventure.

Tom: Man is by instinct a lover, a hunter, a fighter, and none of those instincts are given much play at the warehouse!

Amanda: Man is by instinct! Don't quote instinct to me! Instinct is something that people have got away from! It belongs to animals! Christian adults don't want it!

Tom: What do Christian adults want, then, Mother?

Amanda: Superior things! Things of the mind and the spirit! Only animals have to satisfy instincts! Surely your aims are somewhat higher than theirs! Than monkeys—pigs—

Tom: I reckon they're not.

Amanda: You're joking! However, that isn't what I wanted to discuss.

Tom: (*Rising*) I haven't much time.

Amanda: (*Pushing his shoulders*) Sit down.

Tom: You want me to punch in red at the warehouse, Mother?

Amanda: You have five minutes. I want to talk about Laura.

(Legend: "Plans and provisions")

Tom: All right! What about Laura?

Amanda: We have to be making some plans and provisions for her. She's older than you, two years, and nothing has happened. She just drifts along doing nothing. It frightens me terribly how she just drifts along.

Tom: I guess she's the type that people call home girls.

Amanda: There's no such type, and if there is, it's a pity! That is, unless the home is hers, with a husband!

Tom: What?

Amanda: Oh, I can see the handwriting on the wall as plain as I see the nose in front of my face! It's terrifying!

More and more you remind me of your father! He was out all hours without explanation!—Then *left! Good-bye!*

And me with the bag to hold. I saw that letter you got from the Merchant Marine. I know what you're dreaming of. I'm not standing here blindfolded.

Very well, then. Then *do* it!

But not till there's somebody to take your place.

Tom: What do you mean?

Amanda: I mean that as soon as Laura has got somebody to take care of her, married, a home of her own, independent—why, then you'll be free to go wherever you please, on land, on sea, whichever way the wind blows you!

But until that time you've got to look out for your sister. I don't say me because I'm old and don't matter! I say for your sister because she's young and dependent.

I put her in business college—a dismal failure! Frightened her so it made her sick at the stomach.

I took her over to the Young People's League at the church. Another fiasco. She spoke to nobody, nobody spoke to her. Now all she does is fool with those pieces of glass and play those worn-out records. What kind of a life is that for a girl to lead?

Tom: What can I do about it?

Amanda: Overcome selfishness!

Self, self, self is all that you ever think of!

(Tom springs up and crosses to get his coat. It is ugly and bulky. He pulls on a cap with earmuffs)

Where is your muffler? Put your wool muffler on!

(He snatches it angrily from the closet and tosses it around his neck and pulls both ends tight)

Tom! I haven't said what I had in mind to ask you.

TOM: I'm too late to—

AMANDA: *(Catching his arm—very importunately. Then shyly)* Down at the warehouse, aren't there some—nice young men?

TOM: No!

AMANDA: There *must* be—some . . .

TOM: Mother—*(Gesture)*

AMANDA: Find out one that's clean-living—doesn't drink and—ask him out for sister!

TOM: What?

AMANDA: For *sister!* To *meet!* Get *acquainted!*

TOM: *(Stamping to door)* Oh, my go-osh!

AMANDA: Will you? *(He opens door. Imploringly)* Will you? *(He starts down)* Will you? *Will* you, dear?

TOM: *(Calling back)* YES!

(Amanda closes the door hesitantly and with a troubled but faintly hopeful expression)
(Screen image: Glamor magazine cover)
(Spot Amanda at phone)

AMANDA: Ella Cartwright? This is Amanda Wingfield!
How are you, honey?
How is that kidney condition? *(Pause)*
Horrors! *(Pause)*
You're a Christian martyr, yes, honey, that's what you are, a Christian martyr!
Well, I just now happened to notice in my little red book that your subscription to the *Companion* has just run out! I knew that you wouldn't want to miss out on the wonderful serial starting in this new issue. It's by Bessie Mae Hopper, the first thing she's written since *Honeymoon for Three.*
Wasn't that a strange and interesting story? Well, this one is even lovelier, I believe. It has a sophisticated, society background. It's all about the horsey set on Long Island!

(Fade Out)

SCENE FIVE: *Legend on screen: "Annunciation." Fade with music.*

It is early dusk of a spring evening. Supper has just been finished in the Wingfield apartment. Amanda and Laura in light-colored dresses are removing dishes from the table, in the upstage area, which is shadowy, their movements formalized almost as a dance or ritual, their moving forms as pale and silent as moths.

Tom, in white shirt and trousers, rises from the table and crosses toward the fire-escape.

AMANDA: *(As he passes her)* Son, will you do me a favor?

TOM: What?

AMANDA: Comb your hair! You look so pretty when your hair is combed!
(Tom slouches on sofa with evening paper. Enormous caption "Franco Tri-

umphs") There is only one respect in which I would like you to emulate your father.

TOM: What respect is that?

AMANDA: The care he always took of his appearance. He never allowed himself to look untidy. (*He throws down the paper and crosses to fire-escape*) Where are you going?

TOM: I'm going out to smoke.

AMANDA: You smoke too much. A pack a day at fifteen cents a pack. How much would that amount to in a month? Thirty times fifteen is how much, Tom? Figure it out and you will be astounded at what you could save. Enough to give you a night-school course in accounting at Washington U! Just think what a wonderful thing that would be for you, Son!

(*Tom is unmoved by the thought*)

TOM: I'd rather smoke. (*He steps out on landing, letting the screen door slam*)

AMANDA: (*Sharply*) I know! That's the tragedy of it. . . . (*Alone, she turns to look at her husband's picture*)

(*Dance music: "All the world is waiting for the sunrise!"*)

TOM: (*To the audience*) Across the alley from us was the Paradise Dance Hall. On evenings in spring the windows and doors were open and the music came outdoors. Sometimes the lights were turned out except for a large glass sphere that hung from the ceiling. It would turn slowly about the filter the dusk with delicate rainbow colors. Then the orchestra played a waltz or a tango, something that had a slow and sensuous rhythm. Couples would come outside, to the relative privacy of the alley. You could see them kissing behind ash-pits and telephone poles.

This was the compensation for lives that passed like mine, without any change or adventure.

Adventure and change were imminent in this year. They were waiting around the corner for all these kids.

Suspended in the mist over Berchtesgaden, caught in the folds of Chamberlain's umbrella—

In Spain there was Guernica!

But here there was only hot swing music and liquor, dance halls, bars, and movies, and sex that hung in the gloom like a chandelier and flooded the world with brief, deceptive rainbows. . . .

All the world was waiting for bombardments!

(*Amanda turns from the picture and comes outside*)

AMANDA: (*Sighing*) A fire-escape landing's a poor excuse for a porch. (*She spreads a newspaper on a step and sits down, gracefully and demurely as if she were settling into a swing on a Mississippi veranda*) What are you looking at?

TOM: The moon.

AMANDA: Is there a moon this evening?

TOM: It's rising over Garfinkel's Delicatessen.

AMANDA: So it is! A little silver slipper of a moon. Have you made a wish on it yet?

TOM: Um-hum.

AMANDA: What did you wish for?

TOM: That's a secret.

AMANDA: A secret, huh? Well, I won't tell mine either. I will be just as mysterious as you.

TOM: I bet I can guess what yours is.

AMANDA: Is my head so transparent?

TOM: You're not a sphinx.

AMANDA: No, I don't have secrets. I'll tell you what I wished for on the moon. Success and happiness for my precious children! I wish for that whenever there's a moon, and when there isn't a moon, I wish for it, too.

TOM: I thought perhaps you wished for a gentleman caller.

AMANDA: Why do you say that?

TOM: Don't you remember asking me to fetch one?

AMANDA: I remember suggesting that it would be nice for your sister if you brought home some nice young man from the warehouse. I think that I've made that suggestion more than once.

TOM: Yes, you have made it repeatedly.

AMANDA: Well?

TOM: We are going to have one.

AMANDA: *What?*

TOM: A gentleman caller!

(The annunciation is celebrated with music)
(Amanda rises)
(Image on screen: Caller with bouquet)

AMANDA: You mean you have asked some nice young man to come over?

TOM: Yep. I've asked him to dinner.

AMANDA: You really did?

TOM: I did!

AMANDA: You did, and did he—*accept?*

TOM: He did!

AMANDA: Well, well—well, well! That's—lovely!

TOM: I thought that you would be pleased.

AMANDA: It's definite, then?

TOM: Very definite.

AMANDA: Soon?

TOM: Very soon.

AMANDA: For heaven's sake, stop putting on and tell me some things, will you?

TOM: What things do you want me to tell you?

AMANDA: *Naturally* I would like to know when he's *coming!*

TOM: He's coming tomorrow.

AMANDA: *Tomorrow?*

TOM: Yep. Tomorrow.

AMANDA: But, Tom!

TOM: Yes, Mother?

AMANDA: Tomorrow gives me no time!

TOM: Time for what?

AMANDA: Preparations! Why didn't you phone me at once, as soon as you asked him, the minute that he accepted? Then, don't you see, I could have been getting ready!

TOM: You don't have to make any fuss.

AMANDA: Oh. Tom, Tom, Tom, of course I have to make a fuss! I want things nice, not sloppy! Not thrown together. I'll certainly have to do some fast thinking, won't I?

TOM: I don't see why you have to think at all.

AMANDA: You just don't know. We can't have a gentleman caller in a pig-sty! All my wedding silver has to be polished, the monogrammed table linen ought to be laundered! The windows have to be washed and fresh curtains put up. And how about clothes? We have to *wear* something, don't we?

TOM: Mother, this boy is no one to make a fuss over!

AMANDA: Do you realize he's the first young man we've introduced to your sister?

It's terrible, dreadful, disgraceful and poor little sister has never received a single gentleman caller! Tom, come inside! (*She opens the screen door*)

TOM: What for?

AMANDA: I want to ask you some things.

TOM: If you're going to make such a fuss, I'll call it off, I'll tell him not to come!

AMANDA: You certainly won't do anything of the kind. Nothing offends people worse than broken engagements. It simply means I'll have to work like a Turk! We won't be brilliant, but we will pass inspection. Come on inside. (Tom *follows, groaning*) Sit down.

TOM: Any particular place you would like me to sit?

AMANDA: Thank heavens I've got that new sofa! I'm also making payments on a floor lamp I'll have sent out! And put the chintz covers on, they'll brighten things up! Of course I'd hoped to have these walls repapered.... What is the young man's name?

TOM: His name is O'Connor.

AMANDA: That, of course, means fish—tomorrow is Friday! I'll have that salmon loaf—with Durkee's dressing! What does he do? He works at the warehouse?

TOM: Of course! How else would I—

AMANDA: Tom, he—doesn't drink?

TOM: Why do you ask me that?

AMANDA: Your father *did!*

TOM: Don't get started on that!

AMANDA: He *does* drink, then?

TOM: Not that I know of!

AMANDA: Make sure, be certain! That last thing I want for my daughter's a boy who drinks!

TOM: Aren't you being a little bit premature? Mr. O'Connor has not yet appeared on the scene!

AMANDA: But will tomorrow. To meet your sister, and what do I know about his character? Nothing! Old maids are better off than wives of drunkards!

TOM: Oh, my God!

AMANDA: Be still!

TOM: (*Leaning forward to whisper*) Lots of fellows meet girls whom they don't marry!

AMANDA: Oh, talk sensibly, Tom—and don't be sarcastic! (*She has gotten a hairbrush*)

TOM: What are you doing?

AMANDA: I'm brushing that cow-lick down!

What is this young man's position at the warehouse?

Tom: (*Submitting grimly to the brush and the interrogation*) This young man's position is that of a shipping clerk, Mother.

Amanda: Sounds to me like a fairly responsible job, the sort of a job *you* would be in if you just had more *get-up*.

What is his salary? Have you any idea?

Tom: I would judge it to be approximately eighty-five dollars a month.

Amanda: Well—not princely, but—

Tom: Twenty more than I make.

Amanda: Yes, how well I know! But for a family man, eighty-five dollars a month is not much more than you can just get by on. . . .

Tom: Yes, but Mr. O'Connor is not a family man.

Amanda: He might be, mightn't he? Some time in the future?

Tom: I see. Plans and provisions.

Amanda: You are the only young man that I know of who ignores the fact that the future becomes the present, the present the past, and the past turns into everlasting regret if you don't plan for it!

Tom: I will think that over and see what I can make of it.

Amanda: Don't be supercilious with your mother! Tell me some more about this—what do you call him?

Tom: James D. O'Connor. The D. is for Delaney.

Amanda: Irish on *both* sides! *Gracious!* And doesn't drink?

Tom: Shall I call him up and ask him right this minute?

Amanda: The only way to find out about those things is to make discreet inquiries at the proper moment. When I was a girl in Blue Mountain and it was suspected that a young man drank, the girl whose attentions he had been receiving, if any girl *was*, would sometimes speak to the minister of his church, or rather her father would if her father was living, and sort of feel him out on the young man's character. That is the way such things are discreetly handled to keep a young woman from making a tragic mistake!

Tom: Then how did you happen to make a tragic mistake?

Amanda: That innocent look of your father's had everyone fooled!

He *smiled*—the world was *enchanted!*

No girl can do worse than put herself at the mercy of a handsome appearance!

I hope that Mr. O'Connor is not too good-looking.

Tom: No, he's not too good-looking. He's covered with freckles and hasn't too much of a nose.

Amanda: He's not right-down homely, though?

Tom: Not right-down homely. Just medium homely, I'd say.

Amanda: Character's what to look for in a man.

Tom: That's what I've always said, Mother.

Amanda: You've never said anything of the kind and I suspect you would never give it a thought.

Tom: Don't be so suspicious of me.

Amanda: At least I hope he's the type that's up and coming.

Tom: I think he really goes in for self-improvement.

Amanda: What reason have you to think so?

Tom: He goes to night school.

Amanda: (*Beaming*) Splendid! What does he do, I I mean study?

Tom: Radio engineering and public speaking!

Amanda: Then he has visions of being advanced in the world!

Any young man who studies public speaking is aiming to have an executive job some day!

And radio engineering? A thing for the future!

Both of these facts are very illuminating. Those are the sort of things that a mother should know concerning any young man who comes to call on her daughter. Seriously or—not.

Tom: One little warning. He doesn't know about Laura. I didn't let on that we had dark ulterior motives. I just said, why don't you come and have dinner with us? He said okay and that was the whole conversation.

Amanda: I bet it was! You're eloquent as an oyster.

However, he'll know about Laura when he gets here. When he sees how lovely and sweet and pretty she is, he'll thank his lucky stars he was asked to dinner.

Tom: Mother, you mustn't expect too much of Laura.

Amanda: What do you mean?

Tom: Laura seems all those things to you and me because she's ours and we love her. We don't even notice she's crippled any more.

Amanda: Don't say crippled! You know that I never allow that word to be used!

Tom: But face facts, Mother. She is and—that's not all—

Amanda: What do you mean "not all"?

Tom: Laura is very different from other girls.

Amanda: I think the difference is all to her advantage.

Tom: Not quite all—in the eyes of others—strangers—she's terribly shy and lives in a world of her own and those things make her seem a little peculiar to people outside the house.

Amanda: Don't say peculiar.

Tom: Face the facts. She is.

(The dance-hall music changes to a tango that has a minor and somewhat ominous tone)

Amanda: In what way is she peculiar—may I ask?

Tom: (Gently) She lives in a world of her own—a world of—little glass ornaments, Mother. . . . (Gets up. Amanda remains holding brush, looking at him, troubled) She plays old phonograph records and—that's about all—(He glances at himself in the mirror and crosses to door)

Amanda: (Sharply) Where are you going?

Tom: I'm going to the movies. (Out screen door)

Amanda: Not to the movies, every night to the movies!

(Follows quickly to screen door) I don't believe you always go to the movies! (He is gone, Amanda looks worriedly after him for a moment. Then vitality and optimism return and she turns from the door. Crossing to portieres) Laura! Laura! (Laura answers from kitchenette)

Laura: Yes, Mother.

Amanda: Let those dishes go and come in front! (Laura appears with dish towel. Gaily) Laura, come here and make a wish on the moon!

(Screen image: Moon)

Laura: (Entering) Moon—moon?

Amanda: A little silver slipper of a moon.

Look over your left shoulder, Laura, and make a wish!

(Laura looks faintly puzzled as if called out of sleep. Amanda *seizes her shoulders and turns her at an angle by the door)*

Now!
Now, darling, *wish!*
LAURA: What shall I wish for, Mother?
AMANDA: *(Her voice trembling and her eyes suddenly filling with tears)* Happiness! Good fortune!

(The violin rises and the stage dims out)

(The Curtain Falls)

SCENE SIX: *(Image: High School Hero)*
TOM: And so the following evening I brought Jim home to dinner. I had known Jim slightly in high school. In high school Jim was a hero. He had tremendous Irish good nature and vitality with the scrubbed and polished look of white chinaware. He seemed to move in a continual spotlight. He was a star in basketball, captain of the debating club, president of the senior class and the glee club, and he sang the male lead in the annual light operas. He was always running or bounding, never just walking. He seemed always at the point of defeating the law of gravity. He was shooting with such velocity through his adolescence that you would logically expect him to arrive at nothing short of the White House by the time he was thirty. But Jim apparently ran into more interference after his graduation from Soldan. His speed had definitely slowed. Six years after he left high school he was holding a job that wasn't much better than mine.

(Image: Clerk)

He was the only one at the warehouse with whom I was on friendly terms. I was valuable to him as someone who could remember his former glory, who had seen him win basketball games and the silver cup in debating. He knew of my secret practice of retiring to a cabinet of the wash-room to work on poems when business was slack in the warehouse. He called me Shakespeare. And while the other boys in the warehouse regarded me with suspicious hostility, Jim took a humorous attitude toward me. Gradually his attitude affected the others, their hostility wore off and they also began to smile at me as people smile at an oddly fashioned dog who trots across their path at some distance.
   I knew that Jim and Laura had known each other at Soldan, and I had heard Laura speak admiringly of his voice. I didn't know if Jim remembered her or not. In high school Laura had been as unobtrusive as Jim had been astonishing. If he did remember Laura, it was not as my sister, for when I asked him to dinner, he grinned and said, "You know, Shakespeare, I never thought of you as having folks!"
   He was about to discover that I did. . . .

(Light up stage)
(Legend on screen: "The accent of a coming foot")
(Friday evening. It is about five o'clock of a late spring evening which comes "scattering poems in the sky")
(A delicate lemony light is in the Wingfield apartment)

(*Amanda has worked like a Turk in preparation for the gentleman caller. The results are astonishing. The new floor lamp with its rose-silk shade is in place, a colored paper lantern conceals the broken light fixture in the ceiling, new billowing white curtains are at the windows, chintz covers are on chairs and sofa, a pair of new sofa pillows make their initial appearance*)
(*Open boxes and tissue paper are scattered on the floor*)
(*Laura stands in the middle with lifted arms while Amanda crouches before her, adjusting the hem of the new dress, devout and ritualistic. The dress is colored and designed by memory. The arrangement of Laura's hair is changed; it is softer and more becoming. A fragile, unearthly prettiness has come out in Laura: she is like a piece of translucent glass touched by light, given a momentary radiance, not actual, not lasting*)

AMANDA: (*Impatiently*) Why are you trembling?
LAURA: Mother, you've made me so nervous!
AMANDA: How have I made you nervous?
LAURA: By all this fuss! You make it seem so important!
AMANDA: I don't understand you, Laura. You couldn't be satisfied with just sitting home, and yet whenever I try to arrange something for you, you seem to resist it.

(*She gets up*)

Now take a look at yourself.
No, wait! Wait just a moment—I have an idea!
LAURA: What is it now?

(*Amanda produces two powder puffs which she wraps in handkerchiefs and stuffs in Laura's bosom*)

LAURA: Mother, what are you doing?
AMANDA: They call them "Gay Deceivers"!
LAURA: I won't wear them!
AMANDA: You will!
LAURA: Why should I?
AMANDA: Because, to be painfully honest, your chest is flat.
LAURA: You made it seem like we were setting a trap.
AMANDA: All pretty girls are a trap, a pretty trap, and men expect them to be.

(*Legend: "A pretty trap"*)

Now look at yourself, young lady. This is the prettiest you will ever be!
I've got to fix myself now! You're going to be surprised by your mother's appearance! (*She crosses through portieres, humming gaily*)

(*Laura moves slowly to the long mirror and stares solemnly at herself*)
(*A wind blows the white curtains inward in a slow, graceful motion and with a faint, sorrowful sighing*)

AMANDA: (*Off stage*) It isn't dark enough yet. (*She turns slowly before the mirror with a troubled look*)

(Legend on screen: "This is my sister: Celebrate her with strings!" Music)

AMANDA: *(Laughing, off)* I'm going to show you something. I'm going to make a spectacular appearance!

LAURA: What is it, Mother?

AMANDA: Possess your soul in patience—you will see! Something I've resurrected from that old trunk! Styles haven't changed so terribly much after all. . . .

(She parts the portieres)

Now just look at your mother!

(She wears a girlish frock of yellowed voile with a blue silk sash. She carries a bunch of jonquils—the legend of her youth is nearly revived. Feverishly)

This is the dress in which I led the cotillion. Won the cakewalk twice at Sunset Hill, wore one spring to the Governor's ball in Jackson!
See how I sashayed around the ballroom, Laura?

(She raises her skirt and does a mincing step around the room)

I wore it on Sundays for my gentlemen callers! I had it on the day I met your father—
I had malaria fever all that spring. The change of climate from East Tennessee to the Delta—weakened resistance—I had a little temperature all the time—not enough to be serious—just enough to make me restless and giddy! —Invitations poured in—parties all over the Delta!—"Stay in bed," said Mother, "you have fever!"—but I just wouldn't—I took quinine but kept on going, going!—Evenings, dances!—Afternoons, long, long rides! Picnics— lovely!—So lovely, that country in May—All lacy with dogwood, literally flooded with jonquils!—That was the spring I had the craze for jonquils. Jonquils became an absolute obsession. Mother said, "Honey, there's no more room for jonquils." And still I kept on bringing in more jonquils. Whenever, wherever I saw them, I'd say, "Stop! Stop! I see jonquils!" I made the young men help me gather the jonquils! It was a joke, Amanda and her jonquils! Finally there were no more vases to hold them, every available space was filled with jonquils. No vases to hold them? All right, I'll hold them myself! And then I—*(She stops in front of the picture. Music)* met your father!
Malaria fever and jonquils and then—this—boy. . . .

(She switches on the rose-colored lamp)

I hope they get here before it starts to rain.

(She crosses upstage and places the jonquils in bowl on table)

I gave your brother a little extra change so he and Mr. O'Connor could take the service car home.

LAURA: (*With altered look*) What did you say his name was?
AMANDA: O'Connor.
LAURA: What is his first name?
AMANDA: I don't remember. Oh, yes, I do. It was—Jim!

(Laura *sways slightly and catches hold of a chair*)
(*Legend on screen:* "Not Jim!")

LAURA: (*Faintly*) Not—Jim.
AMANDA: Yes, that was it, it was Jim! I've never known a Jim that wasn't nice!

(*Music: Ominous*)

LAURA: Are you sure his name is Jim O'Connor?
AMANDA: Yes. Why?
LAURA: Is he the one that Tom used to know in high school?
AMANDA: He didn't say so. I think he just got to know him at the warehouse.
LAURA: There was a Jim O'Connor we both knew in high school—(*Then, with effort*) If that is the one that Tom is bringing to dinner—you'll have to excuse me, I won't come to the table.
AMANDA: What sort of nonsense is this?
LAURA: You asked me once if I'd ever liked a boy. Don't you remember I showed you this boy's picture?
AMANDA: You mean the boy you showed me in the year book?
LAURA: Yes, that boy.
AMANDA: Laura, Laura, were you in love with that boy?
LAURA: I don't know, Mother. All I know is I couldn't sit at the table if it was him!
AMANDA: It won't be him! It isn't the least bit likely. But whether it is or not, you will come to the table. You will not be excused.
LAURA: I'll have to be, Mother.
AMANDA: I don't intend to humor your silliness, Laura. I've had too much from you and your brother, both!
So just sit down and compose yourself till they come. Tom has forgotten his key so you'll have to let them in, when they arrive.
LAURA: (*Panicky*) Oh, Mother—*you* answer the door!
AMANDA: (*Lightly*) I'll be in the kitchen—busy!
LAURA: Oh, Mother, please answer the door, don't make me do it!
AMANDA: (*Crossing into kitchenette*) I've got to fix the dressing for the salmon. Fuss, fuss—silliness!—over a gentleman caller!

(*Door swings shut. Laura is left alone*)
(*Legend:* "Terror!")
(*She utters a low moan and turns off the lamp—sits stiffly on the edge of the sofa, knotting her fingers together*)
(*Legend on screen:* "The opening of a door!")
(*Tom and Jim appear on the fire-escape steps and climb to landing. Hearing their approach, Laura rises with a panicky gesture. She retreats to the portieres*)
(*The doorbell. Laura catches her breath and touches her throat. Low drums*)

AMANDA: (*Calling*) Laura, sweetheart! The door!

(*Laura stares at it without moving*)

JIM: I think we just beat the rain.
TOM: Uh-huh. (*He rings again, nervously. Jim whistles and fishes for a cigarette*)
AMANDA: (*Very, very gaily*) Laura, that is your brother and Mr. O'Connor! Will you let them in, darling?

(*Laura crosses toward kitchenette door*)

LAURA: (*Breathlessly*) Mother—you go to the door!

(*Amanda steps out of kitchenette and stares furiously at Laura. She points imperiously at the door*)

LAURA: Please, please!
AMANDA: (*In a fierce whisper*) What is the matter with you, you silly thing?
LAURA: (*Desperately*) Please, you answer it, *please!*
AMANDA: I told you I wasn't going to humor you, Laura. Why have you chosen this moment to lose your mind?
LAURA: Please, please, please, you go!
AMANDA: You'll have to go to the door because I can't!
LAURA: (*Despairingly*) I can't either!
AMANDA: *Why?*
LAURA: I'm *sick!*
AMANDA: I'm sick, too—of your nonsense! Why can't you and your brother be normal people? Fantastic whims and behavior!

(*Tom gives a long ring*)

Preposterous goings on! Can you give me one reason—(*Calls out lyrically*) Coming! Just one second!—why you should be afraid to open a door? Now you answer it, Laura!
LAURA: Oh, oh, oh . . . (*She returns through the portieres. Darts to the victrola and winds it frantically and turns it on*)
AMANDA: Laura Wingfield, you march right to that door!
LAURA: Yes—yes, Mother!

(*A faraway, scratchy rendition of "Dardanella" softens the air and gives her strength to move through it. She slips to the door and draws it caustiously open*)
(*Tom enters with the caller, Jim O'Connor*)

TOM: Laura, this is Jim. Jim, this is my sister, Laura.
JIM: (*Stepping inside*) I didn't know that Shakespeare had a sister!
LAURA: (*Retreating stiff and trembling from the door*) How—how do you do?
JIM: (*Heartily extending his hand*) Okay!

(Laura touches it hesitantly with hers)

JIM: Your hand's *cold*, Laura!
LAURA: Yes, well—I've been playing the victrola. . . .
JIM: Must have been playing classical music on it! You ought to play a little hot swing music to warm you up!
LAURA: Excuse me—I haven't finished playing the victrola. . . .

(She turns awkwardly and hurries into the front room. She pauses a second by the victrola. Then catches her breath and darts through the portieres like a frightened deer)

JIM: *(Grinning)* What was the matter?
TOM: Oh—with Laura? Laura is—terribly shy.
JIM: Shy, huh? It's unusual to meet a shy girl nowadays. I don't believe you ever mentioned you had a sister.
TOM: Well, now you know. I have one. Here is the *Post Dispatch*. You want a piece of it?
JIM: Uh-huh.
TOM: What piece? The comics?
JIM: Sports! *(Glances at it)* Ole Dizzy Dean is on his bad behavior.
TOM: *(Disinterest)* Yeah? *(Lights cigarette and crosses back to fire-escape door)*
JIM: Where are *you* going?
TOM: I'm going out on the terrace.
JIM: *(Goes after him)* You know, Shakespeare—I'm going to sell you a bill of goods!
TOM: What goods?
JIM: A course I'm taking.
TOM: Huh?
JIM: In public speaking! You and me, we're not the warehouse type.
TOM: Thanks—that's good news.
But what has public speaking got to do with it?
JIM: It fits you for—executive positions!
TOM: Awww.
JIM: I tell you it's done a helluva lot for me.

(Image: Executive at desk)

TOM: In what respect?
JIM: In every! Ask yourself what is the difference between you an' me and men in the office down front? Brains?—No!—Ability?—No! Then what? Just one little thing—
TOM: What is that one little thing?
JIM: Primarily it amounts to—social poise! Being able to square up to people and hold your own on any social level!
AMANDA: *(Off stage)* Tom?
TOM: Yes, Mother?
AMANDA: Is that you and Mr. O'Connor?
TOM: Yes, Mother.
AMANDA: Well, you just make yourselves comfortable in there.
TOM: Yes, Mother.
AMANDA: Ask Mr. O'Connor if he would like to wash his hands.

JIM: Aw, no—no—thank you—I took care of that at the warehouse.
Tom—
   TOM: Yes?
   JIM: Mr. Mendoza was speaking to me about you.
   TOM: Favorably?
   JIM: What do you think?
   TOM: Well—
   JIM: You're going to be out of a job if you don't wake up.
   TOM: I am waking up—
   JIM: You show no signs.
   TOM: The signs are interior.

   (Image on screen: The sailing vessel with Jolly Roger again)

   TOM: I'm planning to change. (*He leans over the rail speaking with quiet exhilaration. The incandescent marquees and signs of the first-run movie houses light his face from across the alley. He looks like a voyager*) I'm right at the point of committing myself to a future that doesn't include the warehouse and Mr. Mendoza or even a night-school course in public speaking.
   JIM: What are you gassing about?
   TOM: I'm tired of the movies.
   JIM: Movies!
   TOM: Yes, movies! Look at them—(*A wave toward the marvels of Grand Avenue*) All of those glamorous people—having adventures—hogging it all, gobbling the whole thing up! You know what happens? People go to the *movies* instead of *moving!* Hollywood characters are supposed to have all the adventures for everybody in America, while everybody in America sits in a dark room and watches them have them! Yes, until there's a war. That's when adventure becomes available to the masses! *Everyone's* dish, not only Gable's! Then the people in the dark room come out of the dark room to have some adventures themselves—Goody, goody!—It's our turn now, to go to the South Sea Island—to make a safari—to be exotic, far-off!—But I'm not patient. I don't want to wait till then. I'm tired of the *movies* and I am *about* to *move!*
   JIM: (*Incredulously*) Move?
   TOM: Yes.
   JIM: When?
   TOM: Soon!
   JIM: Where? Where?

   (Theme three music seems to answer the question, while Tom *thinks it over. He searches among his pockets)*

   TOM: I'm starting to boil inside. I know I seem dreamy, but inside—well, I'm boiling!—Whenever I pick up a shoe, I shudder a little thinking how short life is and what I am doing!—Whatever that means, I know it doesn't mean shoes—except as something to wear on a traveler's feet! (*Finds paper*) Look—
   JIM: What?
   TOM: I'm a member.
   JIM: (*Reading*) The Union of Merchant Seamen.
   TOM: I paid my dues this month, instead of the light bill.
   JIM: You will regret it when they turn the lights off.

Tom: I won't be here.

Jim: How about your mother?

Tom: I'm like my father. The bastard son of a bastard! See how he grins? And he's been absent going on sixteen years!

Jim: You're just talking, you drip. How does your mother feel about it?

Tom: Shhh!—Here comes Mother! Mother is not acquainted with my plans!

Amanda: (*Enters portieres*) Where are you all?

Tom: On the terrace, Mother.

(*They start inside. She advances to them.* Tom *is distinctly shocked at her appearance. Even* Jim *blinks a little. He is making his first contact with girlish Southern vivacity and in spite of the nightschool course in public speaking is somewhat thrown off the beam by the unexpected outlay of social charm*)

(*Certain responses are attempted by* Jim *but are swept aside by* Amanda's *gay laughter and chatter.* Tom *is embarrassed but after the first shock* Jim *reacts very warmly, grins and chuckles, is altogether won over*)

(*Image:* Amanda *as a girl*)

Amanda: (*Coyly smiling, shaking her girlish ringlets*) Well, well, well, so this is Mr. O'Connor. Introductions entirely unnecessary. I've heard so much about you from my boy. I finally said to him, Tom—good gracious!—why don't you bring this paragon to supper? I'd like to meet this nice young man at the warehouse!—Instead of just hearing him sing your praises so much!

I don't know why my son is so stand-offish—that's not Southern behavior!

Let's sit down and—I think we could stand a little more air in here! Tom, leave the door open. I felt a nice fresh breeze a moment ago. Where has it gone to?

Mmm, so warm already! And not quite summer, even. We're going to burn up when summer really gets started.

However, we're having—we're having a very light supper. I think light things are better fo' this time of year. The same as light clothes are. Light clothes an' light food are what warm weather calls fo'. You know our blood gets so thick during th' winter—it takes a while fo' us to *adjust* ou'selves!—when the season changes . . .

It's come so quick this year. I wasn't prepared. All of a sudden—heavens! Already summer!—I ran to the trunk an' pulled out this light dress—Terribly old! Historical almost! But feels so good—so good an' co-ol, y' know. . . .

Tom: Mother—

Amanda: Yes, honey?

Tom: How about—supper?

Amanda: Honey, you go ask Sister if supper is ready! You know that Sister is in full charge of supper!

Tell her you hungry boys are waiting for it.

(*To* Jim)

Have you met Laura?

Jim: She—

Amanda: Let you in? Oh, good, you've met already! It's rare for a girl as sweet an' pretty as Laura to be domestic! But Laura is, thank heavens, not only pretty but also very domestic. I'm not at all. I never was a bit. I never could make a thing but angel-food cake. Well, in the South we had so many servants. Gone, gone, gone. All vestige of gracious living! Gone completely! I wasn't prepared for what the future brought me. All of my gentlemen callers were sons of planters and so of course I assumed that I would be married to one and raise my family on a large piece of land with plenty of servants. But man proposes—and woman accepts the proposal!—To vary that old, old saying a little bit—I married no planter! I married a man who worked for the telephone company!—That gallantly smiling gentleman over there! (*Points to the picture*) A telephone man who—fell in love with long-distance!—Now he travels and I don't even know where!—But what am I going on for about my—tribulations?

Tell me yours—I hope you don't have any!

Tom?

TOM: (*Returning*) Yes, Mother?

AMANDA: Is supper nearly ready?

TOM: It looks to me like supper is on the table.

AMANDA: Let me look—(*She rises prettily and looks through portieres*) Oh, lovely!—But where is Sister?

TOM: Laura is not feeling well and she says that she thinks she'd better not come to the table.

AMANDA: What?—Nonsense!—Laura? Oh, Laura!

LAURA: (*Off stage, faintly*) Yes, Mother.

AMANDA: You really must come to the table. We won't be seated until you come to the table!

Come in, Mr. O'Connor. You sit over there, and I'll—

Laura? Laura Wingfield?

You're keeping us waiting, honey! We can't say grace until you come to the table!

(*The back door is pushed weakly open and Laura comes in. She is obviously quite faint, her lips trembling, her eyes wide and staring. She moves unsteadily toward the table*)
(*Legend: "Terror!"*)
(*Outside a summer storm is coming abruptly. The white curtains billow inward at the windows and there is a sorrowful murmur and deep blue dusk*)
(*Laura suddenly stumbles—she catches at a chair with a faint moan*)

TOM: Laura!
AMANDA: Laura!

(*There is a clap of thunder*)
(*Legend: "Ah!"*)
(*Despairingly*)

Why, Laura, you *are* sick, darling! Tom, help your sister into the living room, dear!

Sit in the living room, Laura—rest on the sofa.

Well!

(*To the gentleman caller*)

Standing over the hot stove made her ill!—I told her that it was just too warm this evening, but—

(Tom comes back in. Laura is on the sofa)

Is Laura all right now?

TOM: Yes.

AMANDA: What *is* that? Rain? A nice cool rain has come up!

(She gives the gentleman caller a frightened look)

I think we may—have grace—now. . . .

(Tom looks at her stupidly)

Tom, honey—you say grace!

TOM: Oh . . .

"For these and all thy mercies—"

(They bow their heads, Amanda stealing a nervous glance at Jim. In the living room Laura, stretched on the sofa, clenches her hand to her lips, to hold back a shuddering sob)

God's Holy Name be praised—
              (The Scene Dims Out)

SCENE SEVEN: *A Souvenir.*

Half an hour later. Dinner is just being finished in the upstage area which is concealed by the drawn portieres.

As the curtain rises Laura is still huddled upon the sofa, her feet drawn under her, her head resting on a pale blue pillow, her eyes wide and mysteriously watchful. The new floor lamp with its shade of rose-colored silk gives a soft, becoming light to her face, bringing out the fragile, unearthly prettiness which usually escapes attention. There is a steady murmur of rain, but it is slackening and stops soon after the scene begins; the air outside becomes pale and luminous as the moon breaks out.

A moment after the curtain rises, the lights in both rooms flicker and go out.

JIM: Hey, there, Mr. Light Bulb!

(Amanda laughs nervously)
(Legend: "Suspension of a public service")

AMANDA: Where was Moses when the lights went out? Ha-ha. Do you know the answer to that one, Mr. O'Connor?

JIM: No, Ma'am, what's the answer?

AMANDA: In the dark!

(Jim laughs appreciatively)

Everybody sit still. I'll light the candles. Isn't it lucky we have them on the table? Where's a match? Which of you gentlemen can provide a match?

JIM: Here.

AMANDA: Thank you, sir.

JIM: Not at all, Ma'am!

AMANDA: I guess the fuse has burnt out. Mr. O'Connor, can you tell a burnt-out fuse? I know I can't and Tom is a total loss when it comes to mechanics.

(Sound: Getting up: Voices recede a little to kitchenette)

Oh, be careful you don't bump into something. We don't want our gentleman caller to break his neck. Now wouldn't that be a fine howdy-do?
JIM: Ha-ha!
Where is the fuse-box?
AMANDA: Right here next to the stove. Can you see anything?
JIM: Just a minute.
AMANDA: Isn't electricity a mysterious thing?
Wasn't it Benjamin Franklin who tied a key to a kite?
We live in such a mysterious universe, don't we? Some people say that science clears up all the mysteries for us. In my opinion it only creates more!
Have you found it yet?
JIM: No, Ma'am. All these fuses look okay to me.
AMANDA: Tom!
TOM: Yes, Mother?
AMANDA: That light bill I gave you several days ago. The one I told you we got the notices about?

(Legend: "Ha!")

TOM: Oh—Yeah.
AMANDA: You didn't neglect to pay it by any chance?
TOM: Why, I—
AMANDA: Didn't! I might have known it!
JIM: Shakespeare probably wrote a poem on that light bill, Mrs. Wingfield.
AMANDA: I might have known better than to trust him with it! There's such a high price for negligence in this world!
JIM::   Maybe the poem will win a ten-dollar prize.
AMANDA: We'll just have to spend the remainder of the evening in the nineteenth century, before Mr. Edison made the Mazda lamp!
JIM: Candlelight is my favorite kind of light.
AMANDA: That shows you're romantic! But that's no excuse for Tom.
Well, we got through dinner. Very considerate of them to let us get through dinner before they plunged us into everlasting darkness, wasn't it, Mr. O'Connor?
JIM: Ha-ha!
AMANDA: Tom, as a penalty for your carelessness you can help me with the dishes.
JIM: Let me give you a hand.
AMANDA: Indeed you will not!
JIM: I ought to be good for something.
AMANDA: Good for something? *(Her tone is rhapsodic)* You? Why, Mr. O'Connor, nobody, *nobody's* given me this much entertainment in years—as you have!
JIM: Aw, now, Mrs. Wingfield!
AMANDA: I'm not exaggerating, not one bit! But Sister is all by her lonesome. You go keep her company in the parlor!
I'll give you this lovely old candelabrum that used to be on the altar at the

Church of the Heavenly Rest. It was melted a little out of shape when the church burnt down. Lightning struck it one spring. Gypsy Jones was holding a revival at the time and he intimated that the church was destroyed because the Episcopalians gave card parties.

JIM: Ha-ha!

AMANDA: And how about you coaxing Sister to drink a little wine? I think it would be good for her! Can you carry both at once?

JIM: Sure. I'm Superman!

AMANDA: Now, Thomas, get into this apron!

(The door of kitchenette swings closed on Amanda's gay laughter; the flickering light approaches the portieres)

(Laura sits up nervously as he enters. Her speech at first is low and breathless from the almost intolerable strain of being alone with a stranger)

(The legend: "I don't suppose you remember me at all!")

(In her first speeches in this scene, before Jim's warmth overcomes her paralyzing shyness, Laura's voice is thin and breathless as though she has just run up a steep flight of stairs)

(Jim's attitude is gently humorous. In playing this scene it should be stressed that while the incident is apparently unimportant, it is to Laura the climax of her secret life)

JIM: Hello, there, Laura.

LAURA: *(Faintly)* Hello. *(She clears her throat)*

JIM: How are you feeling now? Better?

LAURA: Yes. Yes, thank you.

JIM: This is for you. A little dandelion wine. *(He extends it toward her with extravagant gallantry)*

LAURA: Thank you.

JIM: Drink it—but don't get drunk!

(He laughs heartily. Laura takes the glass uncertainly; laughs shyly)

Where shall I set the candles?

LAURA: Oh—oh, anywhere . . .

JIM: How about here on the floor? Any objections?

LAURA: No.

JIM: I'll spread a newspaper under to catch the drippings. I like to sit on the floor. Mind if I do?

LAURA: Oh, no.

JIM: Give me a pillow?

LAURA: What?

JIM: A pillow!

LAURA: Oh . . . *(Hands him one quickly)*

JIM: How about you? Don't you like to sit on the floor?

LAURA: Oh—yes.

JIM: Why don't you, then?

LAURA: I—will.

JIM: Take a pillow! *(Laura does. Sits on the other side of the candelabrum. Jim crosses his legs and smiles engagingly at her)* I can't hardly see you sitting way over there.

LAURA: I can—see you.

JIM: I know, but that's not fair, I'm in the limelight. *(Laura moves her pillow closer)* Good! Now I can see you! Comfortable?

LAURA: Yes.

JIM: So am I. Comfortable as a cow! Will you have some gum?

LAURA: No, thank you.

JIM: I think that I will indulge, with your permission. (*Musingly unwraps it and holds it up*) Think of the fortune made by the guy that invented the first piece of chewing gum. Amazing, huh? The Wrigley Building is one of the sights of Chicago—I saw it summer before last when I went up to the Century of Progress. Did you take in the Century of Progress?

LAURA: No, I didn't.

JIM: Well, it was quite a wonderful exposition. What impressed me most was the Hall of Science. Gives you an idea of what the future will be in America, even more wonderful than the present time is! (*Pause. Smiling at her*) Your brother tells me you're shy. Is that right, Laura?

LAURA: I—don't know.

JIM: I judge you to be an old-fashioned type of girl. Well, I think that's a pretty good type to be. Hope you don't think I'm being too personal—do you?

LAURA: (*Hastily, out of embarrassment*) I believe I *will* take a piece of gum, if you—don't mind. (*Clearing her throat*) Mr. O'Connor, have you—kept up with your singing?

JIM: Singing? Me?

LAURA: Yes. I remember what a beautiful voice you had.

JIM: When did you hear me sing?

(*Voice off stage in the pause*)

VOICE (*Off stage*)

> *O blow, ye winds, heigh-ho,*
> *A-roving I will go!*
> *I'm off to my love*
> *With a boxing glove—*
> *Ten thousand miles away!*

JIM: You say you've heard me sing?

LAURA: Oh, yes! Yes, very often. . . . I—don't suppose—you remember me—at all?

JIM: (*Smiling doubtfully*) You know I have an idea I've seen you before. I had that idea soon as you opened the door. It seemed almost like I was about to remember your name. But the name that I started to call you—wasn't a name! And so I stopped myself before I said it.

LAURA: Wasn't it—Blue Roses?

JIM: (*Springs up. Grinning*) Blue Roses!—My gosh, yes—Blue Roses! That's what I had on my tongue when you opened the door! Isn't it funny what tricks your memory plays? I didn't connect you with high school somehow or other.

But that's where it was; it was high school. I didn't even know you were Shakespeare's sister!

Gosh, I'm sorry.

LAURA: I didn't expect you to. You—barely knew me!

JIM: But we did have a speaking acquaintance, huh?

LAURA: Yes, we—spoke to each other.

JIM: When did you recognize me?

LAURA: Oh, right away!

JIM: Soon as I came in the door?

LAURA: When I heard your name I thought it was probably you. I knew that Tom used to know you a little in high school. So when you came in the door—Well, then I was—sure.

JIM: Why didn't you *say* something, then?

LAURA: (*Breathlessly*) I didn't know what to say, I was—too surprised!

JIM: For goodness' sakes! You know, this sure is funny!

LAURA: Yes! Yes, isn't it, though . . .

JIM: Didn't we have a class in something together?

LAURA: Yes, we did.

JIM: What class was that?

LAURA: It was—singing—Chorus!

JIM: Aw!

LAURA: I sat across the aisle from you in the Aud.

JIM: Aw.

LAURA: Mondays, Wednesdays, and Fridays.

JIM: Now I remember—you always came in late.

LAURA: Yes, it was so hard for me, getting upstairs. I had that brace on my leg—it clumped so loud!

JIM: I never heard any clumping.

LAURA: (*Wincing at the recollection*) To me it sounded like—thunder!

JIM: Well, well, well, I never even noticed.

LAURA: And everybody was seated before I came in. I had to walk in front of all those people. My seat was in the back row. I had to go clumping all the way up the aisle with everyone watching!

JIM: You shouldn't have been self-conscious.

LAURA: I know, but I was. It was always such a relief when the singing started.

JIM: Aw, yes, I've placed you now! I used to call you Blue Roses. How was it that I got started calling you that?

LAURA: I was out of school a little while with pleurosis. When I came back you asked me what was the matter. I said I had pleurosis—you thought I said Blue Roses. That's what you always called me after that!

JIM: I hope you didn't mind.

LAURA: Oh, no—I liked it. You see, I wasn't acquainted with many—people. . . .

JIM: As I remember you sort of stuck by yourself.

LAURA: I—I—never have had much luck at—making friends.

JIM: I don't see why you wouldn't.

LAURA: Well, I—started out badly.

JIM: You mean being—

LAURA: Yes, it sort of—stood between me—

JIM: You shouldn't have let it!

LAURA: I know, but it did, and—

JIM: You were shy with people!

LAURA: I tried not to be but never could—

JIM: Overcome it?

LAURA: No, I—I never could!

JIM: I guess being shy is something you have to work out of kind of gradually.

LAURA: (*Sorrowfully*) Yes—I guess it—

JIM: Takes time!

LAURA: Yes.

JIM: People are not so dreadful when you know them. That's what you have to remember! And everybody has problems, not just you, but practically everybody has got some problems.

You think of yourself as having the only problems, as being the only one who is disappointed. But just look around you and you will see lots of people as disappointed as you are. For instance, I hoped when I was going to high school that I would be further along at this time, six years later, than I am now—You remember that wonderful write-up I had in *The Torch?*

LAURA: Yes! (*She rises and crosses to table*)

JIM: It said I was bound to succeed in anything I went into! (*Laura returns with the annual*) Holy Jeez! *The Torch!* (*He accepts it reverently. They smile across it with mutual wonder. Laura crouches beside him and they begin to turn through it. Laura's shyness is dissolving in his warmth*)

LAURA: Here you are in *The Pirates of Penzance!*

JIM: (*Wistfully*) I sang the baritone lead in that operetta.

LAURA: (*Raptly*) So—beautifully!

JIM: (*Protesting*) Aw—

LAURA: Yes, yes—beautifully—beautifully!

JIM: You heard me?

LAURA: All three times!

JIM: No!

LAURA: Yes!

JIM: All three performances?

LAURA: (*Looking down*) Yes.

JIM: Why?

LAURA: I—wanted to ask you to—autograph my program.

JIM: Why didn't you ask me to?

LAURA: You were always surrounded by your own friends so much that I never had a chance to.

JIM: You should have just—

LAURA: Well, I—thought you might think I was—

JIM: Thought I might think you was—what?

LAURA: Oh—

JIM: (*With reflective relish*) I was beleaguered by females in those days.

LAURA: You were terribly popular!

JIM: Yeah—

LAURA: You had such a—friendly way—

JIM: I was spoiled in high school.

LAURA: Everybody—liked you!

JIM: Including you?

LAURA: I—yes, I—I did, too—(*She gently closes the book in her lap*)

JIM: Well, well, well!—Give me that program, Laura.

(*She hands it to him. He signs it with a flourish*)

There you are—better late than never!

LAURA: Oh, I—what a—surprise!

JIM: My signature isn't worth very much right now.

But some day—maybe—it will increase in value!

Being disappointed in one thing and being discouraged is something else.

I am disappointed but I am not discouraged.

I'm twenty-three years old.

How old are you?
LAURA: I'll be twenty-four in June.
JIM: That's not old age!
LAURA: No, but—
JIM: You finished high school?
LAURA: (*With difficulty*) I didn't go back.
JIM: You mean you dropped out?
LAURA: I made bad grades in my final examinations.

(*She rises and replaces the book and the program. Her voice strained*)

How is—Emily Meisenbach getting along?
JIM: Oh, that kraut-head!
LAURA: Why do you call her that?
JIM: That's what she was.
LAURA: You're not still—going with her?
JIM: I never see her.
LAURA: It said in the Personal Section that you were—engaged!
JIM: I know, but I wasn't impressed by that—propaganda!
LAURA: It wasn't—the truth?
JIM: Only in Emily's optimistic opinion!
LAURA: Oh—

(*Legend: "What have you done since high school?"*)
(*Jim lights a cigarette and leans indolently back on his elbows, smiling at Laura with a warmth and charm which lights her inwardly with altar candles. She remains by the table and turns in her hands a piece of glass to cover her tumult*)

JIM: (*After several reflective puffs on a cigarette*) What have you done since high school? (*She seems not to hear him*) Huh? (Laura *looks up*) I said what have you done since high school, Laura?
LAURA: Nothing much.
JIM: You must have been doing something these six long years.
LAURA: Yes.
JIM: Well, then, such as what?
LAURA: I took a business course at business college—
JIM: How did that work out?
LAURA: Well, not very—well—I had to drop out, it gave me—indigestion—

(*Jim laughs gently*)

JIM: What are you doing now?
LAURA: I don't do anything—much. Oh, please don't think I sit around doing nothing! My glass collection takes up a good deal of time. Glass is something you have to take good care of.
JIM: What did you say—about glass?
LAURA: Collection I said—I have one—(*She clears her throat and turns away again, acutely shy*)
JIM: (*Abruptly*) You know what I judge to be the trouble with you?
Inferiority complex! Know what that is? That's what they call it when someone low-rates himself!

I understand it because I had it, too. Although my case was not so aggravated as yours seems to be. I had it until I took up public speaking, developed my voice, and learned that I had an aptitude for science. Before that time I never thought of myself as being outstanding in any way whatsoever!

Now I've never made a regular study of it, but I have a friend who says I can analyze people better than doctors that make a profession of it. I don't claim that to be necessarily true but I can sure guess a person's psychology. Laura! (*Takes out his gum*) Excuse me, Laura. I always take it out when the flavor is gone. I'll use this scrap of paper to wrap it in. I know how it is to get it stuck on a shoe.

Yep—that's what I judge to be your principal trouble. A lack of confidence in yourself as a person. You don't have the proper amount of faith in yourself. I'm basing that fact on a number of your remarks and also on certain observations I've made. For instance that clumping you thought was so awful in high school. You say that you even dreaded to walk into class. You see what you did? You dropped out of school, you gave up an education because of a clump, which as far as I know was practically nonexistent! A little physical defect is what you have. Hardly noticeable even! Magnified thousands of times by imagination!

You know what my strong advice to you is? Think of yourself as *superior* in some way!

LAURA: In what way would I think?

JIM: Why, man alive, Laura! Just look about you a little. What do you see? A world full of common people! All of 'em born and all 'em going to die! Which of them has one-tenth of your good points! Or mine! Or anyone else's, as far as that goes—Gosh! Everybody excels in some one thing. Some in many!

(*Unconsciously glances at himself in the mirror*)

All you've got to do is discover in *what!*
Take me, for instance.

(*He adjusts his tie at the mirror*)

My interest happens to lie in electro-dynamics. I'm taking a course in radio engineering at night school, Laura, on top of a fairly responsible job at the warehouse. I'm taking that course and studying public speaking.

LAURA: Ohhhh.

JIM: Because I believe in the future of television!

(*Turning back to her*)

I wish to be ready to go up right along with it. Therefore I'm planning to get in on the ground floor. In fact I've already made the right connections and all that remains is for the industry itself to get under way! Full steam—

(*His eyes are starry*)

Knowledge—Zzzzzp! Money—Zzzzzzp!—Power!
That's the cycle democracy is built on!

(His attitude is convincingly dynamic, Laura stares at him, even her shyness eclipsed in her absolute wonder. He suddenly grins)

I guess you think I think a lot of myself!
LAURA: No—o-o-o, I—
JIM: Now how about you? Isn't there something you take more interest in than anything else?
LAURA: Well, I do—as I said—have my—glass collection—

(A peal of girlish laughter from the kitchen)

JIM: I'm not right sure I know what you're talking about. What kind of glass is it?
LAURA: Little articles of it, they're ornaments mostly!
Most of them are little animals made out of glass, the tiniest little animals in the world. Mother calls them a glass menagerie!
Here's an example of one, if you'd like to see it!
This one is one of the oldest. It's nearly thirteen.

(Music: "The Glass Menagerie")
(He stretches out his hand)

Oh, be careful—if you breathe, it breaks!
JIM: I'd better not take it. I'm pretty clumsy with things.
LAURA: Go on, I trust you with him!

(Places it in his palm)

There now—you're holding him gently!
Hold him over the light, he loves the light! You see how the light shines through him?
JIM: It sure does shine!
LAURA: I shouldn't be partial, but he is my favorite one.
JIM: What kind of a thing is this one supposed to be?
LAURA: Haven't you noticed the single horn on his forehead?
JIM: A unicorn, huh?
LAURA: Mmm-hmmm!
JIM: Unicorns, aren't they extinct in the modern world?
LAURA: I know!
JIM: Poor little fellow, he must feel sort of lonesome.
LAURA: *(Smiling)* Well, if he does he doesn't complain about it. He stays on a shelf with some horses that don't have horns and all of them seem to get along nicely together.
JIM: How do you know?
LAURA: *(lightly)* I haven't heard any arguments among them!
JIM: *(Grinning)* No arguments, huh? Well, that's a pretty good sign! Where shall I set him?
LAURA: Put him on the table. They all like a change of scenery once in a while!
JIM: *(Stretching)* Well, well, well, well—
Look how big my shadow is when I stretch!
LAURA: Oh, oh, yes—it stretches across the ceiling!
JIM: *(Crossing to door)* I think it's stopped raining.

(*Opens fire-escape door*) Where does the music come from?

LAURA: From the Paradise Dance Hall across the alley.

JIM: How about cutting the rug a little, Miss Wingfield?

LAURA: Oh, I—

JIM: Or is your program filled up? Let me have a look at it. (*Grasps imaginary card*) Why, every dance is taken! I'll just have to scratch some out. (*Waltz music: "La Golondrina"*) Ahhh, a waltz! (*He executes some sweeping turns by himself then holds his arms toward* Laura)

LAURA: (*Breathlessly*) I—can't dance!

JIM: There you go, that inferiority stuff!

LAURA: I've never danced in my life!

JIM: Come on, try!

LAURA: Oh, but I'd step on you!

JIM: I'm not made out of glass.

LAURA: How—how—how do we start?

JIM: Just leave it to me. You hold your arms out a little.

LAURA: Like this?

JIM: A little bit higher. Right. Now don't tighten up, that's the main thing about it—relax.

LAURA: (*Laughing breathlessly*) It's hard not to.

JIM: Okay.

LAURA: I'm afraid you can't budge me.

JIM: What do you bet I can't (*He swings her into motion*)

LAURA: Goodness, yes, you can!

JIM: Let yourself go, now, Laura, just let yourself go.

LAURA: I'm—

JIM: Come on!

LAURA: Trying!

JIM: Not so stiff—Easy does it!

LAURA: I know but I'm—

JIM: Loosen th' backbone! There now, that's a lot better.

LAURA: Am I?

JIM: Lots, lots better! (*He moves her about the room in a clumsy waltz*)

LAURA: Oh, my!

JIM: Ha-ha!

LAURA: Oh, my goodness!

JIM: Ha-ha-ha! (*They suddenly bump into the table.* Jim *stops*) What did we hit on?

LAURA: Table.

JIM: Did something fall off it? I think—

LAURA: Yes.

JIM: I hope it wasn't the little glass horse with the horn!

LAURA: Yes.

JIM: Aw, aw, aw. Is it broken?

LAURA: Now it is just like all the other horses.

JIM: It's lost its—

LAURA: Horn!

It doesn't matter. Maybe it's a blessing in disguise.

JIM: You'll never forgive me. I bet that that was your favorite piece of glass.

LAURA: I don't have favorites much. It's no tragedy, Freckles. Glass breaks so easily. No matter how careful you are. The traffic jars the shelves and things fall off them.

JIM: Still I'm awfully sorry that I was the cause.

LAURA: *(Smiling)* I'll just imagine he had an operation. The horn was removed to make him feel less—freakish!

(They both laugh)

Now he will feel more at home with the other horses, the ones that don't have horns. . . .
JIM: Ha-ha, that's very funny!

(Suddenly serious)

I'm glad to see that you have a sense of humor. You know—you're—well-very different! Surprisingly different from anyone else I know!

(His voice becomes soft and hesitant with a genuine feeling)

Do you mind me telling you that?

(Laura is abashed beyond speech)

I mean it in a nice way. . . .

(Laura nods shyly, looking away)

You make me feel sort of—I don't know how to put it! I'm usually pretty good at expressing things, but— This is something that I don't know how to say!

(Laura touches her throat and clears it—turns the broken unicorn in her hands)
(Even softer)

Has anyone ever told you that you were pretty?

(Pause: Music)
(Laura looks up slowly, with wonder, and shakes her head)

Well, you are! In a very different way from anyone else. And all the nicer because of the difference, too.

(His voice becomes low and husky. Laura turns away, nearly faint with the novelty of her emotions)

I wish that you were my sister. I'd teach you to have some confidence in yourself. The different people are not like other people, but being different is nothing to be ashamed of. Because other people are not such wonderful people. They're one hundred times one thousand. You're one times one! They walk all over the earth. You just stay here. They're common as—weeds, but—you—well, you're—*Blue Roses!*

(Image on screen: Blue roses)

(Music changes)

LAURA: But blue is wrong for—roses. . . .
JIM: It's right for you!—You're—pretty!
LAURA: In what respect am I pretty?
JIM: In all respects—believe me! Your eyes—your hair—are pretty! Your hands are pretty!

(He catches hold of her hand)

You think I'm making this up because I'm invited to dinner and have to be nice. Oh, I could do that! I could put on an act for you, Laura, and say lots of things without being very sincere. But this time I am. I'm talking to you sincerely. I happened to notice you had this inferiority complex that keeps you from feeling comfortable with people. Somebody need to build your confidence up and make you proud instead of shy and turning away and—blushing—
Somebody—ought to—
Ought to—*kiss* you, Laura!

(His hand slips slowly up her arm and her shoulder)
(Music swells tumultuously)
(He suddenly turns her about and kisses her on the lips)
(When he releases her, Laura sinks on the sofa with a bright, dazed look)
(Jim backs away and fishes in his pocket for a cigarette)
(Legend on screen: "Souvenir")

Stumble-john!

(He lights the cigarette, avoiding her look)
(There is a peal of girlish laughter from Amanda in the kitchen)
(Laura slowly raises and opens her hand. It still contains the little broken glass animal. She looks at it with a tender, bewildered expression)

Stumble-john!
I shouldn't have done that—That was way off the beam. You don't smoke, do you?

(She looks up, smiling, not hearing the question)
(He sits beside her a little gingerly. She looks at him speechlessly—waiting)
(He coughs decorously and moves a little farther aside as he considers the situation and senses her feelings, dimly, with perturbation)
(Gently)

Would you—care for a—mint?

(She doesn't seem to hear him but her look grows brighter even)

Peppermint—Life-Saver?
My pocket's a regular drug store—wherever I go . . .

(He pops a mint in his mouth. The gulps and decides to make a clean breast of it. He speaks slowly and gingerly)

Laura, you know, if I had a sister like you, I'd do the same thing as Tom. I'd bring out fellows and—introduce her to them. The right type of boys of a type to—appreciate her.
Only—well—he made a mistake about me.
Maybe I've got no call to be saying this. That may not have been the idea in having me over. But what if it was?
There's nothing wrong about that. The only trouble is that in my case—I'm not in a situation to—do the right thing.
I can't take down your number and say I'll phone.
I can't call up next week and—ask for a date.
I thought I had better explain the situation in case you—misunderstood it and—hurt your feelings. . . .

(Pause)
(Slowly, very slowly, Laura's look changes, her eyes returning slowly from his to the ornament in her palm)
(Amanda utters another gay laugh in the kitchen)

LAURA: *(Faintly)* You—won't—call again?
JIM: No, Laura, I can't.

(He rises from the sofa)

As I was just explaining, I've—got strings on me.
Laura, I've—been going steady!
I go out all of the time with a girl named Betty. She's a home-girl like you, and Catholic, and Irish, and in a great many ways we—get along fine.
I met her last summer on a moonlight boat trip up the river to Alton, on the *Majestic*.
Well—right away from the start it was—love!

(Legend: Love!)
(Laura sways slightly forward and grips the arm of the sofa. He fails to notice, now enrapt in his own comfortable being)

Being in love has made a new man of me!

(Leaning stiffly forward, clutching the arm of the sofa, Laura struggles visibly with her storm. But Jim is oblivious, she is a long way off)

The power of love is really pretty tremendous!
Love is something that—changes the whole world, Laura!

(The storm abates a little and Laura leans back. He notices her again)

It happened that Betty's aunt took sick, she got a wire and had to go to Centralia. So Tom—when he asked me to dinner—I naturally just accepted the invitation, not knowing that you—that he—that I—

(He stops awkwardly)

Huh—I'm a stumble-john!

(He flops back on the sofa)
(The holy candles in the altar of Laura's face have been snuffed out.
There is a look of almost infinite desolation)
(Jim glances at her uneasily)

I wish that you would—say something. *(She bites her lip which was trembling and then bravely smiles. She opens her hand again on the broken glass ornament. Then she gently takes his hand and raises it level with her own. She carefully places the unicorn in the palm of his hand, then pushes his fingers closed upon it)* What are you—doing that for? You want me to have him?—Laura? *(She nods)* What for?
LAURA: A—souvenir . . .

(She rises unsteadily and crouches beside the victrola to wind it up)
(Legend on screen: "Things have a way of turning out so badly!")
(Or image: "Gentleman caller waving good-bye!—gaily")
(At this moment Amanda rushes brightly back in the front room. She bears a pitcher of fruit punch in an old-fashioned cut-glass pitcher and a plate of macaroons. The plate has a gold border and poppies painted on it)

AMANDA: Well, well, well! Isn't the air delightful after the shower? I've made you children a little liquid refreshment.

(Turns gaily to the gentleman caller)

Jim, do you know that song about lemonade?
"Lemonade, lemonade
Made in the shade and stirred with a spade—
Good enough for any old maid!"
JIM: *(Uneasily)* Ha-ha! No—I never heard it.
AMANDA: Why, Laura! You look so serious!
JIM: We were having a serious conversation.
AMANDA: Good! Now you're better acquainted!
JIM: *(Uncertainly)* Ha-ha! Yes.
AMANDA: You modern young people are much more serious-minded than my generation. I was so gay as a girl!
JIM: You haven't changed, Mrs. Wingfield.
AMANDA: Tonight I'm rejuvenated! The gaiety of the occasion, Mr. O'-Connor!

(She tosses her head with a peal of laughter. Spills lemonade)

Oooo! I'm baptizing myself!
JIM: Here—let me—
AMANDA: *(Setting the pitcher down)* There now. I discovered we had some maraschino cherries. I dumped them in, juice and all!
JIM: You shouldn't have gone to that trouble, Mrs. Wingfield.
AMANDA: Trouble, trouble? Why, it was loads of fun!
Didn't you hear me cutting up in the kitchen? I bet your ears were burning!

I told Tom how out-done with him I was for keeping you to himself so long a time! He should have brought you over much, much sooner! Well, now that you've found your way, I want you to be a very frequent caller! Not just occasional but all the time.

Oh, we're going to have a lot of gay times together! I see them coming! Mmm, just breathe that air! So fresh, and the moon's so pretty!

I'll skip back out—I know where my place is when young folks are having a—serious conversation!

JIM: Oh, don't go out, Mrs. Wingfield. The fact of the matter is I've got to be going.

AMANDA: Going, now? You're joking! Why, it's only the shank of the evening, Mr. O'Connor!

JIM: Well, you know how it is.

AMANDA: You mean you're a young workingman and have to keep workingmen's hours. We'll let you off early tonight. But only on the condition that next time you stay later.

What's the best night for you? Isn't Saturday night the best night for you workingmen?

JIM: I have a couple of time-clocks to punch, Mrs. Wingfield. One at morning, another one at night!

AMANDA: My, but you *are* ambitious! You work at night, too?

JIM: No, Ma'am, not work but—Betty! (*He crosses deliberately to pick up his hat. The band at the Paradise Dance Hall goes into a tender waltz*)

AMANDA: Betty? Betty? Who's—Betty!

(*There is an ominous cracking sound in the sky*)

JIM: Oh, just a girl. The girl I go steady with! (*He smiles charmingly. The sky falls*)

(*Legend: "The sky falls"*)

AMANDA: (*A long-drawn exhalation*) Ohhhh . . . Is it a serious romance, Mr. O'Connor?

JIM: We're going to be married the second Sunday in June.

AMANDA: Ohhhh—how nice!

Tom didn't mention that you were engaged to be married.

JIM: The cat's not out of the bag at the warehouse yet.

You know how they are. They call you Romeo and stuff like that.

(*He stops at the oval mirror to put on his hat. He carefully shapes the brim and the crown to give a discreetly dashing effect*)

It's been a wonderful evening, Mrs. Wingfield. I guess this is what they mean by Southern hospitality.

AMANDA: It really wasn't anything at all.

JIM: I hope it don't seem like I'm rushing off. But I promised Betty I'd pick her up at the Wabash depot, an' by the time I get my jalopy down there her train'll be in. Some women are pretty upset if you keep 'em waiting.

AMANDA: Yes, I know—The tyranny of women!

(Extends her hand)

Good-bye, Mr. O'Connor.
I wish you luck—and happiness—and success! All three of them, and so does Laura!—Don't you, Laura?
LAURA: Yes!
JIM: (*Taking her hand*) Good-bye, Laura. I'm certainly going to treasure that souvenir. And don't you forget the good advice I gave you.

(Raises his voice to a cheery shout)

So long, Shakespeare!
Thanks again, ladies—Good night!

(He grins and ducks jauntily out)
(Still bravely grimacing, Amanda closes the door on the gentleman caller. Then she turns back to the room with a puzzled expression. She and Laura don't dare to face each other. Laura crouches beside the victrola to wind it)

AMANDA: (*Faintly*) Things have a way of turning out so badly.
I don't believe that I would play the victrola.
Well, well—well—
Our gentleman caller was engaged to be married!
Tom!
TOM: (*From back*) Yes, Mother?
AMANDA: Come in here a minute. I want to tell you something awfully funny.
TOM: (*Enters with macaroon and a glass of the lemonade*) Has the gentleman caller gotten away already?
AMANDA: The gentleman caller has made an early departure.
What a wonderful joke you played on us!
TOM: How do you mean?
AMANDA: You didn't mention that he was engaged to be married.
TOM: Jim? Engaged?
AMANDA: That's what he just informed us.
TOM: I'll be jiggered! I didn't know about that.
AMANDA: That seems very peculiar.
TOM: What's peculiar about it?
AMANDA: Didn't you call him your best friend down at the warehouse?
TOM: He is, but how did I know?
AMANDA: It seems extremely peculiar that you wouldn't know your best friend was going to be married!
TOM: The warehouse is where I work, not where I know things about people!
AMANDA: You don't know things anywhere! You live in a dream; you manufacture illusions!

(He crosses to door)

Where are you going?
TOM: I'm going to the movies.

AMANDA: That's right, now that you've had us make such fools of ourselves. The effort, the preparations, all the expense! The new floor lamp, the
rug, the clothes for Laura! All for what? To entertain some other girl's fiancé!

Go to the movies, go! Don't think about us, a mother deserted, an unmarried sister who's crippled and has no job! Don't let anything interfere with
your selfish pleasure!

Just go, go, go—to the movies!

TOM: All right, I will! The more you shout about my selfishness to me the
quicker I'll go, and I won't go to the movies!

AMANDA: Go, then! Then go to the moon—you selfish dreamer!

*(Tom smashes his glass on the floor. He plunges out on the fire escape,
slamming the door. Laura screams—cut by door)*

*(Dance-hall music up. Tom goes to the rail and grips it desperately,
lifting his face in the chill white moonlight penetrating the narrow abyss of
the alley)*

(Legend on screen: "and so good-bye . . .")

*(Tom's closing speech is timed with the interior pantomime. The interior
scene is played as though viewed through soundproof glass. Amanda appears to be making a comforting speech to Laura who is huddled upon the
sofa. Now that we cannot hear the mother's speech, her silliness is gone and
she has dignity and tragic beauty. Laura's dark hair hides her face until at
the end of the speech she lifts it to smile at her mother. Amanda's gestures
are slow and graceful, almost dancelike, as she comforts the daughter. At the
end of her speech she glances a moment at the father's picture—then withdraws through the portieres. At close of Tom's speech, Laura blows out the
candles, ending the play)*

TOM: I didn't go to the moon. I went much further—for time is the
longest distance between two places—

Not long after that I was fired for writing a poem on the lid of a shoe-box.

I left Saint Louis. I descended the steps of this fire escape for a last time
and followed, from then on, in my father's footsteps, attempting to find in
motion what was lost in space—

I traveled around a great deal. The cities swept about me like dead leaves,
leaves that were brightly colored but torn away from the branches.

I would have stopped, but I was pursued by something.

It always came upon me unawares, taking me altogether by surprise. Perhaps it was a familiar bit of music. Perhaps it was only a piece of transparent
glass—

Perhaps I am walking along a street at night, in some strange city, before
I have found companions. I pass the lighted window of a shop where perfume is sold. The window is filled with pieces of colored glass, tiny transparent bottles in delicate colors, like bits of a shattered rainbow.

Then all at once my sister touches my shoulder. I turn around and look into
her eyes . . .

Oh, Laura, Laura, I tried to leave you behind me, but I am more faithful
than I intended to be!

I reach for a cigarette, I cross the street, I run into the movies or a bar, I
buy a drink, I speak to the nearest stranger—anything that can blow your
candles out!

(Laura bends over the candles)

for nowadays the world is lit by lightning! Blow out your candles, Laura—
and so good-bye. . . .

(She blows the candles out)

(The Scene Dissolves)

FOR DISCUSSION

1. What is the significance of the title *The Glass Menagerie?*
2. Why does Amanda persist in living in the past?
3. What is the reason for Laura's shyness?
4. What is the theme of the play?
5. If you were adding another act to the play, what would happen to Laura? To Tom? To Amanda?
6. Do you think the screen projections suggested by Williams would add to the effectiveness of *The Glass Menagerie?*
7. Why do you think Amanda is such a domineering person?
8. Why is the father's picture kept on the wall?
9. Does Amanda really think that Laura will have gentlemen callers? Why or why not?
10. How do Jim's attitudes toward life differ from those of the Wingfield family?
11. Why is Laura so afraid of displeasing her mother?
12. Is Amanda in any way a sympathetic character?
13. The story is told from Tom Wingfield's viewpoint. How would it differ if it were told from the viewpoint of Laura or Amanda?
14. What is the significance of the unicorn?
15. Describe the mood of the play.
16. What kind of person is Tom? Discuss.
17. Is Amanda optimistic or pessimistic? What makes you think so?

Arthur Kopit: a different kind of absurdity.

He was born May 10, 1937, in New York City, the son of a business executive. He was graduated from high school in 1955 and enrolled at Harvard University, where he studied engineering. While he was in college, he wrote several plays, including *Oh Dad, Poor Dad, Mamma's Hung You in the Closet and I'm Feelin' so Sad*, and won two playwriting awards as an undergraduate. After he received his B.A. degree in 1959, he went to Europe to study theatre, having been awarded a Shaw traveling fellowship.

Oh Dad, Poor Dad was first presented at the Dunster House Workshop in Cambridge, Massachusetts, by a student cast. The first professional performance was given in New York's Phoenix Theatre on February 26, 1962. That same year, when he was only twenty-four, Kopit won the Vernon Rice Award and the Outer Circle Award for playwriting. In 1965, he published a collection of short plays under the title *The Day the Whores Came Out to Play Tennis and Other Plays*. In 1968 his play *Indians* was produced in London. On May 7, 1969, it opened in Washington, D.C., and that fall moved to New York.

Kopit described *Oh Dad, Poor Dad* as "a pseudoclassical tragifarce in a bastard French tradition." Although the play is often classified as a part of the Theatre of the Absurd, which Kopit no doubt had reference to in his description, it differs markedly from the Absurdist drama as developed by writers like Eugène Ionesco. Ionesco and other playwrights are concerned largely with the absurdity of man's existence in a meaningless world, while Kopit's concern with absurdity lies in a refusal to take human existence seriously. He is parodying Theatre of the Absurd at the same time that he parodies other forms of theatre. One reviewer (of *Oh Dad, Poor Dad*) saw influences of Thornton Wilder, Jean Giraudoux, Jean Anouilh, and Friedrich Duerrenmatt in the play, while *Time* published an article comparing Madame Rosepettle to the domineering females in many of Tennessee Williams' plays. However, Kopit by no means merely copies the styles of other writers, but blends a parody of these styles into a unique and entertaining form all his own.

Oh Dad, Poor Dad parodies the domineering, protective mother who tries to smother her son, and also the son himself, who is too naive and sheltered. Despite the shocking, horrible situations and characters who are too exaggerated to be believable, Kopit still manages to make a serious comment on the problems presented in the play.

Oh Dad, Poor Dad, Mamma's Hung You in the Closet and I'm Feelin' so Sad

THE CHARACTERS

MADAME ROSEPETTLE	COMMODORE ROSEABOVE
JONATHAN	HEAD BELLBOY
ROSALIE	BELLBOYS

SCENES: *The action takes place in Port Royale, a city somewhere in the Caribbean. The play is in three scenes without intermission.*

Oh Dad, Poor Dad, Mamma's Hung You in the Closet and I'm Feeling so Sad

SCENE I

SCENE: *A lavish hotel suite somewhere in the Caribbean.*

AT RISE: *As the curtain goes up, a platoon of* Bellboys *is seen hurrying about. Some are opening the shades on the windows, others are dusting. A group of* Bellboys *enter with extravagant luggage. They march to the master bedroom. Another group enters with duplicate luggage, only smaller. They march to the other bedroom in the suite. Enter* Bellboy *One and Two, carrying a coffin. They look about the room nervously.*

WOMAN'S VOICE: (*Offstage.*) Put it in the bedroom!

BELLBOYS ONE AND TWO: The bedroom.

(*Bellboy* One *goes toward the bedroom at Stage Left.* Bellboy *Two starts toward the bedroom at Stage Right. The handles come off the coffin. It falls to the floor as* Madame Rosepettle *enters, dressed in black, a veil covering her face, with* Jonathan *trailing behind her. The* Bellboys *are frozen with terror.*)

MADAME ROSEPETTLE: *Fools!*

HEAD BELLBOY: Uh—*which* bedroom, Madame?

MADAME ROSEPETTLE: *Which* bedroom? Why, the *master* bedroom, of course. Which bedroom did you think? (*The* Bellboys *smile ashamedly, bow, pick up the coffin, and carry it toward the master bedroom.*) Gently. (*They open the bedroom doors.* Madame Rosepettle *lowers her eyes as the blinding rays of sunlight stream from the room.*) People have no respect for coffins nowadays. They think nothing of the dead. (*Short pause.*) I wonder what the dead think of them? (*Short pause.*) Agh! The world is growing dismal. (*She now proceeds to storm heroically about the room, sweeping over all the furniture in her path. New articles are immediately brought in to replace the broken articles, which are removed.*)

(*After she has demolished the room, the door to the master bedroom opens and* Bellboys *One and Two reappear, coffin still in hand.*)

Reprinted with permission of Farrar, Straus & Giroux, Inc. from OH DAD, POOR DAD, MAMA'S HUNG YOU IN THE CLOSET AND I'M FEELING SO SAD by Arthur L. Kopit, Copyright © 1959, 1960 by Arthur L. Kopit.

BELLBOY ONE: Uh—begging madame's pardon.

BELLBOY TWO: Sorry we must interrupt.

MADAME ROSEPETTLE: Speak up! Speak up!

BELLBOY ONE: Well—you see—

BELLBOY TWO: Yes, you see—

BELLBOY ONE: We were curious.

BELLBOY TWO: Yes. We were curious.

BELLBOY ONE: Uh—just *where* in madame's bedroom would she like it to be put?

MADAME ROSEPETTLE: Next to the *bed,* of course!

BELLBOYS ONE AND TWO: *Of course. (Exit,* Bellboys One *and* Two.)

MADAME ROSEPETTLE: Morons!—*Imbeciles. (Enter two* Bellboys *carrying two large black-draped plants before them. They look about the room, then nod and walk out to the porch.)* Ah, my plants! *(They set the plants down.)* Uh—not so close together. They fight. *(The* Bellboys *move the plants apart.)*

(Bellboy Three *enters carrying a dictaphone on a silver tray and black drapes under his arm.* Bellboys One *and* Two *exit fearfully from the master bedroom.)*

HEAD BELLBOY: The dictaphone, madame.

MADAME ROSEPETTLE: Ah, splendid.

HEAD BELLBOY: Where would madame like it to be placed?

MADAME ROSEPETTLE: Oh, great gods, are you all the same? The center table, naturally. One never dictates one's memoirs from *anywhere* but the center of a room. Any nincompoop knows that.

HEAD BELLBOY: It must have slipped my mind.

MADAME ROSEPETTLE: You flatter yourself.

HEAD BELLBOY: Will there be something else?

MADAME ROSEPETTLE: Will there be something else, he asks? *Will there be something else? Of course* there'll be something else. There's *always* something else. That's one of the troubles with Life.

HEAD BELLBOY: Sorry, madame.

MADAME ROSEPETTLE: Yes, so am I. *(Pause.)* Oh, this talk is getting us nowhere. Words are precious. On bellboys they're a waste. And so far you have thoroughly wasted my time. Now to begin:—

HEAD BELLBOY: Madame, I'm afraid this must end.

MADAME ROSEPETTLE: *(Incredulously.)* I—beg your pardon?

HEAD BELLBOY: I said this must end! I am *not a common* bellboy, madame —I'm a lieutenant. (Notice the stripes if you will.) I am a lieutenant, madame. And being a lieutenant am in charge of other bellboys and therefore entitled, I think, to a little more respect from you.

MADAME ROSEPETTLE: Well—*you* may consider yourself a lieutenant, lieutenant, but *I* consider you a *bore!* If you're going to insist upon pulling rank, however, I'll have you know that I am a Tourist. (Notice the money if you will.) I am a Tourist, my boy.—And being a Tourist am in charge of you. Remember that and I'll mail you another stripe when I leave. As for "respect," we'll have no time for *that* around here. We've got too many important things to do. Right, Albert?

JONATHAN: Ra-ra-ra-rrrright.

MADAME ROSEPETTLE: Now, to begin: you may pick up the drapes which were so ingeniously dropped in a lump on my table, carry them into the master bedroom and tack them over my window panes. I don't wear black in the tropics for my health, my boy. I'm in mourning. And while I'm here in Port Royale, no single speck of sunlight shall enter and brighten the mournful gloom of my heart—at least, not while I'm in my bedroom. Well, go on, lieutenant, go on. Forward to the field of battle, head high. Tack the drapes across my windows and when my room is black, call me in.

HEAD BELLBOY: (*Weakly.*) Yes, madame. (*He picks up the drapes and leaves.*)

MADAME ROSEPETTLE: In Buenos Aires the lieutenant clicked his heels when leaving. That's the trouble with these revolutionaries. No regard for the duties of rank. Remind me, Edward, to have this man fired, first thing in the morning. He'll never do.

(Jonathan *takes a pad of paper out of his pocket and writes with a pencil he has tied on a chain about his neck. Enter* Bellboys One *and* Five *carrying miniature treasure chests.*)

BELLBOY FIVE: The stamp collection, madame.

MADAME ROSEPETTLE: Ah, Robinson! Your fantastic stamp collection. Look! It's arrived.

BELLBOY ONE: Where would madame like it put?

MADAME ROSEPETTLE: Where would you like it put, my love?

JONATHAN: Uh—uh—uh—

MADAME ROSEPETTLE: Now—now, let's not start stammering again.

JONATHAN: Ummmm—

MADAME ROSEPETTLE: My dear, what is wrong with your tongue?

JONATHAN: Uhhhh—

MADAME ROSEPETTLE: But they're *only* bellboys.

JONATHAN: Ummmm—

(*Enter* Bellboys Two *and* Three, *also with miniature treasure chests.*)

BELLBOY TWO: The coin collection, madame. Where would you like it put?

MADAME ROSEPETTLE: Edward, your fabulous collection of coins has just arrived as well. *Now*—where would you like it put?

JONATHAN: Ummmm—

MADAME ROSEPETTLE: Oh, great gods! Can't you for once talk like a normal human being without showering the room with your inarticulate spit!?

JONATHAN: I-I-I-I—I—da—da—

MADAME ROSEPETTLE: Oh, very well. Very well—If you can't muster the nerve to answer—stick out your paw and point.

(He thrusts out his trembling hand and points to a large set of transparent drawers held by an elegant gold frame.)

JONATHAN: If—if—they would—be so kind.

MADAME ROSEPETTLE: Of course they would! They're *bellboys.* Remember that. It's your first Lesson in Life for the day. (*To the* Bellboys.) No! Don't get the stamps in with the coins. They stick!

HEAD BELLBOY: (*He returns from the master bedroom.*) I'm terrible sorry to disturb you, madame, but I find that—that I don't seem to have a—uh—

MADAME ROSEPETTLE: I wondered when you'd ask. (*She takes a huge hammer out of her purse and hands it to him.*)

HEAD BELLBOY: (*Ashamedly.*) Thank you—madame. (*He turns nervously and starts to leave.*)

MADAME ROSEPETTLE: (*Cuttingly.*) *Bellboy?* (*He stops.*) The nails.
HEAD BELLBOY: Yes, of course. How foolish of me.
MADAME ROSEPETTLE: (*She reaches into her purse again and takes out a fistful of nails which she promptly dumps in his hands.*) Keep the extras. (*He exits, once more, into the master bedroom.*) In Buenos Aires the Lieutenant came equipped with a pneumatic drill. *That's* what I call service. Remind me, Robinson darling, to have this man barred from all hotels, everywhere. *Everywhere.* (Jonathan *scratches a large "X" on his pad. The other* Bellboys *have now finished putting the stamps and coins away.* Madame Rosepettle *goes over and dips her hand in the box. To* Bellboy Two.) Here, for your trouble: a little something. It's a Turkish piaster—1876. Good year for piasters. (*To* Bellboy Five.) And for you a—a 1739 Danzig gulden. Worth a fortune, my boy. A *small* fortune, I will admit, but nevertheless a fortune. (*To* Bellboy Three.) And for you we have a—a—1962 DIME! ! Edward— what is a dime doing in here? Fegh! (*She flings the dime to the ground as if it had been handled by lepers. The* Bellboys *leap to get it.*)
JONATHAN: (*Sadly.*) Some—some—some day—it will be—as rare as the others.
MADAME ROSEPETTLE: Some day! *Some day!* That's the trouble with you, Robinson. Always an optimist. I trust you have no more such currency contaminating your fabulous collection. H'm, Albert? Do I assume correctly? H'm? Do I? H'm? Do I? H'm? Do I?
JONATHAN: Ya—yes.
MADAME ROSEPETTLE: Splendid. Then I'll give you your surprise for the day.
JONATHAN: Na—now?
MADAME ROSEPETTLE: Yes, now.
JONATHAN: In—in—front of—*them?*
MADAME ROSEPETTLE: Turn your backs, bellboys. (*She digs into her handbag and picks out a coin in a velvet box.*) Here, Edward, my sweet. The rarest of all coins for your rarest of all collections. A 1572 Javanese Yen-Sen.
JONATHAN: (*Excitedly.*) How—how many—were—were minted?
MADAME ROSEPETTLE: None.
JONATHAN: Na—none?
MADAME ROSEPETTLE: I made it myself. (*She squeezes his hand.*) So glad you like it. (*To the* Bellboys.) You may turn around now. (*The sound of a HAMMER is heard Offstage.*) If you must bang like that, my boy, then please bang with some sort of rhythm. Oh, the Lieutenant in Buenos Aires, remember him, Robinson? How he shook when he drilled. I fairly danced that day. (*She begins to dance, the other* Bellboys *clapping in rhythm.*) That's enough. (*She stops.*)
BELLBOY FOUR: (*He enters pushing a huge treasure chest, on rollers.*) The, uh—book collection, madame.

(Jonathan *leaps up in glee.*)

MADAME ROSEPETTLE: Albert, *look.* Albert! *Look!* Your unbelievable collection of books. *It's arrived.*
JONATHAN: Ca—ca—could they—open it—I—I-I wonder?
MADAME ROSEPETTLE: You want to see them, eh Albert? You really want to see them again? That badly? You really want to see them again, that badly?

JONATHAN: Yyyyyyesssssss.
MADAME ROSEPETTLE: Then let the trunk be opened.

(They open the trunk. Hundreds of books fall onto the floor. Jonathan falls on top of them like a starved man upon food.)

JONATHAN: *(Emotionally.)* Tra-Tra-Trollope—Ha-Haggard—Daudet—Ga-Ga-Gautier—ma-mmmmy old—fffriends. La—lllook at them all. Sh-Sh-Sholokhov—Alain-Fournier—Alighiere—Turturturgenev. My—old friends. *(He burrows into them, reading to himself in wild abandon.)*
MADAME ROSEPETTLE: *(Coldly.)* All right, Albert, that's enough.

(He looks up bewildered. She stares at him disapprovingly.)

JONATHAN: But—
MADAME ROSEPETTLE: That's enough—Get up, get up—Come, off your knees. Rise from your books and sing of love.
JONATHAN: But I—I can't sing.
MADAME ROSEPETTLE: Well, stand up anyway. *(He rises sadly. Short pause.)* All right! Now where's Rosalinda.
THE NEAREST BELLBOY: Who?
MADAME ROSEPETTLE: My fish. I want my fish. Who has my fish?
A VOICE: *(From outside the door.)* I have it, madame.

(Enter Bellboy Two carrying, at arms' length, an object covered by a black cloth. He wears large, thick, well-padded gloves—the sort a snake trainer might wear when handling a newly-caught cobra.)

MADAME ROSEPETTLE: Ah, splendid. Bring it here. Put it here, by the dictaphone. Near my memoirs. Bring it here, bellboy. But set it gently, if you will. *(He sets it down.)* Now. The black shawl of mourning, bellboy. Remove it, if you will. But gently. Gently. Gently as she goes. *(The Bellboy lifts off the shawl. Revealed is a fish bowl with a fish and a cat's skeleton inside.)* Ah, I see you fed it today. *(She reaches into her handbag and extracts a pair of long tongs. She plucks the skeleton from the fish bowl.)* Siamese, I presume.
BELLBOY TWO: No, madame. Alley.
MADAME ROSEPETTLE: *WHAT? A common alley cat?* Just who do you think I am? What kind of fish do you think I have? *Alley cat? Alley cat? Indeed.* In Buenos Aires, I'll have you know, Rosalinda was fed nothing but Siamese *kittens,* which are even more tender than Siamese cats. *That's* what I call consideration! Edward, make note: we will dismiss this creature from the bellboy squad *first thing in the morning!*

(Jonathan scribbles on his pad.)

BELLBOY TWO: Madame, please, there were no Siamese cats.
MADAME ROSEPETTLE: There are *always* Siamese cats!
BELLBOY TWO: Not in Port Royale.
MADAME ROSEPETTLE: Then you should have flown to Buenos Aires. I would have paid the way. Give me back your Turkish piaster. *(He hands back the coin.)* No. Never mind. Keep it. It's not worth a thing except in Istanbul, and hardly a soul uses anything but Traveller's Cheques there anyhow! Shows you should never trust me.

BELLBOY TWO: Madame, *please.* I have a wife.

MADAME ROSEPETTLE: And *I* have a fish. I dare say there are half a million men in Port Royale with wives. But show me one person with a silver Piranha fish and then you'll be showing me something. Your marital status does not impress me, sir. You are common, do you hear? Common! While my Piranha fish is *rare.*

ROSALINDA THE FISH: (*Sadly.*) Glump.

MADAME ROSEPETTLE: Oh, dear thing. You can just tell she's not feeling up to snuff. *Someone will pay for this!*

HEAD BELLBOY: (*Enters from the bedroom.*) Well, I'm finished.

MADAME ROSEPETTLE: You certainly are.

HEAD BELLBOY: I beg your pardon?

MADAME ROSEPETTLE: Edward, make note. First thing in the morning we speak to the chef. Subject: Siamese cats—kittens if possible, though I seriously doubt it here. And make a further note, Albert my darling. Let's see if we can't get our cats on the American plan, while we're at it.

(*Jonathan scribbles on his pad of paper.*)

HEAD BELLBOY: Madame, is there something I can—

MADAME ROSEPETTLE: QUIET! And put that hammer down. (*He puts it down. She puts it back in her purse.*) You have all behaved rudely. If the sunset over Guanabacoa Bay were not so full of magenta and wisteria blue I'd leave this place tonight. But the sunset *is* full of magenta and wisteria blue, and so I think I'll stay. Therefore, beware. Madame Rosepettle will have much to do. She won't have time for hiring and firing people like you. Right, Robinson? (*Jonathan opens his mouth to speak but no words come out.*) I said, *right, Robinson?* (*Again he tries to speak, and again no words come out.*) RIGHT, ROBINSON!? (*He nods.*) There's your answer. Now get out and leave us alone. (*They start to exit.*) No. Wait. (*They stop.*) A question before you go. That yacht in the harbor.

HEAD BELLBOY: *Which* yacht in the harbor?

MADAME ROSEPETTLE: The pink one, of course—187 feet long, I'd judge. Who owns it?

HEAD BELLBOY: Why, Commodore Roseabove, madame. It's a pretty sloop.

MADAME ROSEPETTLE: (*Distantly.*) Roseabove. *Roseabove*—I like that name.

HEAD BELLBOY: Madame realizes, of course, it's the largest yacht at the island.

MADAME ROSEPETTLE: It's also the largest yacht in Haiti, Puerto Rico, Bermuda, the Dominican Republic and West Palm Beach. I haven't checked the Virgin Islands yet. I thought I'd leave them till last. But I doubt if I'll find a larger one there. I take great pleasure, you see, in measuring yachts. My hobby, you might say. (*The Bellboys exit.*) Edward, make note. First thing in the morning we restaff this hotel. (*Jonathan scribbles on his pad of paper. Madame Rosepettle walks over to the French windows and stares wistfully out. There is a short silence before she speaks. Dreamily, with a smile.*) *Roseabove.* I like that name.

ROSALINDA THE FISH: (*Gleefully.*) Gleep.

MADAME ROSEPETTLE: (*Fondly.*) Ah, listen. My lovely little fish. She, too, is feeling better already. She, too. You can tell—you can tell. (Madame Rosepettle, *who is now standing beside her fish, picks up the mouthpiece of her dictaphone.*) *My Memoirs.* Port Royale—Part One—The Arrival. (*Pause, while she thinks of what to say.*) Sorry to say, once again, nothing unusual to report.

(*The LIGHTS now begin to fade on* Madame Rosepettle *as* Jonathan, *standing alone by the porch, sneaks out a little ways and peeks down at the street below. As CARNIVAL MUSIC is heard:*)

the lights fade

SCENE II

(*The place is the same. The time, two weeks later.* Jonathan *is in the room with* Rosalie, *a girl some two years older than he and dressed in sweet girlish pink.*)

ROSALIE: But if you've been here two weeks, why haven't I seen you?
JONATHAN: I've—I've been in my room.
ROSALIE: All the time?
JONATHAN: Yes—all the time.
ROSALIE: Well, you must get out sometimes. I mean, sometimes you simply must get out. You just couldn't stay inside all the time—could you?
JONATHAN: Yyyyyes.
ROSALIE: You never get out at all? I mean, never at all?
JONATHAN: Some-sometimes, I do go out on the porch. M-Ma-Mother has some—Venus-flytraps which she bra-brought back from the rain forests of Va-Va-Va-Venezuela. They're va-very rrrrare and need a—a lot of sunshine. Well, sir, she ka-keeps them on the porch and I—I feed them. Twice a day, too.
ROSALIE: Oh.
JONATHAN: Ma-Ma-Mother says everyone must have a vocation in life. (*With a slight nervous laugh.*) I ga-guess that's—my job.
ROSALIE: I don't think I've ever met anyone before who's fed—uh—Venus-flytraps.
JONATHAN: Ma-Ma-Mother says I'm va-very good at it. I—don't know—if—I am, but—that's—what she says so I—guess I am.
ROSALIE: Well, uh, what do you—feed them? You see, I've never met anyone before who's fed Venus-flytraps so—that's why I don't know what —you're supposed to feed them.
JONATHAN: (*Happy that she asked.*) Oh, I fa-feed them—l-l-lots of things. Ga-ga-green peas, chicken feathers, rubber bands. They're—not very fussy. They're—nice, that way. Ma-Ma-Mother says it it it ga-gives me a feeling of a-co-co-complishment. Iffff you would—like to to see them I— could show them to you. It's—almost fa-feeding time. It is, and—and I could show them to you.
ROSALIE: No. That's all right. (Jonathan *looks away hurt.*) Well, how about later?
JONATHAN: Do-do-do you ra-really wwwwwant to see them?
ROSALIE: Yes. Yes, I really think I would like to see them—later. If you'll show them to me then, I'd really like that. (Jonathan *looks at her and smiles. There is an awkward silence while he stares at her thankfully.*) I still don't understand why you never go out. How can you just sit in—?
JONATHAN: SometimeswhenI'montheporchIdootherthings.

ROSALIE: *What?*

JONATHAN: Sa-sa-sometimes, when I'm—on the porch, you know, when I'm on the porch? Ssssssssome-times I—do *other things,* too.

ROSALIE: What sort of things? (Jonathan *giggles.*) What sort of things do you do?

JONATHAN: Other things.

ROSALIE: (*Coyly.*) What do you mean, "Other things"?

JONATHAN: Other things besides feeding my mother's plants. Other things besides that. That's what I mean. Other things besides that.

ROSALIE: What kind of things—*in particular?*

JONATHAN: Oh, watching.

ROSALIE: Watching?

JONATHAN: Yes. Like—watching.

ROSALIE: Watching what? (*He giggles.*) *Watching what?*

JONATHAN: You.

(*Short pause. She inches closer to him on the couch.*)

ROSALIE: What do you mean—watching me?

JONATHAN: I—watch you from the porch. That's what I mean. I watch you from the porch. I watch you a lot, too. Every day. It's—it's the truth. I—I swear it—is. I watch you ev'ry day. Do you believe me?

ROSALIE: Of course I believe you, Albert. Why—

JONATHAN: Jonathan!

ROSALIE: What?

JONATHAN: Jonathan. Ca-ca-call me Ja-Jonathan. That's my name.

ROSALIE: But your mother said your name was—

JONATHAN: Nooooo! Call—me Jonathan. Pa-pa-please?

ROSALIE: All right—Jonathan.

JONATHAN: (*Excitedly.*) You *do* believe me! You rrrreally do believe me. I-I can tell!

ROSALIE: Of course I believe you. Why shouldn't—?

JONATHAN: You want me to tell you how I watch you? You want me to tell you? I'll bet you'll na-never guess.

ROSALIE: How?

JONATHAN: *Guess.*

ROSALIE: (*Ponders.*) Through a telescope?

JONATHAN: How did you guess?

ROSALIE: I—I don't know. I was just joking. I didn't really think that was—

JONATHAN: I'll bet everyone watches you through a telescope. I'll bet everyone you go out with watches you through a telescope. That's what I'll bet.

ROSALIE: No. Not at all.

JONATHAN: Well, that's how I watch you. Through a telescope.

ROSALIE: I never would have guessed that—

JONATHAN: I thought you were—ga-going to say I—I watch you with—with love in my eyes or some—thing like that. I didn't think you were going to guess that I—watch you through a telescope. I didn't think you were going to guess that I wa-watch you through a telescope on the fa-first guess, anyway. Not on the *first guess.*

ROSALIE: Well, it was just a guess.

JONATHAN: (*Hopefully.*) Do you watch *me* through a telescope?

ROSALIE: I never knew where your room was.

JONATHAN: Now you know. Now will you watch me?

ROSALIE: Well, I—don't have a telescope.

JONATHAN:. (*Getting more elated and excited.*) You can make one. That's how I got mine. I made it. Out of lenses and tubing. That's all you need. Lenses and tubing. Do you have any lenses?

ROSALIE: No.

JONATHAN: Do you have any tubing?

ROSALIE: No.

JONATHAN: Oh. (*Pause.*) Well, would you like me to tell you how I made mine in case you find some lenses and tubing? Would you like that?

ROSALIE: (*Disinterestedly.*) Sure, Jonathan. I think that would be nice.

JONATHAN: Well, I made it out of lenses and tubing. The lenses I had because Ma-Ma-Mother gave me a set of lenses so I could see my stamps better. I have a fabulous collection of stamps, as well as a fantastic collection of coins and a simply unbelievable collection of books. Well, sir, Ma-Ma-Mother gave me these lenses so I could see my stamps better. She suspected that some were fake so she gave me the lenses so I might be—able to see. You see? Well, sir, I happen to have nearly a billion sta-stamps. So far I've looked closely at 1,352,769. I've discovered three actual fakes! Number 1,352,767 was a fake. Number 1,352,768 was a fake, and number 1,352,769 was a fake. They were stuck together. Ma-Mother made me feed them immediately to her flytraps. Well—(*He whispers.*) one day, when Mother wasn't looking—that is, when she was out, I heard an airplane flying. An airplane—somewhere—far away. It wasn't very loud, but still I heard it. An airplane. Flying—somewhere, far away. And I ran outside to the porch so that I might see what it looked like. The airplane. With hundreds of people inside it. Hundreds and hundreds and hundreds of people. And I thought to myself, if I could just see—if I could just see what they looked like, the people, sitting at their windows, looking out—and flying. If I could see—*just* once—if I could see *just once* what they looked like—then I might—know what I—what I . . . (*Slight pause.*) So I—built a telescope in case the plane ever—came back again. The tubing came from an old blowgun. (*He reaches behind the bureau and produces a huge blowgun, easily a foot larger than he.*) Mother brought it back from her last hunting trip to Zanzibar. The lenses were the lenses she had given me for my stamps. So I built it. My telescope. A telescope so I might be able to see. And—(*He walks out to the porch.*) and—and I *could* see. I could! I COULD! I really could. For miles and miles I could see. For miles and miles and *miles!* (*He begins to lift it up to look through but stops, for some reason, before he's brought it up to his eye.*) Only . . . (*He hands it to* Rosalie. *She takes it eagerly and scans the horizon and the sky. She hands it back to him.*)

ROSALIE: (*With annoyance.*) There's nothing out there to see.

JONATHAN: (*Sadly.*) I know. That's the trouble. You take the time to build a telescope that can sa-see for miles, then there's nothing out there so see. Ma-Mother says it's a Lesson in Life. (*Pause.*) But I'm not sorry I built my telescope. And you know why? Because I saw you. Even if I didn't see anything else, I did see you. And—and I'm—very glad. (Rosalie *moves slightly closer to him on the couch. She moistens her lips.*) I—I remember, you were standing across the way in your penthouse garden playing blind man's buff with ten little children. (*After a short pause, fearfully.*) Are—are they by any chance—*yours?*

ROSALIE: (*Sweetly.*) Oh, I'm not married.

JONATHAN: Oh!

ROSALIE: I'm a baby sitter.
JONATHAN: (*With obvious relief.*) Oh.
ROSALIE: I work for the people who own the penthouse.
JONATHAN: I've never seen them around.
ROSALIE: I've never seen them either. They're never home. They just mail me a check every week and tell me to make sure I keep the children's names straight.
JONATHAN: If you could tell me which way they went I could find them with my telescope. It can see for miles.
ROSALIE: They must love children very much, to have so many, I mean. What a remarkable woman she must be. (*Pause.*) There's going to be another one, too! Another child is coming! I got a night letter last night.
JONATHAN: By airplane?
ROSALIE: I don't know.
JONATHAN: I bet it was. I can't see at night. Ma-Mother can but I can't. I'll bet that's when the planes fly.
ROSALIE: (*Coyly.*) If you like, I'll read you the letter. I have it with me. (*She unbuttons the top of her blouse and turns around in a coquettish manner to take the letter from her brassiere. Reading.*) "Have had another child. Sent it yesterday. Will arrive tomorrow. Call it Cynthia."
JONATHAN: That will make eleven. That's an awful lot of children to take care of. I'll bet it must be wonderful.
ROSALIE: Well, they do pay very well.
JONATHAN: They pay you?
ROSALIE: Of course—What did you think? (*Pause. Softly, seductively.*) Jonathan? (*He does not answer but seems lost in thought. With a feline purr.*) Jonathan?
JONATHAN: Yyyyyes?
ROSALIE: It gets very lonesome over there. The children go to sleep early and the parents are never home so I'm always alone. Perhaps—well, Jonathan, I thought that perhaps you might—visit me.
JONATHAN: Well—well—well, you—you see—I—I—
ROSALIE: We could spend the evenings together—at my place. It gets so lonesome there, you know what I mean? I mean, I don't know what to do. I get so lonesome there.
JONATHAN: Ma-ma-ma-maybe you—you can—come over—here? Maybe you you can do—that.
ROSALIE: Why are you trembling so?
JONATHAN: I'm—I'm—I'm—I'm—
ROSALIE: Are you afraid?
JONATHAN: Nnnnnnnnnnnnnnnnnnnno. Whaaaaaaaaaa-why—should I —be—afraid?
ROSALIE: Then why won't you come visit me?
JONATHAN: I—I—I—I—
ROSALIE: I don't think you're allowed to go out. That's what I think.
JONATHAN: Nnnn-o. I—I can—can—can—
ROSALIE: Why can't you go out, Jonathan? I want to know.
JONATHAN: Nnnnnnnnn—
ROSALIE: Tell me, Jonathan!
JONATHAN: I—I—
ROSALIE: I said I want to know! *Tell* me.
JONATHAN: I—I don't—know. I don't know why. I mean. I've— nnnnnnnnnever really thought—about going out. I—guess it's—just natural for me to—stay inside. (*He laughs nervously as if that explained everything.*)

You see—I've got so much to do. I mean, all my sssssstamps and—ca-coins and books. The pa-pa-plane might ffffffly overhead while I was was going downstairs. And then thhhhere are—the plants ta-to feeeeeeed. And I enjoy vvvery much wa-watching you and all yyyyyyour chil-dren. I've—really got so ma-many things—to—do. Like—like my future, for instance. Ma-Mother says I'm going to be great. That's—that's—that's what she says. I'm going to be great. I sssswear. Of course, she doesn't know ex-actly what I'm—going to be great in—so she sits every afternoon for—for two hours and thinks about it. Na-na-naturally I've—got to be here when she's thinking in case she—thinks of the answer. Otherwise she might forget and I'd never know— what I'm ga-going to be great in. You—see what I mean? I mean, I've—I've ggggggot so many things to do I—just couldn't possibly get *anything* done if I ever—went—outside. (*There is a silence.* Jonathan *stares at* Rosalie *as if he were hoping that might answer her question sufficiently. She stares back at him as if she knows there is more.*) Besides, Mother locks the front door.

ROSALIE: I thought so.

JONATHAN: No! You-you don't understand. It's not what you think. She doesn't lock the door to ka-ka-keep me in, which would be malicious. She— locks the door so I can't get out, which is for my own good and therefore— beneficient.

CUCKOO CLOCK: (*From the master bedroom.*) Cuckoo! Cuckoo! Cuckoo!

ROSALIE: What's that?

JONATHAN: (*Fearfully.*) A warning.

ROSALIE: What do you mean, a warning?

JONATHAN: A warning that you have to go. Your time is up.

ROSALIE: My time is what?

JONATHAN: Your time is up. You have to go. Now. At once. Right away. You can't stay any longer. You've got to go!

ROSALIE: Why?

JONATHAN: (*Puzzled; as if this were the first time the question had ever occurred to him.*) I don't really know.

CUCKOO CLOCK: (*Louder.*) Cuckoo! Cuckoo! Cuckoo!

(Jonathan *freezes in terror.* Rosalie *looks at him calmly.*)

ROSALIE: Why did your mother ask me to come up here?

JONATHAN: What?

ROSALIE: Why did your mother ask me—?

JONATHAN: So I—I could meet you.

ROSALIE: Then why didn't you ask me yourself? Something's wrong around here, Jonathan. I don't understand why you didn't ask me yourself.

JONATHAN: Ma-Mother's so much better at those things.

CUCKOO CLOCK: (*Very loudly.*) CUCKOO! CUCKOO! CUCKOO!

JONATHAN: You've got to get out of here! That's the third warning. (*He starts to push her toward the door.*)

ROSALIE: Will you call me on the phone?

JONATHAN: Please, you've got to go!

ROSALIE: Instead of your mother telling me to come, will you come and get me yourself? Will you at least call me? Wave to me?

JONATHAN: Yes-yes—I'll do that. Now get out of here!

ROSALIE: I want you to promise to come and see me again.

JONATHAN: Get out!

ROSALIE: (*Coyly.*) Promise me.

JONATHAN: GET OUT! (*He pushes her toward the door.*)
ROSALIE: Why do you keep looking at the door?
JONATHAN: (*Almost in tears.*) Please.
ROSALIE: Why do you keep looking at that door?
JONATHAN: *Please!* You've got to go before it's too late!
ROSALIE: There's something very wrong here. I want to see what's behind that door. (*She starts toward the master bedroom. Jonathan throws his arms about her legs and collapses at her feet, his faced buried against her thighs.*)
JONATHAN: (*Sobbing uncontrollably.*) I love you.

(Rosalie *stops dead in her tracks and stares down at* Jonathan.*)

ROSALIE: What did you say?
JONATHAN: I-I-I llllllllove you. I love you, I love you, I love you, I—(*The Cuckoo Clock screams, cackles, and goes out of its mind, its call ending in a crazed, strident rasp as if it had broken all its springs, screws and innards. The door to the master bedroom opens. Madame Rosepettle appears. Weakly.*) Too late.
MADAME ROSEPETTLE: Two warnings are enough for any man. Three are enough for any woman. The cuckoo struck three times and then a fourth and still she's here. May I ask why?
ROSALIE: You've been listening at the keyhole, haven't you!
MADAME ROSEPETTLE: I'm talking to my son, harlot!
ROSALIE: What did you say?
MADAME ROSEPETTLE: Harlot, I called you! Slut, scum, sleazy prostitute catching and caressing children and men. Stroking their hearts. I've seen you.
ROSALIE: What are you talking about?
MADAME ROSEPETTLE: Blind man's buff with the children in the garden. The redheaded one—fifteen, I think. Behind the bush while the others cover their eyes. Up with the skirt, one-two-three and it's done. Don't try to deny it. I've seen you in action. I know your kind.
ROSALIE: That's a lie!
MADAME ROSEPETTLE: Life is a lie, my sweet. Not words but Life itself. Life in all its ugliness. It builds green trees that tease your eyes and draw you under them. Then when you're there in the shade and you breathe in and say, "Oh God, how beautiful," that's when the bird on the branch lets go his droppings and hits you on the head. Life, sweet, beware. It isn't what it seems. I've seen what it can do. I've watched you dance.
ROSALIE: What do you mean by that?
MADAME ROSEPETTLE: Last night in the ballroom. I've watched you closely and I know what I see. You danced too near those men and you let them do too much. Don't try to deny it. Words will only make it worse. It would be best for all concerned if you left at once and never came again. Good day. (Madame Rosepettle *turns to leave.* Rosalie *does not move.*)
ROSALIE: Why don't you let Jonathan out of his room?
MADAME ROSEPETTLE: Who?
ROSALIE: Jonathan.
MADAME ROSEPETTLE: Who?
ROSALIE: Your son.
MADAME ROSEPETTLE: You mean Albert? Is that who you mean? Albert?
JONATHAN: Pa-pa-please do-don't.
MADAME ROSEPETTLE: Is that who you mean, slut? H'm? Speak up? Is that who you mean?

ROSALIE: I mean your son.

MADAME ROSEPETTLE: *I don't let him out because he is my son.* I don't let him out because his skin is as white as fresh snow and he would burn if the sun struck him. I don't let him out because outside there are trees with birds sitting on their branches waiting for him to walk beneath. I don't let him out because you're there, waiting behind the bushes with your skirt up. I don't let him out because he is *susceptible.* That's why. Because he is *susceptible.* Susceptible to trees and to sluts and to sunstroke.

ROSALIE: Then why did you come and get me?

MADAME ROSEPETTLE: Because, my dear, my stupid son has been watching you through that stupid telescope he made. Because, in short, he wanted to meet you and I, in short, wanted him to know what you were really like. Now that he's seen, you may go.

ROSALIE: And if I choose to stay?

(Pause.)

MADAME ROSEPETTLE: *(Softly; slyly.)* Can you cook?

ROSALIE: Yes.

MADAME ROSEPETTLE: How well?

ROSALIE: Fairly well.

MADAME ROSEPETTLE: Not good enough! My son is a connoisseur. A connoisseur, do you hear? I cook him the finest foods in the world. Recipes no one knows exist. Food, my sweet, is the finest of arts. And since you can't cook you are artless. You nauseate my son's aesthetic taste. Do you like cats?

ROSALIE: Yes.

MADAME ROSEPETTLE: What kind of cats?

ROSALIE: Any kind of cats.

MADAME ROSEPETTLE: Alley cats?

ROSALIE: Especially alley cats.

MADAME ROSEPETTLE: I thought so. Go, my dear. Find yourself some weeping willow and set yourself beneath it. Cry of your lust for my son and wait, for a mocking bird waits above to deposit his verdict on your whorish head. My son is as white as fresh snow and you are tainted with sin. You are garnished with garlic and turn our tender stomachs in disgust.

ROSALIE: Why did you come to Port Royale?

MADAME ROSEPETTLE: To find *you!*

ROSALIE: And now that you've found me—?

MADAME ROSEPETTLE: I throw you out! I toss you into the garbage can! I heard everything, you know. So don't try to call. The phone is in my room— *and no one goes into my room but me. (She stares at* Rosalie *for a moment, then exits with a flourish.* Rosalie *and* Jonathan *move slowly toward each other. When they are almost together,* Madame Rosepettle *reappears.)* One more thing. If, by some chance, the eleventh child named Cynthia turns out to be a Siamese cat, give it to me. I, too, pay well.

*(*Madame Rosepettle *turns toward her room.* Rosalie *starts toward the door.* Jonathan *grabs her hand in desperation.)*

JONATHAN: *(In a whisper.)* Come back again. Pa-please—come back again.

(For a moment Rosalie *stops and looks at* Jonathan. *But* Madame Rosepettle *stops too, and turning, looks back at both of them, a slight smile on*

her lips. Rosalie, *sensing her glance, walks toward the door, slipping from* Jonathan's *outstretched hands as she does. The LIGHTS FADE about* Jonathan, *alone in the center of the room.*)

CURTAIN

SCENE III

(The hotel room at night, one week later. Jonathan *is alone in the living room. He is sitting in a chair near the fish bowl, staring at nothing in particular with a particular bland expression on his face. A CLOCK is heard ticking softly in the distance. For an interminably long time it continues to tick while* Jonathan *sits in his chair, motionless. After a while the TICKING speeds up almost imperceptibly and soon after, LAUGHTER is heard. At first it is a giggle from the rear of the theatre, then a cough from the side, then a self-conscious laugh from the other side, then a full, gusty belly-roar from all corners of the theatre. Soon the entire world is hysterical. CUBAN DRUMS begin to beat. FIREWORKS explode. ORGIASTIC MUSIC is heard.* Jonathan *continues to sit, motionless. Only his eyes have begun to move. The CLOCK continues to tick. The LAUGHTER grows louder: the laughter of the insane. Suddenly* Jonathan *leaps up and rushes to the French windows, his fingers pressed against his ears. He slams the French windows shut. The noises stop.* Jonathan *closes his eyes and sighs with relief. The French windows sway unsteadily on their hinges. They tip forward. They fall to the floor. They shatter. The LAUGHTER returns.* Jonathan *stares down at them in horror. The* Venus Fly Traps *grow larger and growl.)*

VENUS FLY TRAPS: (*Viciously.*) Grrrrrrrr.

(The piranha fish stares hungrily from its bowl.)

ROSALINDA THE FISH: (*More viciously.*) Grarrgh!

(The Fly Traps lunge at Jonathan *but he walks dazedly past, unaware of their snapping petals, and goes out to the edge of the balcony. He stares out in complete bewilderment. The LAUGHTER and MUSIC of a carnival, the SOUNDS of* People *dancing in the streets fill the air. He looks down at them sadly. Meekly he waves. The sounds immediately grow softer and the* People *begin to drift away. He watches as they leave. Behind him the* Fly Traps *keep growing and reaching out for him, but of this he is unaware. He only stands at the railing, looking down. At last lingering LAUGH is heard somewhere in the distance, echoing. The door to the suite opens. The LIGHTS fade in the room and only the table is lit. The MUSIC grows in brilliance. The* Commodore *and* Madame Rosepettle *waltz into the room. A spot of LIGHT follows them about the floor.)*

THE COMMODORE: How lovely it was this evening, madame, don't you think? (*She laughs softly and demurely and discreetly lowers her eyes. They waltz about the floor.*) How gentle the wind was, madame. And the stars, how clear and bright they were, don't you think? (*She turns her face away and smiles softly. They begin to whirl about the floor.*) Ah, the waltz. How exquisite it is, madame, don't you think? *One-two-three, one-two-three, one-two-three.* Ahhhh, madame, how classically simple. How stark; how strong—how romantic—how sublime. (*She giggles girlishly. They whirl madly about the floor.*) Oh, if only madame knew how I've waited for this moment. If only madame knew how long. How this week, these nights, the nights we shared together on my yacht; the warm, wonderful nights, the almost-perfect nights, the would-have-been-perfect nights had it not been for the crew peeking through the portholes. Ah, those nights, madame, those nights; almost alone but never quite; but now, tonight, at last, we *are* alone. And now, madame, now we are ready for romance. For the night was made for love. And tonight, madame—we will love.

MADAME ROSEPETTLE: (*With the blush of innocence.*) Oh, Commodore, how you do talk.

(*They whirl about the room as the lilting rhythm of the waltzing grows and sweeps on and on.*)

THE COMMODORE: (*Suavely.*) Madame, may I kiss you?

MADAME ROSEPETTLE: Why?

THE COMMODORE: (*After recovering from the abruptness of the question. With forced suaveness.*) Your lips . . . are a thing of beauty.

MADAME ROSEPETTLE: My lips, Commodore, are the color of blood. (*She smiles at him. He stares blankly ahead. They dance on.*) I must say, you dance exceptionally well, Commodore—for a man your age.

THE COMMODORE: (*Bristling.*) I dance with *you*, madame. That is why I dance well. For to dance with you, madame—is to hold you.

MADAME ROSEPETTLE: Well, I don't mind your holding me, Commodore, but at the moment you happen to be holding me too tight.

THE COMMODORE: I hold you too dear to hold you too tight, madame. I hold you close, that is all. And I hold you close in the hope that my heart may feel your heart beating.

MADAME ROSEPETTLE: *One*-two-three, *one*-two-three. You're not paying enough attention to the music, Commodore. I'm afraid you've fallen out of step.

THE COMMODORE: Then lead me, madame. Take my hand and lead me wherever you wish. For I would much rather think of my words than my feet.

MADAME ROSEPETTLE: (*With great sweetness.*) Why certainly, Commodore. Certainly. If that is what you want—it will be my pleasure to oblige. (*They switch hands and she begins to lead him about the floor. They whirl wildly about, spinning faster than they had when the* Commodore *led.*) Beautiful, isn't it, Commodore? The waltz. The Dance of Lovers. I'm so glad you enjoy it so much. (*With a gay laugh she whirls him around the floor. Suddenly he puts his arms about her shoulders and leans close to kiss her. She pulls back.*) Commodore! You were supposed to spin just then. When I squeeze you in the side it means *spin!*

THE COMMODORE: (*Flustered.*) I—I thought it was a sign of affection.

(*She laughs.*)

MADAME ROSEPETTLE: You'll learn. (*She squeezes him in the side. He spins about under her arm.*) Ah, you're learning.

(*He continues to spin, around and around, faster and faster like a runaway top while* Madam Rosepettle, *not spinning at all, leads him about the floor, a wild smile of ecstasy spreading over her face.*)

THE COMMODORE: Ho-ho, ho-ho. Stop. I'm dizzy. Dizzy. Stop, please. Stop. Ho-ho. Stop. Dizzy. Ho-ho. Stop. Too fast. Slow. Slower. Stop. Ho-ho. Dizzy. Too dizzy: Weeeeeeee! (*And, then, without any warning at all, she grabs him in the middle of a spin, and kisses him. Her back is to the audience, so the* Commodore's *face is visible. At first he is too dizzy to realize that his motion has been stopped. But shortly he does, and his first expression is that of shock. But the kiss is long and the shock turns into perplexity and then finally, into panic; into fear. He struggles desperately and breaks free from her arms, gasping wildly for air. He points weakly to his chest, gasping.*) Asthma. (*His chest heaves as he gulps in air.*) Couldn't breathe. Asthmatic. Couldn't get any air. (*He gasps for air. She starts to walk toward him, slowly.*) Couldn't get any ... air. (*She nears him. Instinctively he backs away.*) You—you surprised me—you know. Out—of breath. Wasn't—ready for that. Didn't—expect you to kiss me.

MADAME ROSEPETTLE: I know. That's why I did it. (*She laughs and puts her arm tenderly about his waist.*) Perhaps you'd prefer to sit down for a while, Commodore? Catch your breath, so to speak. Dancing can be so terribly tiring—when you're growing old. Well, if you like, Commodore, we could just sit and talk. And perhaps—sip some pink champagne, eh? Champagne?

THE COMMODORE: Ah, champagne.

MADAME ROSEPETTLE: (*She begins to walk with him toward the table.*) And just for the two of us.

THE COMMODORE: Yes. The two of us. Alone.

MADAME ROSEPETTLE: (*With a laugh.*) Yes. All alone.

THE COMMODORE: At last.

MADAME ROSEPETTLE: With music in the distance.

THE COMMODORE: A waltz.

MADAME ROSEPETTLE: A *Viennese* waltz.

THE COMMODORE: The Dance of Lovers.

MADAME ROSEPETTLE: (*She takes his hand, tenderly.*) Yes, Commodore. The Dance of Lovers. (*They look at each other in silence.*)

THE COMMODORE: Madame, you have won my heart. And easily.

MADAME ROSEPETTLE: No, Commodore. You have lost it. *Easily.* (*She smiles seductively. The room darkens till only a SINGLE SPOT of light falls upon the table set in the middle of the room. The WALTZ plays on.* Madame Rosepettle *nods to the* Commodore *and he goes to sit. But before he can pull his chair out, it slides out under its own power. He places himself and the chair slides back in, as if some invisible waiter had been holding it in his invisible hands.* Madame Rosepettle *smiles sweetly and, pulling out her chair herself, sits. They stare at each other in silence. The WALTZ plays softly. The* Commodore *reaches across the table and touches her hand. A thin smile spreads across her lips. When finally they speak, their words are soft; the whispered thoughts of lovers.*) Champagne?

THE COMMODORE: Champagne.

MADAME ROSEPETTLE: Pour?

THE COMMODORE: Please.

(*She lifts the bottle out of the ice bucket and pours with her right hand, her left being clasped firmly in the* Commodore's *passionate hands. They smile serenely at each other. She lifts her glass. He lifts his. The MUSIC swells.*)

MADAME ROSEPETTLE: A toast?

THE COMMODORE: To you.

MADAME ROSEPETTLE: No, Commodore, to you.

THE COMMODORE: No, madame. To us.

MADAME ROSEPETTLE AND THE COMMODORE: (*Together.*) To us. (*They raise their glasses. They gaze wistfully into each other's eyes. The MUSIC builds to brilliance. The* Commodore *clicks his glass against* Madame Rosepettle's *glass. The glasses break.*)

THE COMMODORE:.   (*Furiously mopping up the mess.*) Pardon, madame! Pardon!

MADAME ROSEPETTLE: (*Flicking some glass off her bodice.*) Pas de quoi, monsieur.

THE COMMODORE: J'etais emporte par l'enthousiasme du moment.

MADAME ROSEPETTLE: (*Extracting pieces of glass from her lap.*) Pas de quoi. (*She snaps her fingers gaily. Immediately a* Waiter *appears from the shadows with a table in his hands and whisks the wet table away. The new table is placed. It is already covered with a table cloth, two champagne glasses, two candelabra (the candles already flickering in them) and a vase with one wilting rose protruding. The* Waiters *disappear into the shadows.* Madame Rosepettle *lifts the bottle of champagne out of the ice bucket.*) Encore?

THE COMMODORE: Si'l vous plait. (*She pours. They lift their glasses in toast. The MUSIC swells again.*) To us.

MADAME ROSEPETTLE: To us, Monsieur—Commodore. (*They clink their glasses lightly. The* Commodore *closes his eyes and sips.* Madame Rosepettle *holds her glass before her lips, poised but not touching; waiting. She watches him. Softly.*) Tell me about yourself.

THE COMMODORE: My heart is speaking, madame. Doesn't it tell you enough?

MADAME ROSEPETTLE: Your heart, monsieur, is growing old. It speaks with a murmur. Its words are too weak to understand.

THE COMMODORE: But the feeling, madame, is still strong.

MADAME ROSEPETTLE: Feelings are for animals, monsieur. Words are the specialty of Man. Tell me what your heart has to say.

THE COMMODORE: My heart says it loves you.

MADAME ROSEPETTLE: And how many others, monsieur, has your heart said this to?

THE COMMODORE: None but you, madame. None but you.

MADAME ROSEPETTLE: And pray, monsieur, just what is it that I've done to make you love me so?

THE COMMODORE: Nothing, madame. And that is why. You are a strange woman, you see. You go out with me and you know how I feel. Yet, I know nothing of you. You disregard me, madame, but never discourage. You treat my love with indifference—but never disdain. You've led me on, madame. That is what I mean to say.

MADAME ROSEPETTLE: I've led you to my room, monsieur. That is all.

THE COMMODORE: To me, that is enough.

MADAME ROSEPETTLE: I know. That's why I did it.

(*The MUSIC swells. She smiles distantly. There is a momentary silence.*)

THE COMMODORE: (*With desperation.*) Madame, I must ask you something. Why are you here? (*Short pause.*)

MADAME ROSEPETTLE: Well, I have to be somewhere, don't I?

THE COMMODORE: But why here, where I am? Why in Port Royale?

MADAME ROSEPETTLE: You flatter yourself, monsieur. I am in Port Royale only because Port Royale was in my way. . . . I think I'll move on tomorrow.

THE COMMODORE: For—home?

MADAME ROSEPETTLE: (*Laughing slightly.*) Only the very young and the very old have homes. I am neither. So I have none.

THE COMMODORE: But—surely you must come from somewhere.

MADAME ROSEPETTLE: Nowhere you've ever been.

THE COMMODORE: I've been many places.

MADAME ROSEPETTLE: (*Softly.*) But not many enough. (*She picks up her glass of champagne and sips, a distant smile on her lips.*)

THE COMMODORE: (*With sudden, overwhelming and soul-rending passion.*) Madame, don't go tomorrow. Stay. My heart is yours.

MADAME ROSEPETTLE: How much is it worth?

THE COMMODORE: A fortune, madame.

MADAME ROSEPETTLE: Good, I'll take it in cash.

THE COMMODORE: But the heart goes with it, madame.

MADAME ROSEPETTLE: And you with the heart, I suppose?

THE COMMODORE: Forever.

MADAME ROSEPETTLE: Sorry, monsieur. The money's enticing and the heart would have been nice, but you, I'm afraid, are a bit too bulky to make it all worth while.

THE COMMODORE: You jest, madame.

MADAME ROSEPETTLE: I never jest, monsieur. There isn't enough time.

THE COMMODORE: Then you make fun of my passion, madame, which is just as bad.

MADAME ROSEPETTLE: But, monsieur, I've never taken your passion seriously enough to make fun of it.

THE COMMODORE: (*There is a short pause. The* Commodore *sinks slowly back in his seat. Weakly, sadly.*) Then why have you gone out with me?

MADAME ROSEPETTLE: So that I might drink champagne with you tonight.

THE COMMODORE: That makes no sense.

MADAME ROSEPETTLE: It makes *perfect* sense.

THE COMMODORE: Not to me.

MADAME ROSEPETTLE: It does to me.

THE COMMODORE: But *I* don't understand. And I *want* to understand.

MADAME ROSEPETTLE: Don't worry, Commodore. You will.

THE COMMODORE: When?

MADAME ROSEPETTLE: Soon.

THE COMMODORE: How soon?

MADAME ROSEPETTLE: Very soon. (*He stares at her in submissive confusion. Suddenly, with final desperation, he grabs her hands in his and, leaning across the table, kisses them passionately, sobbingly. In a scarcely audible whisper.*) Now.

THE COMMODORE: Madame—I love you. Forever. Don't you understand? (*He kisses her hands again. A smile of triumph spreads across his face.*) Oh, your husband—He must have been—a wonderful man—to have deserved a woman such as you. (*He sobs and kisses her hands again.*)

MADAME ROSEPETTLE: (*Nonchalantly.*) Would you like to see him?

THE COMMODORE: A snapshot?

MADAME ROSEPETTLE: No. My husband. He's inside in the closet. I had him stuffed. Wonderful taxidermist I know. H'm? What do you say, Commodore? Wanna peek? He's my very favorite trophy. I take him with me wherever I go.

THE COMMODORE: (*Shaken. Not knowing what to make of it.*) Hah-hah, hah-hah. Yes. Very good. Very funny. Sort of a—um—*white elephant,* you might say.

MADAME ROSEPETTLE: *You* might say.

THE COMMODORE: Well, it's—certainly very—courageous of you, a—a woman still in mourning, to—to be able to laugh at what most other women wouldn't find—well, shall we say—funny.

MADAME ROSEPETTLE: Life, my dear Commodore, is never funny. It's grim! It's there every morning breathing in your face the moment you open your red baggy eyes. Life, Mr. Roseabove, is a husband hanging from a hook in the closet. Open the door too quickly and your whole day's shot to hell. But open the door just a little ways, sneak your hand in, pull out your dress and your day is made. Yet he's still there, and waiting—and sooner or later the moth balls are gone and you have to clean house. Oh, it's a bad day, Commodore, when you have to stare Life in the face, and you find he doesn't smile at all; just hangs there—with his tongue sticking out.

THE COMMODORE: I—don't find this—very funny.

MADAME ROSEPETTLE: Sorry. I was hoping it would give you a laugh.

THE COMMODORE: I don't think it's funny at all. And the reason that I don't think it's funny at all is that it's not my kind of joke. One must respect the dead.

MADAME ROSEPETTLE: Then tell me, Commodore—why not the living, too? (*Pause. She lifts out the bottle of champagne and pours herself some more.*)

THE COMMODORE: (*Weakly, with a trace of fear.*) How—how did he die?

MADAME ROSEPETTLE: Why, I killed him, of course. Champagne? (*She smiles sweetly and fills his glass. She raises hers in toast.*) To your continued good health. (*He stares at her blankly. The MUSIC swells in the background.*) Ah, the waltz, monsieur. Listen. The waltz. The Dance of Lovers. Beautiful—*don't you think?*

(*She laughs and sips some more champagne. The MUSIC grows to brilliance. The* Commodore *starts to rise from his chair.*)

THE COMMODORE: Forgive me, madame. But—I find I must leave. Urgent business calls. Good evening. (*He tries to push his chair back, but for some reason it will not move. He looks about in panic. He pushes frantically. It does not move. It is as if the invisible waiter who had come and slid the chair out when he went to sit down, now stood behind the chair and held it in so he could not get up. And as there are arms on the chair, the* Commodore *cannot slide out at the sides.* Madame Rosepettle *smiles.*)

MADAME ROSEPETTLE: Now you don't *really* want to leave—do you, Commodore? After all, the night is still so young—and you haven't even seen my husband yet. Besides, there's a little story I still must tell you. A bedtime story. A fairy-tale full of handsome princes and enchanted maidens; full of love and joy and music; tenderness and charm. It's my very favorite story, you see. And I never leave a place without telling it to at least one person. So please, Commodore, won't you stay? . . . *Just for a little while?* (*He stares at her in horror. He tries once more to push his chair back. But the chair does not move. He sinks down into it weakly. She leans across the table and tenderly touches his hand.*) Good. I knew you'd see it my way. It would have been such a shame if you'd had to leave. For you see, Commodore, we are, in a way, united. We share something in common—you and I. We share desire. For you desire me, with love in your heart. While I, my dear Com-

modore—desire your heart. (*She smiles sweetly and sips some more cham-*
pagne.) How simple it all is, in the end. (*She rises slowly from her chair and*
walks over to him. She runs her hands lovingly through his hair and down
the back of his neck. The LIGHT on the table dims slightly. Madame Rosepettle *walks slowly away. A SPOT of light follows her as she goes. LIGHT*
on the table fades more. The Commodore *sits, motionless.*) His name was
Albert Edward Robinson Rosepettle III. How strange and sad he was. All the
others who had come to see me had been tall, but he was short. They had
been rich, while he was poor. The others had been handsome but Albert, poor
Albert, he was as ugly as a humid day—(*She laughs sadly, distantly.*) and
just about as wet, too. Oh, he was a fat bundle of sweat, Mr. Roseabove. He
was nothing but one great torrent of perspiration. Winter and summer, spring
and fall, Albert was dripping wet. Yes, he was round and wet and hideous
and I never could figure out how he ever got such a name as Albert Edward
Robinson Rosepettle III. Oh, I must have been very susceptible indeed to
have married Albert. I *was* twenty-eight and that *is* a susceptible year in a
woman's life. And of course I *was* a virgin, but still I—Oh, stop blushing,
Mr. Roseabove. I'm not lying. It's all true. Part of the cause of my condition,
I will admit, was due to the fact that I still hadn't gone out with a man. But
I am certain, Mr. Roseabove, I am certain that despite your naughty glances
my virtue would have remained unsoiled, no matter what. Oh, I had spoken
to men. (Their voices are gruff.) And in crowded streets I had often brushed
against them. (Their bodies, I found, are tough and bony.) I had observed
their ways and habits, Mr. Roseabove. Even at that tender age I had the
foresight to realize I must know what I was up against. So I watched them
huddle in hallways, talking in nervous whispers and laughing when little
girls passed by. I watched their hands in crowded buses and even felt their
feeling elbows on crowded streets. And then, one night, when I was walking
home I saw a man standing in a window. I saw him take his contact lenses
out and his hearing aid out of his ear. I saw him take his teeth out of his
thin-lipped mouth and drop them into a smiling glass of water. I saw him
lift his snow-white hair off his wrinkled, white head and place it on a
gnarled, wooden hat tree. And then I saw him take his clothes off. And when
he was done and didn't move but stood and stared at a full length mirror
whose glass he had covered with towels, then I went home and wept. And
so one day I bolted the door to my room. I locked myself inside, bought a
small revolver just in case, then sat at my window and watched what went
on below. It was not a pretty sight. Some men came up to see me. They came
and knocked. I did not let them in.

> "Hello in there," they said.
> "Hello in there,
> My name is Steven.
> Steven S. (for Steven) Steven.
> One is odd
> But two is even.
> I know you're not
> So I'm not leavin'."

Or something like that. (*Short pause.*) But they all soon left anyway. I think
they caught the scent of a younger woman down the hall.... And so I

listened to the constant sound of feet disappearing down the stairs. I watched a world walk by my window; a world of lechery and lies and greed. I watched a world walk by and I decided not to leave my room until this world came to me, *exactly* as I wanted it. One day Albert came toddling up the stairs. He waddled over to my room, scratched on the door and said, in a frail and very frightened voice, "Will you please marry me?" And so I did. It was as simple as that. (*Pause. Then distantly.*) I still wonder why I did it, though. I still wonder why. (*Short pause. Then, with a laugh of resignation.*) I don't really know why. I guess it just seemed like the right thing to do. Maybe it's because he was the first one who ever asked me. No, that's not right.— Perhaps it's because he was so ugly and fat; so unlike everything I'd ever heard a husband should be. No, that doesn't make much sense, either.— Perhaps it's—yet, perhaps it's because one look at Albert's round, sad face and I knew he could be mine—that no matter where he went, or whom he saw, or what he did, Albert would be mine, my husband, my lover, my own—mine to love; mine to live with:—mine to kill. (*Short pause.*) And so we were wed. That night I went to bed with a man for the first time in my life. The next morning I picked up my mattress and moved myself to another room. Not that there was something wrong with Albert. Oh, no! He was *quite* the picture of health. His pudgy, pink flesh bouncing with glee. Oh, how easily is man satisfied. How easily is his porous body saturated with "fun." All he asks is a little sex and a little food and there he is, asleep with a smile, and snoring. Never the slightest regard for you, lying in bed next to him, your eyes open wide. No, he stretches his legs and kicks you in the shins; stretches his arms and smacks you in the eye. Oh, how noble, how magical, how marvelous is love. So you see, Mr. Roseabove, I had to leave his room. For as long as I stayed there I was not safe. After all, we'd only met the day before and I knew far too little about him. But now that we were married I had time to find out more. A few of the things I wanted to know were: what had he done before we'd ever met, what had he wanted to do, what did he *still* want to do, what was he doing about it? What did he dream about while he slept? What did he think about when he stared out the window? . . . What did he think about when I wasn't near? These were the things that concerned me most. And so I began to watch him closely. My plan worked best at night, for that was when he slept—I would listen at my door until I heard his door close. Then I'd tiptoe out and watch him through his keyhole. When his lights went out I'd open up his door and creep across the floor to his bed, and then I'd listen more. My ear became a stethoscope that recorded the fluctuations of his dream life. For I was waiting for him to speak; waiting for the slightest word that might betray his sleeping, secret thoughts. . . . But, no, Albert only snored and smiled and slept on and on. And *that*, Mr. Roseabove, is how I spent my nights!—next to him; my husband, my "Love." I never left his side, never took my eyes from his sleeping face. I dare you to find me a wife who's as devoted as that. (*She laughs. Short pause.*) A month later I found that I was pregnant. It had happened that first horrible night. How like Albert to do something like that. I fancy he knew it was going to happen all the time, too. I do believe he planned it that way. One night, one shot, one chance in a lifetime and bham! you've had it. It takes an imaginative man to miss. It takes someone like Albert to do something like that. But yet, I never let on. Oh, no. Let him think I'm simply getting fat, I said. And that's the way I did it, too. I, nonchalantly putting on weight; Albert nonchalantly watching my belly grow. If he knew what was happening to me he never let me know it. He was as silent as before. (*Pause.*) Twelve months later my son was born. He was so overdue, when he came out he was already teething. He bit the index finger off the poor doctor's hand and snapped at the nurse till she fainted. I took him home and put him in a cage in the darkest corner of my room. But still I—

THE COMMODORE: Was it a large cage?

MADAME ROSEPETTLE: What?

THE COMMODORE: Was his cage large? I hope it was. Otherwise it wouldn't be very comfortable.

MADAME ROSEPETTLE: I'm sorry. Did I say cage? I meant crib. I put him in a crib and set the crib in a corner of my room where my husband would not see him. For until I'd found out exactly why he'd married me, I would not tell him that a son had been born. (*Pause.*) Shortly after that, Rosalinda came. She was one of Albert's many secretaries. I've always felt there was something star-crossed about those two, for she was the only person I ever met who was equally as ugly as he. It seems that Rosalinda's mother had once owned a laundromat, and she, being a curious child, had taken an exploratory trip through the mangler, with the result that she now resembled nothing more nor less than a question mark. Well, naturally, I never let on that I knew she had come. When she walked in front of me I looked straight through her. When she spoke I looked away. I flatly refused to recognize her presence. And though Albert watched me like a naughty child anxious to see his mother's reaction to a mischievous deed, I disregarded him and continued my life as if nothing had changed. So at night, instead of preparing one, I prepared two beds. Instead of fluffing one pillow I fluffed up two and straightened an extra pair of sheets. I said good night as politely as I could and left them alone—the monster and my husband, two soulmates expressing their souls through sin. And while they lay in bed I listened at the keyhole. And when they slept I crept in and listened more. Albert had begun to speak! After months of my listening for some meager clue he suddenly began to talk in torrents. Words poured forth and I, like some listening sponge, soaked them up and stayed for more. He told her things he never told to me. Words of passion and love. He told her how he worshipped the way she cooked; how he worshipped the way she talked; how he'd worshipped the way she looked now. And this to a hideous, twisted slut of a woman sleeping in sin with him! . . . Words he never told to me. . . . I ask you, Mr. Roseabove, I ask you—how much is a woman supposed to take? (*Short pause.*) Ah, but the signs of regret were beginning to show. And oh, how I laughed when I saw. How little he ate; how little he spoke; how slowly he seemed to move. It's funny, but he never slept any more. I could tell by his breathing. And through the keyhole at night I could see his large, round, empty eyes shining sadly in the dark. (*Pause.*) Then one night he died. One year after she had come he passed on. The doctors didn't know why. His heart, they said, seemed fine. It was as large a heart as they'd ever seen. And yet he died. At one o'clock in the morning his heart stopped beating. (*She laughs softly.*) But it wasn't till dawn that she discovered he was dead. (*She starts to laugh.*) Well, don't you get it? Don't you catch the irony, the joke? What's wrong with you!? He died at one. At ONE O'CLOCK IN THE MORNING! ! DEAD! ! ! Yet she didn't know he was dead till dawn. (*She laughs again, loudly.*) Well, don't you get the point? The point of this whole story? What is wrong with you? He was lying with her in bed for nearly six hours, *dead,* and she never knew it! What a lover he must have been! WHAT A LOVER! ! (*She laughs uproariously, but stops when she realizes he's not laughing with her.*) Well, don't you see? Their affair, their sinfulness—it never even existed! He tried to make me jealous but there was nothing to be jealous of. His love was sterile! He was a child. He was weak. He was impotent. He was *mine!* Mine all the time, even when he was in bed with another, even in death—*he was mine!* (*The Commodore climbs up in his chair and crawls over his arm-rest. He begins to walk weakly toward the doors.*) Don't tell me you're leaving, Commodore. Is there something wrong? (*The Commodore walks weakly toward the door, then runs the last part of the way. In panic he twists the door knob. The door knob comes off. He falls to the ground.*) Why, Commodore, you're on your knees! How romantic. Don't tell me you're going to ask me to marry you again? Commodore, you're trembling. What's wrong? Don't tell me you're afraid that I'll accept?

THE COMMODORE: (*Weakly.*) I—I-I—feel—sa-sorry for your—sssson—that's—all I can—sssssay.

MADAME ROSEPETTLE: And I feel sorrier for you! For you are *nothing!* While my son is mine. His skin is the color of fresh snow, and his mind is pure. For he is safe, Mr. Roseabove, and it is *I* who have saved him. Saved him from the world beyond that door. The world of you. The world of his father. A world waiting to devour those who trust in it; those who love. A world vicious under the hypocrisy of kindness, ruthless under the falseness of a smile. Well, go on, Mr. Roseabove. Leave my room and enter your world again—your sex-driven, dirt-washed waste of cannibals eating each other up while they pretend they're kissing. Go, Mr. Roseabove, enter your blind world of darkness. My son shall have only light!

(*She turns with a flourish and enters her bedroom. The Commodore stares helplessly at the door knob in his hand. Suddenly the door swings open, under its own power. The Commodore crawls out. The door closes behind him, under its own power. From outside can be heard the sound of a CHURCH BELL chiming. The bedroom door reopens and Madame Rosepettle emerges wearing an immense straw hat, sun glasses, tight toreador pants and a short beach robe. She carries a huge flashlight. She is barefoot. She tiptoes across the floor and exits through the main door. The CHURCH BELL chimes thirteen times. Jonathan emerges from behind the Venus Fly Traps. He runs to the door, puts his ear to it then races back to the balcony and stares down at the street below. CARNIVAL LIGHTS flash weirdly against the night sky and LAUGHTER drifts up. The Venus Fly Traps reach out to grab him but somehow he senses their presence and leaps away in time.*)

VENUS FLY TRAPS: (*Gruffly.*) Grrrrrrrr!

(*Jonathan backs up, staring in horror at the now huge leaves which snap at him hungrily, reaching for him. He backs, accidentally, into the table on which the fish and the dictaphone lies. He jars the table in doing so. The DICTAPHONE makes a strange noise and begins to speak.*)

THE DICTAPHONE: (*Madame Rosepettle's voice.*) ". . . And of course, could one ever forget those lovely seaside shops—"

(*Jonathan slams the buttons on the machine. The TAPE stops and starts to play backwards. The PLANTS grow. Jonathan, in horror, slams the buttons again. The TAPE whirls at the wrong speed. The VOICE shrieks wildly. Jonathan stares at it in horror as the TAPE runs out and turns, clicking on its spool. He hits the right button and the MACHINE stops. The FISH giggles. Jonathan stares at it in horror. The PLANTS snarl. Jonathan runs to*) *the wall and smashes the glass case that covers the fire axe. He takes out the axe. He advances cautiously toward the fly traps. He feints and attacks; they follow his movements. He bobs, they weave. It is a cat and mouse game of death. Suddenly Jonathan leaps upon them and hacks them apart till they fall to the floor, writhing, then dead. Jonathan stands above them, victorious, panting, but somehow seeming to breathe easier. Slowly he turns and looks at the fish bowl. His eyes seem glazed, his expression insanely determined. He walks slowly toward the bowl. There are THREE KNOCKS on the door to the suite. He does not hear them. He raises his axe. The door opens. Rosalie enters, pursued by a group of gaily drunken Bellboys. She laughs and closes the door on them. She herself is dressed in an absurdly childish pink party dress, complete with crinolines and frills—the portrait of a girl ten years old at her first "staying-up-late party." Her shoes are black leather pumps and she wears short pink socks. Her cheeks have round circles of rouge on them— like a young girl might have who had never put on makeup before. She carries masks and party favors.)*

ROSALIE: Jonathan! Jonathan! What *have* you done? (*Jonathan stops. He does not look at her but continues to stare at the fish bowl.*) Jonathan! Put down that silly old axe. You might hurt yourself. (*He still does not answer but only stares at the bowl. He does not lower the axe.*) Jonathan! (*Slowly he turns and faces her.*)

JONATHAN: I killed it.

ROSALIE: Ssh. Not so loudly. Where'd you put her body?

JONATHAN: (*Pointing to the plants.*) There.

ROSALIE: Where? I don't see a body. Where is she?

JONATHAN: Who?

ROSALIE: Your mother.

JONATHAN: I haven't killed my mother. I've killed her plants. The ones I used to feed. I've chopped their hearts out.

ROSALIE: (*With an apologetic laugh.*) I thought you'd—killed your mother. (*The Piranha Fish giggles. Jonathan turns and stares at it again. He starts to move towards it, slowly.*) Jonathan, stop. (*He hesitates, as if he were uncertain about what to do. Slowly he raises the axe.*) Jonathan! (*He smashes the axe against the fish bowl. It breaks. The fish screams.*)

ROSALINDA THE FISH: (*Fearfully.*) AAIEEEEEEEEEEEEEE! ! !

ROSALIE: Now look at the mess you've made.

JONATHAN: Do you think it can live without water?

ROSALIE: What will your mother say when she gets back?

JONATHAN: Maybe I should hit it again. Just in case. (*He strikes it again.*)

ROSALINDA THE FISH: (*Mournfully.*) UGHHHHHHHH!

(Jonathan stares in horror at the dead fish. He drops the axe and turns away, sickened and weak. Rosalie walks over and touches him gently, consolingly on the arm.)

ROSALIE: There's something bothering you, isn't there?

(Pause. Jonathan does not answer at first, but stares off into space frightened, bewildered.)

JONATHAN: (*Weakly.*) I never thought I'd see you again. I never thought I'd talk to you again. I never thought you'd come.

ROSALIE: Did you really think that?

JONATHAN: She told me she'd never let you visit me again. She said no one would *ever* visit me again. She told me I had seen enough.

ROSALIE: But I had a key made.

JONATHAN: She—she hates me.

ROSALIE: What?

JONATHAN: She doesn't let me do anything. She doesn't let me listen to the radio. She took the tube out of the television set. She doesn't let me use her phone. She makes me show her all my letters before I seal them. She doesn't—

ROSALIE: Letters? What letters are you talking about?

JONATHAN: Just—letters I write.

ROSALIE: To *whom?*

JONATHAN: To people.

ROSALIE: Other girls? Could they be to other girls by any chance?

JONATHAN: No. They're just to people. No people in particular. Just people in the phone book. Just names. So far I've covered all the "A's" and "B's" up to Barrera.

ROSALIE: What is it you say to them? Can you tell me what you say to them—or is it private? Jonathan, just what do you say to them!?

JONATHAN: Mostly I just ask them what they look like. (*Pause. Suddenly he starts to sob in a curious combination of laughter and tears.*) But I don't think she ever mails them. She reads them, then takes them out to mail. But I don't think she ever does. I'll bet she just throws them away. Well, if she's not going to mail them, why does she say she will? I—I could save the stamps.

ROSALIE: Guess why I had this key made.

JONATHAN: I'll bet she's never even mailed one. From Abandono to Barrera, not one.

ROSALIE: Do you know why I had this key made? Do you know why I'm wearing this new dress?

JONATHAN: She tells me I'm brilliant. She makes me read and re-read books no one's ever read. She smothers me with blankets at night in case of a storm. She tucks me in so tight I can't even get out till she comes and takes my blankets off.

ROSALIE: Try and guess why I'm all dressed up.

JONATHAN: She says she loves me. Every morning, before I even have a chance to open my eyes, there she is, leaning over my bed, breathing in my face and saying, "I love you, I love you."

ROSALIE: Jonathan, isn't my dress pretty?

JONATHAN: But I heard everything tonight. I heard it all when she didn't know I was here. (*He stares off into space, bewildered.*)

ROSALIE: What's the matter? (*He does not answer.*) Jonathan, what's the matter?

JONATHAN: But she must have known I was here. She *must* have known! I mean—where could I have gone? (*Pause.*) But—if that's the case—*why did she let me hear?*

ROSALIE: Jonathan, I do wish you'd pay more attention to me. Here, look at my dress. You can even touch it if you like. Guess how many crinolines I have on. Guess why I'm wearing such a pretty, new dress. *Jonathan!*

JONATHAN: (*Distantly.*) Maybe—it didn't make any difference to her— whether I heard or not. (*He turns suddenly to her and hugs her closely. She lets him hold her, then she steps back and away from him. Her face looks strangely old and determined under her girlish powder and pinkness.*)

ROSALIE: Come with me.
JONATHAN: What?
ROSALIE: Leave and come with me.
JONATHAN: (*Fearfully.*) Where?
ROSALIE: Anywhere.
JONATHAN: Wha'—wha'—what do you mean?
ROSALIE: I mean, let's leave. Let's run away. Far away. Tonight. Both of us, together. Let's run and run. Far, far away.
JONATHAN: You—mean, leave?
ROSALIE: Yes. Leave.
JONATHAN: Just like that?
ROSALIE: Just like that.
JONATHAN: But—but—but—
ROSALIE: You want to leave, don't you?
JONATHAN: I—I don't—don't know. I—I—
ROSALIE: What about the time you told me how much you'd like to go outside, how you'd love to walk by yourself, anywhere you wanted?
JONATHAN: I—I don't—know.
ROSALIE: Yes, you do. Come. Give me your hand. Stop trembling so. Everything will be all right. Give me your hand and come with me. Just through the door. Then we're safe. Then we can run far away, somewhere where she'll never find us. Come, Jonathan. It's time to go.
JONATHAN: There are others you could take.
ROSALIE: But I don't love them.

   (*Pause.*)

JONATHAN: You—you *love* me?
ROSALIE: Yes, Jonathan. I love you.
JONATHAN: Wha-wha-why?
ROSALIE: Because you watch me every night.
JONATHAN: Well—can't we stay here?
ROSALIE: No!
JONATHAN: Wha-wha-whhhhy?
ROSALIE: *Because I want you alone.* (Jonathan *turns from her and begins to walk about the room in confusion.*) I want you, Jonathan. Do you understand what I said? *I want you for my husband.*
JONATHAN: I—I—can't, I mean, I—I want to go—go with you very much but I—I don't think—I can. I'm—sorry. (*He sits down and holds his head in his hands, sobbing quietly.*)
ROSALIE: What time will your mother be back?
JONATHAN: Na—not for a while.
ROSALIE: Are you sure?
JONATHAN: Ya-yes.
ROSALIE: Where is she?
JONATHAN: The usual place.
ROSALIE: What do you mean, "the usual place"?
JONATHAN: (*With a sad laugh.*) The beach. (Rosalie *looks at* Jonathan *quizzically.*) She likes to look for people making love. Every night at midnight she walks down to the beach searching for people lying on blankets and making love. When she finds them she kicks sand in their faces and walks on. Sometimes it takes her as much as three hours to chase everyone away. (Rosalie *smiles slightly and walks toward the master bedroom.* Jona-

than *freezes in fear. She puts her hand on the door knob.*) WHAT ARE YOU DOING!? (*She smiles at him over her shoulder. She opens the door.*) STOP! ! You can't go in there! ! ! STOP! !

ROSALIE: (*She opens the door completely and beckons him to come.*) Come.

JONATHAN: Close it. Quickly!

ROSALIE: Come, Jonathan. Let's go inside.

JONATHAN: Close the door!

ROSALIE: (*With a laugh.*) You've never been in here, have you?

JONATHAN: No. And you can't go in, either. No one can go in there but Mother. It's her room. Now close the door!

ROSALIE: (*She flicks on the light switch. No lights go on.*) What's wrong with the lights?

JONATHAN: There are none. Mother's in mourning. (Rosalie *walks into the room and pulls the drapes from off the windows. Weird COLORED LIGHTS stream in and illuminate the bedroom in wild, distorted, nightmarish shadows and lights. They blink on and off, on and off. It's all like some strange, macabre fun house in an insane amusement park. Even the furniture in the room seems grotesque and distorted. The closet next to the bed seems peculiarly prominent. It almost seems to tilt over the bed. Still in the main room.*) What have you done!? (Rosalie *walks back to the door and smiles to him from within the master bedroom.*) What have you done?

ROSALIE: Come in, Jonathan.

JONATHAN: GET OUT OF THERE!

ROSALIE: Will you leave with me?

JONATHAN: I can't!

ROSALIE: But you want to, don't you?

JONATHAN: Yes, yes. I want to, but I told you—I—I—I can't. I can't! Do you understand? I can't! Now come out of there.

ROSALIE: Come in and get me.

JONATHAN: Rosalie, *please.*

ROSALIE: (*Bouncing on the bed.*) My, what a comfortable bed.

JONATHAN: GET OFF THE BED! ! !

ROSALIE: What soft, fluffy pillows. I think I'll take a nap.

JONATHAN: Rosalie, *please listen to me.* Come out of there. You're not supposed to be in that room. Please come out. Rosalie, *please.*

ROSALIE: Will you leave with me if I do?

JONATHAN: Rosalie—? I'll—I'll show you my stamp collection if you'll promise to come out.

ROSALIE: Bring it in here.

JONATHAN: Will you come out then?

ROSALIE: Only if you bring it in here.

JONATHAN: But I'm not allowed to go in there.

ROSALIE: (*Poutingly.*) Then I shan't come out!

JONATHAN: You've got to!

ROSALIE: Why?

JONATHAN: Mother will be back.

ROSALIE: She can sleep out there. (Rosalie *yawns.*) I think I'll take a little nap. This bed is so comfortable. Really, Jonathan, you should come in and try it.

JONATHAN: MOTHER WILL BE BACK SOON! !

ROSALIE: Give her your room then if you don't want her to sleep on the couch. I find it very nice in here. Good night.

(Pause.)

JONATHAN: If I come in, will you come out?
ROSALIE: If you don't come in I'll never come out.
JONATHAN: And if I do?
ROSALIE: Then I may.
JONATHAN: What if I bring my stamps in?
ROSALIE: Bring them and find out.
JONATHAN: *(He goes to the dresser and takes out the drawer of stamps. Then he takes out the drawer of coins.)* I'm bringing the coins, too.
ROSALIE: How good you are, Jonathan.
JONATHAN: *(He takes a shelf full of books.)* My books, too. How's that? I'll show you my books and my coins and my stamps. I'll show you them all. Then will you leave?
ROSALIE: Perhaps. *(He carries them all into the bedroom and sets them down next to the bed. He looks about fearfully.)* What's wrong?
JONATHAN: I've never been in here before.
ROSALIE: It's nothing but a room. There's nothing to be afraid of.
JONATHAN: *(He looks about doubtfully.)* Well, let me show you my stamps. I have one billion, five—
ROSALIE: Later, Jonathan. We'll have time. Let me show you something first.
JONATHAN: What's that?
ROSALIE: You're trembling.
JONATHAN: What do you want to show me?
ROSALIE: There's nothing to be nervous about. Come. Sit down.
JONATHAN: What do you want to show me?
ROSALIE: I can't show you if you won't sit down.
JONATHAN: I don't want to sit down!

(She takes hold of his hand. He pulls it away.)

ROSALIE: Jonathan!
JONATHAN: You're sitting on Mother's bed.
ROSALIE: Then let's pretend it's my bed.
JONATHAN: It's not your bed!
ROSALIE: Come, Jonathan. Sit down here next to me.
JONATHAN: We've got to get out of here. Mother might come.
ROSALIE: Don't worry. We've got plenty of time. The beach is full of lovers.
JONATHAN: How do you know?
ROSALIE: I checked before I came.

(Pause.)

JONATHAN: Let—let me show you my coins.
ROSALIE: Why are you trembling so?
JONATHAN: Look, we've got to get out! Something terrible will happen if we don't.
ROSALIE: Then leave with me.
JONATHAN: The bedroom?
ROSALIE: The hotel. The island. Your mother. Leave with me, Jonathan. Leave with me now, before it's too late.

JONATHAN: I—I—I—

ROSALIE: I love you, Jonathan, and I won't give you up. I want you . . . all for myself. Not to share with your mother, but for me, alone—to love, to live with, to have children by. I want you, Jonathan. You, whose skin is softer and whiter than anyone's I've ever known. Whose voice is quiet and whose love is in every look of his eye. I want you, Jonathan, and I won't give you up.

(Short pause.)

JONATHAN: *(Softly, weakly.)* What do you want me to do?

ROSALIE: Forget about your mother. Pretend she never existed and look at me. Look at my eyes, Jonathan; my mouth, my hands, my skirt, my legs. Look at me, Jonathan. Are you still afraid?

JONATHAN: I'm not afraid. *(She smiles and starts to unbutton her dress.)* What are you doing!? No!

ROSALIE: *(She continues to unbutton her dress.)* Your mother is strong, but I am stronger. *(She rises and her skirt falls about her feet. She stands in a slip and crinolines.)* I don't look so pink and girlish any more, do I? *(She laughs.)* But you want me anyhow. You're ashamed but you want me anyhow. It's written on your face. And I'm very glad. Because I want you. *(She takes off a crinoline.)*

JONATHAN: PUT IT ON! *Please,* put it back on!

ROSALIE: Come, Jonathan. *(She takes off another crinoline.)* Lie down. Let me loosen your shirt.

JONATHAN: No . . . NO . . . NO! STOP! *Please,* stop!

(She takes her last crinoline off and reaches down to take off her socks. The LIGHTS outside blink weirdly. Wild, jagged MUSIC with a drum beating in the background is heard.)

ROSALIE: Don't be afraid, Jonathan. Come. Lie down. Everything will be wonderful. *(She takes her socks off and lies down in her slip. She drops a strap over one shoulder and smiles.)*

JONATHAN: Get off my mother's bed!

ROSALIE: I want you, Jonathan, all for my own. Come. The bed is soft. Lie here by my side. *(She reaches up and takes his hand. Meekly he sits down on the edge of the bed. The closet door swings open suddenly and the CORPSE of Albert Edward Robinson Rosepettle III tumbles forward stiffly and onto the bed, his stone-stiff arms falling across Rosalie's legs, his head against her side. Jonathan, too terrified to scream, puts his hands across his mouth and sinks down onto the bed, almost in a state of collapse. Outside the MUSIC screams.)* Who the hell is this!?

JONATHAN: It-it-it-it—it—it's—

ROSALIE: What a stupid place to keep a corpse. *(She pushes him back in the closet and shuts the door.)* Forget it, Jonathan. I put him back in the closet. Everything's fine again.

JONATHAN: It's—it's—it's my—my—my—

ROSALIE: *(Kneeling next to him on the bed starting to unbutton his shirt.)* It's all right, Jonathan. It's all right. Sshh. Come. Let me take off your clothes.

JONATHAN: *(Still staring dumbly into space.)* It's—it's my—ffffather.

(The closet door swings open again and the CORPSE falls out, this time his arms falling about Rosalie's *neck.* Jonathan *almost swoons.)*

Rosalie: Oh, for God's sake. *(She pushes him off the bed and onto the floor.)* Jonathan . . . ? LISTEN TO ME, JONATHAN! STOP LOOKING AT HIM AND LOOK AT ME! *(He looks away from his father, fearfully, his mouth open in terror.)* I love you, Jonathan, and I want you *now*. Not later and not as partner with your mother but now and by myself. I want you, Jonathan, as my husband. I want you to lie with me, to sleep with me, to be with me, to kiss me and touch me, to live with me, *forever*. Stop looking at him! He's dead! Listen to me. I'm alive. I want you for my husband! Now help me take my slip off. Then you can look at my body and touch me. Come, Jonathan. Lie down. I want you forever.

Jonathan: Ma-mother was right! You *do* let men do anything they want to you.

Rosalie: Of course she was right! Did you really think I was that sweet and pure? Everything she said was right. *(She laughs.)* Behind the bushes and it's done. One-two-three and it's done. Here's the money. Thanks. Come again. Hah-hah! Come again! *(Short pause.)* So what!? It's only you I love. They make no difference.

Jonathan: You're dirty! *(He tries to get up but can't, for his father is lying in front of his feet.)*

Rosalie: No, I'm not dirty. I'm full of love and womanly feelings. I want children. Tons of them. I want a husband. Is that dirty? Take off your clothes.

Jonathan: NO! !

Rosalie: Forget about your father. Drop your pants on top of him, then you won't see his face. Forget about your mother. She's gone. Forget them both and look at me. Love is so beautiful, Jonathan. Come and let me love you; tonight and forever. Come and let me keep you mine. Mine to love when I want, mine to kiss when I want, mine to have when I want. Mine. All mine. So come, Jonathan. Come and close your eyes. It's better that way. Close your eyes so you can't see. Close your eyes and let me lie with you. Let me show you how beautiful it is . . . love.

(She lies back in bed and slowly starts to raise her slip. Jonathan *stares at her legs in horror. Then, suddenly, he seizes her crumpled skirt the throws it over her face, and smothers her to death. At last he rises and, picking up his box of stamps, dumps the stamps over her limp body. He does the same with his coins and finally, his books, until at last she is buried. Then, done, he throws his hands over his eyes and turns to run. But as he staggers past the corpse of his father, his father's lifeless ARMS somehow come to life for an instant and, reaching out, grab* Jonathan *by the feet.* Jonathan *falls to the floor. For a moment he lies there, stretched across his father's body, too terrified to move. But a soft, ethereal-green LIGHT begins to suffuse the room and heavenly HARP MUSIC is heard in the air. As if his body had suddenly become immortal and weightless* Jonathan *rises up from the floor and with long, slow, dream-like steps (like someone walking under water), he floats through the bedroom door and drifts across the living room, picking up his telescope on the way. He floats out to the balcony and begins to scan the sky. The harp music grows louder and more paradisiacal: Debussy in Heaven. While under the harp music, soft, muffled LAUGHTER can be heard; within the bedroom, within the living room, from the rear of the theatre, LAUGHTER all about. His* Mother *tiptoes into the living room. Her hair is awry, her*

hat is on crooked, her blouse hangs wrinkled and out of her pants. Her legs
are covered with sand.)

MADAME ROSEPETTLE: Twenty-three couples. I annoyed twenty-three couples, all of them coupled in various positions, all equally distasteful. It's a
record, that's what it is. It's a record! *(Breathing heavily from excitement she*
begins to tuck in her blouse and straighten her hair. She notices the chaotic
state of the room. She shrieks slightly.) What has happened!? *(She notices*
the plants.) My plants! *(She notices the fish.)* Rosalinda! Great gods, my fish
has lost her water! ALBERT! ALBERT! *(She searches about the room for her*
son. She sees him standing on the porch.) Ah, there you are, Edward; what
has been going on during my brief absence? What are you doing out here
when Rosalinda is lying in there dead? DEAD!? Oh, God, dead. *(She gives*
her fish artificial respiration but alas, it does not work.) Robinson, answer me.
What are you looking for? I've told you there's nothing out there. This place
is a madhouse. That's what it is. A madhouse. *(She turns and walks into her*
bedroom. An AIRPLANE is heard flying in the distance. Jonathan scans the
horizon frantically. The plane grows nearer. Jonathan follows it with his
telescope. It flies overhead. It begins to circle about. Wildly, desperately,
Jonathan waves his arms to the plane. It flies away. Madame Rosepettle
re-enters the room.) ROBINSON! I went to lie down and I stepped on your
father! I lay down and I lay on some girl. Robinson, there is a woman on my
bed and I do believe she's stopped breathing. What is more, you've buried
her under your fabulous collection of stamps, coins and books. I ask you,
Robinson. As a mother to a son I ask you. *What is the meaning of this?*

BLACKOUT

CURTAIN

FOR DISCUSSION

1. What is Madame Rosepettle's view of life? Do you think it is a realistic view? How does your view of life differ from hers?
2. Describe the importance of the word "susceptible" in the play. How has it affected Jonathan's and Madame Rosepettle's life?
3. Why do you think Mrs. Rosepettle married an "ugly" man?
4. Of what importance are the Venus flytraps to the story? The piranha fish? Are they symbolic? If so, of what?
5. What is the significance of Jonathan's dumping his collections on Rosalie?
6. Why is the airplane so important to Jonathan?
7. Why does everyone's name begin with Rose?
8. Why does Madame Rosepettle call Jonathan by different names?
9. Why does Madame Rosepettle carry her husband's corpse with her?
10. Why couldn't the Commodore get away from the table?
11. Why does Madame Rosepettle spend the evening with the Commodore?
12. Why does Jonathan kill Rosalie?
13. Why do you think Rosalie says she is in love with Jonathan? What makes him attractive to her? What kind of a person is she?
14. What is the significance of Jonathan's collections?
15. Why does Madame Rosepettle allow Jonathan no freedom?
16. What part does exaggeration play in *Oh Dad, Poor Dad?*
17. Why do you think Kopit wrote this play?
18. Is the play believable? Do you like it? Why or why not? Are the characters believable, and do you like them?
19. What is the significance of the title? Who is sad? Why?
20. Why does the corpse fall on Rosalie and later trip Jonathan?
21. What do you think has made Madame Rosepettle the kind of person she is?
22. What is the theme of the play?

West Side Story is a unique collaboration.

As has been the case with many musicals, *West Side Story* was the result of the collaboration of several persons. The original idea came from the choreographer Jerome Robbins. The script was written by Arthur Laurents, and the lyrics by Stephen Sondheim. The music was composed by Leonard Bernstein. The play was first presented in New York on September 26, 1957.

Arthur Laurents was born July 14, 1918, in Brooklyn. He served in the Army and was a lumberjack and a salesman before achieving success as a playwright. His first play to be produced on Broadway was *Home of the Brave*, which opened in 1945. Among his other plays are *The Time of the Cuckoo*, produced in 1952, and *Invitation to a March*, which he also directed and which was presented in 1960 with incidental music composed by Sondheim. Laurents and Sondheim again collaborated on *Gypsy* in 1959, *Anyone Can Whistle* in 1964, and *Do I Hear a Waltz?* in 1965. The latter was based on *The Time of the Cuckoo*, and the director and choreographer was Jerome Robbins. Laurents also wrote the book for the 1967 musical, *Hallelujah, Baby*.

Stephen Sondheim was born in New York City on March 22, 1930, and made his debut as a composer with the incidental music for *The Girls of Summer* in 1956. He wrote the music and lyrics for *A Funny Thing Happened on the Way to the Forum* (1962), for *Company* (1970), and for *Follies* (1971). More recently, Sondheim's work for *Candide* and *A Little Night Music* has been tremendously successful.

Leonard Bernstein was born in Lawrence, Massachusetts, on August 25, 1918. He has composed various pieces for concert performances as well as the one-act opera *Trouble in Tahiti*, first performed in 1955. He and Robbins collaborated on three ballets presented in consecutive years beginning in 1944. Bernstein's first Broadway musical score was written for *On the Town*, which was directed and choreographed by Robbins. This was followed by *Fancy Free*. Bernstein's score for *Candide* in 1956 won the New York Theatre Critics Award. He also composed incidental music for several Broadway plays. In 1959 Bernstein was appointed music director of the New York Philharmonic, a post he held until 1969. He has conducted various operas and most of the major symphony orchestras of the world. His musical score for *Wonderful Town* in 1953 won him the New York Critics Circle Award and an Antoinette Perry (Tony) Award. He is the author of three books, and has made more than a hundred classical recordings. In 1957 Bernstein became director and conductor of the New York Philharmonic's Young People's Concerts, which have been televised throughout the United States and in twenty-nine other countries.

Jerome Robbins, born on October 11, 1918, studied ballet and made his dancing debut in 1937. Although he danced in a variety of notable productions, he has become preeminent as a choreographer and director of a number of Broadway shows, among them *The King and I, Call Me Madam,* and

Fiddler on the Roof. In addition to conceiving the idea for *West Side Story,* he choreographed and directed this production. Two other Broadway shows, *On the Town* and *Look, Ma, I'm Dancin'!* were based on his ideas. In 1954, Robbins adapted, directed, and choreographed Mary Martin's production of *Peter Pan.* His own dance company, Ballet U.S.A., formed in 1958, appeared in several European countries and toured the United States. Robbins directed and choreographed the film version of *West Side Story,* for which he won two Acadamy awards and the Screen Directors Guild Award.

West Side Story has remained a distinguished and popular musical since its opening, perhaps because of the subject matter. Although it is based on the love story of Romeo and Juliet, it has much more immediacy for today's audiences in its story of teenage gang rivalry and prejudice. Not only an entertaining musical but a social commentary, it brings out the all-too-frequent attitudes of those who feel threatened or jeopardized. The Sharks are afraid because they have been transported to a new environment and believe they must fight for survival. The Jets feel threatened by the newcomers who are unpredictable because of their different backgrounds.

The tragic sociological problem of *West Side Story* is one we read about nearly every day. Big city teenage gangs, especially ethnic ones, provide a sort of "family" for their transplanted members. When their territory is threatened, they fight back. Ethnic and racial prejudice gives *West Side Story* much of its impact. As long as this type of prejudice exists, there will be people like the characters in *West Side Story.* Only the Marias and Tonys of the world will dare to look at others as individuals, and dare to love one another.

West Side Story

WEST SIDE STORY *was first presented by Robert E. Griffith and Harold S. Prince, by arrangement with Roger L. Stevens, at the Winter Garden, New York City, September 26, 1957, with the following cast:*

THE JETS
RIFF, *the leader*
TONY, *his friend*
ACTION
A-RAB
BABY JOHN
SNOWBOY
BIG DEAL
DIESEL
GEE-TAR
MOUTHPIECE
TIGER

THEIR GIRLS
GRAZIELLA
VELMA
MINNIE
CLARICE
PAULINE
ANYBODYS

THE SHARKS
BERNARDO, *the leader*
MARIA, *his sister*

ANITA, *his girl*
CHINO, *his friend*
PEPE
INDIO
LUIS
ANXIOUS
NIBBLES
JUANO
TORO
MOOSE

THEIR GIRLS
ROSALIA
CONSUELO
TERESITA
FRANCISCA
ESTELLA
MARGARITA

THE ADULTS
DOC
SCHRANK
KRUPKE
GLAD HAND

SCENE: *The action takes place on the West Side of New York City during the last days of summer.*

ACT ONE

PROLOGUE: THE MONTHS BEFORE

5:00 P.M., *The Street*
5:30 P.M., *A Back Yard*
6:00 P.M., *A Bridal Shop*
10:00 P.M., *The Gym*
11:00 P.M., *A Back Alley*
MIDNIGHT, *The Drugstore*

THE NEXT DAY

5:30 P.M., *The Bridal Shop*
6:00 to 9:00 P.M., *The Neighborhood*
9:00 P.M., *Under the Highway*

ACT TWO

9:15 P.M., *A Bedroom*
10:00 P.M., *Another Alley*
11:30 P.M., *The Bedroom*
11:40 P.M., *The Drugstore*
11:50 P.M., *The Cellar*
MIDNIGHT, *The Street*

Musical Numbers

ACT ONE

PROLOGUE, *Danced by Jets and Sharks*
JET SONG, *Riff and Jets*
"SOMETHING'S COMING", *Tony*
THE DANCE AT THE GYM, *Jets and Sharks*
"MARIA", *Tony*
"TONIGHT", *Tony and Maria*
"AMERICA", *Anita, Rosalia, and Shark Girls*
"COOL", *Riff and the Jets*
"ONE HAND, ONE HEART", *Tony and Maria*
"TONIGHT" (Quintet and Chorus), *Company*
THE RUMBLE, *Riff, Bernardo, Jets and Sharks*

ACT TWO

"I FEEL PRETTY", *Maria, Rosalia, Teresita, Francisca*
"SOMEWHERE", *Danced by Company; Sung by Consuelo*
"GEE, OFFICER KRUPKE", *Action, Snowboy, and Jets*
"A BOY LIKE THAT", *Anita and Maria*
"I HAVE A LOVE", *Anita and Maria*
TAUNTING, *Anita and the Jets*
FINALE, *Company*

West Side Story

ACT I

Scene One.
5:00 p.m. The street.

A suggestion of city streets and alleyways: a brick wall.

The opening is musical: half-danced, half-mimed, with occasional phrases of dialogue. It is primarily a condensation of the growing rivalry between two teen-age gangs, the Jets and the Sharks, each of which has its own prideful uniform. The boys—sideburned, long-haired—are vital, restless, sardonic; the Sharks are Puerto Ricans, the Jets an anthology of what is called "American."

The action begins with the Jets in possession of the area: owning, enjoying, loving their "home." Their leader is Riff: glowing, driving, intelligent, slightly whacky. His lieutenant is Diesel: big, slow, steady, nice. The youngest member of the gang is Baby John: awed at everything, including that he is a Jet, trying to act the big man. His buddy is A-rab: an explosive little ferret who enjoys everything and understands the seriousness of nothing. The most aggressive is Action: a catlike ball of fury. We will get to know these boys better later, as well as Snowboy: a be-spectacled self-styled expert.

The first interruption of the Jets' sunny mood is the sharply punctuated entrance of the leader of the Sharks, Bernardo: handsome, proud, fluid, a chip on his sardonic shoulder. The Jets, by far in the majority, flick him off. He returns with other Sharks: they, too, are flicked off. But the numerical supremacy, the strength of the Jets, is gradually being threatened. The beginnings of warfare are mild at first: a boy being tripped up, or being sandbagged with a flour sack or even being spit on—all with overly elaborate apologies.

Finally, A-rab comes across the suddenly deserted area, pretending to be an airplane. There is no sound as he zooms along in fancied flight. Then over the wall drops Bernardo. Another Shark, another and another appear, blocking A-rab's panicky efforts at escape. They close in, grab him, pummel him, as a Shark on top of the wall is stationed as lookout. Finally, Bernardo bends over A-rab and makes a gesture (piercing his ear); the lookout whistles; Jets tear on, Sharks tear on, and a free-for-all breaks out. Riff goes at once to A-rab, like a protective father. The fight is stopped by a police whistle, louder and louder, and the arrival of a big goonlike cop, Krupke, and a plainclothesman, Schrank. Schrank is strong, always in command; he has a charming, pleasant manner, which he often employs to cover his venom and his fear.

KRUPKE: Knock it off! Settle down.

SCHRANK: All right: *kill each other!* . . . But not on my beat.
RIFF: (*such innocence*) Why if it isn't Lieutenant Schrank!
SEVERAL JETS: (*dancing-class manners*) Top of the day, Lieutenant Schrank.
BERNARDO: (*one with* Riff) And Officer Krupke!
SEVERAL SHARKS: Top of the day, Officer Krupke.
SCHRANK: Boy, what you Puerto Ricans have done to this neighborhood. Which one of 'em clobbered ya, A-rab?

(A-rab *looks to* Riff, *who takes over with great helpful seriousness.*)

RIFF: As a matter of factuality, sir, we suspicion the job was done by a cop.
SNOWBOY: Two cops.
A-RAB: Oh, at least!
KRUPKE: Impossible!
SCHRANK: Didn't nobody tell ya there's a difference between bein' a stool pigeon and cooperatin' with the law?
RIFF: You told us the difference, sir. And we all chipped in for a prize for the first guy who can figure it out.
ACTION: (*indicating* Schrank) Maybe buddy boy should get the prize.
SCHRANK: Don't buddy boy me, Action! I got a hot surprise for you: you hoodlums don't own the streets. There's been too much raiding between you and the PRs. All right, Bernardo, get your trash outa here. (*Mock charm.*) Please.
BERNARDO: Let's go, Sharks.   (*They exit.*)
SCHRANK: (*to the* Jets) If I don't put down the roughhouse, I get put down—on a traffic corner. Your friend don't like traffic corners. So you buddy boys are gonna play ball with me. I gotta put up with them and so do you. *You're gonna make nice with them PRs from now on.* Because otherwise I'm gonna beat the crap outa everyone of ya and *then* run ya in. Say good-bye to the nice boys, Krupke.
KRUPKE: Good-bye, boys.   (*He follows* Schrank *out.*)
SNOWBOY: (*imitating* Krupke) Good-bye, boys.
A-RAB: They make a very nice couple.
ACTION: (*bitterly*) "You hoodlums don't own the streets."
SNOWBOY: Go play in the park!
ACTION: Keep off the grass!
BABY JOHN: Get outa the house!
ACTION: Keep off the block!
A-RAB: Get outa *here!*
ACTION: Keep off the world! A gang that don't own a street is nuthin'!
RIFF: WE DO OWN IT! Jets—square off! Acemen: (Diesel, Action *and* Snowboy *line up at attention.*) Rocketmen: (*three others line up*) Rank-and-file:

(*Sheepishly,* A-rab *trudges into position,* Baby John *behind him.*)

BABY JOHN: (*shocked, to* A-rab) Gee, your ear's got blood on it!
A-RAB: (*proudly*) I'm a casual, Baby John.
BABY JOHN: (*examining the ear*) Them PRs! They branded you!
SNOWBOY: That makes you a Puerto Rican tomato. Cha-cha-cha, señorita?
RIFF: Cut the frabbajabba. Which one of the Sharks did it?

A-RAB: Bernardo. 'Cause I heard him say: "Thees ees for stink-bombin' my old man's store." (*He makes the same gesture* Bernardo *made when he pierced his ear.*)

BABY JOHN: Ouch!

ACTION: You shoulda done worse. Them PRs're the reason my old man's gone bust.

RIFF: Who says?

ACTION: My old man says.

BABY JOHN: (*to* A-rab) My old man says his old man woulda gone bust anyway.

ACTION: Your old man says what?

BABY JOHN: My old man says them Puerto Ricans is ruinin' free ennaprise.

ACTION: And what're we doin' about it?

(*Pushing through the gang comes a scrawny teen-age girl, dressed in an outfit that is a pathetic attempt to imitate that of the* Jets. *Perhaps we have glimpsed her in the fracas before the police came in. Her name is* Anybodys.)

ANYBODYS: Gassin', crabbin'—

ACTION: You still around?

ANYBODYS: Listen, I was a smash in that fight. Oh, Riff, Riff, I was murder!

RIFF: Come on, Anybodys—

ANYBODYS: Riff, how about me gettin' in the gang now?

A-RAB: How about the gang gettin' in—ahhh, who'd wanta!

ANYBODYS: You cheap beast! (*She lunges for* A-rab, *but* Riff *pulls her off and pushes her out.*)

RIFF: The road, little lady, the road. (*In a moment of bravado, just before she goes,* Anybodys *spits—but cautiously.*) Round out! (*This is* Riff's *summoning of the gang, and they surround him.*) We fought hard for this territory and it's ours. But with those cops servin' as cover, the PRs can move in right under our noses and take it away. *Unless* we speed fast and clean 'em up in one all-out fight!

ACTION: (*eagerly*) A rumble! (*A jabbing gesture.*) Chung! Chung!

RIFF: Cool, Action boy. The Sharks want a place, too, and *they are tough.* They might ask for bottles or knives or zip guns.

BABY JOHN: Zip guns . . . Gee!

RIFF: I'm not finalizin' and sayin' they will: I'm only sayin' they might and we gotta be prepared. Now, what's your mood?

ACTION: I say go, go!!

SNOWBOY: But if they say knives or guns—

BABY JOHN: I say let's forget the whole thing.

DIESEL: What do you say, Riff?

RIFF: I say this turf is small, *but it's all we got.* I wanna hold it like we always held it: with skin! But if they say switchblades, I'll get a switchblade. I say I want the Jets to be Number One, to sail, to hold the sky!

DIESEL: Then rev us off. (*A punching gesture.*) Voom-va voom!

ACTION: Chung chung!

A-RAB: Cracko, jacko!

SNOWBOY: Riga diga dum!

BABY JOHN: Pam pam!!

RIFF: OK, buddy boys, we rumble! (*General glee.*) Now protocality calls for a war council to decide on weapons. I'll make the challenge to Bernardo.

SNOWBOY: You gotta take a lieutenant.

Action: That's me!
Riff: That's Tony.
Action: Who needs Tony?

Music starts.

Riff: Against the Sharks we need every man we got.
Action: Tony don't belong any more.
Riff: Cut it, Action boy. I and Tony started the Jets.
Action: Well, he acts like he don't wanna belong.
Baby John: Who wouldn't wanna belong to the Jets!
Action: Tony ain't been with us for over a month.
Snowboy: What about the day we clobbered the Emeralds?
A-rab: Which we couldn't have done without Tony.
Baby John: He saved my ever lovin' neck.
Riff: Right. He's always come through for us and he will now.*(He sings:)*
When you're a Jet,
You're a Jet all the way
From your first cigarette
To your last dyin' day.
When you're a Jet,
If the spit hits the fan,
You got brothers around,
You're a family man!
You're never alone,
You're never disconnected!
You're home with your own—
When company's expected,
You're well protected!
Then you are set
With a capital J,
Which you'll never forget
Till they cart you away.
When you're a Jet,
You stay
A jet!

(He speaks:)
I know Tony like I know me. I guarantee you can count
him in.
   Action: In, out, let's get crackin'.
   A-rab: Where you gonna find Bernardo?
   Riff: At the dance tonight at the gym.
   Big Deal: But the gym's neutral territory.
   Riff: *(sweet innocence)* I'm gonna make nice there! I'm only gonna chal-
lenge him.
   A-rab: Great, Daddy-O!
   Riff: So everybody dress up sweet and sharp. Meet Tony and me at ten.
And walk tall!

(He runs off.)
   A-rab: We always walk tall!
   Baby John: We're Jets!
   Action: The greatest!

(He sings with Baby John:*)*
When you're a Jet,
You're the top cat in town,
You're the gold-medal kid

With the heavyweight crown!

(A-rab, Action, Big Deal *sing:*)

When you're a Jet,
You're the swingin'est thing.
Little boy, you're a man;
Little boy, you're a king!

(*All:*)

The Jets are in gear,
Our cylinders are clickin'!
The Sharks'll steer clear
'Cause every Puerto Rican
'S a lousy chicken!

Here come the Jets
Like a bat out of hell—
Someone gets in our way,
Someone don't feel so well!
Here come the Jets:
Little world, step aside!
Better go underground,
Better run, better hide!
We're drawin' the line,
So keep your noses hidden!
We're hangin' a sign
Says "Visitors forbidden"—
And we ain't kiddin'!
Here come the Jets,
Yeah! And we're gonna beat
Every last buggin' gang
On the whole buggin' street!

(Diesel *and* Action:)

On the whole!

(*All:*)

Ever—!
Mother—!
Lovin'—!
Street!

The Lights Black Out

SCENE TWO.
5:30 P.M. *A back yard.*
    On a small ladder, a good-looking sandy-haired boy is painting a vertical sign that will say: "Doc's." Below, Riff *is haranguing.*
    RIFF: Riga tiga tum tum. Why not? . . . You can't say ya won't, Tony boy, without sayin' why not?
    TONY: (*grins*) Why not?
    RIFF: Because it's me askin': Riff. Womb to tomb!
    TONY: Sperm to worm! (*Surveying the sign.*) You sure this looks like skywritin'?
    RIFF: It's brilliant.
    TONY: Twenty-seven years the boss has had that drugstore. I wanna surprise him with a new sign.
    RIFF: (*shaking the ladder*) Tony, this is important!
    TONY: Very important: Acemen, Rocketmen.

RIFF: What's with you? Four and one-half years I live with a buddy and his family. Four and one-half years I think I know a man's character. Buddy boy, I am a victim of disappointment in you.

TONY: End your sufferin', little man. Why don't you pack up your gear and clear out?

RIFF: 'Cause your ma's hot for me. (Tony *grabs his arm and twists it.*) No! 'Cause I hate livin' with my buggin' uncle uncle UNCLE!

(Tony *releases him and climbs back up the ladder.*)

TONY: Now go and play nice with the Jets.

RIFF: The Jets are the greatest!

TONY: Were.

RIFF: Are. You found somethin' better?

TONY: No. But—

RIFF: But what?

TONY: You won't dig it.

RIFF: Try me.

TONY: OK . . . Every single damn night for the last month, I wake up— and I'm reachin' out.

RIFF: For what?

TONY: I don't know. It's right outside the door, around the corner. But it's comin'!

RIFF: *What* is? Tell me!

TONY: I don't know! It's—like the kick I used to get from bein' a Jet.

RIFF: (*quietly*) . . . Or from bein' buddies.

TONY: We're still buddies.

RIFF: The kick comes from people, buddy boy.

TONY: Yeah, but not from being a Jet.

RIFF: No? Without a gang you're an orphan. With a gang you walk in two's, three's, four's. And when your gang is the best, when you're a Jet, buddy boy, you're out in the sun and home free!

TONY: Riff, I've had it. (*Pause.*)

RIFF: Tony, the trouble is large: the Sharks bite hard! We got to stop them now, and we need *you!* (*Pause. Quietly.*) I never asked the time of day from a clock, but I'm askin' you: Come to the dance tonight . . . (Tony *turns away.*) . . . I already told the gang you'd be there.

TONY: (*after a moment, turns to him with a grin*) What time?

RIFF: Ten?

TONY: Ten it is.

RIFF: Womb to tomb!

TONY: Sperm to worm! And I'll live to regret this.

RIFF: Who knows? Maybe what you're waitin' for'll be twitchin' at the dance!

(*He runs off.*)

TONY: Who knows?

(*Music starts and he sings:*)

Could be! . . .
Who knows? . . .
There's something due any day;
I will know right away
Soon as it shows.
It may come cannonballin' down through the sky,

Gleam in its eye,
Bright as a rose!
Who knows? . . .
It's only just out of reach,
Down the block, on a beach,
Under a tree.
I got a feeling there's a miracle due,
Gonna come true,
Coming to me!

Could it be? Yes, it could.
Something's coming, something good,
If I can wait!
Something's coming, I don't know what it is
But it is
Gonna be great!

With a click, with a shock,
Phone'll jingle, door'll knock,
Open the latch!
Something's coming, don't know when, but it's soon—
Catch the moon,
One-handed catch!

Around the corner,
Or whistling down the river,
Come on—deliver
To me!

Will it be? Yes, it will.
Maybe just by holding still
It'll be there!
Come on, something, come on in, don't be shy,
Meet a guy,
Pull up a chair!

The air is humming,
And something great is coming!
Who knows?
It's only just out of reach,
Down the block, on a beach . . .
Maybe tonight . . .

                    The Lights Dim

SCENE THREE.
6:00 P.M. A bridal shop.
  A small section, enough to include a table with sewing machine, a chair or two.
  Anita, a Puerto Rican girl with loose hair and slightly flashy clothes, is finishing remaking what was a white communion dress into a party dress for an extremely lovely, extremely young girl: Maria. Anita is knowing, sexual, sharp. Maria is an excited, enthusiastic, obedient child, with the temper, stubborn strength and awareness of a woman.

MARIA: (*holding out scissors*) *Por favor,* Anita. Make the neck lower!
ANITA: Stop it, Maria.
MARIA: One inch. How much can one little inch do?
ANITA: Too much.
MARIA: (*exasperated*) Anita, it is now to be a dress for dancing, no longer for kneeling in front of an altar.
ANITA: With those boys you can start in dancing and end up kneeling.
MARIA: *Querida,* one little inch; *una poca poca*—
ANITA: Bernardo made me promise—
MARIA: *Ai!* Bernardo! One month have I been in this country—do I ever even touch excitement? I sew all day, I sit all night. For what did my fine brother bring me here?
ANITA: To marry Chino.
MARIA: When I look at Chino, nothing happens.
ANITA: What do you expect to happen?
MARIA: I don't know: something. What happens when you look at Bernardo?
ANITA: It's when I don't look that it happens.
MARIA: I think I will tell Mama and Papa about you and 'Nardo in the balcony of the movies.
ANITA: I'll rip this to shreds!
MARIA: No. But if you perhaps could manage to lower the neck—
ANITA: Next year.
MARIA: Next year I will be married and no one will care if it is down to here!
ANITA: Down to where?
MARIA: Down to here. (*Indicates her waist.*) I hate this dress!
ANITA: Then don't wear it and don't come with us to the dance.
MARIA: (*shocked*) Don't come! (*Grabs the dress.*) Could we not dye it red, at least?
ANITA: No, we could not. (*She starts to help* Maria *into the dress.*)
MARIA: White is for babies. I will be the only one there in a white—
ANITA: Well???
MARIA: Ahhhh—*sí!* It is a beautiful dress: I love you!

(*As she hugs* Anita, Bernardo *enters, followed by a shy, gentle sweet-faced boy:* Chino.)

BERNARDO: Are you ready?
MARIA: Come in, 'Nardo. (*Whirls in the dress.*) Is it not beautiful?
BERNARDO: (looking only at Maria's *face*) Yes. (*Kisses her.*) Very.
ANITA: I didn't quite hear . . .
BERNARDO: (*kissing* Anita *quite differently*) Very beautiful.
MARIA: (*watches them a second, then turns to* Chino) Come in, Chino. Do not be afraid.
CHINO: But this is a shop for ladies.
BERNARDO: Our ladies!
MARIA: 'Nardo, it is most important that I have a wonderful time at the dancing tonight.
BERNARDO: (*as* Anita *hooks up* Maria) Why?
MARIA: Because tonight is the real beginning of my life as a young lady of America!

(She begins to whirl in the dress as the shop slides off and a flood of gaily colored streamers pours down. As Maria begins to turn and turn, going off-stage, Shark girls, dressed for the dance whirl on, followed by Jet girls, by boys from both gangs. The streamers fly up again for the next scene.)

SCENE FOUR.
10:00 P.M. The gym.
Actually, a converted gymnasium of a settlement house, at the moment being used as a dancehall, disguised for the occasion with streamers and bunting.
Both gangs are jitterbugging wildly with their bodies, but their faces, although they are enjoying themselves, remain cool, almost detached. The line between the two gangs is sharply defined by the colors they wear: the Jets, girls as well as boys, reflecting the colors of the Jet jackets; the same is true of the Sharks. The dancing is a physical and emotional release for these kids.
Maria enters with Chino, Bernardo and Anita. As she looks around, delighted, thrilled by this, her first dance, the Jets catch sight of Bernardo, who is being greeted by Pepe, his lieutenant, and other Sharks. As the music peters away, the Jets withdraw to one side of the hall, around Riff. The Sharks, seeing this, draw to their side, around Bernardo. A brief consultation, and Riff starts across—with lieutenants—to make his challenge to Bernardo, who starts—with his lieutenants—to meet him. The moment is brief but it would be disastrous if a smiling, overly cheerful young man of about thirty did not hurry forward. He is called Glad Hand, and he is a "square."

GLAD HAND: *(beaming)* All right, boys and girls! Attention, please! *(Hum of talk.)* Attention! *(Krupke appears behind Glad Hand: the talk stops.)* Thank you. It sure is a fine turnout tonight. *(Ad libs from the kids.)* We want you to make friends here, so we're going to have a few get-together dances. *(Ad libs: "Oh, ginger peachy," etc.)* You form two circles: boys on the outside, girls on the inside.
SNOWBOY: Where are you?
GLAD HAND: *(tries to laugh at this)* All right. Now when the music stops, each boy dances with whichever girl is opposite, O.K.? O.K. Two circles, kids. *(The kids clap their hands back at him and ad lib: "Two circles, kids," etc., but do not move.)* Well, it won't hurt you to try.
SNOWBOY: *(limping forward)* Oh, it hurts; it hurts; it—

(Krupke steps forward. Snowboy straightens up and meekly returns to his place. Riff steps forward and beckons to his girl, Velma. She is terribly young, sexy, lost in a world of jive. She slithers forward to take her place with Riff. The challenge is met by Bernardo, who steps forward, leading Anita as though he were presenting the most magnificent lady in all the world. The other kids follow, forming the two circles Glad Hand requested.)

GLAD HAND: That's it, kids. Keep the ball rolling. Round she goes and where she stops, nobody knows. All right: here we go!

(Promenade music starts and the circles start revolving. Glad Hand, whistles to his mouth, is in the center with Krupke. He blows the whistle and the music stops, leaving Jet boys opposite Shark girls, and vice versa.

There is a moment of tenseness, then Bernardo reaches across the Jet girl opposite for Anita's hand, and she comes to him. Riff reaches for Velma; and the kids of both gangs follow suit. The "get-together" has failed, and each gang is on its own side of the hall as a mambo starts. This turns into a challenge dance between Bernardo and Anita—cheered on by the Sharks— and Riff and Velma—cheered on by the Jets. During it, Tony enters and is momentarily embraced by Riff, who is delighted that his best friend did turn up. The dance builds wilder and wilder, until, at the peak, everybody is dancing and shouting, "Go, Mambo!" It is at this moment that Tony and Maria—at opposite sides of the hall—see each other. They have been cheering on their respective friends, clapping in rhythm. Now, as they see each other, their voices die, their smiles fade, their hands slowly go to their sides. The lights fade on the others, who disappear into the haze of the background as a delicate cha-cha begins and Tony and Maria slowly walk forward to meet each other. Slowly, as though in a dream, they drift into the steps of the dance, always looking at each other, completely lost in each other; un- aware of anyone, anyplace, any time, anything but one another.)

TONY: You're not thinking I'm someone else?
MARIA: I know you are not.
TONY: Or that we have met before?
MARIA: I know we have not.
TONY: I felt, I *knew* something-never-before was going to happen, had to happen. But this is—
MARIA: (*interrupting*) My hands are cold. (*He takes them in his.*) Yours, too. (*He moves her hands to his face.*) So warm. (*She moves his hands to her face.*)
TONY: Yours, too.
MARIA: But of course. They are the same.
TONY: It's so much to believe—you're not joking me?
MARIA: I have not yet learned how to joke that way. I think now I never will.

(Impulsively, he stops to kiss her hands; then tenderly, innocently, her lips. The music bursts out, the lights flare up, and Bernardo is upon them in an icy rage.)

BERNARDO: Go home, "American."
TONY: Slow down, Bernardo.
BERNARDO: Stay away from my sister!
TONY: . . . Sister?
                                                              (Riff *steps up.*)
BERNARDO: (*to* Maria) Couldn't you see he's one of them?
MARIA: No; I saw only him.
BERNARDO: (*as* Chino *comes up*) I told you: there's only one thing they want from a Puerto Rican girl!
TONY: That's a lie!
RIFF: Cool, boy.
CHINO: (*to* Tony) Get away.
TONY: You keep out, Chino. (*To* Maria:) Don't listen to them!
BERNARDO: She will listen to her brother before—
RIFF: (*overlapping*) If you characters want to settle—
GLAD HAND: Please! Everything was going so well! Do you fellows get

pleasure out of making trouble? Now come on—it won't hurt you to have a good time.

(*Music starts again.* Bernardo *is on one side with* Maria *and* Chino; Anita *joins them.* Tony *is on the other with* Riff *and* Diesel. *Lights emphasizes the first group.*)

BERNARDO: I warned you—
CHINO: Do not yell at her, 'Nardo.
BERNARDO: You yell at babies.
ANITA: And put ideas in the baby's head.
BERNARDO: Take her home, Chino.
MARIA: 'Nardo, it is my first dance.
BERNARDO: Please. We are family, Maria. Go.

(Maria *hesitates, then starts out with* Chino *as the light follows her to the other group, which she passes.*)

RIFF: (*to* Diesel, *indicating* Tony *happily*) I guess the kid's with us for sure now.

(Tony *doesn't even hear; he is staring at* Maria, *who stops for a moment.*)

CHINO: Come, Maria.
                                        (*They continue out.*)
TONY: Maria . . .

(*He is unaware that* Bernardo *is crossing toward him, but* Riff *intercepts.*)

BERNARDO: I don't want you.
RIFF: I want you, though. For a war council—Jets and Sharks.
BERNARDO: The pleasure is mine.
RIFF: Let's go outside.
BERNARDO: I would not leave the ladies here alone. We will meet you in half an hour.
RIFF: Doc's drugstore? (Bernardo *nods.*) And no jazz before then.
BERNARDO: I understand the rules—Native Boy.

(*The light is fading on them, on everyone but* Tony.)

RIFF: Spread the word, Diesel.
DIESEL: Right, Daddy-o.
RIFF: Let's get the chicks and kick it. Tony?
TONY: Maria . . .
                                        (*Music starts.*)
RIFF: (*in darkness*) Tony!
DIESEL: (*in darkness*) Ah, we'll see him at Doc's.
TONY: (*speaking dreamily over the music—he is now standing alone in the light*) Maria . . .
                                        (*Singing softly:*)
The most beautiful sound I ever heard.

VOICES: (*offstage*) Maria, Maria, Maria, Maria . . .
TONY: All the beautiful sounds of the world in a single word:
VOICES: (*off stage:*) Maria, Maria, Maria, Maria . . .

(*Swelling in intensity.*)

Maria, Maria . . .
  TONY:
Maria!
I've just met a girl named Maria,
And suddenly that name
Will never be the same
To me.

Maria!
I've just kissed a girl named Maria,
And suddenly I've found
How wonderful a sound
Can be!

Maria!
Say it loud and there's music playing—
Say it soft and it's almost like praying—
Maria . . .
I'll never stop saying
Maria!
  CHORUS (*offstage, against* Tony's *obbligato:*)
I've just met a girl named Maria,
And suddenly that name
Will never be the same
To me.
Maria—
I've just kissed a girl named Maria,
And suddenly I've found
How wonderful a sound
Can be!
  TONY:
Maria—
Say it loud and there's music playing—
Say it soft and it's almost like praying—
Maria—
I'll never stop saying Maria!
The most beautiful sound I ever heard—
Maria.

(*During the song, the stage behind* Tony *has gone dark; by the time he has finished, it is set for the next scene.*)

SCENE FIVE.
11:00 P.M. A back alley.
    A suggestion of buildings; a fire escape climbing to the rear window of an unseen flat.
    As Tony *sings, he looks for where Maria lives, wishing for her. And she does appear, at the window above him, which opens onto the fire escape. Music stays beneath most of the scene.*

Tony: (*sings:*) Maria, Maria . . .
Maria: Ssh!
Tony: Maria! !
Maria: Quiet!
Tony: Come down.
Maria: No.
Tony: Maria . . .
Maria: Please. If Bernardo—
Tony: He's at the dance. Come down.
Maria: He will soon bring Anita home.
Tony: Just for a minute.
Maria: (*smiles*) A minute is not enough.
Tony: (*smiles*) For an hour, then.
Maria: I cannot.
Tony: Forever!
Maria: Ssh!
Tony: Then I'm coming up.
Woman's Voice: (*from the offstage apartment*) Maria!
Maria: *Momentito*, Mama . . .
Tony: Maria, Maria—
Maria: *Cállate!* (*Reaching her hand out to stop him.*) Ssh!
Tony: (*grabbing her hand*) Ssh!
Maria: It is dangerous.
Tony: I'm *not* "one of them."
Maria: You are; but to me, you are not. Just as I am one of them—(*She gestures toward the apartment.*)
Tony: To me, you are all the—

(*She covers his mouth with her hand.*)

Man's Voice: (*from the unseen apartment*) Maruca!
Maria: *Sí, ya vengo*, Papa.
Tony: Maruca?
Maria: His pet name for me.
Tony: I like him. He will like me.
Maria: No. He is like Bernardo: afraid. (*Suddenly laughing.*) Imagine being afraid of you!
Tony: You see?
Maria: (*touching his face*) I see you.
Tony: See only me.
Maria: (*sings:*)
Only you, you're the only thing I'll see forever.
In my eyes, in my words and in everything I do,
Nothing else but you
Ever!
Tony:
And there's nothing for me but Maria,
Every sight that I see is Maria.
Maria: Tony, Tony . . .
Tony:
Always you, every thought I'll ever know,
Everywhere I go, you'll be.
Maria: All the world is only you and me!

(And now the buildings, the world fade away, leaving them suspended in space.)

Tonight, tonight,
It all began tonight,
I saw you and the world went away.
Tonight, tonight,
There's only you tonight,
What you are, what you do, what you say.
   TONY:
Today, all day I had the feeling
A miracle would happen—
I know now I was right.
For here you are
And what was just a world is a star
Tonight!
   BOTH:
Tonight, tonight,
The world is full of light,
With suns and moons all over the place.
Tonight, tonight,
The world is wild and bright,
Going mad, shooting sparks into space.
Today the world was just an address,
A place for me to live in,
No better than all right,
But here you are
And what was just a world is a star
Tonight!
   MAN'S VOICE: *(offstage)* Maruca!
   MARIA: Wait for me! *(She goes inside as the buildings begin to come back into place.)*
   TONY: *(sings)*
Tonight, tonight,
It all began tonight,
I saw you and the world went away.
   MARIA: *(returning)* I cannot stay. Go quickly!
   TONY: I'm not afraid.
   MARIA: They are strict with me. Please.
   TONY: *(kissing her)* Good night.
   MARIA: *Buenas noches.*
   TONY: I love you.
   MARIA: Yes, yes. Hurry. *(He climbs down.)* Wait! When will I see you? *(He starts back up.)* No!
   TONY: Tomorrow.
   MARIA: I work at the bridal shop. Come there.
   TONY: At sundown.
   MARIA: Yes. Good night.
   TONY: Good night. *(He starts off.)*
   MARIA: Tony!
   TONY: Ssh!
   MARIA: Come to the back door.

TONY: *Sí.* (*Again he starts out.*)
MARIA: Tony! (*He stops. A pause.*) What does Tony stand for?
TONY: Anton.
MARIA: *Te adoro,* Anton.
TONY: *Te adoro,* Maria.

(*Both sing as music starts again:*)

Good night, good night,
Sleep well and when you dream,
Dream of me
Tonight.

(*She goes inside; He ducks out into the shadows just as* Bernardo *and* Anita *enter, followed by* Indio, *and* Pepe *and their girls. One is a bleached-blond, bangled beauty:* Consuelo. *The other, more quietly dressed, is* Rosalia. *She is not too bright.*)

BERNARDO: (*Looking up to the window*) Maria?
ANITA: She *has* a mother. Also a father.
BERNARDO: They do not know this country any better than she does.
ANITA: You do not know it at all! Girls here are free to have fun. She-is-in-America-now.
BERNARDO: (*exaggerated*) But Puerto-Rico-is-in-America-now!
ANITA: (*in disgust*) Ai!
BERNARDO: (*cooing*) Anita Josefina Teresita—
ANITA: It's plain Anita now—
BERNARDO: (*continuing through*)—Beatriz del Carmen Margarita, etcetera, etcetera—
ANITA: Immigrant!
BERNARDO: (*pulling her to him*) Thank God, you can't change your hair!
PEPE: (*fondling* Consuelo's *bleached mop*) Is that possible?
CONSUELO: In the U.S.A., everything is real.
BERNARDO: (*to* Chino, *who enters*) Chino, how was she when you took her home?
CHINO: All right. 'Nardo, she was only dancing.
BERNARDO: With an "*American.*" Who is really a Polack.
ANITA: Says the Spic.
BERNARDO: You are not so cute.
ANITA: That Tony is.
ROSALIA: And he works.
CHINO: A delivery boy.
ANITA: And what are you?
CHINO: An assistant.
BERNARDO: *Sí!* And Chino makes half what the Polack makes—the Polack is American!
ANITA: Ai! Here comes the whole commercial! (*A burlesque oration in mock Puerto Rican accent.* Bernardo *starts the first line with her.*) The mother of Tony was born in Poland; the father still goes to night school. Tony was born in America, so that makes him an American. But us? Foreigners!
PEPE AND CONSUELO: Lice!
PEPE, CONSUELO, ANITA: Cockroaches!
BERNARDO: Well, it is true! You remember how we were when we first came! Did we even think of going back?

BERNARDO AND ANITA: No! We came ready, eager—
ANITA: (*mocking*) With our hearts open—
CONSUELO: Our arms open—
PEPE: You came with your pants open.
CONSUELO: *You* did, pig! (*Slaps him.*) *You'll go back with handcuffs!*
BERNARDO: I am going back with a Cadillac!
CHINO: Air-conditioned!
BERNARDO: Built-in bar!
CHINO: Telephone!
BERNARDO: Television!
CHINO: Compatible color!
BERNARDO: And a king-sized bed. (*Grabs* Anita.) Come on.
ANITA: (*mimicking*) Come on.
BERNARDO: Well, are you or aren't you?
ANITA: Well, are you or aren't you?
BERNARDO: Well, are you?
ANITA: You have your big, important war council. The council or me?
BERNARDO: First one, then the other.
ANITA: (*breaking away from him*) I am an American girl now. I don't wait.
BERNARDO: (*to* Chino) Back home, women know their place.
ANITA: Back home, little boys don't have war councils.
BERNARDO: You want me to be an American? (*To the boys.*) *Vámonos, chicos, es tarde.* (*A mock bow.*) *Buenas noches,* Anita Josefina del Carmen, etcetera, etcetera, etcetera.

(*He exits with the boys.*)

ROSALIA: That's a very pretty name: Etcetera.
ANITA: Ai!
CONSUELO: She means well.
ROSALIA: We have many pretty names at home.
ANITA: (*mimicking*) At home, at home. If it's so nice "at home," why don't you go back there?
ROSALIA: I would like to—(*A look from* Anita.)—just for a successful visit.

(*She sings nostalgically:*)

Puerto Rico . . .
You lovely island . . .
Island of tropical breezes.
    Always the pineapples growing,
    Always the coffee blossoms blowing . . .
    ANITA: (*sings sarcastically*)
Puerto Rico . . .
You ugly island . . .
Island of tropic diseases.
    Always the hurricanes blowing,
    Always the population growing . . .
    And the money owing,
    And the babies crying,
    And the bullets flying.
I like the island Manhattan—
Smoke on your pipe and put that in!

(*all, except* Rosalia:)

I like to be in America!
OK by me in America!

Everything free in America
For a small fee in America!
   ROSALIA: I like the city of San Juan—
   ANITA: I know a boat you can get on.
   ROSALIA: Hundreds of flowers in full bloom—
   ANITA: Hundreds of people in each room!
(All, except Rosalia:*)*

Automobile in America,
Chromium steel in America,
Wire-spoke wheel in America—
Very big deal in America!
   ROSALIA: I'll drive a Buick through San Juan—
   ANITA: If there's a road you can drive on.
   ROSALIA: I'll give my cousins a free ride—
   ANITA: How you get all of them inside?
(All, except Rosalia:*)*

Immigrant goes to America,
Many hellos in America;
Nobody knows in America
Puerto Rico's in America.
(The girls whistle and dance.)

   ROSALIA: When will I go back to San Juan—
   ANITA: When you will shut up and get gone!
   ROSALIA: I'll give them new washing machine—
   ANITA: What have they got there to keep clean?
(All, except Rosalia:*)*

I like the shores of America!
Comfort is yours in America!
Knobs on the doors in America,
Wall-to-wall floors in America!
(They whistle and dance.)

   ROSALIA: I'll bring a TV to San Juan—
   ANITA: If there's a current to turn on.
   ROSALIA: Everyone there will give big cheer!
   ANITA: Everyone there will have moved here!
(The song ends in the joyous dance.)
The Lights Black Out

SCENE SIX.
Midnight. The drugstore.
   A suggestion of a run-down, musty general store which, in cities, is called a drugstore. A door leading to the street outside; another leading to the cellar below.
   Baby John *is reading a comic book;* A-rab *is playing solitaire;* Anybodys *is huddled by the jukebox;* Action *is watching the street door. The atmosphere is tense, jumpy.* Action *slams the door and strides to the dart board.*

   ACTION: Where the devil are they? Are we havin' a war council tonight or ain't we? *(He throws a dart savagely.)*
   BABY JOHN: He don't use knives. He don't even use an atomic ray gun.
   A-RAB: Who don't?
   BABY JOHN: Superman. Gee, I love him.
   SNOWBOY: So marry him.

ANYBODYS: I ain't never gonna get married: too noisy.
A-RAB: You ain't never gonna get married: too ugly.
ANYBODYS: *("shooting" him)* Pow pow!
A-RAB: Cracko, jacko! *(Clutching his belly, he spins to the floor.)* Down goes a teen-age hoodlum.
BABY JOHN: Could a zip gun make you do like that?

(A second of silence. Then Snowboy *slams into the room and they all jump.)*

ACTION: What the hell's a matter with you?
SNOWBOY: I got caught sneakin' outa the movies.
A-RAB: Sneaking' *out?* Whadd'ya do that for?
SNOWBOY: I sneaked in.
ACTION: A war council comin' up and he goes to the movies.
ANYBODYS: And you let him be a Jet!
BABY JOHN: Ah, go walk the streets like ya sister.
ANYBODYS: *(jumping him)* Lissen, jail bait, I licked you twice and I can do it again.

(From the doorway behind the counter a little middle-aged man enters: Doc.*)*

DOC: Curfew, gentlemen. And lady. Baby John, you should be home in bed.
BABY JOHN: We're gonna have a war council here, Doc.
DOC: A who?
A-RAB: To decide on weapons for a big-time rumble!
SNOWBOY: We're gonna mix with the PRs.
DOC: Weapons. You couldn't play basketball?
ANYBODYS: Get with it, buddy boy.
DOC: War councils—
ACTION: Don't start, Doc.
DOC: Rumbles . . .
ACTION: Doc—
DOC: Why, when I was your age—
ACTION: When you was my age; when my old man was my age; when my brother was my age! *You was never my age, none a you!* The sooner you creeps get hip to that, the sooner you'll dig us.
DOC: I'll dig your early graves, that's what I'll dig.
A-RAB: Dig, dig, dig—
DOC: What're you gonna be when you grow up?
ANYBODYS: *(wistfully)* A telephone call girl!

(The store doorbell tinkles as Riff *enters with* Velma.*)*

SNOWBOY: Riff, hey!
ACTION: Are they comin'?
RIFF: Unwind, Action. Hey, Doc, Tony here?
DOC: No, Riff, it's closing time.
ACTION: *(to* Riff*)* What d'ya think they're gonna ask for?
A-RAB: Just rubber hoses, maybe, huh?
RIFF: Cool, little men. Easy, freezy cool.

VELMA: Oo, oo, ooblee—oo.

(*Diesel enters with a would-be grand number:* Graziella.)

DIESEL: They're comin' any minute now!
ACTION: Chung chung!
A-RAB: Cracko, jacko!
VELMA: Ooblee-oo.
RIFF: (*sharply*) Cool!
ANYBODYS: Riff—in a tight spot you need every man you can—
RIFF: No.
GRAZIELLA: (*indicating* Anybodys *to* Velma) An American tragedy.
ANYBODYS: ("*shooting" her*) Pow.
GRAZIELLA: Poo.
VELMA: Ooblee-pooh.

(*They giggle.*)

RIFF: Now when the victims come in, you chicks cut out.
GRAZIELLA: We might, and then again we might not.
DIESEL: This ain't kid stuff, Graziella.
GRAZIELLA: I and Velma ain't kid stuff, neither. Are we, Vel?
VELMA: No thank you-oo, ooblee-oo.
GRAZIELLA: And you can punctuate it?
VELMA: Ooo!

(*They giggle again.*)

ACTION: (*to* Riff) What're we poopin' around with dumb broads?
GRAZIELLA: (*enraged*) I and Velma ain't dumb!
ACTION: We got important business comin'.
DOC: Makin' trouble for the Puerto Ricans?
SNOWBOY: They make trouble for us.
DOC: Look! He almost laughs when he says it. For you, trouble is a relief.
RIFF: We've got to stand up to the PRs, Doc. It's important.
DOC: Fighting over a little piece of the street is so important?
ACTION: To us, it is.
DOC: To hoodlums, it is. (*He goes out through the cellar doorway as* Action *lunges for him.*)
ACTION: Don't you call me hoodlum!
RIFF: (*holding him*) Easy, Action! Save your steam for the rumble.
A-RAB: He don't want what we want, so we're hoodlums!
BABY JOHN: I wear a jacket like my buddies, so my teacher calls me hoodlum!
ACTION: I swear the next creep who calls me hoodlum—
RIFF: *You'll laugh!* Yeah. Now you all better dig this and dig it the most. No matter who or what is eatin' at you, you show it, buddy boys, and *you are dead.* You are cuttin' a hole in yourselves for them to stick in a red-hot umbrella and open it. Wide. You wanna live? You play it cool.

(*Music starts.*)

ACTION: I wanna get even!
RIFF: Get cool.
A-RAB: I wanna bust!
RIFF: Bust cool.
BABY JOHN: I wanna go!
RIFF: *Go cool!*

Boy, boy, crazy boy—   (*He sings:*)
Get cool, boy!

Got a rocket in your pocket—
    Keep coolly cool, boy!
        Don't get hot,
        'Cause, man, you got
        Some high times ahead.
    Take it slow and, Daddy-o,
        You can live it up and die in bed!
Boy, boy, crazy boy—
    Stay loose, boy!
Breeze it, buzz it, easy does it—
    Turn off the juice, boy!
        Go man, go,
        But not like a yo
        Yo school boy—
        Just play it cool, boy,
Real cool!
Easy, Action.
Easy.

(*This leads into a frenetic dance in which the boys and girls release their emotions and get "cool." It finishes, starts again when a* Jet *bounces in with the gang whistle. Everyone but* Riff *and* Velma *stops dancing. A moment, then* Bernardo, Chino, Pepe *and* Indio *enter. The tinkle of the doorbell brings a worried* Doc *back in. Tension—but* Riff *dances a moment longer. Then he pats* Velma *on her behind. Followed by* Graziella, *she runs out, slithering past the* Sharks. Anybodys *is back, huddled by the jukebox, but* Riff *spots her. She gives him a pleading let-me-stay look, but he gestures for her to go. Unlike the other girls, as she exits,* Anybodys *shoves the* Sharks *like a big tough man.*)

RIFF: Set 'em up, Doc. Cokes all around.
BERNARDO: Let's get down to business.
RIFF: Bernardo hasn't learned the procedures of gracious livin'.
BERNARDO: I don't like you, either. So cut it.
RIFF: Kick it, Doc.
DOC: Boys, couldn't you maybe all talk it—
RIFF: Kick it!

(*Doc goes out. The two gangs take places behind their leaders.*)

RIFF: We challenge you to a rumble. All out, once and for all. Accept?
BERNARDO: On what terms?
RIFF: Whatever terms you're callin', buddy boy. You crossed the line once too often.
BERNARDO: You started it.
RIFF: Who jumped A-rab this afternoon?
BERNARDO: Who jumped me the first day I moved here?
ACTION: Who asked you to move here?
PEPE: Who asked you?
SNOWBOY: Move where you're wanted!
A-RAB: Back where ya came from!
ACTION: Spics!

PEPE: Micks!
INDIO: Wop!
BERNARDO: *We accept!*
RIFF: Time:
BERNARDO: Tomorrow?
RIFF: After dark. (*They shake.*) Place:
BERNARDO: The park.
RIFF: The river.
BERNARDO: Under the highway.

(*They shake.*)

RIFF: Weapons:

(*The doorbell tinkles as* Tony *bursts in, yelling.*)

TONY: Hey, Doc!

(*He stops as he sees them. Silence. Then he comes forward.*)

RIFF: Weapons!

(*Doc enters.*)

BERNARDO: Weapons . . .
RIFF: You call.
BERNARDO: Your challenge.
RIFF: Afraid to call?
BERNARDO: . . . Sticks.
RIFF: . . . Rocks.
BERNARDO: . . . Poles.
RIFF: . . . Cans.
BERNARDO: . . . Bricks.
RIFF: . . . Bats.
BERNARDO: . . . Clubs.
RIFF: Chains.
TONY: Bottles, knives, guns! (*They stare.*) What a coop full of chickens!
ACTION: Who you callin' chicken?
BERNARDO: Every dog knows his own.
TONY: I'm callin' all of you chicken. The big tough buddy boys have to throw bricks! Afraid to get close in? Afraid to slug it out? Afraid to use plain skin?
BABY JOHN: Not even garbage?
ACTION: That ain't a rumble.
RIFF: Who says?
BERNARDO: You said call weapons.
TONY: A rumble can be clinched by a fair fight. If you have the guts to risk that. Best man from each gang to slug it out.
BERNARDO: (*looking at* Tony) I'd enjoy to risk that. O.K.! Fair fight!
PEPE: What?
ACTION: (*simultaneously*) No!
RIFF: The commanders say yes or no. (*To* Bernardo.) Fair fight.

(*They shake.*)

BERNARDO: (*to* Tony) In two minutes you will be like a fish after skinnin'.
RIFF: Your best man fights our best man—and we pick him.

(*Claps* Diesel *on the shoulder.*)

BERNARDO: But I thought I would be—
RIFF: We shook on it, Bernardo.
BERNARDO: Yes. I shook on it.

ACTION: (*quickly*) Look, Bernardo, if you wanna change your mind, maybe we could all—

(*One of the* Jets *near the door suddenly whistles. Instantly, they shift positions so they are mixed up: no segregation. Silence; then in comes* Schrank. *During the following, the gangs are absolutely silent and motionless, unless otherwise indicated.*)

DOC: (*unhappily*) Good evening, Lieutenant Schrank. I and Tony was just closing up.

SCHRANK: (*lifting a pack of cigarettes*) Mind?

DOC: I have no mind. I am the village idiot.

SCHRANK: (*lighting a cigarette*) I always make it a rule to smoke in the can. And what else is a room with half-breeds in it, eh, Riff? (Bernardo's *move is checked by* Riff. Schrank *speaks again, pleasantly.*) Clear out, Spics. Sure; it's a free country and I ain't got the right. But it's a country with laws: and I can find the right. I got the badge, you got the skin. It's tough all over. Beat it! (*A second. Then* Riff *nods once to* Bernardo, *who nods to his gang. Slowly, they file out.* Bernardo *starts to whistle "My Country 'Tis of Thee" as he exits proudly. His gang joins in, finishing a sardonic jazz lick offstage.* Schrank, *still pleasant.*) From their angle, sure. Say, where's the rumble gonna be? Ah, look: I know regular Americans don't rub with the gold-teeth otherwise. The river? The park? (*Silence.*) I'm for *you.* I want this beat cleaned up and you can do it for me. I'll even lend a hand if it gets rough. Where ya gonna rumble? The playground? Sweeney's lot? (*Angered by the silence.*) Ya think I'm a lousy stool pigeon? I wanna help ya get rid of them! Come on! Where's it gonna be? . . . Get smart, you stupid hoodlums! I oughta fine ya for litterin' the streets. You oughta be taken down the station house and have your skulls mashed to a pulp! You and the tin-horn immigrant scum you come from! How's your old man's d.t.'s, A-rab? How's the action on your mother's mattress, Action? (Action *lunges for him but is tripped up by* Riff. Schrank *crouches low, ready for him. Quiet now.*) Let him go, buddy boy, just let him go. (Action *starts to his feet but* Diesel *holds him.*) One of these days there won't be nobody to hold you. (Riff *deliberately starts for the door, followed by the others, except* Tony.) I'll find out where ya gonna rumble. But be sure to finish each other off. Because if you don't, I will! (Riff *has stayed at the door until the others have passed through. Now he just looks at* Schrank *and cockily saunters out. Silence,* Schrank *looks at* Doc.) Well, you try keepin' hoodlums in line and see what it does to you.(*He exits.*)

DOC: (*indicating* Schrank) It wouldn't give me a mouth like his.

TONY: Forget him. From here on in, everything goes my way. (*He starts to clean up, to turn out the lights.*)

DOC: You think it'll really be a fair fight.

TONY: Yeah.

DOC: What have you been takin' tonight?

TONY: A trip to the moon. And I'll tell you a secret. It isn't a man that's up there, Doc. It's a girl, a lady. (*Opens the door.*) Buenas noches, señor.

DOC: Buenas noches?! So that's why you made it a fair fight. (Tony *smiles.*) . . . Tony . . . things aren't tough enough?

TONY: Tough? Doc, I'm in love.

DOC: How do you know?

TONY: Because . . . there isn't any other way I could feel.

DOC: And you're not frightened?

TONY: Should I be?

(*He opens door, exits.*)

DOC: Why? I'm frightened enough for both of you. (*He turns out the last light.*)

The Stage is Dark

SCENE SEVEN.

5:30 P.M. The next day. The bridal shop.

Hot late-afternoon sun coloring the workroom. One or two sewing machines. Several dressmaker dummies, male and female, in bridal-party garb.

Maria, in a smock is hand-sewing a wedding veil as Anita *whirls in whipping off her smock.*

ANITA: She's gone! The old bag of a *bruja* has gone!

MARIA: *Bravo!*

ANITA: The day is over, the jail is open, home we go!

MARIA: You go, *querida.* I will lock up.

ANITA: Finish tomorrow. Come!

MARIA: But I am in no hurry.

ANITA: I am. I'm going to take a bubble bath all during supper: Black Orchid.

MARIA: You will not eat?

ANITA: After the rumble—with 'Nardo.

MARIA: (*sewing, angrily*) That rumble, why do they have it?

ANITA: You saw how they dance: like they have to get rid of something, quick. That's how they fight.

MARIA: To get rid of what?

ANITA: Too much feeling. And they get rid of it: after a fight, that brother of yours is so healthy! Definitely: Black Orchid.

(*There is a knock at rear door, and* Tony *enters.*)

TONY: *Buenas noches!*

ANITA: (*sarcastically, to* Maria) "You go, *querida.* I will lock up." (*To* Tony:) It's too early for *noches. Buenas tardes.*

TONY: (*bows*) *Gracias. Buenas tardes.*

MARIA: He just came to deliver aspirin.

ANITA: You'll need it.

TONY: No, we're out of the world.

ANITA: You're out of your heads.

TONY: We're twelve feet in the air.

MARIA: (*gently taking his hand*) Anita can see all that. (*To* Anita:) You will not tell?

ANITA: Tell what? How can I hear what goes on twelve feet over my head? (*Opens door. To* Maria:) You better be home in fifteen minutes.

(*She goes out.*)

TONY: Don't worry. She likes us!

MARIA: But she is worried.

TONY: She's foolish. We're untouchable; we *are* in the air; we have magic!

MARIA: Magic is also evil and black. Are you going to that rumble?

TONY: No.

MARIA: Yes.

TONY: Why??

MARIA: You must go and stop it.

TONY: I have stopped it! It's only a fist fight. 'Nardo won't get—

MARIA: *Any* fight is not good for us.
TONY: Everything is good for us and we are good for everything.
MARIA: Listen and *hear* me. You must go and stop it.
TONY: Then I will.
MARIA: (*surprised*) Can you?
TONY: You don't want even a fist fight? There won't be any fight.
MARIA: I believe you! You *do* have magic.
TONY: Of course, I have you. You go home and dress up. Then tonight,
I will come by for you.
MARIA: You cannot come by. My mama . . .
TONY: (*after a pause*) Then I will take you to my house—
MARIA: (*shaking her head*) Your mama . . .

(*Another awkward pause. Then he sees a female dummy and pushes it
forward.*)

TONY: She will come running from the kitchen to welcome you. She lives
in the kitchen.
MARIA: Dressed so elegant?
TONY: I told her you were coming. She will look at your face and try not
to smile. And she will say: Skinny—but pretty.
MARIA: She is plump, no doubt.
TONY: (*holding out the waist of the dummy's dress*) Fat!
MARIA: (*indicating another female dummy*) I take after my mama; deli-
cate-boned. (*He kisses her.*) Not in front of Mama! (*He turns the dummy
around as she goes to a male dummy.*) Oh, I would like to see Papa in this!
Mama will make him ask about your prospects, if you go to church. But
Papa—Papa *might* like you.
TONY: (*kneeling to the "father" dummy*) May I have your daughter's
hand?
MARIA: He says yes.
TONY: *Gracias!*
MARIA: And your mama?
TONY: I'm afraid to ask her.
MARIA: Tell her she's not getting a daughter; she's getting rid of a son!
TONY: She says yes.
MARIA: She has good taste. (*She grabs up the wedding veil and puts in
on as* Tony *arranges the dummies.*)
TONY: Maid of honor!
MARIA: That color is bad for Anita.
TONY: Best man!
MARIA: That is my Papa!
TONY: Sorry, Papa. Here we go, Riff: Womb to Tomb! (*He takes hat off
dummy.*)
MARIA: Now you see, Anita, I told you there was nothing to worry about.

(*Music starts as she leaves the dummy and walks up to Tony. They look
at each other—and the play acting vanishes. Slowly, seriously, they turn
front, and together kneel as before an altar.*)

TONY: I, Anton, take thee, Maria . . .
MARIA: I, Maria, take thee, Anton . . .
TONY: For richer, for poorer . . .

MARIA: In sickness and in health ...
TONY: To love and to honor ...
MARIA: To hold and to keep ...
TONY: From each sun to each moon ...
MARIA: From tomorrow to tomorrow ...
TONY: From now to forever ...
MARIA: Till death do us part.
TONY: With this ring, I thee wed.
MARIA: With this ring, I thee wed.
TONY: (sings)
Make of our hands one hand,
Make of our hearts one heart,
Make of our vows one last vow:
Only death will part us now.
MARIA:
Make of our lives one life,
Day after day, one life.
BOTH:
Now it begins, now we start
One hand, one heart—
Even death won't part us now.

(They look at each other, then at the reality of their "game." They smile tenderly, ruefully, and slowly put the dummies back into position. Though brought back to earth, they continue to sing.)

Make of our lives one life,
Day after day, one life.
Now it begins, now we start
One hand, one heart—
Even death won't part us now.

(Very gently, he kisses her hand.)

The Lights Fade Out.

SCENE EIGHT.
6:00 to 9:00 P.M. The neighborhood.
Spotlights pick out Riff and the Jets, Bernardo and the Sharks, Anita, Maria and Tony against small sets representing different places in the neighborhood. All are waiting expectantly for the coming of night, but for very different reasons.
JETS: (sing)
The Jets are gonna have their day
Tonight.
SHARKS:
The Sharks are gonna have their way
Tonight.
JETS:
The Puerto Ricans grumble,
"Fair fight."
But if they start a rumble,
We'll rumble 'em right.
SHARKS:
We're gonna hand 'em a surprise
Tonight.

JETS:
We're gonna cut 'em down to size
Tonight.
SHARKS:
We said, "O.K., no rumpus,
No tricks"—
But just in case they jump us,
We're ready to mix
Tonight!
BOTH GANGS:
We're gonna rock it tonight,
We're gonna jazz it up and have us a ball.
They're gonna get it tonight;
The more they turn it on, the harder they'll fall!
JETS:
Well, they began it—
SHARKS:
Well, they began it—
BOTH GANGS:
And we're the ones to stop 'em once and for all,
Tonight!
ANITA:
Anita's gonna get her kicks
Tonight.
We'll have our private little mix
Tonight.
He'll walk in hot and tired,
So what?
Don't matter if he's tired,
As long as he's hot
Tonight!
TONY:
Tonight, tonight,
Won't be just any night,
Tonight there will be no morning star.

Tonight, tonight,
I'll see my love tonight.
And for us, stars will stop where they are.

Today
The minutes seem like hours,
The hours go so slowly,
And still the sky is light . . .

Oh moon, grow bright,
And make this endless day endless night!
RIFF: (to Tony)
I'm counting on you to be there
Tonight.
When Diesel wins it fair and square
Tonight.

That Puerto Rican punk'll
Go down.
And when he's hollered Uncle
We'll tear up the town
Tonight!

MARIA:
Tonight, tonight
Won't be just any night . . .

(She reprises the same chorus Tony has just sung.)

RIFF: So I can count on you, boy?
TONY: All right.
RIFF: We're gonna have us a ball.
TONY: All right . . .

(Regretting his impatience.)

Womb to tomb!

RIFF:
Sperm to worm!
I'll see you there about eight . . .

TONY: Tonight . . .
BERNARDO AND SHARKS: We're gonna rock it tonight! ! !
ANITA: Tonight . . .

(All have been singing at once, reprising the choruses they sang before.)

BERNARDO AND SHARKS:
We're gonna jazz it tonight
They're gonna get it tonight—tonight.
They began it—they began it
And we're the ones
To stop 'em once and for all!
The Sharks are gonna have their way,
The Sharks are gonna have their day,
We're gonna rock it tonight—
Tonight!

ANITA:
Tonight,
Late tonight,
We're gonna mix it tonight,
Anita's gonna have her day,
Anita's gonna have her day,
Bernardo's gonna have his way
Tonight—tonight.
Tonight—this very night,
We're gonna rock it tonight,
Tonight!

RIFF AND JETS:
They began it.
They began it.
We'll stop 'em once and for all
The Jets are gonna have their day,
The Jets are gonna have their way,
We're gonna rock it tonight.
Tonight!

MARIA:
Tonight there will be no morning star.
Tonight, tonight, I'll see my love tonight.
When we kiss, stars will stop where they are.
TONY AND MARIA:
Today the minutes seem like hours.
The hours go so slowly,
And still the sky is light.
Oh moon, grow bright,
And make this endless day endless night,
Tonight!

(*The lights build with the music to the climax, and then blackout at the
final exultant note.*)

SCENE NINE.
9:00 P.M. Under the highway.
   *A dead end: rotting plaster-and-brick walls and mesh wire fences. A street
lamp.*
   *It is nightfall. The almost-silhouetted gangs come in from separate sides:
climbing over the fences or crawling through holes in the walls. There is
silence as they fan out on opposite sides of the cleared space. Then Bernardo
and Diesel remove their jackets, handing them to their seconds: Chino and
Riff.*
   BERNARDO: Ready.
   CHINO: Ready!
   DIESEL: Ready.
   RIFF: Ready! Come center and shake hands.
   BERNARDO: For what?
   RIFF: That's how it's done, buddy boy.
   BERNARDO: More gracious living? Look: I don't go for that pretend crap
you all go for in this country. Every one of you hates every one of us, and
we hate you right back. I don't drink with nobody I hate, I don't shake hands
with nobody I hate. Let's get at it.
   RIFF: OK.
   BERNARDO: (*moving toward center*) Here we go.

   (Diesel *begins to move toward him. There are encouragements called
from each side. The "fair fight" is just beginning when there is an interruption.*)

   TONY: Hold it! (*He leaps over the fence and starts toward* Bernardo.)
   RIFF: Get with the gang.
   TONY: No.
   RIFF: What're you doin'?
   BERNARDO: Maybe he has found the guts to fight his own battles.
   TONY: (*smiling*) It doesn't take guts if you *have* a battle. But we haven't
got one, 'Nardo. (*He extends his hand for* Bernardo *to shake it.* Bernardo
knocks the hand away and gives Tony *a shove that sends him sprawling.*)
   BERNARDO: Bernardo.
   RIFF: (*quiet, strong*) The deal is a fair fight between you and Diesel. (*To*
Tony, *who has gotten up:*) Get with the gang.

(During the following, Bernardo flicks Tony's shirt, pushes his shoulder, pinches his cheek.)

BERNARDO: (to Tony) I'll give you a battle, Kiddando
DIESEL: You've got one.
BERNARDO: I'll take pretty boy on as a warm-up. Afraid, pretty boy?
Afraid, chicken? Afraid, gutless?
RIFF: Cut that—
TONY: I don't want to, Bernardo ...
BERNARDO: I'm sure.
TONY: Bernardo, you've got it wrong.
BERNARDO: Are you chicken?
TONY: You won't understand!
BERNARDO: What d'ya say, chicken?
ACTION: Get him, Tony!
BERNARDO: He is chicken.
DIESEL: Tony—
A-RAB: Get him!
TONY: Bernardo, don't.
BERNARDO: Don't what, pretty little chicken?
RIFF: Tony, don't just stand—
BERNARDO: Yellow-bellied chicken—
RIFF: TONY!
ACTION: Murder him!
SNOWBOY: Kill him!
TONY: DON'T PUSH ME!
BERNARDO: Come on, you yellow-bellied Polack bas—

(He never finishes, for Riff hauls off and hits him. Immediately, the two gangs alert, and the following action takes on the form of a dance. As Bernardo reels back to his feet, he reaches for his back pocket. Riff reaches for his back pocket, and at the same instant each brings forth a gleaming knife. They jockey for position, feinting, dueling; the two gangs shift position, now and again temporarily obscuring the fighters. Tony tries to get between them.)

RIFF: Hold him!

(Diesel and Action grab Tony and hold him back. The fight continues. Riff loses his knife, is passed another by a Jet. At last, he has Bernardo in a position where it seems that he will be able to run him through. Tony breaks from Diesel and, crying out, moves to stop Riff.)

TONY: Riff, don't! (Riff hesitates a moment; the moment is enough for Bernardo—whose hand goes forward with a driving motion, running his knife into Riff. Tony leaps forward to catch Riff. He breaks his fall, then takes the knife from his hand. A free-for-all has broken out as Tony, Riff's knife in hand, leaps at the triumphant Bernardo. All this happens terribly fast; and Tony rams his knife into Bernardo. The free-for-all continues a moment longer. Then there is a sharp police whistle. Everything comes to a dead stop—dead silence. Then a distant police siren: the kids waver, run one way, another, in panic, confusion. As the stage is cleared, Tony stands, horrified, over the still bodies of Riff and Bernardo. He bends over Riff's

body; then he rolls Bernardo's *body over—and stares. Then* Tony *raises his voice in an anguished cry.*)
MARIA!

(*Another police whistle, closer now, but he doesn't move. From the shadows,* Anybodys *appears. She scurries to* Tony *and tugs at his arm. A siren, another whistle, then a searchlight cuts across the playground. Anybodys' insistent tugging brings* Tony *to the realization of the danger. He crouches, starts to run with her to one escapeway. She reaches it first, goes out—but the searchlight hits it just as he would go through. He stops, runs the other way. He darts here, there, and finally gets away as a distant clock begins to boom.*)

The Curtain Falls

ACT II

SCENE ONE.
9:15 P.M. *A bedroom.*

Part of a parlor is also visible. The bedroom has a window opening onto the fire escape, a bed on a wall, a small shrine to the Virgin, and a curtained doorway, rear. There is a door between the bedroom and the parlor.

Gay music for Consuelo, *who is examining herself in the mirror, and for* Rosalia, *who is on the bed, finishing her nails.*

CONSUELO: This is my last night as a blonde.
ROSALIA: No loss.
CONSUELO: A gain! The fortune teller told Pepe a dark lady was coming into his life.
ROSALIA: So that's why he's not taking you out after the rumble!

(*The music becomes festively, humorously Spanish as* Maria *enters through the curtained doorway. She is finishing getting very dressed up.*)

MARIA: There is not going to be a rumble.
ROSALIA: Another fortune teller.
CONSUELO: Where is Chino escorting you after the rumble-that-is-not-going-to-be-a-rumble?
MARIA: Chino is escorting me no place.
ROSALIA: She is just dolling up for us. *Gracias, querida.*
MARIA: No, not for you. Can you keep a secret?
CONSUELO: I'm hot for secrets!
MARIA: Tonight is my wedding night!
CONSUELO: The poor thing is out of her mind.
MARIA: I am: crazy!
ROSALIA: She might be at that. She looks somehow different.
MARIA: I do?
ROSALIA: And I think she is up to something tonight.
MARIA: I am?
CONSUELO: "I do?" "I am?" What is going on with you?
MARIA: (*sings*)
I feel pretty,

Oh, so pretty,
I feel pretty, and witty and bright,
And I pity
Any girl who isn't me tonight.

I feel charming,
Oh, so charming—
It's alarming how charming I feel,
And so pretty
That I hardly can believe I'm real.

See the pretty girl in that mirror there:
Who can that attractive girl be?
    Such a pretty face,
    Such a pretty dress,
    Such a pretty smile,
Such a pretty me!

I feel stunning
And entrancing—
Feel like running and dancing for joy,
For I'm loved
By a pretty wonderful boy!
    ROSALIA *and* CONSUELO
Have you met my good friend Maria,
The craziest girl on the block?
You'll know her the minute you see her—
She's the one who is in an advanced state of shock.

She thinks she's in love.
She thinks she's in Spain.
She isn't in love,
She's merely insane.

It must be the heat
Or some rare disease
Or too much to eat,
Or maybe it's fleas.

Keep away from her—
Send for Chino!
This is not the Maria we know!

Modest and pure,
Polite and refined,
Well-bred and mature
And out of her mind!
    MARIA
I feel pretty,
Oh, so pretty,
That the city should give me its key.
A committee
Should be organized to honor me.

I feel dizzy,
I feel sunny,
I feel fizzy and funny and fine,
And so pretty,
Miss America can just resign!
See the pretty girl in that mirror there:
    ROSALIA *and* CONSUELO: What mirror where?
    MARIA: Who can that attractive girl be?
    ROSALIA *and* CONSUELO
       Which? What? Where? Whom?
    MARIA
       Such a pretty face,
       Such a pretty dress,
       Such a pretty smile,
Such a pretty me!
    ALL
I feel stunning
And entrancing—
Feel like running and dancing for joy,
For I'm loved
By a pretty wonderful boy!
    CHINO: (*offstage*) Maria!
    CONSUELO: It's Chino.
    ROSALIA: The happy bridegroom.
    CHINO: (*closer*) Maria!
    MARIA: Please—
    CONSUELO: Yes, little bride, we're going.

                                     (*She exits.*)
    ROSALIA: They have a quaint old-fashioned custom in this country,
Maria: they get married here *before* the wedding night. (*She follows* Consuelo *out as* Chino *enters from offstage. His clothes are dirty and torn from
the fight; his face is smeared. They shake their heads at him and flounce out.
He closes the outer door.*)
    CHINO: Maria? . . .
    MARIA: I'm in here. I was just getting ready to—(*She is hurriedly trying
to put a bathrobe over her dress.* Chino *comes in before she can finish, so
that she leaves it over her shoulders, holding it closed with her hand.*)
    CHINO: Where are your parents?
    MARIA: At the store. If I had known you were—You have been fighting,
Chino.
    CHINO: Yes. I am sorry.
    MARIA: That is not like you.
    CHINO: No.
    MARIA: Why, Chino?
    CHINO: I don't know why. It happened so fast.
    MARIA: You must wash up.
    CHINO: Maria—
    MARIA: You can go in there.
    CHINO: In a minute. Maria . . . at the rumble—
    MARIA: There was no rumble.
    CHINO: There was.
    MARIA: You are wrong.

CHINO: No; there was. Nobody meant for it to happen ...
MARIA: ... Tell me.
CHINO: It's bad.
MARIA: Very bad?
CHINO: (*nods*) You see ... (*He moves closer to her, helplessly.*)
MARIA: It will be easier if you say it very fast.
CHINO: (*nods*) There was a fight—(*She nods.*) And 'Nardo—(*She nods.*) And somehow a knife—and 'Nardo and someone—(*He takes her hand.*)
MARIA: Tony. What happened to Tony? (*The name stops* Chino. *He drops her hand: the robe opens.*) Tell me! (*Crudely,* Chino *yanks off the robe, revealing that she is dressed to go out.*) Chino, is Tony all right?!
CHINO: He killed your brother. (*He walks into the parlor, slamming the door behind him. A pause.*)
MARIA: You are lying. (Chino *has started to leave the parlor, but turns back now. Swiftly searching behind furniture, he comes up with an object wrapped in material the same color as* Bernardo's *shirt. From the bedroom,* Maria's *voice calls out, louder.*) You are lying, Chino! (*Coldly,* Chino *unwraps a gun, which he puts in his pocket. There is the sound of a police siren at a distance. He goes out. During this,* Maria *has knelt before the shrine on the wall. She rocks back and forth in prayer, some of it in Spanish, some of it in English.*) Make it not be true ... please make it not be true.... I will do anything: make me die.... Only, please—make it not be true. (*As she prays,* Tony *appears at the fire-escape window and quietly climbs in. His shirt is ripped, half-torn off. He stands still, limp, watching her. Aware that someone is in the room, she stops her prayers. Slowly, her head turns; she looks at him for a long moment. Then, almost in one spring, she is on him, her fists beating his chest.*) Killer killer killer killer killer—(*But her voice breaks with tears, her arms go about him, and she buries her face in his chest, kissing him. She begins to slide down his body. He supports her as, together, they go to the floor, he cradling her body in his arms. He pushes her hair back from her face; kisses her hair, her face, between the words that tumble out.*)
TONY: I tried to stop it; I did try. I don't know how it went wrong.... I didn't mean to hurt him; I didn't want to; I didn't know I had. But Riff ... Riff was like my brother. So when Bernardo killed him—(*She lifts her head.*) 'Nardo didn't mean it, either. Oh, I know he didn't! Oh, no. I didn't come to tell you just for you to forgive me so I could go to the police—
MARIA: No!
TONY: It's easy now—
MARIA: No ...
TONY: Whatever you want, I'll do—
MARIA: Stay. Stay with me.
TONY: I love you so much.
MARIA: Tighter.

(*Music starts.*)

TONY: We'll be all right. I know it. We're really together now.
MARIA: But it's not us! It's everything around us!
TONY: Then we'll find some place where nothing can get to us; not one of them, not anything. And—

(*He sings:*)

I'll take you away, take you far far away out of here,
Far far away till the walls and the streets disappear,
Somewhere there must be a place we can feel we're free,
Somewhere there's got to be some place for you and for me.

(As he sings, the walls of the apartment begin to move off, and the city
walls surrounding them begin to close in on them. Then the apartment itself
goes, and the two lovers begin to run, battering against the walls of the city,
beginning to break through as chaotic figures of the gangs, of violence, flail
around them. But they do break through, and suddenly—they are in a world
of space and air and sun. They stop, looking at it, pleased, startled, as boys
and girls from both sides come on. And they, too, stop and stare, happy,
pleased. Their clothes are soft pastel versions of what they have worn before.
They begin to dance, to play: no sides, no hostility now; just joy and pleasure
and warmth. More and more join, making a world that Tony and Maria want
to be in, belong to, share their love with. As they go into the steps of a gentle
love dance, a voice is heard singing.)

OFFSTAGE VOICE: (sings)
There's a place for us,
Somewhere a place for us.
Peace and quiet and room and air
Wait for us
Somewhere.

There's a time for us,
Someday a time for us,
Time together with time to spare,
Time to learn, time to care
Someday!

Somewhere
We'll find a new way of living,
We'll find a way of forgiving
Somewhere,
Somewhere . . .

There's a place for us,
A time and place for us.
Hold my hand and we're halfway there.
Hold my hand and I'll take you there
Someday,
Somehow,
Somewhere!

(The lovers hold out their hands to each other; the others follow suit:
Jets to Sharks: Sharks to Jets. And they form what is almost a procession
winding its triumphant way through this would-be world, as they sing the
words of the song with wonderment. Then, suddenly, there is a dead stop.
The harsh shadows, the fire escapes of the real, tenement world cloud the
sky, and the figures of Riff and Bernardo slowly walk on. The dream
becomes a nightmare: as the city returns, there are brief reenactments of the
knife fight, of the deaths. Maria and Tony are once again separated from each
other by the violent warring of the two sides. Maria tries to reach Bernardo,
Tony tries to stop Riff; the lovers try to reach each other, but they cannot.
Chaotic confusion and blackness, after which they find themselves back in
the bedroom, clinging to each other desperately. With a blind refusal to face
what they know must be, they reassure each other desperately as they sing.)

Tony *and* Maria
Hold my hand and we're halfway there.
Hold my hand and I'll take you there
Someday,
Somehow,
Somewhere!

          (*As the lights fade, together they sink back on the bed.*)

Scene Two.
10:00 p.m. *Another alley.*
   A fence with loose boards; angles between buildings.
   Softly, from behind the fence, the Jet *gang whistle. A pause, then the answering whistle, softly, from offstage or around a corner. Now a loose board flips up and* Baby John *wriggles through the fence. He whistles again, timidly, and* A-rab *comes on.*

A-rab: They get you yet?
Baby John: No. You?
A-rab: Hell, no.
Baby John: You seen Tony?
A-rab: Nobody has.
Baby John: Geez . . .
A-rab: You been home yet?
Baby John: Uh uh.
A-rab: Me, either.
Baby John: Just hidin' around?
A-rab: Uh huh.
Baby John: A-rab . . . did you get a look at 'em?
A-rab: Look at who?
Baby John: Ya know. At the rumble. Riff and Bernardo.   (*Pause.*)
A-rab: I wish it was yesterday.
Baby John: Wadaya say we run away?
A-rab: What's a matter? You scared?
Baby John: . . . Yeah.
A-rab: You cut it out, ya hear? You're only making' me scared and that scares me! (*Police whistle. He grabs* Baby John.) Last thing ever is to let a cop know you're scared or anythin'.
Krupke: (*offstage*) Hey, you two!
A-rab: Play it big with the baby blues.
Baby John: (*scared*) OK.
A-rab: (*gripping him*) Big, not scared, big!

      (*Again a whistle. Elaborately casual, they start sauntering off as* Krupke *appears.*)

Krupke: Yeah, you.
                             (*They stop, so surprised.*)
A-rab: Why it *is* Officer Krupke, Baby John.
Baby John: (*quaking*) Top of the evening, Officer Krupke.
Krupke: I'll crack the top of your skulls if you punks don't stop when I whistle.
A-rab: But we stopped the very moment we heard.
Baby John: We got twenty-twenty hearing.

KRUPKE: You wanna get hauled down to the station house?

BABY JOHN: Indeed not, sir.

KRUPKE: I'll make a little deal. I know you was rumblin' under the high-way—

BABY JOHN: We was at the playground, sir.

A-RAB: We like the playground. It keeps us deprived kids off the foul streets.

BABY JOHN: It gives us comradeship—

A-RAB: A place for pleasant pastimes—And for us, born like we was on the hot pavements—

KRUPKE: OK, wise apples, down to the station house.

BABY JOHN: Which way?

A-RAB: This way! (*He gets down on all fours,* Baby John *pushes* Krupke, *so that he tumbles over* A-rab. Baby John *starts off one way,* A-rab *the other.* Krupke *hesitates, then runs after one of them, blowing his whistle like mad. The moment he is off,* A-rab *and* Baby John *appear through the fence, followed by the other* Jets.) Look at the brass-ass run!

BABY JOHN: I hope he breaks it!

ACTION: Get the lead out, fat boy!

DIESEL: Easy. He'll come back and drag us down the station house.

ACTION: I already been.

SNOWBOY: We both already been.

A-RAB: What happened?

SNOWBOY: A big fat nuthin'!

A-RAB: How come?

SNOWBOY: Cops believe everythin' they read in the papers.

ACTION: To them we ain't human. We're cruddy juvenile delinquents. So that's what we give 'em.

SNOWBOY: (*imitating* Krupke) Hey, you!

ACTION: Me, Officer Krupke?

SNOWBOY: Yeah, you! Gimme one good reason for not draggin' ya down the station house, ya punk.

ACTION: (*sings*)

Dear kindly Sergeant Krupke,
You gotta understand—
It's just our bringin' upke
That gets us out of hand.
Our mothers all are junkies,
Our fathers all are drunks.
ALL
Golly Moses—natcherly we're punks!

Gee, Officer Krupke, we're very upset;
We never had the love that every child oughta get.
We ain't no delinquents,
We're misunderstood.
Deep down inside us there is good!
ACTION
There is good!
ALL
There is good, there is good,
There is untapped good.
Like inside, the worst of us is good.

SNOWBOY: (*imitating* Krupke) That's a touchin' good story.

ACTION: Lemme tell it to the world!

SNOWBOY: (imitating Krupke) Just tell it to the judge.

ACTION: (to Diesel)

Dear kindly Judge, your Honor,
My parents treat me rough.
With all their marijuana,
They won't give me a puff.
They didn't wanna have me,
But somehow I was had.
Leapin' lizards—that's why I'm so bad!

DIESEL: (imitating a judge)

Right!
Officer Krupke, you're really a square;
This boy don't need a judge, he needs a analyst's care!
It's just his neurosis that oughta be curbed—
He's psychologically disturbed!

ACTION: I'm disturbed!

ALL

We're disturbed, we're disturbed,
We're the most disturbed.
Like we're psychologically disturbed.

DIESEL: (speaks, still acting part of judge) Hear ye, Hear ye! In the opinion of this court, this child is depraved on account he ain't had a normal home.

ACTION: Hey. I'm depraved on account I'm deprived!

DIESEL: (as judge) So take him to a headshrinker.

ACTION: (to A-rab)

My father is a bastard,
My ma's an S.O.B.
My grandpa's always plastered,
My grandma pushes tea.
My sister wears a mustache,
My brother wears a dress.
Goodness gracious, that's why I'm a mess!

A-RAB: (as psychiatrist)

Yes!
Officer Krupke, you're really a slob.
This boy don't need a doctor, just a good honest job.
Society's played him a terrible trick.
And sociologically he's sick!

ACTION

I am sick!

ALL

We are sick, we are sick,
We are sick sick sick,
Like we're sociologically sick!

A-RAB: (speaks as psychiatrist) In my opinion, this child don't need to have his head shrunk at all. Juvenile delinquency is purely a social disease.

ACTION: Hey, I got a social disease!

A-RAB: (as psychiatrist) So take him to a social worker!

ACTION: (to Baby John)

Dear kindly social worker,
They say go earn a buck,
Like be a soda jerker,
Which means like be a schmuck.

It's not I'm antisocial,
I'm only antiwork.
Glory Osky, that's why I'm a jerk!
BABY JOHN: (*as female social worker*)
Eek!
Officer Krupke, you've done it again.
This boy don't need a job, he needs a year in the pen.
It ain't just a question of misunderstood;
Deep down inside him, he's no good!
ACTION
I'm no good!
ALL
We're no good, we're no good,
We're no earthly good,
Like the best of us is no damn good!
DIESEL: (*as judge*) The trouble is he's crazy,
A-RAB: (*as psychiatrist*) The trouble is he drinks.
BABY JOHN: (*as social worker*) The trouble is he's lazy.
DIESEL: (*as judge*) The trouble is he stinks.
A-RAB: (*as psychiatrist*) The trouble is he's growing.
BABY JOHN: (*as social worker*) The trouble is he's grown!
ALL
Krupke, we got troubles of our own!
Gee, Officer Krupke,
We're down on our knees,
'Cause no one wants a fella with a social disease.
Gee, Officer Krupke,
What are we to do?
Gee, Officer Krupke—
Krup you!

(*At the end of the song,* Anybodys *appears over the fence.*)

ANYBODYS: Buddy boys!
ACTION: Ah! Go wear a skirt.
ANYBODYS: I got scabby knees. Listen—
ACTION: (*to the gang*) Come on, we gotta make sure those PRs know we're
on top.
DIESEL: Geez, Action, ain't we had enough?
ANYBODYS: (*going after them*) Wotta buncha Old Man Rivers: they don't
know nothin' and they don't say nuthin'.
ACTION: Diesel, the question ain't whether we had enough—
ANYBODYS: The question is: Where's Tony and what party is lookin' for
him.
ACTION: What do you know?
ANYBODYS: I know I gotta get a skirt. (*She starts off, but* Diesel *stops her.*)
DIESEL: Come on, Anybodys, tell me.
SNOWBOY: Ah, what's the freak know?
ANYBODYS: Plenty. I figgered somebody oughta infiltrate PR territory and
spy around. I'm very big with shadows, ya know. I can slip in and out of 'em
like wind through a fence.
SNOWBOY: Boy, is she ever makin' the most of it!
ANYBODYS: You bet your fat A, I am!

ACTION: Go on. Wadd'ya hear?

ANYBODYS: I heard Chino tellin' the Sharks somethin' about Tony and Bernardo's sister. And then Chino said, "If it's the last thing I do, I'm going to get Tony."

ACTION: What'd I tell ya? Them PRs won't stop!

SNOWBOY: Easy, Action!

DIESEL: It's bad enough now—

BABY JOHN: Yeah!

ACTION: You forgettin'? Tony came through for us Jets. We gotta find him and protect him from Chino.

A-RAB: Right!

ACTION: OK then! Snowboy—cover the river! (Snowboy *runs off.*) A-rab —get over to Doc's.

BABY JOHN: I'll take the back alleys.

ACTION: Diesel?

DIESEL: I'll cover the park.

ACTION: Good boy! (*He begins to run off.*)

ANYBODYS: What about me?

ACTION: You? You get a hold of the girls and send 'em out as liaison runners so we'll know who's found Tony where.

ANYBODYS: Right! (*She starts to run off.*)

ACTION: Hey! (*She stops.*) You done good, buddy boy.

ANYBODYS: (*she has fallen in love*) Thanks, Daddy-o.

(*They both run off.*)

The Lights Black Out

SCENE THREE.

11:30 P.M. The bedroom.

The light is, at first, a vague glow on the lovers, who are asleep on the bed. From offstage, faint at first, there is the sound of knocking. It gets louder; Tony stirs. At a distance a police siren sounds, and the knocking is now very loud. Tony bolts upright. Anita comes in from outside and goes to the bedroom door—which is locked—tries the knob.

ANITA: (*holding back tears*) Maria? . . . Maria? (*Tony is reaching for his shirt when Maria sits up. Quickly, he puts his hand, then his lips, on her lips.*) Maria, it's Anita. Why are you locked in?

MARIA: I didn't know it was locked.

ANITA: Open the door. I need you.

(*Maria reaches for the knob, Tony stops her.*)

MARIA: (*a whisper*) Now you are afraid, too.

ANITA: What?

MARIA: (*loud*) One moment.

TONY: (*whispering*) Doc'll help. I'll get money from him. You meet me at his drugstore.

(*In the other room, Anita is aware of voices but unsure of what they are saying.*)

MARIA: At Doc's yes. (*Aloud.*) Coming, Anita!

TONY: (*kisses her*) Hurry!

(*He scrambles out the window as Maria hastily puts a bathrobe on over her slip. In the other room Anita has stiffened and moved away from the door. She stands staring at it coldly as Maria prattles to her through the door.)*

MARIA: Did you see Chino? He was here before, but he left so angry I think maybe he . . . (*She opens the door and sees* Anita's *look. A moment, then* Anita *pushes her aside: looks at the bed, at the window, then turns accusingly to* Maria.) All right: now you know.

ANITA: (*savagely*) And you still don't know: *Tony is one of them!*
(*She sings bitterly:*)

A boy like that who'd kill your brother,
Forget that boy and find another!
One of your own kind—
Stick to your own kind!

A boy like that will give you sorrow—
You'll meet another boy tomorrow!
One of your own kind,
Stick to your own kind!

A boy who kills cannot love,
A boy who kills has no heart.
And he's the boy who gets your love
And gets your heart—
Very smart, Maria, very smart!

A boy like that wants one thing only,
And when he's done he'll leave you lonely.
He'll murder your love; he murdered mine.
Just wait and see—
Just wait, Maria,
Just wait and see!

MARIA: (*sings*)
Oh no, Anita, no—
Anita, no!
It isn't true, not for me,
It's true for you, not for me,
I hear your words—
And in my head
I know they're smart,
But my heart, Anita,
But my heart
Knows they're wrong.

(Anita *reprises the chorus she has just sung, as* Maria *continues her song.)*

And my heart
Is too strong,
For I belong
To him alone, to him alone,
One thing I know:
I am his,
I don't care what he is.

I don't know why it's so,
I don't want to know.
Oh no, Anita, no—you should know better!
You were in love—or so you said.
You should know better . . .

I have a love, and it's all that I have.
Right or wrong, what else can I do?
I love him; I'm his,
And everything he is
I am, too.
I have a love and it's all that I need,
Right or wrong, and he needs me too.
I love him, we're one;
There's nothing to be done,
Not a thing I can do
But hold him, hold him forever,
Be with him now, tomorrow
And all of my life!
    BOTH:
When love comes so strong,
There is no right or wrong,
Your love is your life!
    ANITA: (*quietly*) Chino has a gun . . . He is sending the boys out to hunt for Tony—
    MARIA: (*tears off her bathrobe*) If he hurts Tony—If he touches him—I swear to you, I'll—
    ANITA: (*sharply*) You'll do what Tony did to Bernardo?
    MARIA: I love Tony.
    ANITA: I know. I loved Bernardo.
                      (Schrank *comes into the outer room.*)
    SCHRANK: Anybody home? (*Goes to bedroom door. Pleasantly.*) Sorry to disturb you. Guess you're disturbed enough.
    MARIA: (*gathering her robe*) Yes. You will excuse me, please. I must go to my brother.
    SCHRANK: There are just a coupla questions—
    MARIA: Afterwards, please. Later.
    SCHRANK: It'll only take a minute.
    ANITA: Couldn't you wait until—
    SCHRANK: (*sharply*) No! (*A smile to* Maria.) You were at the dance at the gym last night.
    MARIA: Yes.
    SCHRANK: Your brother got in a heavy argument because you danced with the wrong boy.
    MARIA: Oh?
    SCHRANK: Who was the boy?
    MARIA: Excuse me. Anita, my head is worse. Will you go to the drugstore and tell them what I need?
    SCHRANK: Don't you keep aspirin around?
    MARIA: This is something special. Will you go for me, Anita?
    ANITA: (*hesitates, looks at* Maria, *then nods*) Shall I tell him to hold it for you till you come?
    MARIA: (*to* Schrank) Will I be long?
    SCHRANK: As long as it takes.

MARIA: (*to* Anita) Yes. Tell him I will pick it up myself. (Anita *goes out.*)
I'm sorry. Now you asked?
SCHRANK: (*as the lights dim*) I didn't ask, I told you. There was an argu-
ment over a boy. Who was that boy?
MARIA: Another from my country.
SCHRANK: And his name?
MARIA: José.

The Lights Are Out

SCENE FOUR.
11:40 P.M. The drugstore.
   A-rab *and some of the* Jets *are there as* Anybodys *and other* Jets *run in.*
ACTION: Where's Tony?
A-RAB: Down in the cellar with Doc.
DIESEL: Ya warn him about Chino?
A-RAB: Doc said he'd tell him.
BABY JOHN: What's he hidin' in the cellar from?
SNOWBOY: Maybe he can't run as fast as you.
ACTION: Cut the frabbajabba.
ANYBODYS: Yeah! The cops'll get hip, if Chino and the PRs don't.
ACTION: Grab some readin' matter; play the juke. Some of ya get outside
and if ya see Chino or any PR—

   (The shop doorbell tinkles as Anita *enters. Cold silence, then slowly she
comes down to the counter. They all stare at her. A long moment. Someone
turns on the jukebox; a mambo comes on softly.)*

ANITA: I'd like to see Doc.
ACTION: He ain't here.
ANITA: Where is he?
A-RAB: He's gone to the bank. There was an error in his favor.
ANITA: The banks are closed at night. Where is he?
A-RAB: You know how skinny Doc is. He slipped in through the night-
deposit slot.
ANYBODYS: And got stuck halfway in.
ACTION: Which indicates there's no tellin' when he'll be back. *Buenas
noches, señorita.*
(Anita *starts to go toward the cellar door.*)
DIESEL: Where you goin'?
ANITA: Downstairs—to see Doc.
ACTION: Didn't I tell ya he ain't here?
ANITA: I'd like to see for myself.
ACTION: (*nastily*) Please.
ANITA: (*controlling herself*) . . . Please.
ACTION: *Por favor.*
ANITA: Will you let me pass?
SNOWBOY: She's too dark to pass.
ANITA: (*low*) Don't.
ACTION: *Please* don't.
SNOWBOY: *Por favor.*
DIESEL: *Non comprende.*
A-RAB: *Gracias.*
BABY JOHN: *Di nada.*

ANYBODYS: Ai! Mambo! Ai!
ANITA: Listen, you—(*She controls herself.*)
ACTION: We're listenin'.
ANITA: I've got to give a friend of yours a message. I've got to tell Tony—
DIESEL: He ain't here.
ANITA: I know he is.
ACTION: Who says he is?
A-RAB: Who's the message from?
ANITA: Never mind.
ACTION: Couldn't be from Chino, could it?
ANITA: I want to stop Chino! I want to help!
ANYBODYS: Bernardo's girl wants ta help?
ACTION: Even a greaseball's got feelings.
ANYBODYS: But she wants to help get Tony!
ANITA: No!
ACTION: Not much—Bernardo's tramp!
SNOWBOY: Bernardo's pig!
ACTION: Ya lyin' Spic—!
ANITA: Don't do that!
BABY JOHN: Gold tooth!
DIESEL: Pierced ear!
A-RAB: Garlic mouth!
ACTION: Spic! Lyin' Spic!

(*The taunting breaks out into a wild, savage dance, with epithets hurled at Anita, who is encircled and driven by the whole pack. At the peak, she is shoved so that she falls in a corner. Baby John is lifted up high and dropped on her as Doc enters from the cellar door and yells.*)

DOC: *Stop it!* ... What've you been doing now?
                        (*Dead silence. Anita gets up and looks at them.*)
ANITA: (*trying not to cry*) Bernardo was right ... If one of you was bleeding in the street, I'd walk by and spit on you. (*She flicks herself off and makes her way toward the door.*)
ACTION: Don't let her go!
DIESEL: She'll tell Chino that Tony—
                        (*Snowboy grabs her; she shakes loose.*)
ANITA: Let go! (*Facing them.*) I'll give you a message for your American buddy! Tell the murderer Maria's *never* going to meet him! Tell him Chino found out and—and shot her! (*She slams out. There is a.stunned silence.*)
DOC: What does it take to get through to you? When do you stop? *You make this world lousy!*
ACTION: That's the way we found it, Doc.
DOC: Get out of here!
                        (*Slowly, they start to file out.*)
                        The Lights Fade

SCENE FIVE.
11:50 P.M. The cellar.
   Cramped: a box or crate; stairs leading to the drugstore above; a door to the outside.
   Tony is sitting on a crate, whistling "Maria" as Doc comes down the stairs, some bills in his hand.

Tony: Make a big sale?
Doc: No.
Tony: (*taking the money that* Doc *is holding*) Thanks. I'll pay you back as soon as I can.
Doc: Forget that.
Tony: I won't; I couldn't. Doc, you know what we're going to do in the country, Maria and me? We're going to have kids and we'll name them all after you, even the girls. Then when you come to visit—
Doc: (*slapping him*) *Wake up!* (*Raging.*) Is that the only way to get through to you? Do just what you all do? Bust like a hot-water pipe?
Tony: Doc, what's gotten—
Doc: (*overriding angrily*) Why do you live like there's a war on? (*Low.*) Why do you kill?
Tony: I told you how it happened, Doc. Maria understands. Why can't you?
Doc: I never had a Maria.
Tony: (*gently*) I have, and I'll tell you one thing, Doc. Even if it only lasts from one night to the next, it's worth the world.
Doc: That's all it did last.
Tony: What?
Doc: That was no customer upstairs, just now. That was Anita. (*Pause.*) Maria is dead. Chino found out about you and her—and shot her.

(*A brief moment.* Tony *looks at* Doc, *stunned, numb. He shakes his head, as though he cannot believe this.* Doc *holds out his hands to him, but* Tony *backs away, then suddenly turns and runs out the door. As he does, the set flies away and the stage goes dark. In the darkness, we hear* Tony's *voice.*)

Tony: Chino? *Chino?* Come and get me, too, Chino.

Scene Six.
Midnight. The street.
   The lights come up to reveal the same set we saw at the beginning of Act One—but it is now jagged with shadows. Tony *stands in the emptiness, calling, whirling around as a figure darts out of the shadows and then runs off again.*

Tony: Chino? . . . COME ON: GET ME, TOO!
Anybodys: (*a whisper from the dark*) Tony . . .
Tony: (*swings around*) Who's that?
Anybodys: (*darting on*) Me: Anybodys.
Tony: Get outa here. HEY, CHINO! COME GET ME, DAMN YOU!
Anybodys: What're you doin', Tony?
Tony: I said get outa here! CHINO!
Anybodys: Look, maybe if you and me just—
Tony: (*savagely*) It's not playing any more! Can't any of you get that?
Anybodys: But the gang—
Tony: You're a girl: *be a girl!* Beat it. (*She retreats.*) CHINO, I'M CALLING FOR YOU, CHINO! HURRY! IT'S CLEAR NOW. THERE'S NOBODY BUT ME. COME ON! Will you, please. I'm waiting for you. I want you to—(*Suddenly, all the way across the stage from him, a figure steps out of*

the dark. He stops and peers as light starts to glow on it. He utters an unbelieving whisper.) Maria . . . Maria?

MARIA: Tony . . . *(As she holds our her arms toward him, another figure appears: Chino.)*

TONY: MARIA! *(As they run to each other, there is a gun shot. Tony stumbles, as though he has tripped. Maria catches him and cradles him in her arms as he falters to the ground. During this Baby John and A-rab run on; then Pepe and Indio and other Sharks. Chino stands very still, bewildered by the gun dangling from his hand. More Jets and Sharks, some girls run on, and Doc comes out to stare with them.)* I didn't believe hard enough.

MARIA: Loving is enough.

TONY: Not here. They won't let us be.

MARIA: Then we'll get away.

TONY: Yes, we can. We will. *(He shivers, as though a pain went through him. She holds him closer and begins to sing—without orchestra.)*

MARIA:

Hold my hand and we're halfway there.
Hold my hand and I'll take you there,
Someday,
Somehow . . .

(He has started to join in on the second line. She sings harder, as though to urge him back to life, but his voice falters and he barely finishes the line. She sings on, a phrase or two more, then stops, his body quiet in her arms. A moment, and then, as she gently rests Tony on the floor, the orchestra finishes the last bars of the song. Lightly, she brushes Tony's lips with her fingers. Behind her, Action, in front of a group of Jets, moves to lead them toward Chino. Maria speaks, her voice cold, sharp.)

Stay back. *(The shawl she has had around her shoulders slips to the ground as she gets up, walks to Chino and holds out her hand. He hands her the gun. She speaks again, in a flat, hard voice.)* How do you fire this gun, Chino? Just by pulling this little trigger? *(She points it at him suddenly; he draws back. She has all of them in front of her now, as she holds the gun out and her voice gets stronger with anger and savage rage.)* How many bullets are left, Chino? Enough for you? *(Pointing at another.)* And you? *(At* Action.*)* All of you? WE ALL KILLED HIM; and my brother and Riff. I, too. I CAN KILL NOW BECAUSE I HATE NOW. *(She has been pointing the gun wildly, and they have all been drawing back. Now, again, she holds it straight out at* Action.*)* How many can I kill, Chino? How many—and still have one bullet left for me? *(Both hands on the gun, she pushes it forward at* Action. *But she cannot fire, and she breaks into tears, hurls the gun away and sinks to the ground.* Schrank *walks on, looks around and starts toward* Tony's *body. Like a madwoman,* Maria *races to the body and puts her arms around it, all-embracing, protecting, as she cries out.)* DON'T YOU TOUCH HIM! *(*Schrank *steps back.* Krupke *and* Glad Hand *have appeared in the shadows behind him.* Maria *now turns and looks at* Chino, *holds her hand out to him. Slowly he comes and stands at the body. Now she looks at* Action, *holds out her hand to him. He, too, comes forward, with* Diesel, *to stand by the body.* Pepe *joins* Chino. *Then* Maria *leans low over* Tony's *face. Softly, privately.)* Te adoro, Anton.

(She kisses him gently. Music starts as the two Jets and two Sharks lift

up Tony's body and start to carry him out. The others, boys and girls, fall in behind to make a procession, the same procession they made in the dream ballet, as Baby John comes forward to pick up Maria's shawl and put it over her head. She sits quietly, like a woman in mourning, as the music builds, the lights start to come up and the procession makes its way across the stage. At last, she gets up and, despite the tears on her face, lifts her head proudly, and triumphantly turns to follow the others. The adults—Doc, Schrank, Krupke, Glad Hand—are left bowed, alone, useless.)

The Curtain Falls

FOR DISCUSSION

1. Can you see any similarities between this play and Shakespeare's *Romeo and Juliet?* Discuss.
2. Describe the law officers. What do you think of the way they are characterized in the play? Do you think it is fair?
3. Is the situation in the play realistic? Is it romantic? Discuss.
4. What problem is presented in the play? Is it resolved? In your opinion, can such a problem ever be resolved? Why or why not?
5. Do you sympathize with either the Jets or the Sharks? With both? With neither? Why?
6. Discuss the role of chance in this play.
7. Why did Tony die?
8. Do the characters in the play seem like real people to you? Some of them? All of them? Discuss.
9. What is the theme of *West Side Story?*
10. Why has Tony almost quit the Jets?
11. Why is the character of Doc included in the play? What purpose does he serve?
12. Why does Maria not shoot anyone in the final scene?
13. What does Maria mean when she says, "We all killed him"?
14. Is the trouble between the Jets and the Sharks more a matter of territory or of prejudice? Discuss.

Lorraine Hansberry: a study in courage.

Born May 19, 1930, in Chicago, she became interested in the theatre while in high school. She attended the University of Wisconsin and studied painting before going to New York City. In 1953 she married Robert Nemeroff, a producer, music publisher, and writer. *A Raisin in the Sun,* her first play to be produced, opened in 1959 and was highly successful, winning the New York Drama Critics Circle Award for the best play of the year. It was the first play on Broadway to be written by a black woman and the first in more than fifty years to have a black director, Lloyd Richards. A musical version, entitled *Raisin,* had a successful opening during the 1973–74 Broadway season. The title for *A Raisin in the Sun* comes from a poem, "Harlem," written by Langston Hughes.

Her second Broadway play, *The Sign in Sidney Brustein's Window,* opened on October 15, 1964. The following January Miss Hansberry died of cancer at the age of thirty-four.

In *A Raisin in the Sun* Miss Hansberry, said she did not want to write a black play but only a play about people who happened to be black. She also said she felt that emotional involvement was the key to success in any drama. She wanted to show a clash of old and new in the various "gradations" that exist within one black family. Most important, however, she wanted to depict the courage of blacks.

The central character, of course, is Walter, who, like poor people everywhere, wants to succeed, get ahead. The other three main characters present different types of black women. Mama has battled life and won; Beneatha is a militant before militancy comes to the fore; Ruth only wants to help her husband but doesn't know how to begin. Even though the play ends with the Youngers moving into a white neighborhood, it is not a story of integration but the story of Walter's "gaining his manhood." It just happens that the house that Mama can afford is in a white community. Walter wants much more from life than he has had. True, he defines success in terms of making money, but only because money is a concrete symbol of success.

A Raisin in the Sun also has to do with dignity. Because of the decision he is forced to make, Walter retains his self-respect. He has fought a battle and won; therefore he is a human being and a man.

The play tells the story of a black family, but the story of a poor family, too. It is the story of blacks who have been oppressed, but the story of poor people who want more than they have. These characteristics are what give the play a universal appeal.

A Raisin in the Sun

THE CHARACTERS

RUTH YOUNGER
TRAVIS YOUNGER
WALTER LEE YOUNGER
   (BROTHER)
BENEATHA YOUNGER
LENA YOUNGER (MAMA)

JOSEPH ASAGAI
GEORGE MURCHISON
KARL LINDNER

BOBO
MOVING MEN

The action of the play is set in Chicago's Southside, sometime between World War II and the present.

Act I

SCENE I: *Friday morning.*
SCENE II: *The following morning.*

Act II

SCENE I: *Later, the same day.*
SCENE II: *Friday night, a few weeks later.*
SCENE III: *Moving day, one week later.*

Act III

An hour later

A Raisin in the Sun

ACT I

SCENE I: (*The* Younger *living room would be a comfortable and well-or-dered room if it were not for a number of indestructible contradictions to this state of being. Its furnishings are typical and undistinguished, and their primary feature now is that they have clearly had to accommodate the living of too many people for too many years—and they are tired. Still, we can see that at some time, a time probably no longer remembered by the family (except perhaps for* Mama*) the furnishings of this room were actually select-ed with care and love and even hope—and brought to this apartment and arranged with taste and pride.*

That was a long time ago. Now the once-loved pattern of the couch upholstery has to fight to show itself from under acres of crocheted doilies and couch covers which have themselves finally come to be more important than the upholstery. And here a table or a chair has been moved to disguise the worn places in the carpet; but the carpet has fought back by showing its weariness, with depressing uniformity, elsewhere on its surface.

Weariness has, in fact, won in this room. Everything has been polished, washed, sat on, used, scrubbed too often. All pretenses but living itself have long since vanished from the very atmosphere of this room.

Moreover, a section of this room, for it is not really a room unto itself, though the landlord's lease would make it seem so, slopes backward to provide a small kitchen area, where the family prepares the meals that are eaten in the living room proper, which must also serve as dining room. The single window that has been provided for these "two" rooms is located in this kitchen area. The sole natural light the family may enjoy in the course of a day is only that which fights its way through this little window.

At left, a door leads to a bedroom which is shared by Mama *and her daughter,* Beneatha*. At right, opposite, is a second room (which in the beginning of the life of this apartment was probably a breakfast room) which serves as a bedroom for* Walter *and his wife,* Ruth*.*

At Rise: It is morning dark in the living room. Travis *is asleep on the make-down bed at center. An alarm clock sounds from within the bedroom at right, and presently* Ruth *enters from that room and closes the door behind her. She crosses sleepily toward the window. As she passes her sleeping son she reaches down and shakes him a little. At the window she raises the shade,* and a dusky Southside morning light comes in feebly. She fills a pot with water and puts it on to boil. She calls to the boy, between yawns, in a slightly muffled voice.

Ruth is about thirty. We can see that she was a pretty girl, even exceptionally so, but now it is apparent that life has been little that she expected, and disappointment has already begun to hang in her face. In a few years, before thirty-five, she will be known among her people as a "settled woman."

She crosses to her son and gives him a good, final, rousing shake.)

RUTH: Come on now, boy, it's seven thirty! (Her son sits up at last, in a stupor of sleepiness.) I say hurry up, Travis! You ain't the only person in the world got to use a bathroom! (The child, a sturdy, handsome little boy of ten or eleven, drags himself out of the bed and almost blindly takes his towels and "today's clothes" from drawers and a closet and goes out to the bathroom, which is in an outside hall and which is shared by another family or families on the same floor. Ruth crosses to the bedroom door at right, opens it, and calls in to her husband.) Walter Lee! . . . It's after seven thirty! Lemme see you do some waking up in there now! (She waits.) You better get up from there, man! It's after seven thirty, I tell you. (She waits again.) All right, you just go ahead and lay there, and next thing you know Travis be finished, and Mr. Johnson'll be in there, and you'll be fussing and cussing 'round here like a mad man! And be late, too! (She waits, at the end of patience.) Walter Lee—it's time for you to get up!

(She waits another second and then starts to go into the bedroom, but is apparently satisfied that her husband has begun to get up. She stops, pulls the door to, and returns to the kitchen area. She wipes her face with a moist cloth and runs her fingers through her sleep-disheveled hair in a vain effort and ties an apron around her housecoat. The bedroom door at right opens, and her husband (Walter Lee) stands in the doorway in his pajamas, which are rumpled and mismated. He is a lean, intense young man in his middle thirties, inclined to quick, nervous movements and erratic speech habits— and always in his voice there is a quality of indictment.)

WALTER: Is he out yet?
RUTH: What you mean out? He ain't hardly got in there good yet.
WALTER: (Wandering in, still more oriented to sleep than to a new day.) Well, what was you doing all that yelling for if I can't even get in there yet? (Stopping and thinking.) Check coming today?
RUTH: They said Saturday and this is just Friday and I hopes to God you ain't going to get up here first thing this morning and start talking to me 'bout no money—'cause I 'bout don't want to hear it.
WALTER: Something the matter with you this morning?
RUTH: No—I'm just sleepy as the devil. What kind of eggs you want?
WALTER: Not scrambled. (Ruth starts to scramble eggs.) Paper come? (Ruth points impatiently to the rolled up Tribune on the table, and he gets it and spreads it out and vaguely reads the front page.) Set off another bomb yesterday.
RUTH: (Maximum indifference.) Did they?
WALTER: (Looking up.) What's the matter with you?
RUTH: Ain't nothing the matter with me. And don't keep asking me that this morning.
WALTER: Ain't nobody bothering you. (Reading the news of the day absently again.) Say Colonel McCormick is sick.

RUTH: (*Affecting tea-party interest.*) Is he now? Poor thing.

WALTER: (*Sighing and looking at his watch.*) Oh, me. (*He waits.*) Now what is that boy doing in that bathroom all this time? He just going to have to start getting up earlier. I can't be being late to work on account of him fooling around in there.

RUTH: (*Turning on him.*) Oh, no he ain't going to be getting up no earlier no such thing! It ain't his fault that he can't get to bed no earlier nights 'cause he got a bunch of crazy good-for-nothing clowns sitting up running their mouths in what is supposed to be his bedroom after ten o'clock at night . . .

WALTER: That's what you mad about, ain't it? The things I want to talk about with my friends just couldn't be important in your mind, could they? (*He rises and finds a cigarette in her handbag on the table and crosses to the little window and looks out, smoking and deeply enjoying this first one.*)

RUTH: (*Almost matter of factly, a complaint too automatic to deserve emphasis.*) Why you always got to smoke before you eat in the morning?

WALTER: (*At the window.*) Just look at 'em down there . . . Running and racing to work . . . (*He turns and faces his wife and watches her a moment at the stove, and then, suddenly.*) You look young this morning, baby.

RUTH: (*Indifferently.*) Yeah?

WALTER: Just for a second—stirring them eggs. It's gone now—just for a second it was—you looked real young again. (*Then, drily.*) It's gone now— you look like yourself again.

RUTH: Man, if you don't shut up and leave me alone.

WALTER: (*Looking out to the street again.*) First thing a man ought to learn in life is not to make love to no colored woman first thing in the morning. You all some evil people at eight o'clock in the morning.

(Travis *appears in the hall doorway, almost fully dressed and quite wide awake now, his towels and pajamas across his shoulders. He opens the door and signals for his father to make the bathroom in a hurry.*)

TRAVIS: (*Watching the bathroom.*) Daddy, come on!

(Walter *gets his bathroom utensils and flies out to the bathroom.*)

RUTH: Sit down and have your breakfast, Travis.

TRAVIS: Mama, this is Friday. (*Gleefully.*) Check coming tomorrow, huh?

RUTH: You get your mind off money and eat your breakfast.

TRAVIS: (*Eating.*) This is the morning we supposed to bring the fifty cents to school.

RUTH: Well, I ain't got no fifty cents this morning.

TRAVIS: Teacher say we have to.

RUTH: I don't care what teacher say. I ain't got it. Eat your breakfast, Travis.

TRAVIS: I *am* eating.

RUTH: Hush up now and just eat!

(The boy gives her an exasperated look for her lack of understanding, and eats grudgingly.)

TRAVIS: You think Grandmama would have it?

RUTH: No! And I want you to stop asking your grandmother for money, you hear me?

TRAVIS: (*Outraged.*) Gaaaleee! I don't ask her, she just gimme it some-times!

RUTH: Travis Willard Younger—I got too much on me this morning to be—

TRAVIS: Maybe Daddy—

RUTH: *Travis!*

(*The boy hushes abruptly. They are both quiet and tense for several seconds.*)

TRAVIS: (*Presently.*) Could I maybe go carry some groceries in front of the supermarket for a little while after school then?

RUTH: Just hush, I said. (*Travis jabs his spoon into his cereal bowl viciously, and rests his head in anger upon his fists.*) If you through eating, you can get over there and make up your bed.

(*The boy obeys stiffly and crosses the room, almost mechanically, to the bed and more or less carefully folds the covering. He carries the bedding into his mother's room and returns with his books and cap.*)

TRAVIS: (*Sulking and standing apart from her unnaturally.*) I'm gone.

RUTH: (*Looking up from the stove to inspect him automatically.*) Come here. (*He crosses to her and she studies his head.*) If you don't take this comb and fix this here head, you better! (Travis *puts down his books with a great sigh of oppression, and crosses to the mirror. His mother mutters under her breath about his "slubbornness."*) 'Bout to march out of here with that head looking just like chickens slept in it! I just don't know where you get your slubborn ways ... And get your jacket, too. Looks chilly out this morning.

TRAVIS: (*With conspicuously brushed hair and jacket.*) I'm gone.

RUTH: Get carfare and milk money—(*Waving one finger.*)—and not a single penny for no caps, you hear me?

TRAVIS: (*With sullen politeness.*) Yes'm.

(*He turns in outrage to leave. His mother watches after him as in his frustration he approaches the door almost comically. When she speaks to him, her voice has become a very gentle tease.*)

RUTH: (*Mocking; as she thinks he would say it.*) Oh, Mama makes me so mad sometimes, I don't know what to do! (*She waits and continues to his back as he stands stock-still in front of the door.*) I wouldn't kiss that woman good-bye for nothing in this world this morning! (*The boy finally turns around and rolls his eyes at her, knowing the mood has changed and he is vindicated; he does not, however, move toward her yet.*) Not for nothing in this world! (*She finally laughs aloud at him and holds out her arms to him and we see that it is a way between them, very old and practiced. He crosses to her and allows her to embrace him warmly but keeps his face fixed with masculine rigidity. She holds him back from her presently and looks at him and runs her fingers over the features of his face. With utter gentleness—.*) Now—whose little old angry man are you?

TRAVIS: (*The masculinity and gruffness start to fade at last.*) Aw gaalee—Mama ...

RUTH: (*Mimicking.*) Aw—gaaaaaleeeee, Mama! (*She pushes him, with rough playfulness and finality, toward the door.*) Get on out of here or you going to be late.

TRAVIS: (*In the face of love, new aggressiveness.*) Mama, could I *please* go carry groceries?

RUTH: Honey, it's starting to get so cold evenings.

WALTER: (*Coming in from the bathroom and drawing a make-believe gun from a make-believe holster and shooting at his son.*) What is it he wants to do?

RUTH: Go carry groceries after school at the supermarket.

WALTER: Well, let him go ...

TRAVIS: (*Quickly, to the ally.*) I *have* to—she won't gimme the fifty cents . . .

WALTER: (*To his wife only.*) Why not?

RUTH: (*Simply, and with flavor.*) 'Cause we don't have it.

WALTER: (*To Ruth only.*) What you tell the boy things like that for? (*Reaching down into his pants with a rather important gesture.*) Here, son— (*He hands the boy the coin, but his eyes are directed to his wife's. Travis takes the money happily.*)

TRAVIS: Thanks, Daddy.

(*He starts out. Ruth watches both of them with murder in her eyes. Walter stands and stares back at her with defiance, and suddenly reaches into his pocket again on an afterthought.*)

WALTER: (*Without even looking at his son, still staring hard at his wife.*) In fact, here's another fifty cents . . . Buy yourself some fruit today—or take a taxicab to school or something!

TRAVIS: Whoopee—

(*He leaps up and clasps his father around the middle with his legs, and they face each other in mutual appreciation; slowly Walter Lee peeks abound the boy to catch the violent rays from his wife's eyes and draws his head back as if shot.*)

WALTER: You better get down now—and get to school, man.

TRAVIS: (*At the door.*) O.K. Good-bye. (*He exits.*)

WALTER: (*After him, pointing with pride.*) That's my boy. (*She looks at him in disgust and turns back to her work.*) You know what I was thinking 'bout in the bathroom this morning?

RUTH: No.

WALTER: How come you always try to be so pleasant!

RUTH: What is there to be pleasant 'bout!

WALTER: You want to know what I was thinkin 'bout in the bathroom or not!

RUTH: I know what you thinking 'bout.

WALTER: (*Ignoring her.*) 'Bout what me and Willy Harris was talking about last night.

RUTH: (*Immediately—a refrain.*) Willy Harris is a good-for-nothing loud mouth.

Walter: Anybody who talks to me has got to be a good-for-nothing loud mouth, ain't he? And what you know about who is just a good-for-nothing loud mouth? Charlie Atkins was just a "good-for-nothing loud mouth" too, wasn't he! When he wanted me to go in the dry-cleaning business with him. And now—he's grossing a hundred thousand a year. A hundred thousand dollars a year! You still call *him* a loud mouth!

RUTH: (*Bitterly.*) Oh, Walter Lee . . . (*She folds her head on her arms over the table.*)

WALTER: (*Rising and coming to her and standing over her.*) You tired, ain't you? Tired of everything. Me, the boy, the way we live—this beat-up hole—everything. Ain't you? (*She doesn't look up doesn't answer.*) So tired —moaning and groaning all the time, but you wouldn't do nothing to help, would you? You couldn't be on my side that long for nothing, could you?

RUTH: Walter, please leave me alone.

WALTER: A man needs for a woman to back him up . . .

RUTH: Walter—

WALTER: Mama would listen to you. You know she listen to you more than she do me and Bennie. She think more of you. All you have to do is just sit down with her when you drinking your coffee one morning and talking 'bout things like you do and—(*He sits down beside her and demonstrates graphically what he thinks her methods and tone should be.*)—you just sip your coffee, see, and say easy like that you been thinking 'bout that deal Walter Lee is so interested in, 'bout the store and all, and sip some more coffee, like what you saying ain't really that important to you—And the next thing you know, she be listening good and asking you questions and when I come home—I can tell her the details. This ain't no fly-by-night proposition, baby. I mean we figured it out, me and Willy and Bobo.

RUTH: (*With a frown.*) Bobo?

WALTER: Yeah. You see, this little liquor store we got in mind cost seventy-five thousand and we figured the initial investment on the place be 'bout thirty thousand, see. That be ten thousand each. Course, there's a couple of hundred you got to pay so's you don't spend your life just waiting for them clowns to let your license get approved—

RUTH: You mean graft?

WALTER: (*Frowning impatiently.*) Don't call it that. See there, that just goes to show you what women understand about the world. Baby, don't *nothing* happen for you in this world 'less you pay *somebody* off!

RUTH: Walter, leave me alone! (*She raises her head and stares at him vigorously—then says, more quietly.*) Eat your eggs, they gonna be cold.

WALTER: (*Straightening up from her and looking off.*) That's it. There you are. Man say to his woman: I got me a dream. His woman say: Eat your eggs. (*Sadly, but gaining in power.*) Man say: I got to take hold of this here world, baby! And a woman will say: Eat your eggs and go to work. (*Passionately now.*) Man say: I got to change my life, I'm choking to death, baby! And his woman say—(*In utter anguish as he brings his fists down on his thighs.*)— Your eggs is getting cold!

RUTH: (*Softly.*) Walter, that ain't none of our money.

WALTER: (*Not listening at all or even looking at her.*) This morning, I was lookin' in the mirror and thinking about it . . . I'm thirty-five years old; I been married eleven years and I got a boy who sleeps in the living room—(*Very, very quietly.*)—and all I got to give him is stories about how rich white people live . . .

RUTH: Eat your eggs, Walter.

WALTER: *Damn my eggs . . . damn all the eggs that ever was!*

RUTH: Then go to work.

WALTER: (*Looking up at her.*) See—I'm trying to talk to you 'bout myself —(*Shaking his head with the repetition.*)—and all you can say is eat them eggs and go to work.

RUTH: (*Wearily.*) Honey, you never say nothing new. I listen to you every day, every night and every morning, and you never say nothing new. (*Shrug-*

ging.) So you would rather *be* Mr. Arnold than be his chauffeur. So—I would *rather* be living in Buckingham Palace.

WALTER: That is just what is wrong with the colored woman in this world . . . Don't understand about building their men up and making 'em feel like they somebody. Like they can do something.

RUTH: (*Drily, but to hurt.*) There *are* colored men who do things.

WALTER: No thanks to the colored woman.

RUTH: Well, being a colored woman, I guess I can't help myself none. (*She rises and gets the ironing board and sets it up and attacks a huge pile of rough-dried clothes, sprinkling them in preparation for the ironing and then rolling them into tight fat balls.*)

WALTER: (*Mumbling.*) We one group of men tied to a race of women with small minds.

(*His sister* Beneatha *enters. She is about twenty, as slim and intense as her brother. She is not as pretty as her sister-in-law, but her lean, almost intellectual face has a handsomeness of its own. She wears a bright-red flannel nightie, and her thick hair stands wildly about her head. Her speech is a mixture of many things; it is different from the rest of the family's insofar as education has permeated her sense of English—and perhaps the Midwest rather than the South has finally—at last—won out in her inflection; but not altogether, because over all of it is a soft slurring and transformed use of vowels which is the decided influence of the Southside. She passes through the room without looking at either* Ruth *or* Walter *and goes to the outside door and looks, a little blindly, out to the bathroom. She sees that it has been lost to the Johnsons. She closes the door with a sleepy vengeance and crosses to the table and sits down a little defeated.*)

BENEATHA: I am going to start timing those people.

WALTER: You should get up earlier.

BENEATHA: (*Her face in her hands. She is still fighting the urge to go back to bed.*) Really—would you suggest dawn? Where's the paper?

WALTER: (*Pushing the paper across the table to her as he studies her almost clinically, as though he has never seen her before.*) You a horrible-looking chick at this hour.

BENEATHA: (*Drily.*) Good morning, everybody.

WALTER: (*Senselessly.*) How is school coming?

BENEATHA: (*In the same spirit.*) Lovely. Lovely. And you know, biology is the greatest. (*Looking up at him.*) I dissected something that looked just like you yesterday.

WALTER: I just wondered if you've made up your mind and everything.

BENEATHA: (*Gaining in sharpness and impatience.*) And what did I answer yesterday morning—and the day before that?

RUTH: (*From the ironing board, like someone disinterested and old.*) Don't be so nasty, Bennie.

BENEATHA: (*Still to her brother.*) And the day before that and the day before that!

WALTER: (*Defensively.*) I'm interested in you. Something wrong with that? Ain't many girls who decide—

WALTER *and* BENEATHA: (*In unison.*)—"to be a doctor."

(*Silence.*)

WALTER: Have we figured out yet just exactly how much medical school is going to cost?

RUTH: Walter Lee, why don't you leave that girl alone and get out of here to work?

BENEATHA: (*Exits to the bathroom and bangs on the door.*) Come on out of there, please! (*She comes back into the room.*)

WALTER: (*Looking at his sister intently.*) You know the check is coming tomorrow.

BENEATHA: (*Turning on him with a sharpness all her own.*) That money belongs to Mama, Walter, and it's for her to decide how she wants to use it. I don't care if she wants to buy a house or a rocket ship or just nail it up somewhere and look at it. It's hers. Not ours—*hers*.

WALTER: (*Bitterly.*) Now ain't that fine! You just got your mother's interest at heart, ain't you, girl? You such a nice girl—but if Mama got that money she can always take a few thousand and help you through school too—can't she?

BENEATHA: I have never asked anyone around here to do anything for me!

WALTER: No! And the line between asking and just accepting when the time comes is big and wide—ain't it!

BENEATHA: (*With fury.*) What do you want from me, Brother—that I quit school or just drop dead, which!

WALTER: I don't want nothing but for you to stop acting holy 'round here. Me and Ruth done made some sacrifices for you—why can't you do something for the family?

RUTH: Walter, don't be dragging me in it.

WALTER: You are in it—Don't you get up and go work in somebody's kitchen for the last three years to help put clothes on her back?

RUTH: Oh, Walter—that's not fair . . .

WALTER: It ain't that nobody expects you to get on your knees and say thank you, Brother; thank you, Ruth; thank you, Mama—and thank you, Travis, for wearing the same pair of shoes for two semesters—

BENEATHA: (*Dropping to her knees.*) Well—I *do*—all right?—thank everybody . . . and forgive me for ever wanting to be anything at all . . . forgive me, forgive me!

RUTH: Please stop it! Your mama'll hear you.

WALTER: Who the hell told you you had to be a doctor? If you so crazy 'bout messing 'round with sick people—then go be a nurse like other women —or just get married and be quiet . . .

BENEATHA: Well—you finally got it said . . . It took you three years but you finally got it said. Walter, give up; leave me alone—it's Mama's money.

WALTER: *He was my father, too!*

BENEATHA: So what? He was mine, too—and Travis' grandfather—but the insurance money belongs to Mama. Picking on me is not going to make her give it to you to invest in any liquor stores—(*Underbreath, dropping into a chair.*)—and I for one say, God bless Mama for that!

WALTER: (*To Ruth.*) See—did you hear? Did you hear!

RUTH: Honey, please go to work.

WALTER: Nobody in this house is ever going to understand me.

BENEATHA: Because you're a nut.

WALTER: Who's a nut?

BENEATHA: You—you are a nut. Thee is mad, boy.

WALTER: (*Looking at his wife and his sister from the door, very sadly.*) The world's most backward race of people, and that's a fact.

BENEATHA: (*Turning slowly in her chair.*) And then there are all those prophets who would lead us out of the wilderness—(Walter *slams out of the house.*)—into the swamps!

RUTH: Bennie, why you always gotta be pickin' on your brother? Can't you be a little sweeter sometimes? (*Door opens.* Walter *walks in.*)

WALTER: (*To* Ruth.) I need some money for carfare.

RUTH: (*Looks at him, then warms; teasing, but tenderly.*) Fifty cents? (*She goes to her bag and gets money.*) Here, take a taxi.

(Walter *exits.* Mama *enters. She is a woman in her early sixties, full-bodied and strong. She is one of those women of a certain grace and beauty who wear it so unobtrusively that it takes a while to notice. Her dark-brown face is surrounded by the total whiteness of her hair, and, being a woman who has adjusted to many things in life and overcome many more, her face is full of strength. She has, we can see, wit and faith of a kind that keep her eyes lit and full of interest and expectancy. She is, in a word, a beautiful woman. Her bearing is perhaps most like the noble bearing of the women of the Hereros of Southwest Africa—rather as if she imagines that as she walks she still bears a basket or a vessel upon her head. Her speech, on the other hand, is as careless as her carriage is precise—she is inclined to slur everything —but her voice is perhaps not so much quiet as simply soft.*)

MAMA: Who that 'round here slamming doors at this hour? (*She crosses through the room, goes to the window, opens it, and brings in a feeble little plant growing doggedly in a small pot on the window sill. She feels the dirt and puts it back out.*)

RUTH: That was Walter Lee. He and Bennie was at it again.

MAMA: My children and they tempers. Lord, if this little old plant don't get more sun than it's been getting it ain't never going to see spring again. (*She turns from the window.*) What's the matter with you this morning, Ruth? You looks right peaked. You aiming to iron all them things? Leave some for me. I'll get to 'em this afternoon. Bennie honey, it's too drafty for you to be sitting 'round half dressed. Where's your robe?

BENEATHA: In the cleaners.

MAMA: Well, go get mine and put it on.

BENEATHA: I'm not cold, Mama, honest.

MAMA: I know—but you so thin . . .

BENEATHA: (*Irritably.*) Mama, I'm not cold.

MAMA: (*Seeing the make-down bed as* Travis *has left it.*) Lord have mercy, look at that poor bed. Bless his heart—he tries, don't he? (*She moves to the bed* Travis *has sloppily made up.*)

RUTH: No—he don't half try at all 'cause he knows you going to come along behind him and fix everything. That's just how come he don't know how to do nothing right now—you done spoiled that boy so.

MAMA: Well—he's a little boy. Ain't supposed to know 'bout housekeeping. My baby, that's what he is. What you fix for his breakfast this morning?

RUTH: (*Angrily.*) I feed my son, Lena!

MAMA: I ain't meddling—(*Underbreath; busy-bodyish.*) I just noticed all last week he had cold cereal, and when it starts getting this chilly in the fall a child ought to have some hot grits or something when he goes out in the cold—

RUTH: (*Furious.*) I gave him hot oats—is that all right!

MAMA: I ain't meddling. (*Pause.*) Put a lot of nice butter on it? (Ruth *shoots her an angry look and does not reply.*) He likes lots of butter.

RUTH: (*Exasperated.*) Lena—

MAMA: (*To* Beneatha. Mama *is inclined to wander conversationally sometimes.*) What was you and your brother fussing 'bout this morning?

BENEATHA: It's not important, Mama. (*She gets up and goes to look out at the bathroom, which is apparently free, and she picks up her towels and rushes out.*)

MAMA: What was they fighting about?

RUTH: Now you know as well as I do.

MAMA: (*Shaking her head.*) Brother still worrying hisself sick about that money?

RUTH: You know he is.

MAMA: You had breakfast?

RUTH: Some coffee.

MAMA: Girl, you better start eating and looking after yourself better. You almost thin as Travis.

RUTH: Lena—

MAMA: Un-hunh?

RUTH: What are you going to do with it?

MAMA: Now don't you start, child. It's too early in the morning to be talking about money. It ain't Christian.

RUTH: It's just that he got his heart set on that store—

MAMA: You mean that liquor store that Willy Harris want him to invest in?

RUTH: Yes—

MAMA: We ain't no business people, Ruth. We just plain working folks.

RUTH: Ain't nobody business people till they go into business. Walter Lee say colored people ain't never going to start getting ahead till they start gambling on some different kinds of things in the world—investments and things.

MAMA: What done got into you, girl? Walter Lee done finally sold you on investing.

RUTH: No. Mama, something is happening between Walter and me. I don't know what it is—but he needs something—something I can't give him any more. He needs this chance, Lena.

MAMA: (*Frowning deeply.*) But liquor, honey—

RUTH: Well—like Walter say—I spec people going to always be drinking themselves some liquor.

MAMA: Well—whether they drinks it or not ain't none of my business. But whether I go into business selling it to 'em *is,* and I don't want that on my ledger this late in life. (*Stopping suddenly and studying her daughter-in-law.*) Ruth Younger, what's the matter with you today? You look like you could fall over right there.

RUTH: I'm tired.

MAMA: Then you better stay home from work today.

RUTH: I can't stay home. She'd be calling up the agency and screaming at them, "My girl didn't come in today—send me somebody! My girl didn't come in!" Oh, she just have a fit . . .

MAMA: Well, let her have it. I'll just call her up and say you got the flu—

RUTH: (*Laughing.*) Why the flu?

MAMA: 'Cause it sounds respectable to 'em. Something white people get, too. They know 'bout the flu. Otherwise they think you been cut up or something when you tell 'em you sick.

RUTH: I got to go in. We need the money.

MAMA: Somebody would of thought my children done all but starved to death the way they talk about money here late. Child, we got a great big old check coming tomorrow.

RUTH: (*Sincerely, but also self-righteously.*) Now that's your money. It ain't got nothing to do with me. We all feel like that—Walter and Bennie and me—even Travis.

MAMA: (*Thoughtfully, and suddenly very far away.*) Ten thousand dollars—

RUTH: Sure is wonderful.

MAMA: Ten thousand dollars.

RUTH: You know what you should do, Miss Lena? You should take yourself a trip somewhere. To Europe or South America or someplace—

MAMA: (*Throwing up her hands at the thought.*) Oh, child!

RUTH: I'm serious. Just pack up and leave! Go on away and enjoy yourself some. Forget about the family and have yourself a ball for once in your life—

MAMA: (*Drily.*) You sound like I'm just about ready to die. Who'd go with me? What I look like wandering 'round Europe by myself?

RUTH: Shoot—these here rich white women do it all the time. They don't think nothing of packing up they suitcases and piling on one of them big steamships and—swoosh!—they gone, child.

MAMA: Something always told me I wasn't no rich white woman.

RUTH: Well—what are you going to do with it then?

MAMA: I ain't rightly decided. (*Thinking. She speaks now with emphasis.*) Some of it got to be put away for Beneatha and her schoolin'—and ain't nothing going to touch that part of it. Nothing. (*She waits several seconds, trying to make up her mind about something, and looks at* Ruth *a little tentatively before going on.*) Been thinking that we maybe could meet the notes on a little old two-story somewhere, with a yard where Travis could play in the summertime, if we use part of the insurance for a down payment and everybody kind of pitch in. I could maybe take on a little day work again, few days a week—

RUTH: (*Studying her mother-in-law furtively and concentrating on her ironing, anxious to encourage without seeming to.*) Well, Lord knows, we've put enough rent into this here rat trap to pay for four houses by now . . .

MAMA: (*Looking up at the words "rat trap" and then looking around and leaning back and sighing—in a suddenly reflective mood—.*) "Rat trap"— yes, that's all it is. (*Smiling.*) I remember just as well the day me and Big Walter moved in here. Hadn't been married but two weeks and wasn't planning on living here no more than a year. (*She shakes her head at the dissolved dream.*) We was going to set away, little by little, don't you know, and buy a little place out in Morgan Park. We had even picked out the house. (*Chuckling a little.*) Looks right dumpy today. But Lord, child, you should know all the dreams I had 'bout buying that house and fixing it up and making me a little garden in the back—(*She waits and stops smiling.*) And didn't none of it happen. (*Dropping her hands in a futile gesture.*)

RUTH: (*Keeps her head down, ironing.*) Yes, life can be a barrel of disappointments, sometimes.

MAMA: Honey, Big Walter would come in here some nights back then and slump down on that couch there and just look at the rug, and look at me and look at the rug and then back at me—and I'd know he was down then . . . really down. (*After a second very long and thoughtful pause; she is seeing back to times that only she can see.*) And then, Lord, when I lost that baby—little Claude—I almost thought I was going to lose Big Walter too. Oh, that man grieved hisself! He was one man to love his children.

RUTH: Ain't nothin' can tear at you like losin' your baby.

MAMA: I guess that's how come that man finally worked hisself to death like he done. Like he was fighting his own war with this here world that took his baby from him.

RUTH: He sure was a fine man, all right. I always liked Mr. Younger.

MAMA: Crazy 'bout his children! God knows there was plenty wrong with Walter Younger—hard-headed, mean, kind of wild with women— plenty wrong with him. But he sure loved his children. Always wanted them to have something—be something. That's where Brother gets all these notions, I reckon. Big Walter used to say, he'd get right wet in the eyes sometimes, lean his head back with the water standing in his eyes and say, "Seem like God didn't see fit to give the black man nothing but dreams—but He did give us children to make them dreams seem worth while." (*She smiles.*) He could talk like that, don't you know.

RUTH: Yes, he sure could. He was a good man, Mr. Younger.

MAMA: Yes, a fine man—just couldn't never catch up with his dreams, that's all.

(Beneatha *comes in, brushing her hair and looking up to the ceiling, where the sound of a vacuum cleaner has started up.*)

BENEATHA: What could be so dirty on that woman's rugs that she has to vacuum them every single day?

RUTH: I wish certain young women 'round here who I could name would take inspiration about certain rugs in a certain apartment I could also mention.

BENEATHA: (*Shrugging.*) How much cleaning can a house need for Christ's sakes.

MAMA: (*Not liking the Lord's name used thus.*) Bennie!

RUTH: Just listen to her—just listen!

BENEATHA: Oh, God!

MAMA: If you use the Lord's name just one more time—

BENEATHA: (*A bit of a whine.*) Oh, Mama—

RUTH: Fresh—just fresh as salt, this girl!

BENEATHA: (*Drily.*) Well—if the salt loses its savor—

MAMA: Now that will do. I just ain't going to have you 'round here reciting the scriptures in vain—you hear me?

BENEATHA: How did I manage to get on everybody's wrong side by just walking into a room?

RUTH: If you weren't so fresh—

BENEATHA: Ruth, I'm twenty years old.

MAMA: What time you be home from school today?

BENEATHA: Kind of late. (*With enthusiasm.*) Madeline is going to start my guitar lessons today.

(Mama *and* Ruth *look up with the same expression.*)

MAMA: Your *what* kind of lessons?

BENEATHA: Guitar.

RUTH: Oh, Father!

MAMA: How come you done taken it in your mind to learn to play the guitar?

BENEATHA: I just want to, that's all.

MAMA: (*Smiling.*) Lord, child, don't you know what to do with yourself?

How long it going to be before you get tired of this now—like you got tired of that little play-acting group you joined last year? (*Looking at* Ruth.) And what was it the year before that?

RUTH: The horseback-riding club for which she bought that fifty-five-dollar riding habit that's been hanging in the closet ever since!

MAMA: (*To* Beneatha.) Why you got to flit so from one thing to another, baby?

BENEATHA: (*Sharply.*) I just want to learn to play the guitar. Is there anything wrong with that?

MAMA: Ain't nobody trying to stop you. I just wonders sometimes why you has to flit so from one thing to another all the time. You ain't never done nothing with all that camera equipment you brought home—

BENEATHA: I don't flit! I—I experiment with different forms of expression—

RUTH: Like riding a horse?

BENEATHA: People have to express themselves one way or another.

MAMA: What is it you want to express?

BENEATHA: (*Angrily.*) Me! (Mama *and* Ruth *look at each other and burst into raucous laughter.*) Don't worry—I don't expect you to understand.

MAMA: (*To change the subject.*) Who you going out with tomorrow night?

BENEATHA: (*With displeasure.*) George Murchison again.

MAMA: (*Pleased.*) Oh—you getting a little sweet on him?

RUTH: You ask me, this child ain't sweet on nobody but herself—(*Under-breath.*) Express herself! (*They laugh.*)

BENEATHA: Oh—I like George all right, Mama. I mean I like him enough to go out with him and stuff, but—

RUTH: (*For devilment.*) What does *and stuff* mean?

BENEATHA: Mind your own business.

MAMA: Stop picking at her now, Ruth. (*A thoughtful pause, and then a suspicious sudden look at her daughter as she turns in her chair for emphasis.*) What *does* it mean?

BENEATHA: (*Wearily.*) Oh, I just mean I couldn't ever really be serious about George. He's—he's so shallow.

RUTH: Shallow—what do you mean he's shallow? He's *Rich!*

MAMA: Hush, Ruth.

BENEATHA: I know he's rich. He knows he's rich, too.

RUTH: Well—what other qualities a man got to have to satisfy you, little girl?

BENEATHA: You wouldn't even begin to understand. Anybody who married Walter could not possibly understand.

MAMA: (*Outraged.*) What kind of way is that to talk about your brother?

BENEATHA: Brother is a flip—let's face it.

MAMA: (*To* Ruth, *helplessly.*) What's a flip?

RUTH: (*Glad to add kindling.*) She's saying he's crazy.

BENEATHA: Not crazy. Brother isn't really crazy yet—he—he's an elaborate neurotic.

MAMA: Hush your mouth!

BENEATHA: As for George. Well. George looks good—he's got a beautiful car and he takes me to nice places and, as my sister-in-law says, he is probably the richest boy I will ever get to know and I even like him sometimes—but if the Youngers are sitting around waiting to see if their little Bennie is going to tie up the family with the Murchisons, they are wasting their time.

RUTH: You mean you wouldn't marry George Murchison if he asked you someday? That pretty, rich thing? Honey, I knew you was odd—

BENEATHA: No I would not marry him if all I felt for him was what I feel now. Besides, George's family wouldn't really like it.

MAMA: Why not?

BENEATHA: Oh, Mama—The Murchisons are honest-to-God-real-*live*-rich colored people, and the only people in the world who are more snobbish than rich white people are rich colored people. I thought everbody knew that. I've met Mrs. Murchison. She's a scene!

MAMA: You must not dislike people 'cause they well off, honey.

BENEATHA: Why not? It makes just as much sense as disliking people 'cause they are poor, and lots of people do that.

RUTH: (*A wisdom-of-the-ages manner. To* Mama.) Well, she'll get over some of this—

BENEATHA: Get over it? What are you talking about, Ruth? Listen, I'm going to be a doctor. I'm not worried about who I'm going to marry yet—if I ever get married.

MAMA *and* RUTH: *If!*

MAMA: Now, Bennie—

Beneatha: Oh, I probably will . . . but first I'm going to be a doctor, and George, for one, still thinks that's pretty funny. I couldn't be bothered with that. I am going to be a doctor and everybody around here better understand that!

MAMA: (*Kindly.*) 'Course you going to be a doctor, honey, God willing.

BENEATHA: (*Drily.*) God hasn't got a thing to do with it.

MAMA: Beneatha—that just wasn't necessary.

BENEATHA: Well—neither is God. I get sick of hearing about God.

MAMA: Beneatha!

BENEATHA: I mean it! I'm just tired of hearing about God all the time. What has He got to do with anything? Does he pay tuition?

MAMA: You 'bout to get your fresh little jaw slapped!

RUTH: That's just what she needs, all right!

BENEATHA: Why? Why can't I say what I want to around here, like everybody else?

MAMA: It don't sound nice for a young girl to say things like that—you wasn't brought up that way. Me and your father went to trouble to get you and Brother to church every Sunday.

BENEATHA: Mama, you don't understand. It's all a matter of ideas, and God is just one idea I don't accept. It's not important. I am not going out and be immoral or commit crimes because I don't believe in God. I don't even think about it. It's just that I get tired of Him getting credit for all the things the human race achieves through its own stubborn effort. There simply is no blasted God—there is only man and it is he who makes miracles!

(Mama *absorbs this speech, studies her daughter and rises slowly and crosses to* Beneatha *and slaps her powerfully across the face. After, there is only silence and the daughter drops her eyes from her mother's face, and* Mama *is very tall before her.*)

MAMA: Now—you say after me, in my mother's house there is still God. (*There is a long pause and* Beneatha *stares at the floor wordlessly.* Mama *repeats the phrase with precision and cool emotion.*) In my mother's house there is still God.

BENEATHA: In my mother's house there is still God.

(A long pause.)

MAMA: (*Walking away from* Beneatha, *too disturbed for triumphant posture. Stopping and turning back to her daughter.*) There are some ideas we ain't going to have in this house. Not long as I am at the head of this family.

BENEATHA: Yes, ma'am.

(Mama walks out of the room.)

RUTH: (*Almost gently, with profound understanding.*) You think you a woman, Bennie—but you still a little girl. What you did was childish—so you got treated like a child.

BENEATHA: I see. (*Quietly.*) I also see that everybody thinks it's all right for Mama to be a tyrant. But all the tyranny in the world will never put a God in the heavens! (*She picks up her books and goes out.*)

RUTH: (*Goes to* Mama's *door.*) She said she was sorry.

MAMA: (*Coming out, going to her plant.*) They frightens me, Ruth. My children.

RUTH: You got good children, Lena. They just a little off sometimes—but they're good.

MAMA: No—there's something come down between me and them that don't let us understand each other and I don't know what it is. One done almost lost his mind thinking 'bout money all the time and the other done commence to talk about things I can't seem to understand in no form or fashion. What is it that's changing, Ruth?

RUTH: (*Soothingly, older than her years.*) Now . . . you taking it all too seriously. You just got strong-willed children and it takes a strong woman like you to keep 'em in hand.

MAMA: (*Looking at her plant and sprinkling a little water on it.*) They spirited all right, my children. Got to admit they got spirit—Bennie and Walter. Like this little old plant that ain't never had enough sunshine or nothing —and look at it . . .

(She has her back to Ruth, *who has had to stop ironing and lean against something and put the back of her hand to her forehead.)*

RUTH: (*Trying to keep* Mama *from noticing.*) You . . . sure . . . loves that little old thing don't you?

MAMA: Well, I always wanted me a garden like I used to see sometimes at the back of the houses down home. This plant is close as I ever got to having one. (*She looks out of the window as she replaces the plant.*) Lord, ain't nothing as dreary as the view from this window on a dreary day, is there? Why ain't you singing this morning, Ruth? Sing that "No Ways Tired." That song always lifts me up so—(*She turns at last to see that* Ruth *has slipped quietly into a chair, in a state of semiconsciousness.*) Ruth! Ruth honey—what's the matter with you . . . Ruth!

CURTAIN

Scene II.

(It is the following morning; a Saturday morning, and house cleaning is in progress at the Youngers. *Furniture has been shoved hither and yon and* Mama *is giving the kitchen-area walls a washing down.* Beneatha, *in dungarees, with a handkerchief tied around her face, is spraying insecticide into the cracks in the walls. As they work, the radio is on and a Southside disk-jockey program is inappropriately filling the house with a rather exotic saxophone blues.* Travis, *the sole idle one, is leaning on his arms, looking out of the window.)*

TRAVIS: Grandmama, that stuff Bennie is using smells awful. Can I go downstairs, please?

MAMA: Did you get all them chores done already? I ain't seen you doing much.

TRAVIS: Yes'm—finished early. Where did Mama go this morning?

MAMA: *(Looking at* Beneatha.) She had to go on a little errand.

TRAVIS: Where?

MAMA: To tend to her business.

TRAVIS: Can I go outside then?

MAMA: Oh, I guess so. You better stay right in front of the house, though . . . and keep a good lookout for the postman.

TRAVIS: Yes'm. *(He starts out and decides to give his* Aunt Beneatha *a good swat on the legs as he passes her.)* Leave them poor little old cockroaches alone, they ain't bothering you none. *(He runs as she swings the spray gun at him both viciously and playfully.* Walter *enters from the bedroom and goes to the phone.)*

MAMA: Look out there, girl, before you be spilling some of that stuff on that child!

TRAVIS: *(Teasing.)* That's right—look out now! *(He exits.)*

BENEATHA: *(Drily.)* I can't imagine that it would hurt him—it has never hurt the roaches.

MAMA: Well, little boys' hides ain't as tough as Southside roaches.

WALTER: *(Into phone.)* Hello—Let me talk to Willy Harris.

MAMA: You better get over there behind the bureau. I seen one marching out of there like Napoleon yesterday.

WALTER: Hello, Willy? It ain't come yet. It'll be here in a few minutes. Did the lawyer give you the papers?

BENEATHA: There's really only one way to get rid of them, Mama—

MAMA: How?

BENEATHA: Set fire to this building.

WALTER: Good. Good. I'll be right over.

BENEATHA: Where did Ruth go, Walter?

WALTER: I don't know. *(He exits abruptly.)*

BENEATHA: Mama, where did Ruth go?

MAMA: *(Looking at her with meaning.)* To the doctor, I think.

BENEATHA: The doctor? What's the matter? *(They exchange glances.)* You don't think—

MAMA: *(With her sense of drama.)* Now I ain't saying what I think. But I ain't never been wrong 'bout a woman neither.

(The phone rings.)

BENEATHA: *(At the phone.)* Hay-lo . . . *(Pause, and a moment of recognition.)* Well—when did you get back! . . . And how was it? . . . Of course I've missed you—in my way . . . This morning? No . . . house cleaning and all that and Mama hates it if I let people come over when the house is like this . . . You *have?* Well, that's different . . . What is it—Oh, what the hell, come on over . . . Right, see you then. (*She hangs up.*)

MAMA: (*Who has listened vigorously, as is her habit.*) Who is that you inviting over here with this house looking like this? You ain't got the pride you was born with!

BENEATHA: Asagai doesn't care how houses look, Mama—he's an intellectual.

MAMA: *Who?*

BENEATHA: Asagai—Joseph Asagai. He's an African boy I met on campus. He's been studying in Canada all summer.

MAMA: What's his name?

BENEATHA: Asagai, Joseph. Ah-sah-guy . . . He's from Nigeria.

MAMA: Oh, that's the little country that was founded by slaves way back . . .

BENEATHA: No, Mama—that's Liberia.

MAMA: I don't think I never met no African before.

BENEATHA: Well, do me a favor and don't ask him a whole lot of ignorant questions about Africans. I mean, do they wear clothes and all that—

MAMA: Well, now, I guess if you think we so ignorant 'round here maybe you shouldn't bring your friends here—

BENEATHA: It's just that people ask such crazy things. All anyone seems to know about when it comes to Africa is Tarzan—

MAMA: (*Indignantly.*) Why should I know anything about Africa?

BENEATHA: Why do you give money at church for the missionary work?

MAMA: Well, that's to help save people.

BENEATHEA: You mean save them from *heathenism*—

MAMA: (*Innocently.*) Yes.

BENEATHA: I'm afraid they need more salvation from the British and the French.

(Ruth *comes in forlornly and pulls off her coat with dejection. They both turn to look at her.*)

RUTH: (*Dispiritedly.*) Well, I guess from all the happy faces—everybody knows.

BENEATHA: You pregnant?

MAMA: Lord have mercy, I sure hope it's a little old girl. Travis ought to have a sister.

(Beneatha *and* Ruth *give her a hopeless look for this grandmotherly enthusiasm.*)

BENEATHA: How far along are you?

RUTH: Two months.

BENEATHA: Did you mean to? I mean did you plan it or was it an accident?

MAMA: What do you know about planning or not planning?

BENEATHA: Oh, Mama.

RUTH: (*Wearily.*) She's twenty years old, Lena.

BENEATHA: Did you plan it, Ruth?

RUTH: Mind your own business.

BENEATHA: It is my business—where is he going to live, on the *roof?*

(*There is silence following the remark as the three women react to the sense of it.*) Gee—I didn't mean that, Ruth, honest. Gee, I don't feel like that at all. I—I think it is wonderful.

RUTH: (*Dully.*) Wonderful.

BENEATHA: Yes—really.

MAMA: (*Looking at* Ruth, *worried.*) Doctor say everything going to be all right?

RUTH: (*Far away.*) Yes—she says everything is going to be fine . . .

MAMA: (*Immediately suspicious.*) "She"—What doctor you went to?

(*Ruth folds over, near hysteria.*)

MAMA: (*Worriedly hovering over* Ruth.) Ruth honey—what's the matter with you—you sick?

(*Ruth has her fists clenched on her thighs and is fighting hard to suppress a scream that seems to be rising in her.*)

BENEATHA: What's the matter with her, Mama?

MAMA: (*Working her fingers in* Ruth's *shoulder to relax her.*) She be all right. Women gets right depressed sometimes when they get her way. (*Speaking softly, expertly, rapidly.*) Now you just relax. That's right . . . just lean back, don't think 'bout nothing at all . . . nothing at all—

RUTH: I'm all right . . . (*The glassy-eyed look melts and then she collapses into a fit of heavy sobbing. The bell rings.*)

BENEATHA: Oh, my God—that must be Asagai.

MAMA: (*To* Ruth.) Come on now, honey. You need to lie down and rest awhile . . . then have some nice hot food.

(*They exit,* Ruth's *weight on her mother-in-law.* Beneatha, *herself profoundly disturbed, opens the door to admit a rather dramatic-looking young man with a large package.*)

ASAGAI: Hello, Alaiyo—

BENEATHA: (*Holding the door open and regarding him with pleasure.*) Hello . . . (*Long pause.*) Well—come in. And please excuse everything. My mother was very upset about my letting anyone come here with the place like this.

ASAGAI: (*Coming into the room.*) You look disturbed too . . . Is something wrong?

BENEATHA: (*Still at the door, absently.*) Yes . . . we've all got acute ghettoitis. (*She smiles and comes toward him, finding a cigarette and sitting.*) So—sit down! How was Canada?

ASAGAI: (*A sophisticate.*) Canadian.

BENEATHA: (*Looking at him.*) I'm very glad you are back.

ASAGAI: (*Looking back at her in turn.*) Are you really?

BENEATHA: Yes—very.

ASAGAI: Why—you were quite glad when I went away. What happened?

BENEATHA: You went away.

ASAGAI: Ahhhhhhhh.

BENEATHA: Before—you wanted to be so serious before there was time.

ASAGAI: How much time must there be before one knows what one feels?

BENEATHA: (*Stalling this particular conversation. Her hands pressed together, in a deliberately childish gesture.*) What did you bring me?

ASAGAI: (*Handing her the package.*) Open it and see.

BENEATHA: (*Eagerly opening the package and drawing out some records and the colorful robes of a Nigerian woman.*) Oh, Asagai! . . . You got them for me! . . . How beautiful . . . and the records too! (*She lifts out the robes and runs to the mirror with them and holds the drapery up in front of herself.*)

ASAGAI: (*Coming to her at the mirror.*) I shall have to teach you how to drape it properly. (*He flings the material about her for the moment and stands back to look at her.*) Ah—*Oh-pay-gay-day, oh-gbah-mu-shay.* (*A Yoruba exclamation for admiration.*) You wear it well . . . very well . . . mutilated hair and all.

BENEATHA: (*Turning suddenly.*) My hair—what's wrong with my hair?

ASAGAI: (*Shrugging.*) Were you born with it like that?

BENEATHA: (*Reaching up to touch it.*) No . . . of course not. (*She looks back to the mirror, disturbed.*)

ASAGAI: (*Smiling.*) How then?

BENEATHA: You know perfectly well how . . . as crinkly as yours . . . that's how.

ASAGAI: And it is ugly to you that way?

BENEATHA: (*Quickly.*) Oh, no—not ugly . . . (*More slowly, apologetically.*) But it's so hard to manage when it's, well—raw.

ASAGAI: And so to accommodate that—you mutilated it every week?

BENEATHA: It's not mutilation!

ASAGAI: (*Laughing aloud at her seriousness.*) Oh . . . please! I am only teasing you because you are so very serious about these things. (*He stands back from her and folds his arms across his chest as he watches her pulling at her hair and frowning in the mirror.*) Do you remember the first time you met me at school? . . . (*He laughs.*) You came up to me and you said—and I thought you were the most serious little thing I had ever seen—you said: (*He imitates her.*) "Mr. Asagai—I want very much to talk with you. About Africa. You see, Mr. Asagai, I am looking for my *identity!*" (*He laughs.*)

BENEATHA: (*Turning to him, not laughing.*) Yes—(*Her face is quizzical, profoundly disturbed.*)

ASAGAI: (*Still teasing and reaching out and taking her face in his hands and turning her profile to him.*) Well . . . it is true that this is not so much a profile of a Hollywood queen as perhaps a queen of the Nile—(*A mock dismissal of the importance of the question.*) But what does it matter? Assimilationism is so popular in your country.

BENEATHA: (*Wheeling, passionately, sharply.*) I am not an assimilationist!

ASAGAI: (*The protest hangs in the room for a moment and Asagai studies her, his laughter fading.*) Such a serious one. (*There is a pause.*) So—you like the robes? You must take excellent care of them—they are from my sister's personal wardrobe.

BENEATHA: (*With incredulity.*) You—you sent all the way home—for me?

ASAGAI: (*With charm.*) For you—I would do much more . . . Well, that is what I came for. I must go.

BENEATHA: Will you call me Monday?

ASAGAI: Yes . . . We have a great deal to talk about. I mean about identity and time and all that.

BENEATHA: Time?

ASAGAI: Yes. About how much time one needs to know what one feels.

BENEATHA: You never understood that there is more than one kind of feeling which can exist between a man and a woman—or, at least, there should be.

ASAGAI: (*Shaking his head negatively but gently.*) No. Between a man and a woman there need be only one kind of feeling. I have that for you . . . Now even . . . right this moment . . .

BENEATHA: I know—and by itself—it won't do. I can find that anywhere.

ASAGAI: For a woman it should be enough.

BENEATHA: I know—because that's what it says in all the novels that men write. But it isn't. Go ahead and laugh—but I'm not interested in being someone's little episode in America or—(*With feminine vengeance.*)—one of them! (Asagai *has burst into laughter again.*) That's funny as hell, huh!

ASAGAI: It's just that every American girl I have known has said that to me. White—black—in this you are all the same. And the same speech, too!

BENEATHA: (*Angrily.*) Yuk, yuk, yuk!

ASAGAI: It's how you can be sure that the world's most liberated women are not liberated at all. You all talk about it too much!

(Mama *enters and is immediately all social charm because of the presence of a guest.*)

BENEATHA: Oh—Mama—this is Mr. Asagai.

MAMA: How do you do?

ASAGAI: (*Total politeness to an elder.*) How do you do, Mrs. Younger. Please forgive me for coming at such an outrageous hour on a Saturday.

MAMA: Well, you are quite welcome. I just hope you understand that our house don't always look like this. (*Chatterish.*) You must come again. I would love to hear all about—(*Not sure of the name.*)—your country. I think it's so sad the way our American Negroes don't know nothing about Africa 'cept Tarzan and all that. And all that money they pour into these churches when they ought to be helping you people over there drive out them French and Englishmen done taken away your land. (*The mother flashes a slightly superior look at her daughter upon completion of the recitation.*)

ASAGAI: (*Taken aback by this sudden and acutely unrelated expression of sympathy.*) Yes . . . yes . . .

MAMA: (*Smiling at him suddenly and relaxing and looking him over.*) How many miles is it from here to where you come from?

ASAGAI: Many thousands.

MAMA: (*Looking at him as she would* Walter.) I bet you don't half look after yourself, being away from your mama either. I spec you better come 'round here from time to time and get yourself some decent home-cooked meals . . .

ASAGAI: (*Moved.*) Thank you. Thank you very much. (*They are all quiet, then—.*) Well . . . I must go. I will call you Monday, Alaiyo.

MAMA: What's that he call you?

ASAGAI: Oh—"Alaiyo," I hope you don't mind. It is what you would call a nickname, I think. It is a Yoruba word. I am a Yoruba.

MAMA: (*Looking at Beneatha.*) I—I thought he was from—

ASAGAI: (*Understanding.*) Nigeria is my country. Yoruba is my tribal origin—

BENETHA: You didn't tell us what Alaiyo means . . . for all I know, you might be calling me Little Idiot or something . . .

ASAGAI: Well . . . let me see . . . I do not know how just to explain it . . . The sense of a thing can be so different when it changes languages.

BENEATHA: You're evading.

ASAGAI: No—really it is difficult . . . (*Thinking.*) It means . . . it means One for Whom Bread—Food—Is Not Enough. (*He looks at her.*) Is that all right?

BENEATHA: (*Understanding, softly.*) Thank you.

MAMA: (*Looking from one to the other and not understanding any of it.*) Well . . . that's nice . . . You must come see us again—Mr.—

ASAGAI: Ah-sah-guy . . .

MAMA: Yes . . . Do come again.

ASAGAI: Good-bye. (*He exits.*)

MAMA: (*After him.*) Lord, that's a pretty thing just went out here! (*Insinuatingly, to her daughter.*) Yes, I guess I see why we done commence to get so interested in Africa 'round here. Missionaries my aunt Jenny! (*She exits.*)

BENEATHA: Oh, Mama! . . . (*She picks up the Nigerian dress and holds it up to her in front of the mirror again. She sets the headdress on haphazardly and then notices her hair again and clutches at it and then replaces the headdress and frowns at herself. Then she starts to wriggle in front of the mirror as she thinks a Nigerian woman might. Travis enters and regards her.*)

TRAVIS: You cracking up?

BENEATHA: Shut up. (*She pulls the headdress off and looks at herself in the mirror and clutches at her hair again and squinches her eyes as if trying to imagine something. Then, suddenly, she gets her raincoat and kerchief and hurriedly prepares for going out.*)

MAMA: (*Coming back into the room.*) She's resting now. Travis, baby, run next door and ask Miss Johnson to please let me have a little kitchen cleanser. This here can is empty as Jacob's kettle.

TRAVIS: I just came in.

MAMA: Do as you told. (*He exits and she looks at her daughter.*) Where you going?

BENEATHA: (*Halting at the door.*) To become a queen of the Nile!

(*She exits in a breathless blaze of glory. Ruth appears in the bedroom doorway.*)

MAMA: Who told you to get up?

RUTH: Ain't nothing wrong with me to be lying in no bed for. Where did Bennie go?

MAMA: (*Drumming her fingers.*) Far as I could make out—to Egypt. (*Ruth just looks at her.*) What time is it getting to?

RUTH: Ten twenty. And the mailman going to ring that bell this morning just like he done every morning for the last umpteen years.

(*Travis comes in with the cleanser can.*)

TRAVIS: She say to tell you that she don't have much.

MAMA: (*Angrily.*) Lord, some people I could name sure is tightfisted! (*Directing her grandson.*) Mark two cans of cleanser down on the list there. If she that hard up for kitchen cleanser, I sure don't want to forget to get her none!

RUTH: Lena—maybe the woman is just short on cleanser—

MAMA: (*Not listening.*) —Much baking powder as she done borrowed from me all these years, she could of done gone into the baking business!

(The bell sounds suddenly and sharply and all three are stunned—serious and silent—mid-speech. In spite of all the other conversations and distractions of the morning, this is what they have been waiting for, even Travis, who looks helplessly from his mother to his grandmother. Ruth is the first to come to life again.)

RUTH: *(To Travis.)* *Get down them steps, boy!*

(Travis snaps to life and flies out to get the mail.)

MAMA: *(Her eyes wide, her hand to her breast.)* You mean it done really come?
RUTH: *(Excited.)* Oh, Miss Lena!
MAMA: *(Collecting herself.)* Well . . . I don't know what we all so excited about 'round here for. We known it was coming for months.
RUTH: That's a whole lot different from having it come and being able to hold it in your hands . . . a piece of paper worth ten thousand dollars . . . *(Travis bursts back into the room. He holds the envelope high above his head, like a little dancer, his face is radiant and he is breathless. He moves to his grandmother with sudden slow ceremony and puts the envelope into her hands. She accepts it, and then merely holds it and looks at it.)* Come on! Open it . . . Lord have mercy, I wish Walter Lee was here!
TRAVIS: Open it, Grandmama!
MAMA: *(Staring at it.)* Now you all be quiet. It's just a check.
RUTH: Open it . . .
MAMA: *(Still staring at it.)* Now don't act silly . . . We ain't never been no people to act silly 'bout no money—
RUTH: *(Swiftly.)* We ain't never had none before—*open it!*

(Mama finally makes a good strong tear and pulls out the thin blue slice of paper and inspects it closely. The boy and his mother study it raptly over Mama's shoulders.)

MAMA: Travis! *(She is counting off with doubt.)* Is that the right number of zeros.
TRAVIS: Yes'm . . . ten thousand dollars. Gaalee, Grandmama, you rich.
MAMA: *(She holds the check away from her, still looking at it. Slowly her face sobers into a mask of unhappiness.)* Ten thousand dollars. *(She hands it to Ruth.)* Put it away somewhere, Ruth. *(She does not look at Ruth; her eyes seem to be seeing something somewhere very far off.)* Ten thousand dollars they give you. Ten thousand dollars.
TRAVIS: *(To his mother, sincerely.)* What's the matter with Grandmama —don't she want to be rich?
RUTH: *(Distractedly.)* You go on out and play now, baby. *(Travis exits. Mama starts wiping dishes absently, humming intently to herself. Ruth turns to her, with kind exasperation.)* You've gone and got yourself upset.
MAMA: *(Not looking at her.)* I spec if it wasn't for you all . . . I would just put that money away or give it to the church or something.
RUTH: Now what kind of talk is that. Mr. Younger would just be plain mad if he could hear you talking foolish like that.
MAMA: *(Stopping and staring off.)* Yes . . . he sure would. *(Sighing.)* We got enough to do with that money, all right. *(She halts then, and turns and looks at her daughter-in-law hard; Ruth avoids her eyes and Mama wipes

her hands with finality and starts to speak firmly to Ruth.) Where did you go today, girl?

RUTH: To the doctor.

MAMA: (*Impatiently.*) Now, Ruth ... you know better than that. Old Doctor Jones is strange enough in his way but there ain't nothing 'bout him make somebody slip and call him "she"—like you done this morning.

RUTH: Well, that's what happened—my tongue slipped.

MAMA: You went to see that woman, didn't you?

RUTH: (*Defensively, giving herself away.*) What woman you talking about?

MAMA: (*Angrily.*) That woman who—

(Walter *enters in great excitement.*)

WALTER: Did it come?

MAMA: (*Quietly.*) Can't you give people a Christian greeting before you start asking about money?

WALTER: (*To* Ruth.) Did it come? (Ruth *unfolds the check and lays it quietly before him, watching him intently with thoughts of her own.* Walter *sits down and grasps it close and counts off the zeros.*) Ten thousand dollars —(*He turns suddenly frantically to his mother and draws some papers out of his breast pocket.*) Mama—look. Old Willy Harris put everything on paper—

MAMA: Son—I think you ought to talk to your wife ... I'll go on out and leave you alone if you want—

WALTER: I can talk to her later—Mama, look—

MAMA: Son—

WALTER: WILL SOMEBODY PLEASE LISTEN TO ME TODAY!

MAMA: (*Quietly.*) I don't 'low no yellin' in this house, Walter Lee, and you know it—(Walter *stares at them in frustration and starts to speak several times.*) And there ain't going to be no investing in no liquor stores. I don't aim to have to speak on that again.

(*A long pause.*)

WALTER: Oh—so you don't aim to have to speak on that again? So *you* have decided ... (*Crumpling his papers.*) Well, *you* tell that to my boy tonight, when you put him to sleep on the living-room couch ... (*Turning to* Mama *and speaking directly to her.*) Yeah—and tell it to my wife, Mama, tomorrow when she has to go out of here to look after somebody else's kids. And tell it to *me*, Mama, every time we need a new pair of curtains and I have to watch *you* go out and work in somebody's kitchen. Yeah, you tell me then!

(Walter *starts out.*)

RUTH: Where you going?

WALTER: I'm going out!

RUTH: Where?

WALTER: Just out of this house somewhere—

RUTH: (*Getting her coat.*) I'll come too.

WALTER: I don't want you to come!

RUTH: I got something to talk to you about, Walter.

WALTER: That's too bad.

MAMA: (*Still quietly.*) Walter Lee—(*She waits and he finally turns and looks at her.*) Sit down.

WALTER: I'm a grown man, Mama.

MAMA: Ain't nobody said you wasn't grown. But you still in my house and my presence. And as long as you are—you'll talk to your wife civil. Now sit down.

RUTH: (*Suddenly.*) Oh, let him go on out and drink himself to death! He makes me sick to my stomach! (*She flings her coat against him.*)

WALTER: (*Violently.*) And you turn mine too, baby! (Ruth *goes into their bedroom and slams the door behind her.*) That was my greatest mistake—

MAMA: (*Still quietly.*) Walter, what is the matter with you?

WALTER: Matter with me? Ain't nothing the matter with *me!*

MAMA: Yes there is. Something eating you up like a crazy man. Something more than me not giving you this money. The past few years I been watching it happen to you. You get all nervous acting and kind of wild in the eyes—(Walter *jumps up impatiently at her words.*) I said sit there now, I'm talking to you!

WALTER: Mama—I don't need no nagging at me today.

MAMA: Seem like you getting to a place where you always tied up in some kind of knot about something. But if anybody ask you 'bout it you just yell at 'em and bust out the house and go out and drink somewheres. Walter Lee, people can't live with that. Ruth's a good, patient girl in her way—but you getting to be too much. Boy, don't make the mistake of driving that girl away from you.

WALTER: Why—what she do for me?

MAMA: She loves you.

WALTER: Mama—I'm going out. I want to go off somewhere and be by myself for a while.

MAMA: I'm sorry 'bout your liquor store, son. It just wasn't the thing for us to do. That's what I want to tell you about—

WALTER: I got to go out, Mama— (*He rises.*)

MAMA: It's dangerous, son.

WALTER: What's dangerous?

MAMA: When a man goes outside his home to look for peace.

WALTER: (*Beseechingly.*) Then why can't there never be no peace in this house then?

MAMA: You done found it in some other house?

WALTER: No—there ain't no woman! Why do women always think there's a woman somewhere when a man gets restless. (*Coming to her.*) Mama—Mama—I want so many things . . .

MAMA: Yes, son—

WALTER: I want so many things that they are driving me kind of crazy . . . Mama—look at me.

MAMA: I'm looking at you. You a good-looking boy. You got a job, a nice wife, a fine boy and—

WALTER: A job. (*Looks at her.*) Mama, a job? I open and close car doors all day long. I drive a man around in his limousine and I say, "Yes, sir; no, sir; very good, sir; shall I take the Drive, sir?" Mama, that ain't no kind of job . . . that ain't nothing at all. (*Very quietly.*) Mama, I don't know if I can make you understand.

MAMA: Understand what, baby?

WALTER: (*Quietly.*) Sometimes it's like I can see the future stretched out in front of me—just plain as day. The future, Mama. Hanging over there at the edge of my days. Just waiting for me—a big, looming blank space—full of *nothing*. Just waiting for *me*. (*Pause.*) Mama—sometimes when I'm downtown and I pass them cool, quiet-looking restaurants where them white boys are sitting back and talking 'bout things . . . sitting there turning deals worth millions of dollars . . . sometimes I see guys don't look much older than me—

MAMA: Son—how come you talk so much 'bout money?

WALTER: (*With immense passion.*) Because it is life, Mama!

MAMA: (*Quietly.*) Oh—(*Very quietly.*) So now it's life. Money is life. Once upon a time freedom used to be life—now it's money. I guess the world really do change . . .

WALTER: No—it was always money, Mama. We just didn't know about it.

MAMA: No . . . something has changed. (*She looks at him.*) You something new, boy. In my time we was worried about not being lynched and getting to the North if we could and how to stay alive and still have a pinch of dignity too . . . Now here come you and Beneatha—talking 'bout things we ain't never even thought about hardly, me and your daddy. You ain't satisfied or proud of nothing we done. I mean that you had a home; that we kept you out of trouble till you was grown; that you don't have to ride to work on the back of nobody's streetcar— You my children—but how different we done become.

WALTER: You just don't understand, Mama, you just don't understand.

MAMA: Son—do you know your wife is expecting another baby? (Walter *stands, stunned, and absorbs what his mother has said.*) That's what she wanted to talk to you about. (Walter *sinks down into a chair.*) This ain't for me to be telling—but you ought to know. (*She waits.*) I think Ruth is thinking 'bout getting rid of that child.

WALTER: (*Slowly understanding.*) No—no—Ruth wouldn't do that.

MAMA: When the world gets ugly enough—a woman will do anything for her family. *The part that's already living.*

WALTER: You don't know Ruth, Mama, if you think she would do that.

(Ruth *opens the bedroom door and stands there a little limp.*)

RUTH: (*Beaten.*) Yes I would too, Walter. (*Pause.*) I gave her a five-dollar down payment.

(*There is total silence as the man stares at his wife and the mother stares at her son.*)

MAMA: (*Presently.*) Well—(*Tightly.*) Well—son, I'm waiting to hear you say something . . . I'm waiting to hear how you be your father's son. Be the man he was . . . (*Pause.*) Your wife say she going to destroy your child. And I'm waiting to hear you talk like him and say we a people who give children life, not who destroys them—(*She rises.*) I'm waiting to see you stand up and look like your daddy and say we done give up one baby to poverty and that we ain't going to give up nary another one . . . I'm waiting.

WALTER: Ruth—

MAMA: If you a son of mine, tell her! (Walter *turns, looks at her and can say nothing. She continues, bitterly.*) You . . . you are a disgrace to your father's memory. Somebody get me my hat.

CURTAIN

ACT II.

SCENE I

(Time: Later the same day.

At rise: Ruth *is ironing again. She has the radio going. Presently* Beneatha's *bedroom door opens and Ruth's mouth falls and she puts down the iron in fascination.)*

RUTH: What have we got on tonight!

BENEATHA: *(Emerging grandly from the doorway so that we can see her thoroughly robed in the costume* Asagai *brought.)* You are looking at what a well-dressed Nigerian woman wears—*(She parades for* Ruth, *her hair completely hidden by the headdress; she is coquettishly fanning herself with an ornate oriental fan, mistakenly more like Butterfly than any Nigerian that ever was.)* Isn't it beautiful? *(She promenades to the radio and, with an arrogant flourish, turns off the good loud blues that is playing.)* Enough of this assimilationist junk! (Ruth *follows her with her eyes as she goes to the phonograph and puts on a record and turns and waits ceremoniously for the music to come up. Then, with a shout—.)* OCOMOGOSIAY!

(Ruth jumps. The music comes up, a lovely Nigerian melody. Beneatha *listens, enraptured, her eyes far away—"back to the past." She begins to dance.* Ruth *is dumfounded.)*

RUTH: What kind of dance is that?

BENEATHA: A folk dance.

RUTH: *(Pearl Bailey.)* What kind of folks do that, honey?

BENEATHA: It's from Nigeria. It's a dance of welcome.

RUTH: Who you welcoming?

BENEATHA: The men back to the village.

RUTH: Where they been?

BENEATHA: How should I know—out hunting or something. Anyway, they are coming back now . . .

RUTH: Well, that's good.

BENEATHA: *(With the record.)*
    Alundi, alundi
    Alundi alunya
    Jop pu a jeepua
    Ang gu soooooooooo

    Ai yai yae . . .
    Ayehaye—alundi . . .

(Walter comes in during this performance; he has obviously been drinking. He leans against the door heavily and watches his sister, at first with distaste. Then his eyes look off—"back to the past"—as he lifts both his fists to the roof, screaming.)

WALTER: YEAH . . . AND ETHIOPIA STRETCH FORTH HER HANDS AGAIN! . . .

RUTH: *(Drily, looking at him.)* Yes—and Africa sure is claiming her own tonight. *(She gives them both up and starts ironing again.)*

WALTER: (*All in a drunken, dramatic shout.*) Shut up! . . . I'm digging them drums . . . them drums move me! . . . (*He makes his weaving way to his wife's face and leans in close to her.*) In my *heart of hearts*—(*He thumps his chest.*)—I am much warrior!

RUTH: (*Without even looking up.*) In your heart of hearts you are much drunkard.

WALTER: (*Coming away from her and starting to wander around the room, shouting.*) Me and Jomo . . . (*Intently, in his sister's face. She has stopped dancing to watch him in this unknown mood.*) That's my man, Kenyatta. (*Shouting and thumping his chest.*) FLAMING SPEAR! HOT DAMN! (*He is suddenly in possession of an imaginary spear and actively spearing enemies all over the room.*) OCOMOGOSIAY . . . THE LION IS WAKING . . . OWIMOWEH! (*He pulls his shirt open and leaps up on a table and gestures with his spear. The bell rings. Ruth goes to answer.*)

BENEATHA: (*To encourage Walter, thoroughly caught up with this side of him.*) OCOMOGOSIAY, FLAMING SPEAR!

WALTER: (*On the table, very far gone, his eyes pure glass sheets. He sees what we cannot, that he is a leader of his people, a great chief, a descendant of Chaka, and that the hour to march has come.*) Listen, my black brothers—

BENEATHA: OCOMOGOSIAY!

WALTER: —Do you hear the waters rushing against the shores of the coastlands—

BENEATHA: OCOMOGOSIAY!

WALTER: —Do you hear the screeching of the cocks in yonder hills beyond where the chiefs meet in council for the coming of the mighty war—

BENEATHA: OCOMOGOSIAY!

WALTER: —Do you hear the beating of the wings of the birds flying low over the mountains and the low places of our land—

(*Ruth opens the door. George Murchison enters.*)

BENEATHA: OCOMOGOSIAY!

WALTER: —Do you hear the singing of the women, singing the war songs of our fathers to the babies in the great houses . . . singing the sweet war songs? OH, DO YOU HEAR, MY BLACK BROTHERS!

BENEATHA: (*Completely gone.*) We hear you, Flaming Spear—

WALTER: Telling us to prepare for the greatness of the time—(*To George.*) Black Brother! (*He extends his hand for the fraternal clasp.*)

GEORGE: Black Brother, hell!

RUTH: (*Having had enough, and embarrassed for the family.*) Beneatha, you got company—what's the matter with you? Walter Lee Younger, get down off that table and stop acting like a fool . . .

(*Walter comes down off the table suddenly and makes a quick exit to the bathroom.*)

RUTH: He's had a little to drink . . . I don't know what her excuse is.

GEORGE: (*To Beneatha.*) Look honey, we're going *to* the theatre—we're not going to be *in* it . . . so go change, huh?

RUTH: You expect this boy to go out with you looking like that?

BENEATHA: (*Looking at* George.) That's up to George. If he's ashamed of his heritage—

GEORGE: Oh, don't be so proud of yourself, Bennie—just because you look eccentric.

BENEATHA: How can something that's natural be eccentric?

GEORGE: That's what being eccentric means—being natural. Get dressed.

BENEATHA: I don't like that, George.

RUTH: Why must you and your brother make an argument out of everything people say?

BENEATHA: Because I hate assimilationist Negroes!

RUTH: Will somebody please tell me what assimila-who-ever means!

GEORGE: Oh, it's just a college girl's way of calling people Uncle Toms—but that isn't what it means at all.

RUTH: Well, what does it mean?

BENEATHA: (*Cutting* George *off and staring at him as she replies to* Ruth.) It means someone who is willing to give up his own culture and submerge himself completely in the dominant, and in this case, *oppressive* culture!

GEORGE: Oh, dear, dear, dear! Here we go! A lecture on the African past! On our Great West African Heritage! In one second we will hear all about the great Ashanti enpires; the great Songhay civilizations; and the great sculpture of Bénin—and then some poetry in the Bantu—and the whole monologue will end with the word *heritage!* (*Nastily.*) Let's face it, baby, your heritage is nothing but a bunch of raggedy-assed spirituals and some grass huts!

BENEATHA: *Grass huts!* (Ruth *crosses to her and forcibly pushes her toward the bedroom.*) See there . . . you are standing there in your splendid ignorance talking about people who were the first to smelt iron on the face of the earth! (Ruth *is pushing her through the door.*) The Ashanti were performing surgical operations when the English—(Ruth *pulls the door to, with* Beneatha *on the other side, and smiles graciously at* George. Beneatha *opens the door and shouts the end of the sentence defiantly at* George.)— were still tattooing themselves with blue dragons . . . (*She goes back inside.*)

RUTH: Have a seat, George. (*They both sit.* Ruth *folds her hands rather primly on her lap, determined to demonstrate the civilization of the family.*) Warm, ain't it? I mean for September (*Pause.*) Just like they always say about Chicago weather: If it's too hot or cold for you, just wait a minute and it'll change. (*She smiles happily at this clichés.*) Everybody say it's got to do with them bombs and things they keep setting off. (*Pause.*) Would you like a nice cold beer?

GEORGE: No, thank you. I don't care for beer. (*He looks at his watch.*) I hope she hurries up.

RUTH: What time is the show?

GEORGE: It's an eight-thirty curtain. That's just Chicago, though. In New York standard curtain time is eight forty. (*He is rather proud of this knowledge.*)

RUTH: (*Properly appreciating it.*) You get to New York a lot?

GEORGE: (*Offhand.*) Few times a year.

RUTH: Oh—that's nice. I've never been to New York.

(Walter *enters. We feel he has relieved himself, but the edge of unreality is still with him.*)

WALTER: New York ain't got nothing Chicago ain't. Just a bunch of hustling people all squeezed up together—being "Eastern." (*He turns his face into a screw of displeasure.*)

GEORGE: Oh—you've been?
WALTER: *Plenty* of times.
RUTH: (*Shocked at the lie.*) Walter Lee Younger!
WALTER: (*Staring her down.*) Plenty! (*Pause.*) What we got to drink in this house? Why don't you offer this man some refreshment. (*To* George.) They don't know how to entertain people in this house, man.
GEORGE: Thank you—I don't really care for anything.
WALTER: (*Feeling his head; sobriety coming.*) Where's Mama?
RUTH: She ain't come back yet.
WALTER: (*Looking* Murchison *over from head to toe, scrutinizing his carefully casual tweed sports jacket over cashmere V-neck sweater over soft eyelet shirt and tie, and soft slacks, finished off with white buckskin shoes.*) Why all you college boys wear them fairyish-looking white shoes?
RUTH: Walter Lee!

(*George Murchison* ignores the remark.)

WALTER: (*To* Ruth.) Well, they look crazy as hell—white shoes, cold as it is.
RUTH: (*Crushed.*) You have to excuse him—
WALTER: No he don't! Excuse me for what? What you always excusing me for! I'll excuse myself when I needs to be excused! (*A pause.*) They look as funny as them black knee socks Beneatha wears out of here all the time.
RUTH: It's the college *style,* Walter.
WALTER: Style, hell. She looks like she got burnt legs or something!
RUTH: Oh, Walter—
WALTER: (*An irritable mimic.*) Oh, Walter! Oh, Walter! (*To* Murchison.) How's your old man making out? I understand you all going to buy that big hotel on the Drive? (*He finds a beer in the refrigerator, wanders over to* Murchison, *sipping and wiping his lips with the back of his hand, and straddling a chair backwards to talk to the other man.*) Shrewd move. Your old man is all right, man. (*Tapping his head and half winking for emphasis.*) I mean he knows how to operate. I mean he thinks *big,* you know what I mean, I mean for a *home,* you know? But I think he's kind of running out of ideas now. I'd like to talk to him. Listen, man, I got some plans that could turn this city upside down' I mean I think like he does. *Big.* Invest big, gamble big, hell, lose *big* if you have to, you know what I mean. I'ts hard to find a man on this whole Southside who understands my kind of thinking —you dig? (*He scrutinizes* Murchison *again, drinks his beer, squints his eyes and leans in close, confidential, man to man.*) Me and you ought to sit down and talk sometimes, man. Man, I got me some ideas . . .
MURCHISON: (*With boredom.*) Yeah—sometimes we'll have to do that, Walter.
WALTER: (*Understanding the indifference, and offended.*) Yeah—well, when you get the time, man. I know you a busy little boy.
RUTH: Walter, please—
WALTER: (*Bitterly, hurt.*) I know ain't nothing in this world as busy as you colored college boys with your fraternity pins and white shoes . . .
RUTH: (*Covering her face with humiliation.*) Oh, Walter Lee—
WALTER: I see you all all the time—with the books, tucked under your arms—going to your (*British A—a mimic.*) "clahsses." And for what! What the hell you learning over there? Filling up your heads—(*Counting off on his fingers.*)—with the sociology and the psychology—but they teaching you

how to be a man? How to take over and run the world? They teaching you how to run a rubber plantation or a steel mill? Naw—just to talk proper and read books and wear white shoes . . .

GEORGE: (*Looking at him with distaste, a little above it all.*) You're all wacked up with bitterness, man.

WALTER: (*Intently, almost quietly, between the teeth, glaring at the boy.*) And you—ain't you bitter, man? Ain't you just about had it yet? Don't you see no stars gleaming that you can't reach out and grab? You happy?—You contented son-of-a-bitch—you happy? You got it made? Bitter? Man, I'm a volcano. Bitter? Here I am a giant—surrounded by ants! Ants who can't even understand what it is the giant is talking about.

RUTH: (*Passionately and suddenly.*) Oh, Walter—ain't you with nobody!

WALTER: (*Violently.*) No! 'Cause ain't nobody with me! Not even my own mother!

RUTH: Walter, that's a terrible thing to say!

(Beneatha *enters, dressed for the evening in a cocktail dress and earrings.*)

GEORGE: Well—hey, you look great.

BENEATHA: Let's go, George. See you all later.

RUTH: Have a nice time.

GEORGE: Thanks. Good night. (*To* Walter, *sarcastically.*) Good night, Prometheus. (Beneatha *and* George *exit.*)

WALTER: (*To* Ruth.) Who is Prometheus?

RUTH: I don't know. Don't worry about it.

WALTER: (*In fury, pointing after* George.) See there—they get to a point where they can't insult you man to men—they got to go talk about something ain't nobody never heard of!

RUTH: How do you know it was an insult? (*To humor him.*) Maybe Prometheus is a nice fellow.

WALTER: Prometheus! I bet there ain't even no such thing! I bet that simple-minded clown—

RUTH: Walter—(*She stops what she is doing and looks at him.*)

WALTER: (*Yelling.*) Don't start!

RUTH: Start what?

WALTER: Your nagging! Where was I? Who was I with? How much money did I spend?

RUTH: (*Plaintively.*) Walter Lee—why don't we just try to talk about it . . .

WALTER: (*Not listening.*) I been out talking with people who understand me. People who care about the things I got on my mind.

RUTH: (*Wearily.*) I guess that means people like Willy Harris.

WALTER: Yes, people like Willy Harris.

RUTH: (*With a sudden flash of impatience.*) Why don't you all just hurry up and go into the banking business and stop talking about it!

WALTER: Why? You want to know why? 'Cause we all tied up in a race of people that don't know how to do nothing but moan, pray and have babies! (*The line is too bitter even for him and he looks at her and sits down.*)

RUTH: Oh, Walter . . . (*Softly.*) Honey, why can't you stop fighting me?

WALTER: (*Without thinking.*) Who's fighting you? Who even cares about you? (*This line begins the retardation of his mood.*)

RUTH: Well—(*She waits a long time, and then with resignation starts to put away her things.*) I guess I might as well go on to bed . . . (*More or less to herself.*) I don't know where we lost it . . . but we have . . . (*Then, to him.*) I—I'm sorry about this new baby, Walter. I guess maybe I better go on and do what I started . . . I guess I just didn't realize how bad things was with us . . . I guess I just didn't really realize—(*She starts out to the bedroom and stops.*) You want some hot milk?

WALTER: Hot milk?

RUTH: Yes—hot milk.

WALTER: Why hot milk?

RUTH: 'Cause after all that liquor you come home with you ought to have something hot in your stomach.

WALTER: I don't want no milk.

RUTH: You want some coffee then?

WALTER: No, I don't want no coffee. I don't want nothing hot to drink. (*Almost plaintively.*) Why you always trying to give me something to eat?

RUTH: (*Standing and looking at him helplessly.*) What else can I give you, Walter Lee Younger?

(*She stands and looks at him and presently turns to go out again. He lifts his head and watches her going away from him in a new mood which began to emerge when he asked her "Who cares about you?")*

WALTER: It's been rough, ain't 'it, baby? (*She hears and stops but does not turn around and he continues to her back.*) I guess between two people there ain't never as much understood as folks generally thinks there is. I mean like between me and you—(*She turns to face him.*) How we gets to the place where we scared to talk softness to each other. (*He waits, thinking hard himself.*) Why you think it got to be like that? (*He is thoughtful, almost as a child would be.*) Ruth, what is it gets into people ought to be close?

RUTH: I don't know, honey. I think about it a lot.

WALTER: On account of you and me, you mean? The way things are with us. The way something done come down between us.

RUTH: There ain't much between us, Walter . . . Not when you come to me and try to talk to me. Try to be with me . . . a little even.

WALTER: (*Total honesty.*) Sometimes . . . sometimes . . . I don't even know how to try.

RUTH: Walter—

WALTER: Yes?

RUTH: (*Coming to him, gently and with misgiving, but coming to him.*) Honey . . . life don't have to be like this. I mean sometimes people can do things so that things are better . . . You remember how we used to talk when Travis was born . . . about the way we were going to live . . . the kind of house . . . (*She is stroking his head.*) Well, it's all starting to slip away from us . . .

(*Mama enters, and Walter jumps up and shouts at her.*)

WALTER: Mama, where have you been?

MAMA: My—them steps is longer than they used to be. Whew! (*She sits down and ignores him.*) How you feeling this evening, Ruth?

(*Ruth shrugs, disturbed some at having been prematurely interrupted and watching her husband knowingly.*)

WALTER: Mama, where have you been all day?

MAMA: (*Still ignoring him and leaning on the table and changing to more comfortable shoes.*) Where's Travis?

RUTH: I let him go out earlier and he ain't come back yet. Boy, is he going to get it!

WALTER: Mama!

MAMA: (*As if she has heard him for the first time.*) Yes, son?

WALTER: Where did you go this afternoon?

MAMA: I went downtown to tend to some business that I had to tend to.

WALTER: What kind of business?

MAMA: You know better than to question me like a child, Brother.

WALTER: (*Rising and bending over the table.*) Where were you, Mama? (*Bringing his fists down and shouting.*) Mama, you didn't go do something with that insurance money, something crazy?

(*The front door opens slowly, interrupting him, and* Travis *peeks his head in, less than hopefully.*)

TRAVIS: (*To his mother.*) Mama, I—

RUTH: "Mama I" nothing! You're going to get it, boy! Get on in that bedroom and get yourself ready!

TRAVIS: But I—

MAMA: Why don't you all never let the child explain hisself.

RUTH: Keep out of it now, Lena.

(*Mama clamps her lips together, and* Ruth *advances toward her son menacingly.*)

RUTH: A thousand times I have told you not to go off like that—

MAMA: (*Holding out her arms to her grandson.*) Well—at least let me tell him something. I want him to be the first one to hear . . . Come here, Travis. (*The boy obeys, gladly.*) Travis—(*She takes him by the shoulder and looks into his face.*)—you know that money we got in the mail this morning?

TRAVIS: Yes'm—

MAMA: Well—what you think your grandmama gone and done with that money?

TRAVIS: I don't know, Grandmama.

MAMA: (*Putting her finger on his nose for emphasis.*) She went out and she bought you a house! (*The explosion comes from* Walter *at the end of the revelation and he jumps up and turns away from all of them in a fury.* Mama *continues, to* Travis.) You glad about the house? It's going to be yours when you get to be a man.

TRAVIS: Yeah—I always wanted to live in a house.

MAMA: All right, gimme some sugar then—(Travis *puts his arms around her neck as she watches her son over the boy's shoulder. Then, to* Travis, *after the embrace.*) Now when you say your prayers tonight, you thank God and your grandfather—'cause it was him who give you the house—in a way.

RUTH: (*Taking the boy from* Mama *and pushing him toward the bedroom.*) Now you get out of here and get ready for your beating.

TRAVIS: Aw, Mama—

RUTH: Get on in there—(*Closing the door behind him and turning radiantly to her mother-in-law.*) So you went and did it!

MAMA: (*Quietly, looking at her son with pain.*) Yes, I did.

RUTH: (*Raising both arms classically.*) *Praise God!* (*Looks at* Walter *a moment, who says nothing. She crosses rapidly to her husband.*) Please, honey—let me be glad . . . you be glad too. (*She has laid her hands on his shoulders, but he shakes himself free of her roughly, without turning to face her.*) Oh, Walter . . . a home . . . *a home.* (*She comes back to* Mama.) Well—where is it? How big is it? How much it going to cost?

MAMA: Well—

RUTH: When we moving?

MAMA: (*Smiling at her.*) First of the month.

RUTH: (*Throwing back her head with jubilance.*) *Praise God!*

MAMA: (*Tentatively, still looking at her son's back turned against her and* Ruth.) It's—it's a nice house too . . . (*She cannot help speaking directly to him. An imploring quality in her voice, her manner, makes her almost like a girl now.*) Three bedrooms—nice big one for you and Ruth. . . . Me and Beneatha still have to share our room, but Travis have one of his own—and (*With difficulty.*) I figure if the—new baby—is a boy, we could get one of them double-decker outfits . . . And there's a yard with a little patch of dirt where I could maybe get to grow me a few flowers . . . And a nice big basement . . .

RUTH: Walter honey, be glad—

MAMA: (*Still to his back, fingering things on the table.*) 'Course I don't want to make it sound fancier than it is . . . It's just a plain little old house—but it's made good and solid—and it will be *ours.* Walter Lee—it makes a difference in a man, when he can walk on floors that belong to *him* . . .

RUTH: Where is it?

MAMA: (*Frightened at this telling.*) Well—well—it's out there in Clybourne Park—

(Ruth's *radiance fades abruptly, and* Walter *finally turns slowly to face his mother with incredulity and hostility.*)

RUTH: Where?

MAMA: (*Matter-of-factly.*) Four o six Clybourne Street, Clybourne Park.

RUTH: Clybourne Park? Mama, there ain't no colored people living in Clybourne Park.

MAMA: (*Almost idiotically.*) Well, I guess there's going to be some now.

WALTER: (*Bitterly.*) So that's the peace and comfort you went out and bought for us today!

MAMA: (*Raising her eyes to meet his finally.*) Son—I just tried to find the nicest place for the least amount of money for my family.

RUTH: (*Trying to recover from the shock.*) Well—well—'course I ain't one never been 'fraid of no crackers, mind you—but—well, wasn't there no other houses nowhere?

MAMA: Them houses they put up for colored in them areas way out all seem to cost twice as much as other houses. I did the best I could.

RUTH: (*Struck senseless with the news, in its various degrees of goodness and trouble, she sits a moment, her fists propping her chin in thought, and then she starts to rise, bringing her fists down with vigor, the radiance spreading from cheek to cheek again.*) Well—well!—All I can say is—if this is my time in life—*my time*—to say good-bye—(*And she builds with momentum as she starts to circle the room with an exuberant, almost tearfully happy release.*)—to these Goddamned cracking walls!—(*She pounds the walls.*)—and these marching roaches!—(*She wipes at an imaginary army of marching roaches.*)—and *this* cramped little closet which ain't now or never was no kitchen! . . . then I say it loud and good, *Hallelujah! and good-bye misery . . . I don't never want to see your ugly face again!* (*She laughs joyously, having practically destroyed the apartment, and flings her arms up and lets them come down happily, slowly, reflectively, over her abdomen, aware for the first time perhaps that the life therein pulses with happiness and not despair.*) Lena?

MAMA: (*Moved, watching her happiness.*) Yes, honey?

RUTH: (*Looking off.*) Is there—is there a whole lot of sunlight?

MAMA: (*Understanding.*) Yes, child, there's a whole lot of sunlight.

(*Long pause.*)

RUTH: (*Collecting herself and going to the door of the room* Travis *is in.*) Well—I guess I better see 'bout Travis. (*To* Mama.) Lord, I sure don't feel like whipping nobody today! (*She exits.*)

MAMA: (*The mother and son are left alone now and the mother waits a long time, considering deeply, before she speaks.*) Son—you—you understand what I done, don't you? (Walter *is silent and sullen.*) I—I just seen my family falling apart today . . . just falling to pieces in front of my eyes . . . We couldn't of gone on like we was today. We was going backwards 'stead of forwards—talking 'bout killing babies and wishing each other was dead . . . When it gets like that in life—you just got to do something different, push on out and do something bigger . . . (*She waits.*) I wish you say something, son . . . I wish you'd say how deep inside you you think I done the right thing—

WALTER: (*Crossing slowly to his bedroom door and finally turning there and speaking measuredly.*) What you need me to say you done right for? *You* the head of this family. You run our lives like you want to. It was your money and you did what you wanted with it. So what you need for me to say it was all right for? (*Bitterly, to hurt her as deeply as he knows is possible.*) So you butchered up a dream of mine—you—who always talking 'bout your children's dreams . . .

MAMA: Walter Lee—

(*He just closes the door behind him.* Mama *sits alone, thinking heavily.*)

CURTAIN

SCENE II.

(*Time: Friday night. A few weeks later.*
    At rise: Packing crates mark the intention of the family to move. Beneatha *and* George *come in, presumably from an evening out again.*)

GEORGE: O.K. . . . O.K., whatever you say . . . (*They both sit on the couch. He tries to kiss her. She moves away.*) Look, we've had a nice evening; let's not spoil it, huh? . . . (*He again turns her head and tries to nuzzle in and she turns away from him, not with distaste but with momentary lack of interest; in a mood to pursue what they were talking about.*)

BENEATHA: I'm *trying* to talk to you.

GEORGE: We always talk.

BENEATHA: Yes—and I love to talk.

GEORGE: (*Exasperated; rising.*) I know it and I don't mind it sometimes . . .
I want you to cut it out, see—The moody stuff, I mean. I don't like it. You're
a nice-looking girl . . . all over. That's all you need, honey, forget the atmosphere. Guys aren't going to go for the atmosphere—they're going to go for
what they see. Be glad for that. Drop the Garbo routine. It doesn't go with
you. As for myself, I want a nice—(*Groping.*)—simple (*Thoughtfully.*)—
sophisticated girl . . . not a poet—O.K.?

(*She rebuffs him again and he starts to leave.*)

BENEATHA: Why are you angry?
GEORGE: Because this is stupid! I don't go out with you to discuss the
nature of "quiet desperation" or to hear all about your thoughts—because
the world will go on thinking what it thinks regardless—
BENEATHA: Then why read books? Why go to school?
GEORGE: (*With artificial patience, counting on his fingers.*) It's simple.
You read books—to learn facts—to get grades—to pass the course—to get a
degree. That's all—it has nothing to do with thoughts.

(*A long pause.*)

BENEATHA: I see. (*A longer pause as she looks at him.*) Good night, George.

(George *looks at her a little oddly, and starts to exit. He meets* Mama
coming in.)

GEORGE: Oh—hello, Mrs. Younger.
MAMA: Hello, George, how you feeling?
GEORGE: Fine—fine, how are you?
MAMA: Oh, a little tired. You know them steps can get you after a day's
work. You all have a nice time tonight?
GEORGE: Yes—a fine time. Well, good night.
MAMA: Good night. (*He exits.* Mama *closes the door behind her.*) Hello,
honey. What you sitting like that for?
BENEATHA: I'm just sitting.
MAMA: Didn't you have a nice time?
BENEATHA: No.
MAMA: No? What's the matter?
BENEATHA: Mama, George is a fool—honest. (*She rises.*)
MAMA: (*Hustling around unloading the packages she has entered with.
She stops.*) Is he, baby?
BENEATHA: Yes. (Beneatha *makes up* Travis' *bed as she talks.*)
MAMA: You sure?
BENEATHA: Yes.
MAMA: Well—I guess you better not waste your time with no fools.

(Beneatha *looks up at her mother, watching her put groceries in the
refrigerator. Finally she gathers up her things and starts into the bedroom.
At the door she stops and looks back at her mother.*)

BENEATHA: Mama—
MAMA: Yes, baby—
BENEATHA: Thank you.

MAMA: For what?
BENEATHA: For understanding me this time.

(She exits quickly and the mother stands, smiling a little, looking at the place where Beneatha *just stood.* Ruth *enters.)*

RUTH: Now don't you fool with any of this stuff, Lena—
MAMA: Oh, I just thought I'd sort a few things out.

(The phone rings. Ruth *answers.)*

RUTH: *(At the phone.)* Hello—Just a minute. *(Goes to door.)* Walter, it's Mrs. Arnold. *(Waits. Goes back to the phone. Tense.)* Hello. Yes, this is his wife speaking . . . He's lying down now. Yes . . . well, he'll be in tomorrow. He's been very sick. Yes—I know we should have called, but we were so sure he'd be able to come in today. Yes—yes, I'm very sorry. Yes . . . Thank you very much. *(She hangs up.* Walter *is standing in the doorway of the bedroom behind her.)* That was Mrs. Arnold.
WALTER: *(Indifferently.)* Was it?
RUTH: She said if you don't come in tomorrow that they are getting a new man . . .
WALTER: Ain't that sad—ain't that crying sad.
RUTH: She said Mr. Arnold has had to take a cab for three days . . . Walter, you ain't been to work for three days! *(This is a revelation to her.)* Where you been, Walter Lee Younger? (Walter *looks at her and starts to laugh.)* You're going to lose your job.
WALTER: That's right . . .
RUTH: Oh, Walter, and with your mother working like a dog every day—
WALTER: That's sad too—Everything is sad.
MAMA: What you been doing for these three days, son?
WALTER: Mama—you don't know all the things a man what got leisure can find to do in this city . . . What's this—Friday night? Well—Wednesday I borrowed Willy Harris' car and I went for a drive . . . just me and myself and I drove and drove . . . Way out . . . way past South Chicago, and I parked the car and I sat and looked at the steel mills all day long. I just sat in the car and looked at them big black chimneys for hours. Then I drove back and I went to the Green Hat. *(Pause.)* And Thursday—Thursday I borrowed the car again and I got in it and I pointed it the other way and I drove the other way—for hours—way, way up to Wisconsin, and I looked at the farms. I just drove and looked at the farms. Then I drove back and I went to the Green Hat. *(Pause.)* And today—today I didn't get the car. Today I just walked. All over the South-side. And I looked at the Negroes and they looked at me and finally I just sat down on the curb at Thirty-ninth and South Parkway and I just sat there and watched the Negroes go by. And then I went to the Green Hat. You all sad? You all depressed? And you know where I am going right now—

*(Ruth *goes out quietly.)*

MAMA: Oh, Big Walter, is this the harvest of our days?
WALTER: You know what I like about the Green Hat? *(He turns the radio on and a steamy, deep blues pours into the room.)* I like this little cat they got there who blows a sax . . . He blows. He talks to me. He ain't but 'bout

five feet tall and he's got a conked head and his eyes is always closed and he's all music—

MAMA: (*Rising and getting some papers out of her handbag.*) Walter—

WALTER: And there's this other guy who plays the piano . . . and they got a sound. I mean they can work on some music . . . They got the best little combo in the world in the Green Hat . . . You can just sit there and drink and listen to them three men play and you realize that don't nothing matter worth a damn, but just being there—

MAMA: I've helped do it to you, haven't I, son? Walter, I been wrong.

WALTER: Naw—you ain't never been wrong about nothing, Mama.

MAMA: Listen to me, now. I say I been wrong, son. That I been doing to you what the rest of the world been doing to you. (*She stops and he looks up slowly at her and she meets his eyes pleadingly.*) Walter—what you ain't never understood is that I ain't got nothing, don't own nothing, ain't never really wanted nothing that wasn't for you. There ain't nothing as precious to me . . . There ain't nothing worth holding on to, money, dreams, nothing else—if it means—if it means it's going to destroy my boy. (*She puts her papers in front of him and he watches her without speaking or moving.*) I paid the man thirty-five hundred dollars down on the house. That leaves sixty-five hundred dollars. Monday morning I want you to take this money and three thousand dollars and put it in a savings account for Beneatha's medical schooling. The rest you put in a checking account—with your name on it. And from now on any penny that come out of it or that go in it is for you to look after. For you to decide. (*She drops her hands a little helplessly.*) It ain't much, but it's all I got in the world and I'm putting it in your hands. I'm telling you to be the head of this family from now on like you supposed to be.

WALTER: (*Stares at the money.*) You trust me like that, Mama?

MAMA: I ain't never stop trusting you. Like I ain't never stop loving you.

(*She goes out, and* Walter *sits looking at the money on the table as the music continues in its idiom, pulsing in the room. Finally, in a decisive gesture, he gets up, and, in mingled joy and desperation, picks up the money. At the same moment,* Travis *enters for bed.*)

TRAVIS: What's the matter, Daddy? You drunk?

WALTER: (*Sweetly, more sweetly than we have ever known him.*) No, Daddy ain't drunk. Daddy ain't going to never be drunk again. . . .

TRAVIS: Well, good night, Daddy.

(*The* Father *has come from behind the couch and leans over, embracing his son.*)

WALTER: Son, I feel like talking to you tonight.

TRAVIS: About what?

WALTER: Oh, about a lot of things. About you and what kind of man you going to be when you grow up. . . . Son—son, what do you want to be when you grow up?

TRAVIS: A bus driver.

WALTER: (*Laughing a little.*) A what? Man, that ain't nothing to want to be!

TRAVIS: Why not?

WALTER: 'Cause, man—it ain't big enough—you know what I mean.

TRAVIS: I don't know then. I can't make up my mind. Sometimes Mama asks me that too. And sometimes when I tell you I want to be like you—she says she don't want me to be like that and sometimes she says she does. . . .

WALTER: (*Gathering him up in his arms.*) You know what, Travis? In seven years you going to be seventeen years old. And things is going to be very different with us in seven years, Travis. . . . One day when you are seventeen I'll come home—home from my office downtown somewhere—

TRAVIS: You don't work in no office, Daddy.

WALTER: No—but after tonight. After what your daddy gonna do tonight, there's going to be offices—a whole lot of offices. . . .

TRAVIS: What you gonna do tonight, Daddy?

WALTER: You wouldn't understand yet, son, but your daddy's gonna make a transaction . . . a business transaction that's going to change our lives. . . . That's how come one day when you 'bout seventeen years old I'll come home and I'll be pretty tired, you know what I mean, after a day of conferences and secretaries getting things wrong the way they do . . . 'cause an executive's life is hell, man—(*The more he talks the farther away he gets.*) And I'll pull the car up on the driveway . . . just a plain black Chrysler, I think, with white walls—no—black tires. More elegant. Rich people don't have to be flashy . . . though I'll have to get something a little sportier for Ruth—maybe a Cadillac convertible to do her shopping in. . . . And I'll come up the steps to the house and the gardener will be clipping away at the hedges and he'll say, "Good evening, Mr. Younger." And I'll say, "Hello, Jefferson, how are you this evening?" And I'll go inside and Ruth will come downstairs and meet me at the door and we'll kiss each other and she'll take my arm and we'll go up to your room to see you sitting on the floor with the catalogues of all the great schools in America around you. . . . All the great schools in the world! And—and I'll say, all right son—it's your seventeenth birthday, what is it you've decided? . . . Just tell me where you want to go to school and you'll *go*. Just tell me, what it is you want to be—and you'll *be* it. . . . Whatever you want to be—Yessir! (*He holds his arms open for* Travis.) You just name it, son . . . (Travis *leaps into them.*) and I hand you the world!

(Walter's *voice has risen in pitch and hysterical promise and on the last line he lifts* Travis *high.*)
(*Blackout.*)

SCENE III.

(*Time: Saturday, moving day, one week later.*
Before the curtain rises, Ruth's *voice, a strident, dramatic church alto, cuts through the silence.*
It is, *in the darkness, a triumphant surge, a penetrating statement of expectation:* "Oh, Lord, I don't feel no ways tired! Children, oh, glory hallelujah!"
As the curtain rises we see that Ruth *is alone in the living room, finishing up the family's packing. It is moving day. She is nailing crates and tying cartons. Beneatha enters, carrying a guitar case, and watches her exuberant sister-in-law.*)

RUTH: Hey!

BENEATHA: (*Putting away the case.*) Hi.

RUTH: (*Pointing at a package.*) Honey—look in that package there and see what I found on sale this morning at the South Center. (Ruth *gets up and moves to the package and draws out some curtains.*) Lookahere—hand-turned hems!

BENEATHA: How do you know the window size out there?

RUTH: (*Who hadn't thought of that.*) Oh—Well, they bound to fit something in the whole house. Anyhow, they was too good a bargain to pass up. (Ruth *slaps her head, suddenly remembering something.*) Oh, Bennie—I meant to put a special note on that carton over there. That's your mama's good china and she wants 'em to be very careful with it.

BENEATHA: I'll do it. (Beneatha *finds a piece of paper and starts to draw large letters on it.*)

RUTH: You know what I'm going to do soon as I get in that new house?

BENEATHA: What?

RUTH: Honey—I'm going to run me a tub of water up to here . . . (*With her fingers practically up to her nostrils.*) And I'm going to get in it—and I am going to sit . . . and sit . . . and sit in that hot water and the first person who knocks to tell *me* to hurry up and come out—

BENEATHA: Gets shot at sunrise.

RUTH: (*Laughing happily.*) You said it, sister! (*Noticing how large* Beneatha *is absent-mindedly making the note.*) Honey, they ain't going to read that from no airplane.

BENEATHA: (*Laughing herself.*) I guess I always think things have more emphasis if they are big, somehow.

RUTH: (*Looking up at her and smiling.*) You and your brother seem to have that as a philosophy of life. Lord, that man—done changed so 'round here. You know—you know what we did last night? Me and Walter Lee?

BENEATHA: What?

RUTH: (*Smiling to herself.*) We went to the movies. (*Looking at* Beneatha *to see if she understands.*) We went to the movies. You know the last time me and Walter went to the movies together?

BENEATHA: No.

RUTH: Me neither. That's how long it been. (*Smiling again.*) But we went last night. The picture wasn't much good, but that didn't seem to matter. We went—and we held hands.

BENEATHA: Oh, Lord!

RUTH: We held hands—and you know what?

BENEATHA: WHAT?

RUTH: When we come out of the show it was late and dark and all the stores and things was closed up . . . and it was kind of chilly and there wasn't many people on the streets . . . and we was still holding hands, me and Walter.

BENEATHA: You're killing me.

(Walter *enters with a large package. His happiness is deep in him; he cannot keep still with his new-found exuberance. He is singing and wiggling and snapping his fingers. He puts his package in a corner and puts a phonograph record, which he has brought in with him, on the record player. As the music comes up he dances over to* Ruth *and tries to get her to dance with him. She gives in at last to his raunchiness and in a fit of giggling allows herself to be drawn into his mood and together they deliberately burlesque an old social dance of their youth.*)

BENEATHA: (*Regarding them a long time as they dance, then drawing in her breath for a deeply exaggerated comment which she does not particularly mean.*) Talk about—olddddddddddd-fashionedddddddd—Negroes!

WALTER: (*Stopping momentarily.*) What kind of Negroes? (*He says this in fun. He is not angry with her today, nor with anyone. He starts to dance with his wife again.*)

BENEATHA: Old-fashioned.

WALTER: (*As he dances with* Ruth.) You know, when these *New Negroes* have their convention—(*Pointing at his sister.*)—that is going to be the chairman of the Committee on Unending Agitation. (*He goes on dancing, then stops.*) Race, race, race! . . . Girl, I do believe you are the first person in the history of the entire human race to successfully brainwash yourself. (Beneatha *breaks up and he goes on dancing. He stops again, enjoying his tease.*) Damn, even the N double A C P takes a holiday sometimes! (Beneatha *and* Ruth *laugh. He dances with* Ruth *some more and starts to laugh and stops and pantomimes someone over an operating table.*) I can just see that chick someday looking down at some poor cat on an operating table before she starts to slice him, saying . . . (*Pulling his sleeves back maliciously.*) "By the way, what are your views on civil rights down there? . . ." (*He laughs at her again and starts to dance happily. The bell sounds.*)

BENEATHA: Sticks and stones may break my bones but . . . words will never hurt me!

(Beneatha *goes to the door and opens it as* Walter *and* Ruth *go on with the clowning. Beneatha is somewhat surprised to see a quiet-looking middle-aged white man in a business suit holding his hat and a briefcase in his hand and consulting a small piece of paper.*)

MAN: Uh—how do you do, miss. I am looking for a Mrs.—(*He looks at the slip of paper.*) Mrs. Lena Younger?

BENEATHA: (*Smoothing her hair with slight embarrassment.*) Oh—yes, that's my mother. Excuse me (*She closes the door and turns to quiet the other two.*) Ruth! Brother! Somebody's here. (*Then she opens the door. The man casts a curious quick glance at all of them.*) Uh—come in please.

MAN: (*Coming in.*) Thank you.

BENEATHA: My mother isn't here just now. Is it business?

MAN: Yes . . . well, of a sort.

WALTER: (*Freely, the Man of the House.*) Have a seat. I'm Mrs. Younger's son. I look after most of her business matters.

(Ruth *and* Beneatha *exchange amused glances.*)

MAN: (*Regarding* Walter, *and sitting.*) Well—My name is Karl Lindner . . .

WALTER: (*Stretching out his hand.*) Walter Younger. This is my wife— (Ruth *nods politely.*)—and my sister.

LINDNER: How do you do.

WALTER: (*Amiably, as he sits himself easily on a chair, leaning with interest forward on his knees and looking expectantly into the newcomer's face.*) What can we do for you, Mr. Lindner!

LINDNER: (*Some minor shuffling of the hat and briefcase on his knees.*) Well—I am a representative of the Clybourne Park Improvement Association—

WALTER: (*Pointing.*) Why don't you sit your things on the floor?

LINDNER: Oh—yes. Thank you. (*He slides the briefcase and hat under the chair.*) And as I was saying—I am from the Clybourne Park Improvement Association and we have had it brought to our attention at the last meeting that you people—or at least your mother—has bought a piece of residential property—(*He digs for the slip of paper again.*)—four o six Claybourne Street . . .

WALTER: That's right. Care for something to drink? Ruth, get Mr. Lindner a beer.

LINDNER: (*Upset for some reason.*) Oh—no, really. I mean thank you very much, but no thank you.

RUTH: (*Innocently.*) Some coffee?

LINDNER: Thank you, nothing at all.

(*Beneatha is watching the man carefully.*)

LINDNER: Well, I don't know how much you folks know about our organization. (*He is a gentle man; thoughtful and somewhat labored in his manner.*) It is one of these community organizations set up to look after—oh, you know, things like block upkeep and special projects and we also have what we call our New Neighbors Orientation Committee . . .

BENEATHA: (*Drily.*) Yes—and what do they do?

LINDNER: (*Turning a little to her and then returning the main force to Walter.*) Well—it's what you might call a sort of welcoming committee, I guess. I mean they, we, I'm the chairman of the committee—go around and see the new people who move into the neighborhood and sort of give them the lowdown on the way we do things out in Clybourne Park.

BENEATHA: (*With appreciation of the two meanings, which escape Ruth and Walter.*) Un-huh.

LINDNER: And we also have the category of what the association calls— (*He looks elsewhere.*)—uh—special community problems . . .

BENEATHA: Yes—and what are some of those?

WALTER: Girl, let the man talk.

LINDNER: (*With understated relief.*) Thank you. I would sort of like to explain this thing in my own way. I mean I want to explain to you in a certain way.

WALTER: Go ahead.

LINDNER: Yes. Well. I'm going to try to get right to the point. I'm sure we'll all appreciate that in the long run.

BENEATHA: Yes.

WALTER: Be still now!

LINDNER: Well—

RUTH: (*Still innocently.*) Would you like another chair—you don't look comfortable.

LINDNER: (*More frustrated than annoyed.*) No, thank you very much. Please. Well—to get right to the point I—(*A great breath, and he is off at last.*) I am sure you people must be aware of some of the incidents which have happened in various parts of the city when colored people have moved into certain areas—(Beneatha *exhales heavily and starts tossing a piece of fruit up and down in the air.*) Well—because we have what I think is going to be a unique type of organization in American community life—not only do we deplore that kind of thing—but we are trying to do something about it. (Beneatha *stops tossing and turns with a new and quizzical interest to the* man.) We feel—(*Gaining confidence in his mission because of the interest in the faces of the people he is talking to.*)—we feel that most of the trouble in this world, when you come right down to it—(*He hits his knee for emphasis.*)—most of the trouble exists because people just don't sit down and talk to each other.

RUTH: (*Nodding as she might in church, pleased with the remark.*) You can say that again, mister.

LINDNER: (*More encouraged by such affirmation.*) That we don't try hard enough in this world to understand the other fellow's problem. The other guy's point of view.

RUTH: Now that's right.

(Beneatha *and* Walter *merely watch and listen with genuine interest.*)

LINDNER: Yes—that's the way we feel out in Clybourne Park. And that's why I was elected to come here this afternoon and talk to you people. Friendly like, you know, the way people should talk to each other and see if we couldn't find some way to work this thing out. As I say, the whole business is a matter of *caring* about the other fellow. Anybody can see that you are a nice family of folks, hard working and honest I'm sure. (Beneatha *frowns slightly, quizzically, her head tilted regarding him.*) Today everybody knows what it means to be on the outside of *something.* And of course, there is always somebody who is out to take the advantage of people who don't always understand.

WALTER: What do you mean?

LINDNER: Well—you see our community is made up of people who've worked hard as the dickens for years to build up that little community. They're not rich and fancy people; just hard-working, honest people who don't really have much but those little homes and a dream of the kind of community they want to raise their children in. Now, I don't say we are perfect and there is a lot wrong in some of the things they want. But you've got to admit that a man, right or wrong, has the right to want to have the neighborhood he lives in a certain kind of way. And at the moment the overwhelming majority of our people out there feel that people get along better, take more of a common interest in the life of the community, when they share a common background. I want you to believe me when I tell you that race prejudice simply doesn't enter into it. It is a matter of the people of Clybourne Park believing, rightly or wrongly, as I say, that for the happiness of all concerned that our Negro families are happier when they live in their *own* communities.

BENEATHA: (*With a grand and bitter gesture.*) This, friends, is the Welcoming Committee!

WALTER: (*Dumfounded, looking at* Lindner.) Is this what you came marching all the way over here to tell us?

LINDNER: Well, now we've been having a fine conversation. I hope you'll hear me all the way through.

WALTER: (*Tightly.*) Go ahead, man.

LINDNER: You see—in the face of all things I have said, we are prepared to make your family a very generous offer . . .

BENEATHA: Thirty pieces and not a coin less!

WALTER: Yeah?

LINDNER: (*Putting on his glasses and drawing a form out of the briefcase.*) Our association is prepared, through the collective effort of our people, to buy the house from you at a financial gain to your family.

RUTH: Lord have mercy, ain't this the living gall!

WALTER: All right, you through?

LINDNER: Well, I want to give you the exact terms of the financial arrangement—

WALTER: We don't want to hear no exact terms of no arrangements. I want to know if you got any more to tell us 'bout getting together?

LINDNER: (*Taking off his glasses.*) Well—I don't suppose that you feel . . .

WALTER: Never mind how I feel—you got any more to say 'bout how people ought to sit down and talk to each other? . . . Get out of my house, man. (*He turns his back and walks to the door.*)

LINDNER: (*Looking around at the hostile faces and reaching and assembling his hat and briefcase.*) Well—I don't understand why you people are reacting this way. What do you think you are going to gain by moving into a neighborhood where you just aren't wanted and where some elements— well—people can get awful worked up when they feel that their whole way of life and everything they've ever worked for is threatened.

WALTER: Get out.

LINDNER: (*At the door, holding a small card.*) Well—I'm sorry it went like this.

WALTER: Get out.

LINDNER: (*Almost sadly regarding* Walter.) You just can't force people to change their hearts, son.

(*He turns and puts his card on a table and exits.* Walter *pushes the door to with stinging hatred, and stands looking at it.* Ruth *just sits and* Beneatha *just stands. They say nothing.* Mama *and* Travis *enter.*)

MAMA: Well—this all the packing got done since I left out of here this morning. I testify before God that my children got all the energy of the dead. What time the moving men due?

BENEATHA: Four o'clock. You had a caller, Mama. (*She is smiling, teasingly.*)

MAMA: Sure enough—who?

BENEATHA: (*Her arms folded saucily.*) The Welcoming Committee.

(Walter *and* Ruth *giggle.*)

MAMA: (*Innocently.*) Who?

BENEATHA: The Welcoming Committee. They said they're sure going to be glad to see you when you get there.

WALTER: (*Devilishly.*) Yeah, they said they can't hardly wait to see your face.

(*Laughter.*)

MAMA: (*Sensing their facetiousness.*) What's the matter with you all?

WALTER: Ain't nothing the matter with us. We just telling you 'bout the gentleman who came to see you this afternoon. From the Clybourne Park Improvement Association.

MAMA: What he want?

RUTH: (*In the same mood as* Beneatha *and* Walter.) To welcome you, honey.

WALTER: He said they can't hardly wait. He said the one thing they don't have, that they just *dying* to have out there is a fine family of colored people! (*To* Ruth *and* Beneatha.) Ain't that right!

RUTH AND BENEATHA: (*Mockingly.*) Yeah! He left his card in case—

(*They indicate the card, and* Mama *picks it up and throws in on the floor—understanding and looking off as she draws her chair up to the table on which she has put her plant and some sticks and some cord.*)

MAMA: Father, give us strength. (*Knowingly—and without fun.*) Did he threaten us?

BENEATHA: Oh—Mama—they don't do it like that any more. He talked Brotherhood. He said everybody ought to learn how to sit down and hate each other with good Christian fellowship. (*She and* Walter *shakes hands to ridicule the remark.*)

MAMA: (*Sadly.*) Lord, protect us . . .

RUTH: You should hear the money those folks raised to buy the house from us. All we paid and then some.

BENEATHA: What they think we going to do—eat 'em?

RUTH: No, honey, marry 'em.

MAMA: (*Shaking her head.*) Lord, Lord, Lord . . .

RUTH: Well—that's the way the crackers crumble. Joke.

BENEATHA: (*Laughingly noticing what her mother is doing.*) Mama, what are you doing?

MAMA: Fixing my plant so it won't get hurt none on the way . . .

BENEATHA: Mama, you going to take *that* to the new house?

MAMA: Un-huh—

BENEATHA: That raggedy-looking old thing?

MAMA: (*Stopping and looking at her.*) It expresses *me.*

RUTH: (*With delight, to* Beneatha.) So there, Miss Thing!

(Walter *comes to* Mama *suddenly and bends down behind her and squeezes her in his arms with all his strength. She is overwhelmed by the suddenness of it and, though delighted, her manner is like that of* Ruth *with* Travis.)

MAMA: Look out now, boy! You make me mess up my thing here!

WALTER: (*His face lit, he slips down on his knees beside her, his arms still about her.*) Mama . . . you know what it means to climb up in the chariot?

MAMA: (*Gruffly, very happy.*) Get on away from me now . . .

RUTH: (*Near the gift-wrapped package, trying to catch* Walter's *eye.*) Psst—

WALTER: What the old song say, Mama . . .

RUTH: Walter—Now? (*She is pointing at the package.*)

WALTER: (*Speaking the lines, sweetly, playfully, in his mother's face.*)
     I got wings . . . you got wings . . .
        All God's Children got wings . . .

MAMA: Boy—get out of my face and do some work . . .

WALTER: When I get to heaven gonna put on my wings,
        Gonna fly all over God's heaven . . .

BENEATHA: (*Teasingly, from across the room.*) Everybody talking 'bout heaven ain't going there!

WALTER: (*To* Ruth, *who is carrying the box across to them.*) I don't know, you think we ought to give her that . . . Seems to me she ain't been very appreciative around here.

MAMA: (*Eying the box, which is obviously a gift.*) What is that?

WALTER: (*Taking it from Ruth and putting it on the table in front of Mama.*) Well—what you all think? Should we give it to her?

RUTH: Oh—she was pretty good today.

MAMA: I'll good you—(*She turns her eyes to the box again.*)

BENEATHA: Open it, Mama.

(*She stands up, looks at it, turns and looks at all of them, and then presses her hands together and does not open the package.*)

WALTER: (*Sweetly.*) Open it, Mama. It's for you. (*Mama looks in his eyes. It is the first present in her life without its being Christmas. Slowly she opens her package and lifts out, one by one, a brand-new sparkling set of gardening tools. Walter continues, prodding.*) Ruth made up the note—read it . . .

MAMA: (*Picking up the card and adjusting her glasses.*) "To our own Mrs. Miniver—Love from Brother, Ruth and Beneatha." Ain't that lovely . . .

TRAVIS: (*Tugging at his father's sleeve.*) Daddy, can I give her mine now?

WALTER: All right, son. (*Travis flies to get his gift.*) Travis didn't want to go in with the rest of us, Mama. He got his own. (*Somewhat amused.*) We don't know what it is . . .

TRAVIS: (*Racing back in the room with a large hatbox and putting it in front of his grandmother.*) Here!

MAMA: Lord have mercy, baby. You done gone and bought your grandmother a hat?

TRAVIS: (*Very proud.*) Open it!

(*She does and lifts out an elaborate, but very elaborate, wide gardening hat, and all the adults break up at the sight of it.*)

RUTH: Travis, honey, what is that?

TRAVIS: (*Who thinks it is beautiful and appropriate.*) It's a gardening hat! Like the ladies always have on in the magazines when they work in their gardens.

BENEATHA: (*Giggling fiercely.*) Travis—we were trying to make Mama Mrs. Miniver—not Scarlett O'Hara!

MAMA: (*Indignantly.*) What's the matter with you all! This here is a beautiful hat! (*Absurdly.*) I always wanted me one just like it! (*She pops it on her head to prove it to her grandson, and the hat is ludicrous and considerably oversized.*)

RUTH: Hot dog! Go, Mama!

WALTER: (*Doubled over with laughter.*) I'm sorry, Mama—but you look like you ready to go out and chop you some cotton sure enough!

(*They all laugh except Mama, out of deference to Travis' feelings.*)

MAMA: (*Gathering the boy up to her.*) Bless your heart—this is the prettiest hat I ever owned—(Walter, Ruth and Beneatha *chime in—noisily, festively and insincerely congratulating* Travis *on his gift.*) What are we all standing around here for? We ain't finished packin' yet. Bennie, you ain't packed one book.

(The bell rings.)

BENEATHA: That couldn't be the movers . . . it's not hardly two yet—

(Beneatha goes into her room. Mama starts for door.)

WALTER: *(Turning, stiffening.)* Wait—wait—I'll get it. *(He stands and looks at the door.)*
MAMA: You expecting company, son?
WALTER: *(Just looking at the door.)* Yeah—yeah . . .

(Mama looks at Ruth, and they exchange innocent and unfrightened glances.)

MAMA: *(Not understanding.)* Well, let them in, son.
BENEATHA: *(From her room.)* We need some more string.
MAMA: Travis—you run to the hardware and get me some string cord.

(Mama goes out and Walter turns and looks at Ruth. Travis goes to a dish for money.)

RUTH: Why don't you answer the door, man?
WALTER: *(Suddenly bounding across the floor to her.)* 'Cause sometimes it hard to let the future begin! *(Stooping down in her face.)*
    I got wings! You got wings!
    All God's children got wings!

(He crosses to the door and throws it open. Standing there is a very slight little man in a not too prosperous business suit and with haunted frightened eyes and a hat pulled down tightly, brim up, around his forehead. Travis passes between the men and exits. Walter leans deep in the man's face, still in his jubilance.)

    When I get to heaven gonna put on my wings,
    Gonna fly all over God's heaven . . .

(The little man just stares at him.)

    Heaven—

(Suddenly he stops and looks past the little man into the empty hallway.) Where's Willy, man?

BOBO: He ain't with me.
WALTER: *(Not disturbed.)* Oh—come on in. You know my wife.
BOBO: *(Dumbly, taking off his hat.)* Yes—h'you, Miss Ruth.
RUTH: *(Quietly, a mood apart from her husband already, seeing Bobo.)* Hello, Bobo.
WALTER: You right on time today . . . Right on time. That's the way! *(He slaps Bobo on his back.)* Sit down . . . lemme hear.

(Ruth *stands stiffly and quietly in back of them, as though somehow she senses death, her eyes fixed on her husband.*)

BOBO: (*His frightened eyes on the floor, his hat in his hands.*) Could I please get a drink of water, before I tell you about it, Walter Lee?

(Walter *does not take his eyes off the man.* Ruth *goes blindly to the tap and gets a glass of water and brings it to* Bobo.)

WALTER: There ain't nothing wrong, is there?

BOBO: Lemme tell you—

WALTER: Man—didn't nothing go wrong?

BOBO: Lemme tell you—Walter Lee. (*Looking at* Ruth *and talking to her more than to* Walter.) You know how it was. I got to tell you how it was. I mean first I got to tell you how it was all the way . . . I mean about the money I put in, Walter Lee . . .

WALTER: (*With taut agitation now.*) What about the money you put in?

BOBO: Well—it wasn't much as we told you—me and Willy—(*He stops.*) I'm sorry, Walter. I got a bad feeling about it. I got a real bad feeling about it . . .

WALTER: Man, what you telling me about all this for? . . . Tell me what happened in Springfield . . .

BOBO: Springfield.

RUTH: (*Like a dead woman.*) What was supposed to happen in Springfield?

BOBO: (*To her.*) This deal that me and Walter went into with Willy—Me and Willy was going to go down to Springfield and spread some money 'round so's we wouldn't have to wait so long for the liquor license . . . That's what we were going to do. Everybody said that was the way you had to do, you understand, Miss Ruth?

WALTER: Man—what happened down there?

BOBO: (*A pitiful man, near tears.*) I'm trying to tell you, Walter.

WALTER: (*Screaming at him suddenly.*) THEN TELL ME, GODDAMMIT . . . WHAT'S THE MATTER WITH YOU?

BOBO: Man . . . I didn't go to no Springfield, yesterday.

WALTER: (*Halted, life hanging in the moment.*) Why not?

BOBO: (*The long way, the hard way to tell.*) 'Cause I didn't have no reasons to . . .

WALTER: Man, what are you talking about!

BOBO: I'm talking about the fact that when I got to the train station yesterday morning—eight o'clock like we planned . . . Man—*Willy didn't never show up.*

WALTER: Why . . . where was he . . . where is he?

BOBO: That's what I'm trying to tell you . . . I don't know . . . I waited six hours . . . I called his house . . . and I waited . . . six hours . . . I waited in that train station six hours . . . (*Breaking into tears.*) That was all the extra money I had in the world . . . (*Looking up at* Walter *with the tears running down his face.*) Man, *Willy is gone.*

WALTER: Gone, what you mean Willy is gone? Gone where? You mean he went by himself. You mean he went off to Springfield by himself—to take care of getting the license—(*Turns and looks anxiously at* Ruth.) You mean maybe he didn't want too many people in on the business down there? (*Looks to* Ruth *again, as before.*) You know Willy got his own ways. (*Looks back to* Bobo.) Maybe you was late yesterday and he just went on down there without you. Maybe—maybe—he's been callin' you at home tryin' to tell you what happened or something. Maybe—maybe—he just got sick. He's somewhere—he's got to be somewhere. We just got to find him—me and you got to find him. (*Grabs* Bobo *senselessly by the collar and starts to shake him.*) We got to!

BOBO: (*In sudden angry, frightened agony.*) What's the matter with you, Walter! *When a cat take off with your money he don't leave you no maps!*

WALTER: (*Turning madly, as though he is looking for* Willy *in the very room.*) Willy! . . . Willy . . . don't do it . . . Please don't do it . . . Man, not with that money . . . Man, please, not with that money . . . Oh, God . . . Don't let it be true . . . (*He is wandering around, crying out for* Willy *and looking for him or perhaps for help from God.*) Man . . . I trusted you . . . Man, I put my life in your hands . . . (*He starts to crumple down on the floor as* Ruth *just covers her face in horror.* Mama *opens the door and comes into the room, with* Beneatha *behind her.*) Man . . . (*He starts to pound the floor with his fists, sobbing wildly.*) That money is made out of my father's flesh . . .

BOBO: (*Standing over him helplessly.*) I'm sorry, Walter . . . (*Only* Walter's *sobs reply.* Bobo *puts on his hat.*) I had my life staked on this deal, too . . . (*He exits.*)

MAMA: (*To* Walter.) Son—(*She goes to him, bends down to him, talks to his bent head.*) Son . . . Is it gone? Son, I gave you sixty-five hundred dollars. Is it gone? All of it? Beneatha's money too?

WALTER: (*Lifting his head slowly.*) Mama . . . I never . . . went to the bank at all . . .

MAMA: (*Not wanting to believe him.*) You mean . . . your sister's school money . . . you used that too . . . Walter? . . .

WALTER: Yessss! . . . All of it . . . It's all gone . . .

(*There is total silence.* Ruth *stands with her face covered with her hands;* Beneatha *leans forlornly against a wall, fingering a piece of red ribbon from the mother's gift.* Mama *stops and looks at her son without recognition and then, quite without thinking about it, starts to beat him senselessly in the face.* Beneatha *goes to them and stops it.*)

BENEATHA: Mama!

(Mama *stops and looks at both of her children and rises slowly and wanders vaguely, aimlessly away from them.*)

MAMA: I seen . . . him . . . night after night . . . come in . . . and look at that rug . . . and then look at me . . . the red showing in his eyes . . . the veins moving in his head . . . I seen him grow thin and old before he was forty . . . working and working and working like somebody's old horse . . . killing himself . . . and you—you give it all away in a day . . .

BENEATHA: Mama—

MAMA: Oh, God . . . (*She looks up to Him.*) Look down here—and show me the strength.

BENEATHA: Mama—

MAMA: (*Folding over.*) Strength . . .

BENEATHA: (*Plaintively.*) Mama . . .

MAMA: Strength!

CURTAIN

ACT III.

(An hour later.
At curtain, there is a sullen light of gloom in the living room, gray light not unlike that which began the first scene of Act One. At left we can see Walter within his room, alone with himself. He is stretched out on the bed, his shirt out and open, his arms under his head. He does not smoke, he does not cry out, he merely lies there, looking up at the ceiling, much as if he were alone in the world.
In the living room Beneatha sits at the table, still surrounded by the now almost ominous packing crates. She sits looking off. We feel that this is a mood struck perhaps an hour before, and it lingers now, full of the empty sound of profound disappointment. We see on a line from her brother's bedroom the sameness of their attitudes. Presently the bell rings and Beneatha rises without ambition or interest in answering. It is Asagai, smiling broadly, striding into the room with energy and happy expectation and conversation.)

ASAGAI: I came over . . . I had some free time. I thought I might help with the packing. Ah, I like the look of packing crates! A household in preparation for a journey! It depresses some people . . . but for me . . . it is another feeling. Something full of the flow of life, do you understand? Movement, progress . . . It makes me think of Africa.

BENEATHA: Africa!

ASAGAI: What kind of a mood is this? Have I told you how deeply you move me?

BENEATHA: He gave away the money, Asagai . . .

ASAGAI: Who gave away what money?

BENEATHA: The insurance money. My brother gave it away.

ASAGAI: Gave it away?

BENEATHA: He made an investment! With a man even Travis wouldn't have trusted.

ASAGAI: And it's gone?

BENEATHA: Gone!

ASAGAI: I'm very sorry . . . And you, now?

BENEATHA: Me? . . . Me? . . . Me I'm nothing . . . Me. When I was very small . . . we used to take our sleds out in the wintertime and the only hills we had were the ice-covered stone steps of some houses down the street. And we used to fill them in with snow and make them smooth and slide down them all day . . . and it was very dangerous you know . . . far too steep . . . and sure enough one day a kid named Rufus came down too fast and hit the sidewalk . . . and we saw his face just split open right there in front of us . . . And I remember standing there looking at his bloody open face thinking that was the end of Rufus. But the ambulance came and they took him to the hospital and they fixed the broken bones and they sewed it all up . . . and the next time I saw Rufus he just had a little line down the middle of his face . . . I never got over that . . .

(Walter sits up, listening on the bed. Throughout this scene it is important that we feel his reaction at all times, that he visibly respond to the words of his sister and Asagai.)

ASAGAI: What?

BENEATHA: That that was what one person could do for another, fix him up—sew up the problem, make him all right again. That was the most marvelous thing in the world . . . I wanted to do that. I always thought it was the one concrete thing in the world that a human being could do. Fix up the sick, you know—and make them whole again. This was truly being God . . .

ASAGAI: You wanted to be God?

BENEATHA: No—I wanted to cure. It used to be so important to me. I wanted to cure. It used to matter. I used to care. I mean about people and how their bodies hurt . . .

ASAGAI: And you've stopped caring?

BENEATHA: Yes—I think so.

ASAGAI: Why?

(Walter *rises, goes to the door of his room and is about to open it, then stops and stands listening, leaning on the door jamb.*)

BENEATHA: Because it doesn't seem deep enough, close enough to what ails mankind—I mean this thing of sewing up bodies or administering drugs. Don't you understand? It was a child's reaction to the world. I thought that doctors had the secret to all the hurts. . . . That's the way a child see things— or an idealist.

ASAGAI: Children see things very well sometimes—and idealists even better.

BENEATHA: I know that's what you think. Because you are still where I left off—you still care. This is what you see for the world, for Africa. You with the dreams of the future will patch up all Africa—you are going to cure the Great Sore of colonialism with Independence—

ASAGAI: Yes!

BENEATHA: Yes—and you think that one word is the penicillin of the human spirit: "Independence!" But then what?

ASAGAI: That will be the problem for another time. First we must get there.

BENEATHA: And where does it end?

ASAGAI: End? Who even spoke of an end? To life? To living?

BENEATHA: An end to misery!

ASAGAI: (*Smiling.*) You sound like a French intellectual.

BENEATHA: No! I sound like a human being who just had her future taken right out of her hands! While I was sleeping in my bed in there, things were happening in this world that directly concerned me—and nobody asked me, consulted me—they just went out and did things—and changed my life. Don't you see there isn't any real progress, Asagai, there is only one large circle that we march in, around and around, each of us with our own little picture—in front of us—our own little mirage that we think is the future.

ASAGAI: That is the mistake.

BENEATHA: What?

ASAGAI: What you just said—about the circle. It isn't a circle—it is simply a long line—as in geometry, you know, one that reaches into infinity. And because we cannot see the end—we also cannot see how it changes. And it is very odd but those who see the changes are called "idealists"—and those who cannot, or refuse to think, they are the "realists." It is very strange, and amusing too, I think.

BENEATHA: You—you are almost religious.

ASAGAI: Yes . . . I think I have the religion of doing what is necessary in the world—and of worshipping man—because he is so marvelous, you see.

BENEATHA: Man is foul! And the human race deserves its misery!

ASAGAI: You see: *you* have become that religious one in the old sense.
Already, and rather such a small defeat, you are worshipping despair.

BENEATHA: From now on, I worship the truth—and the truth is that people
are puny, small and selfish. . . .

ASAGAI: Truth? Why is it that you despairing ones always think that only
you have the truth? I never thought to see *you* like that. You! Your brother
made a stupid, childish mistake—and you are grateful to him. So that now
you can give up the ailing human race on account of it. You talk about what
good is struggle; what good is anything? Where are we all going? And why
are we bothering?

BENEATHA: *And you cannot answer it!* All your talk and dreams about
Africa and Independence. Independence and then what? What about all the
crooks and petty thieves and just plain idiots who will come into power to
steal and plunder the same as before—only now they will be black and do
it in the name of the new Independence—You cannot answer that.

ASAGAI: (*Shouting over her.*) *I live the answer!* (*Pause.*) In my village at
home it is the exceptional man who can even read a newspaper . . . or who
ever *sees* a book at all. I will go home and much of what I will have to say
will seem strange to the people of my village . . . But I will teach and work
and things will happen, slowly and swiftly. At times it will seem that
nothing changes at all . . . and then again . . . the sudden dramatic events
which make history leap into the future. And then quiet again. Retrogression
even. Guns, murder, revolution. And I even will have moments when I
wonder if the quiet was not better than all that death and hatred. But I will
look about my village at the illiteracy and disease and ignorance and I will
not wonder long. And perhaps . . . perhaps I will be a great man . . . I mean
perhaps I will hold on to the substance of truth and find my way always with
the right course . . . and perhaps for it I will be butchered in my bed some
night by the servants of empire . . .

BENEATHA: *The martyr!*

ASAGAI: . . . or perhaps I shall live to be a very old man, respected and
esteemed in my new nation . . . And perhaps I shall hold office and this is
what I'm trying to tell you, Alaiyo; perhaps the things I believe now for my
country will be wrong and outmoded, and I will not understand and do
terrible things to have things my way or merely to keep my power. Don't
you see that there will be young men and women, not British soldiers then,
but my own black countrymen . . . to step out of the shadows some evening
and slit my then useless throat? Don't you see they have alway been there
. . . that they always will be. And that such a thing as my own death will
be an advance? They who might kill me even . . . actually replenish me!

BENEATHA: Oh, Asagai, I know all that.

ASAGAI: Good! Then stop moaning and groaning and tell me what you
plan to do.

BENEATHA: Do?

ASAGAI: I have a bit of a suggestion.

BENEATHA: What?

ASAGAI: (*Rather quietly for him.*) That when it is all over—that you come
home with me—

BENEATHA: (*Slapping herself on the forehead with exasperation born of
misunderstanding.*) Oh—Asagai—at this moment you decide to be romantic!

ASAGAI: (*Quickly understanding the misunderstanding.*) My dear, young creature of the New World—I do not mean across the city—I mean across the ocean; home—to Africa.

BENEATHA: *(Slowly understanding and turning to him with murmured amazement.)* To—to Nigeria?

ASAGAI: Yes! . . . *(Smiling and lifting his arms playfully.)* Three hundred years later the African Prince rose up out of the seas and swept the maiden back across the middle passage over which her ancestors had come—

BENEATHA: *(Unable to play.)* Nigeria?

ASAGAI: Nigeria. Home. *(Coming to her with genuine romantic flippancy.)* I will show you our mountains and our stars; and give you cool drinks from gourds and teach you the old songs and the ways of our people—and, in time, we will pretend that—*(Very softly.)*—you have only been away for a day—

(She turns her back to him, thinking. He swings her around and takes her full in his arms in a long embrace which proceeds to passion.)

BENEATHA: *(Pulling away.)* You're getting me all mixed up—

ASAGAI: Why?

BENEATHA: Too many things—too many things have happened today. I must sit down and think. I don't know what I feel about anything right this minute. *(She promptly sits down and props her chin on her fist.)*

ASAGAI: *(Charmed.)* All right, I shall leave you. No—don't get up. *(Touching her, gently, sweetly.)* Just sit awhile and think . . . Never be afraid to sit awhile and think. *(He goes to door and looks at her.)* How often I have looked at you and said, "Ah—so this is what the New World hath finally wrought . . ."

(He exits. Beneatha sits on alone. Presently Walter enters from his room and starts to rummage through things, feverishly looking for something. She looks up and turns in her seat.)

BENEATHA: *(Hissingly.)* Yes—just look at what the New World hath wrought! . . . Just look! *(She gestures with bitter disgust.)* There he is! *Monsieur le petit bourgeois noir*—himself! There he is—Symbol of a Rising Class! Entrepreneur! Titan of the system! (Walter *ignores her completely and continues frantically and destructively looking for something and hurling things to floor and tearing things out of their place in his search.* Beneatha *ignores the eccentricity of his actions and goes on with the monologue of insult.)* Did you dream of yachts on Lake Michigan, Brother? Did you see yourself on that Great Day sitting down at the Conference Table, surrounded by all the mighty bald-headed men in America? All halted, waiting, breathless, waiting for your pronouncements on industry? Waiting for you—Chairman of the Board? (Walter *finds what he is looking for—a small piece of white paper—and pushes it in his pocket and puts on his coat and rushes out without ever having looked at her. She shouts after him.)* I look at you and I see the final triumph of stupidity in the world!

(The door slams and she returns to just sitting again. Ruth comes quickly out of Mama's room.)

RUTH: Who was that?

BENEATHA: Your husband.

RUTH: Where did he go?

BENEATHA: Who knows—maybe he has an appointment at U.S. Steel.
RUTH: (*Anxiously, with frightened eyes.*) You didn't say nothing bad to him, did you?
BENEATHA: Bad? Say anything bad to him? No—I told him he was a sweet boy and full of dreams and everything is strictly peachy keen, as the ofay kids say!

(Mama *enters from her bedroom. She is lost, vague, trying to catch hold, to make some sense of her former command of the world, but it still eludes her. A sense of waste overwhelms her gait; a measure of apology rides on her shoulders. She goes to her plant, which has remained on the table, looks at it, picks it up and takes it to the window sill and sets it outside, and she stands and looks at it a long moment. Then she closes the window, straightens her body with effort and turns around to her children.*)

MAMA: Well—ain't it a mess in here, though? (*A false cheerfulness, a beginning of something.*) I guess we all better stop moping around and get some work done. All this unpacking and everything we got to do. (Ruth *raises her head slowly in response to the sense of the line; and* Beneatha *in similar manner turns very slowly to look at her mother.*) One of you all better call the moving people and tell 'em not to come.
RUTH: Tell 'em not to come?
MAMA: Of course, baby. Ain't no need in 'em coming all the way here and having to go back. They charges for that too. (*She sits down, fingers to her brow, thinking.*) Lord, ever since I was a little girl, I always remembers people saying, "Lena—Lena Eggleston, you aims too high all the time. You needs to slow down and see life a little more like it is. Just slow down some." That's what they always used to say down home—"Lord, that Lena Eggleston is a high-minded thing. She'll get her due one day!"
RUTH: No, Lena . . .
MAMA: Me and Big Walter just didn't never learn right.
RUTH: Lena, no! We gotta go. Bennie—tell her . . . (*She rises and crosses to* Beneatha *with her arms outstretched.* Beneatha *doesn't respond.*) Tell her we can still move . . . the notes ain't but a hundred and twenty-five a month. We got four grown people in this house—we can work . . .
MAMA: (*To herself.*) Just aimed too high all the time—
RUTH: (*Turning and going to* Mama *fast—the words pouring out with urgency and desperation.*) Lena—I'll work . . . I'll work twenty hours a day in all the kitchens in Chicago . . . I'll strap my baby on my back if I have to and scrub all the floors in America and wash all the sheets in America if I have to—but we got to move . . . We got to get out of here . . .

(Mama *reaches out absently and pats* Ruth's *hand.*)

MAMA: No—I sees things differently now. Been thinking 'bout some of the things we could do to fix this place up some. I seen a second-hand bureau over on Maxwell Street just the other day that could fit right there. (*She points to where the new furniture might go.* Ruth *wanders away from her.*) Would need some new handles on it and then a little varnish and then it look like something brand-new. And—we can put up them new curtains in the kitchen . . . Why this place be looking fine. Cheer us all up so that we forget trouble ever came . . . (*To* Ruth.) And you could get some nice screens to put up in your room round the baby's bassinet . . . (*She looks at both of them,*

pleadingly.) Sometimes you just got to know when to give up some things
... and hold on to what you got.

(Walter *enters from the outside, looking spent and leaning against the
door, his coat hanging from him.*)

MAMA: Where you been, son?

WALTER: (*Breathing hard.*) Made a call.

MAMA: To who, son?

WALTER: To The Man.

MAMA: What man, baby?

WALTER: The Man, Mama. Don't you know who The Man is?

RUTH: Walter Lee?

WALTER: *The Man.* Like the guys in the streets say—The Man. Captain
Boss—Mistuh Charley ... Old Captain Please Mr. Bossman ...

BENEATHA: (*Suddenly.*) Lindner!

WALTER: That's right! That's good. I told him to come right over.

BENEATHA: (*Fiercely, understanding.*) For what? What do you want to see
him for!

WALTER: (*Looking at his sister.*) We going to do business with him.

MAMA: What you talking 'bout, son?

WALTER: Talking 'bout life, Mama. You all always telling me to see life
like it is. Well—I laid in there on my back today ... and I figured it out. Life
just like it is. Who gets and who don't get. (*He sits down with his coat on
and laughs.*) Mama, you know it's all divided up. Life is. Sure enough.
Between the takers and the "tooken." (*He laughs.*) I've figured it out finally.
(*He looks around at them.*) Yeah. Some of us always getting "tooken." (*He
laughs.*) People like Willy Harris, they don't never get "tooken." And you
know why the rest of us do? 'Cause we all mixed up. Mixed up bad. We get
to looking 'round for the right and the wrong; and we worry about it and
cry about it and stay up nights trying to figure out 'bout the wrong and the
right of things all the time ... And all the time, man, them takers is out there
operating, just taking and taking. Willy Harris? Shoot—Willy Harris don't
even count. He don't even count in the big scheme of things. But I'll say one
thing for old Willy Harris ... he's taught me something. He's taught me to
keep my eye on what counts in this world. Yeah—(*Shouting out a little.*)
Thanks, Willy!

RUTH: What did you call that man for, Walter Lee?

WALTER: Called him to tell him to come on over to the show. Gonna put
on a show for the man. Just what he wants to see. You see, Mama, the man
came here today and he told us that them people out there where you want
us to move—well they so upset they willing to pay us not to move out there.
(*He laughs again.*) And—and oh, Mama—you would of been proud of the
way me and Ruth and Bennie acted. We told him to get out ... Lord have
mercy! We told the man to get out. Oh, we was some proud folks this
afternoon, yeah. (*He lights a cigarette.*) We were still full of that old-time
stuff ...

RUTH: (*Coming toward him slowly.*) You talking 'bout taking them
people's money to keep us from moving in that house?

WALTER: I ain't just talking 'bout it, baby—I'm telling you that's what's
going to happen.

BENEATHA: Oh, God! Where is the bottom! Where is the real honest-to-
God bottom so he can't go any farther!

WALTER: See—that's the old stuff. You and that boy that was here today. You all want everybody to carry a flag and a spear and sing some marching songs, huh? You wanna spend your life looking into things and trying to find the right and the wrong part, huh? Yeah. You know what's going to happen to that boy someday—he'll find himself sitting in a dungeon, locked in forever—and the takers will have the key! Forget it, baby! There ain't no causes—there ain't nothing but taking in this world, and he who takes most is smartest—and it don't make a damn bit of difference *how.*

MAMA: You making something inside me cry, son. Some awful pain inside me.

WALTER: Don't cry, Mama. Understand. That white man is going to walk in that door able to write checks for more money than we ever had. It's important to him and I'm going to help him . . . I'm going to put on the show, Mama.

MAMA: Son—I come from five generations of people who was slaves and sharecroppers—but ain't nobody in my family never let nobody pay 'em no money that was a way of telling us we wasn't fit to walk the earth. We ain't never been that poor. (*Raising her eyes and looking at him.*) We ain't never been that dead inside.

BENEATHA: Well—we are dead now. All the talk about dreams and sunlight that goes on in this house. All dead.

WALTER: What's the matter with you all! I didn't make this world! It was give to me this way! Hell, yes, I want me some yachts someday! Yes, I want to hang some real pearls 'round my wife's neck. Ain't she supposed to wear no pearls? Somebody tell me—tell me, who decides which women is suppose to wear pearls in this world. I tell you I am a *man*—and I think my wife should wear some pearls in this world! (*This last line hangs a good while and* Walter *begins to move about the room. The word "Man" has penetrated his consciousness; he mumbles it to himself repeatedly between strange agitated pauses as he moves about.*)

MAMA: Baby, how you going to feel on the inside?

WALTER: Fine! . . . Going to feel fine . . . a man . . .

MAMA: You won't have nothing left then, Walter Lee.

WALTER: (*Coming to her.*) I'm going to feel fine, Mama. I'm going to look that son-of-a-bitch in the eyes and say—(*He falters.*)—and say, "All right, Mr. Lindner—(*He falters even more.*)—that's your neighborhood out there. You got the right to keep it like you want. You got the right to have it like you want. Just write the check and—the house is yours." And, and I am going to say—(*His voice almost breaks.*) And you—you people just put the money in my hand and you won't have to live next to this bunch of stinking niggers! . . . (*He straightens up and moves away from his mother, walking around the room.*) Maybe—maybe I'll just get down on my black knees . . . (*He does so;* Ruth *and* Bennie *and* Mama *watch him in frozen horror.*) Captain, Mistuh, Bossman. (*He starts crying.*) A-hee-hee-hee! (*Wringing his hands in profoundly anguished imitation.*) Yasssssuh! Great White Father, just gi' ussen de money, fo' God's sake, and we's ain't gwine come out deh and dirty up yo' white folks neighborhood . . . (*He breaks down completely, then gets up and goes into the bedroom.*)

BENEATHA: That is not a man. That is nothing but a toothless rat.

MAMA: Yes—death done come in this here house. (*She is nodding, slowly, reflectively.*) Done come walking in my house. On the lips of my children. You what supposed to be my beginning again. You—what supposed to be my harvest. (*To* Beneatha.) You—you mourning your brother?

BENEATHA: He's no brother of mine.

MAMA: What you say?

BENEATHA: I said that that individual in that room is no brother of mine.

MAMA: That's what I thought you said. You feeling like you better than he is today? (Beneatha *does not answer.*) Yes? What you tell him a minute ago? That he wasn't a man? Yes? You give him up for me? You done wrote his epitaph too—like the rest of the world? Well, who give you the privilege?

BENEATHA: Be on my side for once! You saw what he just did, Mama! You saw him—down on his knees. Wasn't it you who taught me—to despise any man who would do that. Do what he's going to do.

MAMA: Yes—I taught you that. Me and your daddy. But I thought I taught you something else too . . . I thought I taught you to love him.

BENEATHA: Love him? There is nothing left to love.

MAMA: There is always something left to love. And if you ain't learned that, you ain't learned nothing. (*Looking at her.*) Have you cried for that boy today? I don't mean for yourself and for the family 'cause we lost the money. I mean for him; what he been through and what it done to him. Child, when do you think is the time to love somebody the most; when they done good and made things easy for everybody? Well then, you ain't through learning—because that ain't the time at all. It's when he's at his lowest and can't believe in hisself 'cause the world done whipped him so. When you starts measuring somebody, measure him right, child, measure him right. Make sure you done taken into account what hills and valleys he come through before he got to wherever he is.

(Travis *bursts into the room at the end of the speech, leaving the door open.*)

TRAVIS: Grandmama—the moving men are downstairs! The truck just pulled up.

MAMA: (*Turning and looking at him.*) Are they, baby! They downstairs?

(She sighs and sits. Lindner *appears in the doorway. He peers in and knocks lightly, to gain attention, and comes in. All turn to look at him.*)

LINDNER: (*Hat and briefcase in hand.*) Uh-hello . . . (Ruth *crosses mechanically to the bedroom door and opens it and lets it swing open freely and slowly as the lights come up on* Walter *within, still in his coat, sitting at the far corner of the room. He looks up and out through the room to* Lindner.)

RUTH: He's here.

(A long minute passes and Walter *slowly gets up.*)

LINDNER: (*Coming to the table with efficiency, putting his briefcase on the table and starting to unfold papers and unscrew fountain pens.*) Well, I certainly was glad to hear from you people. (Walter *has begun the trek out of the room, slowly and awkwardly, rather like a small boy, passing the back of his sleeve across his mouth from time to time.*) Life can really be so much simpler than people let it be most of the time. Well—with whom do I negotiate? You, Mrs. Younger, or your son here? (Mama *sits with her hands folded on her lap and her eyes closed as* Walter *advances.* Travis *goes close to* Lindner *and looks at the papers curiously.*) Just some official papers, sonny.

RUTH: Travis, you go downstairs.

MAMA: (*Opening her eyes and looking into* Walter's.) No. Travis, you stay right here. And you make him understand what you doing, Walter Lee. You teach him good. Like Willy Harris taught you. You show where our five generations done come to. Go ahead, son—

WALTER: (*Looks down into his boy's eyes.* Travis *grins at him merrily and* Walter *draws him beside him with his arm lightly around his shoulders.*) Well, Mr. Lindner. (Beneatha *turns away.*) We called you—(*There is a profound, simple groping quality in his speech.*)—because, well, me and my family (*He looks around and shifts from one foot to the other.*) Well—we are very plain people . . .

LINDNER: Yes—

WALTER: I mean—I have worked as a chauffeur most of my life—and my wife here, she does domestic work in people's kitchens. So does my mother. I mean—we are plain people . . .

LINDNER: Yes, Mr. Younger—

WALTER: (*Really like a small boy, looking down at his shoes and then up at the man.*) And—uh—well, my father, well, he was a laborer most of his life.

LINDNER: (*Absolutely confused.*) Uh, yes—

WALTER: (*Looking down at his toes once again.*) My father almost beat a man to death once because this man called him a bad name or something, you know what I mean?

LINDNER: No, I'm afraid I don't.

WALTER: (*Finally straightening up.*) Well, what I mean is that we come from people who had a lot of pride. I mean—we are very proud people. And that's my sister over there and she's going to be a doctor—and we are very proud—

LINDNER: Well—I am sure that is very nice, but—

WALTER: (*Starting to cry and facing the man eye to eye.*) What I am telling you is that we called you over here to tell you that we are very proud and that that is—this is my son, who makes the sixth generation of our family in this country, and that we have all thought about your offer and we have decided to move into our house because my father—my father—he earned it. (Mama *has her eyes closed and is rocking back and forth as though she were in church, with her head nodding the amen yes.*) We don't want to make no trouble for nobody or fight no causes—but we will try to be good neighbors. That's all we got to say. (*He looks the man absolutely in the eyes.*) We don't want your money. (*He turns and walks away from the man.*)

LINDNER: (*Looking around at all of them.*) I take it then that you have decided to occupy.

BENEATHA: That's what the man said.

LINDNER: (*To* Mama *in her reverie.*) Then I would like to appeal to you, Mrs. Younger. You are older and wiser and understand things better I am sure . . .

MAMA: (*Rising.*) I am afraid you don't understand. My son said we was going to move and there ain't nothing left for me to say. (*Shaking her head with double meaning.*) You know how these young folks is nowadays, mister. Can't do a thing with 'em. Good-bye.

LINDER: (*Folding up his materials.*) Well—if you are that final about it . . . There is nothing left for me to say. (*He finishes. He is almost ignored by the family, who are concentrating on* Walter Lee. *At the door* Lindner *halts and looks around.*) I sure hope you people know what you're doing. (*He shakes his head and exits.*)

RUTH: (*Looking around and coming to life.*) Well, for God's sake—if the moving men are here—LET'S GET THE HELL OUT OF HERE!

MAMA: (*into action.*) Ain't it the truth! Look at all this here mess. Ruth, put Travis' good jacket on him . . . Walter Lee, fix your tie and tuck your shirt in, you look just like somebody's hoodlum. Lord have mercy, where is my plant? (*She flies to get it amid the general bustling of the family, who are deliberately trying to ignore the nobility of the past moment.*) You all start on down . . . Travis child, don't go empty-handed . . . Ruth, where did I put that box with my skillets in it? I want to be in charge of it myself . . . I'm going to make us the biggest dinner we ever ate tonight . . . Beneatha, what's the matter with them stocking? Pull them things up, girl . . .

(*The family starts to file out as two moving men appear and begin to carry out the heavier pieces of furniture, bumping into the family as they move about.*)

BENEATHA: Mama, Asagai—asked me to marry him today and go to Africa—

MAMA: (*In the middle of her getting-ready activity.*) He did? You ain't old enough to marry nobody—(*Seeing the moving men lifting one of her chairs precariously.*) Darling, that ain't no bale of cotton, please handle it so we can sit in it again. I had that chair twenty-five years . . . (*The movers sigh with exasperation and go on with their work.*)

BENEATHA: (*Girlishly and unreasonably trying to pursue the conversation.*) To go to Africa, Mama—be a doctor in Africa . . .

MAMA: (*Distracted.*) Yes, baby—

WALTER: Africa! What he want you to go to Africa for?

BENEATHA: To practice there . . .

WALTER: Girl, if you don't get all them silly ideas out your head! You better marry yourself a man with some loot . . .

BENEATHA: (*Angrily, precisely as in the first scene of the play.*) What have you got to do with who I marry!

WALTER: Plenty. Now I think George Murchison—

(*He and* Beneatha *go out yelling at each other vigorously;* Beneatha *is heard saying that she would not marry George Murchison if he were Adam and she were Eve, etc. The anger is loud and real till their voices diminish.* Ruth *stands at the door and turns to* Mama *and smiles knowingly.*)

MAMA: (*Fixing her hat at last.*) Yeah—they something all right, my children . . .

RUTH: Yeah—they're something. Let's go, Lena.

MAMA: (*Stalling, starting to look around at the house.*) Yes—I'm coming. Ruth—

RUTH: Yes?

MAMA: (*Quietly, woman to woman.*) He finally come into his manhood today, didn't he? Kind of like a rainbow after the rain . . .

RUTH: (*Biting her lip lest her own pride explode in front of* Mama.) Yes, Lena.

(Walter's *voice calls for them raucously.*)

MAMA: (*Waving* Ruth *out vaguely.*) All right, honey—go on down. I be down directly.

(Ruth *hesitates, then exits.* Mama *stands, at last alone in the living room, her plant on the table before her as the lights start to come down. She looks around at all the walls and ceilings and suddenly, despite herself, while the children call below, a great heaving thing rises in her and she puts her fist to her mouth, takes a final desperate look, pulls her coat about her, pats her hat and goes out. The lights dim down. The door opens and she comes back in, grabs her plant, and goes out for the last time.*)

CURTAIN

FOR DISCUSSION

1. What kind of person is Beneatha?
2. Do you think Walter gets off too easily for losing Mama's money? Why or why not?
3. What do you think happens after the Youngers move to their house?
4. Why is the plant so important to Mama?
5. What is the theme of the play?
6. Compare the pride and ambition in *Oedipus Rex* with the same qualities in *A Raisin in the Sun.*
7. *A Raisin in the Sun* deals with people's dreams. What dreams do each of the Youngers have? What happens to these dreams?
8. Why is it so important to the Younger family not to accept the money from Lindner? Why does Walter want to accept it at first? Why does he change his mind? What would you have done?
9. Do you think *A Raisin in the Sun* is a good play? Why or why not?
10. Discuss Walter's statement that life is divided between the "takers" and the "tooken."
11. Do you think Beneatha is a selfish person? Walter? Why or why not?
12. What proves to Mama and Ruth that Walter has come into his manhood?
13. Why is this play called *A Raisin in the Sun?*
14. Are the characters true to life? Discuss. Is the play as a whole realistic? Why or why not?

NTC SPEECH AND THEATRE BOOKS

For a current catalog and information about our complete line of language arts books, write:
National Textbook Company,
a division of NTC Publishing Group
4255 West Touhy Avenue
Lincolnwood (Chicago), Illinois 60646-1975 U.S.A.